*A*dventure Guide

Paris

& Ile-de-France

Heather Stimmler-Hall

HUNTER

HUNTER PUBLISHING, INC,
130 Campus Drive, Edison, NJ 08818
☎ 732-225-1900; 800-255-0343; fax 732-417-1744
www.hunterpublishing.com

Ulysses Travel Publications
4176 Saint-Denis, Montréal, Québec
Canada H2W 2M5
☎ 514-843-9882, ext. 2232; fax 514-843-9448

Windsor Books
The Boundary, Wheatley Road, Garsington
Oxford, OX44 9EJ England
☎ 01865-361122; fax 01865-361133

ISBN 1-58843-396-X
© 2004 Hunter Publishing, Inc.

This and other Hunter travel guides are also available as e-books through Amazon.com, NetLibrary.com and other digital partners. For more information, e-mail us at comments@hunterpublishing.com.

Cover photo: Notre Dame Chimera, © *Aileen Ah-Tye*
Back cover photo: Passage Molière, © *Heather Stimmler-Hall*
All other photos courtesy of the author unless otherwise noted.

Maps by Toni Wheeler, © 2004 Hunter Publishing, Inc.

4   3   2   1

Contents

MAPS

About the Author

Heather Stimmler-Hall originally planned on being a news journalist in Washington, DC, but a year of university studying in Paris changed all that, and she's been living and working in France as a full-time writer since 1998 with her British husband and their two Miniature Pinschers (who are from Cannes, of course). Her articles about Paris and the surrounding region can be found in magazines, newspapers and websites in the US, UK, and even China. In January 2001 she created the monthly Secrets of Paris Newsletter (www.SecretsofParis.com) as a way of sharing her latest finds with friends (both French and foreign) living in Paris. Through word of mouth alone it has become a very popular source of alternative information for both residents and visitors to the city. When not writing, Heather can be found leading tours through her favorite hidden corners of Paris and Ile-de-France.

Every effort has been made to provide up-to-date information, but prices and opening hours change frequently, so always check in advance. Updated information for the guide can be found on Heather's website, www.RivieraWriter.com.

Acknowledgements

Special thanks to everyone who helped me during the many, many months of preparing and writing this guide, including fellow travel writer Tom Brosnahan, Travel Journo president Jim Thompson, *Metropole Paris* editor Ric Erickson, and Parisienne Extraordinaire Claire Waddington. I'd like to dedicate this guide to my endlessly patient and enthusiastically supportive husband and partner-in-crime, Mike Hall.

Introduction

Not another guidebook, you say? For many, the Paris they know or imagine is sacred, and there are few who feel the need to see more than the traditional fare of the Louvre, the Latin Quarter and the Moulin Rouge. But Paris is more, so much more. Paris is the leafy suburbs, the colorful ethnic markets,

the modern city-planning projects, the street artists, the strikes, and the techno clubs. The Louvre and Notre Dame aren't going anywhere, but if you want to see aspects of Paris that will probably disappear over the next decade, you'll have to step off the beaten track! This guide offers a mix of classic Parisian sites on every visitor's "must see" list, as well as the modern, multicultural aspects of the city that often go unnoticed. It also reveals a side of Paris that's not always pretty, but will help visitors gain a better understanding of why this city is the way it is, why the paradoxes exist, and why the Parisians can be so endearing and so frustrating at the same time.

As in all Hunter *Adventure Guides*, there's a large section dedicated to helping visitors actively experience Paris as a participant rather than just a spectator. Because, although the city might seem like a historical museum meant for the eyes only, Paris is very much alive. Instead of just learning about what Hemingway or Molière did in Paris, make your own memories, whether through trying your hand at French cooking or keeping up with the thousands of in-line skaters at the Friday Night Fever Skate through the city – the modern Parisian equivalent of running with the bulls! Since some of the best adventures and historical sites are beyond the urban confines of the city, the *Outside Paris* chapter highlights four key areas within 90 minutes of Paris, with detailed information on transportation, sightseeing, adventures, dining, and accommodation.

With so many things to see and do, it's obvious that visitors with limited time will have to make some tough choices on what to leave in and what to leave out. Cramming too many museums and monuments into a few days risks leaving you with a vague, shallow impression of the city. Instead, pick a few places that seem genuinely interesting to you, and spend some time getting to know them well for a much more meaningful – and less stressful – Paris experience.

History

The Early Years

■ From Lutetia to Joan of Arc

Paris might still be a swamp today if it weren't for **Julius Caesar**. In the third century BC, the *Parisii*, a Gallic tribe, settled into an area they called Loukteih (the Celtic word for "a marsh"), where they established a fishing village on the banks of the Ile de la Cité. The various Gallic tribes throughout the region were constantly engaged in war with each other. In 52 BC Julius Caesar put an end to the bickering once and for all at the battle of Alésia, where his armies defeated the Gauls, who had united briefly and unsuccessfully under Vercingétorix. As part of the Roman Empire, Loukteih was given the Latin moniker "Lutetia" (or *Lutèce* in modern French), and soon became an important Roman province.

Roman Influence

Extending the original settlement onto the Left Bank of the Seine, the Romans constructed roads, arenas, the vast catacombs under Montparnasse, and thermal baths (now part of the Cluny Medieval Museum). Protected from the Germanic tribes to the east of the Rhine, the *Parisii* thrived during the Pax Romana (Roman Peace). As the locals became more educated and urbanized, the seeds of a highly cultured French civilization were planted. When Julian the Apostate, Prefect of the Gauls, became the new Roman Emperor in 360 AD, he renamed the city Paris (Civitas Parisiorum, City of the Parisians).

Early Christians

In 451 AD, **Attila** and a half-million of his Huns set their sights on Paris after successfully laying waste to Rheims and Metz. The Parisians started packing their bags to flee the city, only to be stopped by a young Christian girl named **Geneviève**, who convinced them to hold their ground and pray. Whether it was the prayers or the lack of a good map, Attila never made it to Paris, and Geneviève was later named the city's patron saint. Meanwhile, Germanic tribes continued their invasions into Gaul, led by the Visigoths and the Franks. In what may be construed as revenge for the Romans' treatment of Saint Denis (see below), Geneviève converted Clovis, King of the Franks, to Christianity. After his baptism in Rheims in 508 AD, he proceeded to defeat the Roman governor of Gaul and established Paris as the capital of his Frankish kingdom. (He would-

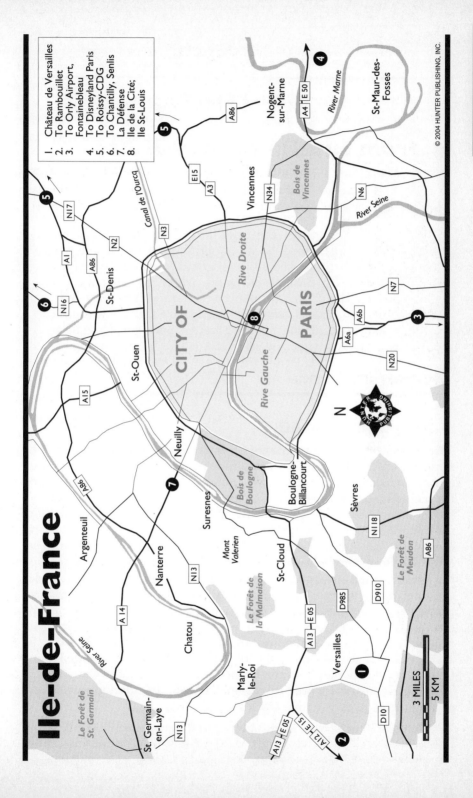

Ile-de-France

1. Château de Versailles
2. To Rambouillet
3. To Orly Airport, Fontainebleau
4. To Disneyland Paris
5. To Roissy-CDG
6. To Chantilly, Senlis
7. La Défense
8. Ile de la Cité; Ile St-Louis

CITY OF PARIS

Rive Droite
Rive Gauche

Le Forêt de St. Germain
St. Germain-en-Laye
Chatou
Nanterre
Argenteuil
St-Ouen
St-Denis
Neuilly
Suresnes
Mont Valerien
St-Cloud
Le Forêt de la Malmaison
Marly-le-Roi
Versailles
Sèvres
Le Forêt de Meudon
Boulogne-Billancourt
Bois de Boulogne
Vincennes
Bois de Vincennes
Nogent-sur-Marne
St-Maur-des-Fosses

River Seine
River Marne
Canal de l'Ourcq

A14
N13
A86
A15
N16
A1
A86
N2
N17
N3
A3
E15
A86
N34
N6
A4 E50
N7
A6b
A6a
N20
N118
D910
D985
A13 E05
A12 E15
A13 E05
D10
N13

N

3 MILES
5 KM

n't be the last king to convert to Catholicism for a throne in Paris.) The Merovingian Dynasty – and the kingdom of France – was born.

SAINT DENIS

St. Denis introduced Christianity to the Gauls around 250 AD, becoming the first bishop of Paris. He was martyred when the Romans beheaded him on a hill outside the city. Most historians think this is the origin of the name "Montmartre" (the hill of the martyr). According to a legend that appeared three centuries later, the slain St. Denis stood back up, picked up his head, and walked all the way to the current site of the Basilica St. Denis, where he collapsed and was buried. The church denounced this story during the 17th century, having come to the conclusion that St. Denis was most likely executed at the spot where he was buried, not at Montmartre. Any time you see a statue of a saint carrying his own head, that's St. Denis (there's one on the façade of Notre Dame).

A Kingdom United

Just two centuries later, the young Christian kingdom was threatened by the northward expansion of Islam, and the Merovingians began to lose control of their provinces. It was one of their powerful chancellors, **Charles Martel**, who reunited the kingdom after defeating the Spanish Moors at the Battle of Poitiers in 732. The Merovingians were now out of the picture as Martel's son, Pepin, was crowned by the pope as the first king of the Carolingian dynasty. Pepin's son was **Charlemagne**, who became the Holy Roman Emperor on Christmas Day 800. After extending the French kingdom's boundaries far beyond what they had been under the Romans, he moved his capital to Aix-la-Chapelle (Aachen, in present-day Germany), leaving Paris to slowly decline. When Charlemagne died without an obvious heir, the entire kingdom split with internal squabbles over who should inherit the throne. In 843 a large chunk of the realm was signed away under the Treaty of Verdun, roughly establishing the present-day border between France and Germany. The Carolingians struggled to sustain power as regional vassals in Aquitaine and Burgundy started to overshadow the king.

Enter **Count Eudes** who, in 885, defended Paris against 30,000 Norman pirates who sailed 700 ships right up the Seine. The French must have remembered this impressive feat, because 100 years later they pledged their loyalty to the new king, Eudes' grand-nephew, Hugh (*Hughes*) **Capet**. The Capetians restored Paris as the French capital, and the city grew in size and prestige as the power of the French kings increased.

ARCHITECTURAL FIRST

Gothic architecture was born in Paris during the 12th century with the construction of the **St-Denis Basilica** just north of the city in 1140. While its arched ceiling rested on two supporting Roman walls, the main load of the Basilica is held by four pillars and external flying buttresses, which allow for a higher, loftier vaulted ceiling. The style was copied throughout Europe, and 20 years later the first stones were laid for Notre Dame, bridging the gap between the early Gothic and High Gothic style of the late 13th century, which incorporated stained glass windows instead of solid masonry walls. It was the artists of the Renaissance who gave Gothic architecture its name, using the word "Goth" to imply that the style was barbaric compared to the clean, noble lines of Roman architecture.

England & France

In order to avoid any further grabs at the throne by powerful lords, the Capetians wisely centralized the administration of the kingdom, establishing France's civil service system with Paris as its center. They also made sure that the king owned the most land, and refused to let the Papacy in Rome push them around. This didn't keep the English from gaining their first major foothold in France in 1152, when Louis VII's arranged marriage to **Eleanor of Aquitaine** ended and she immediately wed Henry of Normandy, a.k.a. **King Henry II of England**. It was King Philippe Auguste (1180-1223), using his friendship with Henry II's estranged son Richard the Lionheart, who was able to reclaim the French lands lost in Normandy and the Loire. Under Philippe Auguste the capital's streets were paved, the city walls were fortified, cathedrals were constructed, and a fortified castle was built on the Right Bank, which would later become the Louvre. The **Latin Quarter** was born on the Left Bank with the opening of the University of Paris in 1215 and the Sorbonne in 1253, attracting notable scholars such as Abélard and St. Thomas Aquinas.

The Capetian dynasty ended in disaster when Philippe IV ("the Fair") died in 1314, quickly followed by his three sons – "the cursed kings" – within a few years. Only his daughter Isabelle survived, giving birth to a son. This is where things get confusing. Isabelle's husband was Edward II of England, which meant the only grandson of Philippe IV of France was England's King Edward III. The French lords therefore put forth their preferred candidate for the throne, Philippe IV's nephew, Philippe de Valois, and the Hundred Years War started. If it had simply been a matter of the French vs. the English, it might not have lasted as long, but it wasn't that simple. As the Valois lost battle after battle (and even one king) to the English, things weren't looking any better for the French on the domestic front. The merchants' Provost of Paris, Etienne Marcel, led a bloody uprising against Charles V, and dukes from the Armagnac and Burgundian families began fighting among themselves for power when it became clear that Charles VI was mad. The English took the opportunity to side with the Burgundians in 1408, and were given control of Paris while the dauphin (the crown prince, the future Charles VII) took refuge in Bourges. This was where the famous young peasant girl, Joan of Arc (*Jeanne d'Arc*), got involved. She rallied the dauphin's troops and managed to win a few battles, but was wounded during the failed siege of Paris in 1429. The six-year-old Henry VI of England was crowned king of France a year later at Notre Dame. Captured by the Burgundians in 1431, Joan was turned over to the English and burned at the stake in Rouen for heresy. In the end, her martyrdom boosted French determination and, by 1436, Charles VII finally defeated the English (and their Burgundian cohorts) at Montereau, then returned triumphantly to Paris. The **Hundred Years War** (which actually lasted over 120 years) was finally over.

UNLUCKY PARIS

During the troublesome Hundred Years War, Parisians had other problems to deal with besides the English occupation. In 1348 the city was hit by famine and the plague. At the height of the epidemic, over 800 Parisians died daily. In 1380 the plague returned, followed by another famine in 1395. Paris flooded twice, in 1410 and 1428. The English brought the smallpox with them in 1422, and hungry wolves managed to enter the city during the winter of 1423. Two years after Charles VII ended the English occupation, over 50,000 Parisians died from yet another bout of the plague, known now as the Black Death. By 1438 the population of Paris was less than half its size before the start of the Hundred Years War.

The Renaissance

■ 16th & 17th Centuries

The Renaissance started off on the right foot. While French military invasions into Italy proved unsuccessful, they got a good glimpse at Italian architecture, inspiring François I in 1515 to transform the Louvre fortress into a Renaissance Palace. Leonardo da Vinci arrived soon after with a certain *Mona Lisa* in his luggage. The first secular educational institution, the **Collège de France**, opened in 1530, while works by Rabelais, Montaigne, Robert Estienne, Marguerite de Navarre, and Diane de Poitiers were available throughout Europe thanks to the arrival of the printing press. The proliferation of new ideas didn't always sit well with the king, and many printers were hanged and burned at Place Maubert for their "blasphemous and seditious" publications. But they couldn't prevent the spread of the Protestant ideas of John Calvin and Martin Luther. By 1562 Paris found itself at the center of France's religious wars.

Catholic & Protestant

In one corner were the French Protestants, known as the **Huguenots**. In the other corner stood the ultra-Catholic faction led by the **Guise** family. Caught up in the middle was **Catherine de Medicis**, regent for her young son, King Henri III. There were many bloody skirmishes during the religious conflict, but nothing matched the horrific **St. Bartholomew's Day Massacre** of 1572. At the wedding of Henri III's sister to the Protestant Henri de Navarre the Duc de Guise and Catherine de Medicis ordered the slaughter of the 3,000 Huguenot guests, throwing their bodies into the Seine, and setting off bloodbaths across the country. Henri de Navarre would eventually get even when Henri III was assassinated in 1589 without an heir, leaving his Protestant brother-in-law as heir to the throne. The Catholics demanded that he renounce his faith and convert to Catholicism before he could rule France. "Paris is worth a mass," he famously pronounced, and Henri de Navarre was crowned King Henri IV of France. As the first king in the Bourbon Dynasty, Henri IV did much to improve Paris, but his most significant contribution was his signature on the Edict of Nantes in 1598. Meant to prevent the kind of tragedy that took place at his own wedding, it granted the Huguenots religious freedom, and put an end to the country's religious wars – for the moment.

In 1610 Henri IV was riding through Paris when his open carriage was blocked on the narrow Rue de la Ferronnerie by the delivery carts of Les Halles. A crazed mystic, Ravaillac, saw an opportunity and leapt into the carriage, assassinating the king with a kitchen knife. Today there's a bronze memorial plaque set in the cobblestones where the event took place (in front of the Café Coeur Couronné).

THE LEGACY OF HENRI IV

 Many of Paris' oldest monuments were built during the reign of Henri IV. He created new squares, such as the **Place Royale** (now Place des Vosges), built the **Hôpital St-Louis** to treat victims of the plague (the oldest working hospital in Paris), and completed the **Pont Neuf** (New Bridge).

The next two kings, Louis XIII and Louis XIV, ruled for over a century, giving Paris enough stability to grow and prosper throughout the 17th century. With their hardworking ministers at the forefront (Richelieu under Louis XIII, Mazarin and Colbert under Louis XIV), the monarchy was able to centralize its power, fend off multiple coups d'états by the aristocracy, and invest heavily in the city's architectural heritage. In the first few decades of the 1600s, Henri IV's widow, Marie de Medicis, built the Luxembourg Palace, Richelieu founded the French language institution called the Académie Française, construction began on the grazing fields of the Ile St-Louis, and Paris became an Episcopal See. The king promoted economic self-sufficiency, and the craftsmen of Paris became known throughout Europe for their fine luxury goods and textiles.

In 1648 Paris was disturbed by the first of a series of civil uprisings – called *Frondes* – in objection to heavy taxation and the absolute authority of the king. Louis XIV decided not to take any further chances with the predictably unpredictable Parisians, and moved his court to the suburbs of Saint-Germain-en-Laye in 1666 while constructing his palace in Versailles, a monumental feat that took 20 years and over 30,000 men to build. The Parisians back in the city were happily kept busy building Les Invalides, while the countryside surrounding Paris, known as *Ile-de-France*, became the new stomping ground for the French royal family, earning it the nickname "the garden of kings."

Louis XIV, known as the Sun King, dominated his kingdom in many ways. *L'état, c'est moi* (I am the State) was his motto, and his taste for extravagance – both at home and in his military campaigns abroad – would eventually drain the royal treasury. In 1685 the king made a bad decision by revoking the Edict of Nantes, removing all privileges from the French Huguenots. Thousands fled the city and joined the League of Augsburg, starting another long and bitter religious war up to the Peace of Rijswijk in 1697.

By the time Louis XIV died (at the ripe old age of 77) in 1715, the Parisians had suffered enough from economic hardship and famine. And they were beginning to think that just maybe it was the monarchy's fault.

The Age of Enlightenment & The Revolution

■ 1715-1799

In the calm before the revolutionary storm, Paris in the 1700s was at the height of its cultural glory, hosting many of the world's finest artists, playwrights and musicians. The city was improved with its first sidewalks, street signs and oil lamps, while its overflowing cemeteries were cleared out and transferred to the empty quarry tunnels known as the *Catacombes*. Louis XV commissioned the **Ecole Militaire**, the **Panthéon** and the square that would become the **Place de la Concorde**.

Most importantly, it was the time when great political thinkers and philosophers such as Voltaire, Rousseau, and Benjamin Franklin would meet in the Paris *salons* to discuss the democratic ideals of the Enlightenment. The monarchy and the clergy made attempts to censor subversive works such as Beaumarchais' *Marriage of Figaro* and Diderot's groundbreaking *Encyclopedia*, which promoted scientific reason over tradition. Ironically, the French monarchy was instrumental in the success of the American Revolution, clandestinely providing the colonists with unlimited funds and military aid even while France was still officially an ally of England.

It was France's own depleted treasury that was the catalyst for the Revolution in 1789. After a long reign by the weak-willed Louis XV, the clergy and feuding aristocrats had regained much of their power lost under the tight control of Louis XIV. In 1774, Louis XVI and his overbearing wife Marie Antoinette inherited a kingdom rife with corruption and on the brink of bankruptcy. This didn't keep them from their own extravagances, however, and by 1788 the royal treasury was almost empty. In May 1789, although the king tried to remedy the problem through fiscal measures, the people were geared up for more sweeping reforms.

At the forefront were the *bourgeoisie* commoners with property and position, but few political rights. Inspired by the success of the American Revolution, they took advantage of the changing times and formed their own representative group, which they called the National Assembly. The king reluctantly legalized the new assembly in June, and then barricaded himself at Versailles hoping the whole thing would blow over.

But the ball was rolling, and on July 14, 1789, in a show of strength, Parisians stormed the royal prison of the Bastille, thus marking the entry of the suffering popular classes into the Revolution. They formed their own municipal government, represented by the tricolor flag, in the Hôtel de Ville. By August 1789 they had succeeded in scaring the nobles and clergy into relinquishing their privileges, putting to an end centuries-old feudal structures. The clergy's lands were nationalized and they were forced to renounce their religious orders and swear allegiance to the state-controlled Civil Constitution of the Clergy.

In October 1789, alarmed by food shortages and suspicious of counter-revolutionary plotting in the courts, a mob went to Versailles and forced the king and queen back to the Tuileries in Paris, where they could keep an eye on them. In 1791 the National Assembly finished drafting the Constitution, which established a limited monarchy with a legislature elected by property-owning voters. For Louis it was the last straw, and in June 1791 he tried to flee the country with his family in order to obtain the aid of foreign monarchs and to restore his authority. But his carriage was captured just outside Paris, and the humiliated king forced to accept the new constitution. Up to this point things were relatively bloodless.

But for many Parisians, even a symbolic monarchy was too much. In August 1792, an insurrection of tradespeople and radical bourgeois known as the Commune forcefully infiltrated the ranks of the National Assembly, and formed the National Convention. Despite its idealistic motto of "Liberté, Egalité, Fraternité," the Convention, dominated by Robespierre and Danton, established a dictatorship of terror, using the justification of preserving the young Republic. When Louis was caught corresponding with royalist armies gathering in Germany, he was convicted of treason and executed by guillotine on January 21, 1793. Under the Reign of Terror over 2,800 suspected royal sympathizers and enemies of the state, including Marie Antoinette, lost their heads. But the Convention soon lost the support of the wealthy land-owning middle classes, who had already gotten what they wanted out of the Revolution – political power. On July 1794, the moderate members of the Convention had Robespierre and his radical Commune members guillotined.

WHO WERE THE SANS-CULOTTES?

The *Sans-Culottes* were the working classes of Paris, deeply patriotic to the democratic ideas of the Revolution and rabidly anti-royalist, who chose to wear pants instead of the fancy breeches of the day known as *culottes*. Too poor to qualify as voters, they finally won a voice in government under the radical Commune leaders of the Convention, and had no small part in influencing the execution of Louis XVI. They're often portrayed in history as the "mob muscle" behind the Revolution.

The Convention drew up yet another constitution and established the Directoire, with a bicameral legislature. But the government was unstable and increasingly dependent on the military to deal with the starving

Parisian mobs and royalist uprisings. At the same time, France's armies were waging war throughout Europe, grabbing territories in the Rhine, the Savoy, and North Africa with mixed results. **General Napoleon Bonaparte** returned to Paris a hero in 1799 after successful campaigns in Italy, and immediately took power in a military coup, replacing the Directoire with the Consulate. Just a decade after the fall of the Bastille, the French Revolution was over. For the moment, the wealthy land-owning classes had come out on top. But, as we'll see in the 19th century, the fallen aristocracy and disgruntled urban masses were just biding their time.

THE REVOLUTIONARY CALENDAR

During the Revolution, a new calendar based on nature and science was officially adopted and used until December 31, 1805. Months were given names such as Brumaire, Thermidor, and Fructidor. The first day of the first month of the fourth year of the Revolution would have been written *1 Vendémiaire IV.*

📖 *David Garrioch's fascinating book,* **The Making of Rev-olutionary Paris** *(University of California Press; September, 2002) is a fascinating anecdotal chronicle of everyday life in Paris, exploring the social and cultural changes in the years leading up to the Revolution with vivid portraits of individual lives.*

The 19th Century

■ 1800-1871

The Emperor Napoleon

As **First Consul** under the Consulate government, Napoleon was actually more authoritarian than Louis XVI, but his sweeping reforms transformed France into an efficient, modern state. He centralized all administration in Paris, made peace with the church (effectively keeping it on a short leash), created the Bank of France, and established the Napoleonic Code as the basis of the new legal system. Napoleon amassed such power that he had the subservient senate proclaim him emperor, and on December 2, 1804 the adoring public watched him place the crown on his own head in Notre Dame Cathedral.

He quickly got to work expanding his empire abroad, while embellishing Paris with monuments such as the **Arc de Triomphe**, the **Vendôme**

Column, and the arcaded **Rue de Rivoli**. War booty from all over Europe was added to the Louvre's collections. Unfortunately, Napoleon's exploits abroad took a turn for the worse and, in March 1814, Paris fell to a coalition of British, Austrian and Prussian armies. Napoleon was packed off to Elba in exile, and Louis XVIII was placed in charge of things while the victors tried to clean up the emperor's mess in Europe. Less than a year later he snuck back into France through Cannes with a group of loyal soldiers. By the time he reached Paris, Louis XVIII had fled, and Napoleon got to work putting his empire back together. At the end of this period, known as the Hundred Days, Napoleon was horribly defeated at the battle of Waterloo and sent as a prisoner of war to the lonely Saint Helena Island, where he died in 1821.

The Restoration

Louis XVIII returned, and reinstated the Bourbons to the French throne in what became known as the Restoration. Things got off to a peaceful start. France's economy recovered and Louis improved the city's infrastructure with the opening of the Canal St-Martin and Canal Ourcq. But when the moderate Louis died in 1824, his reactionary younger brother Charles X took over with the idea of reinstating the rules of the old regime. The middle classes were enjoying their political power and prosperity under the new capitalism, so when Charles censored the press, dissolved the assembly and reduced the electorate in July 1830, the people responded with an armed insurrection. The royal troops were defeated by the Paris barricades and Charles was forced to abdicate.

Despite another chance for a republic, the liberal Duke of Orléans was elected King Louis-Philippe by the popular assembly on July 31, 1830 in what became known as the July Monarchy. Although this "Citizen King" was popular with the bourgeoisie and liberal media, his policies didn't address the needs of the working classes, who were still living in the squalid conditions described in Victor Hugo's novels *Notre Dame de Paris* and *Les Miserables*. After almost 20,000 died in a cholera epidemic, modern sanitary infrastructures were established, including garbage removal and the famous *vespasien* public urinals (named for their inventor, the first-century Roman emperor Vespasian).

Paris continued to attract the leading cultural figures of the time – the writers Balzac and Hugo, the musicians Chopin, Berlioz, Liszt and Wagner, and the artists Delacroix and Ingres. In keeping with the progressive philosophies of the time, public executions and the branding and dismembering of criminals were banned in 1832. A few years later in 1837 the first French railway line opened between Paris and St-Germain-en-Laye.

In 1840 Louis-Philippe had Napoleon's remains returned to Paris and placed in the tomb under the dome of Les Invalides. It was an emotional event for Parisians, who still worshipped their lost emperor, but it did little to boost the king's waning popularity among the royal Legitimists, who supported the senior Bourbon line, and the Leftists, who demanded electoral reform. The king was finally kicked out in February 1848 after attempts to ban a meeting of his political opponents resulted in three days of street fighting and a popular revolution. Louis-Philippe was the last of the French kings.

The 1848 Revolution ushered in the short-lived Second Republic, marred by the first major clashes between the bourgeoisie and the proletarian workers. Driven by high unemployment and influenced by the Communist ideals of Marx and Engels that were spreading throughout Europe, the workers began a bloody, four-day rebellion after the government cut their work subsidies. The revolt was brutally repressed, its leaders executed, but the seeds of class conflict were planted.

Enter the ambitious Louis Napoleon Bonaparte, Napoleon's nephew, who had been exiled and imprisoned during the Restoration for plotting against the monarchy. Riding on the popularity of his name, he essentially followed the path of his uncle: he was elected President of the Assembly in 1848, staged a military coup at the end of his term, and had himself crowned Emperor Napoleon III by 1852. The French welcomed the Second Empire with open arms, hoping it would establish the order, glory and political unity that France had lost.

Paris was rapidly transformed under Napoleon III's authoritarian rule. He commissioned the ruthless **Baron Haussmann** to transform the city from a dirty, overcrowded medieval town into a modern capital worthy of its international reputation. For the next 20 years Paris was one big construction site as Haussmann cut wide boulevards through old neighborhoods, installed a modern sewer system, built train stations, and turned old quarries and garbage dumps into public parks. The new cityscape was equipped with covered markets, street lights, water fountains and public garbage bins (named after their inventor, Monsieur Poubelle). In 1860 the country villages on the outskirts of Paris were annexed to give the population more breathing space, and the city was divided up into 20 new *arrondissements* (districts). Paris hosted the 1855 and 1867 World Expositions, and was at the center of the ground-breaking Impressionist movement led by Edouard Manet, Claude Monet, and Paul Cézanne.

Napoleon's foreign ventures started off well with victory in the Crimean War, commercial trade agreements with Great Britain and the construction of the Suez Canal. But his glory days ended in tragedy on September 1, 1870 when, underestimating Otto von Bismarck's Prussian forces, the emperor was captured on the battlefield at Sedan. When the news reached Paris, the provisional National Assembly of the Third Republic was quickly formed in a bloodless revolution. The Prussian troops surrounded the city on September 19th, and although the Assembly fled to Bordeaux and the French troops were hopelessly outnumbered, Parisians weathered the siege for four months through cold and famine.

The Commune

On January 28, 1871, the National Assembly, represented by the royalist **Adolphe Thiers**, signed an armistice at Versailles to end the Franco-Prussian War. France had to hand over territory in Alsace and Lorraine, and pay an indemnity of about $1 billion within three years (the Prussian troops would remain in Paris until it was paid). The Parisians felt betrayed by the conservative Thiers regime and refused a humiliating surrender. When the government's attempt to disarm the Parisian National Guard failed, Thiers fled back to Versailles. On March 28, 1871, Parisians elected their own municipal government in the deserted Hôtel de Ville and the Paris Commune was born. During their short time in power, the *Communards* enacted labor reforms to benefit the working classes and promoted women's education. But, while the Red Flag flew over the city, the new government rejected radical plans to commandeer private property or allow workers to take over monopolistic factories. Nevertheless, the threat of social change was felt throughout Europe's bourgeoisie. Thiers had to take back control of the city.

On April 11, the neutral Prussian occupiers watched from the sidelines as Thiers' Versailles troops began the second siege of Paris. Heavily fortified by barricades, Paris held out until May 28, when the troops entered the city in what became known as the Bloody Week. The city's defenders, including many women, were executed on the spot as each barrier was destroyed. In a last act of desperation, the Communards killed their hostages (including the Archbishop of Paris) and set fire to the Tuileries Palace, the Hôtel de Ville, and the Palais de Justice. The final bitter fighting took place among the tombs of Père Lachaise Cemetery on the night of May 27. By morning the Commune was defeated, its survivors lined up against the cemetery wall and shot.

WHAT HAPPENED TO NAPOLEON III?

When an armistice ended the Franco-Prussian War in 1871, the defeated emperor was sent into exile in England, joining his wife Eugénie, who had fled Paris after his capture. He died two years later. Their only son, the Prince Imperial, died in 1879 while fighting the Zulus with the British army.

In the following months, reprisals by the victorious Versailles government resulted in the imprisonment, deportation or execution of anyone connected to the Commune. Paris remained under martial law for the next five years, and political activists were routinely arrested. The revolutionary anthem, *Marseillaise*, was strictly outlawed. There is no exact figure, but somewhere between 20,000 and 30,000 Parisians died during the two months of the Commune, far worse than losses during the two months of the Commune, far worse than losses during the Franco-Prussian War or the French Revolution. Although the working class movement was crushed, Karl Marx famously commented: "The principles of the Commune are eternal and indestructible; they will present themselves again and again until the working class is liberated."

The Belle Epoque & Two World Wars

■ 1872-1944

The Third Republic

After the Commune, Thiers tried to return the country to a Constitutional Monarchy under the tricolor flag, but the reactionary Comte Henri de Chambord (the legitimist pretender to the throne) refused to rule under anything but the Bourbon flag. So France remained a republic, albeit with a royalist sympathizer, **Marshal Patrice MacMahon**, elected as its new President.

Under the relative stability of the Third Republic, Paris enjoyed the economic prosperity of the Industrial Revolution and the cultural prestige of the Belle Epoque. New monuments such as the **Opéra Garnier** and **Sacré-Coeur** were completed, while the **Eiffel Tower**, the **Petit** and **Grand Palais**, and the first métro line, decorated with Hector Guimaud's signature Art Nouveau entrances, dazzled visitors at the Universal Expositions of 1889 and 1900. Parisians were introduced to the new pleasures of cinema, telephones, the gramophone, automobiles, and the racy cancan dancers of the Moulin Rouge. In 1911 **Diaghilev's Russian Ballet** moved to Paris and revolutionized the dance world with the artistic collaboration of **Picasso** and music by **Stravinsky**, **Strauss**, **Debussy**, and **Ravel**. The success of **Impressionist artists** such as Renoir and Van Gogh was followed by the birth of **Cubism** at Montmartre's Bâteau-Lavoir, while scientific advances by **Louis Pasteur** and **Pierre and Marie Curie** gained world acclaim.

But the Belle Epoque wasn't just La Vie en Rose, it was also a time of political and social unrest. In 1894 the country was scandalized by the **Dreyfus Affair**, when a Jewish army general was falsely accused and imprisoned for treason. After several appeal hearings that bitterly divided public opinion, Dreyfus was finally released and reinstated in 1906. One of the immediate results of the controversy was the legal separation of church and state in 1905. The event also discredited the monarchists and reactionaries, and brought the Socialists into power for the first time.

THE FLOOD OF 1910

The Seine burst its banks at 10:50 am on January 21, 1910 as the water level rose to 24 feet, flooding much of the Left Bank and cutting the city's electrical power. Streets became rivers, métro and sewer tunnels were flooded, and the trains of the Gare d'Orsay (later to become the Musée d'Orsay) were completely submerged. Parisians spent days building sandbag barriers over a half-mile stretch to save the Right Bank and the Louvre Museum. At one point it looked as if the bridges would go under, but the river finally started to recede on January 28, and Parisians began the long task of cleaning up the debris and pumping out cellars.

First World War

France entered World War I in 1914. Although Paris sustained shelling from German zeppelins, the city was saved from invasion by the Battle of the Marne, and became a temporary home base for convalescing American soldiers. Although France and its allies succeeded in defeating Germany at the end of the war, French casualties numbered almost five million.

THE FIRST PARIS OLYMPICS

Paris is remembered for hosting the 1924 Olympics, immortalized in the 1981 film *Chariots of Fire*. But many forget that the city also hosted the 1900 Olympics, which didn't receive as much publicity because it coincided with the 1900 Universal Exposition; that was the first Olympics where women participated, although adequate sports facilities were lacking and swimming events had to be held in the Seine!

The period between the wars, known as *les années folles* (the mad years), was defined by major artistic and philosophical movements such as **Dadaism**, **Surrealism**, and **Existentialism**. American artists and intellectuals fleeing Prohibition and racism took refuge in the liberal, freethinking atmosphere of Paris. Montparnasse became home to expat writers of the "Lost Generation," as **Gertrude Stein** called them, such as **Ernest Hemingway, Zelda and Scott Fitzgerald, John Dos Passos**, and **Ford Madox Ford.** The Paris jazz scene thrived in the vaulted cellars of St-Germain-des-Prés, and performers like **Josephine Baker** dazzled Parisians in the city's top venues. Other heroes of the era include the modern architect **Le Corbusier** and the pilot **Charles Lindbergh**, who landed in Paris in 1927 after a solo crossing of the Atlantic.

WWII & The Occupation

In the years leading up to World War II, the political mood in Paris was tense, aggravated by the economic depression and the 1937 Stavinsky Affair, a corruption scandal in the Radical Socialist government that led to bloody riots in the streets of Paris by right-wing extremists (primarily royalists). After the 1939 Nazi-Soviet Pact, members of the Communist party were rounded up and interred in camps. Despite the presence of millions of French troops on the defensive Maginot Line, Hitler's 1940 Blitzkrieg caught the Allies by surprise, and German troops entered Paris on June 14. Captured resistance fighters were detained just outside the city at Mont Valérien. The French government, defeatist and deeply divided politically, signed an armistice that allowed Germans to occupy Paris, while leaving 40% of the country free to be governed by Marshal Pétain's administration based in the resort town of Vichy. Seen as a puppet government of the Nazis, Pétain's authority was never internationally recognized. Meanwhile, General Charles de Gaulle escaped to London to organize the French Resistance movement, with a famous BBC broadcast to the French people declaring that the war was not over.

During the occupation, German military forces, including the Gestapo, took over most of the city's prestigious buildings such as the Palais du Luxembourg, the Hôtel Meurice and Hôtel Lutetia. Hitler wasted no time in shutting down the cabarets and clubs, literally sending jazz music underground, with constantly changing locations and passwords – similar to the speakeasies of the US. Parisians were forced to live under a 6 pm curfew, and regular arrests were made of anyone showing patriotic tendencies. Many different groups were involved in clandestine resistance actions, including students of the Sorbonne, who developed a vast espionage and escape network, created false ID papers for Resistance members, and produced an underground newspaper called *Défense de la France*. In 1942 conditions worsened when the Royal Air Force bombed the Renault factories in the suburbs of Boulogne-Billancourt, killing 500 people. On July 16th and 17th, French police collaborators arrested 12,884 Jews in their homes, and held them in the Vélodrome d'Hiver before deporting them to death camps in Poland. By 1943, the Resistance organization was making progress. In May, the National Council of the Resistance met for the first time, bringing together representatives from all of the major Resistance groups working inside and outside the country. Allied bombing intensified in 1944, and although Parisians could see the light at the end of the tunnel, repression was stepped up. By summer they were suffering from severe food shortages and long periods without gas or electricity.

With news of the Allied landing in Normandy, Parisians began a general strike, bringing the city to a halt. By August 18th they set up barricades throughout the city and Resistance fighters occupied the Hôtel de Ville. In the final days, German officers hastily closed up shop and executed or deported the rest of their prisoners. Allied forces expected to see a devastated city when they arrived in Paris, but General von Choltitz couldn't bring himself to follow Hitler's orders to level the city (explosives had even been put into place), and surrendered himself and the remaining German forces to General Leclerc on August 24, 1944. Two days later de Gaulle entered Paris amid a wildly cheering crowd on the Champs-Elysées.

DID YOU KNOW?

DID YOU KNOW? *When the Allies landed in Normandy they were planning on heading straight to Berlin, preferring to avoid a long street battle to liberate Paris. But General de Gaulle finally convinced Eisenhower that the Germans would destroy Paris if they waited any longer. After the city was liberated, the allies took on the extra burden of feeding the starving Parisians.*

Modern Paris

■ Post-War Paris

Spirits were initially high after the war. The new constitution under the Fourth Republic gave women the right to vote in 1946, the same year that **Coco Chanel's** *New Look* wowed the fashion world. But France's bitter loss of their Algerian colony in the 1950s War of Independence not only resulted in the collapse of the Fourth Republic, but also meant the return of over a half-million French colonists, known as the *pieds noirs* (an 18th-century term). Combined with the rural immigration to the cities, Paris was suddenly faced with a serious housing crisis. Not only was there a shortage, the housing that *was* available was in pitiful condition. In 1954 only 10% of French homes had a bath or shower, and only 27% had flushing toilets. Charles de Gaulle came out of retirement to head the Fifth Republic, and launched an emergency building plan. Over the next two decades old buildings in the inner suburbs and outer arrondissements such as the 13th, the 19th and the 20th, were razed to make way for residential towers.

Plans for a modern business district in La Défense were announced, and new buildings for UNESCO and Radio France were completed. When developers began looking toward the older neighborhoods in central Paris, writer and Minister André Malraux stepped in and declared one of the oldest and most historic, the Marais, to be a historic district to save it from destruction. He also convinced the city to fund the cleaning and restoration of the city's major monuments and state-owned buildings.

THE ALGERIAN WAR OF INDEPENDENCE

In 1961 a peaceful demonstration by French Algerians protesting curfews imposed on North Africans during the Algerian War ended in slaughter. Police opened fire on the marchers at the Place de la Concorde, beating them with clubs and throwing the bodies into the Seine. The official word was that three protestors were injured, but independent French media coverage of the massacre was strictly censored by Chief of Police, Maurice Papon. It wasn't until 30 years later, when Papon was brought to trial for his role in the deportation of French Jews during WWII, that investigations into the 1961 protest found evidence that over 200 Algerians had been murdered.

Late 20th Century

The youth scene exploded in Paris in the early 1960s, known as *les années yé-yé*, with American-influenced be-boppers and rockers such as Johnny Hallyday, Eddy Mitchell, France Gall, and Françoise Hardy. It was also the start of Serge Gainsbourg's long and eclectic singing career. Meanwhile, **Jean-Paul Sartre** honed his existentialist ideas in the cafés of St-Germain-des-Prés, and the **Beat Generation's** ex-pat writers, such as Ginsberg, Corso and Ferlinghetti, read their anti-establishment poetry in George Whitman's Latin Quarter bookshop, **Shakespeare & Co.** Influenced by these new ways of thinking, as well as student anti-war protests taking place throughout the world, disillusionment with the establishment began to take root in the Paris universities.

In May 1968 Paris was the scene of a series of riots, protests and strikes that brought the country to a standstill. It all began with the closure of Nanterre University after clashes between right-wing groups and students campaigning against the Vietnam War and American imperialism. On May 3, 600 students protesting the closure were arrested at the Sorbonne, setting off angry marches throughout the Latin Quarter. Parisians watched in horror as police and students clashed in clouds of teargas, with some of the worst violence seen since the war. Over the next few days students set up street barricades and occupied the universities, demanding the release of the prisoners and reforms to the antiquated university structures. Their movement quickly spread to the frustrated working classes, leading to a general strike of over nine million workers throughout the country. Factories and offices were occupied by employees demanding better working conditions, higher pay, and an end to the oppressive management culture.

But the movement suffered from its own spontaneity. Without the support of any major political party or workers' union (even the Communist party leaders were considered "sellouts"), de Gaulle was able to remain in charge. He dissolved the National Assembly and called for new elections, and by June 16th the movement ended as CRS (riot police) cleared out the final barricades. Those still resisting were violently repressed, with one student drowned in the Seine and two workers shot dead in a Peugeot factory. The French were eager for a return to law and order, and the Right came back to power after an overwhelming election victory.

THE AFTERMATH OF MAY 1968

While *les évènements de Mai 1968* fell short of a complete revolution, France was changed forever. Old French institutions loosened up and a more liberal and socialist society developed, giving new momentum to the women's movement and civil rights issues. Even today, the memory of the strikes remains a powerful incentive for government and big businesses to negotiate with trade unions and disgruntled workers.

Charles de Gaulle ended up resigning in 1969 after being defeated in a decentralization referendum, and he was replaced by Georges Pompidou. Paris continued to modernize throughout the 1970s, with the inauguration of the **RER** express train, the **Boulevard Périphérique** ring road, two **international airports** and the construction of the city's first (and last) skyscraper, the **Tour Montparnasse**. The wholesale food market Les Halles was dismantled, moved to the suburbs and replaced with a modern, underground commercial center, the Forum des Halles. Despite initial protests, the brightly colored **Pompidou Center** opened just a few blocks away in the heart of the Beaubourg district.

François Mitterrand continued the building spree when he came to power in 1981, transforming the **Gare d'Orsay** into a museum and the *abattoirs* (slaughterhouses) at **La Villette** into a new park and science museum. Construction continued on the office district at **La Défense**, with the completion of its Grande Arche and the Opéra Bastille for the 1989 French Revolution Bicentennial. Mitterrand's most important *grands travaux* (great works) include the Grand Louvre renovations and the complete overhaul of the Bercy district. A year after his retirement in 1995, the colossal new **François Mitterrand National Library** was inaugurated on the Left Bank of the Seine.

In the 1990s Paris experienced several tragic events, including the 1995 métro bombings by Algerian terrorists that killed eight and seriously injured over 150, and the 1997 death of Diana, Princess of Wales, after her car crashed in a Paris tunnel trying to escape the paparazzi. Domestic politics took a dive when a public service strike by transit workers, postal staff and teachers opposed to social security reforms crippled the city for three weeks in December 1995.

MINITEL VS INTERNET

The famous Minitel was created by France Telecom in 1984, and became a permanent fixture in French households long before the Internet. Made up of a terminal and keyboard that plugs into the phone line, the Minitel serves as a phone and address directory, with links to databases for instant access to daily news, encyclopedias, booking agencies, banking, mail-order shopping, computer dating and even a risqué chat room known as the "Minitel Rose." Fees for usage appear on the phone bill. France Telecom provides the basic terminals for free, although fancier high-tech models are available for a small rental fee. Because of the Minitel, the French were behind the rest of the western world in getting hooked up to the Internet, and only started trying to catch up in 1998. For the moment the two systems live side-by-side, each with its pros and cons, but many predict the eventual demise of Minitel's pioneering information network.

The mood changed for the better in July 1998 when Parisians celebrated the biggest event in the country's sporting history with a Soccer World Cup victory against Brazil in the newly built Stade de France. On the night of December 26, 1999 France was struck by a storm that left many regions without electricity for several weeks, and caused severe damage to many Paris monuments and centuries-old trees. But, despite worldwide paranoia about a Y2K meltdown, Parisians took to the streets to watch the Eiffel Tower countdown to the new Millennium without incident.

Paris Today

Most of the important changes in Paris over recent years are due to efforts by the new Socialist mayor **Bertrand Delanoë** to improve the quality of life for average Parisians. Some of his most successful projects include *Paris Plage*, a beach set up on the banks of the Seine in summer, and the elimination of entrance fees to the municipal museums' permanent collections. He also cut down on traffic and pollution by increasing the numbers of bus and bike lanes, constructing a new tramway, and banning coaches from parking on the Ile de la Cité. Expect to see more improvements over the coming years as Paris puts in a bid to host the 2012 Olympic Games.

The State

National Government

Since the 1789 Revolution brought an end to the French monarchy, the people of France have lived through five republics, two imperial dictatorships, and several experiments in government. The current regime, called the Fifth Republic, was born in 1958 after the Fourth Republic crumbled under the pressures of the Algerian War for Independence. Parliament lured back WWII Résistance hero Charles de Gaulle into a leadership role along with a new constitution offering the President enormous executive powers. He (and, so far, it's always a "he") appoints the Prime Minister and the Council of Ministers, and can dissolve the National Assembly and call for new elections at any time. If that's not enough, the President is also the Commander-in-Chief of the armed forces and has the right to impose dictatorial rule in times of national crisis. With enough pull to carry out personal pet projects, the presidents of the Fifth Republic (notably Mitterrand) have left their marks on the city much in the same fashion as the great French kings, with grandiose architectural and technological projects. Chosen directly by popular vote, the President serves for a five-year term (changed from a seven-year term in 2000), and can be re-elected once.

The Parliament consists of two houses. The lower house – the directly elected **National Assembly** – has 577 members, who serve five-year terms. The Assembly is more powerful than the indirectly elected **Senate**, whose 321 members serve nine-year terms. The Prime Minister's main job is to direct and carry out government policy. Although he is appointed by the President, he answers to the National Assembly, and therefore the President must appoint a Prime Minister of the same political party as the Assembly majority in order to ensure the smooth running of the nation. When the Assembly majority and Prime Minister are of a different political party than the President, this is called "cohabitation." This first happened in 1986, and is considered by some a good way to keep the powers of the President in balance with the Parliament.

Local Government

With the seat of national power in Paris, the city's local governing structure had to be set up differently. Local government in France is normally divided into three levels, with mayors running the cities and villages (*communes*), and elected deputies for each *département* making up the regional council. This is how most of the Ile-de-France is run. But Paris is different. From 1871 until 1977 the national government decided to run the city itself instead of through locally elected officials. This wasn't just for the convenience of centralization. The Parisians had a legacy of insurrection against the French state (1830, 1848, and the Commune of 1871) that needed to be kept "under supervision." So the city was given an assembly without any real powers, a prefect for the police, a prefect for the administration, and government appointed "mayors" of each arrondissement. In 1975, when the Parisians seemed relatively well-behaved, the Prime Minister Jacques Chirac used his majority in Parliament to update the rules: Paris finally got to elect its own mayor.

Today the city is divided into 20 arrondissements with locally elected mayors who all answer to the Mayor of Paris. There are three inner suburban départements and four outer départements that, with Paris, make up the eight départements of the Ile-de-France administrative region, governed by an elected assembly.

 DID YOU KNOW? *The city's coat of arms is based on the seal of the* **Waterman's Guild,** *after the union that once controlled river trading on the Seine. It features a boat motif and the motto* Fluctuat nec mergitur – *"She is buffeted by the waves but does not sink."*

Strangely enough, the election of Paris's first mayor was considered by all the political commentators of the time as a "non event" (from the *Express*, March 1977: "Paris mayoral election: nobody cares"). Former Prime Minister Chirac served as mayor in the Hôtel de Ville for 18 years, pretty much writing his own job description since there were no precedents. His right-hand man Jean Tibéri took over the job when Chirac became President in 1995, and suddenly the administration's dirty secrets were discovered: corruption, money laundering, back-room deals and millions of taxpayers' francs unaccounted for. Tibéri suffered the brunt of the punishment while Chirac hid behind his presidential immunity (and even managed to get re-elected). The 2001 election was definitely an "event," as disgusted voters looking for a change turned out in record numbers to elect the city's first Socialist mayor, Bertrand Delanoë, one of France's few openly gay politicians. With strong ties to *Les Verts* (the Green Party), he immediately declared himself an enemy of traffic congestion and added new bus lanes, cycle lanes, and pedestrian-only streets throughout the capital. But he really won over the Parisians when he created a summer beach – with real palms, sand and striped deck chairs – right on the banks of the Seine in August 2002. This has become an annual event copied by cities throughout Europe.

THE INSIDE STORY

If you want to see the French government in action – or just have a look inside the historic buildings – it's free, but you have to plan a bit in advance.

The **National Assembly** meets in the Palais Bourbon (on the Left Bank across from the Pont de la Concorde). Free tours are on Saturdays at 10am, 2pm and 3pm. If you want to watch an Assembly debate, present yourself with passport ID at least a half-hour before the sessions at 33, Quai D'Orsay, 7th (☎ 01 40 63 99 99 (www.assemblee-nat.fr/english), to see if there are any spaces left (a "casual office" dress code is appropriate).

The **Senate** meets at the Palais du Luxembourg (in Luxembourg Gardens) from September through June. Senate debates are open to the public Tuesday through Thursday (call to check the schedule, ☎ 01 42 34 20 01, or see www.senat.fr). For free passes, show up with photo ID at the Senate, 15 Rue Vaugirard, 6th, 10 minutes before the session starts. Look for the sign saying *Accueil* (Welcome). Ask for the English brochure and try to get a seat in the top row or aisle if you want some leg room. With the look of a grand theater, the sessions take place in the red velvet, gold and marble chamber where Napoleon once officiated.

Guided tours of the **Hôtel de Ville** (Town Hall; in the 4th) are offered Mondays at 10:30 am. You need to call the Friday before to reserve a spot, ☎ 42 76 54 04.

The President's residence, **Le Palais de l'Elysée** (on the Champs-Elysées), and the Prime Minister's residence, **L'Hôtel Matignon** (in the 7th), are only open to the public one weekend a year during the *Journées du Patrimoine* in mid-September (see page 38). Get in line early if you want to see the Prime Minister's beautiful gardens! For more information check out the official Paris tourism web site, www.parisbienvenue.com.

The Party System

Marx once called France a "political nation par excellence," and although things have calmed considerably in the past century, the French still enjoy a good shakeup of the system when they think one's needed. The French have thrown out and rewritten their constitution several times over the past two centuries, so there's no strong sense of loyalty to the current regime. Political debate is a cultural sport in France, and any witty attack on politicians or intelligent questioning of the status quo is well-received. And, because they equate political diversity with political freedom, the multi-party system is still going strong.

Major players include the once-powerful French Communist Party, severely weakened since the end of the Cold War; the Socialist Party of the former President François Mitterrand; the conservative *Rassemblement pour la République* (RPR), founded by Charles de Gaulle and now led by President Chirac; and the *Union pour la Démocratie Française* (UDF), a center-right party usually siding with the RPR. Other prominent parties include the Greens, who successfully teamed up with the Socialists for the 2001 mayoral elections, and Jean-Marie Le Pen's far-right party, the National Front. The smaller splinter parties tend to do better in local elections, although the candidate for the *Lutte Ouvrière* won 5% in the 1995 presidential election after running on the same workers' revolutionary platform since 1974.

POLITICS UNUSUAL

Rising crime and unemployment were the hot topics of the 2002 presidential elections, but everyone was still shocked when the "send 'em back" anti-immigration fanatic Le Pen managed to get through to the second round. Having pushed the favored Socialist candidate and outgoing Prime Minister Lionel Jospin into third place (and therefore out of the game), the voters were left to decide between the incumbent Chirac, who was under investigation for corruption during his tenure as mayor, and Le Pen, a xenophobic extremist who had never before been a viable threat in national elections. While millions of anti-Le Pen protestors flooded the streets of Paris, the international press had a field day filming his supporters marching jubilantly through Marseille. Chirac dismissed the National Front victory as a symbolic protest vote, but still adopted some of Le Pen's more popular rhetoric, promising more police on the streets and a tougher stance on crime. The French went back to the polls and Chirac safely won another five years in office.

In recent times, France has faced a serious economic slowdown, with high unemployment fueled by extremely generous and expensive social benefits. Any attempts to reduce some of these cradle-to-grave benefits result in mass strike actions like the one that paralyzed the country for three weeks in 1995. With its fiscal policy under the constant scrutiny of the European Union, many politicians talk about reducing the bloated bureaucracy. But this is never an easy task when almost everyone has a civil servant in their extended family – and benefits accordingly from the connection.

Even closer to home, the residents of Paris and Ile-de-France have had enough of the skyrocketing violent crime rate, a serious shortage of affordable housing, and overcrowded schools and universities. Racial tensions are running high in certain neighborhoods where newly arrived immigrants (some illegal) are competing for scarce jobs. As all of these issues continue to fester, Paris remains the pilgrimage site for the nation's frustrated citizens. The sight of large crowds marching down the streets brandishing banners and chanting slogans is so commonplace that most Parisians don't even look up from reading their papers on the café terrace.

Parisians have been known throughout history to challenge authority by taking to the streets. But when a rowdy demonstration (*manifestation*) doesn't do the trick, a strike (*un grève*) usually does. Call it a mistrust of the democratic process, or just mistrust of politicians, but it gets results. Whether it's public transport workers looking for safer working conditions, farmers blocking the roads to protest EU competition, or even the unemployed claiming a Christmas bonus benefit payment, the government has shown that it's willing to negotiate (the government doesn't dare step in to break up strikes since the events of May '68).

ORIGINS OF A WORD

The French expression for going on strike, *être en grève* (literally, to be on the strand), dates from the 19th century. During this time, laborers out of work used to meet up on the Place de Grève, a boat landing on the Seine (known today as the Place de l'Hôtel de Ville).

The Economy

 It's hard to overemphasize the role of Ile-de-France as the French economic powerhouse. Its eight départements (**Paris**, **Seine/Saint-Denis**, **Val-de-Marne**, **Hauts-de-Seine**, **Val d'Oise**, **Yvelines**, **Essonne**, and **Seine-et-Marne**) represent 25% of France's national income, with the largest concentration of highly skilled professionals and more than half of the corporate headquarters of France's largest companies. The region benefits from its position as the country's transportation hub, with a well developed high-speed TGV rail network, two international airports, several river ports, and a GDP (gross domestic product) per head for Paris 53% higher than the national average.

The Ile-de-France is the country's most important industrial region, with significant telecommunication, pharmaceutical, publishing, research and defense industries. Heavily dominated by the service sector, Paris generates considerable revenues from business and leisure tourism, and leads the world in fashion and luxury goods sales.

DID YOU KNOW? *All of France is divided into* ***regions***, *and within each region are* ***départements***. *Ile-de-France is a region, Paris is a department within it. Only a few cities in France have* ***arrondissements***.

While public spending accounts for over 50% of France's GDP, the French enjoy low-cost healthcare regardless of income and free public education from kindergarten through university. High unemployment (9.7% in 2003) remains the *bête noir* of the French economy, yet the French are wary of reforms that would lower unemployment at the expense of their quality of life, which places family, health and personal happiness before business, wealth and professional success. They work fewer days than most western nations, with an official 35-hour work week, and an average of five weeks paid vacation each year, plus national holidays. They remain competitive with lower salaries and higher rates of productivity per hour than in the US or UK.

People & Culture

Population

Ile-de-France has a population of 11 million, with two million in Paris alone, making it one of the most densely populated areas in the Western world.

Ile-de-France is home to almost half of the country's immigrant population. In the early 20th century these foreigners were mostly Portuguese, Italian, Polish and Spanish, but since the 1960s most of the newcomers are made up of North Africans from the *Maghreb* (Algeria, Morocco, Tunisia), Africans from former colonies (including Polynesia and the Caribbean), Asians (from Vietnam, Laos, Cambodia), and, more recently, Eastern Europeans and Russians.

Religion

France remains a predominantly Roman Catholic country (over 80%), though only 5% regularly attend church. The second-largest religious group is Muslim (6%), with over 25% regular participation. Less than 2% of the population is Protestant or Jewish, and 7% remain unaffiliated.

The Parisian Identity

There's a popular saying, "You'll never be French, but you can be Parisian." Being Parisian is less about where you're born (or even, some may argue, where you live), and more about attitude. For the average Parisian, life may consist of the "Métro-Boulot-Dodo" routine (to the métro, to work, to bed), but even the most insignificant interaction is an opportunity to display their cleverness or cultural prowess. It's a subtle artistry that takes years for newcomers to really comprehend; that elusive *je-ne-sais-quoi*, which makes Parisians different.

■ The Système D

The *Système D* is a perfect example of this. "D" stands for *démerder*, or to get oneself out of sh—. Parisians have adopted this system of urban survival to get through tough spots, whether it's misleading a bureaucrat, going the wrong way down a one-way street, or completely ignoring the No Smoking signs. And the culture rewards this. If someone cuts into the line at a bank in Paris, the locals are thinking, "I wish I'd thought of that," while newcomers become indignant. It's one thing to be rude – New Yorkers are even famous for it – but breaking the rules just isn't tolerable to most Anglophone visitors. But the *Système D* is how things are done in Paris. After four or five Republics, the French know the rules change all the time, so they don't get too wrapped up in them.

■ La Mode

In France there's a certain power in beauty, and all true Parisians are taught to take advantage of this by making the most of their appearance. Even the children look chic. Fashion has been an unmistakable part of the Parisian identity since the 18th century, weaving its way into all corners of society, from the haute-couture fashion houses to the street. Easily identifiable in a crowd, the Parisian is always immaculately groomed and stylish without being obviously trendy – even in Levis jeans and Nike sneakers. Parisians like the practicality of an all-black wardrobe, rarely consider comfort when buying shoes, and have a way with scarves that will forever baffle the rest of the Western world. Every element of the Parisian's wardrobe says something about that person as clearly as if it were a uniform. In a city where personal appearance is so closely scrutinized, it's no wonder most tourists are discovered before they even open their mouths.

■ Language

During the 18th and 19th centuries Paris was considered to be the social, intellectual, and cultural center of the world. One could cynically say this was also the heyday of the French language, when conversation was elevated to an art form in the salons, and the Académie Française was a literary force to be reckoned with. But no matter how many English words creep into their everyday vocabulary, Parisians are still justifiably proud of their language, mastering its ambiguities and nuances to show off their quick wit or subtly poke fun at others with a play on words. Making an effort to speak the language is a show of respect, no matter how badly you've mangled the pronunciation of the *plat du jour*.

■ Sex & Flirting

Despite the city's worldwide reputation for its liberal attitudes toward sex, visitors still manage to look positively shocked when they first arrive. Full frontal nudity (male and female) is everywhere, from the endlessly repeating métro billboards to prime-time television. For Parisians, sexual innuendo is a welcome part of everyday life. Flirting is an art of mutual flattery (not necessarily a come-on) practiced everywhere from the corner café to the boardroom. The cultural nuances that signal when flirting becomes – well, more – are often unrecognized by newcomers, and the reason behind so many misunderstandings. When it comes to sex, nothing is shocking. Sexual tell-alls by prominent members of society are common, and no one bats an eye if a married politician happens to frequent one of the city's many *échangiste* swingers' clubs. Puritans may cluck in disgust, but one of the most admirable byproducts of this sexual liberty is the sexy older woman. There's nothing more refreshing than seeing a wrinkled, yet confident, woman in her 60s turn heads as she walks down the street.

■ The Youth Culture

Being young in France is hard work. From a very young age students are given hours of homework every night, and there's a lot more emphasis on academic progress than on extra-curricular activities up through university level. Unlike in America, where many look back with nostalgia on their carefree teenage years, French teens can't wait to get out in the world. Once they've done their time in school, they're free to enjoy themselves, knowing the French system practically guarantees them job security for life.

Contemporary French Culture

Paris was considered to be the height of the civilized world in the 19th and early 20th centuries. After barely surviving the effects of German occupation in WWII, the French have been striving to return Paris to its former cultural glory. A generous state-funded arts and music scene dominates the agenda, with performing arts such as opera, theater and dance making the most waves in international circles. There's also a thriving urban underground scene of artists' squats (the term refers to empty buildings that are illegally occupied for living or working quarters; see page 200. Many are legalized *de facto* by the government), and popular graffiti artists whose creations have been displayed in the city's contemporary art museums and galleries.

Public artworks and architecture plays an important role in shaping the Parisian cityscape. Perhaps taking a cue from their great kings and emperors, recent French presidents have put their cultural mark on Paris by commissioning bold monuments such as the Pompidou Center, La Grande Arche de la Défense, the Bibliothèque Nationale-François Mitterrand, and the Musée du Quai Branly, currently under construction near the Eiffel Tower.

Parisian fashion and cuisine fell into a period of stagnation in the late 20th century, getting by on reputation alone until international competition forced designers and restaurants to evolve with the times or get out of the way. Today they're back in form, with top *couture* houses recruiting their artistic directors from abroad and the newly *en vogue* Paris bistro scene offering fresh and innovative cooking at affordable prices.

RECOMMENDED READING

Paris: Capital of the World, by Patrice Higonnet (translated by Arthur Goldhammer; Harvard University Press, 2002)

France in the New Century: Portrait of a Changing Society, by John Ardagh (Penguin, 2000)

The French Exception, by Andrew Jack (Profile Books, 2000)

■ Cultural Paradoxes

In the face of globalization, cultural watchdogs have gone on the defensive, enacting protectionist measures to prevent American culture from dominating their cinemas and radio waves (sheep farmer José Bové became a hero when he demolished a McDonald's being built in the French countryside). But, despite a widespread demonizing of American pop culture, average Parisians still line up to see the latest Hollywood trash and buy Happy Meals for their kids. French television, once the bastion of serious cultural and political talk shows (that nobody watched), is now dominated by reality TV shows that attract record numbers of viewers despite their questionable cultural merit. And even though

EuroDisney (now known as Disneyland Paris) was criticized by the French when it opened in 1992, they now make up over 70% of the park's visitors. Things have calmed a bit since the cross-Atlantic popularity of French films like *Amélie* and music groups like Air have shown that globalization can work both ways.

The Land

Located in the center of northern France, the Ile-de-France (which means *Island of France*) first got its name back in the 14th century, and consisted of the land mass bound by the Seine, Oise, and Marne rivers and their tributaries. Its name also invoked the symbolic importance of Ile-de-France as the cultural, economic and royal capital of the nation. Today the Ile-de-France département extends far past these original physical borders to cover an area of 4,660 square miles.

At its center is the fertile Paris basin where the Oise and Marne join the Seine. The Ile-de-France is relatively flat, with rolling hills that never surpass 650 feet in elevation, and numerous valleys and wetlands carved out by the rivers. Urbanization has replaced the vineyards and forests in Paris but, once you get past the ring of suburban highrises, Ile-de-France is mostly forests and farmland, punctuated by a few villages and urban centers.

Climate

 Ile-de-France has a temperate climate for the most part, with rare extreme temperatures or high winds. July and August are the hottest months, with average highs of 78°F. January and February are the coldest, with average lows of 32°F. Of course, these are just averages. It's not uncommon to have a few days in the low 90s or high 50s in the summer, or a light snow during the winter. Paris tends to be a bit warmer than Ile-de-France, especially in the summer. The traditional rainy season is late spring, with another peak in October, but almost every year over the past decade has been an "exception" to this rule. It's always best to check multiple forecasts before packing, and remember the traveler's mantra: layer, layer, layer...

A WORD TO
THE WISE

TIP: *To convert Celsius to Fahrenheit, see the conversion chart on page 70, or just remember that (°C x 1.8) + 32 = °F, so 20°C = 68°F.*

■ Natural Disasters

The Storm of the Century

On December 26, 1999 a great storm hit France. In just 90 minutes, Paris lost over 150,000 trees in its parks and gardens, and the gardens of Versailles were devastated. Most of the fallen trees were immediately cleared away, but some in the Bois de Boulogne and Bois de Vincennes were left to provide habitat for wildlife and to protect seedlings from pedestrian traffic. The loss of many taller canopy trees meant these seedlings were virtually burned to death during the heatwave that followed a few years later.

The Heat Wave Of The Millennium

A deadly heat wave suffocated Ile-de-France in August 2003, with 10 days of temperatures above 95°F. Since few buildings were equipped with air conditioning, an estimated 15,000 elderly and chronically ill people died from the stifling conditions.

In addition, after months of drought, many of the region's trees dropped their leaves during the 10 days of temperatures over 95°F. Urban parks had to be closed for safety reasons as the branches on older trees dried up and crashed to the ground. Hundreds had to be cut down by the end of the month. The saddest loss was Marie-Antoinette's favorite tree, an oak planted in the gardens of Versailles in 1681.

Flora & Fauna

■ Forests & Parks

Ile-de-France was once covered with deciduous forests consisting primarily of beeches and oaks. Cultivation over the past five centuries, though, either for agricultural purposes or to create hunting grounds for the French kings, has wiped out any virgin woods. The kings were in fact the first conservationists, carefully managing the wildlife populations and replanting damaged areas of the forests with a variety of indigenous and imported seedlings.

The need to protect the natural heritage of the region was recognized as early as the 19th century, when botanists and natural scientists began documenting the different flora and fauna populations. Today, the surviving forests of Ile-de-France are protected within three **National Parks**: *La Vallée de Chevreuse* to the west, *Le Vexin* to the north, and *Le Gâtinais* to the south. These parks, managed by the Office National des Forêts (www.onf.fr), also preserve traditional country activities such as farming as well as the architectural heritage of its many châteaux and historic villages.

Introduction

AUTHOR'S NOTE: *Learn more about the unique characteristics of National Park forests such as* **Fontainebleau** *and* **Rambouillet** *in the* Outside Paris *chapter, pages 359 and 393.*

Today the region's forests are made up of over 80 indigenous and imported tree species, including many varieties of oak and pine, as well as beech, silver birch, hornbeam, chestnut, and linden trees. Heathers, wild broom and ferns cover the forest floor. Locals often spend weekends in the summer and fall collecting wild fruits, nuts and mushrooms from the forests. Blackberries, blueberries, wild strawberries, red currants, wild apples, plums, chestnuts, hazelnuts, mushrooms and linden flowers (for tea) are commonly found throughout Ile-de-France.

ATTENTION! *There are over three dozen varieties of mushroom in the region, but some of them are deadly. To avoid being poisoned, be sure to take your pickings (top and stem intact) to the nearest pharmacy. French pharmacists are trained to identify and distinguish the edible types from the poisonous ones.*

■ Urban Green Spaces

The earliest Parisians lived on and around the Ile de la Cité. As the population grew, the marshes along the river were drained (such as in the Marais) and the hillside vineyards and farms (such as Montmartre, Passy and the Champs-Elysées) were replaced by urbanization. The city's green spaces today consist of the formal, cultivated gardens that once belonged to royal residences (such as the Tuileries and Luxembourg gardens), cemeteries (particularly Père Lachaise) and urban parks created in former quarries or industrial lands (such as the Buttes-Chaumont and André Citroën parks). The city also maintains its famous tree-lined boulevards, with chestnut, plane and elm trees. The former royal hunting grounds in the Bois de Boulogne and Bois de Vincennes are the only forests within the city, although these have been broken up with parks and gardens, sports fields and race tracks, as well as roads open to traffic.

Interpretive Walks

Nature & Découvertes, known for their popular nature stores throughout France, also organize regular interpretive walks (*animations pédagogiques*) in Paris and Ile-de-France. Themes include birdwatching in the Bois de Vincennes, tracking deer and wild boar in the forest of Montmorency, and observing the winter migratory populations in the marshes of the Marne. They're in French only, and cost about

€5 (you need to bring your own binoculars and boots). To see a detailed schedule visit their web site, www.natureetdecouvertes.com.

📖 *For detailed information about the flora and fauna within Paris, check out the* Sentier-Nature *guides. Created by the city's Department of Parks and Gardens, there's a detailed map-guide for each of the 20 arrondissements, the Bois de Boulogne and the Bois de Vincennes (in French; €0.75 each). They can be purchased at the Maison Paris-Nature in the Parc Floral (Bois de Vincennes, 12th), the Maison de l'Air (Parc de Belleville, 20th), or the Chai de Bercy (wine storehouse, Parc de Bercy, 12th).*

■ Wildlife

The wolves and bears that once roamed the forests of Ile-de-France had been eliminated by the 19th century, but native species of deer, stag, roebucks and wild boar have been reintroduced. The best time to see them is at dawn or dusk. Other forest critters include squirrels, bats, foxes and badgers. These can sometimes be seen near larger parks within Paris, although you're more likely to see the occasional métro rat.

DID YOU KNOW? *Hunting (*la chasse*) is still the most popular method for keeping deer and wild boar populations under control. The hunting season is from September through March (except on Wednesdays). There are usually signs posted to indicate that a hunt is underway, but be sure to ask at local tourism or national park offices to be sure.*

There are over 280 species of birds in Ile-de-France, including warblers, swallows, woodpeckers and – especially in urban areas – pigeons and turtledoves. The lakes and marshes are inhabited by ducks, herons, cranes and swans, as well as winter migratory species from Northern Europe. Owls and kestrels are often spotted in bell towers throughout Paris, and larger birds of prey such as falcons and hawks can be observed in semi-liberty at the wild animal preserve, *l'Espace Rambouillet* (see the *Outside Paris* chapter, page 401).

The Seine

The Seine used to be heavily polluted, with many factories dumping their waste directly into the river. By the 1950s there were only four or five species of fish left. Strict environmental regulations and water treatment technology have cleaned up the river, and today there are over three dozen species of fish (mostly silver carp, catfish, pike perch, eels, rainbow trout and perch) and an abundance of aquatic birds and plants. The Seine is still used by commercial shipping barges, although most of the boats passing under the scenic bridges of Paris are pleasure craft – such as sightseeing or dinner cruises.

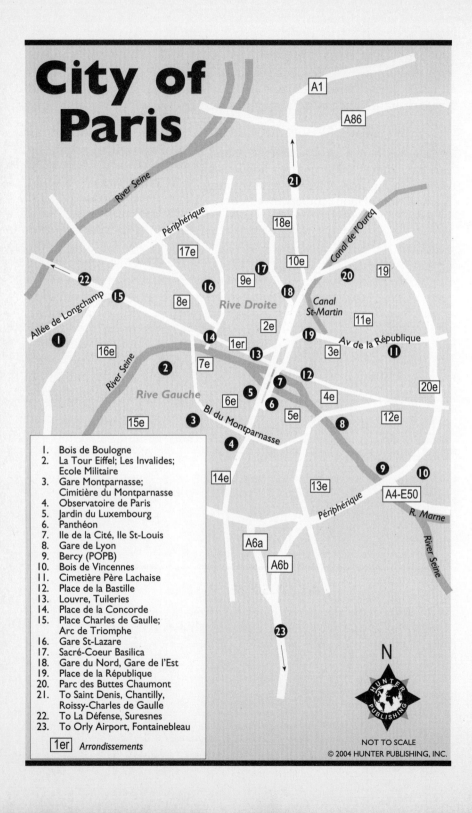

City of Paris

A1

A86

River Seine

Périphérique

21

18e

17e

10e

Canal de l'Ourcq

9e

17

16

8e

20

19

18

Rive Droite

Canal St-Martin

15

22

Allée de Longchamp

1

2e

11e

19

3e

Av de la République

11

14

1er

13

16e

River Seine

2

7e

7

12

20e

Rive Gauche

6e

5

4e

3

6

5e

8

12e

Bl du Montparnasse

4

15e

9

10

14e

13e

A4-E50

R. Marne

Périphérique

A6a

River Seine

A6b

23

1. Bois de Boulogne
2. La Tour Eiffel; Les Invalides;
    Ecole Militaire
3. Gare Montparnasse;
    Cimitière du Montparnasse
4. Observatoire de Paris
5. Jardin du Luxembourg
6. Panthéon
7. Ile de la Cité, Ile St-Louis
8. Gare de Lyon
9. Bercy (POPB)
10. Bois de Vincennes
11. Cimitière Père Lachaise
12. Place de la Bastille
13. Louvre, Tuileries
14. Place de la Concorde
15. Place Charles de Gaulle;
    Arc de Triomphe
16. Gare St-Lazare
17. Sacré-Coeur Basilica
18. Gare du Nord, Gare de l'Est
19. Place de la République
20. Parc des Buttes Chaumont
21. To Saint Denis, Chantilly,
    Roissy-Charles de Gaulle
22. To La Défense, Suresnes
23. To Orly Airport, Fontainebleau

1er *Arrondissements*

N

HUNTER PUBLISHING

NOT TO SCALE
© 2004 HUNTER PUBLISHING, INC.

Planning Your Trip

When To Go

Early fall, known as *la rentrée*, is when Parisians come back from their holidays and the performing arts season starts up again. It's also a time of many important conferences and trade fairs, so book hotel rooms well in advance. November and December can be quite festive as the holiday lights go up around the city and department stores try to outdo each

other with elaborate window displays. It's a time of crowded Christmas markets and ice-skating rinks, nativity scenes in the cathedrals and New Year's Eve feasting. January and February are the coldest months, and the parks and gardens can be quite dreary. But hotel prices are at their lowest, and visitors will enjoy a little more breathing room in the city's museums and monuments. And it's no surprise that Paris is a popular Valentine's Day destination! The weather in spring can be unpredictable, but the city is still relatively uncrowded, apart from the week of Easter vacation (which should be avoided, if possible).

May through October is the best time to visit for anyone hoping to enjoy the many outdoor activities that Ile-de-France has to offer. During these months the countryside is at its best and all of the major attractions are open. Every season has its pros and cons, however, so the best advice is to balance the activities with the season. Summer can be stifling in the city center, so cooking classes in August are out of the question, and winter can be harsh in the small country villages, so forget about spending all day browsing the outdoor markets.

AUGUST IN PARIS

August can be the best and the worst time to visit Paris. It's usually the hottest month of the year, and air conditioning is still an exception to the rule (especially on public transportation). It's the time when most Parisians head for the country, so many smaller shops and restaurants close for the entire month. On the plus side there's less traffic and a more laid-back atmosphere. Many hotels offer special deals in August, and it's the perfect weather to enjoy events such as *Paris Plage* on the Seine.

Celebrations

■ Cultural Events

 Major annual celebrations include the **Chinese New Year** (January/February), with parades in the 13th and 3rd arrondissements; the **Fête de la Musique** (June 21), a 24-hour musical festival throughout France; the **Journées du Patrimoine** (third weekend in September), when France's museums, monuments and state-owned buildings are open to the public for free; the **Nuit Blanche** (first Saturday in October), an all-night culture festival in Paris; and the **Fête du Beaujolais Nouveau** (third Thursday in November) to celebrate the arrival of the first wine of the season. **Halloween** finally crept into the French culture in the late 1990s (they like to focus on the Celtic roots of the holiday), so it's no longer a surprise to see little Parisians decked out in their ghoulish gear as they go trick-or-treating through the city's neighborhoods. See the *Entertainment* section, page 299, for the calendar of annual sporting events and music festivals.

■ Legal & Religious Holidays

Most museums and many shops are closed on these days, called *jours fériés*. When a holiday falls on a Sunday, such as Easter and Pentecost, the legal holiday is on the following Monday.

ANNUAL HOLIDAYS

Nouvel An (New Year's Day) . . . . January 1

Lundi de Pâques (Easter Monday). . . . . . March or April

Fête du Travail (Labor Day) . . . . May 1

Jour de la Victoire (VE-Day WWII). . . . . May 8

Ascension . . . . 6th Thursday after Easter

Pentecôte (Pentecost) . . . . . 2nd Monday after Ascension

Fête Nationale (Bastille Day) . . . . July 14

Assomption . . . . August 15

Toussaint (All Soul's Day) . . . . November 1

Armistice. . . . . November 11

Noël (Christmas) . . . . December 25

Documentation

Passports & Visas

All non-French nationals need a valid passport to enter France. American, Canadian, Australian, New Zealand, and European Union (EU) nationals don't need visas for visits of under 90 days. A long-term visa (*carte de séjour*) is necessary for non-EU citizens staying longer than three months. Get this from the French Consulate in your country of residence prior to departure (be sure to plan ahead, some paperwork takes several weeks). For French consular offices in the US, go to www.info-france-usa.org/intheus/consulates, and search for your state or city. For international locations of French embassies, you can check listings online at www.embassyworld.com/embassy/france1. The web site of the Ministry of Foreign Affairs is www.france.diplomatie.fr/mae (select English from the language choices at the top).

Travel Insurance

Although not required, traveler's insurance is always a good idea. Shop around, since there are many different policies to suit all budgets and needs. Minimum coverage should include trip delays or cancellation (especially if you have purchased non-refundable tickets), lost luggage reimbursement, health coverage and emergency assistance. Be sure to ask if you'll be reimbursed for flights missed due to strikes, which occur frequently in France. Check the fine print on your credit card policy, since many offer insurance coverage on travel purchases (including flights and hotel) for cancellations or lost luggage. French doctors and hospitals don't require patients to have medical insurance, but all bills must be settled immediately.

FOR EU RESIDENTS ONLY

Ask for a "European Form E.111" from your local social security office before leaving home. This allows you to get partially reimbursed for any medical costs, including prescriptions, during your stay in France.

Tourist Information

i The **Paris Convention & Visitors Bureau** (25-27 Rue des Pyramydes, 1st, M° Pyramides, ☎ 08 92 68 30 00, www.paris-touristoffice.com) has a bilingual web site with practical information, current event listings, and basic information for museums, nightlife, shopping, children's amusements, and transportation. Unfortunately, it costs € 0.34/minute to call within France, and it takes an average of three minutes just to get to a human being on the other side. They have smaller offices, or Bureaux d'Accueil (welcome centers) around the city.

AUTHOR'S NOTE: *For basic vocabulary and useful phrases, see the* Glossary, *page 433.*

Bureau d'Accueil Gare de Lyon: M° Gare de Lyon, Boulevard Diderot, open Monday through Saturday, 8am to 6pm. Tourist information, last-minute accommodation assistance, transport and museum-pass sales 20.

Bureau d'Accueil Gare du Nord: M° Gare du Nord, 18 Rue de Dunkerque, beneath the glass roof in the section of the station dedicated to Ile-de-France trains; open daily, 12:30pm to 8pm. Tourist information, last-minute accommodation assistance, transport and museum pass sales, and bookings for shows or excursions.

Bureau d'Accueil Opéra-Grands Magasins: 11 Rue Scribe, 9th, M° Opéra or RER Auber, open Monday through Saturday, 9am to 6:30pm. Tourist information, last-minute accommodation assistance, transport and museum pass sales, and bookings for shows or excursions. Located in the same building as American Express.

Bureau d'Accueil Tour Eiffel: Between the East and North Pillars, M° Bir-Hakeim; open daily, May through September, 11am to 6:40pm. Tourist information only.

The **Ile-de-France Regional Tourism Office** (Carrousel du Louvre, 99 Rue de Rivoli, 1st, M° Palais-Royal/Musée du Louvre, ☎ 08 26 16 66 66 or 01 44 50 19 98, www.francekeys.com/english/region/ile_de_france) provides information for the entire Ile-de-France département, including Paris, Versailles, and Rambouillet, and can sell transportation and museum passes. Open daily, 10am to 7pm.

The **Maison de la France** (www.franceguide.com/prehome.asp) is the country's official tourism office, with locations all over the world. Check out their web site for the latest promotions, practical information and to request brochures. This is a good resource for visitors who will be traveling throughout France, or those who simply want to keep up with the latest cultural news and events. Select the appropriate country from the listing for specific information.

Getting Here

By Air

■ Airports

There are two international airports serving Paris, Roissy-Charles de Gaulle Airport and the smaller Paris-Orly Airport. Both offer full services such as car rental, public transportation links to Paris, tourist information kiosks, shopping, dining, business center, police, hotels, post office, news agents and currency exchange. For detailed information and maps of the terminals see the **Aéroports de Paris** multilingual web site, www.adp.fr/webadp/a, and click on "Welcome." Flight information for both airports (€0.34/minute), ☎ 08 92 68 15 15.

> **TIP:** *To call France from the US or Canada, dial* ☎ *011 and 33 for France, then the telephone number.*

Roissy-Charles de Gaulle

Located 15 miles north of Paris on the A1 motorway, Roissy-Charles de Gaulle (☎ 01 48 62 22 80) is the country's largest airport, with two international terminals (CDG1 & CDG2) and one charter terminal (CDG3, formerly known as T-9).

Paris-Orly

Nine miles south of Paris on the A6 motorway, Orly Airport (switchboard, ☎ 01 49 75 52 52) is the country's second-largest airport, with one international terminal (Orly Ouest) and one charter terminal (Orly Sud).

> **AUTHOR'S NOTE:** *The food available at the Paris airports is surprisingly unappealing and overpriced. Either plan on having a nice (but pricey) meal in one of the few upscale restaurants (such as **Brasserie Flo** at Roissy-CDG 2 or **Maxim's de Paris** at Orly Ouest), or look for one of the **Boulangerie Paul** carts for decent baked snacks to go. Those on their way home can even bring along a last picnic lunch from the open markets in Paris to eat before departure.*

■ International Airlines

All telephone numbers listed are for calls from the US, except where noted. Check online for international information.

Air France. . . . . ☎ 800-237-2747, 800-237-2747

American Airlines . . . . ☎ 800-433-7300

Continental . . . . ☎ 800-231-0856

Delta . . . . ☎ 800-241-4141

Northwest . . . . ☎ 800-447-4747

United . . . . ☎ 800-538-2929

US Airways . . . . ☎ 800-428-4322

Air Canada . . . . ☎ 888-247-2262

British Airways (US/Canada) . . . . ☎ 800-403-0882

British Airways (UK) . . . . ☎ 0870-850-9850

British Midland (BMI; UK). . . . . ☎ 0870-607-0555

Virgin Atlantic (US) . . . . ☎ 800-862-8621

Virgin Atlantic (UK). . . . . ☎ 01293-450-150

Aer Lingus (Ireland) . . . . ☎ 0818-365-000

Aer Lingus (US/Canada) . . . . ☎ 800-474-7424

Aer Lingus (UK) . . . . ☎ 0845-084-4444

KLM (US/Canada) . . . . ☎ 800-447-4747

KLM (UK) . . . . ☎ 0870-507-4074

Lufthansa (US) . . . . ☎ 800-399-5838

Lufthansa (Canada). . . . . ☎ 800-563-5954

Qantas (Australia) . . . . ☎ 13-13-13

Qantas (New Zealand). . . . . ☎ 0800-808-767

■ Regional Airlines

Several discount budget airlines offer no-frills flights between Paris airports and the UK, and only accept reservations on their web sites. Budget airlines come and go all the time in Europe, so keep an eye out for new regional routes to Paris airports on the web.

EasyJet . . . . www.easyjet.com

BMI Baby . . . . www.bmibaby.com

FlyBE . . . . www.flybe.com

■ Discount Travel

It's always worth checking around online to get the best deal on flights to Paris. These are just a few of the many web sites that search for the cheapest prices on major airlines.

- **CheapTickets.com**: Flights from the US and Canada
- **Expedia.com**: Flights from the US, Canada, and the UK
- **Orbitz.com**: Flights from the US
- **Travel.com**: Portal site for flights from the US, Canada, UK, Australia, and New Zealand
- **Opodo.com**: Flights from the UK
- **LastMinute.com**: Portal site for flights from the UK, Australia, and New Zealand

Getting Around

To the City

■ From The Airports

By Taxi & Limo

Licensed taxis can be found lined up outside each terminal. Don't ever accept a ride from anyone who approaches you inside the airport. An average journey during the day and in regular traffic will cost about €40-45 between Paris and Roissy-CDG, €20-30 between Paris and Orly, and €50-55 between Orly and Roissy-CDG. Night rates are slightly higher. Luggage costs an additional €0.90 per suitcase, and for more than three passengers there's a surcharge of €2.60 each. The trip between either airport and Paris with **Airport Limo Services** (☎ 01 40 71 84 62) starts at €100. See page 53 for taxi company listings.

By Shuttle

Shared airport shuttles offer door-to-door service and special rates for multiple travelers. It's absolutely necessary to make reservations at least 48 hours in advance, whether you're arriving or leaving. French hotels don't typically have their own shuttles, but the concierge can usually arrange one on request.

Bee-Shuttle (www.beeshuttle.com), ☎ 01 53 11 01 25. Service daily to all airports 7am to 8pm. Rates €24 for one adult passenger, €14.50 each for two to six adults, €13.50 each for seven or eight adults, and €8 for kids ages seven to 12, free for kids under seven. Pay by cash or credit card on arrival.

Paris Shuttle (www.parisshuttle.com), ☎ 01 53 39 18 18. Service daily to both airports from 7am to 8pm. Rates €25 for one adult passenger, €18 each for two to four adults, €15 each for five to eight adults, and €10 each for kids ages three to 10.

Airport Associate Shuttle (www.airportshuttleparis.com), ☎ 01 58 34 01 26. Service daily to both airports. Rates €20 for one passenger, €13.50 each for two or three, €13 each for four or five, €12.50 each for six to eight. Credit cards accepted on board.

The **Blue Vans** (www.airportshuttle.fr), ☎ 01 30 11 13 00, 0800 BLU VAN. From Roissy-CDG only to Paris 6:15am to 7:30pm; Paris to Roissy-CDG from 4am to 6:30pm. Rates €22 for one passenger, €14.50 each for two or more. Kids under age three ride for free.

By Bus

From Roissy-CDG

 The **RoissyBus (RATP)** has daily service from 6am to 11pm between Roissy-Charles de Gaulle Terminal 2 and the Opéra Garnier (Rue Scribe, in front of the American Express Office, métro Opéra) with departures every 15 to 20 minutes, travel time about one hour. One-way tickets are €8.20 (*Carte Orange* or *Mobilis* zone 5 passes accepted), which can be purchased on the bus, at the airport, or in métro stations in Paris.

The **Cars Air France** (www.carsairfrance.fr), open to passengers of all airlines, are more expensive but have more drop-off/pickup points in Paris. There's regular service from Roissy-CDG to Paris-Orly Airport (every 30 minutes from 6am to 10:30pm, tickets €15.50, €7.75 for kids ages two to 11), to Porte Maillot and the Arc de Triomphe (every 15 minutes from 6am to 11pm, tickets €10, €17 round-trip, €5 for kids ages two to 11), or to Gare de Lyon and Gare de Montparnasse (every 30 minutes from 7am to 9pm, tickets €11.50, €19.55 round-trip, €5.75 for kids ages two to 11). Travel time is approximately 50 minutes.

The **Bus de Nuit** (www.busdenuit.com) offers luxury coach service nightly from 11:40pm to 6am. **Line 1.2** runs between Châtelet (at 90 Rue de Rivoli, 1st) and Roissy-CDG via the Gare du Nord every 30 minutes, tickets €8 (*Carte Orange* or *Mobilis* zone 5 passes accepted). Travel time is approximately 50 minutes.

ATTENTION! *There are five zones for the whole of Paris, with zones 1 and 2 corresponding to the city and some of the nearby suburbs. Make sure you know what zone you are traveling to when you purchase your métro, bus or RER train ticket.*

TRANSPORTATION PASSES

Get around Paris like a Parisian with a **Carte Orange Hebdomadaire** (*hebdomadaire* means weekly) pass, valid for a week of unlimited travel on the métro, bus, tram, and RER. A Carte Orange for zones 1-2 (Paris and immediate suburbs) is €14.50, or €28.90 for zones 1-5 (Paris, much of Ile-de-France, and both airports). You'll receive a plastic holder with your ticket (*coupon*), a mini map, and an orange card with a serial number. Stick your passport-sized photo onto the card (if you didn't bring an extra one, pop into a photo booth in almost any métro station, or have one made on the spot in a photo shop) and copy the serial number from the orange card onto your ticket immediately. The ticket isn't valid without the card. If you have any problems getting through the turnstiles, ask for assistance at the nearest ticket window (the card has unlimited use, but can only go through the same turnstile once to prevent groups from using the same card).

Another option is the **Carte Mobilis**, good for unlimited travel on the RATP network for one day. It costs €5.20 for zone 1-2, €8.75 for zone 1-4, and €12 for zone 1-5. This can be economical if you only need unlimited travel for one or two days.

From Paris-Orly

The **OrlyBus (RATP)** has daily service from 6am to 11:30pm between Paris-Orly and Denfert-Rochereau (outside the RER/métro station) with departures every 15 to 20 minutes. One-way tickets are €5.70 (*Carte Orange* or *Mobilis* zone 4 passes accepted), which can be purchased on the bus, at the airport, or in métro stations in Paris. Travel time is about 30 minutes. If your Paris accommodation is in the 13th or 14th arrondissements, ask the driver about the additional drop-off and pick-up points in these districts (or pick up the OrlyBus brochure at the RATP ticket desk at the airport).

The **Cars Air France** (www.carsairfrance.fr) has regular service from Paris-Orly to Roissy-CDG Airport (every 30 minutes from 6am to 10:30pm, tickets €15.50, €7.75 for kids ages two to 11; travel time is approximately 50 minutes) and between Paris-Orly, Les Invalides, and Gare de Montparnasse (every 15 minutes from 6am to 11pm, tickets €7.50, €12.75 round-trip, €3.75 for kids ages two to 11).

The **Bus de Nuit-Line 1** (www.busdenuit.com) runs nightly between Châtelet (at 90 Rue de Rivoli, 1st) and Paris-Orly via the Gare de Lyon and Place d'Italie every 30 minutes from 11:40pm to 6am, tickets €6 (*Carte Orange* or *Mobilis* zone 4 passes accepted). Travel time is approximately 25 minutes.

By Train

From Roissy-CDG

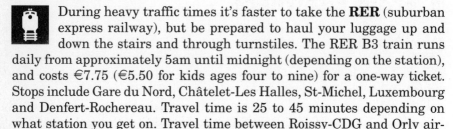 During heavy traffic times it's faster to take the **RER** (suburban express railway), but be prepared to haul your luggage up and down the stairs and through turnstiles. The RER B3 train runs daily from approximately 5am until midnight (depending on the station), and costs €7.75 (€5.50 for kids ages four to nine) for a one-way ticket. Stops include Gare du Nord, Châtelet-Les Halles, St-Michel, Luxembourg and Denfert-Rochereau. Travel time is 25 to 45 minutes depending on what station you get on. Travel time between Roissy-CDG and Orly airport on the RER B is 40 minutes, and costs €16.35.

TIME-SAVING TIP

Some RERs are express to the airport, and others stop at every town along the way. You may get there sooner if you skip the slow train and wait for the next fast one. Check the monitors on the platform to see if all of the stops are lit up for the next train, or just the last few stops, including the airport.

From Paris-Orly

The **Orly-Val** has the most reliable and regular service to Orly Airport, combining the **RER B4** and **Val** monorail to both terminals (take the RER train as far as Antony, then transfer to the monorail). It runs daily, with departures every four minutes from 6am to 11pm, between Antony-Orly and Paris (including Gare du Nord, Châtelet-Les Halles, St-Michel, Luxembourg and Denfert-Rochereau). Approximate travel time between Châtelet-Les Halles and Orly is 35 minutes, tickets are €8.80 (€4.35 for kids ages four to 10), zone 4 transport passes are accepted. Travel time from Orly to Roissy-CDG airport on the RER B train is 55 minutes, and costs €16.35.

The **RER C** train also has service to Orly airport, combining **RER C2** with a **free ADP shuttle**. It runs daily every 15 minutes from 5:30am to 10pm, between Pont de Rungis-Aéroport d'Orly and Paris (stations include Gare d'Austerlitz, St-Michel, Invalides, Javel and Port Maillot).

Travel time is about 40 minutes between Invalides and Orly, one-way tickets cost €5.25. Zone 4 transport passes are accepted.

A WORD TO
THE WISE

TIP: *The best way to get into Paris is to take any of the airport buses into town, then proceed to the hotel by taxi or the nearest métro. The RER train is faster, but can be cumbersome with luggage and unsafe late at night. Families or small groups of travelers may find private airport shuttles to be the most economical.*

■ From Elsewhere

By Train

Paris is at the center of Europe's high-speed train (**TGV**) network, accessible from every corner of France and cities throughout Europe. The **Eurostar** (☎ 08 36 35 35 39, www.eurostar.com) connects the Paris Gare du Nord to London through the Channel Tunnel, and **Thalys** (☎ 08 36 35 35 36, www.thalys.com) connects Paris, Roissy-CDG and Disneyland Paris to cities in Germany, Belgium and the Netherlands.

The six **international train stations** in Paris are the Gare de l'Est (10th), Gare du Nord (10th), Gare Montparnasse (15th), Gare St-Lazare (9th), Gare de Lyon (12th) and the Gare d'Austerlitz (13th). These are connected to the bus, métro and RER networks for quick transfers throughout Paris. Each station provides services such as car rental, baggage lockers, taxis, currency conversion, cash machines, shops and cafés. For general queries contact the French rail company, **SNCF**, ☎ 01 53 90 20 20. For ticketing information from within France, ☎ 08 36 35 35 35, €0.34/minute.

By Coach

The main international bus station is on the edge of the city's 20th arrondissement, at the **Gare Routière Internationale de Paris-Gallieni** (28 Avenue du Général de Gaulle, Bagnolet, M° Gallieni, ☎ 08 36 69 52 52). **Eurolines** (55 Rue St-Jacques, 5th, M° St-Michel, ☎ 01 43 54 11 99, www.eurolines.com), provides regular service between Paris and 28 European countries.

In the City

Paris and Ile-de-France benefit from an excellent public transportation network connecting the métro, RER, regional trains, trams and buses. And with so many bike lanes and inexpensive taxi fares within the city, using a car in Paris is unnecessary and impractical. Ideally, visitors should only need a car to explore the rest of Ile-de-France. Although most major sights outside Paris can be reached by train or RER, a car offers more freedom to discover the countryside.

> **AUTHOR'S NOTE:** *See* Getting Oriented, *page 71, for information about getting around on foot in the city.*

■ By Métro & RER

Routes

The **Paris Métropolitan** (métro) is one of the most efficient and user-friendly subway systems in the world. Its 14 primary lines and two *bis* (secondary or connecting) lines crisscross the city and the immediate suburbs daily from 5:45am to 12:30am, with connections to the RER and international train stations. Each line is designated by a number and its terminus points (e.g., *Line 1: Château de Vincennes-La Défense*). Most stations can be reached with one or two changes at the most. Maps are posted in métro cars, on platforms (*quais*), and next to ticket windows. You can also ask for a free métro map (*un plan*) from any ticket agent.

> **TIP:** *The term "bis" means "secondary," and has two uses. It can refer either to a secondary métro line, as described above, or to a second building or occupant at one street address, as in "1bis Avenue Foch." Another address designation is "ter," or "tertiary," as in "7ter Rue Léonard de Vinci."*

The RER (**suburban express railway**) has five lines (designated RER A, B, C, D and E) with multiple branches (such as RER B2 or C4). The RER isn't just for going to the airport or suburban towns; it's also convenient for crossing Paris since it goes much faster and has fewer stops than the métro. This can be useful for getting quickly from the Parc Montsouris to Gare du Nord (RER B) or from the Champs-Elysées to the Gare de Lyon (RER A). The RER operates during the same hours as the métro, 5:45am to 12:30am, and uses the same tickets as long as you stay within Paris (inside the Péripherique). If you plan on going past zone 2 and you don't have a zone 1-5 pass, then you'll need to buy an individual ticket *before* you enter the RER. A regular métro ticket will allow you to get on any RER within Paris, but if you travel past the zone you won't be able to exit the turnstiles at the other end.

> **AUTHOR'S NOTE:** *Métro stations listed in this guide are abbreviated as **M°** when part of an address, so the St-Michel métro station becomes* M° St-Michel.

Tickets

Tickets can be purchased from automated machines or any RATP (bus) ticket window (tickets are only good for one-way trips, so ask for two tickets to save time if you're coming back the same way). It's important to look at the monitors on the platform to see if your destination is lit up for the incoming train, because express RERs don't stop at every station. When in doubt, ask someone before getting on. And stay at the top end of the platform (RER's arrive from the right, so the top is to the left) because some trains are shorter than others (*train court*) and you'll end up running to catch it.

Individual tickets cost €1.30, or €10 for a *carnet* (set/book) of 10 tickets. Tickets are valid throughout the RATP (☎ 01 44 68 20 20, www.ratp.fr, select "English") network of métro, bus and RER lines within the city and immediate suburbs (zone 1-2). Beyond zone 2, RER fares are higher and require different tickets. Within the métro, a single ticket is good for one journey with unlimited transfers (*correspondences*). Hold on to the ticket until you resurface, as you'll need it to get out and to prove you've paid if the RATP officials do a random check.

A WORD TO THE WISE

ATTENTION! *Keep your ticket accessible while traveling through the métro system, since some stations with RER connections (such as Châtelet-Les Halles) require you to go through multiple turnstiles when changing lines.*

Getting Around With Children

All RATP tickets, carnets and passes are 50% off for children ages four to nine. Kids under age four ride for free. Parents with bulky strollers can avoid the turnstiles by asking agents at the ticket window to open the side gate. Be prepared for long tunnels and numerous stairs throughout the métro and RER.

General Rules & Etiquette

Smoking, eating and drinking on the métro and RER trains are not allowed (although it's usually tolerated on the platform). Don't put your feet or luggage on the seats. The fold-down seats shouldn't be used when the car is crowded (rush hours 6:30am to 9:00am and 4:30pm to 7:00pm). Do not try to jump on at the last second, even if you see daredevil Parisians doing it.

Beware of pickpockets in crowded cars, especially during the jostle of getting on or off. Some people will squeeze in right behind you at the ticket turnstiles to get in without paying; make sure they're not going through your pockets at the same time! If you have any problems, use the yellow emergency call boxes found on every platform. Some métro exits

Planning Your Trip

close early, but there's always at least one open exit. If you come to a closed grill from the inside, look for a button on the wall, which you can push to open it.

RATP SOUVENIRS

The **Métro & Bus Objets du Patrimoine** store is a great place to stock up on gifts and souvenirs such as métro-map umbrellas, RATP-ticket beach towels, T-shirts and Art Nouveau picture frames inspired by the Hector Guimard métro entrances. The boutique is inside the Châtelet-Les Halles RER station, near the exit for Place Carrée and the connection to métro line 4. Open weekdays, 8am to 7:30pm; see www.ratp.fr for a preview.

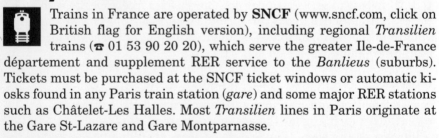

AUTHOR'S NOTE: *The Carte Paris Visite (there's a link on the RATP site) is heavily promoted to tourists, but hardly offers a good deal. It's an expensive transportation pass with a few token discounts to tourist sites (such as 10% off gift shops at Disneyland or a free Moulin Rouge ashtray). See the web site for complete rates (from €8.55 for one day to €26 for five days within Paris). It's better to purchase a **Paris Museum Pass** (see Sightseeing Passes, page 77) and a separate **Mobilis** or **Carte Orange Hebdomadaire** pass.*

■ By Train

Trains in France are operated by **SNCF** (www.sncf.com, click on British flag for English version), including regional *Transilien* trains (☎ 01 53 90 20 20), which serve the greater Ile-de-France département and supplement RER service to the *Banlieus* (suburbs). Tickets must be purchased at the SNCF ticket windows or automatic kiosks found in any Paris train station (*gare*) and some major RER stations such as Châtelet-Les Halles. Most *Transilien* lines in Paris originate at the Gare St-Lazare and Gare Montparnasse.

To find the right platform look for the *Banlieus* or *Transilien* signs (the *Grands Lignes* serve the outer regions of France and the rest of Europe). Just as at the airport, the departure track (*voie*) isn't posted until the last minute, so you'll have to watch the boards. If you're confused, ask at the information kiosk on the platform where you should wait. Tickets *must* be punched in the orange ticket machines located on train platforms before boarding or they are not valid (there are no turnstiles, so it's easy to forget). Tickets are good for a trip, not a particular time or date, so if you miss a train it's still valid for the next one (or even the next day). See the

Getting Around sections for each region in the *Outside Paris* chapter for specific information on local transportation.

■ By Bus

 The RATP bus system is more efficient than it was just five years ago, with many dedicated bus lanes and electronic signs at major stops to indicate the wait time between buses. Most buses operate Monday through Saturday from 7am to 8:30pm, although many major lines are open daily until 1:30am. The signs at each bus stop indicate all of this information, and clearly show the route of each bus, which stops there. If you're not sure, you can ask the driver, but be sure to let other passengers on before doing so.

A WORD TO THE WISE

> **TIP:** *If you're the only person standing at a stop used by different bus lines, be sure to raise your hand or stand at the end of the sidewalk to indicate that you want the approaching bus to stop. Drivers are not supposed to let passengers on or off outside designated stops, but will usually wait if they spot you running down the street.*

Bus tickets are the same as those used on the métro. Drivers can sell single tickets only, no *carnets* or passes (these are available at métro stations or tourist offices). Individual tickets should be punched into the ticket machine. These are only good for one journey on the same bus without transfers. Do *not* punch *Mobilis* or *Carte Orange* tickets into the machine, simply show them to the driver as you board. Newer buses have electronic screens and intercoms that announce the upcoming stop. Push one of the red buttons if you want to get off. Always exit through the back doors (many open automatically; some require you to push a green button).

Special Buses

The **Balabus** (Bb) is a special tourist bus that operates on Sundays and holidays only from mid-April to mid-September, with a particularly scenic route along the Seine between La Défense and Gare de Lyon.

The **Petite Ceinture** (PC1, PC2, PC3) buses do a loop of Paris just inside the *périphérique* ring road.

The **Montmartrobus** circles the Butte de Montmartre between M° Anvers and M° Jules Joffrin, with stops in front of Sacré-Coeur Basilica and Place du Tertre. There's also the **Montmartre Funicular**, a short but steep rail ride up to the foot of Sacré-Coeur in a glass box, for those who can't bear another flight of stairs. All of these accept regular RATP tickets for a single trip without transfers.

Planning Your Trip

The **Batobus** (☎ 01 44 11 33 99, www.batobus.com, select "English") is operated just like a bus on the Seine, with eight stops (see their web site for a map showing locations): **Eiffel Tower** (Port de la Bourdonnais, 7th), **Musée d'Orsay** (Quai Solferino, 7th), **St-Germain-des-Prés** (Quai Malaqui, 6th), **Notre Dame** (Quai de Montebello, 5th), **Jardin des Plantes** (Quai St-Bernard, 5th), **Hôtel de Ville** (Quai de l'Hôtel de Ville, 4th), **Louvre Museum** (Quai du Louvre, 1st) and the **Champs-Elysées** (Port des Champs-Elysées, 8th). Service daily, with 20 minutes between boats, from 10am to 7pm in April, May and October; from 10am to 9pm, June through September; and from 10am to 4pm, November through January 4 (in 2003 at least). The Batobus does not operate between early January and early April. Rates are €7.50 for a one-way trip (€3.50 for kids). Day passes are €10, €5 for kids. Two-day passes are €13, €7 for kids. Discounts are available with Carte Orange.

The RATP's **Noctambus** network operates nightly between 1am and 5am (when the RER and métro are closed). Most of the 18 lettered lines originate at Châtelet, and go all the way out to the suburbs. Individual tickets cost €2.60 (*Carte Orange* and *Mobilis* are accepted for the right zones). You can catch one on the way out or on the way back to Châtelet, where transfers to another Noctambus are allowed on the same ticket. Look for the Noctambus symbol on regular bus stops for network maps, or pick up a map at any RATP ticket office during the day.

ATTENTION! *Châtelet is a métro stop (lines 1, 4, 7, 11, 14). There is also a **Les Halles** métro stop on line 4. **Châtelet-Les Halles** is the RER stop (the RER stops are larger and run below the métro).*

SNCF runs the luxury coaches known as the **Bus de Nuit** (www.busdenuit.com), with three lines (1, 1.2, and 2) operating nightly between midnight and 5:30am, between Châtelet (90 Rue de Rivoli, 1st) and either Versailles, Roissy-CDG Airport, or Paris-Orly Airport. Ticket prices from €3-€11, depending on the journey. These are more comfortable and secure than the Noctambus, but have limited destinations.

■ By Tram

There are two small tramlines on the outskirts of Paris in Saint Denis (T1) and La Défense (T2), but these are rarely used by visitors. More exciting is the new five-mile *Tramway de Marechaux Sud (TMS)* currently under construction (due to open in 2006), which will connect métro stations in the lower 13th, 14th and 15th arrondissements such as Porte d'Ivry, Porte d'Orléans and Porte de Versailles.

TRANSPORTATION STRIKES

The chances of being in France during a *grève* are actually quite high, since they occur on an almost regular basis. Visitors shouldn't panic. Most strikes last only a day or two, and there are almost always a few buses, métros and RERs running, to keep things from completely shutting down (but they can be horrendously crowded), so it may be best to get around on bike or on foot. Your hotel concierge should be able to give you information on getting around and to the airport on time. Otherwise you can check the RATP web site (www.ratp.fr, information in French only) for all service interruptions.

■ By Taxi

 Taxis can be found at airports, train stations, near major tourist sites and on taxi ranks at large intersections. You can also signal for one to stop if you see it passing by (they're easily identifiable by an illuminated sign on the roof). It's almost impossible to find a free taxi on Friday or Saturday night right after the métro closes, so you may have to call for one (some restaurants and bars will call for you).

TAXI COMPANIES

Alpha Taxis	☎ 01 45 85 85 85
Artaxi	☎ 01 42 06 67 10
Taxi G7	☎ 01 47 39 47 39
Taxi Bleus	☎ 08 25 16 10 10
Taxi Bleus (airport)	☎ 08 25 16 66 66
Taxi Parisiens	☎ 06 07 77 33 95
Taxi 7000	☎ 01 42 70 00 42
Km2 Motorcycle Taxi	☎ 01 45 16 28 56

Taxis within Paris during the day are relatively inexpensive (usually €8-€15). If you call a taxi to pick you up, the meter will already be running (all taxis have meters). The minimum fare is €5. Prices are higher at night, (7pm to 7am), in the suburbs, on Sundays and holidays, and if you have luggage (€0.90/each) or a fourth passenger (€2.60). Most taxis only accept cash, so ask in advance if you want to pay by credit card. If you want to tip, it's customary to round up by a euro or two for a short trip.

Planning Your Trip

It helps to have the address written down for the driver, since pronunciation problems can cause confusion. If you need cash, ask the driver to stop at an ATM (*distributeur d'argent*) and wait for you. Always ask for a receipt (*un réçu*) in case you leave something in the taxi or want to file a complaint (see below).

> **AUTHOR'S NOTE:** *If you have a disagreement with your taxi driver, get a receipt and write down the driver's number, which should be posted on the passenger door window. Contact the Préfecture de Police, Service de Taxis, 36 Rue des Morillons, 15th, M° Convention, ☎ 01 55 76 20 00.*

■ By Car

Driving in Paris is not recommended for visitors. Traffic is dense, parking is expensive and almost impossible to find in the center (hotels rarely have private parking), and it's not a very nice way to see the city. But a car can be convenient for exploring the villages, towns, National Parks and countryside of Ile-de-France.

DEFENSIVE DRIVING

Before driving in France, keep in mind this whopping (but useful) generalization: the French have little respect for traffic laws or other drivers. Double parking, going backwards down one-way streets, running red lights and speeding are quite common. Keep your foot near the brake pedal and stay alert. Signal your intentions to turn and, when in doubt, pull over and put your hazards on!

The main ring road or beltway around Paris is called the *périphérique*. The inner ring (*périphérique interieur*) runs clockwise around the city, the outer (*périphérique extérieur*) runs counterclockwise. There are five major motorways in France (*les autoroutes*): the A1 (north network), the A4 (east), A10 (west and southwest), A6 (southeast) and the A13 (northwest to Normandy). Tolls (*péages*) can be paid with coins or credit cards (there are no tolls on motorways surrounding Paris). Major roads are designated as *Routes Nationales* ("RN" or "N1," etc. on maps), and tend to be much slower since they go through town centers, while the smallest roads are the *Routes Départementaux* ("RD" or "D1," etc.).

Paperwork

Drivers must be at least 18 (most car rental companies require drivers to be 25). European Union and Canadian nationals can use their driver's license alone. All other drivers should apply for the International Driver's License (IDL).

INTERNATIONAL DRIVER'S LICENSE

There are many misconceptions about the IDL. There's no test to take because it's basically an official translation of your current *valid* driver's license, and the two must always be carried *together*. You can get an IDL for $10 through any American Automobile Association (AAA) location (or by mail, www.aaa.com). Only AAA and the American Automobile Touring Alliance are licensed to distribute the IDL in the US, so beware of fraudulent web sites selling expensive fakes. Residents from other countries should apply for the IDL through their national Automobile Association.

> **AUTHOR'S NOTE:** *For driving terminology, see* On the Road *in the* Glossary, *page 441.*

Rules & Regulations

The French drive on the right, safety belts are required for all passengers, children under 10 must ride in the back seat, and honking your horn in the city (unless it's to prevent an accident) can result in fines. Do not use the bus lanes, even in heavy traffic. Priority is generally for cars coming from the right (even from smaller roads onto larger ones). In roundabouts, cars already inside have the priority but this is often ignored so watch out. No right turn is allowed at red lights unless there's a blinking yellow arrow. Paris is well-signed, but you should get some literature from your rental agency about the meaning of the various signs and road markings. **Speed limits** are standardized, and are rarely posted except as a reminder. These are the guidelines:

- In towns and urban areas: 50km/h (30mph)
- On main roads: 90km/h (56mph) or 80 km/h in rain or fog
- On motorways: 130km/h (80mph) or 110km/h in rain or fog

> **AUTHOR'S NOTE:** *Before leaving home, check out the free* Moto Europa Guide *(www.ideamerge.com /motoeuropa) for detailed advice on driving in France and other European countries, including common road signs.*

Planning Your Trip

Parking

Do not double-park, park in no-stopping zones, areas reserved for deliveries (*livraisons*) or for the disabled. Street parking in Paris is limited to two hours. The coin-operated parking meters have been replaced by cards, which you can purchase at *tabacs*. Parking is free on Sundays, public holidays, and after 7pm. Parking garages (*parc* or *parking*) can be found throughout the city, and cost from €1-€3/hour.

WHAT'S A TABAC?

A *tabac* is a tobacconist's shop or kiosk, or a counter inside a café or newsagents (look for the red, diamond-shaped TABAC sign outside). They don't just sell tobacco products; this is the place to get stamps, telephone cards, parking meter cards, and lottery scratch cards.

WARNING! *Some streets have free parking, but look carefully for tow-zone signs, usually placed at the ends of the street (with a little pictogram of a tow truck). Other cars may be parked there, but don't let them fool you; Parisians usually know exactly how long they can get away with it. If you get towed, your car will impounded at La Fourrière, ☎ 01 53 71 53 53. You'll need to show proof that it's your car (keep the paperwork on you, not in the car) and pay a fine to get it back.*

Filling Up

There are four types of **gasoline/petrol** (*essence*) in France: *super* (leaded), *sans plomb 98* (unleaded 98), *sans plomb 95* (unleaded 95) and *gazole* (diesel). Be sure you know what kind of gas your rental car takes before filling up! Gasoline is much more expensive in Europe than North America, around €1.15/liter (see page 70 for conversion chart). Diesel fuel is much cheaper, but it may be hard to find a diesel rental car. Gas stations are all self-service; pump your gas and pay inside. Large supermarket gas stations have credit-card operated pumps.

TIP: *Gas is cheaper outside Paris, so wait until you're out of the city to fill up (in the small towns, not at motorway gas stations).*

Car Rental Agencies

Most rental agencies in Ile-de-France have locations at both airports, train stations, throughout Paris and larger towns in the suburbs. It costs €40-€75/day or €200-€275/week to rent a compact car, and €115-€175/day or €450-€500/week for a minivan. Be sure to ask in advance if you require an automatic transmission (most European cars have manual transmission).

Alamo . . . . ☎ 01 48 16 30 33, fax 01 48 16 30 37

Avis . . . . ☎ 08 20 05 05 05, fax 01 46 05 15 73

Budget . . . . ☎ 08 25 00 35 64, fax 1 46 86 22 17

Europcar . . . . ☎ 08 25 35 23 52, fax 01 46 52 02 79

Hertz . . . . ☎ 01 39 38 38 38, fax 01 39 38 35 13

Rent-a-Car . . . . ☎ 08 36 69 46 95

Thrifty . . . . ☎ 01 34 29 86 76

EasyCar . . . . www.easycar.com

A WORD TO
THE WISE

ATTENTION! *The Parisian method of parking usually involves a bit of bumper-car action, and big trucks going down narrow streets often result in nicks, scratches, and crushed side-view mirrors. Keep this in mind when you're discussing what you're insured for on your rental car.*

■ By Scooter & Motorcycle

Unlike their counterparts in the United States, French scooters and motorcycles weave between cars in traffic and always move to the front of the line at red lights. They're also involved in over 50% of the country's traffic accidents. Proceed with caution and remember that helmets are required by law at all times.

Rentals

Free Scoot: 144 Boulevard Voltaire, 11th, M° Voltaire, ☎ 01 44 93 04 03. Rentals by the day or week of bicycles, 50cc scooters (can be rented without a DL), and 125cc maxi-scooters (valid DL necessary). All accessories included. Open Monday through Friday, 9:15am to 7pm; Saturday, 10am to 6pm.

Motorail: 190 Rue de Bercy, 12th, M° Gare de Lyon (in the Gare de Lyon's car rental section, at the corner of Rue Van Gogh), ☎ 01 43 07 08 09, www.motorail.fr. Scooter, motorcycle and bike rental with helmet, gloves, and locks included. You'll need a credit card and ID, and a driver's license for the motorcycles. Rates from €10/day for city cruiser bikes, €29/day for small scooters, and €49/day for light motorcycles (unlimited mileage). There is also a guarded parking lot from €8/day. Open Monday to Saturday, 9:30am to 7pm.

Holiday Bikes: Parking Foch (across from 1*bis* Avenue Foch, 16th, M° Charles de Gaulle-Etoile, ☎ 01 45 00 06 66). This agency rents out a large selection of scooters and motorcycles, including Harley Davidsons, Honda Goldwings and BMWs. Rates from €50-€240 per day. Drivers must be at least 21 years old and have had their driver's license for a minimum of two years. Open daily, 9am to 7pm.

■ By Bike

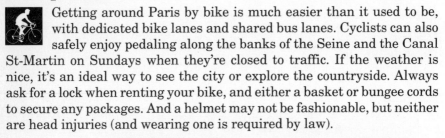 Getting around Paris by bike is much easier than it used to be, with dedicated bike lanes and shared bus lanes. Cyclists can also safely enjoy pedaling along the banks of the Seine and the Canal St-Martin on Sundays when they're closed to traffic. If the weather is nice, it's an ideal way to see the city or explore the countryside. Always ask for a lock when renting your bike, and either a basket or bungee cords to secure any packages. And a helmet may not be fashionable, but neither are head injuries (and wearing one is required by law).

> **AUTHOR'S NOTE:** *See* Adventures On Wheels, *page 178, for a list of bike tour companies and safety tips.*

Rentals

Fat Tire Bike Tours: 24 Rue Edgar Faure, 15th, M° Dupleix, ☎/fax 01 56 58 10 54, www.fattirebiketours.com. Open daily, 9am to 7pm. All ages are welcome, with child seats, kids' bikes, trailers, helmets and rain gear available. You can also rent bikes from €2 per hour to €50 per week. US dollars, euros and traveler's checks accepted (no credit cards).

Paris à Vélo, C'est Sympa: 37 Boulevard Bourdon, 4th, M° Bastille, ☎ 01 48 87 60 01, www.parisvelosympa.com. Open daily, 9am to 6pm (until 7pm in summer, closed 1 to 2pm weekdays). They also rent bikes and tandems: €9.50 for half-day, €12.50 for a day, €24 for the weekend, and €30 for three days.

Maison Roue Libre: Outside the Forum des Halles, 1 Passage Mondétour (at the corner of Rue Rambuteau), 1st, M° Châtelet-Les Halles or Etienne Marcel, ☎ 08 10 44 15 34. Open daily, 9am to 7pm. Weekday rentals are €6/day or €15/five days. Weekend rentals are €3/hour or €12/day. They're all city cruisers with baskets, chain guards and locks (get there early, they run out). Children's bikes, trailers and helmets are available on request. Bikes can also be rented from their **Cyclobus** locations (weekends only, May to October) at Place de l'Hôtel de Ville, Bassin de la

Villette, Bois de Vincennes (M° Porte d'Auteuil), and Bois de Vincennes (M° Château de Vincennes). Photo identity and €150 deposit required.

Cyclo Pouce: 38 Quai Marne, 19th, M° Ourcq, ☎ 01 42 41 76 98. City cruisers, mountain bikes and tandems available for all ages, and includes lock and bungees. They also sell a selection of Paris guidebooks. Open Tuesday to Friday, 10am to 6pm; weekends and holidays, 9:30am to 7pm. From €3.50/hour to €55/week.

Gepetto & Vélos: 59 Rue du Cardinal Lemoine, 5th, M° Cardinal-Lemoine, ☎/fax 01 43 54 19 95, www.gepetto-et-velos.com. Half-day rentals €7.50, full-day rentals €14.

Allo Vélo: 70 Boulevard Strasbourg, 10th, M° Gare de l'Est, ☎ 01 40 35 36 36. Open daily, 9am to 7pm. Bike rental from €2 for 80 minutes during the week to €35 for weekend rental (from Friday noon until Monday noon).

Bike'N'Roller: 38 Rue Fabert, Esplanade des Invalides, 7th, M° Invalides, ☎ 01 45 50 38 27, www.bikenroller.fr. Open daily, 10am to 7pm. Bikes (city cruisers or BMX) are €12 for three hours, €17 for the day, and they even rent out *trotinettes* (like a skateboard with handlebars; electric or push-powered) for €10-€22/hour.

Motorail: 190 Rue de Bercy, 12th, M° Gare de Lyon (in the station's car rental section, at the corner of Rue Van Gogh), ☎ 01 43 07 08 09. Open 9:30am to 7pm, closed Sunday. Rates from €10/day for city cruiser bikes, lock included. Credit card deposit required.

Paris Cycles: ☎ 01 47 47 76 50. Open April to October on Wednesdays and weekends from 10am to 7pm, daily in July and August. This company has bike rental vans parked at the **Bois de Boulogne** (M° Porte Dauphine, on the northeast side of the Lac Inférieur) and **Bois de Vincennes** (M° Porte Dorée, on the northwest side of the Lac Daumesnil). Rates are €5/hour or €12/day.

BIKES ON PUBLIC TRANSPORTATION

 Bikes can be taken on Transilien lines and RER A and B trains, but only in carriages marked with a bicycle symbol, and not during rush hours (weekdays, 6:30am to 9:00am and 4:30pm to 7:00pm). Métro line 1 is open to cyclists on Sundays only until 4:30pm (although you can't get your bike past the turnstiles at La Défense or Louvre-Rivoli). Buses are completely off-limits to bicycles.

Planning Your Trip

Practicalities

Money

■ The Euro

€ On January 1, 2002 the euro (€) became the official currency of France and 11 other EU countries. Although some shops still display prices in Francs, they are no longer accepted as legal currency. You can exchange notes at any **Banque de France** branch until February 17, 2012 (until February 17, 2005 for coins). The main branch in Paris is at 48 Rue Croix des Petits Champs, 1st, M° Palais-Royal, ☎ 01 42 92 39 08. For current exchange rates, check online at www.xe.com/ucc or www.x-rates.com/calculator.

■ Banks

Banks are generally open weekdays 9am to noon and 2pm to 5:30pm. Some are open on Saturday mornings. The best rate for exchanging money or traveler's checks is at the Banque de France (see above). You can get a cash advance with your VISA or MasterCard from most banks; bring your passport for ID. Post offices also handle basic banking transactions and Western Union transfers.

■ Credit Cards

To get a better exchange rate simply use your credit/debit card for purchases or cash advances from automated bank tellers (*distributeurs de billets*). Be sure you know your four-digit code and the maximum daily withdrawal allowance before leaving home. Your own bank may charge €1-€2 per transaction to your account. It's also a good idea to notify your bank of your trip so they don't think your card has been stolen and deactivate it. VISA (also known as *Carte Bleue*) and MasterCard (a.k.a. *EuroCard*) are the most widely accepted credit cards in France, with JCB and Diners Club also widely accepted. Because of the high commission fees, American Express is usually only accepted in larger stores and expensive restaurants; always ask in advance. French credit cards work differently than American cards when making purchases (they have a microchip that recognizes their PIN code instead of the "swipe and sign" method), so don't be surprised if cashiers take a bit longer figuring out how to ring up your purchases.

AUTHOR'S NOTE: *French cash dispensers accept most international bank cards, including ATM and debit cards. If yours doesn't seem to be working at any of the cash machines, don't give up. Try the **BNP Paribas** (72 Rue Monge, 5th, M° Monge), which seems to accept even the most obscure cards.*

■ Traveler's Checks

These can be cumbersome to exchange and commissions are high in the *bureaux de change* found in airports, department stores and near major tourist sights. If you want an emergency back-up in case your credit card doesn't work, exchange them at the **American Express Office** (11 Rue Scribe, 9th, M° Opéra, ☎ 01 47 77 77 58; also at both Paris airports). They exchange traveler's checks from any issuer without commission, and are open Monday to Friday, 9am to 6:30 pm; until 5:30pm on Saturday. The Banque de France will also exchange them without commission.

■ Tipping

There are no set rules on tipping in France, and it's hardly demanded (as in the US), but most people tip hairdressers, tour guides and taxi drivers (10%), bellhops, parking valets and concierges (€0.50-€1.50). The 15% service charge is already included in hotels, cafés and restaurants (*service compris* should appear on the bill), but it's customary to leave the small change (€1-€3, more in *haute-cuisine* restaurants) if the service was good.

OÙ SONT LES TOILETTES?

What to do when nature calls and you're nowhere near your hotel? If there's a busy café or brasserie nearby, they may not notice if you head straight for the toilets and then leave. But since a lot of people try this, some bathrooms require a coin to get in. Public toilets can be found at some métro entrances and outside major monuments, with an actual human being there to collect the small fee before you can go in (always keep a few euro cents handy). All of the major department stores have free restrooms, but smaller shops never have public facilities. As a last resort, there are always the automated public toilet cabins scattered around the city. They're coin-operated, and actually quite clean, since the entire interior is rinsed and disinfected after each use. Experienced travelers know to carry a small tissue packet at all times in case there's no paper.

Customs

■ Import Allowance

Travelers residing outside the EU have to pay duty on general merchandise or gifts valued over €175 (€90 for kids under 15). There are specific duty-free allowances of up to two liters of wine, one liter of alcohol over 22 proof, two liters of alcohol under 22 proof, 200 cigarettes, 100 cigarillos, 50 cigars, 87.5 ounces of tobacco, 17.5 ounces of perfume, 0.25 liters of eau de toilette, 175 ounces of coffee, and 35 ounces of tea.

Residents of EU countries can bring in any amount of goods as long as they're for personal use and not for resale. Taxes apply if you bring in more than 10 liters of hard liquor, 20 liters of fortified wine, 90 liters of wine, 110 liters of beer, 800 cigarettes, 400 cigarillos, 200 cigars, or 350 ounces (one kilo) of tobacco.

A WORD TO
THE WISE

WARNING! *Keep in mind that illegal items include weapons, drugs, plants, endangered species, ivory, and counterfeit goods. Anyone entering or leaving the country with more than €7,600 in cash must declare it to Customs. When in doubt, contact the **French Customs Office** (les Douanes),* ☎ *08 25 30 82 63, www.finances.gouv.fr/douanes.*

■ Export Allowance

US residents must declare everything brought back from abroad, including gifts and duty-free goods. Those who have been in France for at least two days can bring back up to $800 of merchandise duty-free (including $100 for gifts). Everything over this amount will be subject to taxation of about 10%. There's a maximum duty-free allowance of 200 cigarettes, 100 cigars (tobacco products of Cuban origin will be confiscated), and one liter of alcohol (if you're 21 or older). There are no federal limits on the amount of alcohol brought in for personal use, but there may be limits within certain states. Children have the same allowances as adults (except on alcohol), and families can combine their allowances. Keep all receipts and be prepared to unpack the items at the customs desk upon arrival. For more information contact the **US Customs & Border Protection Offices**, ☎ 202-354-1000, www.customs.gov (see "Know Before You Go" section).

ATTENTION! *Aside from baked goods, canned fruits and vacuum-packed cheeses, it's forbidden to bring fresh foods or any meat products (even dried or canned) into the US.*

Residents of Canada have a duty-free allowance of C$750 if you've been out of the country at least seven days, with a limit of 1.5 liters of wine, 40 ounces of hard liquor or 8.5 liters of beer. You may also bring in up to 200 cigarettes, 50 cigars or cigarillos, 200 tobacco sticks, and 200 grams of loose tobacco duty-free. Taxes must be paid on anything above these allowances. Find complete details on the Canadian Customs & Revenue Agency (CRA) web site (www.cra-adrc.gc.ca), or call the Automated Customs Information Service (ACIS), ☎ 800-461-9999 (within Canada), or 204-983-3500 (outside Canada). A list of customs offices is posted at www.cbsa-asfc.gc.ca.

Residents of the UK & Ireland have no real limits to what they can bring back from France provided it's for personal use, although large quantities of alcohol and tobacco may target you as a smuggler (even if you're just taking back extras for friends and family). There are no exact numbers, but officials get suspicious if you have over 10 liters of hard liquor, 20 liters of fortified wine, 90 liters of wine, 110 liters of beer, 3,200 cigarettes, 400 cigarillos, 200 cigars, or 1,050 ounces (three kilos) of tobacco. If you can't justify the large quantities, the goods may be confiscated (and if you're driving across the border, the vehicle can be seized as well). For more information contact the **British Customs & Excise National Advice Service**, ☎ 08 45 010 9000, www.hmce.gov.uk.

In Ireland contact the **Customs & Excise Information Office** in Dublin, ☎ 353 (01) 877 6200.

Australian Customs Service, ☎ 1300 363 263 (from within Australia) or 61 2 6275 6666 (from outside Australia).

New Zealand Customs Service, ☎ 0800 428 786 (within New Zealand) or 09 275 9059 (outside New Zealand).

Embassies & Consulates

American Embassy: 2 Avenue Gabriel, 8th, M° Concorde, ☎ 01 43 12 22 22, www.amb-usa/fr. Open by appointment weekdays, 9am to 6pm.

American Consulate: 2 Rue St-Florentin, 1st, M° Concorde, ☎ 01 43 12 22 22. Open weekdays, 9am to 12:30pm and 1pm to 3pm (consular services are also listed on the embassy site, above).

Canadian Embassy: 35 Ave Montaigne, 8th, M° Franklin D. Roosevelt, ☎ 01 44 43 29 00 (24-hour), www.dfait-maeci.gc.ca/canadaeuropa/france; select "English." Open weekdays, 9am to noon and 2pm to 5pm.

Planning Your Trip

Canadian Consulate: 37 Avenue Montaigne, 8th, ☎ 01 44 43 29 02.

British Embassy: 35 Rue du Faubourg-St-Honoré, M° Concorde, 8th, ☎ 01 44 51 31 00, www.uk.embassyhomepage.com; select "Paris, France" then "English." Open weekdays, 9:30am to 1pm and 2:30pm to 6pm.

British Consulate: 18*bis* Rue d'Anjou, 8th, M° Concorde/or Madeleine, ☎ 01 44 51 31 00. Open weekdays, 9:30am to noon and 2:30pm to 5pm (Tuesday, 9:30am to 4:30pm).

Irish Embassy: 12 Avenue Foch, 16th, M° Charles de Gaulle-Etoile, ☎ 01 44 17 67 00. Open weekdays, 9:30am to 1pm and 2:30pm to 5:30pm.

Irish Consulate: 4 Rue Rude, 16th, ☎ 01 44 19 67 00. Open weekdays, 9:30am to noon.

Australian Embassy: 4 Rue Jean-Rey, 15th, M° Bir-Hakeim, ☎ 01 40 59 33 00, www.austgov.fr. Open weekdays, 9am to 6pm.

New Zealand Embassy: 7*ter* Rue Léonard de Vinci, 16th, M° Victor-Hugo, ☎ 01 45 01 43 43, www.nzembassy.com, click on "France." Open weekdays, 9am to 1pm and 2pm to 5:30 pm (Friday until 4pm; limited hours in July and August).

When In France

■ Time

The French use the 24-hour clock for written times such as business hours and train schedules, so *7h00* is 7 am and *19h00* is 7 pm. France is one hour ahead of Greenwich Mean Time (GMT+1), making Paris six hours ahead of New York (EST) and nine hours behind Sydney.

> **AUTHOR'S NOTE:** *For useful phrases see* Time & Date *and* Around Town *in the* Glossary, *page 433.*

■ Appliances

Any appliances (hair dryers, irons, etc) you bring from home will need a **plug adapter** for the rounded two-prong French plugs. Many hotels can provide these free of charge (ask in advance). The standard European electric current is 220-240 volts. Most US and Canadian appliances are 110 volts and will need an **electricity converter** to avoid being fried (if small print on the power cord says "110-240v" then it doesn't need the converter).

∎ Mail & Shipping

 The **Main Post Office** in Paris (52 Rue du Louvre, 1st, M° Louvre-Rivoli, ☎ 01 40 28 20 00) is open 24 hours. Some windows are reserved for banking transactions, so look for *Envoi de Lettres Et Paquets* or *Toutes Opérations*. Most branch post offices are open weekdays, 8am to 7pm, and Saturdays until noon. You can also get stamps (*timbres*) at tabacs.

If you need to ship packages, you can do so via private international companies such as **DHL** (6 Rue des Colonnes, 2nd, M° Bourse, ☎ 01 55 35 30 30, www.dhl.fr), **Federal Express** (63 Boulevard Haussmann, 9th, M° Havre-Caumartin, ☎ 01 40 06 90 16, www.fedex.com; choose "France," then "English") or **UPS** (107 Rue Réaumur, 2nd, M° Sentier, ☎ 08 00 87 78 77, www.ups.com: select "France," then "English").

∎ Internet

There are plenty of places to check e-mail in Paris for those who don't want to lug around a laptop. Hotels and even youth hostels often have a "pay as you go" terminal in the lobby that can be used with a credit card or coins, but these can be quite pricey and slow. The best option is to drop into one of the city's many Internet cafés, which offer extra services such as printing and QWERTY (American-style) keyboards.

If you want to use your **laptop** to check e-mail, you'll also need a **phone jack adaptor** to plug in the modem (some hotels have dedicated modem lines in the room). Don't forget to **contact your ISP** in advance to find out what the local dial-up number is in France, otherwise you'll be billed for an international call. Wireless Internet access (WIFI) is just starting to catch on in France, particularly in business hotel chains such as Sofitel and Mercure.

Internet Cafés

The **Access Academy** (60-62 Rue St-André-des-Arts, 6th, M° Odéon, ☎ 01 43 25 23 80, www.accessacademy.com) is the largest Internet access center, with 400 flat-screen computers in an air conditioned building (the site is in French; click on "Ou sommes nous" for a map showing their location). There are different rates for use of Microsoft Office or just the Internet, starting at €3/hour, depending on time of day. You need cash to get a password ticket at the front desk. Open daily, 8am to 2am.

The **Café Orbital** (13 Rue de Médicis, 6th, M° Odéon or RER Luxembourg, ☎ 01 43 25 76 77, www.cafeorbital.com/cafe) was one of the first Internet cafés in Paris; it's across from the Jardins du Luxembourg. They have 30 computer stations (Macs, too), WIFI access for laptop users, and a cozy non-smoking café. From €7/hour. Open weekdays, 10am to 8pm; weekends, noon to 8pm.

The **Cybercafé de Paris** (11-15 Rue des Halles, 1st, M° Châtelet, exit Lavandiers or St-Opportune, ☎ 01 42 21 11 11, www.phonebookofthe-world.com/cybercafedeparis.htm) is a small Internet café with multinational keyboards, and you can use your own floppy disk. You get a free hot drink on each visit. From €8/hour. Open Monday through Saturday, 11am to 11pm.

TIP: *If you're not sure how to access your e-mail from a public computer, consider forwarding all of your messages to a free mail account such as Hotmail or Yahoo.*

■ Telephone

French public telephones no longer accept coins, so to make a call you'll need to get a **prepaid phone card** (*carte téléphonique*), approximately €9 for 50 units or €16.50 for 120 units, at main métro stations, post offices, tabacs, newsstands, tourism offices and France Télécom agencies. Most phone booths display the number that lets you receive calls. For **directory information** dial ☎ 12.

Calls within France have a 10-digit number (eg, 01 47 47 00 00). Numbers in Paris and the rest of Ile-de-France always begin with "01," and mobile phones begin with "06."

When calling France from abroad, drop the initial "0" and add the international calling code "33" (for the number above, "33" plus "01" becomes "331").

To call home, dial the French outgoing country code, "33," then "00" and the country code (US/Canada, 00+1; Britain, 00+44; Australia, 00+61; Republic of Ireland, 00+353; New Zealand, 00+64), then the telephone number.

DID YOU KNOW? *To use your calling card or make a collect call from France, contact the **AT&T international operator** (toll-free), ☎ 0 800 99 00 11.*

To use your own **mobile phone** in France, it will need to be GSM compatible. Contact your provider to find out the costs involved for international "roaming" service. It may be worthwhile switching to a French provider during your stay, such as **SFR** (www.sfr.fr.do; click on "International Travellers" section); or **Bouygues Telecom** (www.bouyguestelecom.fr; click on "International Visitors"), so that you can receive calls for free and make inexpensive calls within France. You can also rent mobile phones in Paris from agencies such as **CallPhone** (☎ 01 40 71 72 54, www.call-phone.fr, click on the American/British flag symbol), which include free incoming calls and a charger that you can plug into any French socket without an adapter.

Medical Needs

■ Pharmacies

You can find these all over the city, identifiable by their blinking, neongreen signs. It's always better to stop into a pharmacy before going to the doctor or emergency room. Unlike their American or British counterparts, French pharmacists are permitted to bandage minor wounds and prescribe medicine for common ailments. On the down side, everything in French pharmacies is kept behind the counter, including headache pills, throat lozenges, and condoms. And since brand names of most medicines are different, you'll just have to describe what ails you and hope the pharmacist gives you the right product. If charades aren't your strong point, get over the language barrier at the **Anglo-American Pharmacy** (37 Avenue Marceau, 16th, M° Alma-Marceau, ☎ 01 47 20 57 37); the **Pharmacie Swann** (6 Rue de Castiglione, 1st, M° Concorde, ☎ 01 42 60 72 96); or the **British Pharmacy** (1 Rue Auber, 9th, M° Opéra or RER Auber, ☎ 01 42 65 88 29). Another option, the **Pharmacie Dehry** (84 Avenue des Champs-Elysées, 8th, M° Georges V, ☎ 01 45 62 02 41), is open 24/7.

> **AUTHOR'S NOTE:** *For a list of basic medical terms, see* Where Does it Hurt, *in the* Glossary, *page 433.*

■ Dentists & Doctors

If you need to see a doctor, your hotel or nearby pharmacy should be able to direct you to a generalist in the neighborhood. You can also have a doctor come to you by calling **SOS Médecins** (☎ 08 20 33 24 24 or 01 47 07 77 77), but this costs more, especially at night or on Sundays. For dental emergencies call **SOS Dentistes** (☎ 01 43 37 51 00). It's not necessary to have insurance to see French doctors, but you will have to pay the full bill on the spot.

A WORD TO
THE WISE

> **ATTENTION!** *If you're traveling with prescription drugs, be sure that you have a copy of your doctor's written prescription to show at customs.*

■ Hospitals

If you need urgent care, you can go to any hospital emergency room in Paris such as the **Hôpital Hôtel Dieu** (next to Notre Dame Cathedral, Rue de la Cité, M° Cité, 4th, ☎ 01 42 34 82 32). There are two private hospitals in the suburbs with fully bilingual staff (although the prices are much higher than public hospitals), the **Hôpital Américain** (63 Boulevard Victor Hugo, Neuilly-sur-Seine, ☎ 01 46 41 25 25), and the **Hôpital Franco-Britannique** (3 Rue Barbès, Levallois-Perret, ☎ 01 46 39 22 09).

Personal Safety

■ Theft

Paris is generally safer than other major cities when it comes to violent crime, but visitors should still remain alert and use common sense. **Pickpockets** are a problem, especially in tourist areas and crowded métro cars, so always keep your bags closed and wallets in front pockets. Gypsy children are the most common offenders, but pickpockets may also wear business suits to avoid suspicion. Beware of distractions, especially if you're at a cash machine. And never, ever leave your baggage unattended (if it's not stolen, it could be mistaken for a bomb).

Emergency Numbers

These numbers can be dialed toll-free from any phone:

General Emergency . . . . ☎ 112
Police . . . . ☎ 17
Ambulance (SAMU) . . . . ☎ 15
Fire . . . . ☎ 18

■ Women Alone

Women traveling alone should ride in the front car of the métro or train, nearest to the conductor. Try to avoid the long maze of métro tunnels at Montparnasse, République and Châtelet-Les Halles late at night, which tend to be full of young thugs. There are yellow emergency call boxes on every platform. French men are famous for trying to pick up beautiful women they pass on the street. To avoid unwanted advances, don't smile if you accidentally make eye contact (it's interpreted as a come-on). If you think you're being followed, go into the nearest open café or restaurant and ask them to call you a taxi.

Lost & Found

If you've lost an everyday item, like a **coat** or **hat**, it's worth backtracking to find it. You can also check the *Service des Objets Trouvés* (at the Préfecture de Police, 36 Rue des Morillons, 15th, M° Convention, ☎ 01 55 76 20 20). To report stolen items (which may be necessary for insurance purposes), contact the nearest *Préfecture de Police* (main office at 9 Boulevard du Palais, 4th, M° Cité, ☎ 01 53 71 33 56). To report stolen credit cards, contact VISA (☎ 08 92 70 57 05), MasterCard (☎ 01 45 67 53 53), American Express (☎ 01 47 77 72 00) or Diner's Club (☎ 08 10 31 41 59).

AUTHOR'S NOTE: *See* Common Phrases *and* Remember Your Manners *in the* Glossary, *page 433, for vocabulary and terms to help you smooth the way. A little goes a long way!*

Going Metric

To make your travel through France a bit easier, we have provided the following chart that shows metric equivalets for the measurements you are familiar with.

GENERAL MEASUREMENTS

1 kilometer = .6124 miles

1 mile = 1.6093 kilometers

1 foot = .304 meters

1 inch = 2.54 centimeters

1 square mile = 2.59 square kilometers

1 pound = .4536 kilograms

1 ounce = 28.35 grams

1 imperial gallon = 4.5459 liters

1 US gallon = 3.7854 liters

1 quart = .94635 liters

TEMPERATURES

For Fahrenheit: Multiply Centigrade figure by 1.8 and add 32.

For Centigrade: Subtract 32 from Fahrenheit figure and divide by 1.8.

Centigrade	Fahrenheit
40°	104°
35°	95°
30°	86°
25°	77°
20°	64°
15°	59°
10°	50°

Paris

Paris entered the new millennium looking better than ever. After a push in the 1980s and 1990s to renovate major monuments and clean up historic buildings, the city is now at work rehabilitating older neighborhoods and adding more green spaces and pedestrian-only zones throughout the capital. Some neighborhoods awaiting their turn, especially in

the outer districts of the 10th, 19th and 20th arrondissements, have a mix of deteriorated pre-WWII housing that needs complete renovation and grim 1960s buildings more in need of a serious facelift. For those who really want to get to know Paris, it's important to visit these neighborhoods before they, too, change. **Belleville's** ethnic diversity and the **Butte aux Cailles'** village atmosphere may someday disappear within a more homogenized city. This chapter offers a framework for discovering the major sights of the city's most popular districts as well as the lesser-known, hidden corners of Paris. But no guidebook could cover everything worth seeing in Paris, so don't be afraid to branch out into interesting-looking streets and do a bit of your own exploration.

Getting Oriented

Paris is one of the most user-friendly cities in the world once you understand the basics. It is divided generally into the *Rive Gauche* (Left Bank, to the south of the Seine), and *Rive Droite* (Right Bank, on the river's north side), and then into 20 smaller segments called arrondissements (districts). When listed as part of a street address, these are designated as 1st for first arrondissement, 13th for the 13th arrondissement (as in "11 Rue St-Paul, 4th"). In a mailing address, the arrondissement number is attached to the département code (75 refers to Paris), so the post code for the 12th arrondissement is 75012. The suburbs are called *les Banlieues*, and have different département numbers (e.g., 78 for Yvelines or 92 for Hauts de Seine).

It's not always necessary to have a map to get around the city. Inside every métro (M°) station is a map of the surrounding neighborhood (if the métro has one exit, it's usually just inside; if there are multiple exits, the map is usually along the platform somewhere to show where each exit surfaces). If you know which métro stop is closest to an address, these maps (with street index) should show you how to get there. Once above ground, there are maps of the neighborhood with a *"Vous êtes ici"* (You are here) marker on the back of many signs. Each bus stop also has a mapp showing the immediate area (and shows where all of the surrounding bus stops are located, handy at large intersections).

For those who feel most comfortable with a map on hand at all times, the best one to purchase – the one used by Parisians – is the *Paris Classique: Par Arrondissement*. This little booklet slips easily into a coat pocket, and has detailed maps of every arrondissement, with métro, RER and bus maps, a street index, and even suburbs and airport maps. It shows traffic directions (one way and pedestrian-only streets), and lists major monuments, museums, churches, rental car agencies, even all-night pharmacies and hospitals.

ATTENTION: *Don't get confused by roads with similar names, such as Rue St-Honoré and Rue du Faubourg St-Honoré; Rue de Belleville and Boulevard de Belleville; or Rue du Temple and Rue Vieille du Temple.*

If you get lost, don't hesitate to ask someone for directions. The most polite way to do this is to say *"Excusez moi Monsieur / Madame, où est* [insert what you're looking for here], *s'il vous plait?"* It may seem easier to leave out the beginning and end of that sentence and simply say *"Où est Notre Dame?"* but in French that sounds very rude. You'll probably get a friendlier response from someone on the street rather than asking at newsstand kiosks, since the attendants can get cranky after giving out directions all day long.

THE INSIDE STORY

In France, the ground floor (what is called the "first floor" in the US) is called the *rez de chaussée* ("ray-de-sho-say") or *RDC*. The level above that ("second floor" in the US) is called the *première étage* (first floor), the next is called the *deuxième étage* (second floor), and so on. The basement level is called the *sous-sol*, or *SS*.

Guided Tours in English

There are many companies offering tours of Paris to suit all tastes and budgets, from private, air conditioned shuttle tours that stop at the major monuments and the Moulin Rouge, to small walking tours that focus on historical or cultural themes. Tours where a large group is taken on a set itinerary are usually less expensive than customized tours for private groups. Always call to confirm times for tours where reservations aren't necessary. Any tours that include a lunch or snack break usually don't include the food and drink in the price. Be prepared for outdoor tours with appropriate seasonal clothing and comfortable walking shoes.

ATTENTION! *Many of the web sites listed in this guide are in French, but a good number offer an English-language version. Look for an American or British flag symbol, or the word "English," on the site's homepage.*

DID YOU KNOW?

■ Paris & Ile-de-France

Paris Walkabout (www.pariswalkabout.com) offers private, personalized walking tours with officially licensed, multilingual tour guides of popular Paris neighborhoods such as the Tuileries, St-Michel, Montmartre, the Marais, and the covered passages. They also run museum tours and organize excursions to destinations outside Paris such as Chantilly and Giverny. The Dutch/Indonesian cultural trainer and tour coordinator Yita Hillyard has been living in Paris for the past 20 years. Her tours focus on helping visitors put everything they see into a historical context without overwhelming them with too many facts and figures. Guides also share their knowledge of French lifestyles and Parisian habits. The tour itineraries can be changed at any moment at the whim of the client. For groups of up to five people, three-hour tours are €130, day-trips outside Paris cost €250 and three-hour museum tours cost €130. Prices are higher for larger groups, and transportation and entry fees are not included. Paris Walkabout also has their own native French wine expert offering wine tasting sessions from €260 for two to four people (€30 for each additional person). Check out their web site for contact information and tour descriptions.

AUTHOR'S NOTE: *There are some tour operators (none listed in this guide) who think three hours is enough time to visit destinations outside Paris such as Versailles and Fontainebleau. If you're going to "do the châteaux," do them right and spend the whole day! There's often as much to see in the gardens and surrounding village as in the châteaux themselves. Even if this means you only have time to see one, your in-depth experience will be much more memorable.*

Paris à Pied (☎ 01 46 27 11 56 or 06 64 77 11 56, www.parisapied.com) offers laid-back, three-hour walking tours of central Paris, the Latin Quarter, the Marais and Montmartre for €45 per person. The company is

based out of Minneapolis, but all of the native English-speaking guides
live in Paris. Groups are kept small (eight people max) for comfortable exploration of the city's major monuments and hidden corners.

French Links Tours (☎/fax 01 45 77 01 63, www.frenchlinks.com), offers
a large selection of cultural tours such as Revolutionary Paris, Jewish
Paris, A Woman's History Tour, Children's Paris, and French Links Tours
for the Disabled, as well as fashion, antique and flea-market shopping
tours. The guides are either native English-speakers with advanced degrees in art and history, or trained French guides speaking flawless English. They also conduct tours to other destinations such as Normandy, the
Loire Valley, Vaux-le-Vicomte and Barbizon. All of the French Links tours
are for private groups (pricing is per group, not per person), and are therefore perfect for families and small groups with special needs. This
Franco-American company is run by the expat American Rachel Kaplan,
author of many specialized books on Paris museums and shopping. Tours
are available year-round, even on French holidays. Transportation by
train, chauffeured vehicle or minivan can be arranged for all tours on request. Prices start at $200 for two-hour walking tours (one to four people),
$400 for four-hour shopping tours (one to six people), and $700 for full-day
cultural tours (one to six people). All tours must be pre-booked and prepaid either by a US bank check or by credit card online. Detailed tour information and pricing can be found on their website.

Paris Walks (☎ 01 48 09 21 40, fax 01 42 43 75 51, http://ourworld.compu-
serve.com/homepages/pariswalking) are informal walking tours of the
city's most popular neighborhoods such as the Marais, Montmartre,
St-Germain-des-Prés and Ile de la Cité, with themed tours such as Jeffer-
son's Paris and the French Revolution. Many tours are specially designed
for children. No reservations are needed, just check the schedule online of
daily tours (or ask for a schedule to be mailed), and show up at the meeting point, rain or shine. The two-hour tours cost €10 for adults, €7 for students under 25, and €5 for children. Guides are all either native English
speakers who live in Paris, or perfectly bilingual French citizens. Private
tours and excursions outside Paris are also available on request. Contact
Paris Walks organizers Peter or Oriel Caine for more information.

Anne Hervé's **Walking Tours** (☎ 01 47 90 52 16, fax 01 47 33 94 56,
parisidf@online.fr, www.parisidf.online.fr) explore little-known neighborhoods such as **Batignolles**, the **Port de l'Arsenal**, **La Nouvelle
Athènes**, **Sentier** and the 13th-arrondissement **Chinatown** district.
Anne speaks four languages and was the first French guide to offer tours
in English. Her 90-minute neighborhood walks are €10 per person, no
pre-booking needed. See the web site above (add /Vis_Eng/CatGB98c.htm
for details about the tours and meeting places), or contact Anne directly.
She also organizes private walking or minibus tours.

■ Bus Tours

The **Paris L'OpenTour** (☎ 01 42 66 56 56, www.paris-opentour.com) double-decker-bus tours offer pre-recorded commentary in English of the city's major monuments. A bit on the dry side, but it's a useful way for first-timers in the capital to get their bearings and complete the "checklist." The best part about the Open Tours is that you can get off and on at any of the stops, or just ride around the four different loops all day. The one-day pass is €24, and the two-day pass is just €27. The kids' pass (ages four to 11) is €12 and is good for two days. Kids under age four ride for free. Tickets can be purchased on the bus (keep your headphones until your pass runs out), at tourism offices, RATP (métro or bus) ticket windows or the Open Tour Office (13 Rue Auber, 9th, M° Opéra or RER Auber).

SEE THE SIGHTS

Take a city bus for an inexpensive way to see the city. Avoid the rush hours (8am to 9:30am and 4pm to 7pm) to get a good seat.

- **Bus 21** (until midnight) for a great night-tour, from the Opéra Garnier, past Palais-Royal and the Comédie Française, the Louvre Museum, Ile de la Cité (Notre Dame), St-Michel, the Jardins du Luxembourg and up toward the Rue Mouffetard (get off at Berthollet-Vauquelin).

- **Bus 27** (until 8:30pm) does almost the same route, passing through the Carrousel du Louvre, with a stop at the bottom of Rue Mouffetard, "Monge-Claude Bernard."

- **Bus 29** (Monday-Saturday until 8:30pm) from the Opéra Garnier through the trendy shopping areas around Place des Victoires, along Rue Etienne-Marcel, past the Pompidou Center, into the Marais, and stop at the Place des Vosges or the Place de la Bastille.

- **Bus 63** (until midnight) from the Jardin des Plantes, through the Latin Quarter and St-Germain-des-Prés, past Les Invalides and the Musée d'Orsay, fantastic night views of the Eiffel Tower from Trocadéro.

- **Bus 73** (Monday-Saturday until 8:30pm) from the Musée d'Orsay to the Place de la Concorde, down the Avenue des Champs-Elysées, around the Arc de Triomphe and all the way to the Grande Arche de la Défense.

- **Bus 75** (Monday-Saturday until 8:30pm) from the Pont Neuf to the Parc de la Villette, passing the Hôtel de Ville, Place de la République, and the Parc des Buttes-Chaumont.

- **Bus 96** (Monday-Saturday until 8:30pm) from Montparnasse or Place St-Michel and passing through Châtelet, the Place des Vosges in the Marais, and up to Oberkampf, JP Timbaud, Belleville and Ménilmontant.

■ Specialized Tours

Belleville Insolite (☎ 01 43 57 49 85, www.belleville-insolite.org) is a non-profit organization that conducts insider tours of the eastern neighborhoods of Paris. A tour unlike others, you don't visit monuments or museums, but instead learn about the "underground" world of the Belleville, Ménilmontant, Charonne and Canal St-Martin quarters from the people who live there. Aimed at both locals and visitors, the tours are given by young, multi-lingual and multi-cultural guides. They highlight the side of the city unseen by the typical tourist: its artisans, hidden parks, and multi-cultural heritage (such as Belleville's Chinatown) or historical themes (such as "In the Steps of the Communards.") The 2½-hour tours cost €10 per person; check the web site for the weekly schedule (e-mail them if you need information in English). Reservations can be made by phone weekdays, 9am to 6pm.

Ricki Stevenson's **Black Paris Tours** (☎ 01 46 37 03 96 or 06 62 68 03 96 www.tomtmusic.com, rickis@club-internet.fr) explore the illustrious history of the hundreds of African-Americans who contributed to the cultural heritage of Paris from the 1800s to World War I, and from the days of the Harlem Renaissance to the 1970s. Ricki's personal connections within the Little Africa quarter and the garment district allow her guests to experience – and shop – in places usually off-limits to tourists. Tours Monday through Friday throughout the year, €80 per person for the six- to seven-hour walking-métro-bus tour (note: price does not include lunch). Discounts are available for groups of six or more.

 AUTHOR'S NOTE: *See the* Adventures *section, pages 163-187, for sightseeing cruises, bike tours and nature walks; and* Cultural Adventures, *pages 188-212, for art, photography, shopping and food tours.*

Take the Bus

Use the city buses, getting on and off at different sights if you have time. Start at Place de la Bastille and take **Bus 29** from Boulevard Beaumarchais to Place de l'Opéra (you'll pass by Place des Vosges, the Marais, the Pompidou Center, Rue Etienne-Marcel, and Place des Victoires). Change to **Bus 27** in front of the Café de la Paix (Bus 21 at night) and take it to Monge-Claude Bernard (passing the Palais Royal, Comédie Française, Louvre Museum, Carrousel du Louvre and Pei Pyramid, the Seine, Notre Dame Cathedral, and the Jardins du Luxembourg). Then walk up Rue Mouffetard (the market is open mornings, Tuesday through Sunday) to Place de la Contrescarpe. Turn down the Rue Lacépède, past the Mosquée de Paris (stop in for mint tea if you have time) and into the Jardin des Plantes. Walk all the way through to the exit at Place Valhubert, and cross onto the Quai St-Bernard for the **Batobus**. Take this all the way to the Eiffel Tower. Catch **Bus 42** (direction Gare du Nord) at the corner of Avenue Rapp and Avenue de la Bourdonnais to Place de la Madeleine (passing Avenue des Champs-Elysées, Place de la Concorde and the Tuileries Gardens). End the tour with a stroll over to Place Vendôme and a drink at the Hemingway Bar in the Hôtel Ritz if it's after 6:30pm (or at the more casual Harry's New York Bar nearby at 5 Rue Daunou any time of the day). If you have the evening free, take **métro 12** from Place de la Madeleine, direction Porte de la Chapelle, and get off at Abbesses, the heart of Montmartre, wandering down toward Pigalle on foot for the racy nightlife scene.

Sightseeing Passes

The **Paris Museum Pass** (*Carte Musées-Monuments*) allows free access without standing in line at over 70 museums and monuments in Paris and Ile-de-France (see the full list online at www.museums-of-paris.com /museum-pass). Tickets cost €22 for one day, €38 for three days, and €52 for five days (multiple days must be consecutive). This could be worth the price if you plan on visiting a lot of museums and monuments in a short period of time.

Keep in mind, though, that the Museum Pass doesn't allow access to temporary exhibitions, and that permanent collections of many museums are already free. Students and children usually receive free or discounted entrance. Most museums are closed on Monday or Tuesday, and the first Sunday of the month is usually free. Tickets can be purchased in advance at any participating museum or monument, at the tourism office, or major métro stations.

The **Carte Paris "Visite"** is essentially a public transportation pass with a few discounts to tourist sites. Tickets can be purchased for one, two, three or five days, for either zone 1-3 (Paris and immediate suburbs) or zone 1-5 (Paris, much of Ile-de-France, and airports). See the RATP web site (www.ratp.fr) for complete rate information.

Considering the short list of discounts offered (such as 10% off purchases from the gift shops at Disneyland, or two-for-one entrance to the Arc de Triomphe), it usually makes more sense to purchase a Paris Museum Pass and a separate *Mobilis* day pass (€5.20) or *Carte Orange Hebdomadaire* seven-day pass (€14.50 within Paris, or €28.90 for Paris, Ile-de-France and both airports); remember that kids ages four to 10 travel for half-price on public transportation. See "Transportation Passes" in the *Getting Around* section, page 45, for more information.

Paris by Neighborhood

■ East Right Bank

The Islands

 Begin exploring Paris where the city itself was born: the **Ile de la Cité**. Although virtually wiped clear of its winding medieval streets during Haussmann's reconstruction, the island is still an intriguing showcase of Paris history. At its westernmost tip you'll find the tiny green **Square du Vert Galant**, a popular spot for fishing on the Seine. From here you'll get a good look at the stone arches of the city's oldest bridge, ironically called **Pont Neuf** (New Bridge). Opened by Henri IV in 1603, it was the first bridge in Paris without houses built on it. The **statue of Henri IV** on the platform is actually a replacement commissioned by Louis XVIII after the original dating back to 1614 was torn down by the 1789 Revolutionaries. Cut through the tree-lined **Place Dauphine** (where you get a good view of the Palais de Justice) to the **Quai de l'Horloge**, which brings you to the foot of the medieval **Conciergerie**. Built in the early 14th century, this was part of the first French royal fortress (they later moved to the Louvre) until it became a prison in 1391. During the 1789 Revolution, 2,780 men and women were detained in the Conciergerie while awaiting their trip to the guillotine, including Marie Antoinette, whose personal belongings and prison cell are now open to public viewing. If macabre wax figures in bad wigs don't give you the creeps, the 14th-century vaulted cellars are quite impressive, though a bit empty. Open daily, 10am to 5pm; entry €5.50 (€3.50 for children). Museum Pass accepted. ☎ 01 53 73 78 50.

 AUTHOR'S NOTE: *The oldest clock in Paris is on the façade of the Palais de Justice, at the corner of the Quai de l'Horloge (*horloge *is French for clock) and Pont au Change.*

Today the Conciergerie is part of the **Palais de Justice** complex (HQ of the French judicial system). Policemen and an impressive iron gate guard the entrance along the busy Boulevard du Palais. Almost completely hidden behind the towering walls is the 13th-century **Sainte-Chapelle**. If you are only going to set foot in one religious monument in Paris, this should be the one. There are actually two levels to the chapel: the one upstairs is what you want to see. Built by Louis IX during the zenith of stained glass arts, there are almost 6,500 square feet of stained-glass windows representing 1,134 scenes, including a giant rose window depicting the Apocalypse. Visit on a sunny day to get the brilliant, kaleidoscope

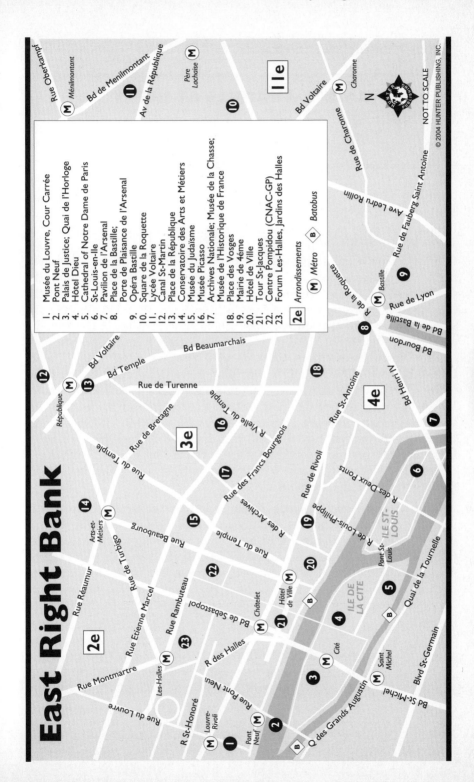

East Right Bank

Key

1. Musée du Louvre, Cour Carrée
2. Pont Neuf
3. Palais de Justice; Quai de l'Horloge
4. Hôtel Dieu
5. Cathedral of Notre Dame de Paris
   St-Louis-en-Ile
6. Pavilion de l'Arsenal
7. Place de la Bastille;
8. Porte de Plaisance de l'Arsenal
   Opéra Bastille
9. Square de la Roquette
10. Lycée Voltaire
11. Canal St-Martin
12. Place de la République
13. Conservatoire des Arts et Métiers
14. Musée du Judaïsme
15. Musée Picasso
16. Archives Nationale; Musée de la Chasse;
17. Musée de l'Historique de France
18. Place des Vosges
19. Mairie de 4éme
20. Hôtel de Ville
21. Tour St-Jacques
22. Centre Pompidou (CNAC-GP)
23. Forum Les-Halles, Jardins des Halles

2e *Arrondissements*

Ⓜ *Métro* Ⓑ *Batobus*

N

NOT TO SCALE

© 2004 HUNTER PUBLISHING, INC.

Paris

effect. Open daily, 10am to 5pm; entry €5.50 (€3.50 for students, free for children). Museum Pass accepted. ☎ 01 53 73 78 51.

SAINTE-CHAPELLE AT NIGHT

Classical music concerts are held most nights throughout the year in Sainte-Chapelle. See the *Entertainment* section, page 303, for more information.

Continue down the Rue de Lutèce, where the imposing **Préfecture de Police** is softened by the lush colors of the **Marché aux Fleurs**, the city's largest flower and plant market. The greenhouses and boutiques are open to the public Monday through Saturday. On Sundays the sidewalks are taken over by a bustling bird and poultry market. Follow the crowds across the street to one of the city's most recognizable monuments, the **Cathedral of Notre Dame**. Don't let the excitement of seeing the famous Gothic portals keep you from looking down: **Place du Parvis**, the square in front of the church, has cobblestones outlining the original streets and shops that stood in front of the church from the Middle Ages before Baron Haussmann later decided the cathedral needed more breathing room. The round, bronze plaque on the ground is known as **Pointe Zéro**, where all measurements in France begin (and which makes for an instantly forgettable photo). Underneath the cobblestones is the **Crypte du Parvis Notre-Dame**, where vestiges of Gallo-Roman streets and housing from the third century were discovered when the city tried to build an underground parking lot there in the 1970s. You still have to pay to go in, but you can't take your car. Open daily, 10am to 5pm, ☎ 01 43 29 83 51. Museum Pass accepted.

If you just saw three busloads of school children enter the cathedral in front of you, take a time-out and duck into the **Hôtel Dieu** next door, a busy Parisian hospital built in 1878 to replace the original crumbling hospital that had stood here since the Middle Ages. It was in this hospital that Pasteur did much of his pioneering research. The quiet courtyard gardens are open to the public. Hôtel Dieu Hospitel (B2 gallery, sixth floor): 1, Place du Parvis-Notre Dame, 4th, ☎ 01 44 32 01 00, fax 01 44 32 01 16.

DID YOU KNOW?

AUTHOR'S NOTE: *You don't have to be ill to get a bed overlooking Notre Dame. In 1992 the top floor of the Hôtel Dieu was converted into hotel rooms. Modest doubles are just under €100.*

Notre Dame Cathedral is one of the most consistent backdrops in the history of Paris. Built on the site of an ancient Roman temple, the first stones were laid by Pope Alexander III in 1163. Even before construction was complete, people came from all over Europe to see this amazing architectural feat. Seven centuries later, we still can't get enough of the flying buttresses, the stained glass windows, and the intricately carved statues on the façade. Pillaged during the 1789 Revolution (the *sans-culottes* smashed the statues of the saints, thinking they were kings) and subsequently turned into a wine depot, it was restored to the church by Napoleon when he was crowned Emperor there in 1804. It survived the Paris Commune of 1871 (supposedly because the *communards* didn't want to burn anything too close to the hospital next door where they took their wounded), although it suffered badly from neglect. When Victor Hugo's *Notre Dame de Paris* (a.k.a. *The Hunchback of Notre Dame*) was published in 1831, Parisians were inspired to shell out for massive renovations. It was only in 1854 that the architect Viollet-le-Duc added the gargoyles and spire to the towers. The cathedral is open daily, 8am to 6:45pm; services are at 9:30am, organ recitals Sundays at 5:30pm. ☎ 01 42 34 56 10.

THE TOWERS

 If you decide to climb the 400 steps to visit the towers of Notre Dame, try to do it as early as possible to avoid "traffic jams" in the claustrophobic corkscrew stairwells. Free guided tours in English are available Wednesday and Thursday at noon, Saturday at 2:30pm, and daily at 2:30pm in August. Don't forget to ask your guide to tap on the 14-ton church bell "Emmanuelle." The tower entrance is on Rue du Cloître-Notre-Dame. Open Monday through Thursday, 9am to 6:45pm; Friday to Sunday, 9am to 9:15pm (10am to 5pm in winter); entry €5.50, €3.50 for students, free at all times for kids and the first Sunday of the month from October through March for everyone else. Museum Pass accepted.

Usually less crowded than the front of Notre Dame, the gardens of **Square Jean XXIII** offer great views of the cathedral and a shady place to rest your feet. Before crossing the Pont St-Louis, take a moment to visit the Square de l'Ile-de-France on the easternmost tip of the island. Once the location of a morgue, it has been home to the emotional **Jewish Deportation Memorial** since 1962 (open daily, 10am to noon and 2pm to 5pm).

Cross over to the **Ile St-Louis** on its eponymous bridge. Once a muddy field full of grazing cows, it was developed into residences and shops in the 17th century, and has hardly changed ever since. The privileged few residents of Ile St-Louis are so happily isolated on their island from modern city life that they even say they're "Going to Paris" whenever they cross the Seine. Despite the many visitors who march through its streets on a daily basis, the atmosphere remains village-like. Let yourself wander the streets, and maybe get a peek into one of the private courtyards.

There's a memorial plaque on the **Hôtel de Jassaud** (Quai d'Anjou), where Camille Claudel lived after leaving her lover and contemporary, the sculptor Rodin. Just next door is the magnificent **Hôtel de Lauzun**. Built in 1656 by Louis Le Vau for a wealthy arms dealer, it was eventually sold to the Duke de Lauzun, one of Louis XIV's favored marshals. Baudelaire supposedly wrote most of his novel *Les Fleurs du Mal* in a room on the third floor. With most of its original décor still intact, it remains the most authentic example of a 17th-century aristocratic residence open to the public. Owned by the City of Paris since 1928, visits are organized by the Caisse des Monuments Historiques, ☎ 01 44 61 20 00.

When walking down the main axis of the island, Rue St-Louis-en-Ile, don't miss the **Eglise Saint-Louis-en-l'Ile**. There's a strange clock built in 1741 that hangs down from the church's entrance like a shop sign. The Baroque church was built between 1644 and 1726. It suffered the same fate as most churches during the Revolution, being shut down and stripped of its artworks. The paintings that decorate the church today were commissioned by the Abbot Bousset from 1864-1888. Concerts take place here almost nightly throughout the summer.

WHO WAS SAINT LOUIS?

 It seems everything on the island is named for Saint Louis. He was Louis IX, one of France's most religious kings. He built **Sainte-Chapelle** as a shrine for the relics he bought from the Emperor of Constantinople: Christ's crown of thorns and a piece of the cross. The sainted king died of the plague at Carthage in 1270 during the eighth Crusade.

St-Paul

Cross over to the Right Bank on the Pont de Sully. Just to the right is the **Pavillon de l'Arsenal** (21 Boulevard Morland, 4th, M° Sully-Morland, ☎ 01 42 76 33 97, www.pavillon-arsenal.com), an information and exposition center for city planning and architecture in Paris. This modern, converted loft space gives visitors a chance to see the current and future urban planning projects for Paris, with a giant floor model of the city (1/2,000th of its actual size), drawings and photographs. On the upper floors you'll find temporary exhibits and proposals for the latest city projects. Free entry; open Tuesday through Saturday, 10:30am to 6:30pm; and Sunday, 11am to 7pm.

As you leave the Pavillon de l'Arsenal, head west and cut through the **Square Henri-Galli**. Most people miss the small stack of masonry stones amid the flowers in this unassuming garden. A small plaque reveals them as the only surviving section of the Bastille's foundations, unearthed during the construction of the métro Line 1 in 1899.

Head away from the Seine on Rue St-Paul to the maze of whitewashed courtyards of the **Village Saint-Paul**, a former city orphanage now populated with charming antique and secondhand shops. If you leave by the other side, at the **Jardins St-Paul**, you can see a section of the 13th-century city fortifications built by Philippe Auguste, now serving as the wall of a high school sports field. Through the Passage Charlemagne around the corner is the only remaining Jesuit church in Paris, **Eglise Saint-Paul-Saint-Louis**. Built as a deliberate snub to the Reformation, this 17th-century church was impressive, with a three-story theatrical façade and rich Baroque interior artworks that were plundered during the Revolution (and now on display in the Louvre). Once just called Eglise St-Louis (after the church's benefactor, Louis XIII), it got its mouthful of a name after the Revolution, when the church absorbed the parish of the destroyed Eglise St-Paul.

KID-FRIENDLY

 Just outside the Village Saint-Paul is the **Museum of Curiosities and Magic** (11 Rue St-Paul, 4th, ☎ 01 42 72 13 26), housed in the 16th-century cellars of a building that once belonged to the Marquis de Sade. Leave your bah-humbug skepticism outside and enjoy the optical illusions, automated antique statues, and the mysterious history of conjuring for an unforgettable visit. There's a continuous magic demonstration from 2 to 7pm. Open Wednesdays, Saturdays and Sundays; entry €7 for adults, €4.60 for kids under 13.

Cut back down the side-street Rue du Prevôt and along Rue du Figuier. You can't miss the fairytale-like **Hôtel de Sens**, one of the rare examples (along with the Musée Cluny) of civil architecture from the Middle Ages. Built in 1475 for the archbishop of Sens, the mansion then passed to Henri IV's ex-wife, Queen Margot. She had the immense fig tree (which the street was named for) cut down so her carriage could pass. The city bought and restored the building in 1916, and today it houses the **Bibliothèque Fourney**, a library dedicated to the decorative arts. Open Tuesday through Friday, 1:30pm to 8pm; and Saturday, 10am to 8:30pm. ☎ 01 42 78 14 60. As you head toward the Rue François Miron, make a detour to the modern world at the **Maison Européenne de la Photographie** (5-7 Rue de Fourcy, 4th, M° St-Paul, ☎ 01 44 78 75 00, www.mep-fr.org). Behind the façade of the typical 18th-century *hôtel*

particulier (once a private house) is a collection of over 15,000 contemporary photos from the 1950s to the present day, from photographers such as Irving Penn, Robert Franck and Raymond Depardon. It's quite a lively place, with a library, exposition center, videothèque and a small café under the old stone vaulted ceilings. Open Wednesday through Sunday, 11am to 8pm. Entry €5 (€2.50 for students and children).

Hôtel de Ville

Going toward the Hôtel de Ville, follow the narrow Rue François Miron, an ancient street full of unique gift shops and art galleries. On the left is the information center for **Paris Historique** (44-46 Rue François Miron, 4th, M° St-Paul, ☎ 01 48 87 74 31, www.paris-historique.org), an organization dedicated to preserving the city's historic buildings. The ground floor houses photo exhibitions of their restoration worksites throughout France, with information on how to become a volunteer. Don't miss the Gothic arches recently excavated in the information center's cellars. Open daily, 2pm to 6pm, free entry. Continuing down the Rue François Miron, it would be hard to miss the rare 15th-century half-timbered houses at the corner of Rue Cloche-Perce (or the unmarked front door to the discreet swingers club inside).

Find more half-timbered buildings around the corner on the pedestrian-only Rue des Barres. On the right is the flamboyant Gothic rear of the 16th-century **Eglise St-Gervais-St-Protais**. Walk around the front to see the Doric, Ionic and Corinthian columns of the façade – the first example of Classic-style architecture in Paris – glowing from a recent restoration. A German bomb was dropped on this church on Good Friday (March 29) 1918, killing 160 parishioners. Today the church is used by the Catholic Community of Jerusalem, whose robed monks and nuns are often seen strolling around the neighborhood. Stop by at 4pm on the first Saturday of the month to hear a free recital on the oldest organ in Paris, built in 1601.

Walk along the Quai de l'Hôtel de Ville to the vast paved square in front of the Paris City Hall, the Hôtel de Ville (a.k.a. *le Mairie de Paris*). The original city hall, dating back to the 16th century, was burned down during the revolt of the Paris Commune in 1871. The current building was completed in 1882, featuring a neo-Renaissance façade with 136 statues of French *grands hommes*. Parisians always gather at the Place-de-l'Hôtel-de-Ville for major events and festivals such as Bastille Day. During the Middle Ages it was the location of public executions (Ravaillac – King Henri IV's murderer – was hanged, drawn and quartered here). Today it's transformed into a beach volleyball court for *Paris Plage* in the summer and into an ice-skating rink in the winter. The elegant interior reception halls, decorated by the leading 19th-century artists, are open to the public on special occasions only. Visitors can pick up free information about the city (usually in French) at the Hôtel de Ville's **Bureau d'Accueil**, which also

Hôtel de Ville (Mairie de Paris) with Chinese Lanterns

Above: Parc de Bagatelle, Bois de Boulogne

Below: Bercy Village

Above: African drummers, Parc de la Villette

Below: Centre Pompidou at night
(Photos © David Henry)

Arc de Triomphe at night (Photo © David Henry)

Opéra Garnier, detail of façade

Music along Canal St-Martin (Photo © David Henry)

Above: Montmartre Streetscape
Below: Rue de Belleville, Chinatown
(Photos © David Henry)

Houses, Butte aux Cailles

hosts fascinating Paris cultural exhibitions throughout the year. Free admission; entrance at 29 Rue de Rivoli; ☎ 01 42 76 43 43.

Across the street is the **Bazaar de l'Hôtel de Ville**, or BHV, the department store beloved by Parisians for its *bricolage* (hardware/do-it-yourself) section in the basement. Those who aren't in the market for a hammer can stop into its **Bricolo' Café**, decorated to look like a vintage tool shed, or take the elevator to the sixth floor and follow signs to the outdoor terrace for views over the Hôtel de Ville. The Gothic tower to the west is the 16th-century **Tour St-Jacques**, all that remains of the church St-Jacques-de-la-Boucherie, torn down in 1802. On top is a statue of the physicist Pascal, who conducted experiments on the weight of air in the tower in 1648. You can't go inside, but there's a nice little park with benches around the base of the tower.

THE ARISTOCRACY LIVES ON!

The French royal family may have ended up at the guillotine more than two centuries ago, but the surviving aristocrats and their royalist supporters still gather, hoping French democracy is just a phase. If you're curious, stop into the royalist HQ, the **Bar des Templiers** (35 Rue de Rivoli, 4th). It may seem like a typical scruffy old Parisian café, but one look at the walls covered in fleurs-de-lis and tributes to Louis XVI will convince you otherwise.

Beaubourg

The Beaubourg neighborhood isn't quite as chic as the Marais, yet it hasn't sold its soul to the fast-food and cheap clothing chains found in Les Halles either. Before the colorful Pompidou Center arrived in the 1970s, the quarter was dominated by the **Eglise St-Merri**, on the corner of Rue de la Verrerie and Rue St-Martin. Like most churches in Paris, this 16th-century flamboyant Gothic church was built to replace a much older chapel dating to the ninth century, and has itself been heavily renovated since the French Revolution. The tower holds the oldest church bell in Paris, built for the original chapel in 1313. Explore the old surrounding streets of Rue du Cloître St-Merri and Rue Brisemiche, where the animated machines of the **Fontaine Stravinsky** (by sculptors Jean Tinguely and Niki de Saint Phalle) ease the transition into contemporary Beaubourg.

AUTHOR'S NOTE: *Fans of Gothic art and architecture can spend a night in the Hôtel St-Merry (78 Rue de la Verrerie, 4th), in the church's restored 17th-century presbytery. See the* Where to Stay *section, page 232, for more details.*

The instantly recognizable **Pompidou Center**, with its controversial "inside-out" architecture, hardly needs an introduction, but a plan of action will make for a better visit. Known officially as the **Centre National d'Art et de Culture Georges Pompidou** (M° Rambuteau or Hôtel-de-Ville, ☎ 01 44 78 12 33, www.cnac-gp.fr/english), this modern center for the arts is made up of the **National Museum of Modern Art**, a **public library** (see below), the **Atelier Brancusi** sculpture studios, plus an art house cinema, concert halls, gift shop, bookstore, café and the trendy **Georges Restaurant** on the top floor. The long lines at the main entrance can be discouraging, especially if it's cold or raining outside. Try to visit after 5 pm, or use one of the sneakier entrances. The red elevator (just to the left of the main entrance) is reserved for those going to the Georges. If you feel that the prices are a bit high (or it's not time to eat yet), enjoy the amazing panoramic views before taking the escalators down to the main lobby.

The public library (**Bibliothèque Publique d'Information**, a.k.a. **BPI**) has its own entrance on the Rue de Renard, with an exit leading directly into the main lobby. Try not to make it too obvious that you're just there for the shortcut! The lobby is where visitors will find the ticket machines, post office, information desk, free cloakroom, bookstore and entrances leading to the Museum, Atelier Brancusi, cinema and concert auditoriums. Overlooking all this action is the mezzanine café and Printemps design boutique.

The Pompidou Center is open daily except Tuesday from 11am to 10pm (until 11pm on Thursday). The Museum is open 11am to 9pm (last admission 8pm), and the Atelier Brancusi is open 2pm to 6pm. Entry to the Centre Pompidou is free; for the Museum and Atelier the fee is €5.50, €3.50 for visitors ages 18 to 25, free for kids under 18. Museum Pass accepted. A combined day pass for the Museum, Atelier Brancusi and temporary exhibits is €10, €8 for visitors 13 to 25, free for kids under 13 (and for everyone the first Sunday of the month). Prices vary for music, dance and theater concerts, cinema screenings, and concerts. Guided tours are Saturdays at 4pm, €4 (plus entrance ticket).

WARNING! *the automated ticket machines at the Pompidou Center only work with French bank cards.*

Back outside, enjoy the lively atmosphere of the **Place Georges Pompidou**, where Parisians and tourists watch the bustling scene of street performers and portrait artists from leafy café terraces. Slip down the narrow Rue de Venise, turning right onto Rue Quincampoix, a quiet pedestrian street lined with art galleries and unique shops. Don't miss the romantic **Passage Molière**, home to the Théâtre Molière (opened in 1791), a tiny bistro and various bric-a-brac shops. Its uneven cobblestones contrast with the slick concrete of the **Quartier Horloge** across the street. Ignore the uninspiring copy shops and have a peek at **Le Défenseur du Temps**, a brass and steel mechanical clock on the wall at the corner of Rue Clairvaux and Passage Brantôme. At noon, 6pm and 10pm, the life-size armored soldier comes to life to battle a dragon, a crab, or a bird with his sword. The dragon's breathing keeps time throughout the day (you can see his belly moving in and out). But don't go too far out of your way to see this clock, since it's frequently out of commission for tune-ups.

Le Marais

The Marais is one of the city's most popular neighborhoods, with an established Jewish population, trendy designer boutiques, and a lively gay scene. The maze of narrow streets hides a mix of medieval architecture and 16th-century *hôtels particuliers*, many converted into museums and government buildings.

FROM CHARLES V TO CHARLES DE GAULLE

 The Marais was once just a soggy marshland (a *marais*). When Charles V built the new ramparts in the 14th century, he brought this neighborhood within the city walls and drained the marshes. After several security incidents at the royal palace on Ile de la Cité, Charles V moved to the Hôtel St-Paul in the Marais. The aristocrats followed, building illustrious private mansions. The Place Royale (today known as **Place des Vosges**; see page 96) was built during the neighborhood's heyday in the 17th century. Gradually, the nobility moved west to the new quarters of the Faubourg St-Honoré and Faubourg St-Germain. After revolutionaries destroyed the Bastille, the quarter was virtually abandoned. By the 1960s, its rat-infested, derelict buildings were destined for the bulldozers. It was Charles de Gaulle's cultural minister, the writer André Malraux, who finally convinced the city to rehabilitate the old buildings instead.

Begin at Rue Rambuteau, a colorful market street, turning left onto Rue du Temple. On the left is the monumental gateway of the 17th-century Hôtel de St-Aignan, now home to the **Musée d'Art et d'Histoire du Judaïsme** (71 Rue du Temple, 3rd, M° Rambuteau, ☎ 01 53 01 86 60, www.mahj.org). Formerly located in Montmartre, this museum features a detailed history of Jewish culture, as well as artworks by Chagall, Modigliani, and Soutine. Open Monday through Friday, 11am to 6pm, and Sunday, 10am to 6pm. Entry to museum and temporary expositions (including multilingual audio guide) €8.50, €6 for visitors 18-26, free for kids under 18.

Follow the Rue des Haudriettes to the Rue des Archives. Note the contemporary wall murals and 17th-century fountain. A short detour to the left will take you to the **Musée de la Chasse et de la Nature** (60 Rue des Archives, 3rd, ☎ 01 53 01 92 40) in the Hôtel de Guénégaud, one of the best restored *hôtels particuliers* in the Marais. The museum displays decorative arts, paintings by Rembrandt and Monet, and various hunting trophies and accessories. Open Tuesday through Sunday, 11am to 6pm; entry €4.60. Back on the Rue des Archives, note the **ancient gateway and turret** across from the intersection of Rue Braque. Built in 1372, they are the only remaining vestiges of the **Hôtel de Clisson**, where the Guise family lived during the French religious wars. It was incorporated into the 16th-century Hôtel de Soubise, today's National Archives, whose entrance is around the corner on the Rue des Francs-Bourgeois.

Made up of the Hôtel de Soubise and the Hôtel de Rohan, the **Archives Nationales** (60 Rue des Francs-Bourgeois, 3rd, M° Rambuteau, ☎ 01 40 27 62 18) was opened by Napoleon in 1808, and houses the French archives from the Merovingians to 1958. Napoleon III later opened the Musée de l'Histoire de France in the same building to present some of the Archives' more prestigious documents to the general public. It's worth a visit to see the formal French gardens and interior architectural details throughout the building. Some rooms are closed during renovations (through Fall 2004), so entrance is free (normally €3). Open weekdays except Tuesday, 10am to 12:30pm and 2 to 5:30pm; weekends, 2 to 5:30pm.

Continue along Rue des Francs-Bourgeois, where many traces of the past can be found. In the corridor at 57*bis*, between the Credit Agricole bank and Les 2 Milles Feuilles boutique, it's possible to see the top of a 12th-century tower from the Philippe Auguste wall (seen earlier in the St-Paul quarter). Overlooking the intersection at Rue Vielle-du-Temple is the elegant turret of the **Hôtel Hérouet**, built around 1500. Opposite the Rue des Hospitalières Saint-Gervais is the creepy looking **Impasse Arbalétriers**, where Charles VI's brother, Louis d'Orléans, was assassinated in 1407 under the orders of the Duke of Burgundy (Jean-sans-Peur), sparking off the civil war between the Bourguignons and the Armagnacs.

Bob and weave through the dense streets between Rue des Hospitalières Saint-Gervais, and Rue St-Croix de la Bretonnerie, arriving back onto the Rue des Archives. The **Cloître des Carmes-Billettes** (24 Rue Archives, 4th) dates back to 1427, and is the only intact cloister in Paris. The entrance seems quite plain, but inside is a courtyard of four galleries and 14 flamboyant Gothic arcades, open to the public for regular arts expositions.

AUTHOR'S NOTE: *The Marais is one of the few Parisian neighborhoods where shops and cafés are open on Sunday.*

From the Rue de la Verrerie, turn left onto the Rue Vieille du Temple, home to some of the Marais' most popular cafés and bars. This leads to the Rue des Rosiers, heart of the Paris Jewish community, lined with kosher delis and falafel stands and, more recently, designer clothing boutiques. At #7 is the **Jo Goldenberg Restaurant**, where a lone bullet hole outlined in the window is a sad reminder of the unsolved terrorist attack that killed six and seriously injured 22 people on August 9, 1982. There are a number of orthodox synagogues on the side-streets off Rue des Rosiers. One of the most famous is the **Agudath Hakehilot** at 10 Rue Pavée, designed by the Art Nouveau architect Hector Guimard, and completely restored after it was dynamited by the Germans in 1940.

Paris

THE JEWISH COMMUNITY

The Marais has been a Jewish quarter off and on since the 12th century. Jews were given full French citizenship after the Revolution, attracting a new wave of immigration. After the horrors of deportation during the Nazi occupation, the Jewish community was re-established by refugees from Central and Eastern Europe in the 1960s and, more recently, by Sephardic Jews from North Africa and the Middle East. To learn more about the Jewish community in Paris, sign up for one of the many specialized tours mentioned at the beginning of this chapter, page 72.

Head back up Rue Pavée past some excellent bookshops (at 17*bis* and #24) to the Rue Payenne. On the left is the entrance to the **Centre Culturel Suédois** (Swedish Culture Center), in the 16th-century Hôtel de Marle. Stop by their café for a snack or relax in the secluded gardens if the weather is nice (closed August). Across the street is a small public garden, the **Square Georges Caïn**, decorated with a salvaged section of the old Tuileries Palace façade.

Turn left on the Rue du Parc Royal for a double museum detour. The **Picasso Museum** (5 Rue de Thorigny, 3rd, M° Chemin Vert or St-Paul, ☎ 01 42 71 25 21, www.musee-picasso.fr) is in the dramatic Hôtel Salé. It's the largest collection of Picasso's works, and includes the artist's personal collection of paintings by Matisse, Renoir and Cézanne, all presented in a minimalist setting. When entering the courtyard, the ticket office is to the right, and the entrance is straight ahead. Don't miss the sculpture garden on the ground floor. Open daily except Tuesday, 9:30am to 5:30pm (until 6pm in summer). Entry €5.50, €4 for visitors 18-25, free for kids under 18. Museum Pass accepted.

The lesser-known **Musée Cognacq-Jay** (8 Rue Elzévir, 3rd, M° Chemin Vert or St-Paul, ☎ 01 40 27 07 21, www.paris-tourism.com/museums/cognacq-jay) features a small collection of 18th-century European paintings and *objets d'art* bequeathed to the city by the founder of the Samaritaine department store in 1928. Located in the Hôtel Donan, it's one of the more intimate Marais museums. Open Tuesday through Sunday, 10am to 6pm; free entry to the permanent collection. An English brochure is available for €4.

Back onto the Rue du Parc Royal, stop by the **Square Leopold-Achille** for picture-pretty views of the **Musée Carnavalet**, a municipal museum dedicated to the history of Paris. The museum entrance is around the corner at 23 Rue de Sévigné (M° Chemin Vert or St-Paul, ☎ 01 44 59 58 58). Since the entry to the vast permanent collection is free, splurge on an English guidebook (€9 in the museum bookshop). The museum uses artworks, scale models and everyday objects to illustrate the city's fascinating and often tragic history from the Gallo-Roman period to the 20th century, with a particular focus on the French Revolution. Allow at least two hours for a full visit. Open Tuesday through Sunday, 10am to 6pm, free entry. Guided tours in English every first Saturday of the month.

Continue down the Rue de Sévigné to the Rue St-Antoine, taking a left at Rue de Jarente for a scenic detour through the **Place du Marché Ste-Catherine**. Back on Rue St-Antoine, duck into the 17th-century **Hôtel de Sully** (62 Rue St-Antoine, 4th), a Renaissance-style mansion once owned by the Duc de Sully, Henri IV's minister of finance. Completely restored, today it houses the offices of the Center of National Monuments and the temporary exhibitions of the Patrimoine Photographique (this collection is scheduled to move to the Jeu de Paume Museum by the end of 2004). The public has free access to the striking garden courtyard, where a small gateway leads directly into the Place des Vosges.

Henri IV commissioned the **Place des Vosges** in the early 17th century as the crowning glory of the fashionable Marais district. Called Place Royale up until the French Revolution, it was briefly dubbed the Place de l'Indivisibilité before receiving its current name by Napoleon in honor of the first French département to pay its taxes. Relax in the grassy square for a moment to admire the symmetrical brick pavilions and arcades, which have hardly changed over the centuries. It's possible to visit the **Maison de Victor Hugo** (6 Place des Vosges, 4th, M° Chemin Vert, ☎ 01 42 72 10 16, www.paris.fr/musees/maison_de_victor_hugo), home of the exiled playwright and novelist from 1832-1848. Ask for the brochure in English at the entrance. Even those unfamiliar with his works, such as *Les Misérables*, will appreciate the period décor and scenic views over the Place des Vosges. Open Tuesday through Sunday, 10am to 6pm, free entry.

DID YOU KNOW? *There used to be another royal palace around the corner, the Palais des Tournelles. Catherine de Medicis had it torn down in 1559 after her husband,* **King Henri II**, *was accidentally killed during a friendly jousting match held just outside on the Rue St-Antoine.*

Temple & Arts-et-Métiers

Just a decade ago, the **Temple Quarter** used to be considered a bit of a "dead" area, with nothing more than wholesale shops and *ateliers* (workshops) for the leather and jewelry industries. But the neighborhood is experiencing a renaissance as art galleries, trendy tearooms and restaurants take over old workshops in the quiet streets off the Rue de Bretagne. Some Parisians even insist on calling it *NoMa*, for North Marais.

BUT WHERE IS THE TEMPLE?

The quarter actually gets its name from the **Knights Templar**, a religious and military order that once owned almost all the land around the Marais. Many artisans and craftsmen took refuge within the Templars' walls, where the monarchy had no jurisdiction to collect taxes. Their impressive wealth and property eventually aroused the resentment of King Philip IV, who decided to get rid of this "state within a state." The Knights Templar were imprisoned in 1307, and their lands confiscated by the Crown. In 1314 they were burned at the stake on the tip of the Ile de la Cité.

Begin at the corner of Rue de Turenne and Rue de Bretagne. You may notice a colorful building at the end of Rue des Filles du Calvaire at the top of the intersection. That's the **Cirque d'Hiver**, an early 19th-century circus still in use today by different visiting circus acts. Continue along the Rue de Bretagne, crossing the Rue Charlot, a street full of many new cafés and shops. Have a stroll through the renovated **Marché des Enfants Rouge** (entrances at 33*bis* Rue Charlot or 39 Rue de Bretagne, 3rd M° Filles du Calvaire). Built in 1612 (making it the oldest covered market in Paris), it reopened in 2000 after many years of neglect, narrowly escaping transformation into a parking garage. Today there are 15 market stands and a wine bar, with the typical fish, bread, fruit and veggie sellers (open Tuesday through Thursday, 9am to 2pm and 4 to 9pm; Friday through Saturday, 9am to 8pm; and Sunday, 9am to 2pm).

Continue along Rue de Bretagne to the Haussmann-era **Square du Temple**, flanked by the majestic **Mairie du 3ème** (the neighborhood's Town Hall) and the **Hôtel de la Garantie** (Assay Office for precious metals). The English-style gardens feature a small duck pond and 19th-century pavilion used for summer concerts. Members of the local Chinese community gather here in the morning to practice tai-chi on the lawn. Follow the Rue Perrée past the Mairie to the **Carreau du Temple**, a covered market of glass and steel built in 1857. Over the past few years it's been mostly empty save for a few uninteresting clothing stands, but the town planners are considering converting the old market into a neighborhood arts and cultural center by the end of 2004.

THE TEMPLAR TOWER

The Carreau du Temple was built on the location of the former Templar Tower, where the royal family was imprisoned during the French Revolution before being sentenced to death. Louis XVI was immediately guillotined, and Queen Marie Antoinette was transferred to the Conciergerie before it was her turn, leaving the *dauphin* alone in the Tower before he eventually died. Recent DNA tests from the gravesite finally put an end to rampant speculation that the real *dauphin* actually escaped. Napoleon had the Tower razed in 1808 to prevent royalist pilgrimages, but a wall plaque on the corner of Rue du Petit Thouars and Rue Eugène Spuller shows exactly where it once stood.

Heading into the Arts-et-Métiers Quarter, take a detour to the **Rue au Mairie**, a narrow street dating back to 1280. Today it's home to one of the city's thriving Wenzhou Chinese communities, with colorful clothing boutiques, authentic restaurants, and exotic food shops. This community, which now extends up to Belleville district, arrived from mainland China as recruited laborers during WWI. They're unrelated to the Teochew Chinese in the 13th (different dialect, foods and customs), who first came to Paris from Vietnam in the 1970s.

Continue up **Rue Volta** (the location of at least one of the oldest houses in Paris) to the **Musée des Arts et Métiers** (60 Rue Réamur, 3rd, M° Arts-et-Métiers, ☎ 01 53 01 82 00, www.arts-et-metiers.net), a museum illustrating humankind's progress in science and technology. Kids will love the full-size flying machine models, and even those not interested in "how things work" will appreciate the beautifully restored 18th-century architecture featuring vaulted, carved-wood ceilings. The whole place has a magical, Jules Verne atmosphere. Don't miss the richly painted interior of the 12th-century **Eglise St-Martin-des-Champs**, where Foucault's pendulum and Bartholdi's Statue of Liberty models are displayed. There is, regrettably, little translated into English (a guidebook can be purchased at the front desk for €9). Open Tuesday through Sunday, 10am to 6pm; Thursday until 9:30pm. Entry to the permanent collection €6.50, €4.50 for students, free for kids under 18. Museum Pass accepted.

TAKE THE SUBMARINE!

The **Arts-et-Métiers** métro station is decorated with copper walls and portholes to resemble the inside of a submarine.

The 10th

The 10th arrondissement is one to watch. Normally known for its traffic-clogged boulevards, train stations and dilapidated quarters, the ethnically diverse communities, village-like quarters, and the tranquility along the Canal St-Martin are things that Parisians are coming to appreciate. Inexpensive lofts are being snatched up by youngish *bobo's* (bourgeois bohemians), with the requisite cafés, bistros, and boutiques that cater to them. If you're looking for urban authenticity, the 10th has it. If you're looking for cute and comfortable, give it another decade (or two).

Boulevard de Strasbourg to the Gare du Nord

Begin at the métro Strasbourg-St-Denis, facing the Gare de l'Est at the far end of Boulevard de Sebastopol. One block to the left is the **Porte St-Denis**, to the right is the **Porte St-Martin**. These mini triumphant arches designate the city's 17th-century fortified gateways, torn down to create the Grands Boulevards in the 19th century.

The Boulevard de Strasbourg is lined with discount stores, hairdressers' supply shops, and street entrepreneurs offering to weave your hair into *tresses* (braids). A hidden gem is the **Musée de l'Eventail**, a museum featuring over 800 fans dating back to the 17th century, displayed in a wood-paneled exposition room built in 1867. The museum is run by the **Atelier Houguet**, the last traditional fan-making and repair workshop in France. 2 Boulevard de Strasbourg, 10th, M° Strasbourg-St-Denis, ☎ 01 42 08 90 20, www.museums-of-paris.com (click on "Decorative Arts" and scroll down the list). Open Monday through Wednesday, 2 to 6pm. Closed August. Entry €5.

Take a left into the **Passage Brady**, a slightly dilapidated covered passage built in 1828. Indian and Pakistani restaurants, shops and hairdressers slowly took over the passage in the 1970s, giving it the nickname

Little Bombay. Stop into the **Bazaar Velan** for incense, spices, and kitsch souvenirs.

Continue up the bustling Rue du Faubourg St-Denis to the **Cour des Petites Ecuries** (at #63), a quiet, cobblestoned passageway where the original **Brasserie Flo** retains its 1910 décor. Turn right at the end of the passage, continuing up Rue Martel to the **Rue de Paradis**. This was once the center for *arts de la table* manufacturing. Today the quarter is better known for its high-tech and film industry firms, but the street is still lined with boutiques selling well-known brands of cutlery, porcelain and glassware. Note the ceramic mosaic façade at the **Galerie Paradis** (number 18), formerly the location of a faïence (earthenware) shop, Magasin de Faïences Boulanger (the passage is closed to the public). The **Pinacothèque de Paris** (30*bis* Rue de Paradis, 10th, M° Poissonière, ☎ 01 53 34 06 70, www.pinacotheque.com) is a privately owned museum recently opened in the Second Empire building formerly home to the Baccarat Museum (now located in the 16th). The temporary expositions focus on rarely seen private collections from around the world (the first exposition featured the collection of Picasso's last wife, Jacqueline). The permanent collection is due to open by fall 2004. Open daily, 10am to 7pm, until 10:30pm Monday and Friday. Entry €12, €8 for visitors 13-25, €6 for kids ages eight to 12. Audio guide, €4.50.

Take Rue d'Hauteville, known for its fur-coat shops, up to the **Eglise St-Vincent-de-Paul**. This church, dedicated to the patron saint of charity who worked with the city's poor in the 17th century, has some beautifully painted woodwork. Continue to the corner of Boulevard de Magenta and Rue de Chabrol to visit the delightful **Marché St-Quentin** (open Monday through Saturday, 8am to 1pm and 3:30 to 7:30pm; Sunday, 8am to 1pm), a beautiful covered market with everything from flowers and produce to antiques and candies.

AUTHOR'S NOTE: *Much like the Brittany crêpe restaurants around the Gare Montparnasse, Alsatian brasseries opened around the Gare de l'Est to welcome immigrants arriving by train from* **Strasbourg** *and* **Alsace**. *Stop by the famous Schmid Delicatessen (76 Boulevard de Strasbourg, 10th) for an authentic soft pretzel (called bretzle in French).*

The somewhat dingy neighborhood between the Gare du Nord and Gare de l'Est is known as **Little Jaffna** for its prominent Tamil community from Sri Lanka. The Rue du Faubourg St-Denis, Rue Cail, and Rue Perdonet are lined with shops selling colorful saris, brass Buddha statues and exotic groceries. The adventurous will find some true bargains here!

Around the Canal St-Martin

 From the Gare de l'Est, take the Rue des Recollets past the Jardin Villemin to the tree-lined **Canal St-Martin**. Napoleon had the canal built to bring drinking water to Paris, but it was mainly used for transporting building materials. Today its nine locks between the Seine and the Bassin de la Villette are mostly used for sightseeing cruises. The Canal is at its best on warm summer weekends, when Parisians of all ages come here to stroll, picnic and even fish along the calm waters.

 **TIP:** *The length of the Canal from the Square des Recollets up to the Parc de la Villette is better explored in the comfort of a cruise boat, or along the smooth cycle paths on bike or in-line skates. The streets along the Canal are completely closed off to traffic every Sunday from May through October.*

On foot, head down the Quai de Valmy past the candy-colored façades of the **Antoine et Lili** boutiques (95 Quai Valmy, 10th), and cross the iron footbridge to the historic **Hôtel du Nord** (102 Quai Jemmapes, 10th). This was where the actress Arletty shouted her famous line "atmosphère, atmosphère..." in the film *Hôtel du Nord* by Marcel Carné. Fans of the recent French hit, *Le Fabuleux Destin d'Amélie Poulain* (titled *Amélie* for American release), will also recognize the Canal St-Martin as the place where Amélie came to skip stones.

Follow the Quai Jemmapes to the Avenue Richerand, which leads to the **Hôpital St-Louis**. One of the oldest hospitals in Paris, it was built in 1607 under Henri IV, with the same brick, stone and dormered slate rooftop architecture seen at the Place des Vosges. Walk around the south side of the hospital to the corner of Rue Alibert and Avenue Claude Vellefaux, where the **Carré St-Louis** offers a few benches for quiet contemplation under the trees. There's an open market here on Sunday mornings.

Make a detour to the **Sainte-Marthe Quarter**. This is the kind of place you'd never find unless you were looking for it, made up of just a handful of streets around the Place Sainte-Marthe. Its narrow *rues* are lined with colorful wooden façades faded with time, hidden artists' ateliers, and crumbling balconies decorated with flower pots and the day's wash hanging out to dry. Combine these humble surroundings with a lively, international population of immigrants from North Africa, Eastern Europe, the Far East and South America, and it's easy to see why many Parisians who live here find it reminiscent of the old quarters of Marseilles.

AUTHOR'S NOTE: See the Where to Eat section, page 267, for dining recommendations in this neighborhood.

Paris

La Villette & Buttes-Chaumont

The two main attractions in the 19th arrondissement are emblematic of the push to rehabilitate the east Paris industrial districts since Napoleon III. In the 1860s, Baron Haussmann created the city's first public park, the **Parc des Buttes-Chaumont**, on an old abandoned quarry site being used as a dump. At the same time, the city's new cattle market and *abattoirs* (slaughterhouses) were built just a few blocks north in La Villette. Obsolete by the 1970s, La Villette was completely redeveloped and opened in 1986 as a modern city park dedicated to science, arts and entertainment. The sleek lines of the **Parc de la Villette** are a stark contrast to the romantic hills of the Parc des Buttes-Chaumont, but both offer a much-needed escape from the surrounding concrete jungle.

The Parc de la Villette (☎ 01 40 03 75 75, www.villette.com) doesn't have any gates or walls. Within its 70 acres of mini-forests, bamboo groves and vast lawns are various museums, concert halls, and whimsical playgrounds. Begin at the métro Porte de la Villette, in front of the imposing **Cité des Sciences et de l'Industrie** (☎ 01 40 05 80 00, www.cite-sciences.fr), a science and technology museum with a section created especially for children. Pass directly through the main entrance to the other side, where the silver sphere of **La Géode Cinéma** (☎ 01 40 05 79 99, www.lageode.fr/fr/geo) mirrors the green grass and blue skies. Follow the covered walkway past the Dragon slide (okay, take a ride on the slide) and cross the **Canal Ourcq** at one of the red *folie* bridges. Continue on the covered pathway alongside the 19th-century glass and iron **Grande Halle**, the only vestige of the former cattle market, now used as an exposition center. Between the **Cité de la Musique** (☎ 01 44 84 44 84, www.cite-musique.fr) concert hall and the **Conservatoire de Paris** is the little red *Folie Information*, where visitors can pick up a detailed map of the park and information on the current concerts and exhibitions. It's possible to spend a whole day at the Parc de la Villette with all there is to see and do. For more detailed information see the *Entertainment* section, page 299.

AUTHOR'S NOTE: *The **Parc de la Villette** has a few refreshment stands, a* Quick *fast-food restaurant, and a rather pricey restaurant at the Cité de la Musique. Le Hublot Restaurant in the Cité des Sciences has* plats du jour *from €8 and a neat aquarium décor. If the weather is nice, plan ahead and bring a picnic to eat on the lawn.*

Leaving the Parc de la Villette, cross the Avenue Jean-Jaurès to the futuristic Holiday Inn (#218-228). The large passageway that goes beneath the hotel leads to the **Allée Arthur-Honegger** and **Allée Darius-Milhaud**, a pedestrian and cycling path built in the early 1990s to connect the Parc de la Villette with the **Parc des Buttes-Chaumont** (M° Botzaris or Buttes-Chaumont).

Although one of the lesser-known Parisian parks, **Buttes-Chaumont** rarely fails to impress with its dramatic landscape of hidden grottos, waterfalls, steep cliffs and suspension bridge (dubbed the *Pont des Suicides*). Get a panoramic perspective from the **Sybille** temple (copied from the Tivoli in Rome) perched 100 feet above a central lake, or join the Parisians on the grassy slopes for a bit of afternoon sunbathing. For a coffee or snack in the park, find a seat on the peaceful terrace of the **Café Weber** on Avenue de la Cascade (near the M° Botzaris entrance).

DID YOU KNOW?

PARISIAN PARK LINGO: Pelouse au Repos *means the lawn is temporarily off-limits while it "rests."*

There are two interesting neighborhoods adjacent to the park. To the east is **La Mouzaïa**, a village of single-story garden bungalows built in 1901 on the tiny cobbled streets around Rue Mouzaïa, Rue Général Brunet, and Rue Miguel-Hidalgo. The best time to visit is late spring, when the creeping wisteria vines are in full bloom. On the other side of the park is the **Butte Bergeyre**, a perched neighborhood of 1920s brick buildings. You'll have to climb some steep stairs (at the Rue Barrelet-de-Ricou, off the Avenue Simon Bolivar). Once you've caught your breath, follow the Rue Georges-Lardennois for fantastic views of Sacré-Coeur Basilica.

Belleville & Ménilmontant

Belleville's narrow streets, ateliers, and garden passages recall the neighborhood's rural and working class roots. Once a wine-making village well outside the city walls, Belleville became known in the 18th century for its *guinguettes* (country cafés), where Parisians would come on Sundays to let their hair down a bit with the help of the plentiful tax-free wine. By the time it was annexed to Paris in the 1860s, Belleville was already heavily populated by the working classes pushed out of their homes by Haussmann's wrecking ball. During the Paris Commune of 1871, the barriers in Belleville were the last in the city to fall to the Versailles troops. Almost half of the devastated neighborhood's 50,000 inhabitants lost their lives.

In the 1900s, Belleville's population grew with the arrival of immigrants from Eastern Europe, Africa, Asia and North Africa. The government started bulldozing the most dilapidated quarters in the 1960s, replacing them with ugly housing projects. Despite these changes, the neighborhood has retained its traditional atmosphere and hidden pockets of history. By the 1990s, the cosmopolitan Belleville attracted a new wave of young artists who set up their ateliers in the old factories and workshops, and middle-class French families looking for inexpensive housing. Today

Paris

Belleville is once again defined by its strong neighborhood solidarity, as well as one of the most lively nightlife scenes in Paris.

Begin at métro Belleville, the heart of the local Chinese community, and walk up the **Rue de Belleville** (not to be confused with the larger Boulevard de Belleville). This street is lined with Chinese grocers, restaurants and shops selling hand-painted porcelain, Buddha statues and firecrackers. Stop into the **Centre Hong Kong** (at #29) to stock up on gifts of green tea, hand-sewn slippers, or colorful paper lanterns. Chinese New Year parades take place in the 13th and 3rd arrondissements in January or February.

Turn right onto Rue Piat, one last hill before the entrance to the **Parc de Belleville**. You're rewarded for your efforts with extraordinary panoramic views over Paris. And considering the absence of tour buses and portrait artists, it certainly beats the view from Montmartre! The Parc de Belleville was created in the 1980s on the site of an old gypsum quarry. Its steep hillside is softened by vine-covered arbors, waterfalls, and even a mini-vineyard in reference to the neighborhood's past. The wooden children's village has unfortunately been closed for safety reasons.

Continue along the Rue Piat to the Rue du Transversaal. At #16 is the **Villa Castel** passage, where Truffaut filmed several scenes of the 1961 film *Jules et Jim*. Take the next right onto the **Passage Plantin**, made up of little cottages originally built for nearby factory workers. Turn left at the Rue de la Mare, to the **Ateliers d'Artistes de Belleville** (32 Rue de la Mare, 20th, M° Jourdain (www.ateliers-artistes-belleville.org). This community art gallery represents over 150 local artists, and organizes an annual *portes ouvertes* in May. Continue via the Rue de Savies to the **Rue des Cascades**, where one of the city's old water points from a Roman aqueduct still stands. This street was the location for another classic French film, *Casque d'Or,* a drama about Belleville's guinguette days of cheap wine bars and dance halls. Follow this street to the Rue de Ménilmontant. The colorful building at the intersection is an artists' squat known as **Le Miroirterie** and its free used clothing boutique. Have a peek in if the door's open (assuming they haven't been booted out by the time you read this). See the *Cultural Adventures* section, page 200, for more information about the city's many art squats.

WHERE'S NEMO?

Keep an eye out for the whimsical stencils of a character called Belleville, created by a local artist named Nemo. His silhouette-man, red umbrella caught in the wind, has been chasing after bouquets of multicolored flowers, birds, butterflies and balloons throughout the neighborhood for over two decades.

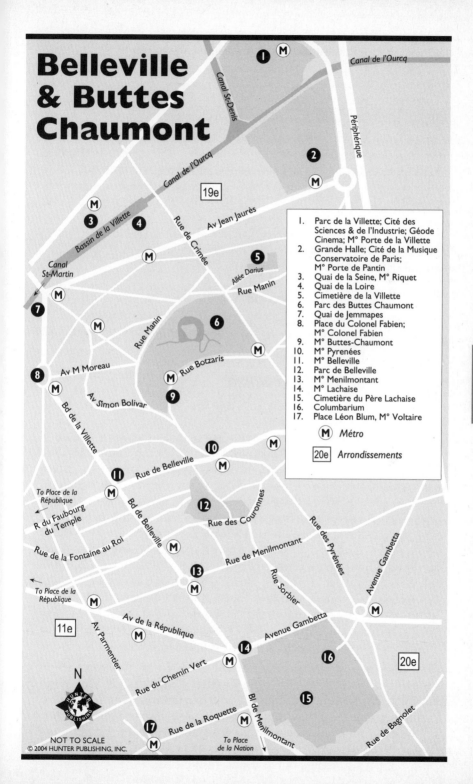

Belleville & Buttes Chaumont

Canal de l'Ourcq

Canal St-Denis

Périphérique

Canal de l'Ourcq

19e

Bassin de la Villette

Av Jean Jaurès

Rue de Crimée

Canal St-Martin

Allée Darius

Rue Manin

Rue Manin

Rue Botzaris

Av M Moreau

Av Simon Bolivar

Bd de la Villette

Rue de Belleville

To Place de la République

R du Faubourg du Temple

Bd de Belleville

Rue des Couronnes

Rue de la Fontaine au Roi

Rue de Menilmontant

Rue des Pyrénées

Rue Sorbier

Avenue Gambetta

To Place de la République

11e

Av de la République

Avenue Gambetta

Av Parmentier

Rue du Chemin Vert

20e

N

Bd de Menilmontant

Rue de la Roquette

Rue de Bagnolet

NOT TO SCALE
© 2004 HUNTER PUBLISHING, INC.

To Place de la Nation

1. Parc de la Villette; Cité des Sciences & de l'Industrie; Géode Cinema; M° Porte de la Villette
2. Grande Halle; Cité de la Musique Conservatoire de Paris; M° Porte de Pantin
3. Quai de la Seine, M° Riquet
4. Quai de la Loire
5. Cimetière de la Villette
6. Parc des Buttes Chaumont
7. Quai de Jemmapes
8. Place du Colonel Fabien; M° Colonel Fabien
9. M° Buttes-Chaumont
10. M° Pyrenées
11. M° Belleville
12. Parc de Belleville
13. M° Menilmontant
14. M° Lachaise
15. Cimetière du Père Lachaise
16. Columbarium
17. Place Léon Blum, M° Voltaire

Ⓜ Métro

20e Arrondissements

Paris

Head down the Rue de Ménilmontant, where, on a clear day, you can see the toy-like Pompidou Center in the distance. Turn right at the Rue Julien Lacroix. On the corner is Ménilmontant's local church **Eglise Notre-Dame de la Croix**. It was here that rebellious soldiers of the 1871 Paris Commune, who had taken over the church as their meeting hall, voted to kill their hostages, including the archbishop of Paris.

Cross the street to the Place Maurice Chevalier and follow the Rue Etienne Dolet to the Boulevard de Belleville. The colorful **Marché Belleville**, one of the city's largest outdoor markets, spreads out along the boulevard every Tuesday and Friday morning with fruits and spices from around the world. Just below is the **Rue Oberkampf**, famous for its lively strip of gritty bars and wild clubs stretching from the métro Ménilmontant to métro Parmentier. But it's also an interesting street to visit during the day, with its mix of typically Parisian food shops, ethnic cafés and quirky boutiques.

 AUTHOR'S NOTE: *See the* Entertainment *and* Where to Eat *sections of this chapter for more information about dining and nightlife in east Paris.*

Père Lachaise & Charonne

The **Cimetière Père Lachaise** (16 Rue du Repos, 20th, M° Père-Lachaise or Philippe Auguste, ☎ 01 55 25 85 10) has been the most fashionable final resting place for Parisians since Napoleon opened it back in 1803. Named for the original landowner, Louis XIV's confessor Père (Father) la Chaise, the cemetery's dramatic landscape of funerary sculptures is somewhat softened by the thousands of trees and flowering hedges. Some visitors are content to stroll the peaceful 110 acres randomly to see what they find. Those looking for a specific grave should pick up a map at the entry, which shows where the more famous residents are buried, including Yves Montand and Simone Signoret, Jim Morrison, Edith Piaf, Chopin, Oscar Wilde, Sarah Bernhardt, Colette, La Fontaine, Modigliani, Gertrude Stein and Alice B. Toklas, Marcel Proust, and Delacroix. One of the more solemn pilgrimage points is the **Mur des Fédérés** (Federalists' Wall, at the southeastern corner of the cemetery), site of the bloody end to the 1871 Paris Commune. The cemetery is open daily from 8am to 5:30pm (from 8:30am on Saturdays, and 9am on Sundays and holidays).

Exit Père Lachaise at the southeastern **Porte de la Réunion** (from Transversale N°2). On the left is the **Jardin Naturel** (120 Rue de la Réunion, 20th, M° Alexandre Dumas), a wild garden with a mini-wetland, prairie and forest to keep the dragonflies and birds happy. Cross the garden and take the Rue de Lesseps to the **Rue de Bagnolet**. Head up the hill, past grafitti'd buildings and the **Flèche d'Or**, a popular nightspot located in an old train depot, to the **Eglise St-Germain-de-Charonne**.

This 12th-century church, with its own parish cemetery around the back, was the center of the old Charonne village before it became part of Paris. Cross the Place St-Blaise to the rehabilitated **St-Blaise quarter**. Some of locals don't like the sterile new look of the neighborhood, but there are still a few interesting corners to explore. Do a little loop through the Passage des Deux Portes to the Rue Florian, where you can get a good look at the Petite Ceinture tracks.

RAILROAD CROSSING

The narrow train tracks you see around the outer edges of the city are part of the old *Petite Ceinture*, a circular passenger railway abandoned in the 1930s. Many proposals have been made over the years to rehabilitate the tracks into a cycle path or greenbelt, but the numerous narrow tunnels pose too many safety issues for the moment. A few of the Petite Ceinture stations have been converted into cafés, such as the Flèche d'Or.

Turn left onto the Rue Vitreuve, crossing the **Place des Grés** (the Maison des Communistes is at #3), to the Rue des Balkans, lined with garden villas typical of this neighborhood. At the top of the street is the large **Jardin Debrousse**, with its charming Pavillon de l'Hermitage, the only remnant of what used to be the Château de Bagnolet, owned by the Duchess of Orléans in the 18th century.

Continue up the Rue de Bagnolet to métro Porte de Bagnolet. If you don't want to end your exploration here, turn left at the large intersection onto the Rue Géo Chavez, and right up the stairs to the charming neighborhood known as **La Campagne à Paris**. These 92 villas with private gardens were built as part of an ownership project for the working classes in 1910. It's no surprise that most of these adorable houses still belong to the same families!

Bastille & Aligre

Don't ever ask a Parisian for directions to "The Bastille." Perhaps the folks back home will fall for the photos of you "in front of the Bastille," but anyone who's read even the most elementary French history book will know that it no longer exists. The French Revolutionaries didn't simply storm the Bastille in 1789, they tore it down.

Built in the 14th century as a fortress outside the city's walls (during the Hundred Years' War), the Bastille (or the **Chastel Saint-Antoine**, as it was originally known) was later used as a prison to demonstrate the monarchy's absolute power. You could only get in – or out – with a letter signed by the king. Famous prisoners included the Man with the Iron Mask, Voltaire (for spreading rumors about the royal family), Fouquet (the finance minister who built Vaux-le-Vicomte), and the Marquis de Sade.

When angry revolutionaries stormed the prison on July 14, 1789, to liberate those oppressed by the king, they found only seven inmates, living in conditions that were far better than the horrid images they'd imagined. Nonetheless, the Bastille was joyfully dismantled, with many of the stones carved into mini-Bastille models and sold as collectors' items. The Place de la Bastille is a popular rallying point today for disgruntled Parisian protest marchers.

The **Colonne de Juillet** now stands in its place, a tribute to those who died in the 1830 and 1848 Paris uprisings, with a crypt below containing their remains and a golden statue of *Liberté* at the top. To see the outline of where the Bastille used to stand, look for the large paving stones set into the cobblestones where the Boulevard Henri IV meets the Place de la Bastille. Try not to get run over by the speeding Parisians!

METRO MURAL

Another historic reminder can be found in the métro Bastille (on the platform for Line 1), where a colorful mural reproduces one of the illustrations published in the French newspapers during the Revolution. Try to spot the humorous anachronism of the female revolutionary wearing very modern glasses.

On the south side of the Place de la Bastille is the **Bassin de l'Arsenal**, a pleasure port for permanent or visiting house-boats. The gardens on the eastern side are a pleasant place to stroll, with a children's playground and small café terrace open in summer. Next door is the imposing **Opéra Bastille** (entry at 130 Rue de Lyon, 12th, ☎ 01 40 01 19 70, www.opera-de-paris.fr), built for the Bicentennial of the French Revolution in 1989. Parisians were not originally impressed with the round, office building look, but the state-of-the-art 112,000-square-foot stage and outstanding acoustics make it the ideal setting for big productions such as *Carmen*. Guided tours cost €10, €5 for visitors under 26. Call for the weekly tour schedule.

Escape from the busy Place de la Bastille through the cobblestoned **Cour Damoye**, turning right at the Rue Daval. The intersection of **Rue de Lapp** and **Rue de la Roquette** is best known for its popular nightlife scene, which is still quite lively despite the migration of its edgier clientele to Belleville and Oberkampf. Farther up the Rue de la Roquette, the **Rue Keller** and **Rue des Taillandiers** are worth a visit for their alternative boutiques and DJ record shops.

SMOKE BREAK

The **Musée du Fumeur** (7 Rue Pache, 11th, M° Voltaire) is worth a detour. Dedicated to the history of smoking, the tiny museum displays vintage prints and antique paraphernalia in an elegant wood-paneled setting. The best part is the cozy café hidden in the back, with its funky psychedelic ceiling mural and healthy menu of organic snacks and fruit smoothies. The boutique sells books in English and French, pipes, cool posters and gifts, and plenty of tobacco and rolling papers. Cannabis (*chanvre* or *haschiche*) gets plenty of air-play as well, on an educational level, but this isn't Amsterdam, so don't ask for it. Open Tuesday through Saturday, 11:30am to 7:30pm; and Sunday, 12:30 to 7:30pm; free. ☎ 01 46 59 05 51.

Continue to the **Rue du Faubourg St-Antoine** via Rue de Charonne. Make an effort to get off the busy main road to peek into the small courtyards and cobblestoned passages of this historic cabinet-making and furniture-manufacturing quarter. Like Belleville, the working-class population of the Faubourg St-Antoine was often on the frontlines of any popular revolt during the 19th century, easily barricading their narrow streets and passageways. Get a feel for the convivial atmosphere of this neighborhood at the traditional **Marché d'Aligre** (Rue d'Aligre, open every morning except Monday), known for its bargain prices and quality produce. The open market has been around since 1777, with the covered section added in 1843. When the market closes on Sunday, locals celebrate with a glass of wine and fresh oysters (in season) at the **Baron Bouge** (at 1 Rue Théophile-Roussel, 12th).

VISITING THE BOIS DE VINCENNES

The **Château de Vincennes** (1 Avenue de Paris, 12th, M° Château-de-Vincennes) was an important royal residence from the 11th through 17th centuries, with the Bois de Vincennes reserved for the king's hunts. When the court moved to Versailles, the Château de Vincennes became a prison and military fortress. Napoleon III turned the Bois into an English-style park and opened it to the public, but the State kept the château, adding an extra military fort to the grounds. Restoration of the 14th-century *donjon* (tower prison) and 16th-century Gothic chapel is ongoing, and won't be finished until the end of 2006, and much of the interior is closed. For more information, see *Family Fun*, page 311.

Follow signs from the market to one of the most interesting newcomers to the neighborhood, the **Viaduc des Arts** (all along Avenue Daumesnil, www.viaduc-des-arts.com). The renovated glass, brick and steel arches used to support the railway linking the Bastille to Vincennes in the late 1800s. The Viaduc was reopened in 1990 with 50 ateliers and boutiques dedicated to art and design. Above the viaduc is the **Promenade Plantée**, a three-mile-long pedestrian greenbelt leading all the way to the Bois de Vincennes (joined by a cycle path at the Jardin de Reuilly). See the *Adventures on Wheels* section, page 178, for information on bike and skate rental in the area.

Bercy

The Bercy district has always been associated with wine. When it was still a rural village outside the city walls, Parisians came to drink cheap, untaxed wine at the many guinguettes along the river. (To have "Bercy fever" was once a popular Parisian euphemism for being drunk.) In the late 19th century Bercy became the center of the French wine market. Its newly created Halles de Bercy, a city within the city, had its own shops, craftsmen, growers and negotiators, working to buy and sell the wine that arrived by rail and boat. Wine was stored in rows of large stone *chais* (storehouses), before being bottled and shipped around the world. Changes in modern transportation and economics slowly made this market obsolete and, by the 1970s, Bercy was an industrial wasteland full of squatter-occupied buildings, rusty railroad tracks, and weeds. City officials decided it would be best to rehabilitate the neighborhood from scratch, and after two decades of massive construction projects, Bercy does indeed look completely different. Despite a few modern eyesores, the overall results are quite impressive, and Bercy has become a genuinely pleasant place to spend the day.

Arrive in Bercy in style on the **Météor**, the city's first driverless métro (line 14), getting off at station Cour St-Emilion. The first thing you see is **Bercy Village** (www.bercyvillage.com), two rows of rehabilitated *chais* (wine storehouses) converted into a pedestrian-only shopping and entertainment center. The boutiques, restaurants and bars aren't really unique (most have branches in other Paris commercial centers), but the converted *chais* add architectural interest, and the café terrace seating along the central cobblestoned pathway provides the perfect setting for an al fresco Sunday brunch. Behind Bercy Village are the **Pavillons de Bercy**, a row of 19th-century mill warehouses currently used by a baking school and the privately owned **Musée des Arts Forains** (53 Avenue Terroirs-de-France, 12th), dedicated to antique fairground arts. Visits are in groups only; send an e-mail in advance to request a spot on the next available tour.

Cross back through Bercy Village to the **Parc de Bercy**. This large park is made up of two sections connected by two arching footbridges. On one side is a romantic-style garden with a duck pond, and on the other side are more formal gardens with themed flower beds, labyrinth and mini-vineyard (for nostalgic purposes). Century-old trees and cobblestoned lanes that used to transport the wine to the Seine have been preserved to give the park an aged feel, and the old tax collection house has been converted into the **Maison de Jardinage**. Stop in to browse through the gardening library or take a break on the sun porch.

At the far end of the park is the former **American Center** building (51 Rue de Bercy, 12th), designed by Frank Gehry (architect of the Bilbao Guggenheim Museum). It closed after just two years when the association, which had prospered for many years at its former Left Bank location, went bankrupt. Empty since 1996, the building is currently being renovated for its future role as the new **Cinémathèque Française** (www.cinemathequefrancaise.com), scheduled to open in 2005.

Continue past the glass-roofed pyramid known as the **POPB** (Palais Omnisports de Paris-Bercy, 2 Boulevard de Bercy, 12th, M° Bercy (www.popb.fr or www.bercy.fr), a modular sports and concert stadium with a public ice-skating rink. On the other side Bercy's frontier is marked by the monstrous **Ministry of Finance** building, its front pillars plunged defiantly into the Seine like an unfinished bridge. It was opened in 1989 to replace the ministry's former premises in the Louvre.

■ West Right Bank

Châtelet-Les Halles & Montorgueil

The **Place du Châtelet** gets its name from the Grand Châtelet fortress that used to guard the bridge to the Ile de la Cité. Today the square is dominated by twin 19th-century theaters, the **Théâtre du Châtelet** and the **Théâtre de la Ville** (formerly known as the Sarah Bernhardt Théâtre), overlooking a sphinx fountain commemorating Napoleon's war victories.

Begin your exploration of the neighborhood at the **Quai de la Mégisserie**, a busy street lined with pet shops and garden boutiques. Cross the street to browse the famous *bouquiniste* stalls selling vintage prints and books. Views of the Conciergerie and Pont Neuf are particularly good from here. Up until the Revolution, this quay was the location

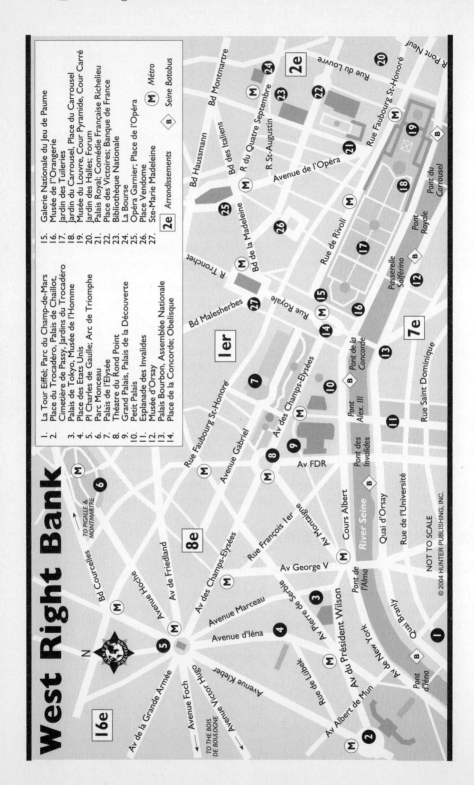

West Right Bank

1. La Tour Eiffel; Parc du Champ-de-Mars
2. Place du Trocadéro, Palais de Chaillot, Cimetière de Passy, Jardins du Trocadéro
3. Palais de Tokyo, Musée de l'Homme
4. Place des Etats Unis
5. Pl Charles de Gaulle; Arc de Triomphe
6. Parc Monceau
7. Palais de l'Elysée
8. Théatre du Rond Point
9. Grand Palais, Palais de la Découverte
10. Petit Palais
11. Esplanade des Invalides
12. Musée d'Orsay
13. Palais Bourbon, Assemblée Nationale
14. Place de la Concorde; Obelisque
15. Galerie Nationale du Jeu de Paume
16. Musée de l'Orangerie
17. Jardin des Tuileries
18. Jardin du Carrousel, Place du Carrousel
19. Musée du Louvre, Cour Pyramide, Cour Carré
20. Jardin des Halles; Forum
21. Palais Royal: Comédie Française Richelieu
22. Place des Victoires; Banque de France
23. Bibliothèque Nationale
24. La Bourse
25. Opéra Garnier; Place de l'Opéra
26. Place Vendome
27. Ste-Marie Madeleine

2e Arrondissements

Ⓜ Métro

◇ Seine Batobus

© 2004 HUNTER PUBLISHING, INC.

NOT TO SCALE

of a public slaughterhouse. Overlooking the bridge is **La Samaritaine** (19 Rue de la Monnaie, 1st), a 1920s department store with excellent Art Deco architecture and an Art Nouveau interior (best seen from the fifth floor). For great views of the city, take the elevator to the ninth floor and then a tiny spiral staircase to the rooftop panoramic terrace.

A WORD TO
THE WISE

TIP: *It's a good idea to pronounce the name of this important transportation hub correctly: Châtelet is pronounced chat-lay, and Les Halles is pronounced lay-al. Don't be tempted to pronounce those final consonants!*

Follow the Rue de l'Arbre Sec around to the **Eglise St-Germain-l'Auxerrois** (Place du Louvre, 1st, M° Louvre-Rivoli). The royal family used this church when they moved to the Louvre beginning in the 14th century. Many of the court's poets, artists, and architects are buried in this church, but it's best known for ringing the bells that gave the signal for the St. Bartholomew's Day Massacre on August 24, 1572.

Take the back streets, Rue de l'Arbre Sec and Rue Sauval (crossing the Rue St-Honoré), to the circular **Bourse du Commerce** (2 Rue de Viarmes, 1st M° Châtelet-Les Halles), home to the French Chamber of Commerce and Commodities Market. The strange 98-foot-high column on the south side of the building is the only remaining vestige of the Grand Hôtel de la Reine built for Catherine de Medicis in 1575. The column's platform was supposedly built for her personal astrologer, Ruggieri. This public display of mysticism probably contributed to the popular belief suspecting her of witchcraft.

Wander through the gardens of the retro-futuristic **Forum des Halles**, a soulless commercial center built in 1971 to replace the city's 800-year-old central food market known as Les Halles. Parisians still mourn the loss of the old glass and iron market halls, if not the inconvenience of having an overgrown wholesale market in the middle of town (it's now near Orly Airport). The stunning **Eglise St-Eustache** (Place du Jour, 1st, M° Châtelet-Les Halles, ☎ 01 42 36 31 05, www.st-eustache.org) was thankfully spared the wrecking ball. Its Gothic architecture and Renaissance décor make it one of the most beautiful – and underrated – churches in Paris. Louis XIV's First Communion took place here, as well as Molière's baptism and funeral service, but St-Eustache is better known for its prestigious organ concerts, including first performances of works by Liszt and Berlioz. Check their web site or stop by for the current schedule of weekly concerts.

Paris

HISTORICAL DETOUR

The horrid chain stores and fast food restaurants crowding the east side of the Forum des Halles are best avoided, but history buffs may want to see the **Fontaine des Innocents** (corner of Rue Berger and Rue Lescot), where the city's most crowded cemetery festered until the late 18th century, when the remains were finally transferred to the Catacombes. Around the corner, on Rue de la Ferronnerie, is a plaque commemorating the assassination of Henri IV. On May 14, 1610, the king was stabbed to death in his carriage outside #11 by the crazed mystic Ravaillac, who believed the king was going to declare war on the pope. The assassin was hanged, drawn and quartered 13 days later.

Behind St-Eustache is the beginning of the **Rue Montorgueil** (pronounced *mon-tor-guy*), a popular pedestrian market street. Across the Rue Etienne-Marcel is the heart of the **Montorgueil district**, renovated in the late 1980s. Its distinctive white cobblestone side-streets hide a number of trendy boutiques and cafés, particularly along Rue Tiquetonne. Don't miss the unique designer creations in the historic **Passage du Grand Cerf**. Do miss the Rue St-Denis if sex shops and loitering ladies of the night (and day) make you uncomfortable.

DID YOU KNOW?

AUTHOR'S NOTE: *North of Rue de Réamur is the Sentier Quarter, heavily dominated by the wholesale clothing industry and a growing hi-tech community optimistically dubbed "Silicon Sentier." The shops are never (officially) open to the public.*

■ Place des Victoires & Palais Royal

Try to visit the recently renovated **Tour de Jean-Sans-Peur** (20 Rue Etienne-Marcel, 2nd M° Etienne-Marcel), the tower where the Duke of Burgundy hid in 1407 after sparking off a war with the Armagnacs (he was the one who arranged for the assassination of the King's brother, Louis d'Orléans). Open Wednesday and weekends, 1:30 to 6pm. Continue along the upscale shopping street Rue Etienne-Marcel to the **Place des Victoires**, dominated by a statue of the Sun King Louis XIV on horseback. Turn right down the small Rue Vide Gousset to **Notre-Dame-des-Victoires Basilica** (Place des Petits-Pères), a popular pilgrimage site with over 40,000 *ex-voto* offerings dedicated to the Virgin on the walls. The basilica also has seven paintings by Van Loo.

Follow the Rue des Petits-Pères to the Rue des Petits-Champs. Immediately on the right is the entrance to one of the city's most beautiful covered passages, the **Galerie Vivienne**, with its mosaic tiled floor and glass-domed rotunda. It connects at the back to the equally beautiful **Galerie Colbert**.

THE PASSAGES

The city's covered passages were built in the early 1800s as pedestrian shopping galleries offering protection from the rain and dangerous carriage wheels (there were no sidewalks yet). Over 140 of these refined passages were originally built, but today only a few dozen remain, primarily in the 2nd and 9th arrondissements (see *Where to Shop*, page 214, for more detailed information).

Exit the passageways onto the Rue Vivienne, behind the 16th-century **Bibliothèque Richelieu** (entrance at 58 Rue de Richelieu, 2nd, M° Bourse ☎ 01 53 79 86 87, www.bnf.fr). This ancient library houses the National Library's specialized collections of prints and photographs, manuscripts, maps, medals and sheet music. It's not really possible to just wander around without a library card. Guided tours (in French) are given the first Tuesday of each month (call to reserve a place), €7.

Cross back over the Rue des Petits-Champs to the Rue de Beaujolais, and pass through the gates of the **Jardins du Palais Royal**. Completely cut off from the outside world, this peaceful formal garden is bordered on three sides by a series of arcades with unique shops. The **Palais Royal** was originally built in 1642 for Richelieu, and then passed around the Royal family for a few generations until it deteriorated into a gambling hall and place of ill-repute. After being burned down by the Paris Commune, it was restored and taken over in 1875 by the current resident, the *Conseil d'Etat* (the highest level of the French legal system, visits not allowed). Be prepared for a visual shock upon entering the main courtyard, where a series of black and white striped columns of differing heights were installed by the artist Daniel Buren in 1980. Just outside the gates is the former Théâtre du Palais-Royal (1 Place Colette, 1st, M° Palais-Royal), where Molière died on stage during a performance in 1673. In 1799 it became the permanent home of the national theater troup **La Comédie-Française**, which was created by Louis XIV in 1680 (☎ 01 44 58 15 00, www.comedie-francaise.fr, "English Version").

The **Place du Palais Royal** is a popular place for freestyle skaters and street performers (if the recent trend of imitating a statue can be considered a performance). On the left is the entrance to the **Louvre des Antiquaires** (2 Place du Palais-Royal, 1st, M° Palais-Royal, www.louvre-antiquaires.com), a sort of luxury shopping mall that brings together 250 professional art and antique dealers.

Paris

METRO ART

The entrance to the métro Palais-Royal on Place Colette was transformed (in 2000) into the *Kiosque des Noctambules*, by the permanent installation of a whimsical cage of colored glass beads, created by the French artist Jean-Michel Othoniel.

The Louvre & Opéra

The Louvre is the largest museum in the world, with a total area of almost 100 acres, including 650,000 square feet of exhibition rooms. To tackle this behemoth efficiently, a bit of preparation is in order.

A Brief History

Countless books have been written on the many aspects of the Louvre's complex and fascinating history (a number of good ones written in English can be found in the museum's bookshop). For casual sightseeing purposes, it's helpful to keep in mind a few essential historical points:

Philippe August built the Louvre as a **fortress** just outside the city walls in the 12th century to protect Paris from Viking raids. This original structure fit inside the Cour Carré. The oldest foundations and moat walls, discovered during construction in the 1980s, have been restored and can be seen throughout the lower ground floor of the museum.

The Louvre didn't become a **royal palace** until the 16th century under François I, who razed the tower and added two new wings. Later that century, Catherine de Medicis had her own palace built in the Tuileries, which Henri IV joined to the Louvre in 1594 to form a monumental double palace.

Louis XIV was the last king to put his mark on the Louvre before virtually abandoning it in 1678, when he moved the royal seat of power to Versailles. The Louvre began its first step toward becoming a **museum** in the 18th century, when the abandoned palace developed as an artists' residence and academy with public exhibitions of the royal collections. After the Revolution, it was officially declared a museum under the First Republic in 1793. In the 19th century, Napoleon I evicted the artists and academics living in the Louvre, and renamed it the Musée Napoleon, stocking it full of "souvenir" artworks pilfered during his various conquests (which the Allies made him return after his defeat at Waterloo in 1815). Improvements to the museum were continued under the Restoration and Napoleon III's Second Empire.

An extensive renovation project spanning the last two decades of the 20th century transformed the museum into the Grand Louvre. Significant changes included the addition of the Pei Pyramid entrance and the Carrousel du Louvre commercial center, the excavation of the medieval foundations, and the opening of the Richelieu Wing (formerly occupied by the Ministry of Finance).

Entrance

The Louvre Museum (☎ 01 40 20 53 17, M° Palais Royal-Musée du Louvre) is open from 9am to 6pm from Thursday through Sunday, and until 9:45pm (main collections only) Mondays and Wednesdays. The main entrance at the **pyramid** (via 99 Rue de Rivoli, 1st) is open from 9am until closing. If you don't want to stand in line outside, enter through the **Carrousel du Louvre** commercial center (open til 10 pm, entrances at 99 Rue de Rivoli, in the Jardins du Carrousel, or directly from the **métro Palais-Royal**, exit 1). The **Porte des Lions** (on the Quai des Tuileries near the Batobus stop) is open 9am to 5:30pm except on Tuesdays and Fridays. And visitors with pre-purchased tickets or museum passes can enter at the **Passage Richelieu** (between the Cour Napoleon and the Place du Palais-Royal), from 9am to 6pm. Please note that the museum is closed on Tuesdays.

A WORD TO
THE WISE

WARNING! *Some collections are only open on certain days of the week. If you're planning on seeing something specific, call or check the web site to make sure it's open.*

Tickets

Tickets to the permanent and temporary collections (except the Hall Napoleon) are €7.50, €5 after 3pm and all day Sunday. Tickets to all the collections, including the Hall Napoleon, are €11.50, €9.50 after 3pm and all day Sunday. The museum is free for kids under 18 and on the first Sunday of the month. Museum Pass accepted. Tickets are valid all day for re-entry. Advance tickets can be purchased at any branch of **FNAC** (a chain of book/electronics/music stores) or **Virgin Megastore**, and department stores **Printemps**, **Galeries Lafayette**, **Le Bon Marché**, and **BHV**. Check the web site for information on advanced purchases from abroad.

DID YOU KNOW? *The Louvre's most famous work of art, Leonardo da Vinci's* Mona Lisa, *is known in Italian as* La Gioconda *(she was the wife of Francesco del Giocondo), and in French as* La Joconde.

Where to Eat

Avoid zombie syndrome with a lunch (or dinner) break and perhaps a stroll through the **Tuileries Gardens**. There are various cafés and restaurants within the museum and a decent food court in the **Carrousel du Louvre** commercial center (www.louvre.fr).

JUST LOOKING, THANKS

 For those who want to see the Louvre – but not necessarily the art collections – enter the **Cour Carré** from the Rue de l'Amiral Coligny, where you can peek through the windows at the statues in the Sully Wing. Continue into the Cour Napoleon and admire I.M. Pei's **pyramid** (have a coffee on the terrace of the **Café Marly**, time permitting). From the Arc de Triomphe du Carrousel you can see the Tuileries Gardens, the Obélisque at the Place de la Concorde, the Arc de Triomphe, and – on a clear day – the Grande Arche de la Défense. Just to the left is the **Carrousel du Louvre** entrance, where you can see the excavated medieval foundations lining the passageway to the museum and commercial center.

Maps & Guides

A free museum map in English can be found at the information desk under the pyramid. More detailed guidebooks can be purchased in the museum's bookshop. Audio guides (with commentary on 1,000 artworks in English) are available at the entrance to each wing for €5, cash or traveler's check only. Guided tours in English are available except on free Sundays; call in advance for the schedule.

The Rohan Wing

The Rohan Wing of the Louvre hosts three museums independently run by the Union Centrale des Arts Décoratifs (105-107 Rue de Rivoli, 1st, M° Palais Royal or Tuileries, ☎ 01 44 55 57 50, www.ucad.fr). The **Musée de la Mode et du Textile** is dedicated to costumes dating from the 16th century; the **Musée des Arts Décoratifs** houses one of the world's largest collections of decorative arts from the Middle Ages to the present day (currently under renovation until the end of 2004; only the Middle Ages and Renaissance sections are open to the public). The **Musée de la Publicité**, opened in 1999, features an international, multimedia collection of objects, posters and commercials from the world of advertising. All three are open Tuesday through Friday, 11am to 6pm (Wednesdays until 9pm); weekends, 10am to 6pm. Entry €2. Museum Pass accepted.

Jardin des Tuileries

Pass through Napoleon's Arc de Triomphe du Carrousel (built in 1806) and the modern Jardins du Carrousel (built during the Grand Louvre renovations) to the entrance of the Jardin des Tuileries. Catherine de Medicis' 16th-century Palais des Tuileries used to stand here, connecting the Louvre's western wings. Even when the court moved to Versailles, the

Tuileries remained the primary royal residence within the city, making it a constant target of revolutionary attacks. It was first sacked in 1791, then burned down by the Commune in 1871. The government of the young Third Republic decided against rebuilding this symbol of absolute power, and had the remains torn down.

They were smart enough to save the palace gardens, which became an instant hit with Parisians. Today the Jardin des Tuileries is one of the city's best-loved public parks, with its cafés and distinctive iron chairs that can be moved around to get the best spot. Many of the original features designed by André Le Nôtre in 1664 still remain, such as the horseshoe terrace overlooking the Place de la Concorde (with great views down the Champs-Elysées) and the large circular fountains, popular with ducks and small children pushing toy boats. As part of a facelift in the 1990s, a number of contemporary sculptures were added, mixing somewhat oddly with the classical statues along the main promenade.

📖 *There's a delightful little boutique dedicated entirely to gardening and landscape books hidden under the horseshoe terrace just inside the entrance to the park at the Place de la Concorde.*

Two of the buildings added by Napoleon III dominate the western terrace of the gardens. The **Musée de l'Orangerie** (☎ 01 42 97 48 16), originally the Tuileries' greenhouse, houses a permanent collection of Impressionist and 20th-century paintings, the main attraction being Monet's *Les Nymphéas* (the museum will be reopening in fall 2004 after extensive renovations). The **Galerie Nationale du Jeu de Paume**, a converted *jeu de paume* court (an ancestor of tennis), was used for many years to host contemporary arts expositions, but is slated to reopen in summer 2004 as the city's new center for photography and photographic imagery (for both of these museums, www.museums-of-paris.com, click on "Modern Art").

Paris

HANDY SHORTCUT

On the Seine side of the Jardin des Tuileries is the pedestrian-only **Passerelle Solferino**, a wood and steel bridge leading directly to the Musée d'Orsay.

Place Vendôme

Exit the Tuileries from the northern terrace, and walk under the elegant arcades of the Rue de Castiglione to the opulent Place Vendôme. Considered the height of 17th-century French architecture, the square has never lost its prestige, though it did lose its statues. The original statue of Louis XIV was destroyed during the Revolution, replaced in 1810 by Napoleon's bronze column cast from canons captured during the Battle of Austerlitz. This in turn was destroyed during the Paris Commune in 1871 (the painter Gustave Courbet was blamed and exiled for supposedly inciting a mob to tear it down), and replaced with a replica during the Third Republic. Today the Place Vendôme is home to the world's most exclusive jewelry boutiques and the famous **Hôtel Ritz**. If there's a crowd of photographers standing by the entrance, get your camera ready – someone famous is about to come out!

Place de L'Opera

Continue up the Rue de la Paix to the Place de l'Opéra, where no amount of traffic can dull the shine of the recently renovated **Opéra Garnier** (Place de l'Opéra, 9th, M° Opéra, ☎ 01 40 01 22 63, www.opera-de-paris.fr). This 19th-century architectural masterpiece by Charles Garnier features an exquisitely decorated interior and ceiling fresco painted by Marc Chagall in 1964. Many scenes from the Hollywood version of the film *Dangerous Liaisons* were filmed here. You can get a free peek at the grand marble staircase and lobby statues from the main entrance (where you'll also find the tiny Opéra boutique). Open daily, 10am to 5pm (until 6pm in August). Access to the rest of the building (without buying a ticket to a show) costs €6, free for kids under 10, and includes entry to the library-museum temporary exhibitions. Guided tours in English are available daily at 10:30am and 12:30pm in summer, and Saturdays at 12:30pm in winter; tickets €10 (€5 for kids under 19).

Place de la Madeleine

Exiting the Opéra, turn right at the corner of the historic **Café de la Paix** onto the Boulevard des Capucines. One of Haussmann's *grands boulevards*, this luxury shopping street leads to the Place de la Madeleine, famous for its gourmet food boutiques such as Hédiard and Fauchon. In the center is the **Eglise de la Madeleine** (www.eglise-lamadeleine.com), a 19th-century church resembling a Greek Temple with its giant Corinthian columns. It's worth braving the three lanes of traffic for the view from the top of the church steps facing the Rue Royale – you can see all the way to the Place de la Concorde and the golden dome of Les Invalides.

CHIC TOILETTES

On the square between the flower market and the church is a little stairway leading to the most beautiful public toilets in town. Built in 1905, they epitomize the Art Nouveau style, with intricate mosaic tiling, carved wooden doors, and stained glass panels. Each stall even has its own period pedestal sink. And don't forget your change – it costs €0.45 for the privilege!

Do a bit of window shopping on the renovated **passages** between the Rue Royal and the Rue Boissy d'Anglas on the way to the **Place de la Concorde**. Originally called the Place Louis XV, it was renamed the Place de la Révolution in 1792, home to the infamous guillotine that would end the lives of Louis XIV, Marie Antoinette and Robespierre, among 1,350 others. After this bloody mess, the Place de la Concorde received its current "neutral" name in 1830, and the original statue of Louis XV (torn down by revolutionaries) was replaced by the two fountains and **Obélisque de Luxor** you see today. A gift from the viceroy of Egypt, the obelisk dates back to 1550 BC, and took two years to reach Paris on a boat specially built to transport the 230-ton monument. The golden symbols on the base were actually instructions on how to re-erect it upon arrival. The gilded top was only recently restored in the early 1990s (some postcards sold in Paris still show the obelisk's formerly unadorned stub). The twin mansions at the north end of the square are occupied by the **Hôtel Crillon**, the **Naval Ministry**, and the **French Automobile Club**. These are flanked on each side by the **American Embassy** and **Consulate**, which accounts for the not-so-subtle concentration of guards in the square.

Paris

NIGHT-LIGHTS

The **Place de la Concorde** should be a more pleasant place considering its magnificent setting, but the square seems to be drowning in its multiple lanes of traffic. City officials have been considering a plan to make it more pedestrian-friendly, perhaps by restricting traffic to buses and taxis only, but so far nothing has been finalized. Try to see the square late at night, when the streets are practically deserted and the fountains are lit up.

The Champs-Elysées

The Avenue des Champs-Elysées is perhaps one of the world's most recognized streets, but its history is actually quite recent. Up until the end of the 18th century it was still just a field with cows. Under the Second Empire it became the height of fashion, lined with private mansions and dance halls. Today it's quite hard to find anything of historical interest, since much of the street's character has been completely transformed by airline offices, cinemas and car showrooms. But despite this modernization, the tree-lined Champs-Elysées remains an impressive avenue framed by the dramatic Arc de Triomphe. Parisians gather here faithfully for annual events such as the Bastille Day parades and the finish of the Tour de France, and to see the sparkling holiday light displays.

The most pleasant area of the Champs-Elysées, between the Rond-Point and the Place de la Concorde, has no shops at all, just leafy gardens, chestnut trees and a few pavilions built for the 1900 Universal Exhibition. One of the nicer buildings, the **Pavillon Elysées** (at the Carré Marigny) was lovingly renovated and reopened in 2003 as a Lenôtre cooking school, café and boutique. Next door is the **Théâtre de Marigny**, designed by Garnier in 1853, where Offenbach performed his popular operettas. The **Marché aux Timbres** (vintage stamps and postcards) takes place outside every Thursday, Saturday and Sunday.

Peeking above the trees on the other side of the avenue is the majestic **Grand Palais**, a 20th-century Art Nouveau exposition center, currently home to the **Palais de la Découverte** interactive science museum and planetarium (Avenue Franklin D Roosevelt, 8th, M° Champs-Elysées-Clémenceau, ☎ 01 56 43 20 21, www.palais-decouverte.fr). Next door is the **Petit Palais**, also built for the 1900 Universal Exhibition. It normally houses the city's Musée des Beaux-Arts, but is closed for major renovations until 2005.

THE PRESIDENT'S HOUSE

Set well back from the Champs-Elysées and surrounded by vast gardens, it's easy to miss the **Palais de l'Elysée** (at the corner of the Avenue Gabriel and Avenue de Marigny). This very private presidential palace is only open to the public once a year during the Journées du Patrimoine (National Heritage Days).

If window shopping isn't your thing, take a short detour up the Avenue Franklin D. Roosevelt to the exquisite **Musée Jacquemart-André** (158 Boulevard Haussmann, 8th, M° St-Philippe-du-Roule, ☎ 01 45 62 11 59, www.musee-jacquemart-andre.com/jandre). Formerly the private mansion of the art-collecting couple Edouard André and Nélie Jacquemart, this museum beautifully presents their original furnishings and impressive collection of 18th-century French, Flemish and Italian masterpieces. There's also an elegant café open for lunch and afternoon tea (11:45am to 6pm). Museum open daily, 10am to 6pm. Tickets €8, €6 for kids ages seven to 17 (includes audio guide).

The Arc de Triomphe

Continue to the top of the Champs-Elysées, where the Arc de Triomphe sits proudly at the intersection of 12 avenues known as the **Place du Général de Gaulle** (although Parisians still refer to it by the original name, *l'Etoile*, which means star). Commissioned by Napoleon in 1806 to honor the Imperial Army, the massive 167-foot arch was finally completed 30 years later, under King Louis-Philippe. The Arc de Triomphe has become the symbolic centerpiece for many important historical events such as the funeral processions of Napoleon and Victor Hugo. The nation still cringes at the memory of Hitler's occupying troops marching beneath the arch in WWII, and the joy when General de Gaulle's liberation forces did the same in 1944. At the base of the arch lies the Tomb of the Unknown Soldier and the Eternal Flame (maintained every evening at 6pm) in honor of those lost in WWI.

UNSPEAKABLE ACTS

The Eternal Flame was extinguished during the 1998 World Cup celebrations when two drunken tourists from Mexico reportedly urinated on it. Just the year before, an Australian tourist was arrested for trying to cook an egg over the flame.

It's definitely worth a visit to the open terrace on top of the Arc de Triomphe. From here you can get the best views of the **Voie Triomphale**, a line of monuments stretching north-south from the Grande Arche de la Défense to the Pyramide du Louvre. This sight is particularly fantastic to watch as the sun sets and the city lights up. Place du Général-de-Gaulle, 8th, M° Charles de Gaulle-Etoile, ☎ 01 55 37 73 77. Open April to September, 9:30am to 11pm; October to May, 10am to 10:30pm. Entry €7, €4.50 for students, free for kids under 18 and the first Sunday of the month. Museum Pass accepted.

A WORD TO THE WISE

WARNING! *Don't try reaching the arch by crossing the busiest intersection in Paris! Use the* **underground pedestrian passages** *from the Avenue des Champs-Elysées or the Avenue de la Grande Armée.*

SHOPPING DE LUXE!

The highest concentration of luxury boutiques and haute couture showrooms can be found in the 8th arrondissement's Golden Triangle, made up of the Avenue des Champs-Elysées, the Avenue Montaigne, and the Avenue George V. Another street dripping with pearls and platinum cards is the Rue du Faubourg St-Honoré, which turns into the slightly hipper Rue St-Honoré after the Rue Royale. See *Where to Shop*, page 214, for more details on the city's top shopping districts.

Parc Monceau

Those with a bit of extra time can take a ride through the luxury residential district of **Courcelles** on **Bus 30** (from the top of Avenue Wagram outside the Arc de Triomphe, direction Gare de l'Est) to the chic Parc Monceau (Boulevard de Courcelles, 16th, M° Monceau), an 18th-century English-style garden with theatrical landscaping touches such as a Corinthian colonnade, Egyptian pyramids and even a Renaissance arcade from the original Hôtel de Ville, which was burned down during the Commune. The gardens, enclosed by a gold-tipped wrought-iron fence, are surrounded by elegant mansions. One of these is the **Musée Nissim de Camondo** (63 Rue de Monceau, 8th, M° Monceau, ☎ 01 53 89 06 50, www.ucad.fr/ ucadgb/nissim_eng), a museum of 18th-century decorative arts set in the private mansion Hôtel Camondo. Open Wednesday through Sunday, 10am to 5pm; entry €4.60, €3.10 for students. Museum Pass accepted.

RUSSIAN CATHEDRAL

The Tsar Alexander II funded the construction in 1861 of the Russian Orthodox Cathédrale St-Alexandre-Nevski (12 Rue Daru, 8th, M° Courcelles, ☎ 01 42 27 37 34), with five golden domes based on the architecture of the St-Petersburg Fine Arts Academy. The interior is richly decorated with mosaics and magnificent icons. Open Tuesday, Friday and Sunday, 3 to 5pm (no shorts or exposed shoulders).

Trocadéro & Passy

Begin your tour of the formal 16th arrondissement at the city's avant-garde center of contemporary art, the **Palais de Tokyo** (13 Avenue du President Wilson, 16th, M° Alma-Marceau or Iéna, ☎ 01 47 23 54 01, www.palaisdetokyo.com). Originally built for the 1937 World's Fair, it served various cultural purposes over the years before reopening in 2002 as the **Site of Contemporary Creation**. Don't be surprised if you walk into what looks like an industrial artists' squat under construction. That's what it's supposed to look like (the French call it *brut*). Even if you don't visit the temporary exhibitions, have a walk around the building. A caged-in shop with art books and magazines, and the boutique Black Block sells the works of the famous Parisian graffiti artist Gilles Dufour, creator of Monsieur André. There's also a restaurant open until 2am, a bar, and a self-serve café downstairs. Open Tuesday through Sunday, noon-midnight. Entry to expositions €6, €4 for students 18-25, free for kids under 18.

The other wing of the Palais de Tokyo houses the **Musée d'Art Moderne de la Ville de Paris** (11 Avenue du President Wilson, 16th, M° Alma-Marceau or Iéna, ☎ 01 53 67 40 80, www.paris.fr/musses, "Modern Art"), closed until October 2004 for much-needed renovations. Check out the web site for information on their temporary exhibitions held in different venues throughout the city. The terrace connecting the two wings of the Palais Tokyo offers more than decent views overlooking the Seine, the Eiffel Tower, and the local skaters practicing their moves on the smooth pavement below. In the summer the terrace becomes a chic open-air bar and restaurant.

Across the street is the aging **Palais Galliera: Musée de la Mode de la Ville de Paris** (10 Avenue Pierre I de Serbie, 16th, M° Alma-Marceau or Iéna, ☎ 01 56 52 86 00, www.paris.fr/musees/musee_galliera), with its collection of over 80,000 articles of clothing and accessories. Because of the fragile nature of the collections, this fashion museum is only open for temporary expositions arranged around a theme or a particular designer. Open during exhibitions Tuesday through Sunday, 10am to 6pm. Tickets €7, €3.5 for students 14-25, free for children under 14. Includes free audio guide in English. Museum Pass accepted.

MARKET DAYS

A large flower and produce market takes place on the central alley along the **Avenue du President Wilson** (just outside the Palais de Tokyo) every Wednesday and Saturday morning, 7am to 2:30pm.

Just one block up the hill is the **Guimet Musée des Arts Asiatiques** (6 Place d'Iéna, 16th, M° Iéna, ☎ 01 56 52 53 00, www.museeguimet.fr). Created over a century ago by the industrialist Emile Guimet, the museum's vast collections are dedicated to the arts and civilization throughout the Asian world, including Japan, China, Cambodia, Tibet, India, Nepal, Pakistan and Afghanistan. A restaurant on the lower level of the museum is open to the public (admission to the museum not required). Open daily except Tuesday, 10am to 6pm; entry to the permanent and temporary collections €7, €5 for students and everyone on Sunday. Free for kids under 18 and for everyone the first Sunday of the month. Free audio guide included. Museum Pass accepted. The museum also has a **Buddhist Pantheon** (entrance at 19 Avenue d'Iéna, 16th, ☎ 01 40 73 88 11) with galleries representing Chinese and Japanese religious art from the fourth to the 19th centuries, and an amazingly peaceful Japanese garden. Open daily except Tuesday, 9:45am to 5:45pm; free admission.

Place des Etats-Unis

Continue up the Avenue d'Iéna to the Place des Etats-Unis, an elegant and peaceful square surrounded by stately townhouses and foreign embassies. Originally called Place de la Bitche (the name of a French town on the Belgian border), it was renamed in 1881 when the US foreign ministry offices moved into #3, both to avoid awkward linguistic situations and to honor the friendship between the two republics. At the center of the square is a statue of generals Lafayette and Washington by Auguste Bartholdi, and a monument to the American volunteers who died for France during World War I.

The square's most illustrious residence, once home to the aristocratic patron of the arts Marie-Laure de Noailles, reopened in October 2003 as the **Maison Baccarat** (11 Place des Etats-Unis, 16th, M° Boissière, ☎ 01 40 22 11 00). Don't miss the sexy new interior, completely redesigned by Philippe Starck with a boutique, show-room, and museum dedicated to the history and future of Baccarat crystal. The Cristal Room Restaurant (open 9am to 1am) serves brunch, lunch, tea and dinner in the Countess' former dining room.

THE COMTESSE DE NOAILLES

Marie-Laure de Noailles was a huge fan of the arts, and generously supported artists such as Cocteau, Bunuel, and Man Ray. She lived at the Place des Etats-Unis from 1920-1970, and hosted fabulous parties and salons frequented by Picasso, Giacometti, Picabia, Balthus, Matisse, and Dali.

Place du Trocadéro

Take the Rue de Lubek back to the Avenue du President Wilson, and continue up the hill to the Place du Trocadéro. Built the same time as the Palais de Tokyo for the 1937 World's Fair, the **Palais de Chaillot** features the same neoclassical architecture, split into two immense wings. The terrace in the center overlooks the elaborate gardens and fountains of the **Jardins du Trocadéro**, with arguably the best view of the Eiffel Tower in town.

 AUTHOR'S NOTE: *Try to visit the terrace at night at least once during your stay, when the powerful cannon fountains shooting up toward the Eiffel Tower are brilliantly illuminated.*

The Palais de Chaillot currently houses two museums (the Cinema Museum closed in 1997 and is scheduled to reopen in the Bercy quarter in 2006). The **Musée de l'Homme** (17 Place du Trocadéro, 16th, M° Trocadéro, ☎ 01 44 05 72 72), managed by the Natural History Museum, is dedicated to the life and history of humankind in France. This somewhat outdated museum is due for complete renovations (the new director has already worked his magic on the Grande Galerie d'Evolution in the Jardin des Plantes) if it hopes to compete with the new Musée du Quai Branly being built across the river (due to open in 2006). Open daily except Tuesday, 9:45am to 5:15pm; tickets €5, €3 for students, kids under 18 free.

The second museum within the Palais de Chaillot is the **Musée Nationale de la Marine** (17 Place du Trocadéro, 16th, M° Trocadéro ☎ 01 53 65 69 53), featuring a collection of naval objects assembled in the 17th century, including scale models of warships and sailing ships. Large windows offer panoramic views over the city. The museum is staying open during renovations, due to finish in 2005. Open daily except Tuesday, 10am to 6pm. Entry €7, €5.40 for students, €3.85 for kids ages six to 18.

CHAILLOT OR TROCADÉRO?

It's easy to get confused by the double moniker for this area. The hill's original name is the Colline de Chaillot. In 1878 the Palais Trocadéro (named after a Spanish fort conquered by the French) was built for the World's Fair, with vast gardens and a square known as the Place du Trocadéro. The building became the Palais de Chaillot in 1937, but the square and gardens held on to the Trocadéro name.

Behind the Place du Trocadéro is the small, yet prestigious **Cimetière de Passy** (2 Rue du Cmdt-Schloesing, 16th, M° Trocadéro, ☎ 01 47 27 51 42). Opened in the aristocratic Passy neighborhood in 1820, this cemetery is the final resting place for Claude Debussy, Edouard Manet and Marcel Renault. Open weekdays 8am to 6pm, from 8:30am Saturdays, and from 9am on Sundays (closes at 5:30pm in winter).

Cross the Square de Yorktown and follow the Rue Vineuse down the hill to the Rue Raynouard. Watch on the left for a tiny passageway called the Rue des Eaux, and follow the stairs down to the bottom. Around the corner to the left is the almost hidden **Musée du Vin** (Rue des Eaux, 16th, M° Passy, ☎ 01 45 25 63 26, www.museeduvinparis.com), a museum dedicated to the history of winemaking, set in ancient quarry tunnels dating back to the 13th century. Passy used to be covered by vineyards in the 18th century, the largest belonging to the Minimes Monastery, who once used these tunnels to store their wine. This is one of the city's most original museums. Open Tuesday through Sunday, 10am to 6pm; entry €6.50 (includes complimentary glass of wine). Read more about the museum and its restaurant in the *Cultural Adventures* section, page 193.

Follow the Rue Charles Dickens to the Avenue Marcel Proust. At the end of the street is a narrow, cobblestone passage, the **Rue Berton**. The back entrance to Balzac's house is at #24. Hunted by creditors, he often used this passage for a quick getaway. Loop around onto the Rue Raynouard to the front entrance of the **Maison de Balzac** (47 Rue Raynouard, 16th, M° Passy, ☎ 01 55 74 41 80). This adorable little house where Honoré de

Paris

Balzac lived and wrote for seven years is the last vestige of what was once Passy village before it became part of the ever-expanding city of Paris in 1860. Even if you're not familiar with Balzac's work (such as *The Human Comedy*), it's definitely worth a stop for the peaceful garden views of the Eiffel Tower. Open Tuesday through Sunday, 10am to 6pm. Free entrance to the permanent collection, €1.60-€3.30 for the temporary expositions.

LADY LIBERTY

If you take the RER C train from the Right Bank to the Left Bank, sit on the right side (and upstairs if it's a bi-level train). When crossing the Seine you'll be able to see the small-scale bronze version of the **Statue of Liberty** on the island off the Allée des Cygnes.

Place de Passy

Cross the street and follow the Rue de l'Annonciation all the way to the Place de Passy. On the left is the **Marché de Passy**, an upscale covered food market. Turn left onto the shopping street Rue de Passy, and follow it past the métro to the **Jardins du Ranelagh** (Chaussée de la Muette, 16th, M° La Muette). This pretty park, opened in 1774, was frequented by Marie Antoinette. Today it's a favorite with kids for its playground, merry-go-round, donkey rides and *marionnettes* (puppet theater). If you've come this far then you'd better not miss the **Musée Marmottan Monet** (2 Rue Louis-Boilly, 16th, M° La Muette, ☎ 01 44 96 50 33, www.marmottan.com). Known for its important collection of Impressionist art, including Monet's *Water Lilies* and *Impression: Sunrise*, this museum set in a former aristocratic hunting lodge also features paintings and furniture from the First Empire, primitive art, and illuminations. Open Tuesday through Sunday, 10am to 6pm. Entry €6.50, €4 for students under 25, free for kids under eight.

The Bois de Boulogne

Once used exclusively as the royal hunting grounds, the vast Bois de Boulogne is one of the "lungs" of Paris, with over 2,000 acres of forested parkland. When it was first opened to the public under Louis XIV, the park had a reputation for sheltering bandits and prostitutes, but eventually attracted high society, who built the mansions and elegant pavilions still surrounding it today. The park deteriorated during the Revolution, and its forests were devastated by the occupying British and Russian army camps in 1815. It was under Napoleon III that it was given its current design with racecourses and wide avenues. He instructed

Haussmann to recreate the same winding paths, ornamental lakes and lush gardens found in London's Hyde Park, and the Bois de Boulogne once again became the favorite strolling grounds for genteel Parisians.

A WORD TO
THE WISE

AUTHOR'S NOTE: *The Bois de Boulogne, like other parks in Paris, lost many trees during the storm of December 1999 and the heat wave of August 2003. Sections of the forest may therefore be closed off to protect newly planted seedlings.*

The Bois de Boulogne is the perfect starting point for discovering the greener side of Paris. But it's not the kind of place where you show up without some sort of plan, because you could wander around in the park all day and still miss the interesting sights. Decide in advance how you'll get around. There are three métro and three RER-C stations – Porte Maillot, Porte d'Auteuil, and Porte Dauphine – on the Paris edge of the park. If you're going to a specific place in the park, it's best to know which is closest (there are also buses that run throughout the park from outside the métro and RER stations). This still involves a lot of walking. The best way to see multiple sights and explore the forest trails is by bicycle (see page 180 for rental information). There's a paved cycle path circling the entire park, but you also have the option of riding on the roads open to traffic and along the unpaved forest trails. The Bois de Boulogne has plenty of snack bars and upscale restaurants, but not much in between. Make like a Parisian and pack a picnic!

Major Sights

The **Lac Inférieur** (Route de Suresnes, M° Porte Dauphine or RER Henri Martin) is the park's largest lake, with two forested islands in the center that can be reached by ferry or rowboat (see *Adventures On Water*, page 175, for information on rowboat rentals). Just below is **La Grande Cascade**, a man-made (yet impressive) waterfall, and the much smaller **Lac Supérieur**.

The romantic **Pré Catalan gardens** (Route de Suresnes, M° Ranelagh or RER Henri Martin) at the center of the park feature shady lawns, a Shakespeare Garden with open-air theater, and some of the oldest trees in the park. The beautiful Belle Epoque pavilion was originally built for Napoleon III, and now houses the Michelin-starred Pré Catalan restaurant.

The **Jardin des Serres d'Auteuil** (corner of Avenue Gordon Bennett and Avenue de la Porte d'Auteuil, M° Porte d'Auteuil, ☎ 01 40 71 75 23) has three beautiful 19th-century glass and wrought-iron tropical greenhouses set in formal French gardens. There are regular musical concerts in the summer. Open daily from 8am on weekdays and 9am on weekends (closing hours vary from 5:30pm in winter to 9:30pm in summer). Entry

Paris

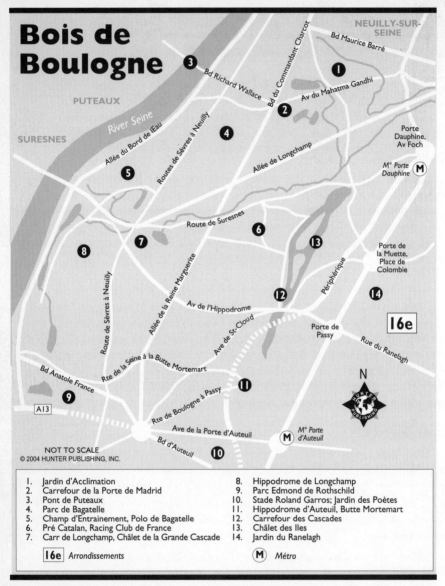

Bois de Boulogne

NEUILLY-SUR-SEINE

PUTEAUX

SURESNES

River Seine

Bd Richard Wallace

Bd du Commandant Charcot

Bd Maurice Barré

Av du Mahatma Gandhi

Allée du Bord de l'Eau

Routes de Sèvres à Neuilly

Allée de Longchamp

Porte Dauphine, Av Foch

Ⓜ M° Porte Dauphine

Route de Suresnes

Route de Sèvres à Neuilly

Allée de la Reine Marguerite

Av de l'Hippodrome

Ave de St-Cloud

Rte de la Seine à la Butte Mortemart

Bd Anatole France

A13

Périphérique

Porte de la Muette, Place de Colombie

16e

Porte de Passy

Rue du Ranelagh

N

Rte de Boulogne à Passy

Ave de la Porte d'Auteuil

Bd d'Auteuil

Ⓜ M° Porte d'Auteuil

HUNTER PUBLISHING

NOT TO SCALE
© 2004 HUNTER PUBLISHING, INC.

1. Jardin d'Acclimation
2. Carrefour de la Porte de Madrid
3. Pont de Puteaux
4. Parc de Bagatelle
5. Champ d'Entrainement, Polo de Bagatelle
6. Pré Catalan, Racing Club de France
7. Carr de Longchamp, Châlet de la Grande Cascade
8. Hippodrome de Longchamp
9. Parc Edmond de Rothschild
10. Stade Roland Garros; Jardin des Poètes
11. Hippodrome d'Auteuil, Butte Mortemart
12. Carrefour des Cascades
13. Châlet des Iles
14. Jardin du Ranelagh

16e Arrondissements   Ⓜ Métro

€1 (€0.50 for students ages seven to 25, free for kids under seven), or €3 (and €1.50) during concerts.

The botanical gardens of the **Parc de Bagatelle** (Route de Sèvres-à-Neuilly or Allée de Longchamp, M° Porte Maillot and Bus 244, ☎ 08 20 00 75 75) hosts the annual international rose competition in June. There are many small paths winding through the greenery, with an adorable vegetable garden and cottage, flower covered pergolas, romantic lakes and an elegant 18th-century château used for garden exhibitions. Ask for a map at the entrance. Open daily from 8am on weekdays and 9am on weekends (closing hours vary from 5:30pm in winter to 9:30pm in summer). Entry €1 (€0.50 for students ages seven to 25, free for kids under seven), or €3 (and €1.50) during concerts.

The **Jardin d'Acclimatation** (M° Porte Maillot, ☎ 01 40 67 90 82, www.jardindacclimatation.fr) is an amusement park open year-round with its own gardens, zoo, museums, pony rides and restaurants (see the *Family Entertainment* section for detailed information). Open daily, 10am to 6pm (until 7pm in summer); entry €2.50.

Sporting venues in the Bois de Boulogne include the **Rolland Garros Tennis Stadium and Tenniseum Museum** (Boulevard d'Auteuil, M° Porte d'Auteuil, ☎ 01 47 43 48 00), the historic **Hippodrome de Longchamp** (Route des Tribunes, M° Porte d'Auteuil or Bus 244, ☎ 08 21 21 32 13) and the **Hippodrome d'Auteuil** (Route des Lacs, M° Porte d'Auteuil, ☎ 08 21 21 32 13). Entrance to the regular season of horseracing is free at both racetracks. See the *Entertainment* section, page 299, for more detailed information on the races and tours of the Rolland Garros Stadium.

WARNING! *It's best to avoid nocturnal cruising along the roads of the Bois de Boulogne if you find the sight of transvestite streetwalkers upsetting (although tough new laws have greatly cut down on this over the past few years).*

Nouvelle Athènes & Grands Boulevards Passages

The vast 9th arrondissement has many personalities, from the luxury shops around the Opéra Garnier and the sex shops below Pigalle to the Orthodox Jewish quarter near the Folies Bergères. Often overlooked is the quiet residential district known as La Nouvelle Athènes, developed in the 1820s for the rising professional classes of the new industrialist era. Influenced by London's urban architecture, the neoclassic houses feature large porches, cast-iron balcony railings and intricate moldings and friezes. Many artists and musicians also lived in the neighborhood, including Berlioz, Jean Cocteau, Delacroix and Guillaume Apollinaire.

Begin from the edge of this peaceful neighborhood at the striking **Eglise de la Sainte-Trinité** (Place d'Estienne d'Orves, 9th, M° Trinité, ☎ 01 48 74 12 77), a neo-Renaissance church built during the Second Empire. The interior is richly painted, with an original Cavaillé-Coll organ built in 1869 (the composer Olivier Messiaen was the church organist from 1931-1992). The church exterior is unique, with one of the tallest bell towers in Paris, and a terraced fountain entrance featuring statues representing Faith, Charity and Hope. The small church park is popular with locals, who relax on benches under the tall shade trees while their children play on the grassy lawn.

Paris

Walk up through Nouvelle Athènes along Rue Blanche, turning right onto Rue la Bruyère and left at Rue Henner. Don't be afraid to peek through the gates of the elegant 19th-century townhouses. At the end of the street is a flowered passage leading to the **Musée de la Vie Romantique** (16 Rue Chaptal, 9th, M° St-Georges, ☎ 01 48 74 95 38). This adorable ivy-covered mansion and cottage-style garden was formerly the home of painter Ary Scheffer, who entertained friends such as George Sand, Chopin, Delacroix, Liszt and Ingres. Regular exhibits highlight the works of Scheffer and other French Romantic artists. Don't miss the lovely garden conservatory tearoom (museum ticket not required). Open Tuesday through Sunday, 10am to 6pm. Tickets €6, €4.50 for students, free for kids under 13. Museum Pass accepted. A small English-language guide to the museum available for €3 in the tiny gift shop.

Turn left outside the museum and right onto the Rue de la Rochefoucauld to visit another artist's-home-turned-museum, the **Musée Gustave Moreau** (14 Rue de la Rochefoucauld, 9th, M° St-Georges or Trinité, ☎ 01 48 74 38 50). This cozy townhouse museum is made up of the artist's living quarters and spacious studios, bequeathed to the French state upon his death in 1898 along with over 7,000 of his carefully organized drawings and paintings. Open daily except Tuesday, 10am to 12:45pm and 2 to 5:15pm. Entry €4, reduced to €2.60 on Sundays or with a ticket from the Musée de la Vie Romantique. Museum Pass accepted.

Make a small detour across the street to the Rue de la Tour-des-Dames, which has some of the best examples of Nouvelle Athènes architecture, then continue down the Rue de la Rochefoucauld and right onto Rue St-Lazare. Turn left onto the Rue Taitbout and enter the passage at #80 (a private entry, sometimes locked on weekends). Pass through the first courtyard and turn left into the **Square d'Orléans**, built in pure English style in 1829 with 46 apartments and six artists' studios. Illustrious former residents include Chopin (#9) and George Sand (#5).

Continue again along the Rue St-Lazare and turn right onto the Rue du Notre-Dame de Lorette. Continue across the Rue de Châteaudun to **Rue du Faubourg Montmartre**. This bustling neighborhood has the second-largest Orthodox Jewish population in Paris after the Marais, concentrated along the Rue Richer. Have a stroll up and down the Rue Cadet, a typically Parisian market street. The austere 1970s building on the right houses a French Masonic museum, the **Grand Orient de la France** (16 Rue Cadet, 9th, M° Cadet, ☎ 01 45 23 20 92, www.godf.org). Open Tuesday through Saturday, 2 to 6pm; entry €2.

Walk back across the Rue du Faubourg Montmartre to the entrance of the **Passage Verdeau** (at 31*bis*), one of the city's historic covered passages. This leads to the **Passage Jouffroy** (cross the Rue de la Grange Batelière), home to the city's wax museum, the **Musée Grévin** (10 Boulevard Montmartre, 9th, M° Grands Boulevards, ☎ 01 47 70 85 05, www.grevin.com). Built in 1882, the museum features scenes from French history (for example, Louis XIV at Versailles) as well as modern French celebrities (Johnny Hallyday and Jean-Paul Gauthier). Open weekdays 10am to 6:30pm, weekends until 7pm. Entry €16, €9 for kids ages six to 14.

Cross the busy intersection of the Boulevard Montmartre to another series of covered passages, the **Passage des Panoramas**. Built in 1800, this old-fashioned passage is a haven for stamp and vintage postcard collectors. It was the first place in Paris to receive gas lighting in 1817. Exit through the Galerie Montmartre on to Rue Montmartre and return to the intersection of Boulevard Montmartre and Boulevard Poissonière. Lined with theaters, night clubs and trendy new restaurants, Haussmann's "Grands Boulevards" have experienced a bit of a renaissance in the new millennium. Relax in the nearest café terrace with a cool drink and watch the world rush by.

Montmartre & Pigalle

Montmartre has always attracted the crowds to its basilica-topped butte. Many come to lose themselves in the historic village atmosphere of cobblestoned passages, secret gardens, and tiny cabarets immortalized by their favorite artists and writers. But Montmartre is more than just a pretty postcard from the past. It's also a lively Parisian neighborhood full of young designer boutiques and trendy local bars. You'll discover here the magical mix of quirky inhabitants, sex shops, and modern romance featured in the film *Amélie*. So admire the view from Sacré-Coeur and drink the local wine at Place du Tertre, but be prepared to do a bit of exploration off the beaten track for a glimpse of the real Montmartre beyond the tour buses and souvenir shops.

Begin at the **métro Abbesses**, with its original 1900 Art Nouveau entrance and a never-ending spiral stairwell decorated top to bottom by local artists. Take the elevator if you must, but those aren't the last stairs you'll see in this neighborhood! Hopeless romantics should visit the **Square Jehan Rictus**, where a 430-square-foot mural created in 2000 is covered with the words *I Love You,* written in 311 languages. Follow the Rue Yvonne Le Tac to the **Place St-Pierre**, at the foot of the Square Willette. This is the heart of the Paris textiles market, with shop after shop of luxurious fabrics sold at wholesalers' prices.

The **Halle St-Pierre**, a former 19th-century covered market of glass and iron, houses the **Musée International d'Art Naïf** (Halle St-Pierre, 2 Rue Ronsard, 18th, M° Abbesses, ☎ 01 42 58 72 89, www.midan.org), a primitive and folk-art museum and library. Open daily, 10am to 6pm; entry €6. There's no fee to stop by the museum's café, where you can enjoy the lovely views of Sacré-Coeur with a cup of tea and a slice of pie.

Continue up Rue Ronsard (or sneak back to the funicular railway, which works with regular métro tickets) to the steps of the Sacré-Coeur Basilica. The panoramic views here are a bit overrated, since perpetual smog and

Paris

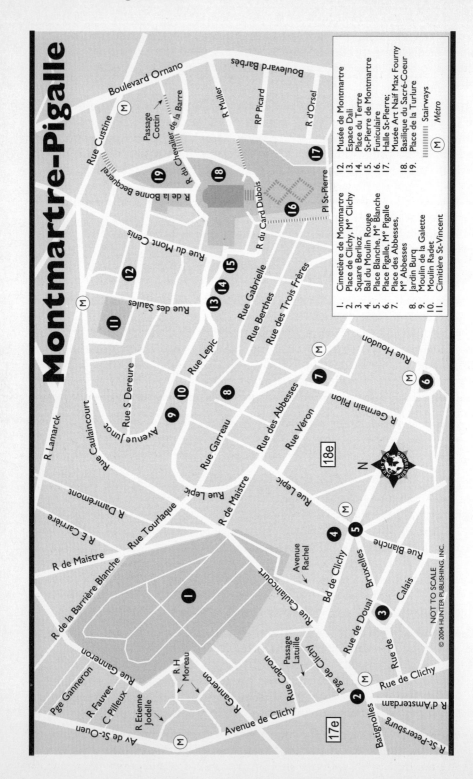

Montmartre-Pigalle

1. Cimetière de Montmartre
2. Place de Clichy, M° Clichy
3. Square Berlioz
4. Bal du Moulin Rouge
5. Place Blanche, M° Blanche
6. Place Pigalle, M° Pigalle
7. Place des Abbesses,
   M° Abbesses
8. Jardin Burq
9. Moulin de la Galette
10. Moulin Radet
11. Cimitière St-Vincent
12. Musée de Montmartre
13. Espace Dali
14. Place du Tertre
15. St-Pierre de Montmartre
16. Funiculaire
17. Halle St-Pierre;
    Musée Art Naïf Max Fourny
18. Basilique du Sacré-Coeur
19. Place de la Turlure
▒▒ Stairways
Ⓜ Métro

NOT TO SCALE
© 2004 HUNTER PUBLISHING, INC.

its distance from central Paris make it hard to distinguish much besides the Eiffel Tower and the Tour Montparnasse.

MONTMARTRE ON WHEELS

If your legs can't bear the stairs, there are two alternative ways of seeing Montmartre. **Le Petit Train de Montmartre** (M° Blanche, ☎ 01 42 62 24 00, €5 adults, €3 kids) leaves from the Place Blanche daily, every 30 minutes from 10am to 7pm, until midnight on weekends and in summer. This 40-minute tour with commentary isn't bad for the price when you consider how much anguish it will save your feet (although your ego may suffer if anyone finds out you were on a toy train ride). The city-run **Montmartrobus** is a cheaper alternative (you just need a regular bus ticket or pass), although there's no commentary. It goes in a loop around Montmartre from the *Mairie* (Town Hall) at Jules Joffrin to Pigalle via Place des Abbesses, the Lapin Agile Cabaret, and the Place du Tertre.

Construction of the Roman-Byzantine **Sacré-Coeur Basilica** (Parvis du Sacré-Coeur, 18th, M° Anvers, ☎ 01 53 41 89 00) began after the Franco-Prussian war of 1870, funded by donations from all over the country by those convinced that the occupation (and subsequent Paris Commune uprising) was a punishment from God for their lack of faith. The grand wedding-cake structure was finally consecrated in 1919. Because of the nature of the stone used to build the basilica, each time it rains it actually gets whiter. The basilica is open daily, 6am to 11pm. The dome (656 feet above sea level) and the crypt can be visited daily, 9am to 5:45pm (entry €4.50).

ATTENTION! *Visitors should always be alert for pickpockets, but make an extra effort in the crowded areas of Montmartre, where distracted tourists are commonly targeted.*

Follow the Rue Azais around to the small **Eglise St-Pierre-de-Montmartre** (2 Rue du Mont-Cénis, 18th), the only surviving vestige of Montmartre's ancient Benedictine Abbey, which was destroyed during the French Revolution. Consecrated in the 12th century, St-Pierre's is one of the oldest churches in Paris (along with St-Germain-des-Prés and St-Martin-des-Champs). The tiny cemetery next door is only open to the public on All Saints' Day (November 1).

Be ready to fend off the roving portrait artists as you enter the Place du Tertre, the historic heart of Montmartre. The official, tax-paying artists are the ones sitting patiently at their easels in the center of the square (you can try haggling a lower price if business is slow). It's best to visit early in the morning, before the café terraces and postcard stands crowd the sidewalks. Be sure to stop into the community-run information center, the Syndicat d'Initiative de Montmartre (21 Place du Tertre, 18th, ☎ 01 42 62 21 21). There's a large binder you can browse through for local information on food, hotels, sightseeing and events. They also sell local maps, detailed history guides, and the rare Clos de Montmartre wine. Open daily, 10am to 7pm.

LA LIBERTÉ

Montmartre has always had a rebellious streak. Newly annexed to Paris in 1860, its anti-conformist ideals and bohemian life-style attracted a number of libertines and artists. But today's visitors may not realize that it was also here that the popular uprising of the Commune was declared in March 1871 (see *History*, page 2). Despite the Commune's bloody repression two months later, the independent spirit of the Butte lives on. In 1920 the Commune Libre du Montmartre was established to preserve the village's community ideals and camaraderie, with its own mayor who performs traditional marriage and baptism ceremonies. They have a number of festive events throughout the year – ask at the information center (above) for more information.

Leave the crowded square by the Rue Poulbot. Devoted Salvador Dali fans won't want to miss the "fantasmagoric universe" known as the **Espace Dali** (11 Rue Poulbot, 18th, M° Abbesses, ☎ 01 42 64 40 10), with over 300 of the Spanish surrealist's prints and sculptures theatrically displayed. Open daily, 10am to 6:30pm, July and August until 9pm. Entry €7.

Explore the photogenic Rue Norvins and Rue St-Rustique, whose **Auberge de la Bonne-Franquette** (on the corner of Rue des Saules) was immortalized in Utrillo's paintings, and frequented in the late 1800s by Pissarro, Cézanne, Monet, Renoir, Van Gogh and the writer Emile Zola. Want to know more about the artists of Montmartre? Just around the corner is the **Musée de Montmartre** (12 Rue Cortot, 18th, M° Anvers, ☎ 01 49 25 89 37, www.museedemontmartre.com), a 17th-century townhouse where Renoir, Dufy and Utrillo once lived, now a museum dedicated to the Butte's Bohemian heyday. Don't miss the great views from the windows. Open Tuesday through Saturday, 10am to 12:30pm and 1:30 to 6pm. Entry €4.50, students €3, free for kids under 10.

Cut back behind the Basilica along the Rue du Chevalier de la Barre to the romantic **Parc de la Turlure**, with its vine-covered pergola and lovely views over the rooftops. Follow the Rue de la Bonne (downhill, at last) to the cobblestoned Rue Saint-Vincent. Across from #14 is the **Jardin Sauvage**, a wildlife preservation garden only open to the public on Saturdays from April to October, 10am to 6pm. Next door is the **Clos du Montmartre**, the symbolic vineyard planted in 1933 to commemorate Montmartre's history as a wine-growing hilltop. The annual grape harvest festival takes place the first week of October (and according to those in the know, the quality of the wine has improved significantly over the past decade).

Across from the vineyard is the historic cottage of the **Cabaret du Lapin Agile** (22 Rue des Saules, 18th, M° Lamarck-Caulaincourt, ☎ 01 46 06 85 87, www.au-lapin-agile.com) once the haunt of Montmartre's artists and now a place to go hear all of the old classic French *chansons* in an authentic cabaret décor (see the *Entertainment* section for more information). Continue along Rue St-Vincent, with a peek into the tiny **Cimetière de St-Vincent** on your right (entrance on Rue Gaulard), where the artist Utrillo and other local parishioners are buried.

Time to head back up the hill along the curve of Avenue Junot. There are some charming townhouses built in the early 1900s at the **Hameau des Artistes** (#11) and **Villa Léandre** (#25). Turn right on Rue Giradon and again at Rue Lepic. Here stand Montmartre's last two windmills, the **Moulin Radet** and the **Moulin de la Galette**, the famous dance hall immortalized in Renoir's *Bal du Moulin de la Galette* (at the Musée d'Orsay). Vincent Van Gogh lived at his brother's flat on the third floor of #54 from 1886-1888, painting the windmills and Montmartre's quickly vanishing wheat fields.

Get ready for a change of scenery at the Place Blanche, where the neon red windmill of the **Moulin Rouge** (82 Boulevard de Clichy, 18th, M° Blanche, ☎ 01 53 09 82 82, www.clubmoulinrouge.com) stands proudly in the center of Pigalle's sex shops, night clubs and peep shows. Although the public adored its frilly petticoated cancan dancers, the Moulin Rouge caused a real scandal in 1890 when the first woman appeared onstage as Cleopatra – completely nude! It's had many ups and downs before evolving to its current Vegas-style show. Read all about it on their web site, or see the *Entertainment* section, page 299, for information on booking a seat.

Just west of the Moulin Rouge is the **Musée de l'Erotisme** (72 Boulevard de Clichy, 18th, M° Blanche, ☎ 01 42 58 28 73) This museum suffers from its seedy location, because it's not just a collection of dirty pictures. There are seven floors dedicated to evolution of eroticism in art, from primitive sculptures and Far Eastern illustrated books to Belle Epoque furniture and contemporary cartoons. Okay, and lots of dirty pictures. The most interesting part of the exhibition presents the glory days of 19th-century Parisian brothels. All of the descriptions are in French and English. The neighborhood may scare off some visitors, but the museum is tastefully done and not at all intimidating, even for solo female visitors. Open daily, 10am to 2am. Entry €7, €5 for students.

NoMo DETOUR

If you haven't already noticed, the north side of Montmartre (NoMo) has quite a different atmosphere than the rest of the Butte. There may not be any museums or ancient winding streets, but this is where actual Parisians eat and shop, without a postcard stand, tour bus, or portrait artist in sight!

Take the stairs down past the métro Lamarck-Caulaincourt to Rue Francoeur, then left down Rue du Mont-Cénis to the Place Jules Joffrin. A tiny microcosm of Parisian life, this bustling square with its Haussmann-style press kiosk and mini merry-go-round is framed dramatically by the neo-Gothic **Notre-Dame de Clignancourt** on one side, and the majestic local town hall, the **Mairie du 18ème**, on the other. Inaugurated in 1892, the Mairie has a beautiful glass and wrought-iron-ceilinged courtyard, which is open to the public. Hidden from sight is one of the most beautiful Salle des Mariages in Paris, with paintings and frescos depicting Montmartre at the beginning of the 20th century. This Mairie is the only town hall in Paris with its own wine cellar, where bottles of the rare Clos Montmartre are carefully stored for special occasions.

Around the corner are the market streets: **Rue Duhesme**, with fresh fruit, vegetable, fish and meat stalls, and the **Rue du Poteau**, with a wide variety of boutiques selling everything from sausages and chocolates to shoes and home decorating supplies (market closed Monday). Don't miss the **Fromagerie de Montmartre** at #9, where they'll vacuum-seal your cheeses for travel. Gather some picnic supplies and head to the tranquil Square de Clignancourt, a small park with children's playground and vintage bandstand, surrounded by listed residential buildings and tall trees.

Back on the Place Jules Joffrin, take the Montmartrobus back up to the Butte, or Bus 85 to the Marché au Puces in St-Ouen (see *Where to Shop*, page 214, for more information).

Continue along the same side of the boulevard to the tiny **Avenue Rachel**, a tree-lined pedestrian street with a few cafés and restaurants spilling out onto the sidewalk in nice weather. At the end of the street is the main entrance to the **Cimetière de Montmartre** (20 Avenue Rachel, 18th, M° Blanche, ☎ 01 53 42 36 30), with the elevated Rue Caulaincourt passing right overhead. Set in the hills, it's deceptively small until you start going up and down the steps. Ask for a printed *plan* at the office just inside, which has the locations of famous residents such Berlioz, Offenbach, Degas, Stendhal, Fragonard and Dalida. Open weekdays 8am to 5:30pm (from 8:30am on Saturday, and 9am on Sunday).

AMELIE FEVER

Baz Luhrmann's modern film version of *Moulin Rouge* may have given the aging cabaret's image a sexy new lease on life, but it's nothing compared to the frenzy of *Amélie* fans who've been flocking to Montmartre by the busload since the release of the 2001 runaway hit *Le Fabuleux Destin d'Amélie Poulain*, titled *Amélie* for American release. The most popular pilgrimage points are the **Brasserie des Deux Moulins** (15 Rue Lepic; the *tabac* counter is gone, but the rest is the same), **Au Marché de la Butte** (56 Rue des Trois Frères; the film's Epicerie Collignon), métro Lamarck-Caulaincourt (where she leads the blind man), and **#56 Rue des Trois Frères**, (Amélie's apartment).

Batignolles

Batignolles hasn't quite made it onto the average sightseeing itinerary, but it's an interesting neighborhood to explore for those looking to escape the souvenir shops and overpriced cafés of nearby Montmartre. Traditionally a working class neighborhood with a diverse ethnic population, Batignolles has recently become a trendy district for young *créateurs* and artists looking for inexpensive working space.

Begin at the **Place de Clichy**, a crazy intersection reminiscent of Times Square with busy traffic intersections and giant cinema billboards. Head up the Avenue de Clichy, where artists of the Ecole des Batignolles such as Pissarro, Renoir, and Degas (known today as the Impressionists) used to live and socialize. Turn left on the **Rue des Dames**, where the bohemian Eldorado Hotel, friendly Lush Bar and traditional Bistro des Dames create a hip and artsy enclave just a few blocks from crazy neon and fast-food joints.

Turn right onto the **Rue des Batignolles**, a pleasant shopping street that leads to the humble **Eglise Ste-Mairie des Batignolles**. The church sits in the center of a charming courtyard with stylish cafés and boutiques. Just behind is the **Square des Batignolles**, a romantic-style garden built in the late 1800s, with a duck pond, children's playgrounds and gently rolling paths for strolling.

Paris

Continue along the Rue des Moines for some window shopping, then cut through the small indoor market at Rue Lemercier to the Rue Brochant. Turn left at Avenue de Clichy and cross the street to enter the **Cité des Fleurs** (the pedestrian gate is usually unlocked), an oasis of elegant, 19th-century townhouses with private gardens and a cobblestoned lane down the center.

Turn right onto Rue de la Jonquière and loop back onto the **Rue Sauffroy**. This colorful commercial street is the center of Batignolles' African community, with the smells and sounds of Brazza, Douala and Kinshasa in the air. Turn left back onto the Avenue de Clichy.

End your exploration of Batignolles with a stroll down the busy avenue (or hop on the bus to La Fourche) to the **Cour St-Pierre** (entrance at 47 Avenue de Clichy, 17th, M° La Fourche), a passage of old horse stables converted into artists' studios and pretty gardens. A sign of great things to come for the Batignolles district?

Barbès & Goutte d'Or

The **Goutte d'Or** (*drop of gold*) gets its name from golden wine produced in the vineyards that covered this hill until the 19th century. It was first developed in 1840 as temporary housing for workers from the provinces, then became the first stop for waves of immigrants from Europe, Africa, Eastern Europe and Asia. Today the neighborhood between Barbès and Château-Rouge is known for its colorful multiethnic community. An ambitious neighborhood rehabilitation program started in the late 1980s is slowly making up for decades of neglect, with mixed reviews. Locals and Parisians welcome a crackdown on street crime and improvements to the infrastructure, but aren't so sure they want to see the exotic boutiques and colorful food markets replaced by chain stores like Virgin Megastore and Footlocker. Take the time to explore this rapidly changing neighborhood before its unique character is modernized beyond recognition.

Start at the **Marché Dejean** (off Rue Poulet, slightly uphill and to the right from M° Château-Rouge), an African market with everything from warm-water fish to spices from the French West Indies. Women dressed in traditional *boubous* sell fresh-baked corn on the cob on the sidewalk (they'll even salt it for you) alongside salesmen hawking very realistic "Gucci" and "Louis Vuitton" bags. Boutiques on side-streets sell handmade African fabrics, Raï music, and mysterious potions and aphrodisiacs from Mali. Turn right down the Rue des Poissonières, left onto Rue Polonceau, and right onto the Rue des Gardes, a.k.a. Rue de la Mode. The local town hall subsidizes this modern block of boutiques to provide an affordable place for up-and-coming designers and artists to exhibit and sell their creations.

SCANDAL

Take a small detour to the 19th-century neo-Gothic church Eglise St-Bernard (follow Rue Polonceau to Rue St-Luc). It became the scene of a scandal in the summer of 1996 when a group of illegal immigrants from Africa took refuge inside to avoid deportation. After several weeks, the national police entered the church and forcibly removed the group despite the protests from the international community.

Continue across the Rue Goutte d'Or and down the Rue Caplat past North Algerian butchers and Tunisian pastry shops. Turn right onto the Boulevard de la Chapelle. The inexpensive **Marché Barbès,** open beneath the elevated métro tracks every Wednesday and Saturday morning, has everything from produce and spices to clothing and souvenirs.

Finish your walk at the recently renovated **métro Barbès-Rochechouart**. This busy intersection is undergoing several changes. Besides the addition of several new mainstream stores, the historic **Luxor Théâtre**, which had been deteriorating from neglect, has been purchased by the city to be transformed into a center for Mediterranean culture and cinema. The outlook for the legendary **Tati** discount store isn't as good. After dominating the intersection for years with its distinctive pink gingham logo, the French discount chain is slowly going out of business, with many other Paris locations already closed in 2003.

■ East Left Bank

While the Right Bank grew with the spread of the royal palaces and aristocratic mansions, the Left Bank, or *Rive Gauche*, has been the stomping grounds of the clergy and their students since the Middle Ages. But the old generalization of the "fashionable Right Bank" and the "*gauche* Left Bank" is not as relevant today, since the 6th and 7th have been taken over by the privileged classes and the most dynamic Right Bank quarters are in the working-class, ethnic enclaves of the 10th, 19th and 20th arrondissements.

The Latin Quarter

Extending over much of the 5th arrondissement, today's *Quartier Latin* remains the center of the city's university life, full of bookshops, literary cafés, art house cinemas and perhaps one too many Greek restaurants. It's also thick with reminders of its past, from the Roman baths ruins to medieval churches and 18th-century gardens. Harder for visitors to image is the Latin Quarter's long track record of political unrest and rebellion, but these narrow streets saw some of the worst fighting of the Paris Commune in 1871, violent clashes between Resistance fighters and Ger-

East Left Bank

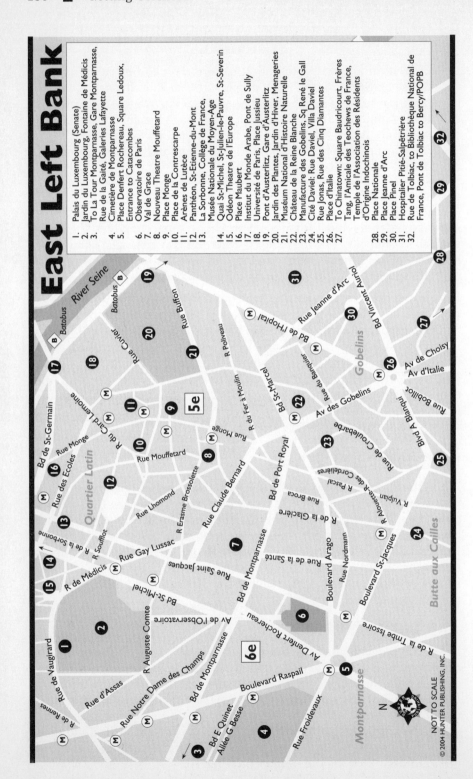

1. Palais du Luxembourg (Senate)
2. Jardin du Luxembourg, Fontaine de Médicis
3. To La Tour Montparnasse, Gare Montparnasse, Rue de la Gaîté, Galeries Lafayette
4. Cimetière de Montparnasse
5. Place Denfert Rochereau, Square Ledoux, Entrance to Catacombes
6. Observatoire de Paris
7. Val de Grace
8. Nouveau Theatre Mouffetard
9. Place Monge
10. Place de la Contrescarpe
11. Arènes de Lutèce
12. Panthéon, St-Etienne-du-Mont
13. La Sorbonne, Collège de France, Musée Nationale du Moyen-Age
14. Quai St-Michel, St-Julien-le-Pauvre, St-Severin
15. Odéon Theatre de l'Europe
16. Place Maubert
17. Institut du Monde Arabe, Pont de Sully
18. Université de Paris, Place Jussieu
19. Pont d'Austerlitz, Gare d'Austerlitz
20. Jardin des Plantes, Jardin d'Hiver, Menageries
21. Museum National d'Histoire Naturelle
22. Château de la Reine Blanche
23. Manufacture des Gobelins, Sq René le Gall
24. Cité Daviel: Rue Daviel, Villa Daviel
25. Rue Jonas, Rue des Cinq Diamantes
26. Place d'Italie
27. To Chinatown: Square Baudricourt, Frères Tang, l'Amicale des Teochews de France, Temple de l'Association des Résidents d'Origine Indochinois
28. Place Nationale
29. Place Jeanne d'Arc
30. Place Pinel
31. Hospitalier Pitié-Salpétrière
32. Rue de Tolbiac, to Bibliothèque National de France, Pont de Tolbiac to Bercy/POPB

NOT TO SCALE

© 2004 HUNTER PUBLISHING, INC.

man police in 1944, and the infamous barricades of the May 1968 student uprising.

 DID YOU KNOW? *Most historians believe the term* Latin Quarter *came from the common language spoken by the neighborhood's clergy and students up until the 1792 Revolution. Others say it was named for the neighborhood's first inhabitants, the Romans.*

Begin at the perpetually crowded **Place St-Michel**, with its dramatic fountain and bronze statue, *Saint Michael Slaying the Dragon*. Walk a short way up the Latin Quarter's main artery, the Boulevard St-Michel (or *Boul' Mich*, as the students call it), to the **Musée National du Moyen Age: Thermes & Hôtel de Cluny** (6 Place Paul-Painlevé, 5th, M° Cluny-La Sorbonne, ☎ 01 53 73 78 00, musee-moyenage.fr). This medieval museum is set within the well-preserved 15th-century Hôtel des Abbés de Cluny, a former Parisian residence for the abbots. The outer walls protect the excavated second-century Gallo-Roman baths, with three mosaic-tiled rooms, the largest used today for medieval music concerts. Founded in 1843, the museum highlights the arts and culture of the Middle Ages, and includes stained glass, altarpieces, ironwork, ceramics, stone and wood carvings, Gothic ivories, embroidery, and the famous Unicorn Tapestries. The mornings are least crowded. Open daily except Tuesday, 9:15am to 5:45pm. Entry €5.50, €4 for visitors ages 18 to 25, free admission daily for kids under 18, and for everyone the first Sunday of the month. Museum Pass accepted. There are English tours (90 minutes) on Saturdays at 11:30am and Sundays at 10am (except on certain holidays, so call to confirm). Tours cost €6 in addition to entry to museum (under 18 just €4.50).

The medieval-inspired **museum gardens** were redone in 2000, divided into different sections representing a unicorn forest, medicinal herb garden, and a prairie. There's also a playground and plenty of good benches for picnicking. Open daily, 9am to 5:30pm in winter, and 9am to 9:30pm in summer. Free entry.

Loop back into the maze of narrow streets off the old Gallo-Roman route known today as **Rue de la Harpe**. Off the Rue de la Parcheminerie, where medieval scribes used to work, is the **Eglise St-Séverin-St-Nicolas** (Rue de Prêtres-St-Séverin), with a 13th-century façade and flamboyant Gothic interior completed in 1530. After crossing the Rue St-Jacques to Rue Galande, take a last look back at the church for a great photo op.

Behind the tiny 13th-century **Eglise St-Julien-le-Pauvre** (a Melkite church since 1889) is the **Square René-Viviani**. Here stands, with the aide of two cement pillars, the oldest tree in Paris supposedly planted in 1602 (although most experts believe it was actually closer to 1680).

Covered in creeping vines, this tree managed to survive having its top lopped off by a shell in WWI as well as the the devastating storm of December 1999. The bronze sculpture in the center of the square was added in 1995 as a tribute to the Saint Julien le Hospitaller, one of three patron saints (all named Julien) of the church.

Explore the tiny streets of Rue de la Bucherie and Rue F. Sauton to the **Place Maubert**. This square was a place of public teaching in the 13th century. The invention of classrooms ended this, and in the 16th century it became a place of public executions. Today its most exciting event is the **outdoor market** (Tuesday, Thursday and Saturday mornings). Across the street is the narrow **Rue de Bièvre**, named for the tributary from the Seine that used to flow openly through the Latin Quarter. Polluted by the tanneries and butchers of Rue Mouffetard, it was finally covered over in the 19th century. The former President François Mitterrand used to live at #22.

Continue onto the **Quai de la Tournelle** for a photogenic view of Notre Dame. Follow the quay to the modern glass and steel building of the **Institut du Monde Arabe** (Place Mohamed V, 1 Rue des Fosses St-Bernard, 5th, M° Jussieu, ☎ 01 40 51 38 38), a museum dedicated to Arab-Islamic arts and history. Designed by the architect Jean Nouvel, the building's south façade is covered in 1,600 panels resembling photographic lenses that open and close to regulate the sunlight. Check out the free views over Paris from the 9th-floor terrace of Le Ziryab, the museum's North African restaurant and tearoom. The museum is open Tuesday through Sunday, 10am to 6pm. Entry €4 (free for kids under 18). Museum Pass accepted.

That ugly, hulking building behind the museum is the **University of Paris' Jussieu** campus. Hastily constructed in the 1960s to accommodate the exploding Baby Boomer population, it remains an eyesore despite several renovations. Leave all that behind with a detour through the modern sculpture gardens of the **Square Tino Rossi** to the **Jardin des Plantes** (entrance Quai St-Bernard or Rue Geoffroy-St-Hilaire, 5th, M° Jussieu or Monge). Founded in 1626 as the king's medicinal garden, it became one of the foremost scientific botanical gardens in the world by the mid-1700s. Today the Jardin des Plantes has over 350 varieties of roses, an alpine garden, tropical and arid greenhouses (open afternoons only; entry €2.50), and winding paths through pines and oaks favored by joggers. The park's *Ménagerie*, one of the world's oldest zoos (open daily, 9am to 5pm; entry €6, €3.50 for kids ages four to 16), has a monkey house, petting farm, lions, and a somewhat sad bear pit. In one grim episode of the 1870 Paris siege, starving Parisians were forced to kill the animals for food.

The 19th-century buildings of the **National Museum of Natural History** serve as an elegant backdrop to the gardens. The **Grande Galerie de l'Evolution** (36 Rue Geoffroy Saint-Hilaire, 5th, M° Jussieu,

☎ 01 40 79 30 00, www.mnhn.fr/Evolution) is the most impressive, both for its well-presented educational content on the evolution of the natural world and its theatrical Jules Verne décor. The 1994 renovations modernized the museum with a completely open floor plan and interactive computer exhibits while preserving the original wrought iron and glass ceiling, wooden floors and stone walls. The low lighting and life-size animal reproductions, from insects and birds to lions and even a prehistoric whale fossil suspended from the ceiling, give the place a magical energy. Start at the top floor where you can get the best view of the museum's architecture, and don't miss the extinct and endangered species gallery on the second floor. Almost everything is in French, but there are English text sheets around the museum in the wooden boxes labeled "Fiches de Lecture." One exhibit features a tigress attacking the carrier basket on an elephant. In 1887 the Duke of Orléans was on safari riding in that basket when the tigress attacked, and got away only because the basket broke under the animal's weight. It was then hunted down, shot, and brought it back to Paris to be stuffed (and later donated to the museum). Make what you want of that evolutionary lesson. If dinosaur fossils are more to your taste, the **Galeries de Paléontologie & Anatomie Comparée** exhibit mammoths, Louis XV's rhinoceros, dinosaurs and austral whales. Open daily except Tuesday, 10am to 6pm. Entry €7, €5 for students under 26, free for kids under age four.

Just outside the park gates is the Alhambra-inspired **Mosquée de Paris** (2*bis* Place du Puits de l'Ermite, 5th, M° Jussieu, ☎ 01 45 35 97 33, www.mosquee-de-paris.com). Built in 1922 around a series of garden courtyards, the mosque features a 108-foot minaret and Muslim cultural center. Open for visits daily except Friday, 9am to noon and 2 to 6pm. The Mosquée's elaborately decorated **tearoom** (entrance at 39 Rue Geoffroy Saint-Hilaire, 5th, ☎ 01 43 31 38 20), is a pleasant place to stop for mint tea and North African pastries (open daily, 9am to 11pm). Try to avoid the crowded weekend afternoons.

Just across the Rue Lacépède are the **Arènes de Lutèce** (Rue de Navarre, 5th, M° Jussieu). Built in the first century, this Roman amphitheater once accommodated up to 15,000 spectators (significantly smaller than the ones in Arles and Nîmes). Discovered during road construction in 1869, *les Arènes* escaped complete demolition thanks to persistent lobbying by Victor Hugo. Today it's primarily used as a *boules* court, a kids' soccer field, and a popular picnic spot.

Crossing Rue Monge, continue up the stairs of Rue Rollin to the **Place de la Contrescarpe**, a lively square surrounded by cafés with perfect people-watching terraces. To the left is the beginning of the animated market street **Rue Mouffetard**, a long, winding street that used to be the main road between Lutèce and Rome. Its village atmosphere described in Hemingway's *A Moveable Feast* (he lived around the corner at #74 Rue du Cardinal Lemoine) has hardly changed over the years, save for perhaps the proliferation of crêpe stands and… more Greek restaurants. The top of the street is dominated by bars (especially around the Rue du Pot de Fer), packed with students after dark. The open market stalls toward the bottom of the street are open Tuesday through Sunday morning (closed at lunch), often to the joyful accompaniment of street musicians on the weekends.

MIRACLE DIRT

As one of the oldest streets in Paris, the Rue Mouffetard figures in many historical anecdotes. One particularly bizarre episode took place in 1732 at the Eglise St-Médard (#141) when the grave of a beloved Jansenist minister in the church cemetery became associated with miraculous cures. It became the site of massive hysteria as sick Jansenists came to eat the dirt, causing Louis XV to close the cemetery with a sign that read, "By decree of the King, no miracles of God may be performed here."

Enjoy an impromptu picnic in the small church garden, or take time to explore the tiny side-streets such as the Rue d'Arbelète. Cut back up the hill via Rue Lhomond and Rue Tournefort. At the corner of the Rue de l'Estrapade you should be able to see the dome of the **Panthéon** (Place du Panthéon, 5th, M° Cardinal Lemoine or RER Luxembourg, ☎ 01 44 32 18 00, www.monum.fr). Originally commissioned by Louis XV in 1744 as a basilica to replace the ruined Abbey Ste-Geneviève, the Panthéon was only finished in 1789 due to funding problems. Two years later the Revolutionary assembly declared it a "Panthéon for great men who died in the period of French liberty," including Rousseau and Voltaire. Over the years it was changed again into a church, then the HQ of the Paris Commune, then finally back to a mausoleum when it received the ashes of Victor Hugo in 1885. Other honored residents include Emile Zola, Louis Braille, Jean Moulin, Marie Curie and Alexander Dumas. Designed by the architect Soufflot, the Panthéon is considered a masterpiece, although the inside is a bit cold and the crypt is downright creepy. Open daily, 10am to 6pm; entry €7, €4.50 for visitors 18-25, free for kids under 18. Museum Pass accepted.

Next door is the **Eglise St-Etienne-du-Mont** (Place St-Geneviève), home to the shrine of Saint Geneviève (the patron saint of Paris) and the city's only surviving roodscreen (a sort of carved stone bridge from which sermons were given in the 15th and 16th centuries).

The Latin Quarter's oldest schools can be found in the maze of streets below. Continue down the Rue de la Montaigne Ste-Geneviève, left at the Rue de l'Ecole Polytechnique, and straight through the pedestrian-only Rue Lanneau to the Place Marcellin-Berthelot. The unique **Collège de**

France (#11) (www.college-de-france.fr) was created by King François I in 1530 to teach secular subjects ignored by the Sorbonne (such as Greek, Hebrew, philosophy and mathematics). To this day, all classes are free and open to the general public. Cross the Rue St-Jacques and walk around the Université de Paris IV to the **Place de la Sorbonne**, the heart of **La Sorbonne**. Most of the school was rebuilt in the 19th century, with the exception of the 17th-century Chapelle de la Sorbonne, with its trademark dome. Have a peek in to see the regular arts and scholarly exhibitions (open Tuesday through Sunday, 1 to 7pm, free entry). End your exploration of the Latin Quarter with a coffee in one of the cafés overlooking the busy square of students, professors, and ever-present street performers.

THE HISTORY OF THE SORBONNE

Created in 1215 with the blessing of Pope Innocent III, the Sorbonne became a prestigious center of western theological study. Over the next seven centuries its role changed many times as the institution evolved. For example, the Sorbonne was originally against any scientific advancement (even denouncing René Descartes), and sided with English and Burgundians in the Hundred Years' War, sending their most imminent scholar to Rouen to prosecute Joan of Arc. The biggest change to the institution came after the Revolution, when the Sorbonne's religious affiliation was dissolved, and it became the seat of centralized, state-run education. After the events of May 1968, the Université de Paris was divided up into 13 independent universities, with the Sorbonne's buildings used by the Université de Paris III and IV. It remains the symbolic heart of the university. Read the full history of the Sorbonne on the school's excellent bilingual web site, www.paris4.sorbonne.fr.

The 13th

Up until the late 1990s, the 13th arrondissement was known only for its 1960s tower blocks and exotic Chinatown district. But as the formerly industrial riverside district is transformed with a stylish, contemporary makeover, visitors are also rediscovering its many historic buildings and hidden village streets, which have escaped modernization.

Gobelins

Begin at the métro Gobelins, right outside the **Manufacture des Gobelins** (42 Avenue des Gobelins, 13th, ☎ 01 44 54 19 33). Originally set up in the mid-1500s as a fabric-dyeing workshop by the artisan Jean Gobelin, it was converted into the royal tapestry manufacturers by King

Louis XIV's minister Colbert in 1662. By the 18th century the Gobelins was famous throughout Europe, and today its tapestries can be found in museums around the world. Tour the workshops, which still operate using 17th-century weaving techniques, every Tuesday, Wednesday and Thursday at 2pm and 2:45pm; entry €8 (€6 for visitors ages seven to 25, kids under age seven free).

Cut around the back of the Gobelins workshops via the Rue Gustave Geoffroy. On the right is the visitor's entrance to the **Château de la Reine Blanche** (18*bis* Rue Berbier du Mets, 13th, M° Gobelins), the *hôtel particulier* built between the 15th and 16th centuries for the Gobelins family, with medieval and Renaissance architectural details such as its twin turrets. Completely renovated in 2002, the listed residence is supposedly named after Philippe VI's widow Blanche d'Evreux, who lived in this location in the 14th century. Tours are available on Wednesday and Sunday afternoons, April through September. Continue up the Rue Berbier du Mets to the **Square René le Gall** (at Rue Croulebarbe), a quiet sunken park with rose gardens, tall shade trees and kids' playgrounds. Turn left onto Rue Corvisart and cross under the métro tunnel to the Boulevard Auguste Blanqui. The local **produce market** takes place every Tuesday, Friday and Sunday. Cross the street to the steps of the Rue Eugène Atget, which cuts through a tiny square before becoming Rue Jonas. At the top of this street is the heart of the Butte aux Cailles neighborhood.

Butte aux Cailles

At an altitude of just over 200 feet, there's hardly a view to speak of (aside from the tall buildings a few blocks away), but the Butte aux Cailles has managed to escape developers' bulldozers, maintaining its authentic village charm. Named after the Cailles family, which once farmed on the hillside, the Butte aux Cailles was covered in windmills until the late 19th century, and was one of the last corners of the city connected to the electric grid. Like many of the working-class hilltop villages annexed to Paris in 1860, it's remembered as one of the strongholds of the Paris Commune of 1871. It wasn't until the late 1960s that the Butte was surrounded by the ugly residential towers that plague most of the 13th (it escaped the same fate because centuries of tunneling into the hillside to excavate stone left the Butte aux Cailles too fragile for buildings more than a few stories tall). Rising prices elsewhere in Paris made the Butte popular with artists, intellectuals, and *Soixant-Huitards* (those involved in the May 1968 strikes). The neighborhood still shows its *populaire* roots, with co-op-owned restaurants and a Socialist mayor, but there are also a number of trendy new bars and bistros, attracting bourgeois executive types eager to buy and "do up" local properties. Only time will tell if the Butte suffers the same Disneyfication of Montmartre.

The **Rue des Cinq-Diamants** and **Rue de la Butte aux Cailles** are pretty much the center of the action after dark. During the day things are a bit quieter, and it's a good time to explore the little streets and their hidden gardens. Turn right at the **Place de la Commune de Paris** and head down to the Rue Daviel to see the Alsace-style cottages of the **Cité Duval** (#7), built to house working-class families in the early 1900s, and the mini gardens of the **Villa Duviel**. Just around the corner and to the left is the virtually undiscovered **indoor flea market** (31 Rue Vergniaud, 13th), which opened in 2003.

Cross back over the hill via Rue de la Butte aux Cailles to the **Place Paul Verlaine**, where you can see the listed façade of the Piscine de la Butte-aux-Cailles (see the *Adventures* section, page 172, for information on this swimming pool). Cross Rue Bobillot and turn right down the pedestrian-only Rue Vendrezanne and Rue Passage du Moulinet. To see more of the little garden villas and interesting architecture, continue across the Rue de Tolbiac to explore the streets around the **Place de l'Abbé Henocque**. Otherwise turn left onto Rue de Tolbiac, which leads straight to the Chinatown district.

Chinatown

Up until the 1950s, this was the least developed part of Paris, with nothing more than makeshift housing surrounded by fields. Desperate to improve living conditions for the post-war baby boom population, the city hastily erected over a dozen residential tower blocks, up to 30 floors tall, in the late 1960s. In the 1970s a wave of refugees and immigrants from Southeast Asia settled in the "Triangle de Choisy," made up of the Avenue de Choisy, Avenue d'Ivry and the Boulevard Masséna. Although the district is known as Chinatown, many of the residents are actually from Cambodia, Vietnam, Laos and Thailand, and speak a different dialect from the Chinese populations in the Arts-et-Métiers and Belleville districts.

Turn right onto **Avenue de Choisy**, with its many Asian restaurants and grocery stores, and turn left onto the pedestrian Rue C. Bertheau. Early in the mornings you can see the elderly residents practicing Tai Chi in the **Square Baudricourt**. Continue through the passage to the **Avenue d'Ivry**, where you'll see the most famous Chinatown store, **Frères Tang** (# 48). Across from the Rue des Frères d'Astier de la Vigerie is the entrance to the vast maze of shops of **Les Olympiades**, with everything from discount electronics to Asian and Vietnamese fabrics. A bit tacky, but fun to browse! Leave the commercial center by the elevators in the left wing of the Galerie d'Oslo to reach the entrance to the Buddhist temple and cultural center, **L'Amicale des Teochews de France** (44 Avenue d'Ivry, 13th, M° Porte d'Ivry, ☎ 01 45 82 06 01). Be sure to remove your shoes before entering. There are regular free music concerts here on Monday, Wednesday and Friday afternoons. Around the corner is the superbly decorated pagoda of the **Temple de l'Association des Résidents d'Origine Indochinoise** (37 Rue du Disque, 13th), hidden in an underground passage that looks like a parking garage entrance (right off 66 Avenue d'Ivry). Continue up the Avenue d'Ivry, with one last stop for tea and pastries at **L'Empire des Thés** (101 Avenue d'Ivry, 13th).

Rive Gauche

Look for **Bus 62** (direction Cours de Vincennes) at the corner of Rue de Tolbiac and Avenue de Choisy, and take this about five stops to the Bibliothèque National de France. You know you're in the right place if it looks like a giant construction site. The **Rive Gauche Project** started in 1988 to renovate 320 acres of industrial wasteland along the Seine between the Gare d'Austerlitz and the Boulevard Masséna. Turn left after the railroad tracks onto the **Avenue de France**, with its neat rows of newly planted trees and central pedestrian and cycle paths. Here you'll find a few cafés with wide sidewalk terraces and the spanking new **Cité de l'Image et du Son MK2**, a cineplex with two restaurants, a café and nightclub, opened in 2003. Just behind, in case you didn't notice, was the first new building in the Rive Gauche project, the monumental mouthful of a library, the **Bibliothèque Nationale de France – site François Mitterrand/Tolbiac** (a.k.a. BnF, or TGB for *très grand bibliothèque*). Opened in 1997, its four towers overlooking the Quai François-Mauriac are supposed to resemble four open books, with façades made entirely of glass (revolving wooden shelves inside can be moved to block the sun). There are some great views from the wooden terrace connecting the buildings, but watch out – those steps are slippery when wet! To go inside you either have to pay the day fee (€3), take a guided tour (in French, call in advance to sign up, ☎ 01 53 79 40 63), or visit the latest cultural exposition in the Grande Galerie (entry €5, ☎ 01 53 79 49 49). For more information check out the web site, www.bnf.fr.

Cross over to the banks of the Seine from the library to the **Quai François Mauriac**, home to many popular floating nightclubs and cafés known as *péniches*. Across the Seine is the Parc de Bercy. (By 2006 there is supposed to be a new footbridge connecting the park to the library.) Continue back toward the Pont de Tolbiac, and turn right onto the Rue de Neuve Tolbiac. Here you can see, surrounded by construction cranes, the only three historical buildings that haven't been torn down. The **Sudac** compressed air factory (1891) and the **Grands Moulins** (1920) flour mills are under renovation to house the library and auditoriums of the new Université de Paris VII (due to open in 2005). After much debate, the graffiti-covered **Les Frigos** (1919) are going to be pretty much left as they are. Originally used as meat lockers, Les Frigos (a.k.a. 91 Quai de la Gare) is one of the city's famous legalized squats, with over 250 artists in residence. They hold two open houses a year; check the web site, www.les-frigos.com, for dates. Stop by to check out the schedule of regular artistic and musical events in their cultural center, **Les Voûtes** (enter by the gardens of Les Frigos).

End your visit to this modern district with a ride back to central Paris on the sleek, driverless **Météor** (line 14; take the steps down from the corner of Rue de Tolbiac and Rue du Chevaleret).

■ West Left Bank

St-Germain-des-Prés

Dominated for centuries by a vast Benedictine abbey, St-Germain-des-Prés came into vogue in the 20th century as the center of intellectual and artistic life, home to smoky jazz clubs and literary cafés. Although the neighborhood's character has forever changed with the recent arrival of couture and designer clothing boutiques, its narrow side-streets and passages are still full of art galleries, bookstores, and cozy café terraces.

Starting from the **Place St-Michel**, take the passage Rue de l'Hirondelle to the Rue Git-le-Coeur, turning right onto the **Quai des Grands Augustins**. This is the oldest quay in Paris, built in 1313. Turn left after the historic restaurant Lapérouse onto the Rue des Grands-Augustins, and explore the Rue Christine, Rue Dauphine and Rue André Mazet. Many of these buildings date back to the 17th century, when the neighborhood surrounding the Abbey at St-Germain-des-Prés became a fashionable place to live. Cross the Rue St-André-des-Arts, a busy street lined with crêpe stands, gift shops, Greek restaurants and art house cinemas, to the **Cour du Commerce-St-André**. This pleasant passage of cafés and gift boutiques was built in 1776 – look out for those uneven cobblestones! On the right is the back door of the country's oldest café, **Le Procope** (13 Rue de l'Ancienne Comédie, 6th, M° Odéon). Opened in 1686, it was popular with actors from the Comédie Française, as well as the young Napoleon Bonaparte and revolutionaries such as Benjamin Franklin and Voltaire. Today it's an upscale restaurant, but sometimes they'll let you stop in for coffee at the lobby bar between 4 and 6pm (use the restrooms upstairs to get a good peek at the restored 18th-century décor).

Loop back up to the Carrefour de Buci, turning left onto the busy market street **Rue de Buci**. This is one of the prime people-watching streets in the neighborhood (particularly from the sidewalk terrace of **Le Bar du Marché**). Take a right onto the Rue de Seine, cutting through the tiny Rue Jacques Callot to the Rue Guénégaud. On the left is the boutique of the **Paris Mint** (2 Rue Guénégaud, 6th). Turn left onto the Quai de Conti to visit the production workshops and coin museum of the **Hôtel des Monnaies** (11 Quai de Conti, 6th, M° Mabillon, www.monnaiedeparis.com). Created by Louis XV in 1775 to mint all of the country's currency,

Paris

West Left Bank

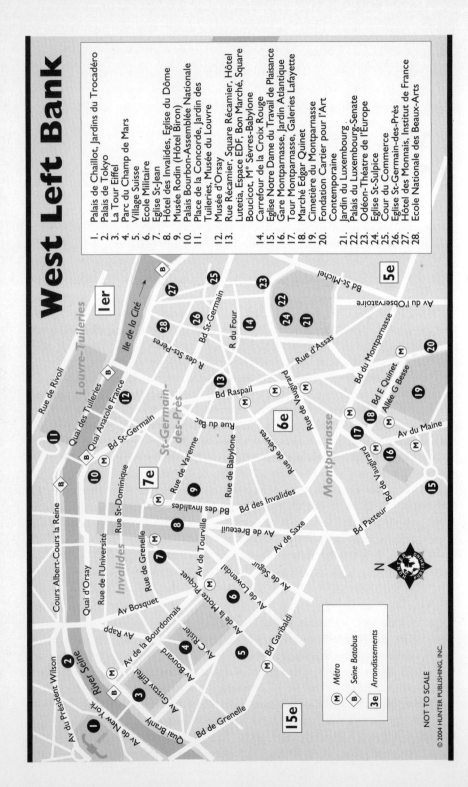

1. Palais de Chaillot, Jardins du Trocadéro
2. Palais de Tokyo
3. La Tour Eiffel
4. Parc du Champ de Mars
5. Village Suisse
6. Ecole Militaire
7. Eglise St-Jean
8. Hôtel des Invalides, Eglise du Dôme
9. Musée Rodin (Hôtel Biron)
10. Palais Bourbon-Assemblée Nationale
11. Place de la Concorde, Jardin des Tuileries, Musée du Louvre
12. Musée d'Orsay
13. Rue Récamier, Square Récamier, Hôtel Lutetia, Espace EDF, Bon Marché, Square Boucicot, Mº Sèvres-Babylone
14. Carrefour de la Croix Rouge
15. Eglise Notre Dame du Travail de Plaisance
16. Gare Montparnasse, Jardin Atlantique
17. Tour Montparnasse, Galeries Lafayette
18. Marché Edgar Quinet
19. Cimetière du Montparnasse
20. Fondation Cartier pour l'Art Contemporaine
21. Jardin du Luxembourg
22. Palais du Luxembourg-Senate
23. Odéon-Théatre de l'Europe
24. Eglise St-Sulpice
25. Cour du Commerce
26. Eglise St-Germain-des-Prés
27. Hôtel des Monnais, Institut de France
28. Ecole Nationale des Beaux-Arts

NOT TO SCALE

© 2004 HUNTER PUBLISHING, INC.

today it's reserved for commemorative pieces and medals. The museum is open Tuesday through Friday, 11am to 5:30pm; and weekends, noon to 5:30pm; entry €8 (includes audio guide). Museum Pass accepted. One-hour guided tours of the workshops are available Wednesdays and Fridays at 2:15pm. Tickets €3, free for kids under 16. Call to reserve a place, ☎ 01 40 46 55 35 or 01 40 46 55 30.

Continue along the quay to the grand **Institut de France** (23 Quai de Conti, 6th, M° Mabillon). This impressive building, with its 17th-century dome by Le Vau, is where the 40 *immortels* of the **Académie Française** gather each year to bemoan the proliferation of *franglais* in the French vocabulary.

PICNIC PLACES

If you're looking for a good spot to eat your picnic lunch, try the Pont des Arts (a.k.a. Passerelle des Arts), a popular pedestrian bridge with some of the best views in town. For a more intimate setting, pass through the little archway in the Institut de France to the Place Gabriel Pierné (corner of Rue de Seine and Rue Mazarine), a quiet garden with benches shaped like open books.

Farther along the quay is the prestigious fine arts academy, the **Ecole Nationale Superieur des Beaux-Arts** (13 Quai Malaquis, 6th, M° St-Germain-des-Prés, ☎ 01 47 03 50 00, www.ensba.fr). There are regular arts exhibitions, and a bookstore that is open to the public Tuesday through Sunday, 1 to 7pm; exhibit entry €4. The rest of the school is off limits to visitors except during the open house in June. Guided tours of the school are available on Mondays during the school year with prior reservations; ☎ 01 47 03 52 15.

Walk down the Rue Bonaparte, with art gallery detours along the Rue des Beaux-Arts and Rue Visconti. Turn left onto Rue Jacob, with its darling little boutiques and bookshops, to the **Rue de Fürstenberg**. This romantic square was originally part of the courtyard for the Palais Abbatial (the brick and stone building you can see at the far end of the street), with stables and housing for servants. Today it's home to upscale interior decorating boutiques and the **Musée Eugène Delacroix** (6 Rue de Fürstenberg, 6th, M° Mabillon, ☎ 01 44 41 86 50). This museum was the painter's last residence, where he died in 1863, offering an intimate look at the artist's work and also personal souvenirs, letters and photographs. Open daily except Tuesday, 9:30am to 5pm. Entry €4, €2.60 for visitors 18-25, free for kids under 18, and everyone the first Sunday of the month. Museum Pass accepted.

Paris

AMERICAN INDEPENDENCE

On September 3, 1783, representatives of the United States
(Benjamin Franklin, John Jay and John Adams) and the King of
England met at 58 Rue Jacob (the **Hôtel de York**) to sign the
Treaty of Paris, in which England officially recognized the inde-
pendence of the 13 colonies. A plaque outside the building com-
memorates this historic event.

Follow the Rue de l'Abbaye to the entrance of the **Eglise St-Germain-
des-Prés** (3 Place St-Germain-des-Prés, 6th, M° St-Germain-des-Prés).
From the Middle Ages up until the Revolution, this entire neighborhood
belonged to the independent Benedictine abbey, with its own houses, stables, chapels, cloisters and prison. It was closed down by the revolutionary Assembly and used for gunpowder storage. An explosion on August
19, 1794 destroyed most of the buildings. Today all that's left of this once
powerful abbey is the Palais Abbatial (converted into government offices)
and the monastic church, St-Germain-des-Prés. The bell tower dates back
to the original construction in the 11th century, although the rest of the
building has been altered throughout the centuries. René Descartes is
buried inside (although his head is actually in the Musée de l'Homme,
page 120).

Overlooking the **Place St-Germain-des-Prés** is the **Café Deux Magots**,
and one block down, the **Café Flore**. These two traditional Parisian cafés
were frequented by artists and writers such as Picasso, Hemingway,
Jean-Paul Sartre, Simone de Beauvoir, Albert Camus, Verlaine, and
Rimbaud. Today they still hang onto their literary roots, although most of
the chic locals and tourists on the terrace don't bother themselves with
anything more existential than a pair of dark sunglasses (the better to
discreetly people-watch, my dear). Across the street is another historic
landmark, the **Brasserie Lipp**, an Alsatian brasserie popular with
French politicians since the 1920s.

Cross the busy Boulevard St-Germain, one of Haussmann's Left Bank
thoroughfares, to the **Rue du Dragon**, a tiny street dating back to the
Middle Ages, known today for its upscale accessories boutiques. At the
end of the street is the **Carrefour de la Croix Rouge**, the crossroads of
the neighborhood's prime shopping streets, punctuated by César's *Cen-
taure* statue. Bear right along the Rue de Sèvres, to the pedestrian-only
Rue Récamier. At the back of the passage is a little garden, the **Square
Récamier**, and the **Espace EDF Electra** (6 Rue Récamier, 6th, M°
Sèvres-Babylone, ☎ 01 53 63 23 45), a former electric station converted
into a contemporary exposition center for the arts run by EDF (the electric company). Open Tuesday through Sunday, noon to 7pm. Free entry.

At the corner of Rue de Sèvres and Boulevard Raspail is the majestic **Hôtel Lutetia**, the Left Bank's only palace hotel (see page 252), and the historic **Bon Marché**, the Left Bank's only department store. Take a well-deserved break in the leafy gardens of the **Square Boucicaut**.

SHOPPING IN ST-GERMAIN-DES-PRES

For those who want to see more of St-Germain-des-Prés, follow the upscale shopping trail from the Bon Marché, up the Rue du Bac, Rue Montalembert, Rue de l'Université and the Rue des Saints-Pères. For more specific shopping ideas, see *Where to Shop*, page 250.

St-Sulpice & Luxembourg

The **Place Saint-Sulpice** is considered a very chic address (Catherine Deneuve lives here), with exclusive designer boutiques slowly edging out the Catholic bookstores selling crosses and statues of the Virgin. But no amount of contemporary glitz can overshadow the real star of the square, the massive **Eglise St-Sulpice**. Commissioned by the abbey in St-Germain-des-Prés for the local parishioners in 1646, it's one of the largest churches in Paris, with several paintings by Delacroix and a world-renowned organ built in 1862. Catch the free recitals on Sunday mornings at 11:30am.

Continue along the Rue St-Sulpice to the **Place de l'Odéon**, via Rue de Condé and Rue Crébillon. The **Odéon-Théâtre de l'Europe** (Place de l'Odéon, 6th, M° Odéon, ☎ 01 44 85 40 40, www.theatre-odeon.fr) was the first national theater, built in 1782 for the Comédie Française troupe. The theater has always been at the center of political discourse, from the premier of Beaumarchais' subversive play *The Marriage of Figaro* to the inflammatory 1968 anti-war play *Paravents*. Today it's considered the place to go for contemporary theater. The elegant 18th-century architecture is under renovation until fall 2005 (see the *Entertainment* section for information on the theater's temporary location).

UNIQUE BOUTIQUE

At the bottom of the street is **Théâtr'Hall** (3 Carrefour de L'Odéon, 6th, M° Odéon, ☎ 01 43 26 64 90, www.cie.theatre-hall.free.fr), a theater costume shop selling high-quality period clothing, capes, hats, wigs and Venetian masks.

Paris

Pass around the east side of the theater to the entrance of the **Jardins du Luxembourg** (Rue de Vaugirard, 6th, M° Odéon). This was originally the private garden of Marie de Medicis' Palais du Luxembourg, built in 1615 after the death of her husband Henri IV. Shortly after moving in she had a fallout with Richelieu over the Franco-Spanish alliance and was banished to Cologne, where she died penniless. The formal garden, tended by a nearby monastery until the Revolution, features a statuary (including a gallery of French queens) surrounding the main fountain, and the dramatic **Fontaine de Medicis** dating back to 1624. Around the edges of the garden are winding English-style paths (find the hidden mini Statue of Liberty), bee houses and trained fruit trees. Open to the public since Napoleon's reign, the gardens are among the most popular in Paris. For kids there are pony rides, playgrounds, marionnettes, and a large basin where they can push around rented toy sailboats. Adults come to relax in the armchairs, enjoy a coffee in the garden café, or get in a bit of jogging. There are also open-air theater productions, free musical concerts, and temporary arts exhibitions held throughout the year. The queen's Italian-style palace is now home to the **French Senate** (www.senat.fr), which oversees prominent arts and culture exhibitions in the **Orangerie** and **Musée du Luxembourg** (entry 19 Rue de Vaugirard, 6th, M° Odéon, ☎ 01 42 34 25 95, www.museums-of-paris.com). Open Friday through Monday, 11am to 10:30pm; Tuesday through Thursday, 11am to 7pm. Entry €9, €6 for visitors 13-25, €4 for kids ages eight to 12. Audio guide in English is €4.50.

AUTHOR'S NOTE: *See the* Inside Story *box in the* Government *section, page 22, for information on visiting the Senate.*

Exit at the south end of the gardens and make a right past the college buildings on Rue Michelet to Rue d'Assas. Turn right, and then watch out on the left for a nondescript passage leading to the **Musée Zadkine** (100*bis* Rue d'Assas, M° Vavin or RER Port Royal, ☎ 01 55 42 77 20). This tiny museum was the home and atelier of the Russian-born artist and sculptor Ossip Zadkine from 1928 until his death in 1967. Open Tuesday through Sunday, 10am to 6pm. Free entry into the permanent collection, temporary exhibits €3.50. Even if you don't go into the museum, have a stroll through the charming sculpture garden at the entrance. While you're in the neighborhood, be sure to stop by the **Lucernaire Forum** (53 Rue Notre-Dame-des-Champs, 6th, ☎ 01 45 44 57 34, M° Vavin, www.lucernaire.fr), a popular neighborhood cultural center, with a cinema, theater, art gallery, rare-book shop, restaurant, bar, and a drama school. The lobby is a charming recreation of an old Parisian street, with bookstalls, fountain, benches, Paris street signs and authentic cobblestones pilfered during the May 1968 student uprising.

Montparnasse

Begin in **Place Pablo Picasso** (M° Vavin), at the noisy intersection of Boulevard Montparnasse and Boulevard Raspail. During the period between the wars known as les années folles, the artists of Montmartre moved into the dirt-cheap ateliers of Montparnasse, and it quickly became the new center of Paris artistic and intellectual life. James Joyce, Hemingway, F. Scott Fitzgerald, Modigliani, Max Ernst, Jean Cocteau and Picasso were among the starving writers, poets, sculptors and painters who frequented the cafés along **Boulevard Montparnasse**, such as the Clôserie des Lilas, Le Dôme, La Rotonde, Le Select and La Coupôle.

> **DID YOU KNOW?** *Montparnasse was home to political exiles such as Trotsky and Lenin.*

The neighborhood still shows signs of artistic life, with young students from around the world toting the weathered portfolios of the serious artist, particularly around the art-supply shops and arts academy of the **Rue de la Grande Chaumière**. Walk down Boulevard Raspail, where many old ateliers have been converted into upscale housing (#240, for example). Man Ray and his muse Kiki lived behind the beautiful ceramic façade at **31 Rue Campagne Première**, and newcomers to the city such as Picabia and Marcel Duchamp stayed next door at the **Hôtel Istria** (#29). Continue down the Boulevard Raspail to the **Fondation Cartier pour l'Art Contemporain** (261 Boulevard Raspail, 14th, M° Raspail, ☎ 01 42 18 56 50, www.fondation.cartier.fr), a contemporary art and culture exhibition center opened in 1994 in a unique glass and steel building by the architect Jean Nouvel. The glassed-in gardens outside are designed to look wild (although sometimes they just look unkempt), with a "fallen tree branch" water fountain and a cedar planted in 1823 by the land's former owner, Châteaubriand. The venue also presents regular Nomadic Nights, devoted to the contemporary performing arts such as dance, music and video, Thursday evenings from 8:30pm (reservations necessary). Open Tuesday-Sunday, noon-6pm; entry €5, €3.50 for visitors 10-25, free for kids under 10. The colorful building across the street is the **Ecole Spéciale d'Architecture**, whose architecture was inspired by the Pompidou Center (closed to the general public).

> **TIME SAVER:** *Those who don't want to walk down Boulevard Raspail can take the Bus 68 from métro Vavin to Place Denfert Rochereau.*

Boulevard Raspail ends at the busy **Place Denfert Rochereau**, with traffic swirling around the bronze **Lion of Belfort** statue by Bertholdi, commemorating one of the few victorious battles of the Franco-Prussian War of 1870. Just behind the statue is a square with one of the old Ledoux city gates. The discreet green cabin around the southern side of the square is the entrance to the **Catacombes** (look for the lines of people), built in the old quarries in the 19th century to accommodate the exhumed remains of over six million Parisians crowding the inner-city cemeteries. See *Adventures*, page 163, for more information on visiting the *Empire de la Mort*.

Take the pedestrian-only Rue de Grancey (from the southwest corner of the Place Denfert Rochereau) to the **Rue Daguerre**. This authentic Parisian market street has a small neighborhood feel to it, where everyone seems to know each other and prices haven't been driven up by tacky souvenir shops... yet. Don't miss the wooden toy shop, **Les Cousins** at #36, the **Chapellerie Divine** hat boutique at #39, and **Paris Accordéon** at #80, a shop and museum dedicated to the humble accordion (they give lessons, too).

UNIQUE RELIGIOUS ARCHITECTURE

Take a detour to the Eglise Notre-Dame-du-Travail de Plaisance (36 Rue Guilleminot, 14th, M° Pernety), a church built in 1900 for the working classes. From the outside it looks like any Paris church, but the inside is constructed of vaulted steel arches in the style perfected by Gustave Eiffel. The priest who commissioned the church wanted it to resemble the modern factories where so many members of his congregation worked.

Turn right on the Avenue de Maine to enter the **Cimetière du Montparnasse** from the corner of Rue Froidevaux (the main entrance is at 3 Boulevard Edgar Quinet, 14th, M° Edgar Quinet, ☎ 01 44 10 86 50). Opened in 1824, this cemetery can't match Père Lachaise in size or fame, but it certainly has its fair share of prestigious inhabitants, including Samuel Beckett, Simone de Beauvoir and Jean-Paul Sartre, Charles Garnier, Eugene Ionesco, Man Ray, Serge Gainsbourg, George Sand and Jean Seberg. Some of the more interesting sculptures include a polychrome cat by Niki de Saint Phalle and a birdman by Tinguely.

Exit the cemetery from the Allée Principale, turning left onto the **Boulevard Edgar Quinet**. There's an open-air produce market in the central alley of the boulevard every Wednesday and Saturday morning (7am to 2:30pm), and an arts fair every Sunday (10am until sunset). There are still a few surviving vestiges of Montparnasse's cabaret glory days down narrow **Rue de la Gaîté**, although many of the old theaters have evolved into neon peep shows like those found in Pigalle. Streets such as the **Rue d'Odessa**, **Rue du Montparnasse**, **Rue Delambre** and **Rue du Maine** are lined with authentic Breton *crêperies* left over from the days when the

Gare Montparnasse was the main station for passengers arriving in Paris from the Brittany coast.

MONTPARNASSE

There used to be a small hill in Montparnasse, created by the debris from centuries of quarrying the Left Bank. Back when it was outside the city walls, it was a favorite place for students to recite poetry. They nicknamed the hill Mont Parnassus, from the mountain of the mythological poet-god, Apollo. In the 18th century, Haussmann leveled the hill to make room for the Boulevard de Montparnasse, but the name lived on.

Ready to tackle the beast? The 688-foot-tall **Tour Montparnasse** (33 Avenue du Maine, 15th, ☎ 01 45 38 52 56, www.tour-montparnasse.com) opened in 1973 to so much criticism that Parisians voted to never allow another skyscraper to tarnish their historic skyline. An elevator can take you to the 56th-floor terrace (glassed in) in just 38 seconds. Proceed all the way to the 59th floor, the only place in Paris with a panoramic view of the city that does not include La Tour! Open daily to the public 9:30am to 11:30pm (winter until 10:30pm). Entrance on the Rue de l'Arrivée. Entry €8, €6.80 for students, €5.50 for kids under 14. Free for kids under five.

Paris

IN A HURRY?

Most moving walkways in the Paris métro reach the speed of only 1.8 mph, but a new fast-moving walkway in the métro Montparnasse-Bienvenue goes three times as fast. Great fun if you don't fall down, so pay attention (because the only signs are in French): grab the handrail, step on, and then *stop moving your feet* – the rolling beads move you automatically onto the conveyor belt (then it's okay to walk). When you get to the end, the blinking shoe sign means to stop walking again – the belt slides you onto the rollers, where you'll slow down enough to step off onto solid ground.

If you prefer to stay closer to earth, climb the stairs on the corner of Rue du Départ and Boulevard du Montparnasse to the terrace on top of the Maine-Montparnasse Commercial Center. From here you get free views over the billboard-covered buildings and cinemas of the Place du 18 Juin 1940 – the Parisian version of Times Square! For a more peaceful stroll, visit the elevated **Jardin Atlantique** (enter from the Rue du Commandant René Mouchotte or from within the train station), with more than eight acres of gardens built in 1994 over the tracks of the Gare Montparnasse.

The 7th: Orsay, Invalides & Eiffel Tower

After spending time in the narrow, winding streets of the Marais or Latin Quarter, the 7th arrondissement's grand monuments, wide boulevards and vast open lawns can be a real visual breath of fresh air. But what horror for the feet! Make the most of the flat sidewalks (and general lack of pedestrians) by exploring this elegant district on the wheels of your choice (see *Adventures*, page 180, for nearby bike, scooter and skate rental companies).

Begin at one of the city's most popular museums, the **Musée d'Orsay** (Quai Anatole France, 7th, M° Solferino or RER C station Musée d'Orsay, ☎ 01 40 49 48 48, www.musee-orsay.fr). Originally a train station built for the Universal Exhibition of 1900, it was closed in 1939 because modern trains grew too large for the station. After almost being torn down, it re-opened as a museum in 1986 to house a permanent collection of mostly French art from the period 1848-1914, including Art Nouveau, Impressionism, Rodin sculptures, a new photography gallery, and models of architectural arts such as the Opéra Garnier (including a replica of the original ceiling fresco covered by Chagall's modern painting in 1964).

The main hall still has the feel of a train station, especially with the giant glass and iron clock on the arched glass wall. The side rooms are more intimate and group paintings and decorative arts by style. Don't miss the ornately gilded Salle des Fêtes, which was once part of the hotel built adjacent to the train station.

The same décor of wooden floors, marble columns, ceiling frescos and crystal chandeliers can be found in the romantic museum **restaurant** overlooking the Seine (lunch 11:30am to 2:30pm, tearoom 3:30 to 5:40pm excluding Thursdays, dinner Thursdays 7 to 9:30pm). There's also a more simply decorated **café** and a self-service **snack bar** on the upper level.

Some great panoramic views of the Louvre, Tuileries, and Sacré-Coeur can be seen from the windows on the fifth floor, notably from rooms 33, 31 and 28. Visitors could easily see the entire collection in this museum in a half-day; but arrive at opening time to avoid long lines. Open Tuesday, Wednesday, Friday and Saturday, 10am to 6pm (from 9am mid-June to mid-September); Sunday, 9am to 6pm; and Thursday, 10am to 9:45pm. Entry €7; €5 for visitors ages 18 to 25, and for everyone after 4:15pm (after 8pm Thursdays) and on Sunday; free for kids under 18, and everyone on first Sundays. Museum Pass accepted. Audio guides €5. Guided tours in English twice a day Tuesday through Saturday, €6 extra. English guidebooks to the museum can be purchased in the bookshop for €8.

Follow the Quai Anatole France to the **Palais Bourbon**, home of the **Assemblée Nationale** (main entrance 33 Quai d'Orsay, 7th, M°

Assemblée Nationale, ☎ 01 40 63 64 08, www.assemblee-nat.fr). The public can visit **Le Kiosque** (entrance on Rue Aristide Briand, closed August), for books and souvenirs of the French Parliament. Nothing is in English, but the multilingual web site has a detailed history of the Assemblée Nationale and the Palais Bourbon. To attend one of the parliamentary sessions, see the box in the *Government* section, page 22.

Continue down the Rue Aristide Briand to the Rue de Bourgogne, and make a right on Rue de Varenne. On your left is the Hôtel Biron, home to the **Musée Rodin** (75 Rue de Varenne, 7th, M° Varenne, ☎ 01 44 18 61 10, www.musee-rodin.fr). This elegant, state-owned mansion dating from 1731 is completely surrounded by gardens; it is where one of France's greatest sculptors, Auguste Rodin, once lived and worked. By 1909 it was a crumbling shadow of its former 18th-century glory, having been occupied by a religious order from the time of Napoleon, and then used as inexpensive housing for artists. Rodin donated all of his sculptures, private drawings and personal collections to the state on the condition that the mansion was turned into a museum. It opened in 1919 with over 600 sculptures, including *The Thinker* and *The Kiss*. The gardens, which can be accessed independent of the museum for €1, have many of his most famous sculptures, and a café open in nice weather. Open Tuesday through Sunday, 9:30am to 5:45pm (October-March until 4:45pm). Entry €5, €3 for students, free for kids under 18. Museum Pass accepted.

Continue along the Rue de Varenne to one of the city's grandest monuments, the **Hôtel des Invalides** (entrance on the Avenue de Tourville, 7th, M° Invalides or St-François-Xavier, ☎ 01 44 42 38 77, www.invalides.org). The imposing Invalides complex was built by Louis XIV in the 17th century as a military hospital and retirement home for up to 4,000 soldiers. It included the vast grass esplanade stretching to the Seine, the soldiers' church St-Louis-des-Invalides, and the royal chapel Eglise du Dôme. In 1840, Napoleon's exhumed remains were placed in the tomb under the chapel's golden dome, almost 20 years after the emporer's death in exile on St-Helena. Today Les Invalides is home to the **Musée de l'Armée**, one of the world's largest collections of military weapons and uniforms from antiquity through WWII, and the **Musée de l'Ordre de la Libération**, an in-depth look at France during the Occupation (including the Free French forces fighting in Africa, the Résistance movement within France, the deportations by the Vichy government, and the liberation of Paris in August 1944). There is limited information in English. Count on a full morning to see everything. You can leave for lunch and return, but skip the sterile Invalides' cafeteria and opt for a picnic on the grassy **Esplanade** or lunch at one of the many reasonable brasseries nearby (such as the **Brasserie la Source** on 49 Boulevard de la Tour Marbourg or **Café Thoumieux** at 79 Rue St-Dominique). Open daily 10am-5pm (until 6pm April to September), closed holidays and first Monday of the month. Entry €6, includes both museums, temporary exhibitions, and Napoléon's tomb at the Eglise du Dôme. Museum Pass accepted. Free for kids under 18.

 DID YOU KNOW? *On July 14, 1789, the rebellious citizens of Paris looted the armory at Les Invalides for over 28,000 rifles on their way to the Bastille.*

Exit Les Invalides on the north side of the building to get a good view of the Esplanade and the gilded statues of the **Pont Alexandre III**, built for the 1900 World's Fair. Turn left onto the Rue de Grenelle, which leads into the only neighborhood in the 7th built on a human scale, with artisan workshops and small boutiques in the side-streets and passages. Have a rest in the gardens of the charming old Lutheran church **Eglise St-Jean** (147 Rue de Grenelle, 7th), then visit the gourmet food shops and cafés of the popular market street **Rue Cler**.

Return to the land of large landmarks with a right turn onto the Avenue de la Motte Piquet, following it until you're at the foot of the Champ-de-Mars, between the Ecole Militaire and the Eiffel Tower. Napoleon Bonaparte is one of the many illustrious graduates of the **Ecole Militaire**, considered one of the finest examples of French 18th-century architecture. Built in 1751, it's still used today as a military academy by the French Ministry of Defense. The vast park of the **Champ-de-Mars** used to be the school's training grounds. In 1790 Parisians gathered here to celebrate the first anniversary of the Revolution, and it remains a popular place to watch the annual Bastille Day fireworks. The glass and steel sculpture at the top of the gardens is the **Wall of Peace**, erected in 2000 with the word *peace* inscribed in 32 different languages.

ANTIQUES VILLAGE

Antiques hunters should take a detour down the Avenue de la Motte Piquet to the **Village Suisse** (78 Avenue de Suffren, 15th), which has over 150 antiques dealers, decorators and art galleries housed in a village built for the 1900 World's Fair.

The Eiffel Tower

Continue to the end of the Champ-de-Mars, where Gustave Eiffel's grand monument needs no introduction. Inaugurated in 1889 with as much criticism as praise, **La Tour Eiffel** quickly became the internationally recognized symbol of Paris. No first-time visitor to the city can resist the monument's magnetic pull, so go ahead and stand between the pillars, take photos from strange angles, and check the line for the elevators (keeping in mind that if you want to go all the way to the top, you'll have to switch elevators on the second floor). There are four options for visiting the tower: walk up the stairs to the first floor (€3.30), take an elevator to the first floor (€3.70, €2.30 for kids ages three to 12), take an elevator to the second floor (€7, €3.90 for kids three to 12), take an elevator to the top floor (€10.50, €5.50 for kids three to 12). The first and second floors are equipped with restaurants (**Altitude 95** and the **Jules Verne**), snack bars, souvenir shops and expositions on the history and engineering of the tower. There's also a post office on the first floor where you can get your mail stamped "Eiffel Tower – Paris." The top floor is much, much smaller (which makes it more uncomfortable for claustrophobics than those suffering from vertigo), divided into a lower, glassed-in platform and an upper, caged-in outdoor platform. Be warned: the cage makes taking sweeping panoramic photos rather difficult. The best time to visit is first thing in the morning, when there are no lines (preferably on a clear day). Be sure to travel light; there is no baggage-check service. For information, ☎ 01 44 11 23 23. Open daily, September to mid-June, 9:30am to 11pm (stairs close at 6:30pm); and mid-June through August, 9am to midnight.

A NEW MUSEUM

The massive construction project on the Quai Branly is the future Musée du Quai Branly, designed by the architect Jean Nouvel. The museum, due to open in 2006, will bring together arts and civilization collections from Africa, Asia, Oceania, and the Americas.

South Side Parks

Paris has three parks that are very much off the beaten path, yet each one offers something unique that makes it worth the trek.

The **Parc Montsouris** (RER Cité Universitaire) was commissioned by Haussmann in the 1860s, with 50 acres of scenic English-style gardens divided into two sections by the RER tunnel. The west side is dominated by huge open lawns (popular with sunbathing Parisians) and a meteorological observatory, while the more romantic east side features an artificial lake with waterfalls, a gourmet restaurant and a small café (the park's engineer reportedly committed suicide after the lake mysteriously drained on opening day). Take a stroll on the nearby streets to the west of the park to see the charming artists' houses built during the early 1920s, particularly along the **Square Montsouris**, **Rue George Braque**, **Villa Nansouty** and **Villa Seurat**.

The **Parc Georges-Brassens** (Rue des Morillons, 15th, M° Convention), named for the French singer who lived nearby, was built in 1975 to replace the former Vaugirard *abattoir*, and offers a vineyard, rose gardens, playground, bee houses, and a forested hill with panoramic views. Vestiges of the slaughterhouse have been incorporated into the design, with the bronze bull statues on guard at the main entrance, the original belfry overlooking the ornamental lake, and the renovated horse market that now hosts a weekend book fair (see *Where to Shop*, page 224, for more information).

CITE UNIVERSITAIRE

Fans of 1920s architecture should visit the Cité Universitaire (19-21 Boulevard Jourdan, 14th, RER Cité Universitaire, www.anglais.ciup.org). Built to accommodate the growing international student population after World War I, the campus is made up of 37 halls of residence, each with a unique architectural style to represent different countries. Contributing architects include le Corbusier (Fondation Suisse), Willem Marinus Dudok (Collège Néerlandais) and Claude Parent (Fondation Avicenne.

Originally a wine pavilion salvaged from the 1900 World's Fair, **La Ruche** (the beehive) was rebuilt in the Passage Dantzig (west of the park) as cheap housing and studios for artists in 1902. Famous lodgers include Fernand Leger, Chagall, Modigliani, Lipchitz and Brancusi. After several threats by developers in the 1970s, La Ruche was declared a historical monument. It's only open to the public during the annual Heritage Days (Journées du Patrimoine).

The **Parc André Citroën** (Quai André Citroën, 15th, M° Balard or Javel) is the most avant-garde of the Paris parks, opened in 1992 on the site of a former Citroën automobile factory. The center of the garden has two contemporary greenhouses overlooking a manicured lawn (kid friendly, dogs forbidden) that stretches down to the Seine. Hidden from immediate view are several themed gardens (such as a bamboo jungle and wild flower prairie) perfect for escaping the crowds. Water plays an important role in the design, with fountains, waterfalls and streams connecting the different sections of the park. One of the entertainment features is the giant Eutelsat hot air balloon (permanently tethered above the park) offering panoramic views of the city (see the *Adventures* section, page 187, for more information).

Suburban Sights

Although the suburbs (*les banlieus*) can be a bit dull compared to Paris, there are several sights worth the short trip, all of which can be reached using public transportation.

AUTHOR'S NOTE: *See the* Outside Paris *chapter for more elaborate excursions in the Ile-de-France region.*

■ Saint-Denis

Saint-Denis isn't the prettiest of Parisian suburbs. Living conditions in the historic center had deteriorated so badly by the 1970s that most of it was razed and rebuilt. A few buildings managed to escape the wrecking ball besides the Basilica, including the Hôtel de Ville and the 17th-century Carmelite convent (now home to an art and history museum). The city's open market, first established under the reign of King Dagobert, is one of the biggest and liveliest in the Ile-de-France (Tuesday, Thursday and Sunday mornings). Stop by the tourism office (1 Rue de la République, Saint-Denis, ☎ 01 55 87 08 70) if you'd like to explore the lesser known sights of Saint-Denis.

The prestigious **Basilica of Saint-Denis** (1 Rue de la Légion, St-Denis, M° Basilique St-Denis, ☎ 01 48 09 83 54) is known as the royal necropolis of France, where all but three of the French monarchs since King Dagobert in the seventh century have been buried. The current basilica was built in the 12th century on the burial site of St-Denis, the martyred patron saint of France. Important renovations under Saint-Louis (King Louis IX) in the 13th century turned the basilica into one of the finest examples of Gothic architecture, copied throughout Europe. Its funerary art is impressive, with many tombs from the 12th to the 16th centuries decorated with life-sized statues of the recumbent kings and queens. Revolutionary mobs ransacked the tombs in 1793, throwing the remains into mass graves. When the Bourbons returned to power briefly in 1817, Louis XVIII recovered the bodies of Marie Antoinette and Louis XVI, and transferred the remains from the mass graves to the basilica's crypt.

Entrance to the basilica is free. Don't miss the small chapel on the left displaying Louis XVIII's funeral robes and a replica of Charlemagne's crown. To enter the necropolis and the crypt, you need to exit the basilica on the right and buy a ticket at the small booth (entry €6.10, €4.10 for kids; free on the first Sundays, October through March). Museum Pass accepted. Audio guides cost €4 for one or €5.50 for two. There's also a visitor's center with restrooms here if you need them. Open daily, 10am to 6:15pm (open Sunday from noon; closes 5:15pm October to March).

The **Musée Bouilhet-Christofle** (112 Rue Ambroise Croizat, St-Denis, M° St-Denis-Porte-de-Paris, ☎ 01 49 22 40 40) is set in the silversmith workshops opened by Charles Christofle in 1874. The museum presents over 2,000 examples of silverware and *objets d'art*, including royal and imperial commissions, with demonstrations of the different techniques and styles of silversmithing. Parts of the building are still used for manufacturing, making it one of the few remaining 19th-century manufactur-

Paris

ers still in the same family. The museum is overlooking the Seine near the Stade de France. If you arrive by métro, look for the signs (about 10 minutes on foot). If you arrive by car from the Péripherique, take the A1 from the Porte de la Chapelle, exit St-Denis-Grand Stade and follow the signs. Free parking. Open Monday through Friday, 9:30am to 5:30pm. Entry €5, €3 for students, free for kids under 16.

 AUTHOR'S NOTE: *See the* Entertainment *section, page 317, for information on visiting the* **Stade de France** *in Saint-Denis.*

■ La Défense

The neighborhood was originally named after a statue called *La Défense de Paris*, installed in 1883 to commemorate the Parisian resistance during the Franco-Prussian War of 1870-1871 (it's now outside the Espace Info). In 1958 President de Gaulle revealed plans to transform the area into the largest business center in Europe. The modern office buildings, commercial center and residential towers are built around a central pedestrian esplanade (all traffic flows through tunnels beneath), decorated with fountains and modern sculptures by artists such as César, Miro, and Calder. For more information about the individual buildings or the Petit Train tours of La Défense, stop into the Espace Information (15 Place de la Défense, ☎ 01 47 74 84 24), open weekdays 10am to 6pm.

La Grande Arche de la Défense (1 Parvis de la Défense, Paris-La Défense, M° La Défense Grande Arche, ☎ 01 49 07 27 57, www.grande-arche.com). This contemporary Arch of Triumph is perfectly aligned with the original Arc de Triomphe, the Champs-Elysées, the Place de la Concorde, and the Pei Pyramid at the Louvre. There are office buildings built into the sides of the open cube, and a viewing platform at the top. Built by the Danish architect Otto van Spreckelsen, the glass and white marble Arche, inaugurated in 1989, measures 360 feet and could fit Notre Dame Cathedral within its walls. Tickets to the top also include entrance to the exhibition center dedicated to up-and-coming contemporary artists. Open daily, 10am to 6:30pm, tickets €7.50, €6 for students and kids.

 AUTHOR'S NOTE: *The RER A train also goes to the La Défense-Grande Arch station, but it's in zone 3, which means you need to buy a separate ticket (standard RER / métro / bus tickets are only good for two zones), or get off one station early, at the Esplanade de la Défense.*

■ The American Cemetery in Suresnes

The American Military Cemetery was donated to the United States by the city of Suresnes and inaugurated by President Woodrow Wilson in 1919. Located on seven acres on a hillside below the Fort du Mont Valérien (five miles west of Paris), the cemetery contains the graves of 1,541 American servicemen from WWI, as well as 24 unknown soldiers from WWII. Bronze tablets in the memorial chapel commemorate the 974 Americans lost at sea in 1917. To get there by car, drive into Suresnes through the Bois de Boulogne, cross the Pont de Suresnes, turn right onto Avenue Charles de Gaulle, left onto Avenue Franklin Roosevelt, and left again onto Boulevard Washington (or just follow the signs for *Cimetière Militaire Américain*). To get there using public transportation, take the Transilien urban train from Gare St-Lazare to the Suresnes Mont Valerien station (then a 10-minute walk up the hill). Ask at the Visitor Center for assistance finding a particular grave or memorial site. Open daily, 9am to 5pm, closed December 25 and January 1. ☎ 01 46 25 01 70.

Fort du Mont Valerien

Built as part of the city's fortifications in 1840, the fort was unable to prevent the Prussians from surrounding Paris in 1871. But when the Commune erupted a few months later, the fort was instrumental in helping the Versailles troops gain the upper hand and crush the insurrection, with over 15,000 cannonballs fired over the two-month period. During World War II, German troops executed over 1,000 Resistance fighters and hostages outside the fort's walls. A memorial was inaugurated in 1960, the **Mémorial de la France Combattante** (open to the public daily, 9am to noon and 2 to 5pm, in summer until 7pm). The fort is currently home to 8th Signals Regiment, and only open to the public during annual Heritage Days (Journées du Patrimoine).

■ Château de Malmaison

Napoleon Bonaparte lived at the Château de Malmaison (Avenue du Château de Malmaison, Rueil-Malmaison, ☎ 01 41 29 05 55, www.chateau-malmaison.fr) with his first wife, Joséphine, from 1800-1809. It's been restored to look as it did during the Consulate, when Malmaison was the seat of the French Government. In the years before the Empire, Napoleon made many important decisions in Malmaison's library and its tent-like council chamber, including the creation of the Civil Code, the basis for France's current laws. After divorcing in 1809, Joséphine continued to live in Malmaison, attending to her rose gardens until her death in the upstairs bedroom on May 29, 1814. It went through many owners, including Napoléon III, until falling into ruin after the Franco-Prussian War of 1870. A wealthy philanthropist, Daniel Osiris Iffla, bought

Malmaison and donated it to the state, which opened it as a museum in 1906. It's a beautifully restored house, with painted ceilings, luxurious fabric wall coverings, and many fine works of art such as one of the three copies by David of the painting "Napoléon Crossing the Alps." The smaller pavilions in the gardens are not always open, including the Pavillon des Voitures, which houses Napoléon's landau captured by the Prussians during the battle at Waterloo (they later graciously donated it to the museum). When visiting, ask for the English descriptions at the entry to the Château (or better yet, stop into the gift shop on the left before entering the Château if you want a full photo guide in English, €8.50). If you walk through the large open park to the left of the parking lot, you'll see Joséphine's second mansion, the Château du Bois Préau, closed indefinitely for renovations. Open weekdays except Tuesday 10am to noon and 1:30 to 4:30pm (5pm in summer), weekends 10am to 5pm (5:30pm in summer). Entry €4.50, €3 for visitors 18-25 and everyone on Sunday, free for kids under 18. Museum Pass accepted. To get there on public transportation, take Line 1 to Grande Arche de la Défense, switch to Bus 258 and get off at "Le Château." To get there by car follow the RN13 7.5 miles northwest of Paris.

■ Ile des Impressionnistes

The **Impressionists' Island** at Chatou is the heart of the Impressionists' Trail, which highlights many locations where the Impressionists of the 19th century – such as Renoir, Monet, Pissarro, Sisley and Vlamink – lived and painted. Today the island remains a manicured tribute to the past amid modern urbanization, and makes a pleasant day-trip for its museum, restaurants, riverside hiking trails and old-fashioned boat tours. The best time to visit is in spring or early summer when the flowers are in bloom and the weather is good for a stroll or boat ride. To get there take the RER A direction St-Germain-en-Laye to the station Rueil Malmaison, and walk five minutes in the direction of Chatou (access from the river bridge). To get there by car take the RN13 toward Nanterre and then the N190 to the island.

The **Maison Fournaise** (Ile des Impressionnistes, ☎ 01 34 80 63 22) is known to art lovers as the place where Pierre-Auguste Renoir painted *The Luncheon of the Boating Party* in 1881. Overlooking the Seine from the scenic Ile des Impressionnistes, the restaurant and hotel of the Maison Fournaise were at the heart of the action, with painters documenting the lively riverside atmosphere much in the way modern paparazzi hover outside the latest trendy Parisian hotspots. After falling into ruin in the early 20th century, La Fournaise became a listed monument in 1982 and reopened its restaurant and new museum in the 1990s after being restored to its former glory. The museum doesn't own any major Impressionist paintings, but has regular expositions on the spirit of the Impressionist period (and they sell traditional straw bowler hats). Museum open

Wednesday through Friday, 10am to noon and 2 to 6pm; weekends, 11am to 6pm; entry €4, (€3 for children). The restaurant is open daily for lunch and dinner, ☎ 01 30 71 41 91.

HISTORIC RIVER TOUR

Enjoy an hour-long Impressionist History tour of the Seine on an old-fashioned wooden boat called *Le Dénicheur*. Electrically powered, it glides silently down the river with up to 12 passengers. Tours are run weekends, May through October, from 3 to 6pm; €7 (€5 for children under 12). Reserve in advance if possible; they close two weekends in August. Tours are operated by **Sequana**, a non-profit river-conservation group (☎ 06 16 01 07 92, http://perso.club-internet.fr/jdutert/sequana) based out of the the Gare de l'Eau, adjacent to the Rives de la Courtille restaurant (☎ 01 34 80 92 62) on the Ile des Impressionistes.

Urban Adventures

Parisians may not have a worldwide reputation for their sportiness, but don't tell them that! Just under a decade ago they used to eye joggers and in-line skaters with typical Gallic suspicion, but after a slow start the Parisians have enthusiastically embraced the idea of urban adventure in all forms – especially if the outfits are cool! Paris in the new millennium is a city of climbing walls, bike lanes, and free weekly group skates for thousands of participants of all ages and abilities. The less athletically inclined can enjoy a boat cruise out to the countryside, go for a swim in an historic Art Deco swimming pool, or join a guided nature tour of the city's parks and gardens. Parisians love to walk, and have even designated ideal hiking routes though the city with traditional trail markers. So go ahead and join them in taking advantage of the many adventurous possibilities!

AUTHOR'S NOTE: *See the* Outside Paris *chapter, page 337, for more adventures in the countryside.*

Paris

On Foot

■ Walking & Hiking

Become a True Flâneur

The French verb *flâner* is loosely defined as "to wander," somewhere between structured strolling and disinterested loafing. Parisians have it down to an art, and so should anyone who wants a unique insight into the city. It goes like this: spend a day – or at least half a day – wandering around the city without a map, simply going down any street that looks interesting. It helps if you start in a place you're not familiar with at all. It's really quite simple in concept, but most time-and-schedule-driven Anglo-Saxon types find it impossible to leave their exploration to fate. But it will all be worth it when you discover that little café with the most amazing cappuccino, a shady courtyard hidden from the main road, or a dusty shop where locals-in-the-know stock up on handcrafted copper pots. Even the most insignificant-seeming places hold surprises if you keep your eyes open – and don't walk too fast! And when you're ready to return to the familiar, use your best French and ask someone *"Où est le métro, s'il vous plâit?"*

BE PREPARED

For those not used to walking six to eight hours a day (especially with the inevitable backpack full of necessary supplies), Paris can do a number on the feet. Anyone with an ambitious sightseeing plan should buy the most comfortable pair of walking shoes, and – most importantly – break them in before coming to Paris! Companies like Mephisto and Timberland make stylish walking shoes, and even Birkenstocks have come back into fashion in Europe (sandals are always okay, but without the socks if you're under 75). Almost anything is preferable to those big, snow-white sneakers that scream "American tourist"! By all means bring your dress shoes, but save them (and your toes) for your night on the town.

Where to Walk

Where not to walk?! Paris is a walker's paradise, and most visitors end up clocking in a few dozen miles without even trying. There's so much to see, so many mysterious passages, tiny *rues*, steep staircases, and hidden courtyards off-limits to those on wheels. Parisian gardens, even the more formally designed ones, always have their secluded little trails and grottos. Rainy days are the perfect time to check out the city's 19th-century covered passages for a bit of vintage-boutique window shopping. The most interesting ones can be found in the intersection of the 2nd, 9th and 10th arrondissements. With a bit of planning and a good map, it's possible to go from passage to passage with minimal time outside.

Those looking for an authentic peek into Paris life should wander around the residential neighborhoods far from the city's crowded museums and monuments. See the *Paris by Neighborhood* section, page 78, for more detailed information about the covered passages and recommended neighborhoods off the beaten track.

RAINY DAY WALKING

The covered *passages* and *galeries* of Paris were designed by the city architect Baron Haussmann at the beginning of the 19th century to give window-shopping pedestrians protection from carriage traffic, muddy streets and the elements.

Urban Hiking Trails

There are marked hiking trails, courtesy of the **Fédération Française de Randonnée Pédestre**, crisscrossing France and neighboring European countries called the *Grandes Randonnées* (Grand Hikes), shortened to "GR" and the number of the trail (ie GR8). Three of these trails go right through Paris, using the same markers found on the forests trails (see below). Those who like a bit of a challenge can follow the markers from one end of Paris to the other (each one is approximately 12 miles long). One east-west trail goes from the Bois de Boulogne to the Bois de Vincennes via the Jardins du Luxembourg. The second east-west trail goes from Porte Maillot to the Porte Dorée via Montmartre and the Parc des Buttes-Chaumont (lots of hills!). The north-south trail goes from Porte de la Villette to the Cité Universitaire via Notre Dame. For street-by-street directions pick up a map of the *Traversée de Paris* at the IGN Map Store (Espace IGN, 107 Rue la Boétie, 8th, M° Franklin-D-Roosevelt, ☎ 01 43 98 85 10) or check out the *Grandes Randonnées* web site, www.gr-infos.com (scroll down to "Walking in Paris").

TIP: *In the city, trail markers are usually painted onto lampposts, telephone poles, walls or directly onto buildings. They may be different colors, but the shapes are always the same.*

Paris

Hiking to the Top

The best panoramic views of Paris can only be reached on foot, and not always with an elevator, either! Burn off those extra *éclairs* on the 387 spiral steps of the **Notre Dame Cathedral Towers** (1st, M° Cité; entry €5.50, free for kids under 18 and for everyone from October to March), the 290 steps leading to the **Sacré-Coeur Basilica Dome** (18th, M° Abbesses; entry €4.50), or the 300-plus steps up to the rooftop of the **Arc de Triomphe** (8th, M° Charles-de-Gaulle-Etoile; entry €7, free for kids under 18). It's also possible to take the open stairs up to the first and second levels of the **Eiffel Tower** (7th, M° Bir Hakeim, stair entry €3.30; you have to take the elevator if you want to go all the way up).

AUTHOR'S NOTE: *For a list of adventuresome vocabulary, see* Out-Of-Doors, *in the* Glossary, *page 433.*

Nature Walks

Informal, monthly hikes into the Ile-de-France countryside are organized by Canadian Brian Spence, owner of the **Abbey Bookshop** (29 Rue de la Parcheminerie, 5th, M° St-Michel, www.abbeybookshop.com). There's no fee for the walk, but hikers should bring a packed lunch, water, and enough cash to pay their own entrance fees for any monument or château visits. The day-long walks are from 20-30 miles. Give Brian a call for more details, ☎ 01 46 33 16 24.

The **Paris Garden Guild Tours** are led by native English-speaking landscape designers, artists, and architectural historians with a passion for gardens. The tours combine historical and design commentary with practical advice for those who want to try the same thing back home. At just €10 per person (€5 for children) for a one-hour tour, why not try more than one? For the schedule or reservations contact director Robin Watson, ☎/fax 01 47 41 21 59, or parisgarden@free.fr.

The **Randonneurs d'Ile-de-France** (www.rifrando.asso.fr) is a non-profit hiking association that specializes in day hikes around the Ile-de-France. Although it's normally only open to members, visitors are welcome to go on a free "sample hike" (participants pay their own train transportation and food costs). There are several hikes almost every day of the year to choose from. Check out their bilingual web site for more details, or simply stop by their office to sign up: 92 Rue du Moulin Vert, 14th, M° Pernety, ☎ 01 45 42 24 72.

Anyone with an understanding of French should sign up for one of the various outings organized by the nature store chain **Nature et Découvertes** (☎ 01 39 56 70 44). Their *balades natures* include bird watching in the Jardin des Plantes or sunset walks in the Bois de Vincennes, and cost from €5-€10. Check the *animations* schedule on their web site, www.natureetdecouvertes.com, for more information. Walks usually fill up about a month in advance.

> **AUTHOR'S NOTE:** *See* Cultural Adventures, *page 195, for nature drawing hikes with RandoCroquis.*

■ Running

Where to Run

Unless you run at dawn, the streets of Paris can be a bit hectic for joggers. Parisians tend to run in the larger parks such as the **Jardins du Luxembourg** (6th), **Parc Monceau** (8th), **Jardin des Tuileries** (1st), the **Parc de Bercy** (12th), and the **Champ-de-Mars** (7th). Those who like hills go jogging in the **Jardin des Plantes** (5th), the **Parc des Buttes-Chaumont** (19th), and the **Parc Montsouris** (14th). The largest green spaces are in the **Parc de la Villette** (19th), the **Bois de Vincennes** (12th), and the **Bois de Boulogne** (16th).

The smooth sidewalks along the Canal St-Martin (east Paris) are better for running than the ankle-twisting cobblestones along the banks of the Seine. From March through November the nicely paved roads along the Seine are closed to traffic on Sundays and holidays between 9am and 5pm, and all day long during *Paris Plage* (mid-July to mid-August). This is the best time to run along the river, although joggers have to share the streets with in-line skaters, pedestrians and cyclists.

Paris Marathons

The 26-mile (42-km) **Marathon de Paris** (www.parismarathon.com) takes place each year on the first Sunday in April, starting from the Avenue des Champs-Elysées and passing through all of the most scenic areas of Paris. It's open to men and women of all nationalities (runners must be at least 20 years old and provide a medical certificate at registration). The fee is €62, €42-€52 if you register early (online registration available from September). The marathon is limited to 30,000 runners, so sign up as early as possible to get a place. Check out the bilingual web site for the complete rules and registration forms.

The shorter 13-mile (21.1-km) **Semi-Marathon de Paris** (www.parismarathon.com/semi/2004/us) takes place each year on the first Sunday in March in the Bois de Vincennes and eastern neighborhoods of Paris. It's open to men and women of all nationalities (runners must be at least 18 years old and provide a valid medical certificate at registration). The fee is €27, or €20-€23 for advance registration. The Semi-Marathon is only open to 16,000 runners, so it fills up fast!

The annual **La Parisienne** (☎ 01 40 71 08 51, www.la-parisienne.net), a women's four-mile (6.5-km) run around the Eiffel Tower and Les Invalides

quarter, takes place on the second Sunday of September to raise awareness about breast cancer. Prizes are awarded in many different categories, including Mothers, Grandmothers and Mother-Daughter teams, and
each participant receives a rose and commemorative medal at the finish
line. There's a weekend festival surrounding the race open to the general
public, with information tents and activities to promote women's health
and well-being. Registration is limited to 5,000 women, age 15 and up
(with a health certificate). The entry fee is €20 (€12 for early registration).

There's also the annual **Paris-Versailles** (www.parisversailles.com), a
10-mile (16.3-km) run/walk on the last Sunday in September, which goes
from Paris to the town of Versailles. Registration costs €20 (plus a medical certificate less than a year old). There are also 500 places open on the
morning of the race for last-minute registrations. There are no shuttles
for returning to Paris, so plan on taking a very crowded RER C, the
slightly less-crowded train from the Gare Versailles-Rive Droite, or
reserve a hotel in town for the night. Every participant gets a commemorative medal at the finish line and a diploma sent in the mail.

Running Clubs

If you're already familiar with the **Hash House Harriers**
(www.parishash.net) you'll be happy to know there are four groups in the
region, two in Paris, one in the western suburbs, and one in Fontainebleau. Known worldwide as the "drinking club with a running problem,"
these local chapters are run by a mixed group of native English-speakers
and French converts who welcome visitors of all fitness levels on their
runs. Most groups have a few walkers, and some also have cyclists ("bash-
ers").

Paris HHH: "Je hashe....donc je suis" (I hash, therefore I am.). Hashes
every other Saturday, always in a different place, with plenty of drinking
and eating afterwards (a €5 donation requested). Bashes are held occasionally throughout the year as and when some gullible person steps up to
set the trail. Contact Hairy Mary or email hairymary@buchelay.com.

Fool Moon HHH: Meets once a month for a full moon hash.
http://jase.free.fr/foolish, hairymary@buchelay.com.

Sans Clue HHH: The name of this group, based in the western suburb of
Saint-Cloud, is a pun: *Saint* sounds a bit like *sans* ("without"), and *Cloud*
is pronounced like "clue," so in *Franglais* the name means "without a
clue". Hashes every Sunday, meet at Garches SNCF train station 2pm
sharp (take the 137pm Transilien from Gare St-Lazare, direction
St-Nom-la-Breteche, get off at Garches-Marnse-la-Coquette). €5 donation covers the trail marking, drinks and food. For more information call
Caitlin, ☎ 06 87 55 60, or sansclue@yahoo.com.

Fontainebleau HHH: Hashes every other Saturday morning. Contact
Yvonne, ☎ 01 64 99 31 00.

■ Urban Climbing

There are no natural cliffs or boulders to climb inside the city, but before you start eyeing the historical monuments, check out these two indoor climbing centers. They're good places to get in some practice climbs in a safe environment before heading out to the real thing in Fontainebleau (see page 374 in the *Outside Paris* chapter for outdoor climbing opportunities).

Antrebloc: 5 Rue Henri Barbusse, Villejuif (94), M° Villejuif-Léo-Lagrange, ☎ 01 47 26 52 44, www.antrebloc.com. Open Monday through Friday, noon to 10:30pm; weekends and holidays, 10am to 7pm.

This 10,700-square-foot climbing and fitness center is just south of the 13th arrondissement in the suburb of Villejuif. Climbing sessions cost €10, €5.50 for kids under 12. Hiking shoes and climbing equipment rental is €4.50. Beginners' initiations are every Friday at 7:30pm and cost €25, and private sessions can be reserved for €40 (English spoken). Antrebloc also organizes hiking trips around France. Call or e-mail for more details.

Mur Mur: 55 Rue Cartier Bresson, Pantin (93), M° Aubervilliers-Quatre Chemins, ☎ 01 48 46 11 00. Open Monday through Friday, noon to 11pm; weekends and holidays, 9:30am to 6:30pm.

Mur means "wall" in French, and Mur Mur has over 16,600 square feet of climbable surfaces, with 250 different courses from 28 to 56 feet high, and 100 rope lines. Non-residents who already know how to climb can ask for a free temporary membership card (*carte provisoire*), paying just the session fees of €6-€12 (includes equipment rental). Beginners must sign up for the €41 climbing initiation (reserve a spot two days in advance). There's a small snack bar for those climbing-induced munchies as well.

■ Golf

Golf du Bois de Boulogne: At the Hippodrome d'Auteuil (entry off the Route d'Auteuil aux Lacs), 16th, M° Porte d'Auteuil, ☎ 01 44 30 70 00, www.golfduboisdeboulogne.fr. Open daily, 8am to 8pm; until 9pm from May through September (closed on race days).

Opened in 1999, this golf club next to the racetrack is the largest of its kind inside Paris, with training, putting and driving ranges, club house, pro shop and restaurant. There are no membership requirements. €4 per bucket of balls, Crazy Golf €4/half-hour. One-on-one lessons with a pro cost €22/hour. Club rental is available from the pro shop with a deposit. Visit their bilingual web site for more information and opening times (closed during horse racing events).

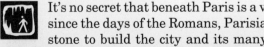

DID YOU KNOW? *Some of the best golf courses in France can be found in the Ile-de-France region. See the* Outside Paris *chapter, pages 351, 383 and 430, for more information.*

■ Tennis

Le Racing Club de France (www.racingclubdefrance.org) is one of the most prestigious sports clubs in France, with five locations in Paris and Ile-de-France for tennis, golf, fencing, badminton, swimming, rugby and other sports. Guests can use the tennis courts at the **Club de Saussure** (154 Rue Saussure, 17th, M° Pereire-Levallois, ☎ 01 47 63 99 26) or the **Centre Eblé** (5 Rue Éblé, 7th, M° St-François-Xavier, ☎ 01 45 67 55 86) for €26/hour.

To play on the **municipal courts** found in the city's parks and gyms, it's necessary to get a **Pass Tennis** from the *Mairie* (at the Hôtel de Ville), which costs about €10. This card allows you access to the courts for €6/hour in the day, €8/hour at night (for lighting), and €12/hour for the indoor courts.

AUTHOR'S NOTE: *For spectator sports, check the* Entertainment *section, page 299, for information on major sporting events and venues in Paris.*

■ Subterranean Tours

The Sewers

The Parisians are quite proud of their sewer system, originally designed by Napoleon III, with over 1,300 miles of tunnels named after the streets above them. Back in the old days there were boat tours of *les égouts*, but today's visitors stay on solid ground. The tours consist of an audio-visual show on the history of the sewers, models of the machinery used, and a short walk along the, uh, open streams. These tours are perfect for anyone interested in modern urban waste treatment and "how things work." Do they smell? Not as bad as you'd think, but don't plan on eating right away. **Musée des Egouts de Paris**, entry opposite #93 Quai d'Orsay, 7th, M° Alma-Marceau, ☎ 01 53 68 27 81. Open Saturday through Wednesday, 11am to 4pm; closed for two weeks in January. Tickets €3.80, free for kids under age five.

The Catacombes

It's no secret that beneath Paris is a veritable city of tunnels. Ever since the days of the Romans, Parisians have been excavating the stone to build the city and its many ramparts, mostly from the Left Bank. By the late 18th century it was obvious that something had to be done to prevent the city from collapsing in on itself. A special team of quarry inspectors and engineers were assigned to reinforce the tunnels, many of which were later used as part of the vast sewer and métro system.

At the same time, Parisian cemeteries were overflowing. The largest cemetery in the center of Paris, the *Cimetière des Innocents* at Les Halles, had six centuries of graves, attracting vermin and causing the spread of deadly diseases like the plague. The king's advisors decided to close the cemeteries inside the city walls, moving the bones to the tunnels at Mont Rouge, the area just outside the city gates known today as Place Denfert-Rochereau. Consecrated in 1786 by the Archbishop of Paris, the *Catacombes de Paris* contain the remains of over six million people, some over 1,300 years old. Although bodies were added up until 1871, the *Catacombes* have been open to the public since 1800, with various closures over the years to improve security and air circulation. Visitors descend a narrow spiral staircase into a gallery featuring temporary photo exhibitions, then go through a long tunnel before reaching the actual catacombs, a one-way maze of artfully stacked bones and skulls. There are plaques marking the names of the cemeteries from which each group of bones was unearthed.

CATAPHILES

Humans are a curious bunch, and they've been sneaking around in these tunnels since they were first created. The Résistance famously used the Catacombes to operate right underneath the Germans' noses. Today there are the diehard addicts – called *cataphiles* – who regularly descend into the tunnels through the latest "unknown" entry, play elaborate hide and seek games, decorate the walls, pull pranks on each other, or give tours to the uninitiated. This is obviously completely illegal and potentially dangerous, with the police and tunnel inspectors constantly trying to seal up the various entrances

---

The 118,000 square feet of Catacombes open to the public make up only a small fraction of the city's tunnels. Those not used for the métro and sewer systems have been blocked off, accessible only to city workers in case of ruptured pipes. To get a good look at what lies under the surface risk-free, check out the **Urban Adventure** web site (www.urbanadventure.org; do a search for "Paris"). This is the best site in English for photos and commentary on the various abandoned train stations and métro tunnels, and the catacomb network of graffiti-covered rooms, galleries, and meeting places where the *cataphiles* hang out.

The tunnels are obviously chilly, although the ceilings don't drip with condensation as much as they used to since renovations in the late 1990s. Avoid wearing nice shoes that might get mucked up by the chalky white gravel on the ground. **Les Catacombes de Paris,** 1 Place Denfert-Rochereau, 14th, M° Denfert-Rochereau, ☎ 01 43 22 47 63. Open Tuesday, 11am to 5pm; Wednesday through Sunday, 9am to 5pm (entry until 4pm). Tickets €5, €2.50 for students ages 14 to 26, free for kids under 14. Get there early in the day to avoid lines.

On the Water

The Seine is at the center of Paris' growth as a city, with many of its prestigious monuments overlooking the river. The river's economic importance is reflected in the city's seal – created in the 13th century – which features a merchant riverboat. Paris started turning its back on the Seine in the 20th century, with express roads cutting pedestrians off from the river and many quays reduced to parking lots. Aside from the sightseeing cruises, there was little life on the Seine. But things have changed over the past five years. *Péniche* boats moored along the Seine have been converted into trendy restaurants, bars, and clubs, with dancing and picnicking Parisians spilling onto the quays during the warmer months. Roads are closed off to traffic for pedestrians and cyclists on Sundays and turned into a beach – ***Paris Plage*** – in summer. Parisians have rediscovered the Canal St-Martin and the Bassin de la Villette, and although it's still not possible to swim in the Seine, there are more opportunities than ever to enjoy the city from the water's edge.

SWIMMING IN THE SEINE

Going for a swim in the Seine is not permitted, but not because it's unclean. Dumping waste into the Seine was banned in the 1970s, when only three species of fish were left and the water was regularly smelly and full of trash. Today there are over 23 species of fish living in the Seine. So why is swimming *interdite*? First, it's dangerous because of the barge traffic and a strong undercurrent, and second, there's a naturally occurring bacteria in the water that doesn't sit well with the human digestive system if swallowed.

■ Paris Plage

Cynics laughed and automobilists growled when Paris' newly elected Socialist mayor Bertrand Delanoë decided to close the Seine's riverbanks to traffic for six weeks in summer 2002 to set up a temporary *plage* (beach) complete with sand, parasols, lounge chairs, palm trees and grassy picnic spots. Of course it became the surprise hit of the summer as visitors and Parisians who couldn't get out of town for the annual August exodus enjoyed the laid-back seaside atmosphere. *Paris Plage 2003* was even bigger, stretching almost two miles along the Right Bank, with sand volleyball courts in front of the Hôtel de Ville, a climbing wall, bike rental hut, water misters and a floating stage with nightly concerts. Best of all, it's completely free. As cities around Europe scramble to copy the idea, the future of *Paris Plage* as a regular summer event looks bright, indeed! Look for it from mid-July through August, from the Quai des Tuileries to the Quai Henri IV.

■ Cruises

On the Seine

The **Batobus** (☎ 01 44 11 33 99, www.batobus.com) was created in 1989 as part of the city's public transport system, and works just like a bus on the Seine. There are eight stops (20 minutes between boats) at the Eiffel Tower (Port de la Bourdonnais, 7th), Musée d'Orsay (Quai Solferino, 7th), St-Germain-des-Prés (Quai Malaqui, 6th), Notre Dame (Quai de Montebello, 5th), Jardin des Plantes (Quai St-Bernard, 5th), Hôtel de Ville (Quai de l'Hôtel de Ville, 4th), Louvre Museum (Quai du Louvre, 1st) and the Champs-Elysées (Port des Champs-Elysées, 8th). Service daily from 10am to 7pm in April, May, October and November; and from 10am to 9pm, June through September. Closed December to March. €2.50 per stop. Day passes are €12, €6 for kids. Two-day passes are €13, €7 for kids.

Smaller boats and live commentary distinguish the **Bâteaux Vedettes du Pont Neuf** (☎ 01 46 33 98 38, www.pontneuf.net) from the rest of the Seine river cruise operators. Their hour-long tours take off from the Square du Vert Galant, (on the western tip of the Ile de la Cité, M° Pont Neuf or Cité), doing a circular tour past the Eiffel Tower, Musée d'Orsay, Louvre Museum, Place de la Concorde, Notre Dame Cathedral and the Hôtel de Ville. Hourly tours from 10:30am to 10:30pm, March to October; from 10am to 10pm, November through February. Tickets €9, €4.50 for children under nine (check their web site for printable discount coupons).

WINE MUSEUM & CRUISE

You can get a combined ticket for the Musée du Vin and a Seine sightseeing cruise with **Vedettes de Paris** for €10, including a complementary glass of wine. Ask about the **Croisière de Bacchus** (Bacchus Cruise) at the Musée du Vin (Rue des Eaux, 16th, M° Passy, ☎ 01 45 25 63 26, www.museeduvinparis.com, open Tuesday through Sunday, 10am to 6pm), or Vedettes de Paris (Port de Suffren, 7th, ☎ 01 47 05 71 29).

Le Calife (3 Quai Malaquais, Pont des Arts, 6th, M° Pont Neuf, ☎ 01 43 54 50 04, www.calife.com) offers romantic **dinner cruises** aboard one of the most beautiful wooden barges on the Seine. Traditional French menu or Middle Eastern menu for €60 (not including drinks); and a special set menu for €35. The two-hour cruises take place Tuesday through Saturday nights from 8:30pm (return at about 11pm). They also have regular **live music cruises** from €80, call or check their web site for the schedule.

AUTHOR'S NOTE: *See the* Outside Paris *chapter, page 379, for information on renting a houseboat or motorboat without a permit, or visit the official web site for the Paris Ports, www.paris-ports.fr.*

On the Canal & Marne

Paris Canal (☎ 01 42 40 96 97, www.pariscanal.com) conducts half-day cruises from the Musée d'Orsay to the Parc de la Villette via the **Canal St-Martin**. Daily 9:30am departure at the Quai Anatole France (outside the Musée d'Orsay, 7th, M° Solferino), arrives at the Parc de la Villette at about 12:15pm. Departs at 2:30pm from the Parc de la Villette (meet at the "Folie des visites du parc" at the intersection of the canals, 20th, M° Porte de la Villette), arrives at the Musée d'Orsay at 5pm. Tickets are €16 (€9 for kids under 12). There are also full-day **countryside cruises** along the Seine and Marne rivers every Saturday and Sunday. Meet at 9:45am and return at 5pm at the Quai Anatole France. Tickets are €32 per person, lunch not included (pack a picnic or eat at one of the restaurants at the rest point). **Reservations** are required for all cruises.

Canauxrama (☎ 01 42 39 15 00, www.canauxrama.com) offers cruises along the **Canal St-Martin** between the Port de l'Arsenal to the Bassin de la Villette with a musical storyteller recounting the canal's history in French and English. The 2.5-hour cruises depart daily at 9:45am and 2:30pm from the Port de l'Arsenal (across from 50 Boulevard de la Bastille, 11th, M° Bastille) or at 9:45am and 2:45pm at the Bassin de la Villette (13 Quai de la Loire, 19th, M° Jaurès). Tickets cost €13 (€8 for children under 12; no discount weekend afternoons and holidays).

Actors bring the great French poetic works to life for the romantic evening **Poetic Cruises**, every Thursday at 6:30pm from mid-July through mid-October from the Bassin de la Villette. Tickets are €28, refreshments included. There are also round-trip day-cruises through the guinguette countryside of the Marne River with a stop for lunch in Bry-sur-Marne. Cruises every Thursday, Saturday and Sunday at 9am from the Port de l'Arsenal, €33, lunch not included (not recommended for kids). Reservations are necessary for all cruises.

AUTHOR'S NOTE: *Read about the history of the guinguettes of the Marne River in the* Entertainment *section, page 332.*

■ Boating

There's nothing more romantic than rowing around the scenic lakes of the Bois de Boulogne and Bois de Vincennes, especially if you can get your partner to do most of the rowing! In the **Bois de Boulogne** boat rental is available on the north end of the **Lac Inférieur** (M° Porte Dauphine) from March through October on weekdays, noon to 5:30pm; and week-ends, 10am to 6:30pm. The boats cost €9.50/hour (€30 deposit) for up to five passengers. In the **Bois de Vincennes**, rowboats are available on the **Lac Daumesnil** (M° Porte Dorée) daily from 9am until sundown, March through October; €9/hour for one to two passengers, €10/hour for three to four passengers (€10 deposit). Don't forget the wine and cheese, and an umbrella for a bit of shade on sunny days.

ROWING EVENTS

There are two annual rowing races on the Seine the last Sunday in September. French national rowing clubs compete for the **Grand National en Huit** (Grand National Eights) in the morning between the Ile aux Cygnes (16th) and the Pont de Bercy (13th). Later in the morning is the **Traversée de Paris**, part of the **Randon'Aviron EDF** rowing outings (these are open to the general public). To watch the action, get a good spot along the Seine by 8am (the Pont des Arts and Passerelle Solferino are the most popular bridges). To participate, contact the **Ligue Ile-de-France d'Aviron** (LIFA), 17 Boulevard de la Marne, 94736 Nogent-sur-Marne Cedex, ☎ 01 48 75 79 17, fax 01 48 75 79 32, http://aviron-iledefrance.org.

■ Swimming

Historic Architecture

Piscine de la Butte-aux-Cailles: Place Paul Verlaine (corner of Rue Bobillot and Rue du Moulin-des-Près), 13th, M° Place d'Italie, ☎ 01 45 89 60 05. Entry €2.50. Opening times change seasonally, so call ahead.

The Piscine de la Butte-aux-Cailles has a brick, Art Deco façade built in the 1920s. The interior pool is beautifully tiled, with a dramatic vaulted ceiling made up of seven arches. Fed by an underground hot spring, the temperature is always a cozy 82°F. There are also two smaller, outdoor pools open in summer. The pool is most crowded Wednesday afternoons, weekends in summer, and every day in August. Get there early to avoid lines.

Piscine Pontoise: 19 Rue de Pontoise, 5th, M° Maubert-Mutualité, ☎ 01 55 42 77 88, www.clubquartierlatin.com. Entry €3.80, €2.90 for kids under 16, €6.70 for night swimming. Private changing rooms €0.45. Opening times change seasonally, so call ahead or check the web site.

This beautiful 1930s pool, often used in photo shoots and films, measures 108 feet long by 50 feet wide, with two mezzanine levels of private changing rooms. For an indoor pool, it's surprisingly airy and spacious, and the water is heated to a regular 82°F. Convenient for early and late swimmers, the pool is open weekdays at 7am to 8:30am and 9 to 11:45pm (the hours in between and on weekends change seasonally).

A WORD TO THE WISE

IMPORTANT NOTE: *Public hygiene laws in France require men to wear fitted, racing-style bathing suits in municipal pools. Swim trunks that resemble shorts are not allowed. Some pools also require swimming caps, which can be purchased inexpensively at any large sports shop in Paris.*

Ritz Health Club Pool: Hôtel Ritz Paris, 15 Place Vendôme, 1st, M° Concorde, ☎ 01 43 16 30 60, www.ritzparis.com. Open daily, 9am to 10pm.

You don't have to be a guest of the legendary Ritz Paris to enjoy their fabulous health club. Anyone who can cough up €150 has access to the luxurious swimming pool decorated with frescoes and mosaic tiling reminiscent of ancient Greek or Roman baths. The mezzanine bar overlooking the pool serves light meals throughout the day, and is a very chic place in Paris to brunch on Sundays. It may be an indoor pool, but don't forget your sunglasses for discreet star spotting.

Great Views

Piscine Jean Taris: 16 Rue Thuin, 5th, M° Cardinal Lemoine, ☎ 01 43 25 54 03. Open Tuesday through Sunday; call for opening hours. Entry €2.50.

Just a few steps from the Sorbonne, this municipal pool has bay windows overlooking a leafy garden, with the top of the Panthéon peeking out over the trees.

Piscine Waou Porte de Sèvres: 22nd floor of the Hôtel Sofitel, 8 Rue Louis Armand, 15th, M° Ballard (or take Bus 39 to be dropped off right outside), ☎ 01 45 54 79 00. Open Monday through Friday, 8am to 10pm; Saturday, 9am to 7pm; Sunday, 9am to 3pm. Entry for non-members €40.

The Sofitel is a soulless chain hotel in a particularly bland part of the 15th near the Porte de Versailles. But up on the top floor is an exclusive fitness club called *Waou* (pronounced "wow" when you say it with a French accent), featuring panoramic views of Paris from the heated swimming pool and two sunbathing terraces. The high-tech gym equipment isn't bad either. Avoid lunchtime, when every corporate worker in the neighborhood tries to squeeze in a few laps between noon and 2pm. Next door is **Aquaboulevard**, the largest indoor water park in Paris (see *Theme Parks*, pages 313-315, for more information).

THE FLOATING POOL

The famous Piscine Deligny, a floating swimming pool moored to the banks of the Seine, was first built in the late 1700s as a cleaner option for swimming than the river. It was rebuilt many times over the years, becoming bigger and more luxurious each time, finally measuring almost 30,000 square feet, with 340 changing cabins and 13 private salons, one reserved for princes. It was considered one of the coolest places to see and be seen in Paris – until it mysteriously sank one evening in July 1993. After a decade of mourning, plans for its replacement have been approved by the city officials. The new floating pool is tentatively scheduled to open by 2006 at the foot of the National Library (*Bibliothèque Nationale-François Mitterand*) in the 13th.

■ Fishing

Pêche Extrême (☎ 01 47 57 17 32, www.peche-paris.com) organizes fishing trips for giant catfish, pike and carpe on the Seine just outside Paris (by small motorboat), from April through the end of October. They also organize freshwater fly-fishing for trout in a lake at the Bois de Boulogne (from September). It costs €122-€183 (extra €30 for non-fishing companion) for eight hours of "no-kill" (catch-and-release) fishing with a licensed, bilingual guide, and includes the day permit and all materials. Lunch isn't included. Their office and meeting place is right on the edge of Paris at the **Maison de la Pêche et de la Nature**, 22 Allée Claude Monet, Ile-de-la-Jatte, Levallois (92). M° Pont de Levallois-Bécon. Open Monday through Friday, 10:30am to 5:30pm.

On Ice

■ Outdoors

There are three outdoor skating rinks in Paris, and these are open mid-December through February. The most popular one is at the **Place de l'Hôtel de Ville** (4th), which is absolutely magical at night when the Hôtel de Ville (Paris Town Hall) is lit up. The other rinks are at the **Place**

Raoul Dautry (15th, at the foot of the Tour de Montparnasse) and at the **Place de la Bataille de Stalingrad** (19th, at the Bassin de la Villette). Free entry, skate rental €5, double-bladed skates for kids are free. Weekday mornings are usually reserved for school groups, and then it's open to the public from early afternoon to 10pm. Weekends, 9am till 10pm; open until midnight Friday and Saturday. For more information check the Town Hall's web site (www.paris.fr) or look in the December issue of *Pariscope* for "Patinoire."

■ Indoors

The only indoor skating in Paris is the **Patinoire Sonja Henie** at the Palais Omnisports de Paris-Bercy (a.k.a. POPB, Porte 28, 12th, M° Bercy, ☎ 01 40 02 60 60, www.bercy.fr). It's open Wednesday from 3 to 6pm; Friday from 9:30pm to 12:30am; Saturday from 3 to 6pm and 9:30pm to 12:30am; and Sunday from 10am to noon and 3 to 6pm. Entrance is €3-€6, skate rental €3, helmet and pads €1 each. The rink itself has been used for competitions and private training since 1984, and was only opened to the general public in October 2002 with a make-over and a new café.

On Wheels

■ Biking

Cycling in Paris isn't just for Lycra-clad couriers or Tour de France trainees. It isn't rare to see an elegantly dressed woman gliding between cars with Hermès scarf flying, or an elderly Frenchman working his way up a hill with his groceries in the basket and a Gauloise hanging from the corner of his mouth. Paris is an ideal city to explore by bike. You can sail through traffic, cover a lot of ground, and benefit from the wide, scenic boulevards that were built to connect and highlight the city's major monuments. Motorists might grumble, but the city's roads have become safer for cyclists and skaters since Mayor Delanoë increased the number of bike lanes and traffic-free zones in Paris. And when you've got a bike, there are no worries about métro strikes, parking, or wearing out the soles of your shoes. Whether you join one of the many guided tours or set out on your own with rented equipment and a good map, you'll find yourself discovering Paris in a whole new light.

On Your Own

Paris is relatively flat at the center, although Montmartre, Belleville and the Butte aux Cailles should be avoided if you're averse to hills. Get a copy of the free cycling map, "Carte Vélo à Paris" (at any Mairie or tourism office), which helps you navigate the one-way maze of bike lanes and find the most scenic routes. But don't just stick to the roads with cycle lanes. Having a bicycle also gives you the freedom to explore the narrow roads of the Marais and the Latin Quarter.

 AUTHOR'S NOTE: *Sunday morning is usually the best time to cycle around the capital, when the few cars on the road aren't likely to be in a hurry.*

Urban Cycling

Cyclists are allowed in the bus lanes, but it's advisable to speed up or get out of the way if one starts bearing down on you (let the bus pass you on the right so you don't get trapped in the gutters). To compete with the Indy-racing cars and pedestrians chattering away obliviously on their cell phones, quick reflexes and a bit of attitude go a long way. Always point to where you're going, look out for parked cars pulling out or opening doors, and always wear a helmet (though you might think no one else in Paris does). In most cases, you should stay off the sidewalks, give way to pedestrians in traffic-free zones, and obey the same traffic rules as cars.

CYCLING TIPS

An American cyclist known as "Q. May" has created a very useful web site (www.mayq.com) for urban cyclists in Paris, with safety info, vocabulary and pronunciation tips, and cycling routes to get out of Paris and into the suburbs (not as easy as you'd think), with plenty of photos.

Cycling in the Great Outdoors

You don't have to go far to escape the crowds and traffic congestion of the city. Paris's 2,100-acre **Bois de Boulogne** (16th) and 2,400-acre **Bois de Vincennes** (12th) have paved and unpaved cycling trails that pass through quiet forested areas and around scenic lakes and gardens. The best time to go is late spring through late fall, when the forests and gardens look their best. Be sure to ask for a free map when renting a bike (see the *Bike Rental* section below for information), since it's easy to get lost on the more secluded trails. A lock is also necessary in case you want to stop for lunch or do a bit of sightseeing (the gardens and museums in both parks are off-limits to bikes). The nicest trail in the Bois de Boulogne is the **Route St-Denis**, running almost parallel to the Allée de Longchamp from the Porte de Maillot to the Pré Catalan gardens, continuing to the Grande Cascade. In the Bois de Vincennes, the most scenic trails are between the **Parc Floral** and the **Lac Daumésnil**. The trails around the hippodrome have nothing more scenic than sport training fields, and tends to be favored by Lycra-clad speed cyclists. For the best scenery in both Bois, stick to the cycle trails that go into the forest and not alongside the roads open to traffic. And don't be afraid to explore the dirt trails as long as they're not for horse riding (designated by a sign with a boot in a horse stirrup). See the *Paris by Neighborhood* section, page 78, for more information on what to see in the Bois de Boulogne and Bois de Vincennes.

Sunday Riders

From March through November, *Operation Paris Respire* (Paris Breathes) closes off certain roads to traffic on Sundays and holidays between 9am and 5pm. These areas include the quays of the Seine, Rue Mouffetard, the Nationale neighborhood, along Bassin de la Villette, and along Canals St-Martin and L'Ourcq. The Left Bank of the Seine between the Ile St-Louis and the Louvre is also closed to traffic mid-July through mid-August for *Paris Plage*. Cyclists and skaters should still give way to pedestrians.

BIKES ON PUBLIC TRANSPORTATION

You can take your bike on the RER lines A and B, but only in carriages marked with a bicycle symbol (look on the platform ahead of time for a sign on the ground), and not during rush hours (weekdays, 6:30am to 9:00am and 4:30 to 7:00pm). Métro line 1 is open to cyclists on Sundays only until 4:30pm (although you can't get your bike past the turnstiles at La Défense or Louvre-Rivoli). Exceptions are made for cyclists with a flat tire or injury depending on the mood of the ticket agent (hamming it up a bit helps). Buses are completely off-limits to bicycles.

Bike Rental & Touring Companies

Fat Tire Bike Tours: 24 Rue Edgar Faure, M° Dupleix, 15th, ☎/fax 01 56 58 10 54, www.fattirebiketours.com. Open daily, 9am to 7pm.

Fat Tire Bike Tours offer the most enjoyable English bike tours in Paris, with day-trips to Versailles (€50), the Loire Valley (see web site) and Monet's Gardens in Giverny (€65) as well. Their Paris Day Tour includes a stop at the Berthillon ice cream shop (€24) and the Night Tour includes a Seine boat cruise with wine (€28; both tours €48). The three- to four-hour tours are easy going, with stops every few hundred yards for commentary and photo opportunities. All ages are welcome, with child seats, kids' bikes, trailers, helmets and rain gear available. You can also rent bikes from €2 per hour to €50 per week. The shop (formerly known as Mike's Bike Tours), run by friendly Texas native David Mebane, is a short walk from the Eiffel Tower; it's an English-speaking oasis with a satellite TV in the lounge area, Starbucks coffee, lots of Paris guidebooks

Typical Paris Passage

Parc de Bercy

Sacré-Coeur Basilica

Montmartre Streetscape

Ile de la Cité from the Pont des Arts

Marché aux Fleurs

Frank Gehry building, Bercy

Chair, Paris park

to read, cheap Internet access, telephone cards and pay phone, clean bathrooms, and Bailey (David's fluffy dog). Visitors can book a hotel, store luggage, meet other travelers, and pick up the latest copies of the *Paris Voice* or *Paris Time Out* magazines. Student discounts available. US dollars, euros and traveler's checks accepted (no credit cards).

> **AUTHOR'S NOTE:** *Fat Tire's Day and Night Tours meet* under the Eiffel Tower, *not at the shop.*

Paris à Vélo, C'est Sympa: 37 Boulevard Bourdon, 4th, M° Bastille, ☎ 01 48 87 60 01, www.parisvelosympa.com. Open daily, 9am to 6pm (until 7pm in summer, closed from 1 to 2pm weekdays). This company was founded by a Belgian woman who fell in love with Paris. Different three-hour tour themes include Paris at dawn and unknown corners of eastern Paris around the 13th/14th and 19th/20th arrondissements. There are also day-tours of Versailles and the Marne River. Rates (includes bike, guide, insurance) from €30 (€16 for children under 12; minimum age 10 years). They also rent bikes and tandems: €9.50 for half-day, €12.50 for a day, €24 for the weekend, and €30 for three days.

Maison Roue Libre: Outside the Forum des Halles, 1 Passage Mondétour (at the corner of Rue Rambuteau), 1st, M° Châtelet-Les Halles or Etienne Marcel, ☎ 08 10 44 15 34, open daily, 9am to 7pm.

The Maison Roue Libre is run by the public transport system to encourage Parisians to use bicycles instead of cars in the city center, so the rates are particularly low. Weekday rentals are €6/day or €15/five days. Weekend rentals are €3/hour or €12/day. They're all city cruisers with baskets, chain guards and locks (get there early, they run out). Children's bikes, trailers and helmets are available on request. There are also multilingual guided tours of Paris, Versailles, and the Ile-de-France from €21 (90 minutes) to €29 (full-day tours). Call for the schedule. Bikes can also be rented from their **Cyclobus** locations (in service weekends May to October) at Place de l'Hôtel de Ville, Bassin de la Villette, Bois de Vincennes (M° Porte d'Auteuil), and Bois de Vincennes (M° Château de Vincennes). Photo ID and €150 deposit required.

Cyclo Pouce: 38 Quai Marne 19th, M° Ourcq, ☎ 01 42 41 76 98. This non-profit neighborhood association recovers and repairs bicycles, then rents them out at a very reasonable rate. City cruisers, mountain bikes and tandems available for all ages, and includes lock and bungees. They also sell a selection of Paris guidebooks. Open Tuesday through Friday, 10am to 6pm; weekends and holidays, 9:30am to 7pm. From €3.50/hour to €55/week.

Gepetto & Vélos: 59 Rue du Cardinal Lemoine, 5th, M° Cardinal-Lemoine, ☎/fax 01 43 54 19 95, www.gepetto-et-velos.com. Half-day rentals €7.50, full-day rentals €14.

Paris

Allo Vélo: 70 Boulevard Strasbourg, 10th, M° Gare de l'Est, ☎ 01 40 35 36 36, www.allovelo.com. Open daily, 9am to 7pm. Bike rental from €2 for 80 minutes during the week to €35 for weekend rental (Friday noon until Monday noon).

Bike'N'Roller: 38 Rue Fabert, Esplanade des Invalides, 7th, M° Invalides, ☎ 01 45 50 38 27, www.bikenroller.fr. Open daily, 10am to 7pm. This bike and skate shop handles rentals, sales, repairs and even skating lessons. In-line skates and old-fashioned four-wheel skates are €9/day, bikes (city cruisers or BMX) are €12 for three hours, €17 for the day, and they even rent out *trotinettes* (like a skateboard with handlebars; electric or push-powered) for €10-€22/hour.

Motorail: 190 Rue de Bercy, 12th, M° Gare de Lyon (in the Gare de Lyon's car rental section, at the corner of Rue Van Gogh), ☎ 01 43 07 08 09, www.motorail.fr. Open 9:30am to 7pm, closed Sunday. Motorail offers scooter, motorcycle and bike rental. Rates from €10/day for city cruiser bikes, €29/day for small scooters, and €49/day for light motorcycles (unlimited mileage; includes helmet, gloves, and locks). You'll need a credit card and ID, and a driver's license for the motorcycles. They can also keep your car in a guarded parking lot from €8/day.

Paris Cycles: ☎ 01 47 47 76 50. Open April to October on Wednesdays and weekends from 10am to 7pm, daily in July and August. This company has bike rental vans parked at the **Bois de Boulogne** (M° Porte Dauphine, on the northeast side of the Lac Inférieur) and **Bois de Vincennes** (M° Porte Dorée, on the northwest side of the Lac Daumesnil). Rates are €5/hour or €12/day.

TOUR DE FRANCE

Racing fever in Paris is at an all-time high after Lance Armstrong (one of France's favorite American heroes) won his fifth straight victory at the 2003 Centennial Tour de France. Anyone in Paris during the third week in July can watch the race's finish along the Avenue des Champs-Elysées (get there early for a good spot). To get a bit closer to the action, join one of the specialized tour companies that follow the race, such as France Off the Beaten Path (www.traveloffthebeatenpath.com) or DuVine Adventures (www.duvine.com).

Free Bike Tours

Paris Rando Vélo (☎ 06 20 11 40 10, www.parisrandovelo.com) organizes free Friday night bike tours of the city; meet up at 9:30 pm at the Hôtel de Ville, 4th, M° Hôtel de Ville. In summer, you can rent a bike on the spot if you get there early enough (look for the cyclobus); other times of the year you'll need to rent from a bike shop. The ride starts at 10pm sharp and goes in a circular scenic route around Paris, returning to the start at about 1am. There's also a daytime ride every third Sunday of the month, beginning at 10:30 am, at the same location.

Paris Bike Tour (☎ 01 43 90 80 80, www.parisbiketour.com) offers three-hour multilingual guided bike tours of Paris (Right or Left Bank). They also rent out bikes for €13/half-day or €22/day (lock, map, helmet and rain poncho included), delivered directly to any address or hotel within Paris. Call at least 24-hours in advance to reserve.

■ Paris by Segway

Segways are the coolest new way to get around Paris. They glide by silently on two wheels, battery-powered and controlled by high-tech gyroscope sensors. When the driver leans forward, the Segway moves forward, stopping when the driver leans back. A little knob on the handle turns it to the left or right. The futuristic Segways take a bit of time to get used to, and they can't go up and down steps, but they're perfect for gadget addicts interested in turning heads all over town!

Paris Segway Tours (☎ 01 56 58 10 54, www.parissegwaytours.com) are run by the friendly folks at Fat Tire Bike Tours (see above), with four- to five-hour tours in the day or night, €70 each. They include a 30-minute practice session and snack break. Riders must be at least 14 years old and weigh between 100 and 250 pounds. Tours are available March through November. Reserve as early as possible, since they sell out quickly!

To speed around without a guide, stop by the **Vinci Car Park** (entrance outside 88 Avenue des Champs-Elysées, 8th, www.vincipark.com) to rent a Segway for €6-€10/hour or €30/day. You'll also need to purchase a €15 permit and take their 45-minute training session before zooming off.

■ Skating

As recently as the mid-1990s, in-line skating was still considered an alternative sport for teens and extreme-sports enthusiasts. The transportation strikes in the fall of 1995 changed all that when daily commuters strapped on their newly purchased skates to get to work, and haven't looked back since. It may have taken Parisians a while to warm up to in-line skating, but they've certainly made up for lost time! Today roller-parks can be found in all corners of the city, and organized skates through the city regularly attract thousands of Parisians of all ages. If you want to try your hand at skating in Paris, you won't have a hard time finding wide, smooth sidewalks, especially around Les Invalides and the Eiffel Tower. And, with all the exercise, you can enjoy those heavenly Parisian pastries guilt-free!

Paris

HISTORICAL NOTE

Roller skating first became popular in Paris in the early 1800s, when a special "summer skating" rink was created at Nouveau Tivoli, between Rue de Clichy and Rue Blanche. The first real rink, the 6,500-square-foot Skating Palace, was built in 1875 in the Bois de Boulogne, complete with floral decorations, sparkling lights and a full orchestra.

Where to Skate

If you're looking for large expanses of smooth, traffic-free surfaces, try the **Esplanade des Invalides** (7th), the **Parc de la Villette** (19th), the new **Rue de Bercy** (13th), or the **Parvis de la Défense**. The streets along the Seine and canals are closed to traffic every Sunday in season (see *Sunday Riders* box in *Biking* section, page 180), and many of the city's gardens allow skaters on the paths (watch out for baby strollers). You can skate high above the cars and smog on the **Promenade Plantée**, a paved garden trail created on top of the Viaduc des Arts all the way to the **Bois de Vincennes** (12th) or dodge pedestrians on the famous Champs-Elysées. You can watch both amateur and pro stunt skaters show off their jumps, slides and other acrobatics the **Esplanade du Trocadéro** (16th), **Place du Palais Royal** (1st) and on the steps of the **Parc Omnisports de Paris-Bercy** (12th). Younger skaters can try the 1,300-square-foot paved skating area at the **Square Tino-Rossi** (Quai St-Bernard, 5th) or **Parc Monceau** (8th), which has a railing for tiny hands to hold onto.

Skate Rentals & Lessons

Nomades Roller Shop: 37 Boulevard Bourdon, 4th, M° Bastille, ☎ 01 44 54 07 44, www.nomadeshop.com. Open Monday through Friday, 11am to 1pm and 2 to 7pm. No credit cards. This in-line skating headquarters rents out skates with protection and helmets for €5-8 half day, €7-11 full day, €15-18 on weekends, and €25-35 for the week. This shop is the meeting place for the *Rollers et Coquillages* Sunday afternoon skate (see below). If you want to be sure to have skates for Sunday, you can pick them up Saturday afternoon before 6pm without an extra fee. The **Roller Club de France** gives lessons here from €14 for one 90-minute group class, or €30 per hour for private lessons. For classes in English ask for Ben.

Ilios Roller Shop: 4 Allée Vivaldi, 12th, M° Michel Bizot, ☎ 01 44 74 75 76. Open daily, 10am to 8pm. In-line skate rentals from €5/hour or €12.50/day. One-hour lessons are available for €15.50, four people max. The shop is conveniently located right at the trail entrance of the Promenade Plantée (paved walking and cycling trail through gardens) going all the way to the Bois de Vincennes.

Bike'N'Roller: 38 Rue Fabert, Esplanade des Invalides, 7th, M°
Invalides, ☎ 01 45 50 38 27, www.bikenroller.fr. Open daily, 10am to 7pm.
In-line skates and old-fashioned four-wheel skates are €9/day. Group lessons for people who already have some experience on skates are Sundays
at 11am and 2pm, €20-€24 per lesson. Individual lessons are by reservation during the week, from €10-€32/hour, including equipment rental.
Children's lessons are Wednesdays at 2pm, €17-€20 per session.

Rollerparc Avenue: 100 Rue Léon Geffroy, Z.I. Les Ardoines,
Vitry-sur-Seine (by car or RER C, station Les Ardoines), ☎ 01 47 18 19 19,
www.rollerparc.com. See web site for their rather complicated opening
hours. Entry €10 (€8 for kids under 10), €7 weekdays after 4pm.

This is the second-largest indoor/outdoor skate park in Europe, with
107,000 square feet of ramps, tubes, hockey courts, speed track and
smooth, flat surfaces for beginners. There's also a snack shop, pro shop,
and lounge area. Rent all types of in-line skates and skateboards (€4 and
up, includes protection). Group classes for all levels are every Saturday
morning from 10:30am to noon (€20 + entry fee), and on Sunday and
Tuesday with reservations. Individual lessons are €30 + entry for one
person or €45 + entry for two. It's about 20 minutes outside Paris, but
worth the trip for real skating fanatics of all ages.

Get Equipped

If you need to stock up on any sporting equipment, clothing or just want a
new pair of sneakers for your power-walks around Paris, check out
Citadum (50-56 Rue Caumartin, 9th, M° Havre-Caumartin, ☎ 01 55 31
74 00), a four-level superstore just around the corner from the Grands
Magasins of Boulevard Haussmann. Other major sporting goods chains
include **Go Sport** (Forum des Halles, level 3, Porte Lescot, 1st, M° Les
Halles, www.go-sport.com), **Decathlon** (les Trois Quartiers, level 1, 23
Boulevard de la Madeleine, 1st, M° Madeleine, www.decathlon.com), and
Au Vieux Campeur (38 Rue St-Jacques, 5th, M° Maubert-Mutualité,
☎ 01 43 25 23 57, www.au-vieux-campeur.fr).

Group Skates

Anyone who thinks they're gifted in a pair of skates shouldn't miss **Friday Night Fever** when up to 15,000 skaters fly *en masse* through the
streets of the city. Police close off the streets to traffic and ambulances
stand by for the inevitable injuries. It's free for anyone who can handle
steep hills on cobblestones (more importantly, you need to be able to
brake). The organizers **Pari-Roller** (www.pari-roller.com) highly recommend full protection and valid insurance for all participants. Unless it's
raining, the skate begins at 10pm every Friday in front of the Tour
Montparnasse at Place Raoul-Dautry (M° Montparnasse), for a
three-hour tour. Check the Pari-Roller web site for the route map the
Thursday morning before, or just follow the crowd!

Paris

SKATING ETIQUETTE

Pedestrians always have the right of way, and since they can't hear you coming you should be extra vigilant. If you're good enough to skate with the Paris motorists, follow the same rules as a cyclist would (hand signals, thank you). Finally, keep your shoes in your backpack if you plan on using public transportation or going into any cafés or shops – skates are for outdoor use only!

For a relatively laid-back and family-friendly experience, try the Sunday afternoon skate (***Randonée du Dimanche***) organized by **Roller et Coquillages** (www.rollers-coquillages.org). With more than 30,000 skaters during the high season, it's the largest group skate in the world. The skate starts at Boulevard Bourdon (in front of the Nomades Shop near the Place de la Bastille), at 2:30pm, and lasts about three hours. Skaters should already have some experience, and ideally be at intermediate level.

The **Roller Squad Institut** (☎ 01 56 61 99 61, www.rsi.asso.fr) organizes free group skates for beginners on Sundays at 2:45pm and for more experienced skaters on Saturdays at 2:45pm. The group meets on the Esplanade des Invalides, across from the Air France building, 7th. Most of the skating is done on sidewalks that are relatively smooth and flat.

Planète Roller (www.planetroller.com) organizes long-distance skates around Paris and Ile-de-France, including the indoor skate park **Rollerparc Avenue** (www.rollerparc.com) in Vitry (southern Paris suburb). Check out their web site (in French only) for the latest calendar of rides and contact info.

In the Air

 You can fulfill your dream of flying over Paris, although flights of planes, helicopters and hot air balloons are strictly regulated to the air "corridors" on the immediate outskirts of the city. This still allows birds-eye views of many of the city's monuments such as the Eiffel Tower, Sacré-Coeur, the Arc de Triomphe, Les Invalides and the Tour Montparnasse. Consider supplementing any flight with a detour over the many châteaux of the Ile-de-France, such as Versailles and Vaux-le-Vicomte, for some truly magnificent views.

■ Balloon Flights

Enjoy the panoramic views of the Eiffel Tower and the Seine from the **Eutelsat hot-air balloon**. Tethered permanently at the Parc André

Citroën, the balloon can take up to 30 passengers 495 feet above the park in a secure, extra-large basket. No reservations are needed, but call in the morning if the weather is uncertain. Flights daily at the **Parc André Citroën**, 9am until 30 minutes before the park closes; 2 Rue de la Montagne de la Fage, 15th, M° Javel or Ballard, ☎ 01 44 26 20 00, www.aeroparis.com. Tickets €12 (€10 weekdays), €10 for kids ages 12 to 17 (€9 weekdays), €6 for kids ages three to six (€5 weekdays), free for children under three. Views are clearest on cool, crisp mornings.

AUTHOR'S NOTE: *See the* Outside Paris *chapter, pages 382, 405 and 426, for hot-air balloon* (montgolfière) *flights throughout the Ile-de-France (some operators offer shuttle service from Paris).*

■ Helicopter Tours

HeliParis (☎ 08 25 82 60 04, www.heliparis.com) offers helicopter tours around Paris (€119 per person) and Paris-Versailles (€199 per person). Flights take off conveniently from the **Héliport de Paris** (Porte de Sèvres, 15th). They also have piloting initiations for anyone at least 15 years old (from the heliport at Toussus le Noble, near Versailles), and Porsche 911 driving on a race track. The web site is currently only in French, so call or e-mail particuliers@heliparis.com for more information.

Paris en Hélicoptère (☎ 01 48 35 90 44, www.helifrance.fr) organizes Sunday helicopter flights from Le Bourget airport around Paris (€122, €110 for kids) and Paris-Versailles (€149, kids €140). They also have flights around Paris-Versailles-Abbaye des Vaux-de-Cernay from the Héliport de Paris (Porte de Sèvres, 15th), with a free one-hour visit of the Abbey, for €185 (€152 for kids).

■ Kite Flying

Kids of all ages who prefer to keep both feet on the ground can try flying a kite. You'll have to go out to the Bois de Boulogne (16th) or Bois de Vincennes (12th) to find enough space free of cars and trees. Kids with small (non-acrobatic) kites can fly in the Parc de la Villette (19th) or on the fields of the Cité Universitaire across from the Parc du Montsouris (14th). For inspiration, check out the **Maison du Cerf-Volant** (House of Kites), 7 Rue Prague, 12th, M° Ledru Rollin, ☎ 01 44 68 00 75, open Tuesday through Saturday, 11am to 2pm and 3 to 7pm, with displays of beautiful, hand-made kites of all shapes and sizes, as well as advice on where to fly them. Have a peek next door in the atelier of **Pan Gang** (☎ 01 43 41 88 88), an expert craftsman of traditional Chinese kites. Two other notable kite shops include **Vire Volé** (31 Rue Raymond Losserand, 14th, M° Pernety, ☎ 01 43 20 15 38) and **Le Ciel est à Tout le Monde** (10 Rue Gay

Paris

Lussac, 5th, M° Luxembourg, ☎ 01 46 33 21 50). And the best part is that they don't weigh too much to take home!

AIR & SPACE MUSEUM

France is quite proud of its contribution to the aeronautics industry, and has a whole museum – the **Musée de l'Air et de l'Espace** – dedicated to aircraft, space objects and life-size rocket replicas. Exhibitions highlight the first balloon ascent, vintage flying machines, and the now-retired Concorde. There is also a planetarium, and a 3-D cinema with a 12-minute flight-simulation film.

The museum is about five miles north of Paris at Le Bourget Airport (follow signs from the A1 motorway or take Bus 350 from Gare de l'Est). ☎ 01 49 92 71 99, www.mae.org. Open every day except Monday from 10am to 5pm (until 6pm May to October). Tickets €7, €5 for students, free for kids under 18, €2 extra to tour the Boeing 747.

Cultural Adventures

Don't just visit Paris, experience it. Make meaningful connections with the Parisians, pick up a few of their cooking tips and wine-tasting *savoir faire*. Learn to dance your first tango in Paris, get pampered in luxury spas, or sketch the skyline with local artists. Take home something besides a statue of the Eiffel Tower: the souvenirs of your own adventure!

Culinary

■ Private Cooking Classes

Paule Caillat's Promenades Gourmandes begin with a market tour of her northern Marais neighborhood for the day's supplies. As the small group of up to six guests goes from bakery to butcher shop to cheese store, Paule explains how to choose the best produce, which cuts of meat to buy, and the difference between buying fresh or aged French cheeses. Then it's back to her large kitchen, where everyone gathers around a large wooden table, each armed with a clean apron and a printout of the day's three-course menu.

Paule specializes in contemporary *cuisine bourgeoise*, with recipes that are impressive enough for entertaining, but simple enough to prepare for everyday dining. The atmosphere is very laid-back and convivial, with lots of hands-on participation and time for questions.

After lunch, Paule leads the group on a gourmet walking tour that combines sightseeing anecdotes, secret culinary addresses to stock your own kitchen, and a peek behind-the-scenes of a popular Parisian bakery. Paule also teaches in California, so not only is her English faultless, she also provides a list of substitute ingredients and cooking supplies for the US (essential for getting those French recipes perfect). Class fees vary from €220-300, or €100 for just the gourmet walking tour; ☎ 01 48 04 56 84, www.promenadesgourmandes.com.

AUTHOR'S NOTE: *Most cooking schools take a break in August, when most market shops are closed and the kitchens are too hot.*

Samira Hradsky's Food Unites the World cooking classes are held in her lovely Parisian apartment just off the Champs-Elysées. Early in the morning she takes her small group of students to the local open-air market to gather the essential ingredients for the day, from fresh salmon and Roma tomatoes to pungent cheeses and an armful of warm baguettes. Back at her modern, custom-built kitchen Samira hands out the aprons and gets everyone started on slicing, chopping and mixing (with plenty of spoon licking), while answering questions and surveying the boiling pots. Originally from Jordan, Samira has lived all over the world, so her cooking classes combine traditional French cooking with international flavors from North Africa, Spain, Italy, China and Eastern Europe. A self-taught cook, Samira doesn't fuss over exact measurements. She thinks cooking should be fun, and tries to pass that onto her students. She also believes that you "eat with your eyes before your stomach," and shows students a few presentation tricks during the class. The day ends with a five-course feast and wine enjoyed around Samira's dining room table. The day-long classes are €180, €30 for market tours only. ☎ 01 45 00 08 31, www.foodunitestheworld.com.

A graduate of the Ecole Hôtelière de Toulouse, **Françoise Meunier** started her **Cours de Cuisine** to help demystify traditional French cooking. Classes take place in her private, loft-style kitchen near La Bourse, with up to 12 students from Paris and around the world. Françoise switches easily between French and English (she also speaks Spanish and a bit of Japanese) as she combines tips such as knife-handling or fish-boning with vocabulary lessons and light teasing of the students too squeamish to pull the heads off the giant shrimp. Students are given a print-out of the recipes (with bilingual translation and ingredient conversions for the pastries), where they can take notes as they go along. After the three-course meal is finished, students set the table and sit down together to taste the outcome of their traditional French meal. Three-hour

Paris

classes are €90, or €360 for five classes. ☎ 01 40 26 14 00, www.fmeun-ier.com.

Since 1975, Marie-Blanche de Broglie's **La Cuisine de Marie-Blanche** has helped students discover the secrets of French gastronomy and the traditional art of entertaining *à la Française* adapted for today's lifestyle. Classes such as pastry baking, dining etiquette, or cheese tasting take place in Marie-Blanche's elegant apartment in the 7th arrondissement, in French and English, for up to six students. Individual cooking classes are €145, or five classes for €550. Six-week and three-month diploma courses are also available. ☎ 01 45 51 36 34, www.cuisinemb.com.

CHOCOLATE & BAKERY TOURS

Indulge your sweet tooth in a customized tour of the city's top bakeries and pastry boutiques with American cookbook author and pastry chef David Lebovitz. His six-hour tours are a feast of warm croissants and *pain au chocolat*, behind-the-scenes peeks at a famous bread bakery, sampling heavenly gold-flecked pralines and meltingly smooth ganache-filled chocolates at the latest *artisan* boutique, and David's favorite addresses for Tarte Tatin and creamy rice pudding. And as a graduate of French and Belgian cooking schools, he knows exactly which cooking ingredients and kitchen supplies you won't be able to find outside France, and where to get them before you leave. Tours to Lyon and the Basque region are also available. Check his web site for more information: www.davidlebovitz.com.

■ Cooking Schools

Even before we watched Audrey Hepburn learn to bake a soufflé at **Le Cordon Bleu** in the1950s film *Sabrina*, this Paris cooking school was already famous worldwide, counting American chef **Julia Child** among its alumni. Today's Cordon Bleu is a modern, international school that welcomes students and visitors from around the world. The building buzzes with the young chefs of tomorrow slaving away for their diplomas, and tourists who've come for the hands-on pastry and cooking workshops, wine-tasting classes or the weekly Chef's Secrets demonstrations. Geared toward all ability levels, the classes are relaxed, with silver-haired chefs in tall white hats often cracking jokes that leave the translators blushing. Even if you're an absolute beginner in the kitchen, it's worth the trip, especially for the €39 demonstrations that include a tasting with wine at the end. You can also pick up souvenir Cordon Bleu aprons, kitchen utensils and cookbooks from the boutique at the school's entrance. Classes cost €115 to €850 for week-long gourmet sessions. Open daily, 8:30am to 7pm,

8 Rue Léon-Delhomme, 15th, M° Vaugirard, ☎ 01 53 68 22 50, www.cordonbleu.edu.

The well-known **Lenôtre Ecole de Cuisine et Pâtisserie** moved its cooking school into the historic Pavillon Elysée in 2003, offering a regular schedule of bilingual cooking demonstrations (€46), cuisine and pastry classes (€100-105), wine and food combining courses (€98), and workshops for children and young teens (€38-90). The Pavillon is in the gardens of the Champs-Elysées, and includes the Café Lenôtre restaurant and a gourmet food and kitchen boutique. Call or stop by for the complete program of classes. Pavillon Elysée, 10 Avenue des Champs-Elysées, 8th, M° Champs-Elysées-Clémenceau, ☎ 01 42 65 97 68.

■ For Wine Lovers

Wine Tastings

Learning about and enjoying fine wine is a hobby in most countries; in France it's a way of life. Those with a limited knowledge of wine tasting will find no better place than Paris to pick up a few essential lessons, while seasoned wine connoisseurs will find unlimited opportunities for enjoying the finest vintages from France and all over the world. In addition to wine classes, many wine shops hold regular *dégustations* (wine tastings) on Saturdays, often with the grower present if it's from a small or independent *domaine*.

AUTHOR'S NOTE: See the Where to Shop section, page 225, for more recommended Paris wine caves.

Legrand Filles & Fils (1 Rue de la Banque or 12 Galérie Vivienne, 2nd, M° Bourse) opened in 1919 as a spice shop, and expanded into the wine industry in the 1960s, specializing in hard-to-find wines from small *domaines*. The original shop and its 1880 façade on Rue de la Banque still carries gourmet food products, but through the back passageway visitors will see the wine shop has taken over both sides of the lovely Galerie Vivienne (one of Paris's historic covered shopping passages) with an accessory and gift boutique across from the *Espace Dégustation* (don't call it a wine bar). Stop by anytime for a selection of wines by the glass, served with plates of cheese and cold meats, or sign up for the Tuesday night *Soirées Dégustation du Mardi* with a bilingual presentation of carefully chosen wines (€80-€150 depending on the wine). Call to reserve, ☎ 01 42 60 07 12 12.

Opened in 2002, Europe's biggest wine shop, **Lavinia** (3-5 Boulevard Madeleine, 1st, M° Madeleine, ☎ 01 42 97 20 20, open 10am to 8pm), is completely different from any other Parisian wine shop. Designed to be accessible to the masses, yet still temperature- and humidity-controlled, it presents neatly labeled wines, liqueurs and liquors from 43 countries on three floors, with special designations for the house sommeliers' favorites and bottles under €10. There's also a bookshop, accessories boutique and a wine bar where you can drink any bottle purchased in the store without a corkage fee. Public *dégustations* take place Friday and Saturday, 11am to 7pm, or if your French isn't too rusty, there are regular *Cours d'Initiation à la Dégustation* (€50-€140 per session) for learning the basics to wine tasting.

Other wine shops that offer regular *dégustations* include **Caves Taillevent** (199 Rue du Faubourg St-Honoré, 8th, M° Charles-de-Gaulle-Etoile, ☎ 01 45 61 14 09, every Saturday), the famed wine cellar for the Michelin-starred Restaurant Taillevent; **La Dernière Goutte** (6 Rue Bourbon-le-Château, 6th, M° Mabillon, ☎ 01 43 29 11 62, every Saturday), a Left Bank American-owned shop specializing in small, independent *domaines* and organically grown wines; and **Le Vin en Tête** (30 Rue des Batignolles, 17th, M° Rome, ☎ 01 44 69 04 57; Saturdays 4 to 8:30pm), a recently opened wine shop in the Batignolles neighborhood, which invites a different grower each weekend to present their wines.

WHAT DOES A GOOD BOTTLE COST?

The French make – and drink – a lot of wine, which translates into lower prices for good bottles than you'll find in the US or UK. Any average wine shop in Paris will have a selection of very enjoyable wines for under €10. It's even possible to find some genuinely decent wines under €5. Bottles with screw-off tops are generally used for cooking. It's always better to purchase wines from an actual wine shop (and not the supermarket), where you'll receive expert advice on choosing a bottle to suit your tastes and budget.

Wine Classes

The **Centre d'Information, de Documentation et de Dégustation (CIDD)** was founded in 1982 by Alain Ségelle, an award-winning Parisian wine sommelier who was named the Best Nose in Europe in 1988. Courses are on all levels and some are held in English and Japanese, most of them with Segelle himself. If you can, try to take the classes in French, since there are more courses to choose from (and c'mon, wine just *sounds* better in French). Individual courses are €53, with lower rates if you sign up for more than one. E-mail or call Alain to receive the schedule, as well as the calendar of monthly wine dinners, vineyard visits, and *portes ouvertes* (open houses). CIDD, 30 Rue de la Sablière, 11th, M° Pernety, ☎ 01 45 45 44 20, alainsegelle.wines@wanadoo.fr.

Wine Dinners

If you really want to splash out on a special occasion, **Wine Dinners** (☎ 01 41 83 80 46, www.wine-dinners.com) organizes gourmet meals in two- or three-star Michelin restaurants, with a selection of 10 vintage wines. Really vintage. Most of the bottles are at least 30 years old, and quite a few are more than a half-century old. One on the list is even from 1828. Wine like this doesn't come cheap, so expect to pay anywhere from €650-€5,300. A real once-in-a-lifetime treat (or twice if you can stand it). English-speaking guests get to sit next to the bilingual François Audouze if translation are needed. Have a look at the past and futures wine dinners planned by the group on their web site, or contact François directly for more information and dates for the next dinners (be sure to plan ahead, there's only room for 10 guests at each dinner).

Wine Museum

Located in an exceptional setting, the **Musée du Vin** (Rue des Eaux, 16th, M° Passy, ☎ 01 45 25 63 26, www.museeduvinparis.com, open Tuesday through Sunday, 10am to 6pm) was built within the ancient limestone quarries mined between the 13th and 18th centuries to provide the stone to build Paris. In the 16th and 17th centuries, the Friars of the Minimes Monastery used the cool quarries to store the wine they made in the vineyards that once occupied the surrounding land. Today, exhibits are creatively set up in the maze of tunnels, and a restaurant offers a four-course/four-wines menu for lunch (€50, reservations necessary). The museum visit and a glass of wine costs €6.50 (free for restaurant guests). An English guidebook is available for €2 in the boutique. You can purchase a combined ticket for the Musée du Vin and a **Seine sightseeing cruise** with the Vedettes de Paris (Port de Suffren, 7th) for just €10 (ask at the museum for more information).

Wine Festivals

Vineyards in Paris may be few and far between, but they sure know how to celebrate the annual Grape Harvest Festival. The best-known is the **Fête des Vendanges de Montmartre** (www.fetedesvendangesde-montmartre.com), which takes place around the **Clos Montmartre** vineyard (corner of Rue des Saules and Rue St-Vincent, 18th) on the second weekend in October. You can purchase a bottle of the *Clos Montmartre* only at the Syndicat d'Initiative de Montmartre (21 Place du Tertre, 18th) or from the wine cellar of the *Mairie* of the 18th (Place Jules Joffrin, M° Jules Joffrin), with the funds going to local charities. On a smaller, but no less festive scale is the vine (there's only one) at **Jacques Mélac's Wine Bistro** (42 Rue Léon Frot, 11th, M° Charonne, ☎ 01 43 70 59 27, www.melac.fr), which, planted in the bistro's cellar in the 70s, grows up and along the façade, producing enough grapes for 35 bottles. Mélac's

Fête des Vendanges usually takes place the first weekend in October with a big block party and grape-crushing in wooden vats.

AUTHOR'S NOTE: *See the* Where to Eat *section, page 282, for more Paris wine bar listings.*

The annual **Beaujolais Nouveau Festival**, on the third Thursday of November, is a celebration welcoming the first wine of the year, Beaujolais Nouveau. Since the 1960s it's been celebrated around the world with much fanfare as everyone races to serve the new wine first. A wise man once said that the arrival of the Beaujolais Nouveau is like the arrival of a new baby. When it comes, you don't worry about whether it's smart or good looking, you celebrate because it's arrived. The point is to enjoy the Beaujolais Nouveau and wait until the morning to decide whether it was worth it or not. If you're lucky enough to be in Paris, park yourself at the nearest wine bar and you'll be guaranteed a good time (if not a good wine)!

Wine Fairs

Wine fairs (*foires* and *salons*) are the ideal places to test and purchase wines direct from growers from around the world. After paying a small entrance fee (and sometimes even receiving your own personal wine glass), you're free to browse the stands to sample different wines. Some stands are simple affairs run by the growers themselves, others are big and flashy stands sponsored by familiar names like Moët-Chandon. There are often food stands and entertainment as well, making it a nice day out. Check *Pariscope* or ask at the tourism office for the schedule of annual fairs. The two biggest ones are the **Foire de Paris** (the largest fair in Paris, not just for wine; www.foiredeparis.fr), for five days the end of April, and the **Salon des Vignerons Indépendant** (Independent Wine Growers, www.vigneron-independant.com), which takes place twice a year, at the end of November and the beginning of April.

WARNING! *If you're there to shop, use those buckets (to spit out the wine), or else you may find by the end of the day that you can hardly tell the difference between a glass of Cabernet and a glass of grape juice!*

■ For Cigar Aficionados

For some, fine wine and fine food just wouldn't be the same without a fine cigar at the end of the evening. **La Casa del Habano** (169 Boulevard St-Germain, 6th, M° St-Germain-des-Prés, ☎ 01 45 49 24 30, fax 01 45 44 65 64) combines a cigar shop with a *fumoir* (cigar bar), art gallery and cigar club. Every Tuesday and Thursday afternoon from 2 to 4:30pm you can drop by for a *dégustation* of the cigar of the day, with a bit of *eau-de-vie* (liqueur) and an espresso, for €35. Their *Institut du Cigare* organizes personalized, bilingual workshops that cover anything from history and fabrication of cigars to different methods of smoking them, for beginners or experienced cigar aficionados. Sessions from €95, or €300 for a four-session cycle (all food, drink and cigars included). Call or stop by for the dates and program.

Cigar Bars

These bars are all noteworthy for their selection of fine cigars chosen by knowledgeable barmen, as well as their dignified décor. The location of these popular cigar bars in Paris hotels makes one wonder if perhaps cigars are less of a Parisian thing and more of an imported pastime.

Regency Bar at the Hôtel Prince des Galles: 33 Avenue George V, 8th, M° George V, ☎ 01 53 23 77 77.

Ernest Bar at the Hôtel Lutétia: 45 Boulevard Raspail, 6th, M° Sèvres-Babylone, ☎ 01 49 54 46 46.

Duke's Bar at the Hôtel Westminster: 13 Rue de la Paix, 2nd, M° Opéra, ☎ 01 42 61 57 46.

Hemingway Bar at the Hôtel Ritz: 15 Place Vendôme, 1st, M° Concorde, ☎ 01 43 16 30 30 (particularly Wednesday nights).

Bar of the Hôtel Normandy: 7 Rue de l'Echelle, 1st, M° Pyramides, ☎ 01 42 60 30 21.

Artistic

Many of the world's finest artists have made Paris their home over the past three centuries. Follow in their footsteps by picking up a brush, a sketchpad, a camera… there's no lack of inspiration!

■ Sketching

A sketchbook and a solid pair of walking shoes are the essential supplies for an outing with **RandoCroquis** (☎ 01 47 07 50 54, www.randocroquis.com), a group that combines light hiking (*rando*) with sketching (*croquis*). The focus is on nature sketching along the Seine, in Paris parks or nearby forests, with total walking time of one to three hours. It's open to all levels, with qualified artist guides to offer tips and advice on technique. There are also regular night-sketching outings within Paris. It's a casual, fun way to see a bit of the city from a different perspective. Weekly half-day (€23) or full-day (€38) hikes are organized throughout the year (less in August) in Paris as well as other cities in France. To check the schedule or reserve a spot, call Cyrille (he speaks some English) on Monday or Tuesday, 10am to 2pm.

The **Académie de la Grande Chaumière** (14 Rue de la Grande Chaumière, 6th, M° Vavin, ☎ 01 43 26 13 72) is a scruffy little Montparnasse arts academy with an illustrious list of alumni, including Picasso and Modigliani. Visitors can attend the afternoon sketching sessions (*atelier croquis*) with a live model on weekdays, 2 to 5pm, and Saturdays, 1 to 5pm. The fee is €15 (less if you attend more than once), with an instructor who offers individual advice if needed. Open to all levels. Call ahead or just show up a few minutes early. Sketchbooks and pencils are available at the art-supply stores on the same street as the Académie.

> **AUTHOR'S NOTE:** *There are many places to buy art supplies in Paris, especially in Montparnasse.*

Those inspired by the medieval arts can join the **Carnet de Dessins** sessions at the Musée National du Moyen Age (Thermes & Hôtel de Cluny, 6 Place Paul-Painlevé, 5th, M° Cluny La-Sorbonne, ☎ 01 53 73 78 16), where visitors of all artistic abilities are guided by a professional artist in sketching the museum's treasures. The cost is €12 per person, no supplies needed, and you get to keep your sketchbook afterwards. The instruction is in French, so basic French comprehension is helpful. The two-hour sessions take place Saturdays from March through September; call in advance to reserve a place.

Contemporary Brazilian artist **Saulo Portela** opens his private atelier just off the Canal St-Martin (10th) for weekly sketching sessions with a live model. These aren't classes, but more of an artists' social group; each participant does their own thing with some advice if they ask, in a very casual environment. There's also some outdoor sketching around the Canal. The group is made up of all ages, nationalities, and artistic abilities, and provides a unique glimpse into a real artist's life in Paris. Sessions from €15 (and participants split the model's fee). Call Saulo (he speaks very good English) for more information, ☎ 01 40 68 74 46.

TERMS TO KNOW

The word *cours* means class, either for the whole academic year or just one day. When looking for short-term classes of a day or week, look for the word *stage*, which means workshop or internship. Another helpful word is *baptême*, which literally means baptism, but in an activity context means initiation.

■ Painting

Complete beginners can pick up some painting skills at the art gallery **Paris Loisirs Culturels** (11 Rue Saint Maur, 11th, M° Voltaire, ☎ 01 43 70 70 26), run by a bilingual instructor. Students choose a well-known painting that they like, and learn by imitation. About €40 covers the materials and instruction, and you get your painting as a souvenir. Regular classes held September through July; call for details.

For those who would like to try something a bit more advanced, the **Atelier du Temps Passé** (5 Avenue Daumesnil, 12th, M° Bastille, ☎ 01 43 07 72 26, www.atelier-re-naissance.com) offers week-long painting workshops in the beautifully renovated glass and vaulted stone studios of the Viaduc des Arts. An expert at restoring paintings, instructor André Fisch teaches students of any artistic ability how to paint using the techniques of the great masters such as Van Gogh or Rembrandt. Most students are French, but André also speaks English, and most of the training is one-on-one. Classes are available in February, April, June and July and cost about €335, all materials provided.

Learn the art of porcelain painting at the **Atelier des Buttes-Chaumont** (☎ 01 42 02 40 78, www.porcelain-painters.com). Indian-born artist Anjana Gogel teaches one- to three-day courses in her tiny, but spotless, Paris studio just a block from the bucolic Parc des Buttes-Chaumont. There is a course for absolute beginners, as well as courses for intermediate-level artists. In July she also gives oil painting classes, helping each student develop their own style. Anjana speaks perfects English, and has students of all ages and nationalities. Check the web site for schedule and pricing.

■ Sculpture & Pottery

Matisse's former atelier in the 14th, a jumble of sculptures, pottery, sketches and paintings, is today part of the **Ateliers Terre et Feu** (37*bis*, Villa d'Alésia, 14th, M° Alésia, ☎ 01 45 42 36 13, www.terre-et-feu.com), where students can learn to throw a pot or create a sculpture based on a live model (€170 for 18 hours over six days). It's also possible to work independently in the *ateliers libres* for €5/hour plus clay purchase. Two other ateliers, at République (3rd) and Villiers (17th) offer drawing and painting workshops from €16 per session. For more info, stop by **Villa d'Alésia** in the afternoon or call the office in the morning, ☎ 01 45 77 10 10 (closed annually from the end of July through August).

■ Printmaking & Photography

The **Association Pour l'Estampe et Pour l'Art Populaire** (49*bis* Rue des Cascades, 20th, M° Jourdain, ☎ 01 43 49 19 80) is a community artists' association with the goal of making the arts accessible to the average person, without an elitist gallery atmosphere. Behind their Belleville gallery is a printmaking (*gravure*) atelier offering weekend workshops (four people max in each six-hour session), for about €55, all inclusive. Each participant should have one or two sketches prepared in advance. Call the atelier's friendly, multilingual instructor Julien Pelletier for more information and schedules.

Tired of returning home with yet another pile of so-so vacation photos featuring your thumb in the foreground? Join the transplanted American Linda Mathieu on her **Paris Photo Tours** (☎ 01 44 75 83 80, www.paris-phototours.com) to discover the secret corners of the city and, more importantly, how to capture them perfectly with your camera. Tours (limited to four people) focus on specific areas of the city such as Montmartre, or on themes such as gastronomy, women-only, or language-immersion tours with Linda's French colleague, Christine. These are fun, relaxed tours geared toward first-time visitors. See the web site for more information.

THE NINE LIVES OF LA GAÎTE LYRIQUE

La Gaîté Lyrique dates back to 1759, when it was just a tiny dance hall. It became a grand theater in the 1800s, in the Italian style popular at the time. The theater gained presitge over the years, even hosting Diaghilev's Russian Ballet in the 1920s, but by the 1960s it was falling apart. The city had no budget for renovations; after a few failed attempts to keep it going, the theater closed for good in 1974. In 1983, a French company was given permission to change the place into an indoor amusement park for children. The listed façade and Empress Eugénie Reception Hall were restored, but the rest of the theater, including the Italian marble staircase and grand stage, were demolished. The amusement center, Planète Magique, opened for 12 days and went immediately out of business when the rides didn't work.

Ten years later the building was once again opened, tentatively, to be used as an exposition center for multimedia art installations. The dusty amusement park decoration provided a surreal setting, but not exactly a safe one, so work has slowly begun to renovate La Gaîté Lyrique once again. The plan is to transform it into a Center for Multimedia Creation by 2006.

In the meantime, there are regular artistic, musical and theatrical expositions, concerts, debates and installations open to public *only with a reservation* (free visit; e-mail them your name and telephone and date you want to visit: visite@la-gaite-de-paris .info). Check the web site or stop by to pick up the schedule of events, or just sign up for a tour of the building. It's worth seeing what the inside looks like now, before it's changed forever once again. 3 Rue Papin, 3rd, M° Réaumur-Sébastopol or Arts-et-Métiers (visitor's entrance around the back at 70 Rue Réaumur), http://la-gaite-de-paris.info.

■ Floral Design

Learn the art of French flower arranging at the exclusive **L'Ecole des Fleurs** (☎ 01 55 90 59 60, www.ecoledesfleurs.com), run by famous floral designer Christian Tortu. In a bright classroom overlooking the inner courtyard at the Hôtel Crillon, students learn techniques in a hands-on environment (with English and Japanese translators available), and get to take their bouquets with them at the end of the class. Different themes are available; "Country Bouquet" or "Dining Room Table Arrangements" are popular. Prices start at €100 for *découverte* classes, to €350 for a full day of four courses plus brunch. Limited space, so reserve as far in advance as possible (no classes in August).

■ Art Tours

If you're interested in cutting edge art and artists in Paris, either as a buyer or simply out of curiosity, try one of the **WysiwygArt Tours** (What you see is what you get) by Art Process (☎ 01 47 00 90 85, info@art-process.com). For the past five years they've taken groups to see artist studios, unknown galleries, artist squats, and private shows all over Paris. They speak multiple languages, and can also be hired for private tours on request. Their monthly group tours take place the third Saturday of every month, and fill up quickly (€50 per person). Contact ArtProcess PAC (Personal Artistic Coach), Eric Mézan for more information.

Banish any ideas of being herded through the Louvre in a large group, barely able to hear the dry, scripted commentary. **Paris Muse** offers intimate, interactive tours to make your museum visit "the contemplative experience art was intended to provide." Run by art history teacher and PhD graduate student Ellen McBreen, Paris Muse opens up the Paris art world for both knowledgeable art lovers and those who just want to know what they're looking at, for groups of no more than four. She offers both in-depth tours of specific artists or periods, and general "best of" tours in art galleries, museums, or current expositions. They also do kids' tours with a special treasure hunt. All guides are teachers or PhD students in their areas of expertise, not tour guides, so it's like going on a tour with a good friend who is very knowledgeable. Prices vary from €60-110, depending on the length of the tour and the number of people. Check out the web site (www.parismuse.com) or call Ellen, ☎ 06 73 77 33 52, for more information.

■ Visiting The Ateliers

Every Paris neighborhood with a large number of artists' ateliers organizes an annual *portes ouvertes*, where the artists open their doors for a few days for the public. These are usually well-publicized around town, with the Mairie or a local artists' association providing maps and information. These open days are a great way to see what Paris art studios are really like, to chat with the artists themselves, and maybe – if you see something you like – take home a unique work of art.

Les Frigos (corner of Quai Panhard & Levassor and Rue Neuve Tolbiac, www.les-frigos.com) is one of the city's most successful legalized squats, with about 100 artists living and working in an abandoned 1920s meat-packing warehouse. There are *portes ouvertes* the last weekends in May and November, as well as regular concerts and cultural events at **Les Voûtes** (ground floor, enter by the garden).

The **Ateliers d'Artistes de Belleville** (32 Rue de la Mare, 20th, M° Jourdain, ☎ 01 46 36 44 09, www.ateliers-artistes-belleville.org; open Wednesday through Saturday, 2 to 6pm) is a collective gallery for the many artists of Belleville. They organize the annual *portes ouvertes* for five days the last week in May, with over 120 artists' ateliers open to the public.

Other regular *portes ouvertes* to look out for include **Montmartre-aux-Artistes** (in the 18th, every December, www.montmartre-aux-artistes.org), **Le 6ème Atelier d'Artistes** (artists of the 6th, every November, ☎ 01 45 48 02 29), **Gros Caillou-Quartier d'Arts** (7th, monthly, ☎ 01 47 05 94 07), **Artistes à la Bastille** (11th, every October, www.artistesalabastille.com), **Ateliers d'Artistes du 14ème** (14th, late May to early June, ☎ 01 45 45 67 14), **Goutte d'Or-Carré d'Art** (18th, every June, ☎ 01 42 23 56 56) and **Les Ateliers de Ménilmontant** (20th, every September, ☎ 01 46 36 47 17, www.artotal.com/menil).

LIVE JAZZ PAINTING

In the heart of Belleville is a tiny artist's studio and gallery run by the friendly Tunisian-born painter, Asnour. During the day he sets up a few tables for afternoon tea and snacks, and on Thursday nights he hosts live events such as poetry slams, music, and short films. Don't miss his performance painting to live jazz music on the first Thursday of the month (€2 donation requested). L'Atélier d'Asnour: 6 Rue Julien Lacroix, 20th, M° Ménilmontant, ☎ 01 46 36 19 15, www.asnour.org, closed Mondays.

■ Artist Squats

The squatting movement has taken over Paris, with artists too poor to afford studio space setting up shop in abandoned buildings, often decorating them to taste (which, needless to say, is not always in line with the neighbors'). In addition to Les Frigos (mentioned above), there are few other "tolerated" squats.

Chez Robert (Electrons Libres 59 Rue de Rivoli, 1st, M° Châtelet, www.59rivoli.org) has become recognized by city officials as the third most-visited contemporary art center in Paris. Visitors are welcome to wander through the artists' colorfully decorated studios (and there's plenty of art for sale if you see something you like). Tuesday through Sunday, 1:30 to 7:30pm. Closed August.

Théâtre de Verre (6 Impasse Barrier, via the Rue de Citeaux, 12th, M° Reuilly-Diderot). Not far from the Marché d'Aligre, this legalized artists' squat has regular open days on Sunday afternoons, often with a bit of a reception or barbecue (those who arrive with a bottle of wine are particularly welcome).

La Miroiterie (88 Rue de Ménilmontant, 20th, M° Ménilmontant) has an "on your honor" store open during the day, usually without a soul in sight, with used clothing and home items neatly stacked for purchase or trade. The actual building is usually open to the public on the first Sunday of the month at 7:30pm.

A WORD TO
THE WISE

AUTHOR'S NOTE: *Squats are, by nature, a bit fleeting, so these listings could change. The most reliable source of information about the latest occupations and expulsions can be found at www.inter-face.net and www.artetsquats.com.*

■ Archeology & Restoration

There are plenty of opportunities to volunteer on *chantiers* (worksites) throughout Ile-de-France. They usually require a minimum commitment of 14 days (but there are a few weekend camps), and cost from €12/day for food and board in camping facilities. Most volunteers are young (but it's not a requirement), and come from all over the world. This isn't a luxury gig, but volunteers get to help restore a piece of French heritage. The web site is partly bilingual, but the chantier listings are all in French. If you don't understand, it's best to call and talk to them directly. **Rempart,** 1 Rue des Guillemites, 4th, M° St-Paul, ☎ 01 42 71 96 55, fax 01 42 71 73 00, www.remparts.com.

There are two specific *chantiers* in Ile-de-France run by the French heritage society **Paris Historique** (www.paris-historique.org): the **Maison de Fontainier**, a historic building that housed the arrival point of the 17th-century Medici aqueduct, and the 16th-century **Maison d'Ourscamp**. They organize monthly restoration weekends, with a donation of €4 per day to cover lunch (you need appropriate shoes and clothing for a work site). Call or stop by the information center (44-46 Rue François Miron, 4th, M° St-Paul, ☎ 01 48 87 74 31. Open Monday through Saturday, 2pm to 6pm) and ask for Karine Mourot or Franck Garnier. Their volunteers also conduct regular tours of historical sites around Paris.

Fashion & Beauty

■ Fashion Culture

The Birth of Haute Couture

Paris has been the fashion capital of the world since the great age of Louis XIV, when the whims and extravagances of his Versailles court set the tone for every boudoir in Europe. Haute couture was established in Paris when an English tailor, Charles Frederick Worth, set up his studio near the Paris Opéra in 1858 with the original idea of presenting his creations on live models. The fashion show was born and, soon after, an elite trade union formed to set the strict guidelines for the "haute couture" designation. France has been the yardstick for fashion ever since, even while gratefully borrowing foreign talent. There are 18 houses of haute couture in France today: Balmain, Pierre Cardin, Carven, Chanel, Christian Dior, Louis Féraud, Givenchy, Lecoanet Henant, Christian Lacroix, Lapidus, Guy Laroche, Hanae Mori, Paco Rabanne, Nina Ricci, Yves Saint Laurent, Jean-Louis Scherrer, Torrente, and Emanuel Ungaro.

UP-AND-COMING DESIGNERS

You'll find unique, hand-made clothing and accessories at affordable prices from the city's *jeune créateurs*, young designers who sell their creations direct to the public while they work toward their haute-couture dreams.

Two sure bets: the **Créateurs du Forum des Halles** (Porte Berger at the Forum des Halles, 1st) and the **Créateurs Goutte d'Or** (Rue des Gardes, 18th) the first street in Paris entirely devoted to young designer fashion. Enjoy the one-of-a-kind pieces, and just maybe one day you'll see something similar on the cover of *Vogue*!

Fashion Week

There are four Fashion Weeks in Paris each year: January and July for haute couture, March and October for prêt-à-porter (Ready-to-Wear). Designers camp out in the city's most prestigious hotels such as the Ritz and Hôtel Costes, models are seen at hotspots like La Suite and Le Cab, and fashion editors invade the boutiques of their favorite stomping ground, the Rue St-Honoré. Enjoy the electric atmosphere but, unless you're friends with Anna Wintour or on Chanel's client list, forget about trying to get into a show. Well, those shows anyway. Mere mortals looking for hints on the latest trends can attend one of the free weekly fashion shows held throughout the year at the Printemps (www.printemps.com) and Galeries Lafayette (www.galerieslafayette.com) department stores on Boulevard Haussmann. And, if you like what you see, you know where to find it! Sign-up at the stores' Welcome Desk or online.

Fashion & Costume Museums

Musée de la Mode et du Textile: At the Musée du Louvre, 107 Rue de Rivoli, 1st, M° Palais-Royal, ☎ 01 44 55 57 50, www.ucad.fr. Open Monday through Friday, 11am to 6pm (Wednesday until 9pm); Saturday and Sunday, 10am to 6pm. Entry €2.

Located in the Rohan wing of the Louvre, this museum showcases the evolution of female fashion and costume from the Middle Ages to the grand couturiers of the present day. A specialized fashion documentation library is open to the public by request (☎ 01 44 55 58 57).

Musée de la Mode de la Ville de Paris: At the Musée Galliera, 10 Avenue Pierre Ier de Serbie, 16th, M° Alma Marceau, ☎ 01 56 52 86 20. Open Tuesday through Sunday, 10am to 6pm. Entry €7, €3.50 for students under 25, free for kids under 13.

This museum, set in a Renaissance-style palace, has over 80,000 costumes and accessories, and 40,000 fashion prints and photographs collected from the past three centuries. Exhibitions showcase a specific part of the collections to the public, changing every six months. Closed between exhibitions.

Musée Hermès: 24 Rue du Faubourg Saint-Honoré, 8th, M° Concorde, ☎ 01 40 17 48 23.

Hermès' fashion house was founded in 1831 by an artisan shoemaker originally from Germany. The museum collection includes his collectibles and artworks from this time period, and houses temporary exhibits. An elegant place to visit, but don't expect a scarf museum!

Musée de la Parfumerie Fragonard: 9 Rue Scribe, 9th, M° Opéra ☎ 01 47 42 93 40, www.fragonard.com. Open Monday through Saturday, 9am to 5:30pm. Free guided tours.

Fragonard has been making perfume since 1926. Their museum retraces the history of perfume-making over the past three centuries (and steers you conveniently into their boutique when you're done).

■ Parisian Pampering

Parisians see spa treatments as a necessity, not a luxury, so you'll find many of the traditional spas to be quite reasonable. Thanks to a significant immigrant population, Paris also has a good selection of authentic *hammams* (also known as Turkish baths). Always call ahead to check on the hours for men and women (some days are mixed, you'll need a bathing suit). And leave your Puritan modesty in the locker room; the French don't bother covering up their naked bodies!

LESSONS IN PERFUME

Run by the French fragrance house L'Artisan Parfumeur, students at the **Atelier du Parfum** learn the secrets of perfume in their whimsical boutique classroom just across from the Louvre. Groups of up to 12 people are taught how to recognize the different essences, top notes and base notes, by comparing the primary natural ingredients with the final bottled fragrance. After a gourmet snack break, students learn about how a scent is brought to the public, from the original concept down to the actual bottle shape. Students leave with a certificate from the course, a booklet with everything they've learned, perfume testers from L'Artisan Parfumeur, discount certificates for the boutique, and a surprise gift. Classes in English and French, €95 per person; 2 Rue de l'Amiral Coligny, 1st, M° Louvre-Rivoli, ☎ 01 44 88 27 50, www.artisanparfumeur.com.

Hammams (Oriental Baths)

Hammam de la Mosquée, 39 Rue Geoffroy-Saint-Hilaire, 5th, M° Place Monge, ☎ 01 43 31 18 14.

If you dream of the Alhambra, you won't want to miss the baths inside this authentic 1920s Moroccan-style mosque. Entry to the *hammam* and heated pools costs €15. For €55, you also get a body scrub, massage, lunch and mint tea in the elaborately decorated tearoom when you're done. If you hate crowds, give Saturday a miss.

- Women only: Monday, Wednesday and Thursday, 10am to 9pm; and Friday, 2 to 9pm
- Men only: Tuesday, 2 to 9pm; and Sunday, 10am to 9pm

Les Bains du Marais, 31-33 Rue des Blancs Manteaux, 4th, M° Rambuteau, ☎ 01 44 61 02 02, www.lesbainsdumarais.com.

A very trendy Marais crowd comes here for the traditional steam baths and sauna in a relaxing marble-and-wood setting. There's also a hair salon, restaurant, tanning beds, and manicure/pedicure services. Towels, robe and shoes included, but don't forget your bathing suit on mixed days. Entry to the steam baths, sauna, pool and relaxation rooms, €30. Exfoliating scrub and massage, €30.

- Women only: Monday, 11am to 8pm; Tuesday, 11am to 11pm; and Wednesday, 10am to 7pm

- Men only: Thursday, 11am to 11pm; Friday, 10am to 8pm; Saturday, 10am to 8pm
- Mixed: Wednesday, 7 to midnight; Sunday, 11am to 11pm

Day Spas

Institut Guerlain, 68 Avenue des Champs-Elysées, 8th, M° Franklin D. Roosevelt, ☎ 01 45 62 11 21, www.guerlain.fr. Open Monday through Saturday, 9:30am to 6:45pm.

Reserve well in advance for this historic beauty institute. Renovated in 2002, its sumptuous, gilded beauty palace above the perfume boutique is frequented by Paris's lucky pampered ladies. Facials are from €75 for the *express* (one hour) or from €170 for face, eyes, neck and décolletage (two hours). They also do makeup, body treatments, pedicures, manicures, and hair removal.

Centre de Bien-être Caudalie, Hôtel Meurice, 228 Rue de Rivoli, 1st, M° Concorde, ☎ 01 44 58 10 77.

This luxury spa in the five-star Hôtel Meurice offers *vinothérapie* treatments, once only available at the famed Caudalie spa in Bordeaux, made from crushed grape-seed extract. Try the "Pulp Friction" massage or the "Crush Cabernet" scrub of grape seeds, honey and essential oils for €95. All treatments in the 9,900-square-foot spa give you access to the sauna, *hammam* and Jacuzzi. Complete the pampering with afternoon tea and cakes in the hotel's Art Nouveau-style Winter Garden.

Cinq Mondes Spa, 6 Square de l'Opéra, 9th, M° Opéra, ☎ 01 42 66 00 60, www.cinqmondes.com.

This is one of the newer spas to open in Paris, with its own range of all-natural spa products sold in the city's department stores. The spa takes its inspiration from around the world (*Cinq Mondes* means Five Worlds). Japanese, Indian, Brazilian, Middle Eastern and Chinese methods are combined for a very Zen experience in a very nature-friendly setting. Perfect for the inner tree-hugger in everyone. Facials, body treatments, Oriental hair removal, massages, yoga sessions and steam bath treatments from €45. The three-hour Anti-Stress Anti-Jetlag Ritual Treatment is €210.

La Sultane de Saba, 8*bis* Rue Bachaumont, 2nd, M° Sentier or Etienne-Marcel, ☎01 40 41 90 95, www.lasultanedesaba.com. Open Monday through Friday, 10am to 7:30pm; Saturday, 10am to 6pm.

La Sultane de Saba is a Moroccan beauty spa for men and women with its own line of products sold all over France. Treatments in the relaxing, exotic spa include facials (€39-54), henna tints (€10-25), body scrubs (€15-60), traditional oriental pedicures and manicures (€23-30), and oriental hair removal (€5-31). There are half-day packages for €100-170. All treatments include access to the *hammam*.

Paris

AUTHOR'S NOTE: *See also the* Where to Shop *section, page 226, for top Parisian beauty shopping spots!*

For Men Only

Marc Delacre, 17 Avenue Georges V, 8th, M° Georges V, ☎ 01 40 70 99 70.

Popular with French politicians, this men's salon is decorated in pale marble and brown leather, and private *cabines* equipped with phone and fax machine for busy professionals. Treatments include manicures, pedicures, UV tanning, massage, and special hair treatments.

Nickel, 48 Rue Francs Bourgeois, 3rd, M° Rambuteau, ☎ 01 42 77 41 10, www.nickel.fr. Open Monday through Friday, 11am to 7:30pm (Wednesday and Thursday until 9pm); Saturday, 10am to 7:30pm.

Nickel sells its men's skin and hair products all over the world. This Marais institute offers treatments such as facials, massages, and hair removals for the perfect swimmer's chest or cyclist's legs. Their second institute at the Printemps department store (Boulevard Haussmann, 9th) is decorated to look like the interior of a futuristic submarine. They also offer men's products from Acqua di Parma, Aramis Lab Series, Dolce & Gabbana, and Comme des Garçons.

Alain Maître Barbier, 8 Rue Saint Claude, 3rd, M° Chemin Vert, ☎ 01 42 77 55 80. Open daily, 9:15am to 7pm.

This old-fashioned barber shop specializes in clean shaves and beard or moustache trims, with lots of vintage shaving implements and photographs for decoration.

KIDS' CUTS

A paradise for children and frazzled parents, **Au Pays d'Oscar** (16 Rue Vavin, 6th, ☎ 08 26 00 06 16, www.au-pays-d-oscar.fr) specializes in children's hair, with cotton candy or *pain au chocolate* to make kids happy, and special family discounts to make parents happy. There are also special cocktails-and-cuts for moms and dads. Call the friendly, bilingual staff or check out the web site for more information. Open Monday, Tuesday and Friday, 10am to 9pm; Thursday, 10am to 7pm; Wednesday and Saturday, 9:30am to 6:30pm.

Parisian Makeovers

Ever wonder how to capture that elusive French allure? Jacqueline Sablayrolles, a chic, Swiss-born image consultant living in Paris since 1989, has been helping women of all nationalities do just that through her company, **La Mode – Le Club** (☎ 01 45 05 17 29, www.lamode-leclub.com).

She helps clients get the most flattering look that suits their personality and lifestyle, hand-picking top professional hairdressers and makeup artists, and knowing all the best Parisian shopping addresses for clothing and accessories. Jacqueline talks to the clients on the phone ahead of time to determine expectations and if they have specific shops they want to see. She decides which hairdresser will suit the personality of the client, whether it's a trendy stylist with models everywhere or a more discreet session in a private *cabine*, and acts as a buffer between clients and sales staff when shopping so there's no pressure to make purchases (she doesn't receive commissions from any shops). Jacqueline and her English-speaking staff make sure the clients always feel comfortable. The full Fashion Day costs €750 (€600 for hair and makeup only, €300 for just shopping). See the web site to learn about other services available through La Mode – Le Club, or call Jacqueline to arrange for your Parisian transformation!

DID YOU KNOW? *Did you think the term "fashion police" was just a cheeky description of someone who criticizes others' outfits? Not at all! The term came about in the late Middle Ages after laws restricting or regulating extravagance in dress (on religious or moral grounds) were passed by nobles to ensure that certain fabrics and styles were reserved for those who had the right to wear them. Fashion police patrolled the streets, fining or imprisoning dress-code violators.*

Most of the major Paris department stores have a personal shopper and image consultant who can help you find flattering clothes or suggest the right hairstyle and color. But if you're looking for a complete makeover and wardrobe fix (for men and women), put yourself in the hands of **Josy Mermet** and her expert team at Printemps department store (on the fourth floor of the "Printemps de la Mode," Boulevard Haussmann, 9th, M° Havre-Caumartin, ☎ 01 42 82 64 23, www.josymermet.com). She has been helping bring out the "inner you" in clients for over 25 years, focusing on hair, makeup and clothing style suited perfectly to the client's personality, lifestyle, and budget. Josy has a very flamboyant style of the classic sexy Parisian woman, but doesn't attempt to clone herself. Using a technique she calls *chromopsychology*, she takes about an hour asking the client questions about him or herself, while directing the stylist's sketches based on clients' hair texture, the way of moving, temperament, character, and bone structure. The stylist's sketches include recommended hairstyle, colors, textures, and clothing shapes. Her one-hour sessions are €120, which includes personal shopping selections but not the hair stylist (you can choose to take your artist's style sketches to your own hair dresser or use the one in the department store). Clients can e-mail Josy anytime afterwards for advice or shopping tips. If you're still not convinced, check out the before and after shots on her web site!

Tattoos & Piercing

Beauty is in the eye of the beholder!

Tin-Tin Tatouages, 37 Rue Douai, 9th, M° Blanche, ☎ 01 40 23 07 90, www.tin-tin-tattoos.com. Open Monday through Saturday, noon to 8pm.

A tattoo is the ultimate souvenir! And they've already done an Eiffel Tower, so don't be shy. Around since 1985, this spotless shop near Pigalle has a multilingual staff headed by the Chilean Tin-Tin.

Abraxas Paris, 9 Rue St Merri, 4th, M° Châtelet or Hôtel de Ville, ☎ 01 48 04 33 55, www.abraxas.fr. Open Monday, 11am to 8pm; Tuesday through Thursday, 11am to 9pm; Friday and Saturday, 11am to 10pm; and Sunday, 1 to 8pm.

Tattoos and piercing in a very elegant boutique that looks more like a jewelry shop than a tattoo parlor. They also hold regular art expositions.

■ Shopping Adventures

Tours

Shop like a Parisian with **Chic Shopping Paris** (☎ 06 14 56 23 11, www.chicshoppingparis.com), a custom-tailored shopping service by bilingual American Francophiles David, Nicole and Rebecca. Whether it's the finest French linens, one-of-a-kind gifts or the best chocolate truffles in town, these guides can help you find it. They have a selection of themed tours such as "Made in France" and "Très Tasty," or a tour can be customized based on a client's taste and budget. Reasonably priced at just €75 for a four- to five-hour tour, guides also provide lively sightseeing commentary during the tours, and can recommend their favorite restaurants and cafés (all completely unbiased – the guides don't receive commissions).

 AUTHOR'S NOTE: *Check out* Where to Shop, *pages 214-231, for detailed listings of top Paris shops and markets.*

Rachel Kaplan's **French Links Shopping Tours** (☎/fax 01 45 77 01 63, www.frenchlinks.com) are based on different themes such as Discount Designer Shopping, Art de Vivre, Food & Wine, Art & Antiques, and the "Pretty Woman" Beauty and Shopping Tour. Rachel is the author of *Best Buys to French Chic in Paris*, and has been giving sightseeing and shopping tours of her adopted country for over six years. The tours cost €400-€850 for up to six people. French Links can also arrange special tours of French wholesalers and exporters for fashion buyers. Check out the web site for the very detailed descriptions of each tour.

📖 *Suggested Reading:* Paris Fashion: A Cultural History, *by* Valerie Steele, *Berg Pub. Ltd., 1998.*

Auctions

Bitten by the eBay bug? Try the real thing at the Paris auction houses, or just go for the show! There are many auction houses in Paris, but the **Hôtel Drouot** is the one with the most prestigious history (for example, King Louis-Philippe's estate was auctioned off here in 1852). The crowd is full of experts, buyers, sellers, tourists and people who come regularly for the "show." The best spot is usually up front to the side so you can see, but people tend to move around, coming and going, in case you want to change seats. The *manettes* – plastic crates full of the kind of junk you'd find at a garage sale, from clothing to dishes to books – are usually sold off first from €10-50, a bit of potluck on the contents! Payment in cash or by French check only; a convenient cash machine is just outside). There's a free guide at the welcome desk that explains how it all works (in French only, so ask if you have any questions). Information can also be found at www.franceantiq.fr. There are no auctions in August.

Hôtel Drouot, 9 Rue Drouot, 9th, M°Richelieu-Drouot, ☎ 01 48 00 20 00. Open Tuesday through Friday, preview 11am to noon, auctions at 2pm. For the monthly schedule check www.gazette-drouot.com. This is the best place to start, with 16 auction rooms and a range of prices. The building itself is of little interest, built during the late 1970s to replace the original building when it became too crowded.

Drouot-Montaigne, 15 Avenue Montaigne, 8th, M° Alma Marceau, ☎ 01 48 00 20 99. This site is reserved for the prestigious international auctions of very high estimations. Go to watch, if not to buy.

Christie's, 9 Avenue Montaigne, 8th, M° Franklin D. Roosevelt, www.christies.com. Another exclusive auction house, Christie's also has regular classes on art and antique appraisal.

Salle de Ventes des Domaines, 17 Rue Scribe, 9th, M° Opéra, ☎ 01 44 94 78 78. Unclaimed items, customs seizures, and state-owned items for sale!

Artcurial, Hôtel Dassault, 7 Rond-Point des Champs-Elysées, 8th, M° Champs-Elysées-Clémenceau, ☎ 01 42 99 20 20 or 01 42 99 16 19, www.artcurial.com. The newest auction house in Paris also houses a library, gallery and café (open Monday through Saturday, 10:30am to 7pm). Stop by to browse the catalogs or visit the web site for upcoming auctions.

Paris

Language & Literature

One of the best ways to feel less like a tourist and more like a world traveler is to interact with the locals in a meaningful way (ie, more than just ordering dinner). Native English speakers living in Paris (a.k.a. expatriates, or *expats*) provide a strong and permanent link between their visiting compatriots and the French, bringing them together for modern literary salons, French-English conversation sessions, or simply for casual socializing in a friendly environment. By making an effort to meet and converse with Parisians, you'll get a real inside look at the city and its people – and maybe even make some new friends!

■ Dinner Groups

New Orleans-native **Jim Haynes** is a professor at the Sorbonne and former Swingin' Sixties editor of *Suck* magazine in London. For the past 30 years, Jim has been hosting **Sunday night dinners** for up to 70 at his converted artist's atelier in Montparnasse (Atelier A-2, 83 Rue de la Tombe Issoire, 14th, M° Denfert-Rochereau, ☎ 01 43 27 17 67 or 01 43 27 19 09, fax 01 43 20 41 95, jim_haynes@wanadoo.fr). People from all over the world mingle and exchange stories and Paris experiences. All you have to do to get invited is call up and reserve a spot (a €20 donation is requested). It's definitely a Parisian experience not to be missed!

Patricia Laplante-Collins hosts a **21st-Century Parisian Salon** every Sunday night at her apartment on the Ile St-Louis (35 Quai d'Anjou, 4th, M° Pont Marie, ☎ 01 43 26 12 88, fax 01 45 86 40 59, parissoirees@noos.fr), with dinner and guest speakers ranging from artists, musicians and authors to storytellers, shaman healers and wine experts. The goal of the group is to simply meet new people in a safe and culturally stimulating atmosphere. Call or e-mail Patricia to reserve your spot (a €20 donation is requested).

■ French-English Conversation

Conversation is an art in Paris, and what better way to get your high-school French up to speed? There are French-English conversation groups for all levels, both formal and informal. Check the free magazines *FUSAC* (France-USA Contacts, published twice monthly, www.fusac.org) or the monthly *Paris Voice* (www.parisvoice.com) for regular listings.

> **AUTHOR'S NOTE:** FUSAC *and* Paris Voice *are available at any English-language bar, bookshop, church or shop in Paris.*

Conversation Groups

Some groups are structured around improving your French (and for the French, their English). Others are more of a social gathering where you can chat and meet people without any pressure.

Michael and Véronique host **Teatime = Talktime** (☎ 01 43 25 86 55), a conversation group in their own home on Saturday evenings from 5:30 to 8:30 with snacks, tea, soft drinks and free-form conversation. The first half of the evening is conversation in any language (usually English), then Michael signals when everyone has to start speaking only French. €10 donation requested. Call to reserve a spot and get directions.

PONT DES ARTS PICNICS

Michael and Véronique (see above) also host Thursday night picnics on the Left Bank end of the Pont des Arts footbridge from spring through early fall. There's no need to call ahead, but everyone should bring something to drink and snacks (cups and a bottle opener will win you Brownie points). Call Michael if you have any questions, ☎ 01 43 25 86 55.

Parler Parlor (☎ 01 40 27 97 59 or 01 44 19 76 61, www.parlerparlor.com) offers free-form conversation in French and English four times a week at a local language school. Hostess Adrian Leeds creates groups balancing Anglophones and Francophones to speak 45 minutes in French and 45 minutes in English. The first session is free, then from €10 per session.

One-on-One Conversation

There are plenty of Parisians out there desperate to practice their English with real people (ie, not teachers). You'll find ads for conversation exchanges in the *FUSAC*. People usually meet up in cafés or other public places and chat informally. Just beware of "conversation *et plus si affinité*" ads (meaning, we'll do more than talk if we fancy each other).

■ Literary Readings

The schedule and locations of the city's many literary readings changes each season. The most reliable place to find current listings for poetry, novel and play readings in English is in the *Paris Voice* magazine. The English bookstores in Paris also host regular readings. **WH Smith** (248 Rue de Rivoli, 1st, M° Concorde, ☎ 01 44 77 88 99) regularly invites authors for readings and book signings, while the less formal **Shakespeare & Co** (37 Rue de la Bûcherie, 5th, M° St-Michel, ☎ 01 43 26 96 50) has literary readings every Wednesday evening at 4pm.

■ Writing Workshops

The English-language continuing-education center, WICE (www.wice-paris.org), offers an internationally renowned **Paris Writers Workshop** every summer for poetry, short story writing, creative nonfiction, and novel development. The week-long workshop costs €400, €320 for Early Bird registration.

For longer-term studies during the academic year, the University of London's British Institute in Paris has **Creative Writing Workshops** (www.bip.lon.ac.uk, look under "Advanced Courses") for poets and fiction writers (€355 per semester). The students produce the twice-annual literary journal, *Pharos*.

ENGLISH-LANGUAGE JOURNALS

Artists, writers and musicians have always found the culture-rich Parisian air conducive to artistic creation. English-language literary journals based out of Paris such as *FRANK* (www.readfrank.com), *Upstairs at Duroc* (from WICE; see below for information) and *Double-Change* (www.doublechange.com) provide poets, writers and artists from France, the US and around the world an outlet for their works. Interested in contributing that ode to the Paris métro? Check their submission guidelines online.

Dance & Dramatic Arts

■ Dance Instruction

 Le Centre de Danse du Marais: 41 Rue du Temple, 4th, M° Hôtel de Ville, ☎ 01 42 72 15 42, www.parisdanse.com. Open daily, 9am to 10:30 pm.

This is one of the most popular dance schools in Paris, offering classes for all levels in baroque dance, tango, African dance, Irish tap, ballroom dancing, salsa, Oriental dance, Egyptian dance, classic ballet, flamenco, jazz, hip-hop, rock-and-roll (swing), yoga, and even Japanese Buto. The entrance is at the end of a courtyard next to the Café de la Gare theater. Most instructors speak English. Sign-up fees include €8 for insurance and registration for one year; each course costs from €16 for one session to to €110 for 10. A "passport" lets you sample five different courses for €62, and there are summer deals, too. Those with an excess of talent should check out the professional audition notices posted in the hallway directly across the courtyard from the reception.

L'Ecole de Danse RMP, 40 Rue Quincampoix, 4th, M° Châtelet-Les Halles (in the courtyard, take the door to the left and go down the stairs), ☎ 06 83 01 96 41 or 01 69 39 30 28, www.salsarmp.com.

Learn real Cuban Salsa with Rogelio Martinez Piloto, from Havana, or Miami-style salsa classes with LeeRoy. Open for all levels, there are different hours scheduled for beginner, intermediate and advanced salsa dancers in a laid-back, informal atmosphere (instructors speak English, too). From €11 per class, less if you sign up for more than one.

Danse Centre Momboye, 25 Rue Boyer, 20th, M° Gambetta or Ménilmontant, ☎ 01 43 58 85 01, www.ladanse.com/momboye.

This unique dance center teaches many different African dance styles accompanied by live percussionists. Learn dance styles from Mali, Côte d'Ivoire, Burkina Faso, modern Afro-Latin, and even Oriental dance and polyphonic chanting. Classes for all levels throughout the week, all year long, and you don't have to speak French to understand. Rates from €14 per 90-minute class, lower rates for multiple classes. Children's classes available as well. Check the web site or send an e-mail for more info: centremomboye@wanadoo.fr.

La Casa del Tango, 11 Allée Darius-Milhaud, 19th, M° Ourcq, ☎ 01 40 40 73 60, www.lacasadeltango.net.

Ready for your first tango in Paris? The "House of Tango" organizes classes, workshops, tango balls, tea-time dances and acts as a cultural center for tango lovers from all over the world, with exhibitions and literary events in a very "Buenos Aires" atmosphere, right across from the Parc des Buttes-Chaumont. Initiation courses from €10 per session or €50 for six sessions. Check the web site for the latest schedule, events, and open house days.

Paris

■ Theater Workshops

The **Franco Américaine Cinéma et Théâtre** (FACT; 65 Rue de Reuilly, 12th, ☎/ fax 01 43 44 76 98, www.chez.com/fact/) has short-term **Bilingual Acting Workshops** every summer, and ongoing **American Acting in Paris** classes in English throughout the year.

YOU DON'T SAY!

You can take a five-day mime workshop at the **Ecole Internationale de Mimodrame de Paris** (17 Rue René Boulanger, 10th, ☎ 01 42 02 32 82), the school founded by the most famous mime in the world, Marcel Marceau. They take place throughout the year and have different themes; each session is limited to 20 people, so call well ahead of time to register.– €350 for the five-day sessions, or €600 for two five-day sessions; must be at least 18.

Acting International (☎ 01 42 00 06 79, fax 01 42 00 16 71, www.act-ing-international.com) teaches European and American acting methods and theatrical training. Full- and part-time classes are taught in both French and English; summer workshops start at €390 per week.

Where to Shop

Paris is one of the few cities in the world where shopping has been elevated to an art form and a venerable cultural pursuit. Americans may have been born to shop, but Parisians live for it. Their boutiques and markets are among the best in the world, whether you're looking for exclusive luxury goods or secondhand flea-market bargains. Sure, you can find many of the same things back home thanks to globalization, but in Paris it's the whole shopping experience that counts, with creative window displays to lure you in, and divinely wrapped packaging to carry your purchases home.

There are very few places in Paris where you can't shop, with interesting boutiques hidden in even the most obscure little streets and passages. Of course, too much of a good thing can cause no little anxiety in visitors who simply don't know where to start. Focus on what you can't get anywhere else, such as antiques, vintage garments and exclusive designers, art and handmade crafts, and gourmet food products.

SERIOUS SHOPPERS TAKE NOTE

 It would be impossible to list every noteworthy Parisian boutique in just one chapter, so anyone planning on doing some serious shopping may want to invest in a specialist guide. You'll find a good, up-to-date selection of shopping guides in the Englishlanguage bookshops (see page 231). Don't bother with any guide over two years old, since shopping information changes so quickly. Rachel Kaplan's *Best Buys to French Chic in Paris* (www.frenchlinks.com) is an electronic guide, so the listings are constantly updated. Clotheshorses should check out *Where To Wear Paris*, by Jill Fairchild and Gerri Gallagher, or Alicia Drake's *A Shopper's Guide to Paris Fashion*.

See the *Cultural Adventures* section, page 202, for information about customized shopping tours.

Practicalities

■ Opening Hours

Most shops are open 10am to 7pm, Monday through Saturday. Smaller boutiques may close at lunch, on Mondays and for all or part of the month of August. Many shops in the Marais are open on Sundays, and the larger stores on the Champs-Elysées remain open until midnight every night of the week.

■ How to Pay

Department stores and luxury shops are well-equipped for international traveler's checks and American Express, but be prepared to pay in cash or with VISA/MasterCard at the average boutique. Sales tax is already included on the price tag (so it's easy to know exactly what the final cost will be).

> **AUTHOR'S NOTE:** *Some shops will ask if you have* "monnaie" *(change) if you try to pay with a large-denomination note.*

■ VAT Refunds

Non-EU residents who spend at least €175 in one store (on the same day) can claim a 12-15% tax refund (called *détaxe*). The shop assistant will fill out a special form (you'll need your passport or a copy), which you'll need to have stamped at the airport customs desk before leaving the EU. Mail this back to the store (many provide pre-addressed envelopes for this) within three months to receive the refund by credit card or check.

■ Sales

The twice-annual clothing sales, called *les soldes,* take place for five weeks in late January and again in late June, with discounts of 30-60% off the regular prices. Parisians line up outside their favorite shops on the opening day of the sales, and by the final weeks there's hardly anything left!

■ Etiquette

Parisian shop assistants are famous for being rude, even to other Parisians, so don't take it personally. Hold up your end by adhering to a few basic rules: always, always, always say *Bonjour, Madame/Monsieur* when entering a shop, and *Merci, au revoir Madame/Monsieur* when leaving. If you just want to look around without any assistance, just say

Paris

Je regarde, merci. No matter what happens, remember to be patient – the customer may always be right in the US, but in France a shop owner would often rather lose a sale than lose face in an argument.

Shopping by Neighborhood

In Paris, the best shopping streets happen to be in the top sightseeing districts, making it easy to do a bit of both!

■ St-Germain-des-Prés and St-Sulpice (6th)

This prime shopping district combines upscale galleries, old-fashioned boutiques, and popular mainstream shops. Antiques, art galleries, and chic home décor shops are concentrated along the **Quai Voltaire**, **Rue de Baune**, **Rue de Lille**, **Rue des Beaux Arts**, **Rue Jacob**, **Rue Bonaparte**, **Rue de Seine**, and the **Rue de Bac**. Designer and trendy clothing stores can be found around the **Place St-Germain-des-Prés** (Dior, Vuitton), **Boulevard St-Germain**, **Rue du Four**, **Rue St-Sulpice**, and **Rue de Sèvres**, **Rue de Rennes** (Céline, Kenzo), and **Rue des Saints Pères** (Paco Rabanne, Prada, Ferragamo, Sonyia Rykiel, Barbara Bui, Yoji's Y). Discount clothing shops are grouped around the **Rue St-Placide**, **Rue du Cherche-Midi** and the lower end of **Rue de Rennes**.

■ The Marais & St-Paul (4th)

The narrow streets of the Marais are packed with trendy clothing and accessories stores, art galleries and charming gift boutiques. It's one of the few neighborhoods where shops are open on Sundays. Almost any street in the area between **Rue des Francs Bourgeois, Rue Roi de Sicile, Rue de Turenne** and **Rue du Temple** is worth exploring, but the **Rue des Rosiers** remains the most popular, with its mix of kosher delis and designer boutiques (Issey Miyake, Bill Torrade, Annick Goutal). The St-Paul quarter is known for its antiques shops, concentrated around the **Rue St-Paul** and its antique village. There are also art galleries and unique shops along the **Rue François Miron**.

■ Rue Etienne Marcel (2nd)

This whole street is lined with hip clothing stores and designer boutiques, culminating in the upscale **Place des Victoires** (Thierry Mugler, Yoji Yammamto, Cerruti Jeans, Kenzo). Some of the funkier addresses can be found on the side-streets behind **St-Eustache** and off the **Rue Montorgueil** (Diesel, Gas, Paul & Joe, Kabuki).

■ Covered Passages

The covered shopping galleries of Paris, dating from the early- to mid-19th century, are a pleasure to shop; each has its own distinct personality and features quaint boutiques selling everything from secondhand books and artisan accessories to antique toys and gourmet treats.

Galeries du Palais Royal (Jardins du Palais Royal, 1st, M° Palais-Royal): Three galleries around the Jardins du Palais Royal, with vintage-artifact collectors' shops, antiques, art galleries and upscale clothing and beauty boutiques.

Galerie Véro-Dodat (19 Rue J.J. Rousseau, 1st, M° Palais-Royal): A small passage with gift boutiques and the Capia antique doll shop.

Passage Choiseul (44 Rue des Petits-Champs, 2nd, M° Quatre-Septembre): Nothing fancy, just a bazaar of practical shops and gift boutiques in a passage that has been virtually unchanged since it was created in 1827.

Galerie Vivienne (4 Rue des Petits-Champs, 2nd, M° Bourse): The most luxurious of the covered passageways, with the famous Legrand wine boutique, a toy shop, tearoom, clothing boutiques.

Galerie Colbert (6 Rue des Petits-Champs, 2nd, M° Bourse) Another luxury passage with upscale designers and gift boutiques.

Passage du Grand-Cerf (4 Rue Dussouds, 2nd, M° Etienne-Marcel): Artisan boutiques and hand-made accessories.

Commerce St-André (130 Boulevard St-Germain, 6th, M° Odéon): Gift boutiques and cafés.

Passage des Panoramas (11 Boulevard Montmartre, 2nd, M° Grands-Boulevards): Vintage postcards and stamp collectors' shops, little restaurants.

Passage Jouffroy (10 Boulevard Montmartre, 9th, M° Grands-Boulevards): Secondhand books and vintage-gifts shops.

Passage Verdeau (31*bis* Rue du Faubourg Montmartre, 9th, M° Le Pelletier): Collectors' items and antique cameras.

Passage Brady (46 Rue du Faubourg St-Denis, 10th, M° Château d'Eau): Split by Boulevard Strasbourg, half of the passage is occupied by Indian/Pakistani shops and restaurants, half by costume shops.

■ St-Honoré & Rivoli (1st)

Favorite stomping grounds of the fashionista pack, the classic Parisian shops of the ancient **Rue St-Honoré** rub elbows with some of the hottest designer concept stores of the moment (Colette, Gucci, Christian Lacroix, John Galliano). The price tags go up as you head west of the Palais Royale, skyrocketing at the luxury jewelry boutiques on the **Place**

Vendôme (Bulgari, Chaumet, Fred, Cartier, Bregnet, Boucheron). Cost-conscious young Parisians get the right look on a budget at the trendy clothing chains along **Rue de Rivoli** (Zara, H&M, Etam, Kookaï, Sephora, Promod).

■ Madeleine (8th)

Gourmet food stores, designer boutiques, and posh interior décor boutiques dominate the **Place de la Madeleine** and the **Rue Royal** (Swarovski, Pierre Cardin, Cerruti). Casual shopping is over once you reach the couture houses and exclusive art galleries of the **Rue du Faubourg St-Honoré** (Hermès, YSL, Missoni, Gucci, Prada, Bottega Veneta, Lanvin).

■ Champs-Elysées (8th)

The Golden Triangle has the highest concentration of luxury designer boutiques and couture houses in Paris. This window-shopping wonderland is made up of the **Avenue Georges V** (Givenchy, Jean-Paul Gaultier, Balenciaga, YSL), **Avenue Matignon** (Thierry Mugler, Prada, Inès de la Fressange, Pucci, Dolce & Gabbana, Louis Vuitton, Dior, Jean Louis Scherrer, Escada, Valentino, Nina Ricci, Chanel), and the **Avenue des Champs-Elysées** (Gucci, Carven, Torrente, Lancel, Boss, Louis Vuitton).

■ Rue de Passy (6th)

This narrow winding street is one of the most pleasant shopping areas of the posh 16th, with a mix of prêt-à-porter shops and designer accessory boutiques (Kenzo, Christofle, Lancel, Caroll, Kookai, Et Vous, Ferragamo, Gerard Darel, MAC, Bouchara, Lulu Castagnette, Sephora, Wolford, Anne Fontaine, Joseph, Furla).

■ Montmartre (18th)

Forget about the souvenir shops at the Place du Tertre. There are plenty of up-and-coming designers, vintage-clothing shops, and imaginative gift boutiques along the **Rue des Abbesses, Rue Vieuville** and **Rue des Trois Frères**.

■ Alternative Shopping Areas

Looking for something completely different? Those willing to brave the city's lesser-known neighborhoods and ethnic enclaves will find some unusual boutiques and excellent deals. **Rue des Taillandiers, Rue de Charonne** and **Rue Keller** (11th, M° Ledru-Rollin) are full of punk and skate shops, DJ record stores and funky vintage-clothing boutiques. **Rue**

Oberkampf and Rue J.P. Timbaud (11th, M° Parmentier) are full of edgy young designers, discount shops, and typical Parisian butchers, bakeries and bistros. Toward **Rue de Ménilmontant** and all along **Boulevard de Belleville** (11th/20th, M° Ménilmontant) are North African bazaars and French Caribbean food markets. **Rue de Belleville** (19th/20th, M° Belleville) is lined with Chinese gift shops and grocery stores. Venture in to the African clothing boutiques, Moroccan music shops and Algerian delis around **métro Barbès-Rochechouart** (18th), including **Rue Dejean** and **Rue de la Goutte d'Or**.

SHOPPING MALLS

There are actually quite a few indoor shopping malls in Paris, but most of them are small, outdated and full of identical chain stores. They may be convenient for Parisians, but visitors can find much nicer places to spend their limited time (and euros).

Department Stores

Known in France as *les grands magasins*, Paris's department stores offer one-stop shopping for everything from clothing and gifts to books and music, and often have their own cafés and restaurants. Handy services include coat check, tax refund desk, currency exchange, and a ticket agent for major shows and museum passes. Even the smaller department stores usually have a service desk to help international customers. Whether you're in a hurry or trying to stay out of the rain, these are sure bets for shopping success.

■ La Samaritaine

Quai du Louvre, 1st, M° Pont Neuf (direct access) or Louvre-Rivoli, ☎ 01 40 41 20 20, www.lasamaritaine.com. Open Monday through Saturday, 9:30am to 7pm (Thursday until 9pm, Saturday until 8pm). This is a medium-sized department store overlooking the Seine, with a separate building for the men's department. It has an Art Deco exterior, Art Nouveau interior, and a popular rooftop café with great views.

■ Bazar de l'Hôtel de Ville (BHV)

52 Rue de Rivoli, 4th, M° Hôtel de Ville (direct access), ☎ 01 42 74 90 00, www.bhv.fr. Open Monday through Saturday, 9:30am to 7pm (Wednesday and Friday until 8:30pm). BHV is the department store where Parisians go for everyday shopping, since it's better-known for its interior décor and

Paris

home improvement departments than anything else. Don't miss the Bricolo Café on the lower-level, decorated to look like a vintage tool shed.

■ Bon Marché

24 Rue du Sèvres, 7th, M° Sèvres-Babylone, ☎ 01 44 39 80 00, www.lebon-marche.fr. Open Monday through Saturday, 9:30am to 7pm (open later on Thursday and Saturday; closed Sunday). This elegant department store near St-Germain-des-Prés is the most typically Parisian of all the Grands Magasins, best known for its beauty and fashion departments. There are regular cultural expositions on the second floor. Just behind (connected by a skyway) is the **Grand Epicerie** (☎ 01 44 39 81 00, www.lagrande-epicerie.fr, or click on the link on the Bon Marché site; both have English versions), a gourmet supermarket open Monday through Saturday, 8:30am to 9pm.

■ Le Printemps

64 Boulevard Haussmann, 9th, M° Havre-Caumartin, ☎ 01 42 82 50 00, www.printemps.com. Open Monday through Saturday, 9:35am to 7pm (Thursday until 10pm). Printemps Haussmann is one of the city's largest department stores, spread out over three buildings (*Homme, Mode* and *Beauté & Maison*). Their revamped beauty department, opened in November 2003, is supposedly the largest in the world. The best time to visit is weekday mornings, otherwise be prepared for massive crowds. Free fashion shows are held every Tuesday at 10am for the international clientele. If power shopping isn't your thing, head to the top floor of the *Beauté & Maison* building for fantastic panoramic views.

■ Galeries Lafayette

40 Boulevard Haussmann, 9th, M° Havre-Caumartin, ☎ 01 42 82 34 56. Open Monday through Saturday, 9:30am to 7:30pm (Thursday until 9pm). Galeries Lafayette is so popular with international visitors that they've even got their own double-decker-bus tours of Paris (the *Cars Rouges*). Built in 1912, the store features a stunning neo-Byzantine stained glass dome and Art Nouveau architectural details. Their free fashion show takes place every Tuesday at 11am (it's possible to sign up on their web site). Next door is a smaller building housing the men's department and the Lafayette Gourmet food store.

■ Franck et Fils

80 Rue de Passy, 16th, M° Muette, ☎ 01 44 14 38 00. Open Monday through Saturday, 10am to 7pm (until 7:30pm Saturday). This tiny women's department store caters to the chic ladies of the 16th with luxury brands like Tods, Burberry and Chanel. There's a young designer's sec-

tion, a particularly nice lingerie department, and they even stock the must-have Diptyque candles. On the top floor (past the bridal section) is a little café for lunch or afternoon tea.

Antiques, Art & Crafts

Louvre des Antiquaires: 2 Place du Palais Royal, 1st, M° Palais-Royal. Over 205 high-end antiques dealers, completely indoors.

CSAO (*Compagnie du Sénégal et de l'Afrique de l'Ouest*), 1-3 Rue Elzévir, 3rd, M° Chemin Vert, ☎ 01 44 54 55 88. A large boutique selling traditional and contemporary crafts from recycled materials by a collective of West African artists. Open Monday through Saturday, 11am to 7pm; Sunday, 2 to 7pm. CSAO also has an African arts gallery down the street at 15 Rue Elzévir, open Monday through Saturday, 11am to 7pm.

Village St-Paul, between Rue St-Paul and Rue Charlemagne, 4th, M° St-Paul. About 60 vintage-clothing boutiques and antiques shops in a series of cobblestoned courtyards. Open 10am to 7pm, closed Tuesday and Wednesday.

L'Atélier 74, 74 Rue de la Verrerie, 4th, M° Hôtel-de-Ville, ☎ 01 42 72 34 84. A collective of 12 artisans sell their hand-crafted jewelry, clothes, décor, gifts and art at this small boutique. Open weekdays, 11am to 8:30pm; Saturdays until 11pm; Sundays from 2 to 8pm.

Toast Gallery, 3 Rue de l'Estrapade, 5th, M° Place Monge, ☎ 01 44 07 04 22. This is the ready-to-wear of art galleries, destined to bring art to the masses. Paintings and photographs are sold in a non-snobby atmosphere where you can browse by style, size, artist or price (everything is priced between €50 and €915). Wednesday through Sunday, 11am to 8:30pm

Carré Rive Gauche, A collective of art galleries and antique dealers in the area bordered by the Quai Voltaire, Rue de l'Université, Rue des Saints-Pères, and Rue du Bac. 6th, M° Rue-du-Bac.

Viaduc des Arts, 1-129 Avenue Daumesnil, 12th, M°Gare de Lyon or Bastille. Over 50 artisans and designers in atelier-boutiques under the restored brick arches of a former elevated railway.

Marché Parisien de la Création, Boulevard Edgar Quinet (at foot of Montparnasse), 14th, M° Montparnasse. An open-air market of over 120 artists and designers selling paintings and crafts. Open Sundays, 10am to dark.

TIP: *Check with the Paris Convention & Visitors Bureau (www.paris-touristoffice.com) or the weekly* Pariscope *magazine for the schedule of current and upcoming art fairs.*

Paris

Boutique de l'Artisanat Monastique, 68 Avenue Denfert-Rochereau, 14th, M° Denfert-Rochereau or RER Port Royal, ☎ 01 43 35 15 76. A large boutique selling linens, foods, and crafts made in French monasteries and convents all over the country. Open weekdays, noon to 6:30pm; Saturdays, 2 to 7pm.

Village Suisse, 78 Avenue de Suffren, 15th, M° La Motte-Piquet-Grenelle. Over 150 antique dealers, interior decorators and art galleries in an open village. Open 11am to 7pm, closed Tuesday and Wednesday.

Flea Markets

Also known as the *marché aux puces*, the Paris flea markets are legendary. The Puces de St-Ouen are certainly the largest, but better deals may be found for low-budget items in the smaller flea markets.

A WORD TO
THE WISE

AUTHOR'S NOTE: *When shopping the flea markets, always carry cash, take an empty shopping bag to carry small items home and don't be afraid to haggle (rainy days are the best for getting good deals).*

Marché aux Puces de St-Ouen: Located just outside the city limits since 1885, this is the largest flea market in the world (over 17 acres), divided into 13 specialized markets (some indoors) and over 2,000 individual dealers. The oldest is the **Marché Vernaison**, a real maze of surprises and bargains among the china, silverware, toys, furniture and clothing, with the lively Chez Louisette bistro hidden in the back. You can take the métro (M° Porte de Clignancourt), but you'll have to walk through the temporary, crowded stalls of new junk and street entrepreneurs trying to sell authentic Rolex's before getting to the real market on the other side of the elevated highway. It's best to arrive by Bus 85 (from Luxembourg Gardens via the Louvre), which stops in the heart of the Puces at the Marché Paul Bert (except Sundays). Here you'll find the local tourism office (☎ 01 58 61 22 90), where you can pick up a free map – highly recommended! Open Saturday, Sunday, Monday, 9:30am-6pm (don't arrive too early, since most shops open slowly). Many shops are closed in August. The market has public toilets (at the Marché Jules-Valles), parking garages (not free), cash machines, international shipping companies, currency exchange bureaus, and plenty of cafés and snack bars. See the brilliantly helpful bilingual web site for maps and details.

Puces de la Porte de Vanves: Avenue Georges Lafenestre and Avenue Marc Sangnier, 14th, M° Porte-de-Vanves. This outdoor market is more laid-back than the one at St-Ouen, and much smaller. Typical items include paintings, antiques, old toys, vintage magazines, knick-knacks and secondhand books. Open Saturday and Sunday, 7am to 1pm (the afternoon market is for new clothing and household items).

USEFUL TERMS

Brocante is basically anything secondhand or vintage (even the junk found at garage sales), and a *brocanteur* is someone who sells it. An *antiquaire* sells actual antiques, called *antiquités*, and the prices reflect this difference. Don't get duped. A chair *d'époch Louis XIV* was around during the Sun King's reign, while a chair in the *style Louis XIV* could have been made yesterday.

Marché Beauvau, Place d'Aligre, 12th, M° Ledru-Rollin. This small covered market has a few flea-market stands of vintage clothing, antiques, crockery and fun junk within the much larger food market. Considered one of the least expensive markets in town. Open Tuesday through Saturday, 8am to 1pm and 4 to 7:30pm; Sunday, 8am to 1pm.

Orphelins-Apprentis d'Auteuil, 40 Rue la Fontaine, 16th, M° Jasmin, ☎ 01 44 14 75 75. Set inside the marvelous garden sanctuary of a children's home, this virtually unknown boutique (similar to a Salvation Army shop) sells clothing, furniture, lace, jewelry and books donated by Parisians to support the charity. Open weekdays and the first Saturday of the month, 2:30 to 6pm. Closed August.

DID YOU KNOW?

AUTHOR'S NOTE: *Temporary neighborhood flea markets are advertised as* Brocante *or* Vide-Grenier, *and are usually made up of locals who've emptied out their closets (although some professionals sneak in as well). Look for signs posted on street corners or check the Paris Convention & Visitors Bureau web site (www.paris-touristoffice.com).*

Specialized Markets

■ Stamps

Marché des Timbres, Avenue Matignon, Rond-Point des Champs-Elysées, 8th, M° Franklin-D-Roosevelt. An outdoor stamp- and postcard-collector's market. Open Thursdays and weekends, 9am to 7pm.

■ Books

Marché aux Livres, Parc Georges Brassens, 15th, M° Convention. Over 60 antique and secondhand book vendors. Open weekends, 9am to 6pm.

AUTHOR'S NOTE: *The bouquinistes have been selling secondhand books, magazines and vintage prints along the Seine for over 200 years. Look for their green boxes along the Quai de Conti or Quai de la Tournelle on the Left Bank, and Quai de l'Hôtel de Ville or Quai de la Mégisserie on the Right Bank.*

■ Food Markets & Gourmet Shops

Outdoor Markets

Rue Montorgueil (2nd, M° Etienne-Marcel or Sentier). Old-fashioned pedestrian market street open daily (some shops closed Sundays).

Rue Rambuteau (3rd, M° Rambuteau). Market street in the Marais, shops normally open Tuesday through Saturday.

Rue Mouffetard (5th, M° Censier-Daubenton or Place Monge). A historic market street with an open market toward the bottom, open Tuesday through Sunday morning (stands close for lunch).

Marché du Boulevard Raspail (6th, M° Rennes). This large covered market between the Rue du Cherche Midi and the Rue de Rennes is open Tuesday and Friday, 7am to 1:30pm. On Sunday there's an organic market (*marché bio*), 9am to 1pm.

Rue de Buci (6th, M° Odéon). A traditional market street in the chic St-Germain-des-Prés district, with open market stands, Tuesday through Sunday (stands close for lunch).

Rue Cler (7th, M° Ecole-Militaire). Traditional market street in a stylish neighborhood, shops open Tuesday through Saturday.

Rue du Faubourg St-Denis (10th, M° Château d'Eau or Strasbourg-St-Denis). This busy market street has a mix of traditional and ethnic food shops. Some great bargains. Shops open Tuesday through Saturday, and Sunday morning.

Marché Bastille (11th, M° Bastille or Breguet-Sabine). This large market extends along the Boulevard Richard Lenoir on Thursday and Sunday mornings. Prices get cheaper as you get closer to the Place de la Bastille.

Marché Belleville (11th/20th, M° Couronnes). Selling produce and spices from around the world, this exotic market stretches all the way from métro Belleville to métro Ménilmontant. Open Tuesday and Friday mornings.

Rue Daguerre (14th, M° Denfert-Rochereau). Traditional market street, open Tuesday through Sunday, with open food market stalls on Sunday.

Rue Poteau (18th, M° Jules Joffrin). This traditional market street has a small outdoor market in the mornings (on the corner of Rue Duhesme). Shops open Tuesday through Saturday.

Rue Dejean (18th, M° Château Rouge). This is the city's largest African market, with great deals in the shops and market stalls, open daily.

 AUTHOR'S NOTE: *There are over 75 neighborhood markets in Paris. Be sure to ask your hotel concierge where to find the closest one in your neighborhood.*

Covered Markets

Marché des Enfants-Rouges (39 Rue de Bretagne, 3rd, M° Temple). This is the oldest covered market in Paris, dating back to 1612 and completely renovated in 2002. There are a small number of stands with traditional market products. Open Tuesday through Thursday, 9am to 2pm and 4 to 9pm; Friday and Saturday, 9am to 8pm; and Sunday, 9am to 2pm.

Marché St-Quentin (85*bis* Boulevard Magenta, 10th, M°Poissonière or Gare de l'Est). A lovely historic covered market of iron and glass, with produce, flowers, gifts, food products, bakery, and some flea-market stands. Open Monday through Saturday, 8am to 1pm and 3:30 to 7:30pm; Sunday, 8am to 1pm.

Marché Beauvau (Place d'Aligre, 12th, M° Ledru-Rollin). The open market has existed since 1777 (the covered market was built a century later), with both flea-market and produce stands, and rock-bottom prices. Open Tuesday through Saturday, 8am to 1pm and 4 to 7:30pm; Sunday, 8am to 1pm.

Marché de Passy (1 Rue Bois le Vent, 16th, M° La Muette). Smack in the center of the chic Passy shopping district, this covered market features gourmet produce and deli stands. Open Tuesday through Saturday, 8am to 1pm and 4 to 7:30pm; Sunday, 8:30am to 1pm.

Food & Wine Boutiques

The two of the largest gourmet supermarkets with everything from wines and cheeses to produce and dry goods are **Gourmet Lafayette** and **La Grande Epicerie du Bon Marché** (see *Department Stores* section above).

The Place de la Madeleine (8th) is home to many famous gourmet food boutiques, including **Fauchon** (#26-30), **Hédiard** (#21), the **Boutique Maille** (#6), and the **Maison de la Truffe** (#19). Just up the road is **Lavinia** (3-5 Boulevard de la Madeleine, 1st, M° Madeleine, ☎ 01 42 97

20 20), the largest wine boutique in France, with wines and spirits from France and around the world.

> **DID YOU KNOW?** *Fauchon, at Place de la Madeleine, sells little pots of honey made by bees kept on the Opéra Garnier rooftop!*

For smaller, independently run boutiques, try **Izraël** (30 Rue François Miron, 4th, M° St-Paul, ☎ 01 42 72 66 23), an exotic *épicerie* opened in 1947 with products from every corner of the earth; **Goumanyat** (3 Rue Dupuis, 3rd, M° Temple, ☎ 01 44 78 96 74), a specialist in gourmet spices and cooking ingredients in a former 19th-century apothecary (call ahead, very irregular hours); or **G. Detou** (58 Rue Tiquetonne, 2nd, M° Etienne-Marcel, ☎ 01 42 36 54 67), a wholesale boutique for baking ingredients (including beautiful edible flowers), open to the public.

Legrand Filles et Fils (1 Rue de la Banque or Galerie Vivienne, 2nd, M° Bourse, ☎ 01 42 60 07 12) is an historic, family-run wine boutique with a tiny *épicerie* selling gourmet teas, coffees and candies. The relatively new **L'Epicerie & Le Champagne** (12 Rue Parrot, 12th, M° Gare de Lyon, ☎ 01 46 28 13 50) specializes in Champagnes at all prices, as well as foie gras, Andalucian hams, caviar, and candies. They are near the Viaduc des Arts. Supplier to the palace hotels and Michelin restaurants, **Da Rosa Epicerie** (62 Rue de Seine, 6th, M° Odéon, ☎ 01 40 51 00 09) now sells the same high-quality wines, hams, oils, truffles and cheeses direct to the public. **Au Roi de Bretagne** and **Coop Breizh** (10 & 12 Rue du Maine, 14th, M° Montparnasse, ☎ 01 43 20 84 60) specialize in cider, whiskey, sea salt, Quimper faïence and foods from Brittany.

> **AUTHOR'S NOTE:** *Stock up on French kitchen supplies like copper pots and Peugeot salt and pepper grinders at La Bovida (36 Rue Montmartre, 2nd, M° Etienne Marcel, ☎ 01 42 36 09 99); or down the street at Mora (13 Rue Montmartre, 2nd, ☎ 01 45 08 19 24). The pros shop here!*

Specialty Stores

■ Fashion & Beauty

Trendy Boutiques & Concept Stores

Colette, 213 Rue St-Honoré, 1st, M° Tuileries, ☎ 01 55 35 33 90, www. colette.fr. This is where Parisian fashion editors come to find out what will be "in" next season. All the latest clothing for men and women, home design objects, shoes, accessories, books, music and the famous Water Bar. Come during Fashion Week for some great people-watching.

L'Eclaireur, 3ter Rue des Rosiers, 4th, M° St-Paul, ☎ 01 48 87 10 22, www.leclaireur.com. The same concept as Colette but with an edgier, down-to-earth style. This is the flagship store, with other locations at 7 &10 Rue Hérold, 1st; 12 Rue Malher, 4th (men's only); 26 Avenue des Champs-Elysées, 8th; and 129-133 Galerie de Valois (Palais Royal), 1st.

Agnès b., Rue du Jour, 1st, M° Etienne-Marcel or Châtelet-Les Halles, ☎ 01 45 08 56 56, www.agnesb.fr. The classic French designer of timeless, comfortable clothes has locations all over the world, but the Rue du Jour might as well be the Rue Agnès b., because it has five different boutiques on one street for men, women, babies, children, and sportswear.

Scooter, 10 Rue de Turbigo, 1st, M° Etienne-Marcel, ☎ 01 45 08 50 54, www.scooter.fr. Modern, ethnic-inspired clothing, accessories and home décor objects by the designer Zaza make this boutique popular with the arts and music crowd. There's a second, smaller shop on Rue du Dragon, 6th.

Kenzo, 1 Rue du Pont Neuf, 1st, M° Pont-Neuf, ☎ 01 73 04 20 00, www.kenzo.fr. This new flagship store, opened summer 2003 in one of the renovated Samaritaine buildings, houses the designer's entire line of accessories, perfume, women's clothing (including the less expensive Jeans and Jungle lines), children's clothing and men's clothing, on four floors. At the top is the Philippe Starck-designed **Kong** restaurant and bar, a crazy hot-pink and Plexiglass paradise with views over the Seine, and the lower-level **Lô Sushi** bar designed by Andrée Putman.

John Galliano Boutique, 384 Rue St-Honoré, 1st, M° Madeleine, ☎ 01 55 35 40 40, www.johngalliano.com. One of the most provocative designers of the decade, Galliano opened his only ready-to-wear boutique in Paris in 2003, with the entire women's collection and accessories on two floors in what he describes as "high-tech romance" décor. If the price tags are a bit steep, pick up one of the delicious-smelling Dyptique "Essence of Galliano" candles for under €40.

Le Shop, 3 Rue d'Argout, 2nd, M° Sentier, ☎ 01 40 26 07 75. This alternative, mini-department store on two levels has everything from streetwear and clubwear clothing and accessories to a tattoo/piercing parlor, CD shop and live DJ. A great place to pick up Paris clubbing flyers.

Agatha Ruiz de la Prada, 9 Rue Guénégaud, 6th, M° Odéon, ☎ 01 43 25 86 88, www.agatharuizdelaprada.com. This Spanish designer's concept store is about color and happy shapes like flowers and hearts – not one thing is black! Find clothing, children's toys, notebooks, décor and gifts in an upbeat shop on two floors.

Antoine et Lili, "Le Village," 95 Quai de Valmy, 10th, M° Jacques-Bonsergent, ☎ 01 40 37 34 86, www.antoineetlili.com. This is the heart of the Antoine et Lili empire of trendy kitsch, with two colorful bou-

Paris

tiques (clothing/accessories and interior décor) and an adorable tearoom overlooking the Canal St-Martin.

Stella Cadente Living Room, 93 Quai de Valmy, 10th, ☎ 01 42 09 66 60. Romantic women's clothing, accessories and home décor in a girly boutique on the Canal St-Martin. There's also a little tearoom in the back open in the afternoons, and a second address at 4 Quai Célestins, 4th, M° Sully-Morland.

Les Créateurs: Up-and-Coming Designers

Forum des Halles, 1-7 Rue Pierre Lescot, 1st, M° Châtelet-Les Halles (direct access), ☎ 01 44 76 96 56, www.forum-des-halles.com. Open Monday through Saturday, 10am to 7:30pm. Despite a recent facelift, the Forum des Halles is still a dark, slightly creepy mall full of teenagers and the shops that cater to them. Its only redeeming value is the **Espace Créateurs** (at the Porte Berger, level 1, along the Grand Balcon), a group of eight boutiques where up-and-coming designers rent space to showcase their collections of clothing, accessories, bags and artwork. Come here to browse the one-of-a-kind outfits and funky handmade accessories in a laid-back setting.

Créateurs Goutte d'Or, 4 Rue des Gardes, 18th, M° Barbès Rochereau. Dubbed "Rue de la Mode," this street houses 13 young designer boutiques (subsidized by the city to bring a creative element to the neighborhood) selling fabulous hand-made clothing and accessories that would be twice as expensive if this were the Marais. Most boutiques are open in the afternoon, Monday through Saturday.

Omiz, 8 Rue des Abbesses, 18th, M° Abbesses, ☎ 01 42 52 13 30. This funky Montmartre boutique has a good selection of young designer brands, with men's and women's clothing and *très cool* accessories at affordable prices.

Vintage, Secondhand & Outlet Shops

The Paris flea markets are the first place to look for vintage and secondhand clothing, but there are also a lot of excellent deals to be found on the streets around the Pompidou Center and Les Halles. The closet-sized boutique **Iglaïne** (12 Rue de la Grande-Traunderie, 1st, ☎ 01 42 36 19 91) specializes in vintage clothing and accessories, while the much larger **Kiliwatch** (64 Rue Tiquetonne, 2nd, ☎ 01 42 21 17 37) has a mix of old and new, neatly organized and priced slightly higher (the shop also has a great collection of fashion and design magazines and club flyers).

For vintage *couture*, visit the three Palais Royal boutiques of **Didier Ludot** (20-24 Galerie Montpensier and 125 Galerie de Valois, Jardin du Palais Royal, 1st, ☎ 01 42 96 06 56, www.didierludot.com), including one completely dedicated to little black dresses. St-Germain-des-Prés also has

Paris Plage along the Seine

Above: Maison Balzac
Below: Shops along the Canal St-Martin

Restaurant La Bohème, Barbizon

Above: Château Fontainebleau, façade

Below: Château Fontainebleau, reflection
(Photos courtesy of Fontainebleau Tourism Office)

Above: Château Fontainebleau, Etang des Carpes

Below: Château Fontainebleau, carriage ride
(Photos courtesy of Fontainebleau Tourism Office)

Above: Forêt de Fontainebleau, desert

Below: Forêt de Fontainebleau, rock formations
(Photos courtesy of Fontainebleau Tourism Office)

Above: Forêt de Fontainebleau, path

Below: Forêt de Fontainebleau, Gorges d'Appremont
(Photos courtesy of Fontainebleau Tourism Office)

Millet studio, Barbizon

a few collectors' addresses, including **Ragtime** (23 Rue de l'Echaudé, 6th, ☎ 01 56 24 00 36), with vintage clothing dating from the 1860s to the 1970s, and **Le Dépot Vente de Buci** (4-6 Rue de Bourbon-le-Château, 6th, ☎ 01 46 34 28 28), selling some very 1980s clothing and accessories.

Discount outlets can be found nearby around métro Rennes, including the **Chercheminippes** empire for men, women, and babies (102, 109, 110, 111, and 124 Rue du Cherche-Midi, 6th, ☎ 01 42 22 45 23), **Mouton à Cinq Pattes** (8 and 18 Rue Saint Placide, 6th, ☎ 01 45 48 86 26), and **Stock Carroll** (30 and 51 Rue Saint-Placide, 6th, ☎ 01 45 48 83 66).

The best street for designer outlets is the **Rue d'Alésia**, down in the 14th arrondissement (M° Alésia) with big names such as Sonyia Rykiel (#64), Carven (#107) and Cacharel (#114). If you're looking for high-end designer outlets, it's worth the trek out to **La Vallée** (in Marne-la-Vallée, RER A4 Val d'Europe, www.lavalleeoutletshoppingvillage.com), with at least a third off regular prices in stylish boutiques such as Anne Fontaine, Kenzo, Diesel, Lancel, MaxMara, Nina Ricci, Mandarina Duck, Versace, Camper and Charles Jourdan (drop the kids at Disneyland Paris, just one RER stop away).

La Beauté

There are very few French beauty products that can't be found back home these days (and sometimes even less expensively). But let's face it, buying a tube of Chanel lipstick at the airport duty-free shop just isn't the same as buying it at Chanel (and the freebies are much better). It's also worth stopping by the major design houses such as Dior, Guerlain and Lancôme, who regularly produce limited-edition perfumes that are never sold outside France.

Les Salons du Palais Royal Shiseido, 142 Galerie de Valois, Jardins du Palais Royal, 1st, M° Palais-Royal, ☎ 01 49 27 09 09, www.salons-shiseido.com. This sumptuous, violet-colored boutique would be worth visiting for its décor alone, but it's also the only place you can buy Serge Luten's exclusive perfumes. For an extra fee, they'll even etch your initials onto the perfume bottle.

Caron, 34 Avenue Montaigne, 8th, M° Alma-Marceau, ☎ 01 47 23 40 82. Founded in 1904, the Caron boutique is a jewel box of a perfume store on this luxury shopping street. Clients get to fill their own perfume bottles from the Baccarat crystal urns containing the house's signature scents, some dating back to 1919 (and sold exclusively in this boutique).

Boutique Guerlain, 68 Avenue des Champs-Elysées, 8th, M° Franklin-D-Roosevelt, ☎ 01 45 62 52 57. Given a face lift in 2003, Guerlain's Champs-Elysées boutique is simply the most luxurious address on the Avenue to buy your cosmetics and perfumes. Founded in 1828, they still sell l'Eau de Cologne Imperiale created in 1853 for Napoleon IIIs wife, the Empress Eugénie.

La Grande Boutique de l'Artisan Parfumeur, 2 Rue de l'Amiral de Coligny, 1st, M° Louvre-Rivoli, ☎ 01 44 88 27 50. This is the flagship store for the whole Artisan Parfumeur line of perfumes, interior scents and whimsical gift items.

DISCOUNT COSMETICS

One budget brand worth remembering is Chanel's, **Bourjois** line, found on the shelves in major department stores and Monoprix locations.

Institut Lancôme, 29 Rue du Faubourg St-Honoré, 8th, M° Concorde, ☎ 01 42 65 30 74. This boutique and beauty spa has many exclusive products in the Lancôme cosmetics and perfume line not sold anywhere else. They also have classes on makeup application and a full range of spa treatments. Hours are Monday through Saturday, 10am to 7pm; see the web site, www.lancome.com, for prices.

By Terry, 21-36 Galerie Véro-Dodat, 1st, M° Louvre-Rivoli, ☎ 01 44 76 00 76. Set in a lovely covered passage, these three boutiques sell the products of the catwalk makeup guru Terry de Gunzburg: personalized cosmetics blended in the **Haute Couture** boutique, off-the-shelf (and less expensive) cosmetics line in the **Prêt-à-Porter** boutique, and home décor objects in the **Home** boutique.

Stephane Marais, 217 Rue St-Honoré, 1st, M° Tuileries, ☎ 08 25 82 56 85, www.stephanemarais.com. This funky cosmetics line from Shiseido's artistic director is sold in a cutting edge boutique that's completely redone every three months to follow the current fashions. Makeup classes are possible for small groups.

Galerie Noémie, 92 Avenue des Champs-Elysées, 8th, M° Georges V, ☎ 01 45 62 78 27, www.galerienoemie.com. Created by a young French artist (the painting kind, not the cosmetics kind), Noémie's makeup boutiques look almost like art-supply stores with little palettes to mix the perfect shade of foundation, tiny pots of liquid eye color, and all of the necessary brushes and artist's tools. And the best part – you won't go broke in here. Drop in for a "flash" makeup application session for under €20. Great idea before a night on the town.

Chanel, 31 Rue Cambon, 1st, M° Concord, ☎ 01 42 86 28 50, www.chanel.com. There are several Chanel locations in Paris; this boutique carries the cosmetics line.

AUTHOR'S NOTE: See the Cultural Adventures section, page 203, for Parisian day spas and makeover artists.

■ English Bookshops

The Abbey Bookshop, 29 Rue de la Parcheminerie, 5th, M° St-Michel or Cluny-La Sorbonne, ☎ 01 46 33 16 24. This independent bookshop in the Latin Quarter specializes in new and used books from Canada (in French and English), the UK and the US. The friendly Canadian owner helps newcomers navigate the densely stacked shelves, and always has a hot pot of coffee – with maple syrup sweetener!

DISCOUNTS ON FRENCH BOOKS

Browse the Latin Quarter bookshops for French classics or art and design books on sale. A good place to start is under the ubiquitous yellow canopies of the **Gibert Jeune** stores (M° St-Michel), with several stores dominating the intersection at Place St-Michel. Many of the discounted books are stacked on tables outside, but there's also a small English-language section (look for a shop called *Langues et Lettres*, 10 Place St-Michel). This is a great place to get inexpensive French notebooks and stationery, as well.

Shakespeare & Company, 37 Rue de la Bucherie, 5th, M° St-Michel, ☎ 01 43 26 96 50, www.shakespeareco.org. Open since 1951, this independent, secondhand bookshop is the successor of Sylvia Beach's original Shakespeare & Co. in St-Germain-des-Prés, which closed during the Nazi occupation. The expatriate American owner George Whitman and his daughter, Sylvia Beach Whitman, still provide free bunk space in the shop's library for visiting artists and writers.

Tea & Tattered Pages, 24 Rue Maynet, 6th, M° Duroc, ☎ 01 40 65 94 35. This tiny, independent bookshop is a bit off the beaten bath, but they've got some of the best deals on new and used English-language books, and a tearoom serving up authentic brownies and apple pie.

Brentano's, 37 Avenue de l'Opéra, 2nd, M° Pyramides or Opéra, ☎ 01 42 61 52 50, www.brentanos.fr. Brentano's is the largest independent English-language bookstore in Paris, open since 1895. They specialize in the latest British-American best-sellers, with a large selection of international magazines. Check the web site under "Events, Calendar" for the schedule of upcoming readings and book signings.

Galignani, 224 Rue de Rivoli, 1st, M° Tuileries, ☎ 01 42 60 76 07. This elegantly old-fashioned French-English bookshop opened in 1802, and claims to be the first English bookseller on the Continent. They stock classic French literature, best-sellers, English travel books, international magazines and contemporary art and design books.

Paris

The Red Wheelbarrow, 22 Rue St-Paul, 4th, M° St-Paul, ℅ 01 42 77 42 17. This cozy, independently owned bookstore in the St-Paul district sells a large assortment of new books, holds regular author readings and book signings, and even has a piano hidden among the stacks for the musically inclined. Their children's bookshop is just around the corner at 13 Rue Charles V.

■ For Kids

 Notsobig, 38 Rue Tiquetonne, 2nd, M° Etienne-Marcel, ☎ 01 42 33 34 26. This is the Colette of the infant world, a concept store with the latest designer trends in children's clothing and toys. Grownups can find some fun objects for themselves, too, such as cookie-scented candles and bath gel. Needless to say, it's *notsocheap*.

Village JouéClub, 3-5 Boulevard des Italiens, 2nd, M° Richelieu-Drouot, ☎ 01 53 45 41 41. If you're looking for a more mainstream toy store, this is the largest in Paris (almost 22,000 square feet on two levels), inside the Passage des Princes. They have everything from dolls and Legos to board games and model kits. There's even a kids' hair salon.

Pixi & Cie, 6 Rue de l'Echaudé, 6th, M° Odéon, ☎ 01 46 33 88 88. This tiny boutique in St-Germain-des-Prés specializes in *Le Petit Prince* (Antoine de St-Exupéry's *The Little Prince*) collectibles.

Bonpoint, 42 Rue de l'Université, 7th, M° Rue du Bac, ☎ 01 40 20 10 55. This is the end-of-season outlet store for the ultra-classic French kids' clothing brand, Bonpoint.

Au Nain Bleu, 406-410 Rue St-Honoré, 8th, M° Concorde, ☎ 01 42 60 39 01. Open since 1836, this is the oldest toy store in Paris, with a famous annual catalogue of old fashioned (and modern) toys from the high end of the market. This is where you can buy the same toy sailboats that Parisian kids push around the fountains in the Luxembourg and Tuileries gardens.

There are two adorable kids' boutiques on the Rue Dauphine (6th, M° Odéon). **Bois de Rose** (#30, ☎ 01 40 46 04 24) sells embroidered dress clothes, newborns' smocks, and wedding outfits for little boys and girls; and **Le Monde en Marche** (#34, ☎ 01 43 29 09 49, http://www.le-monde-en-march.com) sells old-fashioned toys made by hand.

Where to Stay

Finding the right hotel is one of the most difficult challenges for first-time visitors who aren't familiar with the city's neighborhoods or French hotel particularities. The choices are endless, from youth hostels and budget no-frills hotels to four-star historic monuments and private furnished apartment rentals. The hotels listed here were chosen for their location, price, style, or comfort, with a preference for those that are independently owned or typically Parisian in character. Also included are agency listings for those who would like to rent a furnished Parisian apartment or stay in a bed & breakfast.

Practicalities

ACCOMMODATIONS PRICE SCALE	
The following price scale represents rates charged for a double room per night during high season, including taxes. Breakfast isn't included except where noted. All prices are quoted in euros. Credit cards accepted unless noted.	
€	Under €70
€€.	€70-€100
€€€	€101-€150
€€€€	€151-€250
€€€€€.	over €250

Paris

■ Booking & Reservations

The best deals can be found during the low season, typically January-February and July-August (when most Parisians head to the country). The most difficult time to find a room is during the Easter vacation and in early fall, when many conferences and conventions take place. Book well in advance for these periods.

Many hotels have special deals for bookings done through their web site, so always check there first before calling a hotel directly. Web sites like Expedia and RatestoGo (see next page) advertise rooms well below the rack rate. But be warned: much like the airline system of upgrades, hotels are likely to give the best rooms, with the fantastic views, to guests who've paid full price.

A WORD TO THE WISE

TIP: *To dial French telephone/fax numbers from abroad, dial the outgoing country code (US is "1"), then the country code for France, which is "33," then the 10-digit number,* without *the first "0."*

Policies on children vary by hotel, but the most common practice is to allow kids under 12 to stay for free in the same room as the parents (with a rollout bed). Be sure to ask about this in advance, since some hotel rooms are too small for rollouts.

Always get a confirmation of your reservation in writing, either by fax or e-mail, specifying the arrival and departure dates, and number of beds. And be sure to notify the hotel in advance if you will be arriving later than 6pm, or they could give your room to someone else (check-in/check-out time is usually around noon).

 ATTENTION! *In France, dates are written as they are spoken, with the day* **before** *the month – day / month / year – so* **10/12/04** *is* **le 10 December**, *2004, not October 12, 2004.*

■ Finding a Hotel Online

In addition to the hotels reviewed in this guide, visitors can find accommodations through the Internet, many of which offer rates below the published "rack rate" of major hotels. Here are a few noteworthy sites:

The **Paris Tourism Office** (☎ 08 92 68 30 00, €0.34/minute; www.parisbienvenue.com) can help travelers find rooms in the city's hotels, youth hostels and furnished apartment for all budgets, even at the last minute. Those who show up in town without anywhere to stay should go here first, or use their online search engine. Avoid calling, since it's expensive and often busy. The main location is next to the **American Express Office**, 11 Rue Scribe, 9th M° Opéra. There are other locations at the **Gare de Lyon** and **Gare du Nord**.

Paris Hotels (www.parishotels.com) has over 180 "charming hotels" in Paris, with an easy search engine by price, location, or star-rating. They guarantee the lowest prices, charge no agency fees, and allow you to book immediately using their real-time online reservation system.

Paris By (www.parisby.com) has a good database of Paris hotels with plenty of photos and detailed room information, organized by location or star-rating. Rooms can be booked directly online.

Expedia (www.expedia.com) lists major Paris hotels with full descriptions and competitive rates, searchable by neighborhood or star-rating. Rooms can be booked directly through the Expedia web site (hotel addresses are listed, but not telephone numbers or web sites).

EuroCheapo (www.eurocheapo.com/paris) is an independent budget hotel reviewer that gives the lowdown on Paris' least expensive rooms and hostels, with a focus on popular tourist neighborhoods such as the Marais and the Latin Quarter. Some hotels can be booked directly through their web site, but for most you'll have to contact the hotel yourself.

Rates to Go (www.ratestogo.com) offers discounts up to 60% off hotel rooms for last-minute bookings (up to 20 days in advance). Hotels are fully described with photos, address, and amenities, and include consumer reviews. If possible, check here before booking your room directly with the hotel. Reservations can be made immediately online with a credit card (15% deposit taken). There is a small booking fee of €4.

■ Parisian Hotel Peculiarities

Many Parisian hotels are in centuries-old buildings, which means that rooms tend to be smaller than North American standards, often with odd shapes, cramped bathrooms and elevators that can barely squeeze in two people. If space is important, ask for the largest room (it will usually cost more). Of course, some are willing to pay extra for the attic rooms with exposed wooden ceiling beams (and very little headroom).

Like the rooms, bathrooms in many Parisian hotels are quite small. A room with a bathtub may cost more than a shower, and often there is only a handheld shower attachment in the tub for "sit-down" showers. All of the hotels listed here (except for hostels) have rooms with private facilities, but many budget hotels also have cheaper rooms available for those willing to share facilities down the hall.

Many budget hotels have no elevator, so the less athletic may want to request rooms on the lower floors, though these are generally noisier (especially if facing a busy road) and receive less sunlight. Don't forget that in France the ground floor is the *rez de chaussée (RDC)*, with numbering starting on the next floor (so the second floor to Americans is the first floor in France, a.k.a. *première étage*).

Paris

SKIP BREAKFAST

One of the best ways to save money in Paris hotels is to avoid the breakfast (which is rarely included in the price). Paying €5-€15 for croissants, juice and coffee is a bit steep, and guests can usually find the same thing cheaper and with a better view at any local café. Buffets are usually a bit more elaborate (and expensive), with fruit, cereal and cold meats. If you are still hesitating, don't commit until after the first morning, when you've had a chance to peek at the breakfast room and see what's available.

Finally, rooms within the same hotel can differ in décor, size, comfort or view, so if you're absolutely horrified on arrival, never hesitate to ask – politely – if it's possible to switch to a "different" room for the same rate. It's more effective to imply that you heard the rooms were fantastic and would like a better one, than to say outright that your room is awful. Honey, not vinegar, works best with the French.

AUTHOR'S NOTE: *See* Appliances, *page 64, for explanations of voltage differences, plugging in laptops, etc.*

Hotels

■ The Islands, Beaubourg & the Marais

Hôtel Henri IV, 25 Place Dauphine, 1st, M° Cité or Pont-Neuf, ☎ 01 43 54 44 53 (€). No credit cards. Breakfast included.

Located in a 17th-century building overlooking the tree-lined Place Dauphine (at the western end of the Ile de la Cité), this budget hotel is so popular it's usually necessary to book two months in advance. And that's no easy task: you need to call at least a month in advance, then send payment by money order or traveler's check to confirm the reservation. There's no fax, no e-mail, and no credit cards accepted. The reception room (and the hotel's only direct-dial phone) is up a narrow flight of steps, with a corner for the continental breakfast service. There are 20 rooms on the floors above, the least expensive ones have no bathroom facilities (shower and toilets down the hall). The décor is threadbare but functional.

> **WARNING!** *Those with lots of luggage will not appreciate the old, narrow staircase (no elevators).*

Hôtel du Séjour, 36 Rue du Grenier St-Lazare, 3rd, M° Rambuteau or Etienne-Marcel, ☎ 01 48 87 40 36, fax 01 48 87 40 36 (€).

This hotel has 20 sunny rooms with basic décor (no phone or TV). The rooms on the fifth floor are the most spacious (but beware, no elevator). Less expensive rooms are available without bathroom facilities (toilets in each hall, showers on the 3rd floor, €4). The owners are friendly and the hotel is well-placed (next to a police station) just above the Pompidou Center, only five minutes' walk to the Marais.

Hôtel de Roubaix, 6 Rue Greneta, 3rd, M° Arts-et-Métiers, ☎ 01 42 72 89 91, fax 01 42 72 58 79, Hotel.de.Roubaix@wanadoo.fr (€).

This hotel near Arts-et-Métiers and the Pompidou Center has a faded, old-fashioned elegance that wouldn't look out of place at grandma's house. Its 53 spacious rooms, with satellite TV and direct-dial phone, have vintage furnishings and spotless, modern bathrooms. Triples available for €71. This is one of the few budget hotels in town with an elevator, so book early!

Hôtel Moderne Caron, 3 Rue Caron, 4th, M° Bastille or St-Paul, ☎ 01 48 87 97 05, fax 01 48 87 97 05, hotel.moderne.caron@wanadoo.fr (€).

Completely renovated in 2002, this small hotel is on a tiny street just off a beautiful cobblestoned square lined with bistros, and just two minutes' walk to the Place des Vosges or Place de la Bastille. Rooms are basic and clean, with modern tiled bathrooms. Less expensive rooms are available if you don't mind using shared bathrooms. Continental breakfast served in the lounge. Reception is usually closed by 2am, so try to get a key before heading out for the evening.

Hospitel Hôtel Dieu, 1 Place du Parvis Notre Dame (Galerie B2, sixth floor) 4th, M° Cité or RER St-Michel-Notre Dame, ☎ 01 44 32 01 00, fax 01 44 32 01 16, www.hotel-hospitel.com (€€).

This unique hotel is in the historic Hôtel Dieu, a Parisian hospital on the same square as Notre Dame Cathedral. The 14 rooms are simple but comfortable, with TV, private bathroom, telephone, safe and hairdryer or fan on request. It's amazingly quiet, and all guests have access to the peaceful courtyard gardens. Room service – for those who want to see what French hospital food is like – is available for breakfast, lunch and dinner (full meals from €10). There's no curfew, but after 10pm you have to retrieve your key at the ER entrance (a.k.a. *Urgences* in French). Other sights on the Ile de la Cité include the colorful Marché aux Fleurs, the Conciergerie, and Sainte-Chapelle.

Hôtel de Nice, 42*bis* Rue de Rivoli, 4th, M° Hôtel-de-Ville, ☎ 01 42 78 55 29, fax 01 42 78 36 07 (€€).

This delightfully eclectic hotel is decorated in a mismatch of antiques and flea-market finds, vintage prints and old paintings. Funky and romantic for some, suffocating and gaudy for others. Most of the 23 rooms are quite small, but have their own bathroom (shower or tub), satellite TV and direct-dial phone. Rooms on the top floor, which guests can reach by elevator, have great views over the city. You'd hardly notice this little hotel unless you were looking for it, but its prime location right across from the Hôtel de Ville is perfect for exploring the Marais, Beaubourg and the islands.

Grand Hôtel Jeanne d'Arc, 3 Rue de Jarente, 4th, M° St-Paul, ☎ 01 48 87 62 11, fax 01 48 87 37 31, www.hoteljeannedarc.com (€€).

This pretty budget hotel is just off the charming and somewhat secluded Place du Marché Ste-Catherine. The 36 rooms are decorated simply in warm colors, with large windows, diverse wooden furnishings, satellite TV, telephone, and private bathrooms (bathtub or shower) with hair dryer. The lobby is tiny, with a large mosaic tile mirror and 17th-century stone staircase leading up to the rooms. Overall, it's a pleasantly clean and comfortable hotel within easy walking distance of the Marais and the Bastille nightlife districts. It's possible to book rooms directly on their web site.

Hôtel du 7ème Art, 20 Rue St-Paul, 4th, M° St-Paul, ☎ 01 44 54 85 00, fax 01 42 77 69 10, hotel7art@wanadoo.fr (€€).

Just around the corner from the Village St-Paul antiques shops, this quirky hotel has developed quite a cult following over the years. Run by an old film buff, vintage cinema posters decorate the hotel's 23 rooms, its lounge, breakfast room, hallways, and even the tiny basement gym. Despite the somewhat frumpy furniture, the rooms are comfortable, with private bath or shower, cable TV, telephone, and in-room safe. Rooms on the top floors are more spacious, and therefore a bit pricier. There are also a few budget rooms with shared facilities in the hall. The cozy lounge has leather club chairs and a fireplace.

Hôtel Caron de Beaumarchais, 12 Rue Vieille-du-Temple, 4th, M° St-Paul or Hôtel-de-Ville, ☎ 01 42 72 34 12, fax 01 42 72 34 63, www.carondebeaumarchais.com (€€€).

Named for the playwright Beaumarchais (who penned the *Marriage of Figaro* a few doors away in 1786), this dollhouse of a hotel in the heart of the Marais perfectly recreates the atmosphere of an 18th-century Parisian townhouse. Each of the 19 soundproofed rooms is decorated in pretty fabrics and hand-painted tiles, with exposed wooden beam ceilings and vintage framed prints. They're equipped with en-suite bathroom, Internet connections, satellite TV, hair dryer, and minibar. Air conditioning and an elevator bring this hotel comfortably into the 21st century. Continental breakfast can be served in the guest rooms. A hotel this adorable fills up fast at these prices. Ask about promotions when booking.

Hôtel du Jeu de Paume, 54 Rue St-Louis-en-Ile, 4th, M° Pont Marie, ☎ 01 43 26 14 18, fax 01 40 46 02 76, www.jeudepaumehotel.com (€€€€).

This extraordinary hotel on the Ile St-Louis is in a former 17th-century *Jeu de Paume* (indoor tennis) court. It was lovingly converted into a stylish and bright modern hotel while preserving the original wooden beam and stone architecture. There are 28 rooms (and two apartments) accessible by a glass elevator, each with its own unique contemporary style and views overlooking the interior patio garden. They're each equipped with satellite TV, telephone, minibar, modem Internet access, in-room safe, and hair dryer. The hotel also has a fitness room with sauna and Jacuzzi, a comfortable lounge bar, library, and billiard room with *fumoir*. The hotel has a breakfast room, but no restaurant. But this is no problem, since the island has everything from bakeries and ice-cream shops to wine bars and traditional French bistros. Rooms can be booked online.

Hôtel du Bourg Tibourg, 19 Rue du Bourg-Tibourg, 4th, M° Hôtel de Ville, www.hoteldubourgtibourg.com, ☎ 01 42 78 47 39, fax 01 40 29 07 00 (€€€€).

Decorated by style guru Jacques Garcia (of Hôtel Costes fame), this painfully hip boutique hotel in the heart of the Marais is both funky and modern, a rare mix in this part of town. Crazy jungle prints mix with Oriental lacquered furnishings in the lounge bar, softened by an interior garden, while the rooms have more of a contemporary *bastide* (country house or manor) atmosphere with warm colors and luxurious fabrics. The 31 cozy rooms have en-suite bathrooms with hair dryer, direct-dial phone with modem Internet connections, satellite TV, minibar and in-room safe. What they lack in size they certainly make up for in personality! The hotel is air conditioned and has an elevator. There's no restaurant, but breakfast is served each morning in the lounge or in the guest rooms. Rooms can be booked online.

Hôtel Saint-Merry, 78 Rue de la Verrerie, 4th, M° Châtelet or Hôtel-de-Ville, ☎ 01 42 78 14 15, fax 01 40 29 06 82, www.hotelmarais.com (€€€€).

The magnificent 17th-century Gothic-style interior of this hotel, all carved wood, stone and wrought iron, was once the presbytery of the neighboring Eglise St-Merri. The bed in room nine is tucked right under one of the stone flying buttresses holding up the church. Each of the 11 rooms has a private bathroom, hair dryer, and telephone. This is the perfect place to escape the modern world! Located in the Beaubourg quarter around the corner from the Pompidou Center, this hotel is just a few minutes' walk from the Marais and Notre Dame Cathedral. Breakfast is served in the guestrooms only. Check the web site for promotional off-season rates.

■ Louvre, Palais Royal & Tuileries

Hôtel de Rouen, 42 Rue Croix des Petits Champs, 1st, M° Palais Royal-Louvre, ☎ 01 42 61 38 21, fax 01 42 61 38 21 (€).

This tiny hotel has 22 rooms on five floors (no elevator), with private bathrooms and TVs. The décor is modern and bright, but very basic. Stay here for the price, the privacy, and the excellent location between the Place des Victoires and the Louvre. Quads available for €55.

Hôtel Tiquetonne, 6 Rue Tiquetonne, 2nd, M° Etienne-Marcel, ☎ 01 42 36 94 58, fax 01 42 36 02 94 (€). Closed August.

This hotel is on a pedestrian-only street in the Montorgueil neighborhood, near hip cafés and trendy vintage-clothing boutiques. It's perfectly safe, just stay away from the seedy Rue St-Denis. The Louvre and the Pompidou Center are less than 10 minutes on foot. There are 44 rooms with basic décor (no phone or TV). Doubles have a private bathroom with shower (bathroom facilities in the hall for less expensive rooms). Some rooms face the noisy Rue de Turbigo, so ask for a room on the Rue Tiquetonne side.

Hôtel Agora: 7 Rue de la Cossonnerie, 1st, M° Etienne-Marcel, ☎ 01 42 33 46 02, fax 01 42 33 80 99 (€€-€€€).

Paris

This is one of the rare charming hotels around Les Halles, with 29 rooms decorated just like grandma's house in old-fashioned wallpaper, vintage furnishings and oil paintings. Amenities include telephone, satellite TV, in-room safe and private bathroom (shower or bathtub). Some rooms (particularly on the second and fifth floors) have views over the St-Eustache church. There's a narrow staircase leading to the reception desk on the first floor, then a tiny elevator to take you to your room.

Hôtel Louvre Ste-Anne: 32 Rue Sainte Anne, 1st, M° Bourse or Pyramides, ☎ 01 40 20 02 35, fax 01 40 15 91 13, www.louvre-ste-anne.fr (€€€).

This friendly hotel is right around the corner from the Palais Royal and Paris' famous covered passages. The hotel's 20 air conditioned rooms, decorated in discreet pastel prints and pale wood furnishing, are equipped with satellite TV, direct-dial phone with modem jack, minibar, marble bathroom with complimentary toiletries, towel warmer and hair dryer. There's also a small lobby lounge, vaulted stone breakfast room, and an elevator.

Grand Hôtel de Champagne: 17 Rue Jean-Lantier (corner of 13 Rue des Orfèvres), 1st, M° Châtelet, ☎ 01 42 36 60 00, fax 01 45 08 43 33, www.hoteldechampaigneparis.com (€€€-€€€€).

Those looking to immerse themselves in historic Paris will adore this charming hotel centrally located on a quiet street between Notre Dame and the Louvre. The building itself dates back to 1562, has six floors decorated in the styles of different periods from Louis XIII to Louis XVI, with exposed wooden beams, stone walls, Jouy prints and rich fabrics. Modern amenities include direct-dial telephone, satellite TV, bathroom (bathtub or shower), hairdryer and air conditioning. The elevator only goes to the fifth floor. Check their web site for regular low-season specials.

Hôtel du Louvre: Place Andre Malraux, 1st M° Palais-Royal, ☎ 01 44 58 38 38, fax 01 44 58 38 01, www.hoteldulouvre.com (€€€€€).

Behind the Hôtel du Louvre's formal, 19th-century palace façade is a richly decorated boutique hotel that combines modern style with Directoire architecture and carved wooden ceilings. Each of the 177 completely soundproofed rooms is decorated differently, with views over the neighboring Louvre, Opéra Garnier and Comédie Française. All are equipped with satellite TV, direct-dial phone with modem access, individually controlled air conditioning, minibar, digital safe, and marble bathrooms with heated towel racks and designer toiletries by Annick Gouttal. The hotel also has a 24-hour business/computer center and small fitness room with machines and free weights. Guests can enjoy breakfast in the hotel's typically Parisian brasserie, with a terrace overlooking the Place du Palais Royal. Cocktails and light meals are available in the more intimate setting of the lounge bar. This hotel is perfect for those who like top quality service and comfort in a discreet and cozy atmosphere. Check the hotel's online booking system for good promotional rates.

Jolly Hôtel Lotti: 7 Rue de Castiglione, 1st, M° Concorde, ☎ 01 42 60 37 34, fax 01 40 15 93 56, www.jollyhotels.com (€€€€€).

Despite the merry moniker, the Italian-owned Hôtel Lotti is a seriously elegant hotel with a prestigious location between the Place de la Concorde and the Place Vendôme. Its Italian roots show in the Tuscan-style lounge bar, with mosaic tiled floors, potted palms and stained glass ceiling. The hotel's 128 spacious rooms are decorated with delicate antique furniture and oil paintings, and are equipped with extra closet space, climate control, satellite TV, minibar, bathroom phone extension, in-room safe, and dial-up Internet access (for a fee). The Italian marble bathrooms have heated towel racks, bathrobes, combined shower/tub, and bidet. Guests can dine in the hotel's Michelin-starred Italian restaurant, Gualtiero Marchesi, open for lunch and dinner (the buffet breakfast is also served here). A full-service concierge desk can handle anything from booking shows to hiring babysitters. Renovations, including a new gym and business center, should be finished by mid-2004. Check the hotel's web site for off-season and last-minute promotions of 50% off the rack rate.

Hôtel Clarion St James & Albany: 202 Rue de Rivoli, 1st M° Tuileries, ☎ 01 44 58 43 21, fax 01 44 58 43 11, www.clarionsaintjames.com (€€€€€).

A former royal residence dating from the 17th century, this grand hotel across from the Jardin des Tuileries features a truly stunning private garden courtyard and a newly opened spa and fitness center with indoor pool. Completely buffered from the noise of the busy Rue de Rivoli, the hotel's 196 air conditioned guest rooms are decorated in cherry-wood Louis-Philippe furnishings and warm colors, with modem Internet access, satellite TV, pay movies, minibar, in-room safe, large desk and abundant closet space. The modern bathrooms have a second phone and combined shower/bathtub. The hotel is actually made up of five buildings, the oldest being the Château, which overlooks the garden courtyard. The hotel has a restaurant and a laid-back lounge bar, and in warmer weather there are tables set up on the garden patio for breakfast *al fresco*. The St. James & Albany hotel is grand without being stuffy, and is ideally located within five minutes of the Louvre, St-Germain-des-Prés, and the Champs-Elysées.

■ Opéra & Madeleine

Hôtel Richmond: 11 Rue du Helder, 9th, M° Opéra or Chaussée d'Antin, ☎ 01 47 70 53 20, fax 01 48 00 02 10, www.richmond-hotel.com (€€€).

This elegant and spacious hotel is on a side-street between the Opéra Garnier and the Boulevard Haussmann department stores. It has an Empire-style lobby and lounge with stained glass ceilings, marble pillars, and comfortable armchairs for relaxing with an afternoon coffee or complementary newspapers. The 59 air conditioned rooms are decorated in Louis XV-style with minibar, in-room safe, direct-dial phone with voicemail and modem jack, tiled bathroom with hair dryer, and satellite TV. The hotel has an elevator and Internet station in the lobby. Strangely, the web site still has rates posted in Francs.

Hôtel Opal: 19 Rue Tronchet, 8th, M° Madeleine, ☎ 01 42 65 77 97, fax 01 49 24 06 58, www.hotelopal.com (€€€€).

This elegant Parisian boutique hotel just off the Place de la Madeleine is perfect for those wanting a peaceful retreat right in the center of the Right Bank's lively theater and shopping district. There are 34 soundproofed and air conditioned rooms, decorated in classic Parisian style using cream and mauve tones, with antique furnishings, thick draperies, chandeliers, floor-to-ceiling windows, upholstered chairs, and hardwood floors. Amenities include private bathroom with hair dryer, minibar, cable TV, and in-room safe. The hotel has the feel of a private Parisian townhouse, with ivory stone archways, fine art and antiques, stained-glass windows, and a mix of comfortable furnishings, with an elevator, stylish breakfast lounge, and WiFi wireless Internet access for guests with laptop computers.

Hôtel Westminster: 13 Rue de la Paix, 2nd, M° Opéra or Madeleine, ☎ 01 42 61 57 46, fax 01 42 60 30 66, www.warwickwestminsteropera.com (€€€€€).

Despite its exclusive location between the Place Vendôme and the Opéra Garnier, the Hôtel Westminster has a particular warmth and coziness often lacking in the neighborhood. It has the comfortable luxury of a private Parisian mansion, with a refined Michelin-stared restaurant and laid-back British-style bar with deep leather chairs, fireplace, and live jazz on the weekends. State-of-the-art touches include WiFi Internet access in public areas and a business/computer center. The bright rooftop spa and fitness center (opened in 2002) features a beautifully tiled steam room and views over the city. The 102 soundproofed guest rooms are decorated in classic Parisian style with period furniture and marble fireplaces. They're equipped with satellite TV, duvet comforters, minibar, bathrobes, cordless phones with voice mail, high-speed Internet access, and marble bathrooms with heated towel racks and designer toiletries. Some rooms also have a bidet and double sink. If they got rid of the Astroturf on the first inner courtyard it would be perfect. It's possible to find good promotional rates for this hotel on the web.

Concorde St-Lazare: 108 Rue Saint Lazare, 8th, ☎ 01 40 08 44 44, fax 01 42 93 01 20, M° St-Lazare, www.concordestlazare-paris.com (€€€€€).

This typically Parisian *fin-de-siecle* luxury hotel is right across from the Gare St-Lazare, a few blocks from the department stores along Boulevard Haussmann, the Opéra Garnier, and the Place de la Madeleine. The hotel's 19th-century Gustave Eiffel-inspired lobby is a historic landmark, and the high ceilings, marble pillars, and sculptures look much as they have for over a century. All 300 rooms were refurbished in 2001 with complete soundproofing, double doors, air conditioning, minibar, in-room safe, phone with voice mail and Internet modem jack, and cable TV. The spacious bathrooms (with combined bath/shower) have separate toilet, hair dryer, and Annick Goutal toiletries. The hotel has all of the four-star services such as room service, laundry, concierge, business center (with computer station), and valet parking. Guests have access to a fitness center three blocks away. The Belle Epoque brasserie *Café Terminus* and sultry Golden Black Bar were both styled by the fashion designer Sonia Rykiel.

■ Montmartre & Pigalle

Le Régent Montmartre: 37 Boulevard Rochechouart, 9th, M° Anvers, ☎ 01 48 78 24 00, fax 01 48 78 25 24, www.leregent.com (€).

Located at the foot of Montmartre, some of the rooms in this budget hotel even have views of Sacré-Coeur. The 60 rooms are simple but comfortable, with private bathrooms, double-glazed windows and TV. Irons and hair dryers can be borrowed. The hotel has an elevator, 24-hour reception desk with safety deposit box, newspapers and Internet access (for a fee). There are also budget rooms (from €50 for a double) for those who don't mind using the shared bathroom facilities.

Hôtel Caulaincourt Square: 2 Square Caulaincourt (between 63 and 65 Rue Caulaincourt), 18th, M° Lamarck-Caulaincourt ☎ 01 46 06 46 06, fax 01 46 04 46 16, www.caulaincourt.com (€).

This lively budget hotel is perfect for those looking for privacy and a good location, but not necessarily a peaceful family hotel. It has 50 rooms with TV and private bath or shower, and basic décor. There are nice views over the rooftops of Paris (on the north side) or a leafy boulevard. Less expensive rooms (including a few dorm rooms) are available with use of shared facilities. Breakfast is served in the lobby lounge, which stays open until 2 am for the late-night revelry of the backpacking crowd. The hotel is perched on the edge of a steep hill on the north side of Montmartre, far from the tourist masses but close to typical Parisian bistros and cafés. It's best to take a taxi – there are a *lot* of steps.

Style Hôtel: 8 Rue Ganneron, 18th, M° Place de Clichy or La Fourche, ☎ 01 45 22 37 59, fax 01 45 22 81 03 (€).

This cheap and cheerful hotel right around the corner from Montmartre Cemetery has 36 rooms in an Art Deco style with mirrored armoires and tulip-shaped lampshades. Rooms have private bathrooms with shower. The hotel has an elevator, patio garden, and a charming bistro-style breakfast room.

Paris

Hôtel Regyn's Montmartre: 18 Place des Abbesses, 18th, M° Abbesses, ☎ 01 42 54 45 21, fax 01 42 23 76 69, www.regynsmontmartre.com (€€).

Located right outside the métro Abbesses, this hotel is in the heart of Montmartre. There are 22 rooms with private bathroom (bath or shower), in-room safe, cable TV, and telephone. The décor is bright and modern with simple furnishings and pastel colored fabrics. Rooms on the fifth floor have the best views over Paris (don't worry, there's an elevator), but cost a bit more. The lobby and breakfast room are on the plain side, but with the many cafés, bistros and boutiques of Montmartre right outside, it doesn't really matter.

Hôtel Roma Sacré-Coeur: 10 Rue Caulaincourt, 18th, M° Lamarck-Caulaincourt, ☎ 01 42 62 02 02, fax 01 42 54 34 92 57 (€€).

This family-run hotel on the tourist-free side of Montmartre has an old Parisian ambience. The hotel has a stylish lobby with marble floors and red velour armchairs, elevator and safe-deposit box. Forget the depressing breakfast room; have it delivered to your room or enjoy your croissants and coffee at one of the many nearby cafés. The 57 rooms have bright blue walls and white bedspreads, with direct-dial phone, satellite TV, minibar, radio, in-room safe and private bathroom (with shower) and hair dryer. Ask for rooms on the top floors for the best views. Don't miss the trendy restaurant next door, **Ginette de la Côte d'Azur**.

Hôtel Royal Fromentin: 11 Rue Fromentin, 9th, M° Blanche, ☎ 01 48 74 85 93, fax 01 42 81 02 33, www.hotelroyalfromentin.com (€€€).

Located on a quiet street near the racy Pigalle district, it's no surprise that this elegant hotel once housed a popular cabaret, *Le Don Juan*. The owners have preserved the 1930s character and masculine décor, with its dark-wood paneling and rich green and burgundy colors. There's a zinc bar, stained glass ceilings, and metal-caged wooden elevator. The 47 spacious rooms feature rich colors and quality artworks, with private bathroom, hair dryer, satellite TV, double-glazed windows, and room service. Many rooms have views of Sacré-Coeur and balconies. Internet access in the lobby. Quads (two double beds) available for €184.

■ Grands Boulevards

Hôtel des Arts: 7 Cité Bergère, 9th, M° Grands Boulevards, ☎ 01 42 46 73 30, fax 01 48 00 94 42 (€).

The family-run Hôtel des Arts offers one of the best deals in this area. Its 26 rooms are small but functional, decorated in pastel colors and equipped with private bathroom (shower or bath) and direct-dial telephone. There's an elevator, cozy lounge (with an aquarium), and a breakfast room that looks like a greenhouse with its jungle of plants. Triple rooms available from €90. It's centrally located, with quick access to Montmartre, Bastille, Palais Royal and the Opéra Garnier.

Hôtel Chopin: 46 Passage Jouffroy (off 10 Boulevard Montmartre), 9th, M° Grands Boulevards, ☎ 01 47 70 58 10, fax 01 42 47 00 70 (€€).

Anyone who likes the old-fashioned 19th-century atmosphere of the city's covered passages will adore this charming hotel in Passage Jouffroy, once frequented by Frederic Chopin. Opened in 1846, the hotel has an elevator, 36 rooms with private bath (bathtub with handheld shower), and satellite TV. The romantic décor is a mix of vintage wooden architectural detail and modern furnishings (and, it must be said, slightly garish salmon walls and green carpets). There's a breakfast room and drinks dispenser. It's a bustling neighborhood during the day, just off the hectic *grands boulevards*, but the passage closes to the public at night so there's no noise in the rooms. The location is at the center of the Right Bank, with direct access to two métro lines and several bus lines. It's a good location for clubbing night-owls.

■ Arc de Triomphe & Trocadéro

Hôtel Keppler: 12 Rue Keppler, 16th, M° George V, ☎ 01 47 20 65 05, fax 01 47 23 02 29, www.hotelkeppler.com (€€).

The family-run Hôtel Keppler is one of the few budget hotels in the swanky Champs-Elysées neighborhood. Its 49 rooms are spacious and brightly decorated with blue and gold fabrics and pale walls, and are equipped with in-roof safe, phone with dial-up Internet access, satellite TV, and private bathrooms (shower or bath) with hair dryer. The hotel has room service, elevator and a large lounge bar just off the lobby with wooden parquet floors. Continental breakfast is served in a separate dining room or in guest rooms.

Au Palais de Chaillot: 35 Avenue Raymond Poincaré, 16th, M° Trocadéro, ☎ 01 53 70 09 09, fax 01 53 70 09 08, www.chaillotel.com (€€€).

This bright and modern hotel a stone's throw from the Eiffel Tower has 28 soundproofed rooms with private bathroom (shower), hair dryer, in-room safe, dial-up Internet access, satellite TV, and plenty of space. The hotel has an elevator, room service, and laundry service. Breakfast can be served in the guest rooms or the comfortable lounge. This hotel is best known for its friendly, multilingual staff.

Hôtel Pergolèse: 3 Rue Pergolèse, 16th, M° Argentine, ☎ 01 53 64 04 04, fax 01 53 64 04 40, www.hotelpergolese.com (€€€€).

This sleek designer boutique hotel near the Champs-Elysées features the latest contemporary design and luxury amenities, without a sky-high price tag. There are 40 soundproofed and air conditioned rooms equipped with Bang & Olufsen television, minibar, in-room safe, direct-dial phone, parquet-wood furniture, luxury linens and sparkling white tiled bathrooms with chrome sink. Guests can order 24-hour room service. The hotel also has an attractive bar decorated with contemporary artworks, a small garden, and a bright breakfast room designed by Philippe Starck. Ask for a courtyard-facing room, and opt for the Superior Double if you want some extra space.

Hôtel du Rond-Point de Longchamp: 86 Rue de Longchamp, 16th, M° Trocadéro or Victor Hugo, ☎ 01 45 05 13 63, fax 01 47 55 12 80, www.rd-pt-longchamp.fr (€€€€).

The Eiffel Tower is in full view right outside the front door of this elegant hotel in the Trocadéro district. There are 58 soundproofed rooms decorated in classic contemporary style with air conditioning, minibar, marble bathroom, hairdryer, satellite TV, and direct-dial phone. A few rooms actually have balcony views of Gustave Eiffel's masterpiece. The hotel also has an intimate bar, billiards room, and English or American à la carte breakfast. Torcadéo is pretty quiet after dark, but the Champs-Elysées is just five minutes away by taxi or métro.

■ The Latin Quarter

Hôtel Esmeralda: 4 Rue St-Julien-le-Pauvre, 5th, M° Maubert-Mutualite, ☎ 01 43 54 19 20, fax 01 40 51 00 68 (€). No credit cards.

This is one of the city's most popular budget hotels, with eclectic flea-market décor, wooden beam ceilings and views overlooking Notre Dame. The building itself is so old that space is an issue (no elevator), so unless you fork out for a larger room with a bathtub, you'll be forced to squeeze into tiny closets to shower or relieve yourself. Still, it has lots of charm and personality lacking in most budget hotels. The friendly owner recommends booking at least three months in advance to secure one of the 19 rooms.

Hôtel St-Jacques: 35 Rue des Ecoles, 5th, M° Maubert-Mutualité, ☎ 01 44 07 45 45, fax 01 43 25 65 50, www.hotel-saintjacques.com (€€).

This Latin Quarter hotel has plenty of charm and comfort. The elegant 19th-century-style lobby and breakfast room is decorated with painted murals, a crystal chandelier, antique staircase, molded ceilings and dainty furnishings. An elevator leads to the 35 soundproofed rooms, each equipped with satellite TV, telephone, private bathrooms with shower or bathtub, hair dryer, in-room safe, and modem Internet access. Many rooms have views over the Panthéon and Notre Dame, and room #25 even has a corner balcony. Some people may not like the hotel's location on the busy Rue des Ecoles, but it's ideally located for those who want to be in the center of the Latin Quarter.

Hôtel Marignan: 13 Rue du Sommerand, 5th, M° Maubert-Mutualité, ☎ 01 43 54 63 81, fax 01 43 25 16 69, www.hotel-marignan.com (€€).

This hotel is a bit like a hostel (without the dorm rooms), with a friendly, service-oriented staff, free breakfast, laundry room, fully equipped kitchen, Internet access and a library full of guidebooks. There are 30 rooms, including quads and quintuples, each with functional furniture and a sink, and either private or shared shower and toilet facilities. The hotel is on a small street near the Sorbonne and the Panthéon, just 10 minutes from Notre Dame, the Jardins du Luxembourg or St-Germain-des-Prés. Rates vary throughout the year; check the web site for current promotions.

Hôtel des Grandes Ecoles: 75 Rue Cardinal Lemoine, 5th, M° Cardinal Lemoine, ☎ 01 43 26 79 23, fax 01 43 25 28 15, www.hotel-grandes-ecoles.com (€€€).

Looking for floral cottage ambience? Then this adorable hotel with its cobblestone courtyard entrance and window boxes is a must. The hotel has 51 rooms (and an elevator), all lovingly decorated in Laura Ashley prints, with en-suite bathrooms, hair dryer, and direct-dial phone (sorry, no TVs). Continental breakfast (€8) is served in a bright dining room with parquet floors and crochet lace tablecloths, or out in the garden during warmer weather. Indoor parking is available for €30. The hotel is just a few blocks from the Panthéon, the Sorbonne, and the most adorable market street in Paris, Rue Mouffetard (open every day except Monday and Sunday afternoon).

Hôtel Sully St-Germain: 31 Rue des Ecoles, 5th, M° Maubert-Mutualité, ☎ 01 43 26 56 02, fax 01 43 29 74 42, www.hotel-paris-sully.com (€€€€).

This Latin Quarter hotel pleases those who want a bit of medieval atmosphere without sacrificing modern comforts such as air conditioning and private parking (€26). The hotel has a fitness room with sauna and Jacuzzi, and 61 bright rooms with private bathroom, hair dryer, minibar, cable TV, direct-dial phone (some with modem connections), and in-room safe. The buffet breakfast is served in the lounge, but there's no restaurant. Guests have access to the billiards room in the sister hotel next door. Check the web site for seasonal promotions.

■ St-Germain-des-Prés & Luxembourg

Hôtel de Nesle: 7 Rue de Nesle, 6th, M° Odéon, ☎ 01 43 54 62 41, fax 01 43 54 31 88, www.hoteldenesle.com (€€).

The quirky Hôtel de Nesle (pronounced *nell*) features 20 themed guest rooms, individually decorated with colorful wall murals and names like Notre Dame de Paris, Molière, and a Hammam room completely tiled like a Turkish bathhouse. Some rooms face the hotel's tiny private garden, and are equipped with a bathtub, shower, or shared facilities in the hall. But that's where the mod con's stop. There are no TVs, no phones in the rooms, no elevator and no breakfast service. The backpacking and bohemian clientele come for the artsy atmosphere and prices almost unheard of for the St-Germain-des-Prés district. Reservations by phone only, one week in advance. Visit their web site to choose which room you'd like.

Delhy's Hôtel: 22 Rue de l'Hirondelle, 6th, M° St-Michel, ☎ 01 43 26 58 25, delhys@wanadoo.fr (€€).

This small hotel is on a quiet passage right off the busy Place St-Michel. The décor is not particularly noteworthy, although some rooms have exposed wooden-beam ceilings, and the breakfast room has an old-fashioned bistro feel. All 21 rooms have satellite TV, direct-dial telephones, and sinks. If you don't want to share facilities be sure to reserve a room with en-suite shower well in advance (the toilets are on each floor, and shared showers are on the ground floor, and cost €4).

Hôtel du Lys: 23 Rue de Serpente, 6th, M° St-Michel or Odéon, ☎ 01 43 26 97 57, fax 01 44 07 34 90, www.hoteldulys.com (€€€).

This old-fashioned Paris hotel set in a 17th-century building has 22 rooms with exposed wooden beams, antique furniture and floral printed wallpaper. Private bathrooms have either a bathtub or shower, and a hair dryer. There's no elevator and the rooms can be tiny (ask for 8, 11, 13 or 18 for more space), but there's satellite TV, in room safes, and breakfast is included in the price. The location alone, on a quiet side-street between St-Germain-des-Prés and the Latin Quarter, is enough to woo fans of historic Paris.

Hôtel Lenox: 9 Rue de l'Université, 7th, M° Rue du Bac, ☎ 01 42 96 10 95, fax 01 42 61 52 83, www.lenoxsaintgermain.com (€€€).

Located on a quiet street that becomes Rue Jacob, this hotel pays tribute to the jazz heritage of St-Germain-des-Prés with its 1930s-style Lenox Club bar. The 34 rooms are bright, with a classic contemporary décor, private bathroom (bath or shower), hair dryer, air conditioning, in-room safe, satellite TV, and phone with dial-up Internet access. The attic rooms are larger, with exposed wooden ceiling beams. The hotel has an elevator, laundry service, and vaulted stone cellar breakfast room.

Le Clos Médicis: 56 Rue Monsieur-le-Prince, 6th, M° Cluny-La Sorbonne or RER Luxembourg, ☎ 01 43 29 10 80, fax 01 43 54 26 90, www.closmedicis.com (€€€€).

The Clos Médicis is a stylish and intimate hotel between St-Germain-des-Prés and the Latin Quarter, just a block from the Jardins du Luxembourg. The 38 air conditioned rooms are decorated in chic neutral tones, dark wood furnishings and textured fabrics, with minibar, flat screen TV with cable, in-room safe, dedicated modem line, and tiled bathrooms (shower or bath) with terra cotta floors and hair dryer. Most rooms have high ceilings or exposed wooden beams. The country-style breakfast salon has exposed ceiling beams and French doors opening onto a private garden patio. A roaring fire greets guests in the comfy lobby lounge, with a small corner bar, Internet station, and complementary newspapers. Check out their web site for regular last-minute and low-season specials.

Hôtel Luxembourg Parc: 42 Rue de Vaugirard, 6th, M° Odéon or RER Luxembourg, ☎ 01 53 10 36 50, fax 01 53 10 36 59, www.hotelluxparc.com (€€€€).

This elegant hotel successfully combines Left Bank history and charm with ample space and luxury service. Located directly across from the Jardins du Luxembourg, the hotel has a peaceful inner courtyard with a sculpture fountain, a cozy library lounge with fireplace, and is equipped with an elevator and air conditioning. There are 23 rooms with en-suite bathroom, cable and satellite TV, 24-hour room service, Internet and e-mail access, and fax service. The period décor is more stylish than stuffy, with period furnishings, original artworks, rich fabrics, and exposed beam ceilings. St-Germain-des-Prés and the Latin Quarter are a five-minute stroll from the hotel.

L'Hôtel: 13 Rue des Beaux Arts, 6th, M° St-Germain-des-Prés, ☎ 01 44 41 99 00, fax 01 43 25 64 81, www.l-hotel.com (€€€€€).

This is where Oscar Wilde famously died "above his means" in 1900. Completely redone by the designer Jacques Garcia, it's now a sumptuous Baroque paradise that the decadent writer would have adored, with rich fabrics, gilded mirrors, mahogany wood, fluffy robes and Hermès toiletries... not for minimalists! Each of the 20 rooms is individually designed with its own personality – Art Deco, Empire, Oriental, etc. – equipped with private bathroom and all of the modern luxuries such as cable TV, air conditioning, in-room safe, room service, minibar, high-speed Internet connection and fax machine. Attention: the elevator doesn't go to the sixth floor. The hotel has private parking, laundry service, and a small swimming pool and sauna below ground. Le Belier restaurant and bar are open to the public (closed Sunday and Monday and all of August). See the web site for photos of the different style rooms.

Paris

■ Invalides & Eiffel Tower

Hôtel de l'Empereur: 2 Rue Chevert, 7th, M° Ecole-Militaire or La Tour Maubourg, ☎ 01 45 55 88 02, fax 01 45 51 88 54, www.hotelempereur.com (€€).

Built in the 1700s, this original hotel is completely dedicated to Napoleon Bonaparte, with tasteful Empire décor in every room. A view of the Invalides Dome, where the Emperor now lies, is available from rooms 12, 22, 32, and 42. The 38 rooms are smallish in size, but each has its own tiled bathroom with shower and hair dryer; rooms also have direct phone line for Internet access, satellite TV, minibar, and in-room safe. There's an elevator, laundry and room service, and baby cribs available.

Hôtel du Champ-de-Mars: 7 Rue du Champ-de-Mars, 7th, M° Ecole Militaire, ☎ 01 45 51 52 30, fax 01 45 51 64 36, www.hotel-du-champ-de-mars.com (€€).

This family-run hotel is right at the foot of the Eiffel Tower, near Invalides, the Rodin Museum, and the Rue Cler market. Each of the 25 rooms is individually decorated with a Provençal floral theme and stenciled walls, and is equipped with satellite TV, direct-dial phone, and private bathroom with hair dryer. Two rooms on the ground floor overlook private, flowered courtyards. The hotel has a cozy breakfast room and lobby lounge. Of course, for comfort at these prices you'll need to book well in advance!

Hôtel la Bourdonnais: 111 Avenue de la Bourdonnais, 7th, M° Ecole-Militaire, ☎ 01 47 05 45 42, fax 01 45 55 75 54, www.hotellabourdonnais.com (€€€).

Resembling a typical French bourgeois townhouse, this cozy hotel has had the same owner since 1962; it has a friendly, family-run atmosphere and a loyal following. The hotel is on a quiet, tree-lined street between the Eiffel Tower and Les Invalides, two blocks from the Rue Cler market street. The 60 guest rooms are decorated in rich colors with antiques and Persian rugs, with private bathroom (bath or shower), hair dryer, air conditioning, soundproofing, direct-dial phone, in-room safe, and dial-up Internet access. The main lobby opens onto a leafy winter garden and patio where guests enjoy breakfast, or snacks throughout the day. There's also an intimate lounge for reading the daily newspapers, enjoying a cup of tea, or checking e-mail at the Internet station. Triples and quads are also available.

■ Palace Hotels

Paris has many legendary four-star deluxe "palace hotels," renowned for their posh period décor, state-of-the-art facilities, Michelin-starred restaurants, and superbly trained multilingual staff. With typical rates between €500 and €800 per night for standard rooms these are beyond the average traveler's budget, but if you have occasion to splurge you have your choice of some of the best – and best known – hotels anywhere.

Hôtel Ritz Paris: 15 Place Vendôme, 1st, M° Concorde, ☎ 01 43 16 30 70, fax 01 43 16 36 68, www.ritzparis.com. From €680, 106 rooms (smallest rooms are 323 square feet), 18th-century décor, kid-friendly services, no pets.

Always in style, this Grande Dame on the Place Vendôme simply oozes glitz and glamour, with stretch limos and paparazzi parked permanently at the front door. The hotel is home to the **Ritz Escoffier Culinary Academy**, the famous **Hemingway Bar** and the new **Cambon Champagne Bar** (all open to visitors).

BONUS: *Guests have access to the members-only Ritz Club restaurant and nightclub, as well as the hotel's luxurious health club (with a La Prairie beauty institute and a poolside lounge bar).*

Hôtel de Crillon: 10 Place de la Concorde, 8th, M° Concorde, ☎ 01 44 71 15 00, fax 01 44 71 15 02, www.crillon.com. From €585, 95 rooms, Louis XV décor, walk-in closets.

Built in 1775 and turned into a luxury hotel in 1909, the imposing façade of the Crillon dominates the busy Place de la Concorde, next to the American Embassy, the Jardin des Tuileries and the Champs-Elysées. Its lavish interior of Italian marble and crystal chandeliers was completely renovated in 2003, with a new Guerlain spa and fitness center.

BONUS: *The hotel has complimentary services for solo female travlers, children from tots to teens, and even pets, who receive a souvenir Crillon collar. The hotel also hosts floral-design workshops, organized by star floral designer Christian Tortu, which are open to visitors.*

Hôtel Plaza Athénée: 25 Avenue Montaigne, 8th, M° Alma-Marceau, ☎ 01 53 67 66 67, fax 01 53 67 66 66, www.plaza-athenee-paris.com. From €875, 145 rooms decorated in Louis XVI or Regency style; two floors in Art Deco style. Remote-controlled air conditioning and heating.

The Plaza Athénée has been open since 1911, but has become one of the most stylish hotels in Paris since its sexy new renovation in 1999. Models and media types adore the hip **Bar Athénée** as well as the hotel's location on one of the most luxurious shopping streets in Paris.

BONUSES *include a trendy restaurant run by star chef Alain Ducasse, and a fitness center with a personal trainer on duty.*

Hôtel Meurice: 228 Rue de Rivoli, 1st, M° Tuileries, ☎ 01 44 58 10 10, fax 01 44 58 10 15, www.meuricehotel.com. From €720, 160 very spacious rooms decorated in different styles, from Empire to Louis XVI; kid-friendly services.

"Le Meurice" is under the stone arcades of the busy Rue de Rivoli, overlooking the Jardin des Tuileries. Its opulent Louis XVI décor and intricate mosaic tiled floors were spruced up during its recent extensive remodeling. Although always popular with movie stars and royalty, this Parisian institution has been wooing a younger, trendier clientele (the classical pianist in the lobby was replaced with a lounge DJ).

Paris

> **BONUSES** *include the Art Nouveau* **Winter Garden** *and a 3,000-square-foot spa with Les Sources de Caudalie "vinotherapie" treatments.*

Hôtel Prince des Galles: 33 Avenue Georges V, 8th, M° George V, ☎ 01 53 23 77 77, fax 01 53 23 78 78, www.luxurycollection.com. From €500, 138 rooms decorated with classic French period furnishings and Art Deco marble bathrooms; guest rooms also have CD and DVD player, VCR, game console and fax machine.

Built during the 1920s, this discreetly elegant hotel is just off the Champs-Elysées on the busy Avenue George V. It has a comfortable, family-friendly atmosphere, with period furnishings, pale wood paneling and a cozy British-style bar with a no-smoking policy – rare in Paris!

> **BONUSES** *include complimentry minibars in the guest rooms and the gorgeous* **Jardin des Cygnes** *gourmet restaurant, decorated with Italian frescoes and floor-to-ceiling windows overlooking the mosaic-tiled courtyard.*

Hôtel Lutetia: 46 Boulevard Raspail, 6th, M° Sèvres-Babylone, ☎ 01 49 54 46 46, fax 01 49 54 46 00, www.lutetia-paris.com. From €480, 250 soundproofed rooms (smallest rooms are 215 square feet) in Art Deco style, with Annick Goutal's toiletries.

The Lutetia is not only the first Art Deco hotel built in Paris, dating from 1910, but it is also the only palace hotel on the left bank. It's across from the historic Bon Marché department store, just a few blocks from St-Germain-des-Prés and Invalides. Its jazzy atmosphere is popular with artists and musicians.

> **BONUSES** *include the Art Deco style* **Brasserie Lutetia**, *famous for its seafood and Sunday brunch; and the live jazz Wednesday through Saturday nights in the cozy Ernst Bar, which has its own cigar club. There are great promotions on the suites off-season through the hotel's web site.*

Hôtel Le Bristol: 112 Rue de Faubourg St-Honoré, 8th, M° Miromesnil, ☎ 01 53 43 43 00, fax 01 53 43 43 01, www.lebristolparis.com. From €580, 173 rooms, classic period décor featuring blue and gold fabrics and pale walls.

On a street famous for art galleries and haute couture boutiques, the discreetly exclusive Bristol is a favorite of Parisians in the know. Opened in 1924, the Gustave Eiffel-inspired building is decorated with Gobelins tapestries and Baccarat crystal chandeliers. There's a live catwalk show of top designers' fashions every Saturday in the tearoom.

 BONUSES *include the 13,000-square-foot gardens in the center of the hotel, and the sixthfloor sundeck and heated swimming pool with panoramic views of Paris.*

Hôtel Royal Monceau: 37 Avenue Hoche, 8th, M° Charles de Gaulle-Etoile, ☎ 01 42 99 88 00, fax 01 42 99 89 90, www.royalmonceau.com. From €480, 203 rooms featuring elegant furnishings and pale colors, with high-tech amenities such as video game consoles.

Opened at the height of the Roaring Twenties, the Royal Monceau has all of the luxury and modern amenities expected of a palace hotel. Although the hotel is just 350 yards from the Arc de Triomphe and the Champs-Elysées, it feels worlds away from the bustling Parisian streets, making it popular with families, as well as distinguished guests who value their privacy.

BONUSES *are **Le Jardin**, a restaurant set in a glassed-in garden conservatory, and **Les Thermes**, a spa and fitness center overlooking the hotel gardens.*

Le Grand Hôtel Intercontinental: 2 Rue Scribe, 9th, M° Opéra, ☎ 01 40 07 32 32, fax 01 42 66 12 51, www.paris.intercontinental.com. From €400, 477 rooms decorated in Napoleon III style, with high mahogany beds and wall prints in gold, royal blue or burgundy; no pets.

Le Grand is the better known of the two Intercontinental hotels in Paris (the other, known as the Intercontinental Paris, is in a former monastery on Rue Castiglione). Built in 1862 and completely renovated in 2003, it overlooks the Palais Garnier Opéra, two blocks from the Place Vendôme and major department stores. This is a large hotel, with an entire wing for conferences and a brand new health club. In the center of the hotel is an iron and glass atrium lounge, which is so large that you feel as if you are outside. A pianist performs in the evenings.

BONUSES *include watching Paris go by from the all-season terrace of the hotel's famous **Café de la Paix**, or escaping the crowds in the low-lit **Bar du Grand Hotel**.*

Four Seasons Hôtel George V: 31 Avenue George V, 8th, M° George V, ☎ 01 49 52 70 00, fax 01 49 52 70 10, www.fourseasons.com. From €680 245 rooms (smallest rooms are 398 square feet) decorated in Louis XV style, featuring marble bathrooms with deep tub and separate shower. Guest room amenities include video game console and stereo; kid friendly.

Paris

This classic Paris hotel dating from 1928 was completely remodeled in 2002. Its opulent décor features pale marble, rich fabrics, and crystal chandeliers throughout. The Four Seasons name attracts a well-heeled clientele from around the world to its location off the Champs-Elysées, just a block from the designer boutiques of Avenue Montaigne.

> **BONUS:** *Dine at "Le Cinq's" haute cuisine restaurant and summer terrace, or chill out in the luxurious spa's relaxation rooms or the indoor pool surrounded by trompe l'oeil gardens.*

Park Hyatt Paris-Vendôme: 5 Rue de la Paix, 2nd, M° Opéra, ☎ 01 58 71 12 34, fax 01 58 71 12 35, http://paris.vendome.hyatt.com. From €525, 177 rooms decorated in mahogany and neutral colors, with touches of silk and bronze; limestone bathrooms have under-floor heating; walk-in closets.

Those looking for something more modern will appreciate the sleek new Hyatt opened in 2002 just off the Place Vendôme. The designer crowd comes for the white leather booths and trendy open-kitchen design of the hotel's **Le Park** restaurant.

> **BONUSES** *include a spa and fitness center with Carita beauty treatment rooms, and a Bang & Olufsen entertainment center in each guestroom.*

■ Neighborhood Hotels

These hotels are often overlooked by foreign tourists because they're in unfamiliar areas of town. But staying in one of these less "touristy" accommodations can give visitors a peek into a real Parisian neighborhood. Most are less expensive, and are no more than 10 minutes from the center by métro.

Les Chansonniers, 113 Boulevard de Ménilmontant, 11th, M° Ménilmontant or Père-Lachaise, ☎ 01 43 57 00 58, fax 01 48 05 03 78 40, leschansonniers@caramail.com (€).

This 1960s-retro hotel is dedicated to the legendary figures of French *chanson* such as Edith Piaf and Charles Trenet. It has 40 bright rooms on three levels, all equipped with a private shower or bath, hair dryer, satellite TV, minibar, and direct-dial phone with modem Internet access. Non-smoking rooms and free children's beds available on request. The hotel is in the heart of Eastern Paris – ideal for those who want to explore Belleville, Père Lachaise, La Villette and the Oberkampf-Ménilmontant nightlife scene.

> **BONUS:** *The colorful **Marché Belleville** (see page 225) takes place right outside Les Chansonniers twice a week.*

L'Hôtel des Voyageurs: 22 Rue Boulard, 14th, M° Denfert-Rochereau, ☎ 01 43 21 08 20, fax 01 43 21 08 21, hotel.des.voyageurs2@wanadoo.fr (€).

This friendly hotel near the Rue Daguerre market street is a popular hangout for local artsy types. The main attraction of this hotel is the breakfast lounge overlooking a private garden courtyard. The 35 rooms are pretty basic, with simple, modern décor and private bathrooms (bath or shower). Some overlook the Fondation Cartier. Free Internet access in the lobby.

> **BONUS:** *RER B (direct to both airports) and the OrlyBus are right around the corner from L'Hôtel des Voyageurs.*

Hôtel Eldorado: 18 Rue des Dames, 17th, M° Place de Clichy, ☎ 01 45 22 35 21, fax 01 43 87 25 97 (€).

This is one of the hippest budget hotels in town, embodying the counter-cultural spirit of the up-and-coming Batignolles neighborhood. Decorated with flea-market finds and colorful ethnic fabrics, this former bordello attracts an eclectic clientele of artists, models and musicians. Some rooms overlook the hotel's private courtyard garden, where guests hang out during warmer weather. There's also a billiards room in the basement. Book far, far in advance.

> **BONUS:** *The Hôtel Eldorado is flanked on either side by the Brit-owned **Lush Bar** and the typically French **Bistro des Dames**.*

Hôtel Langlois (formerly *Hôtel des Croisés*): 63 Rue Saint-Lazare, 9th, M° Trinité, ☎ 01 48 74 78 24, fax 01 49 95 04 43, hotel-descroises@wanadoo.fr (€€).

This late 19th-century bank was turned into a hotel in 1896, and has retained many of its beautiful Belle Epoque architectural details such as the retro wooden elevator and vintage front desk. The 27 spacious rooms – some with 15-foot-high ceilings – are decorated in Art Nouveau or Art Deco style, with elegant fabrics and period furnishings. The beautifully tiled bathrooms are decorated with ornamental fireplaces. Modern comforts include direct-dial phones with Internet dial-up access, minibar, and satellite TV. Top floor rooms have views of Sacré-Coeur. The hotel is a bit off the beaten tourist track in the residential Nouvelle Athènes district, just 15 minutes on foot to Montmartre or Opéra Garnier.

> **BONUS:** *The **Museé de la Vie Romantique** and **Musée Gustave Courbet** are right around the corner from the Hôtel Langlois.*

Hôtel Beaumarchais: 3 Rue Oberkampf, 11th, M° Filles du Calvaire or Oberkampf, ☎ 01 53 36 86 86, fax 01 43 38 32 86, www.hotelbeaumarchais.com (€€).

Pompidou Center fans take notice! This bright and modern hotel between the Marais and the hip Oberkampf district combines contemporary kitsch décor and curvy Ikea-style furnishings with warm, Mediterranean colors. The 31 air conditioned rooms have private, mosaic tiled bathrooms (bath or shower) with hair dryer, satellite TV, in-room safe and double-glazed windows. The hotel has room service, and an adorable little patio garden where guests can eat breakfast in warmer weather.

> **BONUS:** *The historic **Marché des Enfants Rouges** is just two blocks from the Hôtel Beaumarchais.*

Le Vert Galant: 41-43 Rue Croulebarbe, 13th, M° Gobelins or Corvisart, ☎ 01 44 08 83 50, fax 01 44 08 83 69 (€€).

This friendly, family-run hotel is in a quiet neighborhood across from a large park. Its 15 bright and modern rooms, simple yet comfortable, overlook an inner garden courtyard and are equipped with cable TV, minibar, in-room safe, telephone with dial-up Internet access, and private bathroom (bath or shower). Six rooms have little kitchenettes (burners, mini fridge, utensils) for those who want to save a bit on dining out costs. Located on the south side of the Latin Quarter, the hotel is within easy walking distance of the Rue Mouffetard market street or the charming Butte aux Cailles district.

> **BONUS:** *Next door to Le Vert Galant is a fantastic Basque restaurant, **L'Auberge Etchegorry** (run by the same family), with a cozy country atmosphere.*

Hôtel Istria: 29 Rue Campagne-Première, 14th, M° Raspail, ☎ 01 43 20 91 82, fax 01 43 22 48 84, hotelistria@wanadoo.fr (€€).

Located right around the corner from the Fondation Cartier and Montparnasse Cemetery, this cozy hotel was once home to Francis Pacabia, Man Ray and other artists during Montparnasse's heyday of the 1930s. It has 26 rooms decorated in warm colors and dark wood furniture, with private bathroom (shower or bath), air conditioning, direct-dial phone and TV and in-room safe. Four rooms overlook the inner courtyard. Breakfast is served in a vaulted stone cellar.

BONUS: *The **Jardins du Luxembourg** is just two blocks away from the Hôtel Istria.*

Eden Hôtel: 19 Rue Ordener, 18th, M° Jules-Joffrin, ☎ 42 64 61 63, fax 42 64 11 43, www.edenhotel-montmartre.com (€€).

This comfortable hotel is in a typically Parisian neighborhood on the north side of Montmartre, just 10 minutes' walk to the Sacré-Coeur Basilica and a direct bus to the Marché aux Puces. The 35 comfy rooms are decorated with pastel colors and pale wood furniture, and are equipped with direct-dial phone, satellite TV, and tiled bathroom (shower or tub) with hair dryer. The hotel has an elevator, 24-hour reception desk, safe-deposit box and hot/cold drink dispenser. Breakfast can be served in your room.

BONUS: *There are a number of restaurants and cafés near the Eden, and an open market around the corner each morning.*

Hôtel Mayet: 3 Rue Mayet, 6th, M° Duroc, ☎ 01 47 83 21 35, fax 01 40 65 95 78, www.mayet.com (€€€). Breakfast included.

Budget-conscious visitors looking for a fresh, contemporary hotel on the Left Bank should check out the Hotel Mayet, in the bottom of the 6th on a quiet side-street near Montparnasse and the shopping street Rue Cherche-Midi. The décor is a mix of sleek lines and neutral tones with splashes of bold color and funky accessories. Rooms are equipped with ceiling fans, direct-dial telephone, cable TV, and private bathrooms (shower or bath) and hair dryer. The hotel has an elevator, lobby bar with graffiti mural, and a vaulted stone breakfast room.

BONUS: *The English bookshop-and-tearoom **Tea & Tattered Pages** is on the same street as the Hôtel Mayet.*

Le Hameau de Passy: 48 Rue de Passy, 16th, M° Passy or Muette, ☎ 01 42 88 47 55, fax 01 42 30 83 72, www.hameaudepassy.com (€€€).

Located on the chic, west Paris shopping street Rue de Passy, this oasis of a hotel offers great value. Overlooking an inner garden courtyard, the 32 rooms have a modern décor with light colors, private bathroom, direct-dial telephone with dial-up Internet access, cable TV and alarm clock. A fax and safe-deposit boxes are available at the front desk. A continental breakfast – included in the price – is served in the bright dining room or in the guestroom on request.

Paris

> **BONUS:** *Museums near the Hameau de Passy include the* **Musée du Vin**, **Maison de Victor Hugo**, *and the* **Musée Marmottan-Monet**.

Apart'hotels & Furnished Rentals

Renting a furnished apartment in Paris is not only a good way to save money (primarily by being able to cook your own meals), it also allows visitors a chance to live like real Parisians by shopping at local markets. For those who would still like to have the services of a hotel, apart'hotels combine the best of both worlds (although they can feel a bit more sterile).

Paris Furnished Apartments: ☎ 01 42 74 07 07, fax 01 42 74 01 01, www.parisfurnishedapartments.com. This agency lists furnished apartment rentals, house rentals and a few rooms in shared private residences. There are good photos and plenty of information. They can also provide airport shuttles and babysitting services.

Paris Lodging: www.parislodging.fr. This bi-lingual site suffers a bit from *franglais* (when it says a flat comes with "towel," it means "linens"), but there's a good selection of private studios and one- or two-bedroom flats, most with photos. The reservation fee is a steep €43 for one to two guests, €85 for three or more guests. Can be reserved online.

Inter-Logement: ☎ 01 45 66 66 88, fax 01 45 67 04 22, www.inter-logement.com. This agency is recommended by the Paris Convention & Visitors Bureau, with furnished studios and flats (up to five bedrooms) to rent for the week, 15 days or month. The selection and photos are good, but the low rates are offset a bit by the agency fee (20%) and the annual "membership fee" of €25.

Paris Appartements Services: ☎ 01 40 28 01 28, fax 01 40 28 92 01, www.paris-appartements-services.fr. Run a bit like a hotel, this agency lets customers reserve the size and neighborhood, but not a specific apartment. However, they are all supposedly three-star level (with prices to match), and have the same services and equipment. They can also provide for Continental breakfast delivery to the apartment each morning.

Citadines Apart'hotels: ☎ 08 25 01 03 34, www.citadines.com. These modern accommodations are fully equipped studios and apartments for up to six guests with kitchen (fridge, dishwasher, coffee maker, microwave, etc.), bathroom with hair dryer, cable TV and a mini-stereo. They also have optional services such as babysitting, breakfast and laundry. Most have a lounge area with Internet computer station, some are air conditioned. Popular with business travelers and large families, there are locations all over Paris (and several other locations in Europe), with different rates (€100-€300/night) depending on the season and length of stay. Two well-placed Citadines are in Montmartre, on a quiet passage next to Montmartre Cemetery, and at the Louvre, right next to the Comédie Française.

Bed & Breakfasts

 Alcove et Agape, ☎ 01 44 85 06 05, fax 01 44 85 06 14, www.al-cove-et-agapes.com, info@paris-bedandbreakfast.com. This bed & breakfast agency manages about 40 properties throughout Paris. Listings are classified into four different categories. A room in a modest Parisian apartment with shared facilities is about €48/night, and a large room with private en-suite bathroom in a prestigious mansion with garden is about €120/night. They have very strict standards, so there's usually a very good price/quality ratio. And you get to enjoy true Parisian hospitality!

Bed & Breakfast France: ☎ 01491 578803 (UK), fax 01491 410806 (UK), www.bedbreak.com. Based in Britain, this agency lists and rates B&Bs throughout France, with a large selection of Paris properties. The symbols on the web site can be confusing, and there are many properties without photos, but overall this is a very useful site for Englishspeaking travelers, with attentive customer service.

Youth Hostels

Parisian youth hostels are among the most expensive in Europe, but can still be a good deal for solo travelers and anyone who enjoys the social interaction. Most of the hostels have private doubles, but these can end up costing the same as a double in a hotel. Below are a few well-located hostels. No matter where you go, be sure to confirm ahead of time whether there's a membership fee or age restrictions, if the breakfast and linens are included, if there's a curfew or lockout, and what time you need to check in.

Les Maisons Internationales de la Jeunesse et des Etudiants (MIJE): 6 Rue de Fourcy, 4th, M° St-Paul or Hôtel-de-Ville, ☎ 01 42 74 23 45, fax 1 40 27 81 64, www.mije.com. Dorm beds €24-€26, breakfast and linens provided. Annual membership fee €2.50.

The MIJE has three hostels, in fully restored 17th-century townhouses in the Marais, open to guests 18-30 years old. The setting, with exposed wooden beams and cobblestone courtyards, puts other hostels to shame! Each dorm has four beds and a bathroom with shower and sink (toilets in the hall). Double and single rooms can be rented as well (€30-€47 per person). The vaulted dining hall is in the Fourcy MIJE, and serves full meals for €10.50. Reserve at least a week in advance through the web site, or show up in the morning between 7 am and 11 am. Lockout is noon to 3 pm, curfew is 1 am to 7 am. Free lockers. The other locations are around the corner at 12 Rue des Barres and 11 Rue Fauconnier (all in the St-Paul area of the Marais).

Young & Happy Hostel: 80 Rue Mouffetard, 5th, ☎ 01 45 35 09 53, fax 01 47 07 22 24, www.youngandhappy.fr. Dorm beds €22, doubles €23/person, includes breakfast. Linen rental €5.

The age limit is a bit "fluid" at this tiny hostel, on a cobblestoned market street in the Latin Quarter, near plenty of student bars and cheap crêpe stands. Dorms have four or five beds each and a private bathroom with sink and shower (more showers and toilets down the hall). The building itself is quite old, with exposed wooden beams and stone walls. Continental breakfast (baguette with butter and jam, OJ and coffee or tea) is served in the stone cellar (the kitchen down there is fully equipped for those who want to cook themselves). The lobby has a small bar, daily papers, and an Internet kiosk (which always seems to be out of service). Reserve online or by fax, or show up in the morning between 8 and 11am. Lockout 11am to 5pm, curfew 2 to 7am.

Peace & Love Youth Hostel and Bar: 245 Rue de la Fayette, 10th, M° Jaures, ☎ 01 46 07 65 91, www.paris-hostels.com. Dorm beds €21, doubles €25/person, included linens and breakfast.

Although slightly off the beaten track, this modern hostel has no curfew, no lockout, and its lobby bar has cheap beer and satellite TV. Needless to say, it attracts the party crowd, which, along with the busy traffic outside, can be quite noisy (not ideal for light sleepers). There are cooking facilities and free safety deposit boxes. Rates are slightly cheaper off-season or if you just want a mattress on the floor. The hostel is at the intersection of three métro lines close to the Gare de l'Est and Gare du Nord, and the Canal St-Martin. Reserve via the web or call in advance.

Auberge de Jeunesse – Jules Ferry: 8 Boulevard Jules Ferry, 11th, M° République, ☎ 01 43 57 55 60, fax 01 43 14 82 09, www.hostels-in.com, paris.julesferry@fuaj.org. Dorm beds €19.50, including breakfast and linens. Annual membership fee €2.50.

This hostel at the crossroads of the Marais, Oberkampf and Bastille quarters has no age limits, and doesn't accept advance reservations. There's a laundry room and free lockers, but no cooking facilities (just a microwave). Each dorm room has two to six beds and a bathroom with shower. The reception desk is open 24 hours (no curfew), but there is a lockout from 10am to 4pm. It's a small hostel in a good location, so get there early in the morning for a room.

Le Village Hostel: 20 Rue d'Orsel, 18th, M° Anvers, ☎ 01 42 64 22 02, fax 01 42 64 22 04, www.villagehostel.fr. Dorm beds €21.50, doubles €25/person, including breakfast. Linen rental is extra (small fee). No age limits.

This Montmartre hostel is famous for its private terrace with views of Sacré-Coeur. Like most hostels, it has old stone walls and exposed wooden beams, with metal-framed bunk beds and modern bathrooms. The reception and café are open until 2 am (curfew), lockout 11am to 4pm. A small kitchen is available for light cooking. Dorm rooms have up to five beds, but there are also singles and doubles, all with their own bathroom facilities and telephone. Reserve a room by web or fax, or show up early in the morning.

Auberge de Jeunesse – Le d'Artagnan: 80 Rue Vitreuve, 20th, M° Porte de Bagnolet, ☎ 01 40 32 34 56, fax 01 40 32 34 55, www.hostels-in.com, paris.le-dartagnan@fuaj.org.

Dorm beds €20.60, doubles €21.50/person, includes breakfast and linens. Annual membership fee €2.50. No age limits.

This is the largest hostel in France, with over 400 beds in a modern building in the St-Blaise Quarter (near Père Lachaise Cemetery and Belleville. It's open 24 hours (rooms closed noon to 3pm), with a cafeteria, game room, mini-movie theater, and a bar (open 8pm to 2am). No cooking facilities (outside food must be eaten in the rooms). Dorm rooms have up to eight beds. Lockers, laundry and Internet access available. Because of the size, this hostel gets a lot of groups, and the staff rarely seem to have time to be overly helpful to individual guests. It's right up the street from the popular Flèche d'Or Café, and is well-placed for anyone wanting to explore the eastern quarters of Paris, but families may be put off by the slightly "rough" look of the area.

Camping

Camping du Bois de Boulogne: Allée du Bord de l'Eau, 16th, M° Porte Maillot, ☎ 01 45 24 30 00, www.mobilhome-paris.com.

Although this campsite is right on the Seine, the views of the industrial park across the river aren't exactly ideal. Otherwise, the forest location isn't bad for nature lovers who want easy access to Paris. It costs €18-€24 to pitch a tent. Mobile home rentals are €62-€76 (sleeps four, some with A/C or TV). There's a shuttle bus to the nearest métro station (Porte Maillot) from 8:30am to 1am. The gates close from 2am to 6am. Other services include a restaurant and café, shop, game area and billiard table, playground and tourism desk. To get there by car, follow signs throughout Bois de Boulogne toward the Pont de Suresnes. (Look under *Camping* in the *Outside Paris* chapter for camping sites in Versailles (page 358), Fontainebleau (page 387), Haute Vallée de Chevreuse (page 410) and Chantilly (page 430).)

Where to Eat

Practicalities

■ Choosing a Restaurant

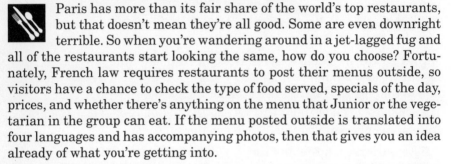 Paris has more than its fair share of the world's top restaurants, but that doesn't mean they're all good. Some are even downright terrible. So when you're wandering around in a jet-lagged fug and all of the restaurants start looking the same, how do you choose? Fortunately, French law requires restaurants to post their menus outside, so visitors have a chance to check the type of food served, specials of the day, prices, and whether there's anything on the menu that Junior or the vegetarian in the group can eat. If the menu posted outside is translated into four languages and has accompanying photos, then that gives you an idea already of what you're getting into.

The establishments listed in this guide were chosen for their good value. Sometimes the Price-Food-Atmosphere ratio weighs heavier in one category than another, but they all have something special, something memorable. The *International* section is a mere hint of the rich diversity a cosmopolitan city like Paris has to offer, from Moroccan tearooms and Italian *trattorie* to Scandinavian delis and Thai restaurants. There's also a selection of sandwich and healthy takeout shops listed, so no one has to resort to the soulless fast-food chains.

This isn't by any means meant to be an exhaustive list. Entire books have been written about Parisian restaurants! For the advice of a professional food critic, I recommend Patricia Wells' *Food Lover's Guide to Paris*. She's been the Paris food journalist for *L'Express* and the *International Herald Tribune* for years, and updates her guides on a regular basis. For a different perspective, the annual *Time Out Paris: Eating & Drinking* comes in a handy magazine format, with an irreverent, edgy slant to their restaurant, café and bar reviews. There's a list of basic dining vocabulary in the *Glossary* (see page 433); if you absolutely need to know what every word on the menu means, try *World Food France* (part of the World Food Guides series), which describes every region's specialties and wines, and includes a detailed, cross-referenced dictionary, or the *Bon Appetit: French English Menu Dictionary* by Judith White.

■ Opening Hours

Regular restaurant hours are noon to 2:30pm for lunch and 7 to 10:30pm for dinner. Many restaurants close for all or part of August, or shorten the opening hours, so be sure to call ahead if you're going out of your way.

Cafés usually serve snacks such as *croques monsieur* or other sandwiches throughout the day, and most brasseries are open all day and night (see *Dining After Midnight*, page 298).

■ Reservations

Always a good idea, especially if there are more than two in your group. Many places listed in this guide have a limited number of tables, so it's noted that reservations are a must. Trendy bistros may need to be booked up to a week in advance, rising to several months for the haute-cuisine restaurants in high season. It's also a good time to confirm whether they have non-smoking sections and if they accept credit cards, since this information tends to change frequently.

■ A La Carte vs. Le Menu

English words that look like French words but mean something completely different are called *faux amis* (false friends). Americans usually know that *à la carte* means "from the menu," therefore *la carte* is the menu (it also means "map," which isn't completely illogical). We get in trouble when we see the French word *menu*, and think it means the same thing. But it's a false friend. Make it your new best friend. Ordering a *menu* is always cheaper than ordering *à la carte*, especially at lunch. It's a fixed-price, three-course meal that includes a starter, main dish and dessert. In some places these courses are already decided, so if you ask for the *menu*, you're done ordering. More often you get a limited selection to choose from for each course. On a similar note is the *formule*, which consists of two-courses (main dish and either starter or dessert), and sometimes includes coffee or a glass of wine.

Another false friend is the word *entrée*. In the US, the entrée is the main dish. In France it's the appetizer (*entrer* means "to start"), and the *plat* is the main dish. At least we all agree on dessert!

■ Beverages

Wine

Woe is the tourist who orders a bottle of wine without knowing the price. This usually happens when, in a moment of linguistic panic, the client nods in agreement with whatever the server recommends. Avoid nasty surprises by asking them to point it out on the wine menu. There's no shame in ordering the house wine (*vin maison*) by the pitcher (*un pichet*), which can also come in ¼- or ½-bottle sizes. In finer restaurants, the sommelier should be able to suggest a bottle within your specified price limits. At lunch it's normal to order wine by the glass, especially when dining alone.

Paris

Apéritifs

Typical *apéritifs* are a *kir* (white wine with blackcurrant syrup) a *kir royal* (the same, but made with Champagne instead of wine), a *pastis* (a Provençal favorite of anisette liqueur, like Pernod, mixed with water), or possibly a small beer. The French don't drink hard liquors or cocktails before eating because they think it dulls the taste buds.

Coffee & Tea

The least expensive beverage on any café or restaurant menu is normally *un café* (espresso). The price goes up if you want it with steamed milk or cream (*café crème*). You can also order a *noisette* (an espresso with a drop of milk), a *décaféiné* (decaffeinated, also called *déca*), a *café serré* (extra strong shot of espresso) or a *café allongé* (watered-down espresso). In a restaurant, the coffee comes after the dessert unless you ask the server to bring them at the same time. Sugar is always on the side, sometimes with a square of dark chocolate, too. The flavored coffees of Starbucks haven't made it to France yet, but you can still find *cappuccino* and hot chocolate at any given Parisian café. The French drink *café au lait* (half-coffee, half-milk served in a bowl) at home for breakfast, so you'll get strange looks ordering it in a restaurant. *Thé nature* is just plain black tea. You can also order it with milk (*avec du lait*) or lemon (*avec citron*). If you want non-caffeinated herbal tea, ask for a *tisane* or *infusion*. In tearooms the selection is obviously much more elaborate.

Water

Une carafe d'eau (du robinet) means "pitcher of tap water," which is perfectly fine to drink in Paris, and a good idea if you're on a budget. If you don't like the taste you can order *eau plat* (still mineral water like Evian) or *eau gazeuse* (sparkling mineral water like Perrier). Don't say *eau plat* if you mean *une carafe* (even though tap water *is* still) or you'll end up with bottled water and a bigger bill.

Milk & Juice

It's rare for adults in France to drink milk by the glass. The milk typically used in cafés for coffee is UHT, or long-conservation milk that comes in a box and doesn't have to be refrigerated until opened. If you want to order a fresh glass of milk, ask if they have *lait frais*. Semi-skimmed is called *demi-écrémé* and skimmed is called *écrémé*. Similarly, if you order an orange juice or tomato juice in a café, odds are you'll get the preserved, bottled juices that just don't taste as good as the real thing. If you want fresh OJ, ask if they have *jus d'orange pressé* (in a café you'll see the orange squeezer on the counter). It's typically served in a half-filled glass with a pitcher of water and sugar on the side (the French like to dilute and sweeten their juice).

AUTHOR'S TIP: *In a café you can drink whatever you please, but with meals, wine is the default beverage. If you don't want wine with your meal, a small bottle of mineral water is the most acceptable substitute, followed by a Coca-light for madame. You could order a fruit juice or Orangina, but you'll get a few raised eyebrows, since the French think these are reserved for kids.*

■ Dining Etiquette

Don't ever call a waiter *garçon* unless you want a bowl of hot onion soup dropped on your lap. French food usually comes with the condiments already applied to the chef's liking. Aside from salt and pepper, which are usually on the table, you'll have to ask if you want mustard, ketchup or mayonnaise. In general, it's not possible to request substitutions or changes to a dish, so if you do, be as charming as possible, making up an allergy if necessary (*allergique*, conveniently).

Don't take it personally if your server is brusque, or worse, invisible. Even the French think that Parisian servers are rude. It's part of the act, like New York taxi drivers. No matter what happens, keep repeating the mantra *patience, patience, patience....*

When you order meat, the server won't usually ask how you want it cooked. If the sight of pink (or even red) meat makes you queasy, ask for it *bien-cuit*, which means well-done. It will probably arrive medium-rare anyway. This isn't because the French are trying to give you food poisoning. The chef simply doesn't want to "ruin" his carefully prepared dish. The French eat rare and raw beef (*steak tartare*) every day, so the standards of meat-handling are much higher than in the US, where E. coli outbreaks are blamed on undercooked food. If you're still not convinced, go ahead and ask the server to take your plate back to the kitchen. And cross your fingers it doesn't come back as a lump of charcoal.

■ Paying & Tipping

Cash is still king in French restaurants, especially smaller cafés and bistros. Larger establishments usually accept credit cards, primarily VISA (*Carte Bleue* in France) and MasterCard, but rarely American Express. It's almost impossible to use traveler's checks in restaurants. When in doubt, call ahead or carry cash.

In most restaurants you won't get the bill until you ask for it (*l'addition, s'il vous plait*), even if you finished your dessert and coffee ages ago. The tax and service charge (tip) are always included in the total, although you may not get an itemized bill in smaller establishments. Don't be afraid to ask if you think there's been a mistake, but don't over-react if there is. In busy places where the servers rely on memory when taking your order, there can be errors – sometimes in your favor.

To tip or not to tip? The short answer is no, you don't have to tip, since service is already included. When paying by credit card, there's no line to add a tip, but the French tend to leave the loose change behind when they pay in cash. Since the servers aren't expecting it, they won't be calculating the percentage to see if you're a cheapskate or not!

What's In a Name?

In the United States the terms *bistro*, *brasserie* and *café* seem to be interchangeable terms for any place serving food, but in France these titles mean something, and knowing these meanings will make it a lot easier to predict what kind of dining experience you will have.

■ Bistros

The typical bistro is a small, simple establishment with limited opening hours and honest, home-style cooking. Although many new bistros today feature stylish décor and chic clientele, the focus is still on a cozy atmosphere and traditional cuisine made with the highest quality, seasonal ingredients. The average Parisian bistro is an excellent value, with budget *menus* and well-priced wine lists.

■ Brasseries

Brasseries are bigger, open longer (sometimes 24 hours), and are generally less expensive than bistros. They're usually set in beautiful, late-19th-century dining rooms, yet have an informal atmosphere, with no dress code and a flexible menu allowing guests to order one course or many, any time of the day. The first brasseries were opened in Paris by Alsatians who fled their German-occupied region after the Franco-Prussian War, bringing with them their specialty beers and pork-based dishes such as *choucroute* (sauerkraut and sausages). Other typical brasserie fare includes fresh seafood platters, *cassoulet* and onion soup.

■ Cafés & Salons de Thé

Cafés are the most difficult to pin down. They are generally casual places to have a drink, with light snacks such as *croques-monsieur* or salads available throughout the day. They're the kind of places where you can spend the day people-watching or reading a book. Regulars tend to congregate at the bar, where coffee and drinks are cheaper than at tables. Sometimes a bistro or a restaurant will also call itself a café if it has seating for those just stopping in for a drink. Sometimes a café is a bar, sometimes it's a restaurant. When in doubt, don't sit down for a drink if every table is set for eating. Tearooms have become very popular in the past few years. Some serve only tea and pastries throughout the day, others have full lunch menus with tea service limited to the afternoon. Tearoom cooking is typically a choice of light but refined salads, quiches and *tartes*.

■ Restaurants

Whether formal or low-key, a restaurant is where you go to have a lingering, three-course (or more) meal, typically with wine, cheese and coffee at the end. Go to a restaurant when you have the time and the appetite to enjoy the entire experience. Sometimes an establishment is called a restaurant if it doesn't fit into any other category.

■ Wine Bars

Also called a *bistro à vin* (wine bistro), these establishments are typically informal, and offer a limited selection of *charcuterie* (cold meats and cheeses) and *tartines* (open sandwiches) to accompany the carefully chosen wines. The best wine bars serve high-quality wines for all budgets, making them ideal places for sampling wines you've never tried before. Some upscale establishments call themselves wine bars, but are really more like restaurants with extensive (and often expensive) wine lists.

RESTAURANT PRICE SCALE
The following price scale represents the cost of an average meal for one person, not including drinks.
€ . . . . Under €15
€€ . . . . €16-€25
€€€ . . . . €26-€40
€€€€ . . . . €41-€60
€€€€€ . . . . over €60

Dining Recommendations

■ Haute Cuisine

These classic temples to haute cuisine, many of them inside luxury palace hotels, offer the best in service, décor and, of course, French cuisine. For those who would like to taste a bit of heaven on a budget, lunch menus during weekdays are significantly less expensive (otherwise, *à la carte* dinners average €200 per person). Always re-

Paris

serve for these restaurants, and if you would like a romantic corner don't be afraid to ask for one. Most of these restaurants require men to be in a suit jacket, especially for dinner. Dressing up is part of the fun!

Lapérouse: 51 Quai des Grands Augustins, 6th, M° St-Michel, ☎ 01 43 26 68 04, Traditional French (€€€€€). Open Monday through Friday, noon to 2:30pm and 6 to 10pm; and Saturday, 6 to 10pm. Valet parking.

First opened in 1766, Lapérouse combines traditional French haute cuisine with a luxurious Belle Epoque interior overlooking the Seine. It's really one of those places that seem to have popped right out of a period film. It was a popular literary café during its heyday, and became famous for its private *salons particuliers* where couples could dine undisturbed (these can be reserved for €110 per person). There's a lunch *menu découvert* (discovery menu) for €30 and a *menu dégustation* (tasting menu) for €84.

L'Atelier de Joël Robuchon: Hôtel Pont Royal, 5 Rue de Montalembert, 7th, M° Rue du Bac, ☎ 01 42 84 70 00. Modern French (€€€€). Open daily, 11:30am to 3pm and 6:30 to 11pm. No reservations accepted. 100% non-smoking.

After spending a few years in retirement, French "Chef of the Century" Joël Robuchon wanted to try something completely different in the world of haute cuisine. The result is L'Atelier, a black, red and chrome restaurant where diners sit on barstools around a central open kitchen to watch the master (occasionally) and his chefs at work. Since its 2003 opening, much has been said in the press about its no-reservation policy, which means the hungry end up waiting on the sidewalk for the next available stool. But the affordable prices, high-quality cuisine and enforced non-smoking rule make up for the wait. It's the perfect place for solo diners and those who would like to try fine French cooking without the whole starched-tablecloths-and-set-menu routine.

Jardin des Cygnes: Prince de Galles Hôtel, 33, Avenue George V, 8th, M° George V, ☎ 01 53 23 78 50. French/Mediterranean (€€€€). Open daily. Valet parking.

This elegant restaurant has Mediterranean-inspired décor, with hand-painted frescos, and immense floor-to-ceiling windows overlooking the lush vegetation and intricate mosaic tiling of the courtyard garden (opened for *al-fresco* dining in the summer). The food takes a similar approach, with a southern touch to the fine French cuisine, and a reasonably priced wine list. The best deals are the evening set *menu-carte* of €59, or the weekday lunch *menu* for €46, which includes dessert and coffee. Sunday brunches are accompanied by a jazz pianist.

Alain Ducasse au Plaza Athénée: Hôtel Plaza Athénée, 25 Avenue Montaigne, 8th, M° Alma-Marceau, ☎ 01 53 67 65 00, www.alainducasse.com. Modern French (€€€€€). Open Monday through Wednesday, 8 to 10:30pm; Thursday and Friday, 1 to 2:30pm and 8 to 10:30pm. Closed for August and December holidays.

The multi-Michelin-starred Alain Ducasse is one of the hottest chefs in Europe, with virtual demi-god status in Paris (the master himself won't be in the kitchen, he leaves that to his talented protégé Jean-François Piège). His restaurant in the Hôtel Plaza Athénée serves French classics with a modern twist , and an extensive international wine list. Popular with entertainment industry executives with large expense accounts and models booked into the suites upstairs.

Les Elysées du Vernet: Hôtel Vernet, 25 Rue Vernet, 8th, M° George V, ☎ 01 44 31 98 98, www.hotelvernet.com. French traditional (€€€€€). Open for lunch Tuesday through Friday, for dinner Monday through Friday. Closed August.

Les Elysées is a classic French restaurant in a boutique hotel just off the Champs-Elysées. Its intricate stained-glass ceiling by Gustave Eiffel gives the dining room a fresh, winter garden feel. Lobster and truffles feature heavily on the chef's *terroir* menu, but the €45 lunch *menu* of fresh market dishes (and dessert) is considered one of the best deals in town, so book well in advance. Dinner guests should stop by the hotel's India-inspired **Jaïpur Bar** for an intimate *digestif* or exotic cocktail.

Pierre Gagnaire: 6 Rue Balzac, 8th, M° George V, ☎ 01 58 36 12 50, www.pierre-gagnaire.com. Nouvelle cuisine (€€€€€). Open Monday through Friday, noon to 1:30pm and 7:30 to 9:30pm. Closed mid-July through mid-August. Valet parking.

Chef Pierre Gagnaire's culinary creativity may not be for everyone, but this is *the* place for those who appreciate daring flavor combinations. The décor is classic contemporary, comfortable without distracting diners from what's on their plate. Reservations (a month in advance, ideally) can be made on the web site.

Lucas Carton: 9 Place de la Madeleine, 8th, M° Madeleine, ☎ 01 42 65 22 90, www.lucascarton.com. Modern French (€€€€€). Open for dinner Monday through Saturday, and for lunch Tuesday through Friday. Closed August.

Those who don't believe in the art of food and wine pairing will change their minds once they've tried Chef Alain Senderens's cuisine, renowned for its ability to complement perfectly the fine vintages from the hand-picked wine list. The sumptuous 1890 Art Nouveau dining room is a listed historical monument, but for those appreciating a more modern atmosphere, the **Cercle** dining room upstairs has an Uptown New York décor. The lunch menu is available for €79.

Le Train Bleu: Gare de Lyon, 12th, M° Gare de Lyon, ☎ 01 43 43 09 06, www.le-train-bleu.com. Traditional French (€€€€). Bar open weekdays, 7:30am to 11pm, weekends, 9am to 11pm. Restaurant open daily, 11:30am to 3pm and 7 to 11pm.

Paris

Le Train Bleu is a Second-Empire-style restaurant built as part of the Gare de Lyon for the 1900 Universal Exposition in Paris. Its luxurious, gilded interior features 42 frescoes of the destinations served by the railway at the turn of the 20th century. Located just across from the train platforms, the restaurant bar is an ideal place to stop for a coffee or pre-departure cocktail. Le Train Bleu also has a non-smoking room and a children's menu for €15.

Montparnasse '25: Le Meridien Montparnasse, 19 Rue du Commandant Mouchotte, 14th, M° Montparnasse, ☎ 01 44 36 44 25. Modern French (€€€€€). Closed weekends and August.

Hidden on an upper floor of the Le Meridien Montparnasse hotel, the low-lit dining room of Montparnasse '25 has an '80s-jazz-club atmosphere with plenty of black lacquer, smoked glass and artists' photographs of local legends lining the walls. The creative, modern cuisine is complemented by an international wine list, but be sure to leave room for the cheese! The monumental cartload of matured cheeses, chosen by the restaurant's in-house cheese expert Gérard Poulard, is considered to be the finest in town.

■ Brasseries & Fine Dining

Le Dôme du Marais: 53*bis* Rue des Francs-Bourgeois, 4th, M° Rambuteau, ☎ 01 42 74 54 17. Trendy gourmet (€€€). Open Tuesday through Saturday for lunch and dinner.

The amazing interior of this converted church has an engraved glass dome ceiling for a magical ambiance, with high-quality French cuisine favored by the local gallery owners and society-page types. The unique children's *menu* is charged according to age (€1.60 for each year).

Le Procope: 13 Rue de l'Ancienne-Comédie, 6th, M° Odéon, ☎ 01 40 46 79 00. Historic brasserie (€€€). Open daily, noon to 1am. Reservations recommended.

Supposedly the oldest café in the world (opened in 1686 by an Italian immigrant), Le Procope was once a popular meeting place for the artistic, literary and political high fliers such as Voltaire, Balzac, La Fontaine, Diderot and Benjamin Franklin. Today it's a brasserie serving elaborate seafood platters and prime cut pepper steaks in richly decorated 17th-century dining rooms. It's possible to stop by in the late afternoon (between 3:30pm and 6pm) for a coffee or tea at the small bar (a trip to the restrooms upstairs is recommended to get a good look around).

Café Lenôtre at the Pavillon Elysée: Espace Marigny, 10 Avenue des Champs-Elysées, 8th, M° Champs-Elysées-Clémenceau, ☎ 01 42 65 85 10, www.lenotre.fr. Trendy gourmet (€€€). Open daily, 8:30am to 11pm. Reservations recommended weekends.

Lenôtre opened their latest café-boutique-cooking school in the beautiful setting of the historic Pavillon Elysée, under the trees of the "nice" end of the Champs-Elysées. There's a bar inside overlooking the gourmet food and kitchen boutique, with the restaurant under a giant glass pavilion and terrace seating in warmer weather. The décor is both modern and elegant, much like the clientele. Food choices range from dainty salads and quiches for small appetites to traditional steak fillet and *foie gras* dishes. Save room for the famous Lenôtre desserts. Sunday brunch is particularly popular for people watching, so be sure to reserve your seat and wear your Sunday best.

Brasserie Flo: 7 Cour des Petites Ecuries (entrance at 63 Rue du Faubourg St-Denis), 10th, M° Château d'Eau, ☎ 01 47 70 13 59, www.floparis.com. Alsace brasserie (€€-€€€). Open daily, noon to 3pm and 7pm to 1am. Valet parking evenings.

This is the first of the Brasseries Flo dotted all over Paris. This one is hidden down a long pedestrian passage in a neighborhood known more for its Indian restaurants than traditional Alsatian brasseries. Inside is a step back into the early 1900s, with intricate wood paneling and stained glass windows. The professional, attentive staff serve up huge platters of seafood and hearty pork and sauerkraut dishes from Alsace. There's a €23 *formule* available at lunch and after 10pm.

L'Oulette: 15 Place Lachambeaudie, 12th, M° Cour St-Emilion, ☎ 01 40 02 02 12. French gourmet (€€€€). Open Monday through Friday, noon to 2:15pm; and Monday through Saturday, 8 to 10pm.

This contemporary restaurant is off the beaten track, hidden on a small square dominated by a Gothic church, Notre-Dame-de-Bercy. It's worth seeking out for the top quality gourmet cuisine of Mediterranean and Southwestern specialties praised in all the French food guides. For budget diners there's a lunch *menu* for €28.

Le Dôme: 108 Boulevard du Montparnasse, 14th, M° Vavin, ☎ 01 43 35 25 81. Historic brasserie (€€€€). Open daily for lunch and dinner until midnight. Reservations recommended.

This may not be the trendiest Montparnasse brasserie, but it's definitely one of the most authentic, with its 1930s spirit still heavy in the air. But don't just come for the history, Le Dôme is the place to be if you're looking for some serious seafood. The *megasole meuniere* will set you back €35, but the five-kilo fish just isn't the same elsewhere, and people travel from all over the world for the *bouillabaisse*.

Pavillon Montsouris: Parc Montsouris, 20 Rue Gazan, 14th, M° Cité Universitaire, ☎ 01 43 13 29 00, www.pavillon-montsouris.fr. Gourmet French (€€€€). Open daily for lunch, Monday through Saturday for dinner (dinner reservations recommended). Valet parking.

Dine in the bucolic setting of the Parc Montsouris, overlooking the lake, at this late-19th-century pavilion. Completely renovated in 2002, it has a subtle colonial décor with pale colors and floor-to-ceiling windows. The traditional French gourmet cooking has a southern influence with Mediterranean flavors. Everyone gets a *menu* (€49; €15.50 for kids), with fish, meat and vegetarian options, cheese platter included. The summer terrace is particularly romantic at night.

Le Châlet des Iles: Lac Inférieur du Bois de Boulogne, 16th, M° Rue de la Pompe or RER Henri Martin (then take the boat from the *Embarcaderie* at the east side of the Lac Inférieur), ☎ 01 42 88 04 69, www.lerivercafe.net. Trendy/modern (€€€€). Open Monday through Saturday for lunch and dinner, Sunday non-stop noon to 5pm. Valet parking.

As soon as the first days of spring arrive, this island restaurant in the Bois de Boulogne becomes packed with Parisians and affluent suburbanites in designer-sunglasses. Originally built by Napoleon III for his wife, the Châlet des Iles has been beautifully restored to its period décor. The menu includes modern interpretations of traditional seafood, meat and pasta dishes, with an affordable *Formule Châlet* for just €23 (Monday through Saturday). Be sure to reserve a seat on the terrace.

Au Claire de la Lune: 9 Rue Poulbot, 18th, M° Abbesses, ☎ 01 42 58 97 03. Traditional (€€€€). Open for lunch Tuesday through Saturday, and dinner Monday through Saturday until 11:30pm. Reservations recommended for dinner.

This popular Montmartre restaurant is on a quiet street around the corner from the Espace Dali museum. Classically prepared French dishes are served by attentive staff in a comfortable dining room decorated with murals depicting Parisian life. It's a nice, if pricey, escape from the frenzied atmosphere of the Place du Tertre.

■ Hip & Hype

Carpé Diem Café: 21 Rue des Halles, 1st, M° Châtelet, ☎ 01 42 21 02 01. Trendy French (€€). Open Monday through Thursday, 9am to 2am; Friday and Saturday, 9am to 4am. Full menu at lunch and dinner.

This former Irish bar now attracts a young and *branché* (hip) clientele with its cozy, low-lit jazz atmosphere and live DJs on the weekend. The food isn't bad, either, with yummy treats like warm camembert with caramelized syrup and Poilâne bread. The Saturday brunch (11am to 3pm) is a good deal at just €12, with free espresso refills. Stop by later in the evening to test out the cocktails under the sparkly-starred ceiling.

L'Alcazar: 62 Rue Mazarine, 6th, M° Odéon, ☎ 01 53 10 19 99. Trendy fusion (€€€). Open daily for lunch and dinner (until 1am Thursday through Saturday). Reservations recommended.

One of the most stylish brasseries on the Left Bank, L'Alcazar features slick, modern design and Franco-British fusion cuisine by UK restaurant magnate Terence Conran. Dine on *steak tartare* with fries or grilled salmon in anisette sauce, with groovy lounge music from the Mezzanine Bar in the background. Sunday brunch €26, kids' brunch €13.

Colette Water Bar: 213 Rue St-Honoré, 1st, M° Tuileries, ☎ 01 55 35 33 90. Trendy/light (€). Open Monday through Saturday, 11am to 7pm.

The Colette concept boutique, copied many times over around town, is still *the* place to find the latest must-have fashions. The Water Bar on the lower level is more than just a gimmick: the menu features over 70 kinds of bottled waters from around the world. Seriously thin models and stiletto'd fashion editors lounge at the vast, communal tables sipping their *eau du jour* and nibbling salads or barely-there sandwiches. There's also organic, pre-packaged food and juices to go.

Anahi: 49 Rue Volta, 3rd, M° Arts-et-Metiers, ☎ 01 48 87 88 24. Trendy Argentinean (€€€). Open daily, 8pm to 2am (seating until midnight). Reservations a must.

It may look like a condemned building from the outside (no sign, either; look for the entrance on the corner of Rue Vertbois), but ever since it opened in the 1980s, this Argentinean restaurant in a former butcher shop attracts the beautiful crowd looking for fantastic steaks and tango tunes. Come later in the evening for the best atmosphere.

404: 69 Rue des Gravilliers, 3rd, M° Rambuteau or Arts-et-Métiers, ☎ 01 42 74 57 81. Upscale Morrocan (€€€). Open daily for lunch and dinner (seating until midnight). Reservations a must.

The international jet-set's favorite Moroccan restaurant is a small and intimate affair, with mood lighting and subtle oriental décor. Everyone keeps one discreet eye on the VIP mezzanine in case Madonna or Galliano stop by, but the food and service are enough to make for a memorable meal if they don't.

L'Envue: 39 Rue Boissy d'Anglas, 8th, M° Madeleine or Concorde, ☎ 01 42 65 10 49. Trendy modern (€€€). Open Monday through Saturday, 8am to 2am.

Seafood platters and vegetarian dishes such as warm goat cheese salads and baby spinach with ricotta highlight the menu at this chic restaurant decorated in feminine mauve and pink tones. You can watch Fashion TV on the flat-screen monitors over the bar or dine with the fashion crowd at pastel glass tables in the quiet upstairs dining room. This is a good place to stop in for hot chocolate and croissants at breakfast or fresh juice during a shopping break.

L'Appart: 9-11 Rue du Colisée, 8th, M° Franklin-D-Roosevelt, ☎ 01 53 75 42 00. Trendy modern (€€€). Open daily for lunch and dinner. Bar open 7pm to 2am. Reservations recommended.

This restaurant on two levels is decorated to look like a stylish Parisian apartment. The modern French cuisine is based on Mediterranean and *terroir* flavors (with a few vegetarian options). Join the chic locals and their matching children for the Sunday brunch (12:30 to 3pm), with special kids' *menu* and cooking demonstrations to keep them entertained. The lower-level bar has a good selection of cigars and cocktails.

Poona Lounge: 25 Rue Marbeuf, 8th, M° Franklin-D-Roosevelt, ☎ 01 40 70 09 99. Trendy Indian fusion (€€€). Open daily, 9am to 3am, Friday and Saturday until 5am.

How many Buddha-statued restaurants can one city take? Apparently quite a few, judging by the success of the latest Bollywood-inspired Poona Lounge. Its intimate interior is colorful and cozy, and the French-Indian fusion food is actually very well prepared (unlike the food in many of its nearby competitors). There's a Poona Express lunch for just €20, but it's more relaxing to lounge upstairs on the long cushions late into the night accompanied by appropriately themed DJ mixes.

Asian: 30 Avenue George V, 8th, M° George V, ☎ 01 56 89 11 00, www.asian.fr. Trendy Asian mix (€€€). Open daily (except Saturday lunch), noon to 2am. Kitchen open non-stop until 1am.

The fashionable Asian restaurant features a mix of Far Eastern flavors and a modern-but-intimate Zen décor on two levels. There is seating for up to 400 and an indoor bamboo "forest." Food is served anytime of day by the models-in-waiting, and a large selection of teas is available for afternoon *dégustations*. You can also sit at the bar upstairs for sake and fresh sushi prepared in front of you.

Le Martel: 3 Rue Martel, 10th, M° Château-d'Eau, ☎ 01 47 70 67 56, Trendy North-African (€€). Open for lunch Monday through Friday, for dinner Monday through Saturday. Reservations recommended.

Tucked between kebab shops and wholesalers, this hardly seems to be the kind of place that attracts every big name in fashion and music, and yet, it is. Run by an ex-waiter from 404 (one of Madonna's favorite Paris restaurants), Le Martel serves up North African and French fusion cuisine, with couscous, *tangines* (a traditional Moroccan dish) and giant salads on the menu.

Chai 33: 33 Cour St-Emilion 12th, M° Cour St-Emilion, ☎ 01 53 44 01 01, www.chai33.com. Upscale wine bar (€€€). Restaurant open daily, noon to 3pm and 7:30pm to midnight. Bar open from 7pm.

Chai 33 (pronounced "shay") is a trendy wine shop, lounge bar and restaurant set in the restored wine warehouses of Bercy Village, with a modern loft décor of steel, glass and sandblasted stone. As the coolest kid on the block, it's popular with the *branché* (connected) see-and-be-seen crowd, but when the novelty has worn off, it's the unique concept that keeps people coming back. The wines are arranged by flavor, not region, so if you know you like dry whites or fruity, young reds, you can't mess up. Restaurant guests follow the sommelier down to the cave to pick their own bottle with as much or as little advice as needed. The international wine list is accompanied by traditional French cuisine. When the weather is nice, be sure to reserve a table at one of the two terraces overlooking the pedestrian-only Bercy Village.

Apollo: 3 Place Denfert-Rochereau, 14th, M° Denfert-Rochereau, ☎ 01 45 38 76 77. Modern fusion (€€€). Open daily for lunch and dinner until midnight.

Is this ultra-modern restaurant in a former train depot (right next to the RER entrance) hip or hype? It depends on personal taste. If you like funky, design-heavy décor – and are willing to pay extra for it – give this unique place a try. There's a private terrace that is actually pretty quiet, even when the RER goes past. The tables overlooking the traffic-jams at Place Denfert-Rochereau are only interesting if you're waiting for the next airport shuttle. The cuisine is a fusion of international flavors and traditional French dishes.

L'Entrepôt: 7-9 Rue Francis de Préssensé 14th, M° Pernety, ☎ 01 45 40 60 70, www.lentrepot.fr. Modern French (€€€). Open daily, 10am to midnight for lunch and dinner.

At the back of the Entrepôt independent cinema and bar is a magical restaurant with a huge glassed-in terrace and one of the best private gardens in Paris. Sitting under the trees on a warm day, it's hard to believe you're still in the city. The organic French cuisine includes warm goat cheese salad, grilled salmon, and an absolutely sinful *fondant chocolate*. Reserve for Sunday brunch, 11:30am to 4pm.

R: 6-8 Rue de la Cavalerie, 15th, M° La Motte-Piquet-Grenelle, ☎ 01 45 67 06 85. Bar-restaurant-lounge (€€€€). Open Monday through Saturday for lunch and dinner. Reservations a must.

Get one of the best views of the sparkling Eiffel Tower from this trendy penthouse restaurant. Located at the top of a 1930s building (with an elevator, fortunately), "R" is decorated in a hip neo-'70s style and serves decent Asian-fusion cuisine. Be sure to reserve a spot on the glassed-in terrace with unobstructed views of La Tour, especially after dark when the city lights sparkle, even through the smog.

La Villa Corse: 164 Boulevard de Grenelle, 15th, M° Cambronne or La Motte-Piquet-Grenelle, ☎ 01 53 86 70 81. Stylish Corsican (€€€). Open Monday through Saturday for lunch and dinner. Reservations highly recommended.

Don't let the boring location in the shadow of the elevated métro tracks put you off. La Villa Corse is a chic and comfortable restaurant with three dining areas around a central bar, including a salon with bookcases and leather club chairs, and the mezzanine with Mediterranean-style wrought-iron furniture. The menu focuses on fresh and modern Corsican-Mediterranean cuisine, expertly cooked and accompanied by an international wine list.

Tokyo Idem: Palais de Tokyo, 13 Avenue du Président-Wilson, 16th, M° Iéna, ☎ 01 47 20 00 29. Contemporary self-service (€-€€). Open Tuesday through Sunday, noon to 11:30pm.

If you know nothing about the Palais de Tokyo, you may think you've mistakenly walked onto a construction site. Welcome to the Space for Contemporary Creation, part gallery, part museum exhibition space. Turn left at the entrance and you'll see the flower-power floor painting of the self-service cafeteria, Tokyo Idem. Kids love this place, with its curvy plastic furniture and wide open spaces. There's certainly no danger of breaking anything. Grab a tray at the counter for a selection of real food (not sandwiches in a plastic box), and try to find a place to sit down, which can prove difficult during the weekday lunch rush. If you want something a bit more refined (as refined as concrete and exposed electrical wiring can be), there's a full-service restaurant on the ground floor past the boutique.

Ginette de la Côte d'Azur: 101 Rue Caulaincourt, 18th, M° Lamarck-Caulaincourt, ☎ 01 46 06 01 49. Trendy bistro (€€). Open daily for lunch and dinner (until midnight).

Parisians on the quieter side of the Butte (Montmartre) have fallen in love with the terrace at this stylish bistro, but the unique, art-gallery interior isn't bad either. House specialties include salmon *tartare*. Reservations recommended (especially for the *fabu* terrace).

ON THE MENU: See the Glossary, page 433, for useful restaurant and menu terms.

■ Traditional French Cuisine

La Fresque: 100 Rue Rambuteau, 1st M° Etienne Marcel or Les Halles, ☎ 01 42 33 17 56 (€€). Closed Sunday at lunch. Seating for dinner until midnight.

La Fresque serves traditional French dishes (including a few vegetarian options) in two separate, shot-gun-style dining rooms. The one on the right of the entrance has an old-fashioned look with a large fresco on the wall (thus the name), and the second dining room has a more modern look with ceiling fans for a bit of summertime relief. Service is friendly, but a bit on the slow side, so avoid this restaurant if you're in a hurry.

Le Père Fouettard: 9 Rue Pierre Lescot, 1st, M° Les Halles or Etienne-Marcel, ☎ 01 42 33 74 17 (€). Food served daily, 11:30am to 1am.

Les Halles, with its fast-food chains and crêpe stands, is normally not the best place to go when you're looking for a good meal, but this place is an exception. Its tobacco-stained old-fashioned interior and huge all-season

Banks of the River Loing, Moret-sur-Loing

Mill at Moret-sur-Loing

Above: Château de Breteuil
Below: Gardens at Château de Rambouillet

Above: Potager des Princes, Chantilly
Below: Parc de Chantilly

Above: Hippodrôme de Chantilly (Photo © R&B Presse)
Below: Horseback Riding (Photo © Eric van Ees Beeck)

Notre Dame de Senlis (© Claude Laroussinie)

terrace are packed every day with local shop employees who enjoy the hearty *pot au feu* and rotisserie beef (there are also vegetarian options). A large selection of wines by the glass, attentive friendly service and down-to-earth prices make this restaurant one of the best deals the neighborhood.

Le Palet: 8 Rue de Beaujolais, 1st, M° Palais Royal, ☎ 01 42 60 99 59 (€€). Open Monday through Friday, noon to 2pm; and Monday through Saturday, 7 to 11pm.

This French restaurant just behind the Jardins du Palais Royal is known for its excellent quality traditional French cuisine and low prices. Reserve a table downstairs, where a series of stone vaulted cellars are decorated to resemble the inside of a 19th-century Pullman train complete with wooden luggage racks overhead.

Café Louis-Philippe: 66, Quai de l'Hôtel de Ville, 4th, M° St-Paul or Pont-Marie, ☎ 01 42 72 29 42. Traditional brasserie (€€). Open daily for lunch and dinner. Reservations recommended for dinner.

This romantic Old Paris restaurant has a bright décor with white-washed wood trim and a leafy garden terrace overlooking the Seine. Downstairs you can enjoy well-prepared traditional French pasta, salad, fish and meat dishes. Upstairs, there's an intimate tea-room salon with lighter fare and a panoramic view of Notre Dame. Kids' menus are available for €9.

Le Petit Prince de Paris: 12 Rue Lanneau, 5th, M° Maubert-Mutualité, ☎ 01 43 54 77 26. French/Mediterranean (€€). Open nightly 7:30 to 11:45pm (last orders), until 12:15am Friday through Saturday. Reservations a must.

This wonderfully romantic bistro is open for dinner only, with a low-lit Tuscan-inspired dining room on two levels, gilded mirrors, garden statues, terra-cotta walls and exposed wooden beams. The staff are not only friendly, they actually seem to be having a good time. The service, presentation and quality of the food normally cost twice as much in this town. Lucky for us it doesn't!

L'AOC: 14 Rue des Fossés St-Bernard, 5th, M° Jussieu, ☎ 01 43 54 22 52. Regional French (€€€). Open Tuesday through Saturday for lunch and dinner. Reservations recommended.

AOC stands for *appellation d'origine contrôlée*, usually a designation for wine whose pedigreed origins are well-documented. What that means at L'AOC is finest *terroir* cuisine such as *andouillette* and roast meats, and a wine list to match. In summer there is a small terrace overlooking the towering Institut du Monde Arabe.

L'Ecurie: 2 Rue Laplace, 5th, M° Maubert-Mutualité, ☎ 01 46 33 68 49. (€-€€). Open daily, 7pm to midnight; and noon to 3pm daily except Tuesday and Sunday.

Paris

Former 17th-century stables are now a cozy restaurant just behind the Panthéon offering freshly grilled veggies and meats with generous complimentary servings of sangria and Calvados liqueur. There's seating on a small terrace in the summer, and a vaulted stone cellar with long wooden tables for small groups.

Chez Lena et Mimile: 32 Rue Tournefort, 5th, M° Censier-Daubenton, ☎ 01 47 07 72 47. Romantic bistro (€€€). Open Tuesday through Friday, noon to 2:30pm; and Monday through Saturday, 7:30 to 11:30pm. Reservations recommended.

A block away from the student bars and kebab stands of Rue Mouffetard is a romantic little French bistro overlooking a cobblestoned square. Classic country dishes like roasted rabbit and grilled fish are served by a friendly and efficient staff. Reserve one of the few tables on the summer terrace for dinner accompanied by the tinkling of the medieval fountain.

Chez Maitre Paul: 12 Rue Monsieur-le-Prince, 6th, M° Odéon, ☎ 01 43 54 74 59. Regional French (€€€). Open Monday through Saturday for lunch and dinner, closed Mondays in August. Reservations recommended.

This restaurant around the corner from the Jardins du Luxembourg has been serving hearty country cooking from the Jura and Franche-Comté regions of France for over 50 years. On the menu: roast chicken, foie gras, terrines, sausages, hard cheeses and the "golden" wines of the Jura.

Chartier: 7 Rue du Faubourg-Montmartre, 9th, M° Grands Boulevards, ☎ 01 47 70 86 29. Traditional (€). Open daily, 11:30am to 3pm and 6:30 to 10pm.

This turn-of-the-century (the one before last) worker's canteen remains a frenzy of fast, hearty, and cheap food for the masses. A large menu has many selections, very typical French dishes for a very cheap price, written up by your hurried server on the paper tablecloth. It's a great place to come with kids, but not for a quiet, relaxing meal.

Restaurant GR5: 19 Rue Gustave-Courbet, 16th, M° Trocadero or Pompe, ☎ 01 47 27 09 84. Traditional Savoyard (€€). Open lunch and dinner Monday through Saturday.

The GR5 is part of the *Grande Randonée*; it's a cross-country hiking trail passing through the Savoy region of France. The restaurant's owner is a fan of hiking, and has decorated this place like a hiking refuge, with cozy alpine touches and the food to match: cheese and potatoes are the main staples, and couples can share gooey fondue or raclettes with white wines to wash it down.

Au Casque d'Or: 51 Rue des Cascades, 20th, M° Pyrénées, ☎ 01 43 58 44 55. Regional French (€€). Open Monday through Friday, 11:30am to 3pm; and Monday through Saturday, 7 to 11pm. Named after the 1951 cult film by Jacques Becker, made a few steps away with Simone Signoret, this Auverne restaurant serves *terroir* specialties like stuffed goose neck, roast piglet and sausage dishes in a cozy, country-style dining room. The large tables and laid-back atmosphere make this a popular family restaurant.

Chez Louisette: Marché Vernaison, 132 Avenue Michelet, Puces de St-Ouen (93), M° Porte de Clingancourt or Bus 85, ☎ 01 40 12 10 14. Musical bistro (€€). Open Saturday through Monday for lunch. Closed August. Reservations highly recommended.

Hidden all the way in the back of the Marché Vernaison, the oldest part of the Marché aux Puces, Chez Louisette is a holdover from another era, full of Gauloises-smoking Parisians and Edith Piaf wannabe's singing soulfully to a rowdy crowd. The décor is a bit kitsch with its checkered floor and Christmas garlands on the walls, and the traditional food may be a bit pricier than that in the neighboring market restaurants, but it has an unmatched atmosphere, and the kids can finally relax.

■ Bistros

Aux Lyonnais: 32 Rue St-Marc, 2nd, M° Richelieu-Drouot, ☎ 01 42 96 65 04. Traditional Lyonnais (€€€). Open for lunch and dinner, Tuesday through Friday; Saturday for dinner only.

Set in an authentic 19th-century bistro, this Alain Ducasse restaurant is one of the famous chef's most accessible (regarding the price), with modern interpretations of traditional Lyon specialties. The service and quality of the food are worth the trek out to this quiet part of town.

Potager du Marais: 22 Rue Rambuteau, 3rd, M° Rambuteau, ☎ 01 44 54 00 31. Organic/vegetarian (€€). Open daily, noon to 3pm and 7pm to midnight.

This restaurant may be 100% organic, but – with plenty of fish specialties – it's not just for vegetarians. The uncomplicated daily specials are presented on the blackboard alongside regular menu items such as vegetarian lasagna. The dining room is long and narrow, with old fashioned wooden benches and unpretentious décor overlooking a busy market street between the Pompidou Center and the Marais.

A Deux Pas du Trois: 101 Rue Vieille du Temple, 4th, M° Filles-du-Calvaire, ☎ 01 42 77 10 52. Modern bistro (€€). Open Tuesday through Friday for lunch, Tuesday through Saturday for dinner. Reservations recommended.

It may have been a gay bistro at one time, but with good value meals, cozy décor and exclusive views over the Hôtel Salé (Musée Picasso), it's hard to keep the rest of the world away. A sure bet in this neighborhood, with tasty, modern bistro specialties and a €13.50 lunch *menu*.

7ème Sud: 159 Rue de Grenelle, 7th. M° LaTour Maubourg, ☎ 01 44 18 30 30. Mediterranean (€€). Open daily for lunch and dinner.

This is a good choice for lunch after a morning at the Marché Cler or visiting Napoleon's tomb. It has exotic and light North African/Mediterranean specialties in a Moroccan dining room that's cozy and stylish. They have another location in Passy at 56 Rue Boulainvilliers, 16th.

Chez Casimir: 6 Rue de Belzunce, 10th, M° Gare du Nord, ☎ 01 48 78 28 80. Country bistro (€€€). Open Monday through Friday for lunch and dinner, closed August. Reservations recommended.

This small annex to Chez Michel serves huge portions of fresh, country-style cuisine with chunky bread in a stylish neo-bistro dining room. Everything from the *terrine de campagne* to the mashed potatoes is made from scratch with top quality ingredients, accompanied by a wine list of small, independent vineyards and home-made desserts.

Chez Michel: 10 Rue Belzunce, 10th, M° Gare du Nord, ☎ 01 44 53 06 20. Brittany bistro (€€€). Open Tuesday through Saturday for lunch and dinner (until midnight), closed August. Reservations recommended.

Located on a quiet street behind St-Vincent-de-Paul church, this bistro attracts Parisians from all the way across town with its authentic Brittany cuisine, carefully picked wine list and its excellent value. Expect a lot of rich dishes featuring seasonal game, roasted potatoes, and fresh cream. Even if you don't have room for an authentic Brittany dessert, you'll leave with a pocket full of their traditional soft caramels.

Le Galopin: 34 Rue Ste-Marthe, 10th, M° Belleville or Goncourt, ☎ 01 53 19 19 55. Traditional bistro (€). Open Tuesday through Sunday for lunch and dinner. No credit cards.

This small and friendly bistro overlooks the Square Sainte-Marthe, the heart of the gritty-but-charming Sainte-Marthe neighborhood just west of Belleville. The food is traditional and filling, with main dishes like *magret de canard* accompanied by gratin potatos, steamed veggies and rice, and tasty bread. Reservations are recommended since there are only a few tables.

Le Sporting: 3 Rue des Récollets, 10th, M° Jacques Bonsergent, ☎ 01 46 07 02 00. Bistro/café (€€). Open Tuesday through Sunday, 11am to 2am, food served noon to 3pm and 7 to 11:30pm.

One of the Canal St-Martin's successful neo-bistros, popular with local artists and musicians, Le Sporting has an open, light-filled dining room with wooden floors and crystal chandeliers. Specials are written on a chalkboard hung on the wall. Simple bistro dishes include steak filets, grilled fish, soups, and meaty salads. It's always packed, even on weekdays, so be sure to get there a bit early or call ahead.

Swann & Vincent: 7 Rue St-Nicolas, 12th, M° Ledru-Rollin, ☎ 01 43 43 49 40. Italian bistro (€€). Open daily for lunch and dinner (until 11:45pm). Reservations and patience a must.

At lunchtime this trendy 1930s-style Italian bistro is bustling with nearby office workers, artists and famous clothing designers. At night it's a bit less hurried, but the ambiance is still lively and the food and wine so tasty, that even with a reservation you may have to wait around for a table to free up (the gracious staff will offer their apologies and an *aperitif* while you wait).

Le Petit Porcheron: 3 Rue de Prague, 12th, M° Ledru-Rollin, ☎ 01 43 47 39 47. Stylish bistro (€€). Open daily, 8am to 2am (service noon to 2pm, 8 to 11pm).

Not far from the Marché d'Aligre, this modern bistro with terra-cotta walls, dark-wood furniture and lush plants serves bistro food livened up with exotic flavors to the local *bobo* (bourgeois bohemian) crowd. At night it has more of a trendy bar atmosphere.

Les Cailloux: 58 Rue des Cinq Diamants, 13th, M° Corvisart, ☎ 01 45 80 15 08. Italian bistro (€€). Open Tuesday through Saturday for lunch and dinner. Closed August. Dinner reservations recommended.

Part Italian *trattoria*, part wine bar, this trendy bistro sits right at the heart of the Butte aux Cailles neighborhood. A long list of Italian wines accompanies carefully cooked *panna cotta* and linguini dishes in a bright dining room with wooden floors and bay windows.

La Bonne Heure: 72 Rue du Moulin-des-Prés, 13th, M° Tolbiac, ☎ 01 45 89 77 00. Organic/vegetarian (€€). Open Tuesday through Sunday for lunch and dinner.

Located on an adorable little street between the Rue de la Butte aux Cailles and the Place d'Italie, this laid-back organic food bistro serves vegetarian and fish specialties to a loyal following of self-aware locals. If organic cola isn't your thing, there's a decent organic wine list.

L'Avant-Goût: 26 Rue Bobillot, 13th, M° Place d'Italie, ☎ 01 53 80 24 00. Modern bistro (€€). Open Tuesday through Saturday for lunch and dinner, closed August. Reservations a must.

This popular Butte aux Cailles bistro is known for its cooking, excellent wine list and the chef's special *pot-au-feu*. There's a weekday lunch *formule* with wine for €11, but the €23 *menu* is a great value for the quality and quantity of food. All of the food can be ordered for takeout if you can't get a table. Kid-friendly.

Sasso: 36 Rue Raymond-Losserand, 14th, M° Gaité, ☎ 01 42 18 00 38. Italian bistro (€€). Open Tuesday through Saturday for lunch and dinner. Reservations recommended.

If this Italian restaurant with the industrial-loft décor reminds you of Les Cailloux on the Butte aux Cailles, it's because they have the same owner. The Italian chef cooks up fresh pasta and grilled vegetables, served with Parma ham and thinly sliced carpaccio for the laid-back but demanding regulars who keep the place packed day and night.

Paris

Le Bistrot des Pingouins: 79 Rue Daguerre, 14th, M° Denfert-Rochereau or Gaîté, ☎ 01 43 21 92 29. Chic bistro (€€). Open Monday through Friday, noon to 3:30pm; and Monday through Saturday, 7:30pm to midnight.

No penguins in sight, just a stylish neo-bistro with convivial atmosphere and small groups of regulars comfortably ensconced at the roomy tables. The cuisine is focused on fresh seasonal produce and light variations on traditional French cooking. The dining room is packed at lunch for the €11 *formule*.

Le Kiosque: 1 Place de Mexico, 16th, M° Trocadero, ☎ 01 47 27 96 98. Traditional bistro (€€€). Open daily for lunch and dinner until 11pm.

There are few places in this neck of the woods where you can be sure to eat well for a reasonable price. Le Kiosque is a local favorite with a French regional menu that changes weekly, printed in newspaper style (the owner was a former editor-in-chief of various French publications). There's a carpaccio-lovers' brunch Saturday and Sunday, noon to 3pm, for €25.

Le Piston Pélican: 15 Rue de Bagnolet, 20th, M° Alexandre-Dumas, ☎ 01 43 70 35 00. World-food bistro (€). Open daily, 8am to 2am (opens at 10am Sunday), kitchen open noon to midnight.

This popular bistro not too far from Père Lachaise cemetery serves "world food" from around the globe in an authentic 1930s décor and zinc bar that recalls Paris of old films (the locals say it used to be a brothel). At night it has more of a bar atmosphere with a DJ on some nights, and any time of day you can stop in for a drink and a snack.

FRENCH DRESSING

If there's one thing that surprises French people when they visit a restaurant in the States, it's the salad dressing options. In France, the salad comes with the dressing that the chef believes goes with it. In traditional establishments, this will be a light mustard vinaigrette. Creamy dressings are rare, and French dressing doesn't exist. Don't ever expect to be given a choice of dressings, or the option of having it on the side unless you're feeling very brave and the server is particularly friendly.

■ Wine Bars

Le Baromètre: 17 Rue Charlot, 3rd, M° Rambuteau, ☎ 01 48 87 04 54 (€-€€). Open Monday to Friday, 7:30am to 11pm; kitchen open from noon to 3pm and 8 to 10:30pm. Closed August.

An old-fashioned wine bar and bistro with specialties like *andouillette* or *tartare* served at lunch and dinner. Or you can just pull up to the bar and order a *tartine* of Poilâne bread and cheese and a glass of wine anytime of day.

La Réserve de Quasimodo: 4 Rue de la Colombe, 4th, M° Cité, ☎ 01 46 34 67 67 (€€-€€€). Open Tuesday through Saturday, noon to 9pm.

Tucked into a 12th-century building on the Ile de la Cité between Notre Dame and the Quai aux Fleurs, this wine bar and adjoining wine boutique have a real Old Paris atmosphere. There are also special evenings with live entertainment such as storytelling or magic acts. If you're not up for a full meal, it's possible to order the dessert and wine *menu* for €9.50.

L'Escale: 1 Rue des Deux Ponts, 4th, M° Pont Marie, ☎ 01 43 54 94 23 (€). Open Tuesday through Sunday, 7:30am to 9pm; kitchen open noon to 3pm. Closed August.

This family-run wine bar on the lovely Ile St-Louis has a comfortable mix of loyal regulars ordering "the usual" and tourists warily eying up the *tartare*. When in doubt on what to drink, try the excellent value *vin du mois*, sold by the bottle for under €15. If you're just stopping in for a drink, avoid lunchtime and come instead after 6pm to unwind with the Parisians.

Fish – La Boissonerie: 69 Rue de Seine, 6th, M° Odéon, ☎ 01 43 54 34 69 (€€€). Open Tuesday through Sunday, noon to midnight, kitchen open noon to 3pm and 7 to 11pm. No Amex cards, no cigars.

Owned by a New Zealander who owns the Cosi sandwich shop across the street and an American who own a wine shop around the corner, this casual wine bar with the colorful mosaic façade and wooden benches serves fresh and creative Mediterranean cuisine and strong French wines. Popular with the local French *bobo's* as well as the expat Anglophone crowd and tourists wandering by, so be sure to reserve a table if you've come to eat.

Lavinia: 3-5 Boulevard de la Madeleine, 8th, M° Madeleine, ☎ 01 42 97 20 20 (€€€). Open Monday through Saturday, noon to 3pm; tapas served 3 to 8pm lunch. Strictly non-smoking.

Choose a bottle from the cellars of the largest wine store in Paris and head upstairs to smoked salmon or Spanish hams. At lunchtime you can order main dishes of veal and filet steak if you're really hungry, or come by in the afternoon for tapas and *dégustations* of not only wine, but fine spirits as well. A bit pricey, but the selection and staff recommendations can't be beat.

Le Griffonnier: 8 Rue des Saussaies, 8th, M° Champs-Elysées-Clémenceau, ☎ 01 42 65 17 17, www.traditionduvin.com (€€). Open Monday through Friday, 7:30am to 9:30pm; Thursday until 11pm; hot food served noon to 3pm, until 10:30pm on Thursday. Cold dishes served all day.

This traditional wine bar across from the Ministry of the Interior is packed at lunch with suited bureaucrats and politicians enjoying the fine country cuisine. Come later in the afternoon to quietly enjoy the terrines, paté and smoked sausages with reasonably priced Beaujolais or Loire Valley wines.

Le Coin de Verre: 38 Rue de Sambre-et-Meuse, 10th, M° Belleville or Colonel Fabien, ☎ 01 42 45 31 82 (€). Open Monday through Saturday, 8pm to midnight. No credit cards.

Going to this tiny wine bistro is a bit like going to a private French home. Ring the bell and one of the friendly owners will let you in if there's room (reservations are recommended). The hidden back room is the coziest, with diners crammed in next to each other at large wooden tables. French *terroir* specialties and hearty salads complement the carefully chosen wines (served by the bottle, €10-15), usually along the lines of cheese or meat platters, or large salads served with baskets of country bread. You will not find cola or fries on the menu, so leave the kids with a babysitter, and don't even think of asking for a non-smoking table.

AUTHOR'S NOTE: *To learn more about the wonderful world of wine, check out the* Cultural Adventures *section for courses,* dégustations *(wine tasting), and annual wine festivals.*

Le Baron Bouge: 1 Rue Théophile-Roussel, 12th, M° Ledru-Rollin, ☎ 01 43 43 14 32 (€). Open Monday, 5 to 10pm; Tuesday through Friday, 10am to 2pm and 5 to 10pm; Saturday, 10am to 10pm; and Sunday, 10am to 3:30pm.

Stallholders from the Aligre market, local artists and transplanted New Yorkers snack on Corsican *charcuterie* and wines from all over France at the unpretentious wooden bar of the Baron Bouge (often mistakenly called the Baron Rouge). The colorful crowd is at its liveliest after the market closes on evenings and Sunday afternoons, especially for the fresh oysters, available October through April.

Le Rallye-Peret: 6 Rue Daguerre, 14th, M° Denfert-Rochereau, ☎ 01 43 22 57 05 (€€). Open Tuesday through Saturday, 9am to 11:30pm; Sunday and Monday, 11am to 8pm.

Almost a century old, this typical Parisian wine bar and café is most interesting for its covered terrace overlooking the pedestrian-only market street. Food is traditional, home-cooked meals like stuffed vegetables, snails and salads, with giant signs proclaiming "no vacuum-packed dishes, no frozen food." Except for the Berthillon ice cream, of course.

Vin des Rues: 21 Rue Boulard, 14th, M° Denfert-Rochereau, ☎ 01 43 22 19 78 (€€). Open Monday through Saturday for lunch, 12:30 to 2:30pm; and Wednesday, Friday and Saturday from 9pm until around midnight; reservations required. No credit cards.

A '50s-style historic wine bar with zinc bar and *Gitane*-puffing regulars right out of a Doisneau photograph. On the menu are herrings, sausages from Lyon and roast lamb. Come on Thursday after 8pm for a raucous night of old-fashioned live accordion music, cold meat and cheese platters, and some of the best Beaujolais in town. Not for those trying to quit secondhand smoking.

■ International Cuisine

 Joe Allen: 30 Rue Pierre Lescot, 1st, M° Etienne Marcel or Les Halles, ☎ 01 42 36 70 13, www.joeallenrestaurant.com. American Fusion (€€). Open daily with non-stop service noon to 1am.

Opened in Paris in 1972, this authentic, low-lit New York-style restaurant features starched white tablecloths, wooden floors and brick walls covered in Broadway posters and photographs. Classic American favorites like Louisiana fried chicken with honey sauce, chili con carne and grilled T-bone steaks are complemented by grilled tuna with pesto sauce and fresh pasta with chanterelle mushrooms. The bar is stocked with international wines, beers, and spirits. Reservations are a good idea, especially if you want a terrace seat in the summer.

Harry's New York Bar, 5 Rue Daunou, 2nd, M° Opéra, ☎ 01 42 61 71 14, www.harrysbar.fr. Casual American (€). Lunch is served Monday through Saturday, noon to 3pm.

This historic, American-style cocktail bar is a Parisian legend (see *Nightlife*, page 319, for more information). During the daytime it's taken over by financial executives and theater workers who come for the club sandwiches, clam chowder, the daily English newspapers and friendly bar staff. Kid-friendly.

Gli Angeli: 5 Rue St Gilles, 3rd, M° Chemin Vert, ☎ 01 42 71 05 80. Trendy Italian (€€€).

This stylish Italian *cucina* has high-quality cuisine and a boisterous atmosphere as the regulars exchange *bises* with the owner and everyone else in the room they recognize. And no problem if your French isn't up to speed, because the menu, like most of the clientele, is Italian.

Ziryab: Institut du Monde Arabe, 1 Rue des Fossés-St-Bernard Institut Arabe, 5th, M° Jussieu, ☎ 01 53 10 10 16. Modern Moroccan (€€€€). Open Tuesday through Saturday for lunch and dinner, Sunday for lunch only, tearoom Tuesday through Sunday, 3 to 5:30pm. Dinner reservations required.

On the ninth floor of the high-tech Institut du Monde Arabe is a Moroccan restaurant with terrace views over the Seine and Notre Dame. The dining room is a bit like a giant glass box, with potted palms and garden-style furniture giving it a greenhouse feel (a cotton canopy keeps the sunlight off guests in the summer); it opens onto the wooden-decked terrace. The cuisine is is a modern take on Moroccan dishes such as couscous, *pastilla* and lamb, accompanied by a French/Moroccan wine list heavy on the rosé. In the afternoon you can come for the views and a pot of mint tea.

Le Café Maure de la Mosquée: 39 Rue Geoffry-St-Hilaire, 5th, M° Place Monge, ☎ 01 43 31 18 14. Moroccan café (€-€€). Open daily, 9am to 11pm.

Built across from the Jardin des Plantes in 1927 with heavy inspiration from the Alahambra in Spain, the Paris Mosque includes steam baths, a restaurant and the popular tearoom and terrace. The interior is amazing in colorful tiled walls and round brass tables. Pastries and mint tea are served in the tearoom to the right of the entrance, and between meal-times. The restaurant menu consists of classics like tangines and couscous. Try to avoid weekend afternoons and lunchtime if you're looking for a quiet moment to enjoy your tea. The service is brusque, but the setting is worth it.

Le Quincampe: 76 Rue de Quincampoix, 3rd, M° Rambuteau, ☎ 01 40 27 01 45. Moroccan restaurant/tearoom (€-€€). Open Monday through Friday, noon to 11pm; Saturday, 6 to 11pm.

Le Quincampe has a wonderfully cozy dining room, with club chairs, exposed wooden beams, open fireplace, and a lounge area piled high with colorful cushions. They serve delicious Moroccan specialties such as tangines and *pastilla*, or you could just stop in for a steaming pot of real mint tea. Reservations on weekends recommended for dining.

L'Osteria: 10 Rue de Sévigné 4th, M° St-Paul, ☎ 01 42 71 37 08. Gourmet Italian (€€€-€€€€). Open Tuesday through Friday for lunch, Monday through Friday for dinner. Reservations a must.

Parisians come to this elegant restaurant for classic Italian dishes and wines, and some of the best *gnocchi* in town. You'll have to look hard for the entrance (there's no sign), but once inside you'll receive a warm welcome and attentive service.

Le Bonza: 19 Rue Ste-Marthe, 10th, M° Belleville, ☎ 01 42 03 27 97. Australian fusion (€€). Open Wednesday through Sunday, 6pm to 2am.

Smack in the center of the multicultural Sainte-Marthe neighborhood is an Australian restaurant unlike many others. Instead of "outback" theme décor and satellite TV rugby matches, Le Bonza instead focuses on creating high-quality cuisine combining Australian, Asian and French flavors. You can watch the Australian cooks at work in the open kitchen or have the friendly owner mix up a mean *mojito* at the bar.

Le Pooja: 91 Passage Brady, 10th, M° Château-d'Eau, ☎ 01 48 24 00 83. Indian (€€). Open Tuesday through Sunday for lunch and dinner.

The Passage Brady is like a small piece of India right in the center of Paris, with Indian grocery stores, hair dressers, clothing boutiques and restaurant. Le Pooja is consistently rated the best of the bunch for its fresh, quality cooking, even if the décor leaves much to be desired. Lunch *menus* are under €10 and include vegetarian options.

La Mer de Chine: 159 Rue du Château-des-Rentiers, 13th, M° Nationale, ☎ 01 45 84 22 49. Chinese (€€€). Open daily (except Tuesday) for lunch and dinner until 1am.

This restaurant is a bit off the Chinatown beaten track, but it's worth the trek and extra cost for top-quality Chinese cuisine in an elegant setting.

Tricotin: 15 Avenue de Choisy, 13th, M° Porte de Choisy, ☎ 01 45 84 74 44. Chinese/Thai canteen (€). Chinese side open 9am to 11pm non-stop, Thai side open for lunch and dinner, closed Tuesday.

Cheap and cheerful, the two side-by-side Tricotin restaurants are constantly packed full of both Asian and French locals. On the left is the Thai restaurant, and on the right is the Chinese restaurant, although both have Chinese, Cambodian, Thai and Vietnamese dishes on the menu. At prices this low, you could try both. There's usually a wait, but it's very short, since the service is lightning-fast. There are a few round tables for families, but most people are seated cafeteria-style at long tables with chopsticks and condiments in the center. Reserve a table if you have a large group.

Sukho Thaï: 12 Rue du Père-Guérin, 13th, M° Place d'Italie, ☎ 01 45 81 55 88. Thai (€€). Open Monday through Saturday, noon to 2:30pm and 5 to 10pm. Closed August.

This authentic Thai restaurant at the foot of the Butte aux Cailles neighborhood has a cozy, low-lit dining room. Reservations are recommended for dinner, be sure to specify if you'd like a table in the non-smoking section.

Specialités Antillaises Ménilmontant "Chez Max": 14-16 Boulevard de Belleville, 20th, M° Belleville, ☎ 01 43 58 31 30. French West Indies (€€). Restaurant open daily, noon to 3:30pm.

Get an authentic taste of the French West Indies at this family-run bistro overlooking the busy Marché Belleville. If you take a liking to the home-made rum punch and aromatic spices, you can buy them in the attached food shop and deli counter.

■ Tearooms & Cafés

Autour d'un Café: 55 Boulevard Sébastopol, 1st, M° Châtelet-Les Halles, ☎ 01 42 21 42 47. Coffeehouse (€). Open Monday through Saturday, 9am to 5pm.

If you're craving a real caramel latte or *mochaccino*, Autour d'un Café is an American-style coffee house with fresh baked goods, a couch and plenty of reading material to browse. Eat-in or take-out salads, sandwiches, quiches, muffins and home-made cookies.

Appart'Thé: 7 Rue Charlot, 3rd, M° St-Sebastien-Froissart, ☎ 01 42 78 43 30, Trendy tearoom (€). Open daily, noon to 9pm.

In a quiet northern Marais street is a discreet tearoom with deep red walls, plush chairs, and no sign on the door. But don't be shy. This is the perfect romantic place to sip Mariage Frères teas and nibble dainty pastries. At lunchtime there are also quiches and *tartines* with foie gras or salmon, and on Sunday, full brunch for €20.

Café Parisien at Images de Demain: 141 Rue St-Martin, 4th, M° Rambuteau, ☎ 01 44 54 99 99. Casual tearoom (€). Open Monday through Saturday, 10:30am to 5pm.

Just across from the Pompidou Center is a poster-and-framing boutique with postcard stands on the sidewalk, similar to many on the street. However, this one has a darling tearoom upstairs with delicate armchairs, lots of lovely framed art and ceramics to take home, and views over the square in front of the Pompidou Center. The whitewashed wooden beams and tiled floor gives it a bit of a country Bastide look, and the mellow music and friendly service make it the perfect place for afternoon tea and cakes.

Café Hugo: 22 Place des Vosges, 4th, M° Chemin Vert or St-Paul, ☎ 01 42 72 64 04. Typical café (€€). Open daily, 8am to 2am.

Places des Vosges isn't short on fine dining options, but when you just want to sit down with the daily paper, a coffee, and maybe a ham and cheese *croque monsieur*, head to Café Hugo. Enjoy a quiet morning or afternoon under the arcades watching the world go by as the friendly staff, in traditional dark vests and long white aprons, shuttle back and forth between the café bar and dining room next door (open for lunch and dinner).

Au Petit Fer à Cheval: 30 Rue Vieille du Temple, 4th, M° St-Paul, ☎ 01 42 72 47 47. Traditional café/bar (€). Open 9am to 2am, food served noon to 1am.

An institution in the Marais with its horseshoe-shaped zinc bar, the Petit Fer à Cheval is a great place to read the paper with a glass of red wine or people-watch on the tiny terrace with a cold beer. Behind the bar is a dining room serving country-style salads and uncomplicated *plats du jour*. It's always packed on weekends and for lunch, so get there early or call ahead to reserve a table.

Le Bricolo' Café: BHV, 52 Rue de Rivoli, 4th, M° Hôtel-de-Ville, ☎ 01 42 74 90 00. Boutique café. Open Monday through Saturday, 9:30am to 6:30pm.

Anyone bit by the home improvement bug will enjoy a shopping break at this little café in the ground floor of the BHV department store. Decorated to resemble an old tool shed, it has cold and hot drinks, quiches, sandwiches, muffins, and do-it-yourself books on the shelf. Each day at 4pm is a free class in the café on home improvement projects (in French). When the weather is clear you can also head up to the top floor terrace to see if the snack carte is open. If not, you can still enjoy rooftop views of the Hôtel de Ville and Tour St-Jacques.

Le Loir dans la Théière: 3 Rue des Rosiers, 4th, M° St-Paul, ☎ 01 42 72 90 61. Traditional tearoom (€). Open Sunday through Thursday, 11am to 7pm; Friday and Saturday, 10am to 7pm.

Get comfortable on the worn leather club chairs and distressed wooden tables and dive into the home-made quiches, savory tartes, and the tallest slice of lemon meringue pie in town. There's a large selection of teas and hot chocolate in three flavors that doesn't come from a powder mix.

Mariage Frères: 30 Rue du Bourg-Tibourg, 4th, M° Hôtel-de-Ville, ☎ 01 42 72 28 11, www.mariagefreres.com. Upscale tearoom (€€). Lunch noon to 3pm, tearoom 3 to 7pm.

This is the main address for the upscale tea empire of Mariage Frères, with a colonial-style tearoom, boutique and tiny exhibition upstairs on the history of tea. Although it's been listed in every guidebook ever printed, it still remains a very chic place where the clientele dress up a bit for lunch or afternoon tea in style. Full brunch served Sunday, reservations highly recommended.

La Fourmi Ailée: 8 Rue du Fouarre, 5th, M° Maubert-Mutualité, ☎ 01 43 29 40 99. Casual tearoom (€-€€). Open daily, noon to midnight.

This cozy tearoom across the river from Notre Dame has old books lining the walls, a fireplace, and a small mezzanine balcony with skylight. There are quiches, salads and vegetarian dishes, or you can just come by for an afternoon *apfelstreudel* and glass of white wine.

Flamant: 8 Place de Furstenberg, 6th, M° St-Germain-des-Prés, ☎ 01 56 81 12 40. Boutique café (€). Open 11am to 5:30pm, lunch served noon to 2:30pm, tearoom open from 2:30pm.

On a lovely square next to the Delacroix Museum, the stylish Belgian home décor company Flamant has a large boutique set up like a home, where you go from room to room to see the furnishings and decorations. The café is in the elegant, Victorian-style kitchen with fresh flowers on each table and home decorating magazines on the shelves. Choose from Poilâne sandwiches made with Brie and walnut or roast eggplant and tomatoes, or fresh salads made right in front of you. To drink, there's a selection of wines by the glass, artisan apple juice and even pear cider. If you're still craving something sweet, stop by the gourmet chocolate and candy counter next to the boutique's side entrance.

Deux Magots: 6 Place St-Germain-des-Prés, 6th, M° St-Germain-des-Prés, ☎ 01 45 48 55 25. Historic café (€-€€). Open daily, 7:30am to 1:30am.

If you must go here – and everyone does ever since Sartre, Hemingway, Picasso and de Beauvoir first put it on the map – try to go when you've got a few hours free to hang out, and make sure you're in a prime

Paris

people-watching location on the terrace. After all, that €6 doesn't just pay for a *café crème*, it also pays for that little bit of real estate you get to occupy. Sandwiches, *charcuterie* and salads are available throughout the day in case you get the munchies.

Le Lucernaire: 53 Rue Notre-Dame-des-Champs, 6th, M° Notre-Dame-des-Champs or Vavin, ☎ 01 45 48 91 10, www.lucernaire.fr. Arthouse café (€). Open daily, noon to 2pm and 7pm to midnight (bar open until 1am).

In the back of this Montparnasse cultural center and cinema is a casual café and bar serving inexpensively priced meals and light snacks for the student and theater crowd. A unique location, with authentic cobblestones from the May '68 uprising paving the courtyard entrance.

La Palette: 43 Rue de Seine, 6th, M° St-Germain-des-Prés, ☎ 01 43 26 68 15. Typical café (€-€€). Open Monday through Saturday, 8am to 2am; closed three weeks in August.

Reserve your table on the terrace to lunch under the trees at this classic St-Germain-des-Prés café, or hang out at the *zinc* (café bar) alongside local gallery owners, Beaux-Arts students and well-heeled locals. Simple *plats du jour* are available for lunch along with inexpensive *croque monsieurs*, salads and wines by the glass.

Amorino: 4 Rue de Buci, 6th, M° Odéon, ☎ 01 43 26 57 46, Italian ice cream (€). Open Sunday through Thursday, noon to midnight; Friday and Saturday, noon to 1am. Takeout only.

There's always a crowd lined up at this Italian *gelato* shop. The freshly made sorbets and ice creams are labeled in Italian, and the adventurous can ask for up to four different flavors arranged expertly onto a cone to resemble a gigantic creamy flower. Their second location on Ile St-Louis (at 47 Rue St-Louis-en-Ile) is rapidly convincing former Berthillon addicts to switch camps.

Ladurée: 21 Rue Bonaparte, 6th, M° St-Germain-des-Prés, ☎ 01 44 07 64 87. Historic tearoom (€-€€). Open daily for breakfast 8am to 11am, lunch noon to 3pm, tearoom 3 to 7pm, and dinner 7 to 11:30pm. Reservations for lunch and dinner recommended.

This is the first Left Bank location for the classic Ladurée tearoom (the original is on the Champs-Elysées), opened in a former antiques boutique with Imperial Napoleon III décor. It includes the tearoom, pastry shop and chocolate boutique. If you don't have time for a sit-down meal, pick up a few of their famous macaroons at the pastry shop, where even the croissants are wrapped and packaged for you in high style. The candles and teas make great gifts.

Forêt Noire: 9 Rue de l'Eperon, 6th, M° Odéon, ☎ 01 44 41 00 09. German tearoom (€). Open Monday through Saturday, 11am to 7pm.

It's no surprise that the specialty in this casual tearoom is the German owner's own Black Forest cake. There's also cheese cake and gâteau aux leégumes (savory veggie cake), and some serious gourmet French teas from Mariage Frères and Contes de Thé.

Martine Lambert, 192 Rue de Grenelle, 7th, M° Ecole Militaire, ☎ 01 45 51 25 30. Home-made ice cream. Daily, 10am to 8pm

After 15 years of scooping out her home-made ice cream at the seaside resort of Deauville, Martine Lambert has opened a tiny boutique just around the corner from the Marché Cler. The ice cream and sorbet are made fresh each day with fewer than six ingredients. The tiramisu wins hands-down as the most popular flavor.

Café du Musée Jacquemart-André: 158 Boulevard Haussmann, 8th, M° St-Philippe-du-Roule, ☎ 01 45 62 11 59. Museum tearoom (€). Open daily with service for lunch, 11:45am to 3pm; and for tea, 3 to 5:30pm. Sunday brunch, 11am to 3pm. Reservations recommended.

One of the most beautiful museums in Paris is also endowed with one of the most beautiful tearooms. It's set in the former dining room of the Jacquemart-André family, with Brussels tapestries, ceiling frescos and views over the formal courtyard gardens. Lunch includes salads, quiches and *plats du jour*. Home-made pastries and ice cream are served for afternoon tea. The Sunday brunch (€23) includes fresh orange juice, smoked salmon, bread basket, salad, poached eggs and dessert.

La Terrasse Flo: Printemps de la Maison (ninth floor), 64 Boulevard Haussmann, 9th, M° Havre-Caumartin, ☎ 01 42 82 62 76. Rooftop café (€-€€). Open Monday through Saturday, 9:35am to 7pm.

There are at least seven different places to eat in the maze of buildings that makes up Printemps department store, but the best one is La Terrasse Flo. Not for its cafeteria-style self-service food, but for the amazing panoramic views of Paris. The café's windows look over western Paris, including the Eiffel Tower. Go out onto the terrace (you can eat out there in the summer) and you'll also be able to see the roof of the Palais Garnier and a full-size view of Sacré-Coeur Basilica (you'll kick yourself if you've run out of film). You could always just skip eating and go straight to the terrace, where a few benches are set up for weary shoppers to rest their feet.

Café de la Musée de la Vie Romantique: 16 Rue Chaptal, 9th, M° St-Georges, ☎ 01 48 74 95 38. Museum tearoom (€). Open Tuesday through Sunday, 11:30am to 5:30pm.

In the heart of the St-Georges neighborhood is the Musée de la Vie Romantique, a charming house covered in ivy and set back from the street, surrounded by a cottage-style garden. It was once home to painter Ary Scheffer, who entertained friends such as George Sand, Chopin, Delacroix, Liszt and Ingres. Most enjoyable is the tearoom overlooking the gardens, run by Cakes de Bertrand, with tea and cakes, savory tarts, and Sunday brunch. On sunny spring mornings when no one else is around, it feels like your own private piece of paradise.

Paris

La Cantine Antoine et Lili: 95 Quai de Valmy, 10th, M° Jacques Bonsergent or Gare de l'Est, ☎ 01 40 37 34 86, www.antoineetlili.com. Kitsch tearoom (€-€€). Open Monday and Tuesday, 11am to 7pm; Wednesday through Saturday, 11am to 11pm; Sunday, noon to 6:30pm.

This colorful tearoom on the Canal St-Martin is part of the Antoine et Lili empire of clothing and home décor boutiques scattered around Paris. There's a selection of teas, including mint tea, cakes, sandwiches and quiches for all appetites. A great place for kids, with a friendly, Bohemian crowd, when it's not packed.

La Passerelle: 3 Rue St-Hubert, 11th, M° St-Maur ☎ 01 43 57 04 82 Latin-American café (€€). Open Tuesday through Thursday, 3pm to 1am; Friday and Saturday, 3pm to 2am; Sunday, 4 to 10pm.

This literary café and restaurant serves Latin American specialties in a Spanish villa décor of terra-cotta walls, wrought iron balcony and soaring vaulted ceilings, with a fountain on the patio. They also sell books from small, independent publishers, hold regular acoustic concerts, literary readings, and art expositions. There are a few couches for those seeking a good place to spend the afternoon with a book and a glass of Argentinean wine.

L'Empire des Thés: 101 Avenue d'Ivry, 13th, M° Tolbiac, ☎ 01 45 85 66 33. Chinese tearoom (€). Open Tuesday through Sunday, 11am to 7:30pm for the tearoom, until 8pm for the boutique.

Right in the heart of Chinatown, this Zen tearoom has more than 200 Chinese teas, served with lovely pastries. The knowledgeable staff will patiently help you choose one that suits your tastes. Smoking not allowed.

Phinéas: 99 Rue de l'Ouest, 14th, M° Pernety, ☎ 01 45 41 33 50. Modern café (€). Open Tuesday through Sunday, 11:30am to 3:30pm; and Tuesday through Saturday, 7:30 to 11pm.

Curl up with one of the comic books lying around and a slice of the home-made lemon tart (*tarte au citron*) in this kitsch paradise run by authentic hippies, Joy and Phinéas. Quiches and savory tartes are also available, with brunch on Sundays.

Café Mauve: Franck et Fils, 80 Rue de Passy, 16th, M° Muette, ☎ 01 44 14 38 00. Boutique tearoom (€€). Open Monday through Saturday, 11:30am to 6:30 pm. Lunch served noon to 2:30pm.

This girly café on the top floor of the elegant Franck et Fils department store (past the bridal department) is the perfect place to stop for lunch or afternoon tea if you're in the Passy neighborhood. At lunch there are salads and classic dishes like grilled meats with steamed veggies, or you can sit at the booths in the salon for tea, hot chocolate and the home-made desserts in the afternoon.

Pâtisserie Carette: 4 Place du Trocadéro, 16th, M° Trocadéro, ☎ 01 47 27 98 85. Traditional tearoom (€). Open daily.

This cute, old-fashioned tearoom and pastry shop is situated between a few more modern brasseries on the busy Place du Trocadéro, but is worth a stop if you're dying for a proper cup of tea (and for €5.50 you get enough hot water to pour yourself four cups from the dainty silver service). Their macaroons have been considered among the best in Paris since 1927. In summer the terrace is packed and an ice-cream stand is set up.

Café du Halle St-Pierre: 2 Rue Ronsard, 18th, M° Anvers, ☎ 01 42 58 72 89, www.hallesaintpierre.org. Tearoom/café (€). Open daily, 10am to 6pm.

The Halle St-Pierre houses the Naive Art Museum and library, and has a lovely little café with views of leafy Montmartre through the large glass windows of the former 19th-century covered market. Quiches, salads, teas and cakes are served non-stop on tiny tables, with a selection of art magazines and newspapers on hand for browsing. Kid-friendly.

Lou Pascalou: 14 Rue des Panoyaux, 20th, M° Ménilmontant, ☎ 01 46 36 78 10. Old-fashioned café (€). Open daily, 9am to 2am, food served noon to 2am.

After just 20 years, this Ménilmontant café has become a legend, the café that every new "authentic East Paris café" tries to copy. It's the neighborhood artistic and cultural center, the cool place to hang out for a beer and a game of chess, and it has one of the most enviable terraces in town. Dress down and plan on hanging out for a few hours to enjoy a real piece of Parisian village life (after all, no one actually comes for the food, but it's there, and it's reasonably priced). Don't miss the futuristic toilets.

CAFE CULTURE

Some Americans find it very odd that all of the chairs on café terraces face the street, but in France people-watching is considered half the fun of hanging out in a café (the other half being the fun of just hanging out, another concept the ever-productive Anglophones seem to find bewildering). If being a voyeur makes you squeamish, put on a pair of sunglasses and pretend you're reading the paper. And remember: the French *expect* to be watched, they put a lot of effort into the way they look!

■ Museum Cafés

Some museum cafés are only open to those actually visiting the museum. Among these are **Le Café du Jeu de Paume** (Musée du Jeu de Paume, 1 Place de la Concorde, 8th, M° Concorde, ☎ 01 40 20 00 77; open Wednesday through Friday, noon to 6pm; Thursday until 8:30pm; Saturday and Sunday, 10am to 6pm), with just a few tables and excellent pastries. **La Cafétéria de la Musée Rodin** (75 Rue de Varenne, 7th, M° Invalides or

Varenne, ☎ 01 45 50 42 34, open Tuesday through Sunday, 9:30am until 6:30pm from April to September, and until 4:30pm from October to March) isn't a cafeteria at all, but a lovely café set in the sculpture gardens of the museum, serving inexpensive hot and cold sandwiches, salads and desserts under the trees. Very kid-friendly, and there's a reduced entrance fee if you're just visiting the gardens.

For something on a much grander scale, try the turn-of-the-19th-century dining room of the **Musée d'Orsay Restaurant**, which was once part of the hotel built adjacent to the train station. It has wooden floors, marble columns, ceiling frescoes and crystal chandeliers, and a view of the Seine. There's even a live pianist on Sunday afternoons. Quai Anatole France, 7th, M° Solferino, ☎ 01 45 49 47 03, www.musee-orsay. (For hours and other details about the restaurant and the café, click on "English," "Practical Information" and then "Café & Restaurant.")

■ Snacking & Takeout

Certains L'Aiment Bio: 37 Rue Mauconseil, 1st, M° Etienne Marcel or Les Halles, ☎ 01 42 36 52 17. Organic/vegetarian (€). Open 10:30am to 6pm, Monday through Friday.

This little deli on a pedestrian side-street off Rue Montorgueil serves organic and vegetarian sandwiches, soups, quiches, smoothies and desserts to eat in or take out. On warmer days a mini-terrace is set up outside.

Amici Miei: 53 Rue Beaumarchais, 3rd, M° Chemin Vert or Bastille, ☎ 01 42 71 82 62. Gourmet pizza (€€). Open Tuesday through Saturday, noon to 2:30pm; and Monday through Saturday, 7:45 to 11pm. No reservations.

Get here early unless you want to be stuck in a line going out the door. This Sicilian *trattoria* specializes in gourmet pizza, including *pizza blanches* (without tomato sauce), as well as antipasti, *fougasse* (the French version of focaccia) and fresh pastas. If you don't feel like waiting for one of the few tables, get your pizza to go and find a spot on the lawn of the nearby Place des Vosges.

TERMS TO REMEMBER

Takeout (to go). . . . . *à emporter*
Eat in. . . . . *sur place*

Au Duc de Montmorency: 46 Rue de Montmorency, 3rd, M° Rambuteau, ☎ 01 42 72 18 10. Organic deli (€). Open Monday through Friday, 9am to 9pm; Saturday, 9am to 5pm.

Owned by the medieval Nicolas Flamel restaurant across the street, this tiny organic deli with a 1960s new-age décor sells simple, inexpensive dishes and light wines to go. There are also a few tables in the corner for on-site enjoyment if it's not too crowded.

Adolis: 15 Rue du Grenier St-Lazare, 3rd, M° Rambuteau, ☎ 01 42 77 46 77. Lebanese takeout (€). Open daily, 11am to midnight.

The heavenly scents coming from this Lebanese deli make it hard to pass by without ordering one of the falafels or sandwiches, made with high-quality, fresh ingredients (the deli actually shares a kitchen with the Lebanese restaurant around the back).

BEST PICNIC SPOTS

Picnicking has become quite the rage in France over the past few years, with periodic "neighborhood picnics" organized in parks or open squares. Head to the nearest open market to stock up on supplies, or any *traiteur* or *épicerie* (deli) counter for prepared meals to go. And thanks to the absence of "open-container" laws in France, it's possible to bring along a nice bottle of rosé. Just don't forget the bottle opener! Anywhere along the Seine or the Canal St-Martin is ideal for boat watching. The pedestrian-only bridges, **Passerelle Solferino** (7th) and **Pont des Arts** (6th), are always lined with picnickers on summer evenings, and offer the best views of the sparkling Eiffel Tower and the illuminated Pont Neuf. Parks where you're allowed to picnic on the grass include the **Champ-de-Mars** (7th), for sunset picnics after 6pm, when the park guards have gone home, **Parc André Citroën** (15th), and **Parc de la Villette** (19th).

Le Petit Jean Bart: 84 Rue St-Antoine, 4th, M° Bastille or St-Paul ☎ 01 42 72 04 41 Brittany Crêpes (€-€€). Open daily from 11am to midnight, closed two weeks in August.

Almost directly across from the St-Paul-St-Louis church, this charming little Breton restaurant and *crêperie* has a huge selection of crêpes, pastas, soups, sandwiches, salads, hot dishes like *steak-frites*, and desserts served in a whimsical seaside décor. The prices are amazingly low for the service and quality, and everything can be ordered to go.

Le Pain Quotidien: 136 Rue Mouffetard, 5th, M° Censier-Daubenton, ☎ 01 55 43 91 99. Country brunch (€-€€). Open daily, 7am to 7pm. Non-smoking.

Okay, there's a branch of this chain in LA, but it's still one of the best places in town for brunch. This one overlooks the historic Marché Mouffetard and the Eglise St-Médard, with signature communal wooden

Paris

tables and takeout bakery counter. For those eating in, there are organic salads, hearty sandwiches, vegetarian dishes, and a selection of teas and coffees to go with your brunch.

Le Pot au Lait: 41 Rue Censier, 5th, M° Censier-Daubenton, ☎ 01 42 17 15 69. Takeout crêperie (€). Open Tuesday through Saturday, 11:30am to 2:30pm and 6:30 to 10:30pm.

Generous crêpes (sweet or savory) and friendly service, just a few steps from the markets of Rue Mouffetard.

La Buvette des Marionnettes: Jardins de Luxembourg, 6th, M° Odéon or RER Luxembourg, ☎ 01 43 26 33 04. Park café (€). Open daily, 8:30am to 7pm.

Have a salad or *croque monsieur* on Poilâne bread while kids watch the marionnette show in the beautiful Luxembourg Gardens.

Nils: 10 Rue de Buci, 6th, M° Mabillon, ☎ 01 46 34 82 82. Scandinavian takeout (€). Open daily, 10:30am to 10pm.

This Danish deli has Scandinavian sandwiches, salads, and smoked fish platters to take out or eat in at the tiny bar that resembles an IKEA store restaurant. Beverages include Nordic specialties like *glögg* (mulled wine), and beers from Finland and Denmark. There's a second location on Rue Montorgueil in the 1st.

Cosi: 54 Rue de Seine, 6th, M° Mabillon, ☎ 01 46 33 35 36. Gourmet sandwiches (€). Open daily, noon to 11pm.

Order from a menu of tasty sandwiches or have one custom-made with the wholesome and original ingredients and piping hot bread. They can be wrapped to go or eaten in the bright dining room upstairs. Lines stretch onto the sidewalk between noon and 2pm, so try to get there earlier or later in the afternoon to have the best selection of ingredients.

La Grand Epicerie du Bon Marché: 38 Rue de Sèvres, 7th, M° Sèvres-Babylone, ☎ 01 44 39 81 00. Gourmet deli (€-€€). Open Monday through Saturday, 8:30am to 9pm.

This high-end gourmet supermarket attached to the Bon Marché department store is the perfect place to put together a picnic basket with fresh baked goods, antipasti and charcuterie at the deli counter, and the perfect bottle of wine. At lunch and dinner there's also an Asian fast-food counter open for takeout rice, veggies and meats cooked the way the client wants (steamed, grilled or fried). The only danger in this store is that you'll end up with a whole cartload of food!

BE: 73 Boulevard de Courcelles, 8th, M°Monceau, ☎ 01 46 22 20 20. Trendy deli (€€). Open Monday through Saturday, 8am to 8pm, closed August.

BE stands for *boulangerie-epicerie*, an Alain Ducasse-owned gourmet deli with minimalist décor and designer packaging for the takeout sandwiches, salads, fruit juices and picnics (you could try to eat in-house, but there's rarely enough room). Popular with local *bobo's* who double-park their Mercedes 4x4s outside the front door.

 AUTHOR'S NOTE: *Check out the* Where to Shop *section, pages 223-226, for gourmet food boutiques.*

La Butik du Flora Danica: 142 Avenue des Champs-Elysées, 8th, M° Etoile, ☎ 01 44 13 86 26. Danish deli (€). Open daily, 9am to 10pm.

There's not much in the way of healthy takeout on the Champs-Elysées, but this Danish deli, attached to the Maison du Danemark's gourmet restaurant, is the perfect place for herrings, soups, sandwiches and smoked salmon to go. Prices are slightly higher if you decide to take a seat on their vast terrace overlooking the Champs-Elysées.

Bert's: 4 Avenue du Président Wilson, 8th, M° Alma Marceau, ☎ 01 47 23 43 37. Trendy sandwich bar (€). Open Monday through Saturday, 8am to 8pm.

This deluxe breakfast and organic sandwich bar serves salads, sandwiches and soups in a fashionably hip eggplant-colored dining room and sidewalk terrace. There are comfy club chairs, bar seating, and plenty of reading material for solo diners. Service at the counter, whether you're eating in or ordering to go. Other locations at 6 Rue de Ponthieu, 8th, and 5 Rue de Presbourg, 16th.

Des Crêpes et des Cailles: 13 Rue de la Butte aux Cailles, 13th, M° Corvisart, ☎ 01 45 81 68 69. Brittany crêpes (€). Open daily at lunch and dinner.

Located in the center of the Butte aux Cailles, this is the only authentic Brittany *crêperie* in this part of Paris. A selection of dinner or dessert crêpes can be eaten on-site with a mug of cider or ordered from the window to go.

Pizzeria Enzo; 72 Rue Daguerre, 14th, M° Denfert-Rochereau, ☎ 01 43 21 66 66. Modern pizzeria (€€). Open for lunch Monday through Saturday, dinner Monday through Friday.

A neighborhood favorite, this tiny Italian café is always full. Call ahead if you'd like to order a pizza to go (€7-€10): the *Enzo Speciale* is highly recommended.

Aquavence: 17 Rue Desaix, 15th, M° Dupleix, ☎ 01 53 86 70 45. Organic deli (€). Open Monday through Friday, 8am to 6pm; Saturday, 9:30am to 5pm.

Just a few steps from the Champ-de-Mars is an organic deli selling healthy sandwiches, soups and salads to take out or eat in the small dining room with counters overlooking the street. Perfect for a healthy picnic lunch at the foot of the Eiffel Tower.

Pend'Art: 14 Rue Ruisseau, 18th, M° Lamarck-Caulaincourt, ☎ 01 42 62 06 72. Organic pizzeria (€). Open daily (dinner only), 7pm to 1:30am.

Just north of Montmartre is a *bijou* restaurant where hearty salads, gooey desserts and gourmet pizzas with toppings like seaweed are made with fresh, completely organic ingredients of the highest quality. Artsy locals squeeze into vintage cinema seats in the low-lit interior, or spill out onto the sidewalk when the weather is agreeable. Pizzas can also be ordered to go.

■ Dining After Midnight

 It's no longer very difficult to find a bar or club open into the wee hours of the morning, but for those who need a full meal after midnight, it's best to stick to the Champs-Elysées (8th) and Les Halles (1st), where traditional brasseries and a few typically French bistro-bars have been keeping the masses of the night well fed for years.

La Poule au Pot: 9 Rue Vauvilliers, 1st, M° Les Halles, ☎ 01 42 36 32 96. Traditional brasserie (€€€). Open Tuesday through Sunday, 7pm to 5am.

This intimate little brasserie near Les Halles has been serving its famous *poule-au-pot* since 1935! Hearty stews, friendly service and great after-midnight ambiance make this a favorite for all hungry night-owls.

Le Tambour: 41 Rue Montmartre, 2nd, M° Les Halles or Sentier, ☎ 01 42 33 06 90. Vintage bistro (€€). Open 24/7, dinner served 8pm to 2am.

Le Tambour has an amusing Alpine chalet exterior and a mildly claustrophobic bric-a-brac interior that somehow makes it a very comfortable place to be at 4am. It's usually full to bursting by midnight with down-to-earth locals and night owls who have lost their way. The beer is cheap, and the solid bistro cooking, served until 2am, isn't bad for the price.

L'Enfance de Lard: 21 Rue Guidard, 6th, M° Mabillon, ☎ 01 46 33 89 65. Traditional French (€€). Open Tuesday through Saturday, 7pm to 4am (last orders); and Sunday and Monday, 7 to 11:30pm.

Deep in the heart of the Latin Quarter, this old-fashioned restaurant is popular with the French regulars for its friendly service (at any hour) and festive atmosphere (helped along by the wine in the early hours). Try not to translate the name of this restaurant literally, lest you lose your appetite.

L'Alsace: 39 Avenue des Champs-Elysées, 8th, M° Franklin D Roosevelt, ☎ 01 53 93 97 00. Alsatian brasserie (€€€). Open 24/7.

This authentic Alsatian brasserie with early-1900s décor serves hearty foods like sauerkraut, seafood platters and seasonal game, with Alsace white wines or tall beers to accompany them. Being right on the Champs-Elysées, it's almost as crowded at 4am as it is at lunch.

La Cloche d'Or: 3 Rue Mansart, 9th, M° Blanche, ☎ 01 48 74 48 88. Traditional French (€€). Open Monday through Saturday for lunch and dinner until 5am (last service at 4am), Sunday until 1am. Closed August.

This is one of the only all-night restaurants near Montmartre-Pigalle, serving onion soup, *escargots* and *andouillettes* in a cozy, Norman *auberge* setting.

Viaduc Café: 43 Avenue Daumesnil, 12th, M° Gare de Lyon, ☎ 01 44 74 70 70. Trendy café (€€). Open daily, 9am to 4am, service noon to 3pm, 7pm to 3am, non-stop Saturday and Sunday.

Tucked under the arches of the Viaduc des Arts, the Viaduc Café has a spacious, converted loft dining room with mezzanine, which can make for noisy dining when the place is packed. Brunch with live jazz on Sundays.

Entertainment

Event Listings

First thing to do on arriving in Paris is to pick up the weekly *Pariscope* (€0.40; it's in French, but there's an English section at the very back written by the *Time Out Guide*). It has cinema and theater listings, concerts and museum exhibitions, gallery shows and nightlife, and comes out every Wednesday. If you understand French, then check the *Zurban* (€0.80, also each Wednesday), a slightly more detailed version of *Pariscope*, with shopping ideas, restaurant reviews, club soirées, children's activities and general goings-on in Paris and Ile-de-France for casually hip, youngish locals. There are a few free English-language guides that come out monthly: *The Connexion*, *The Voice* (www.parisvoice.com), *Funky Paris* (www.funkymaps.com), and the twice monthly *FUSAC*, all of which can usually be found in the English-language bookshops (WH Smith, Abbey Bookshop, or Shakespeare & Co.) or expat bars around town (see the *Bars & Clubs* section below), with events listings and bar ads targeting English-speaking readers.

The monthly magazine *Paris Capital* (at most newsstands and some hotels) is a luxury restaurant and nightlife magazine with Paris society pages and ads for expensive watches. Their web site (www.leclubparis.com) is free and partially translated into English. Listings include clubs, cabarets, hotels, bars and the latest trendy restaurants.

The **Paris Tourism Office** bilingual web site (www.parisbienvenue.com) highlights festivals and events such as the annual Techno Parade and Jazz Festival, as well as more family-friendly entertainment options such as zoos and circuses. There are club and bar addresses, but no descriptions.

Finally the **What's On When?** (www.whatsonwhen.com) web site lists events from sports matches to classical music concerts to religious celebrations that can be searched by city, month, theme or specific venue, along with star ratings for each listing and detailed contact information. It's a great site to browse before arriving in Paris.

Ticket Agents

Le Kiosque Théâtre: To buy tickets at half-price on the day of the show stop by one of the two theater kiosks at Place de la Madeleine (8th) and Esplanade de la Tour Montparnasse (14th). Open Tuesday through Saturday, 12:30 to 7:45pm; and Sunday, 12:30 to 4pm. Anyone under 26 can get even steeper discounts from the theater kiosks at 25 Boulevard Boudon (M° Bastille, 4th) or 91 Boulevard St-Michel (5th).

FNAC Billetterie: ☎ 08 25 02 00 20 (bookings by phone Monday through Saturday, 9am to 8pm), www.fnac.com. Most FNAC store locations around Paris also sell tickets to local events. Forum des Halles (1st), and 19 Avenue de l'Opéra (1st).

Virgin Megastore: ☎ 08 25 02 30 24 (telephone bookings Monday through Saturday, 10am to 6pm). There are multiple locations around Paris, including inside the Galerie du Carrousel du Louvre (1st) and 52 Avenue des Champs-Elysées (8th).

Cultural Events

■ Performing Arts

Paris, being the undisputed cultural capital of Europe, has an appropriately mind-boggling choice of theater, dance, opera and classical music concerts throughout the year. Thanks to generous government subsidies, many small and independently run theaters and production companies survive right alongside the two national operas and four national theaters. Headline performing artists from around the world come to stage their productions in the city's top venues such as the historic Palais Garnier or the modern Cité de la Musique. Whether it's classic ballet or avant-garde theater, experimental dance or Baroque concerts, there's something to suit all tastes. The contemporary dance scene is particularly well-regarded, while there's always at least one venue paying tribute to the glory days of French *chanson* with Piaf and Brel on the repertoire. Check out the weekly *Pariscope* or *Zurban* guides for the latest offerings, keeping in mind that many theaters are closed in July and August.

Opéra Garnier: Place de l'Opéra, 9th, M° Opéra, ☎ 08 92 89 90 90, www.opera-de-paris.fr. This beautiful theater, the Palais Garnier, is home to the Ballet de l'Opéra (see below), and is devoted almost exclusively to ballet and dance productions, both classic and contemporary, with a smaller selection of musical concerts and lesser-known operas throughout the year. Completely restored to all its gilded glory in the late 1990s, the Palais Garnier has over 2,000 seats. During intermission it's possible to wander around the different reception rooms and marble halls, peek into the private box seats, or strike a pose on the grand staircase with a glass of wine from the bar. There are usually no productions in August. Tickets €6-€100.

HISTORICAL NOTE

The Sun King, Louis XIV, not only created the first official ballet and opera company in 1661 (they performed at court, of course), he was an accomplished dancer himself. He opened the Académie Royale de la Danse in 1669 to establish dance as an official profession, and today the Ballet de l'Opéra is considered the best in the world, whose dancers train almost exclusively at the (renamed) Ecole de Danse de l'Opéra.

Opéra Bastille: Place de la Bastille, 12th, M° Bastille, ☎ 01 40 01 19 70, www.opera-de-paris.fr. The uber-modern Opéra Bastille was inaugurated in 1989 for the bicentennial of the French Revolution. Despite all the grumbling about its sterile, airport-like interior, the 2,700-seat auditorium has superb acoustics, state-of-the-art stage equipment (and an exact replica of the main stage for rehearsals), and its own costume and scenery workshops. Home of the Opéra National de Paris, the annual opera program runs from well-loved classics to modern (even avant-garde) productions. The Opéra Bastille also hosts the *Etoiles* (stars) from the Ballet de l'Opéra (from the Palais Garnier) and musical concerts in its smaller auditoriums. The season runs from September through July. Tickets €6-€100.

OPERA CONFUSION

The **Opéra Bastille** and **Opéra Garnier** are known collectively as the Opéra de Paris, sharing a web site and ticket sales. Be sure you confirm the location of the production when purchasing your seats.

Opéra Comique: Place Boieldieu, 2nd, M° Richelieu-Drouot, ☎ 08 25 00 00 58, www.opera-comique.com. This "Théatre Musical Populaire" hosted the première of *Carmen* in its beautiful interior. Today it specializes in operettas and musical comedies. Tickets €7-€100.

Théâtre de la Ville: 2 Place du Châtelet, 4th, M° Châtelet-Les Halles, ☎ 01 42 74 22 77, www.theatredelaville-paris.com. Tickets €11-27. Once run by Sarah Bernhardt (the brasserie outside has been named after her in tribute), the Théâtre de la Ville is known for its contemporary dance productions, but also stages regular world music, theater and classical music concerts. Many of the theater and world music productions take place in the company's second theater, **Les Abbesses** (31 Rue des Abbesses, 18th, M° Abbesses). Be sure to confirm the location when purchasing your tickets.

Théâtre des Champs-Elysées: 15 Avenue Montaigne, 8th, M° Franklin-Roosevelt, ☎ 01 49 52 50 50, www.theatrechampselysees.fr. This elegant theater, built in 1913, is known for its star-packed seasonal program, with top opera, dance, orchestra, and vocal artists from around the world. A bit more expensive (no state funding), but worth every euro for its sumptuous décor and quality programming. Tickets €6-110.

La Comédie-Française: Salle Richelieu, 2 Rue de Richelieu, 1st, M° Palais-Royal, ☎ 01 44 58 15 15, www.comedie-francaise.fr. Founded in 1680, the Comédie Française is France's oldest theater company. During the French Revolution the actors occupied the royal theater of the Palais Royal, where the troupe took up official residence in 1799. The repertoire includes classics by Molière, Racine, Shakespeare and Victor Hugo, along with contemporary pieces. Note: Some productions take place in the second location, the **Théâtre du Vieux-Colombier** (21 Rue du Vieux-Colombier, 6th, M° St-Sulpice). Tickets €10-40.

OPEN-AIR PRODUCTIONS

There are regular performances of Shakespeare's plays (in French) from spring through fall at the Bois de Boulogne's Théâtre de Verdure, in the Jardin Shakespeare, with seating for 500 (☎ 01 40 19 95 33, tickets €10-€20), and open-air opera concerts, usually Mozart each June, in the Jardins du Luxembourg (☎ 01 56 33 70 10, www.akouna.com/operaenpleinair).

■ Theater in English

Odéon-Théâtre de l'Europe: Place de l'Odéon, 6th, M° Odéon, ☎ 01 44 85 40 40, www.theatre-odeon.fr. Tickets €13-26. Built in 1782 as the home of the Comédie-Française, the Odéon, with its classic 18th-century architecture, is just outside the Jardins du Luxembourg on the Left Bank. In 1990 it was renamed the Théâtre de l'Europe, dedicated to working together with Europe's top theater troops, directors and playwrights. The annual program features mostly modern and contemporary pieces, with at least one production in English each season.

> **ATTENTION:** *Due to the extensive and ongoing restoration work at the Théâtre de l'Europe, performances will take place in the Ateliers Berthiers (8 Boulevard Berthier, 17th, M° Porte-de-Clichy) through the fall of 2005.*

One World Actors (www.oneworldactors.com) produces weekly Monday-night English-language theater at UNESCO's 130-seat auditorium (7 Place Fontenoy, 7th, M° Ségur). The repertoire includes everything from Shakespeare to Mamet. Shows are at 8:15 pm, tickets €18. For more information call ☎ 01 48 28 00 46.

Other theaters that often have at least one seasonal production in English include the **Théâtre de Nesle** (8 Rue de Nesle, 6th, M° Odéon, ☎ 01 46 34 61 04), and the **Sudden Theater** near Montmartre (14*bis* Rue Sainte-Isaure, 18th, M° Jules-Joffrin, ☎ 01 42 62 35 00).

FOR A LAUGH

Catch the hottest stand-up comedians from around the world (in English) at the historic Art Deco **Hôtel du Nord** (102 Quai de Jemmapes, 10th, M° Goncourt or Jaurès, ☎ 01 53 19 98 88) overlooking the Canal St-Martin. Tickets €15-€20. The production company **Laughing & Music Matters** (www.anythingmatters.com) appears here and at other venues around Paris. Check their web site for the current schedule.

■ Classical Music

Concert Halls

Cité de la Musique: Parc de la Villette, 19th, M° Porte-de-Pantin, ☎ 01 44 84 45 45, www.cite-musique.fr. This music cultural center houses the Paris National Conservatory, several concert halls and the Musée de la Musique. All styles of music are on the annual program from classical string quartets and jazz festivals to Pink Floyd laser shows and traditional Irish dancing. Tickets from €3.50-€34.

Théâtre du Châtelet (Théatre Musical de Paris): 1 Place du Châtelet, 1st, M° Châtelet, ☎ 01 40 28 28 40, www.chatelet-theatre.com. Tickets €9-€150. The recently renovated Théâtre du Châtelet, built in 1862, presents classical and contemporary music concerts, teaming up with the Maison Radio-France and the Paris Philharmonic Orchestra, as well as ballet, opera and vocal recitals. The Midi-Musicaux lunchtime concerts take place every Monday, Wednesday and Friday at 12:45pm in the Grand Foyer at a reduced rate, and the Sunday matinées are €24.

Churches

Spend an enchanting evening listening to classical music in some of the most beautiful churches, chapels and cathedrals in Paris such as Sainte-Chapelle, Eglise St-Julien-le-Pauvre, and Eglise de la Madeleine. Look for posters throughout town or check out the schedule at www.ampconcerts.com (you can reserve seats and pay for them on arrival). Ticket prices from €15-25. Tickets can also be purchased in advance through FNAC ticket offices.

FREE CONCERTS

It's always worth a peek into the lesser-known churches and cathedrals of Paris if passing by, since you may catch the organist or church choir in rehearsal. There are free organ recitals at **Notre Dame Cathedral** every Sunday at 4:30pm, and at the **Eglise St-Sulpice** (Place St-Sulpice, 6th) on Sundays at 11:30am. Bell-ringing concerts take place at the **Eglise St-Germain-l'Auxerrois** (Place du Louvre, 1st) on Wednesdays from 2 to 3pm. Up-and-coming young musicians give classical, Baroque and gospel concerts every Tuesday, 12:15 to 1:15pm, at the **Eglise St-Roch** (24 Rue St-Roch, 1st, M° Pyramides); and at the **Eglise St-Merri** (78 Rue St-Martin, 4th, M° Rambuteau), every Saturday at 9pm and Sunday at 4pm.

■ Music Festivals

There are so many musical festivals in Paris that they tend to overlap each other! Some are free and informal open-air concerts held in various garden kiosks or small churches, others are internationally renowned and feature top names, so tickets need to be purchased far in advance. Stop by or check the web sites for current and upcoming festivals at the Paris Tourism Office (www.parisbienvenue.com) or the Mairie (Hôtel de Ville, www.paris.fr). Here are just a few of the more popular festivals in Paris:

Paris Jazz Festival: Pull up a deck chair or just lie on the grass at the Parc Floral de Paris (Bois de Vincennes) for the free jazz concerts every weekend at 3pm from mid-May through July; www.paris.fr, ☎ 08 20 00 75 75. Entry to the park is €3 (€1.50 for students age seven to 26).

Fête de la Musique: The longest day of the year – June 21 – is celebrated throughout France with an all-night midsummer musical festival in the streets, bars, concert halls, and parks. Schedules can be found at the tourism office, town halls and in most weekly entertainment guides and newspapers, or just be spontaneous and follow your ears around the city.

Festival Musique en l'Ile: This annual church music festival takes place each summer (June through September) in the churches of St-Louis-en-L'Ile (Ile St-Louis, 4th) and St-Germain-des-Pres (6th). There are guest ensembles and choirs from around the world playing both early and Baroque sacred masterpieces, and music from different religious traditions such as gospel or Gregorian chant. Tickets €22-€26. Information at the Paris Tourism Office (www.parisbienvenue.com).

Solidays: Hippodrome de Longchamp, Bois de Boulogne www.solidarite-sida.org. This annual music festival (first weekend in July) is dedicated to raising money and awareness for AIDS and HIV organizations in France and around the world. There are three stages, a campsite, hundreds of information stands and a generally convivial Woodstock-like atmosphere about the place. Headliners over the years have included Earth, Wind & Fire and Indochine, as well as many alternative and underground groups. Tickets for the two days are €35, campsites (tent provided) are €5 per night; reserve early for a place.

Paris Quartier d'Eté: From July 15 to August 15, the gardens, squares and parks of Paris host a wide range of international music concerts, dance, and theater productions; www.quartierdete.com, ☎ 01 44 94 98 00.

Chamber Music at the Orangerie de Bagatelle: The group *Octuor de France* performs classical and contemporary music concerts each August at the Orangerie de Bagatelle in the Bois de Boulogne; www.octuorde-france.com, ☎ 01 42 29 07 83.

Festival Classique au Vert: Free classical music concerts at the Parc Floral (Bois de Vincennes) every weekend at 4pm in August and September; www.paris.fr, ☎ 08 20 00 75 75. Entry to the park is €3 (€1.50 for students age seven to 26).

Festival d'Automne à Paris: An annual festival of contemporary performing arts from mid-September through December, in venues throughout Paris; www.festival-automne.com, ☎ 01 53 45 17 00.

Techno Parade: This noisy and colorful parade of floats blasting every kind of electronic music from techno to trance takes place every third Saturday in September; www.technopol.net, ☎ 01 42 47 84 75.

■ Performance Venues

Paris-Bercy (a.k.a. Palais Omnisport Paris-Bercy, or POPB): Rue de Bercy, 12th, M° Bercy, ☎ 08 92 69 23 00, www.bercy.fr. This glass-covered pyramid seats up to 17,000 for major sporting events, music concerts and shows such as *Riverdance*, *Disney on Ice*, and *Carmina Burana*.

Paris

Le Zénith Paris: Parc de la Villette, 19th, M° Porte-de-Pantin, ☎ 01 42 08 60 00, www.le-zenith.com/paris. This modern concert hall seats up to 6,400 spectators. Not very big, but considered to be one of the best Paris venues by top musicians and rock stars looking for a more "intimate" atmosphere (so book early to see Bob Dylan, Christina Aguilera or Renaud). Tickets from FNAC and other regular outlets.

L'Olympia: 28 Boulevard des Capucines, 9th, M° Madeleine, ☎ 08 92 68 33 68, www.olympiahall.com. Even more intimate than the Zénith, this small and exclusive concert hall was originally solely a bastion of French artists, but more and more international acts such as Blur and Elton John are scheduling their Paris concerts here instead of at the big stadiums.

Le Bataclan: 50 Boulevard Voltaire, 11th, M° Oberkampf or Richard Lenoir, ☎ 01 43 14 35 35. Built in 1864 as a theater with an odd Chinese pagoda façade, the Bataclan had many ups and downs over the years, eventually falling into disrepair and neglect in the 1950s. Today little of its original historical charm is intact, but it lives on anyway as a popular concert hall hosting international musicians playing everything from rock and heavy metal to jazz and world music with seating for up to 1,100 people. The hall also transforms into a dance club on some nights, throwing fabulous themed soirées.

L'Elysée Montmartre: 72 Boulevard Rochechouart, 18th, M° Anvers, ☎ 01 42 23 46 50, www.elyseemontmartre.com. Going strong since 1807, this Parisian nightlife landmark has seen everything from can-can dancers to rave parties. Today this compact venue in the heart of the Pigalle district plays host to DJ dance parties, fashion shows, top international musicians, and the traditional monthly Bal Elysée (old-fashioned dancing to a full orchestra).

Cinema

Despite the proliferation of American-style multi-screen cineplexes in certain areas of Paris, there are still many tiny theaters hidden throughout the city in unlikely places, some with just one screening room. Some are owned by mainstream distributors such as Gaumont or UGC, others are independent, showing foreign films, art films, old French films, or simply cult classics. Check *Pariscope* for weekly listings. New films usually come out on Wednesdays.

■ Multi-screen Cineplexes

UGC Ciné Cité (Cinéma at the Forum des Halles), 1st, M° Châtelet-Les-Halles, ☎ 08 92 70 00 00. Tickets €8.90, €5.50 for kids under 12; €4.50 for all films before noon. This cineplex is the largest in Paris, with 16 screens of varying sizes (the first three have extra-large screens), showing current films in their original language. Monitors above the ticket booths show how many places are left for each screening.

MK2 Bibliothèque (outside the Bibliothèque François Mitterand): 128 Avenue de France, 13th, M° Quai de la Gare or Bibliothèque. Tickets €9, €4.90 before noon. This brand new cineplex in the constantly changing Rive Gauche neighborhood has the latest films in VO, and is attached to two new cafés, a trendy bar and chic restaurant. The best deal is the Café M's "Formule Ciné," where you get salad, sandwich, dessert, drink and cinema voucher for €13. Open daily, 10:30am to 10:30pm, with a pleasant terrace for afternoon sun.

Gaumont Grand Ecran Italie: 30 Place d'Italie, 13th, M° Place d'Italie, ☎ 08 92 69 66 96. Tickets €9 (€5.50 matinées). This is one of the most "high-tech" of Paris cinemas, with an 80-foot-tall screen. They usually show both VF and VO versions of films in different rooms (be sure to ask) as well as a three-minute 3D laser show before each screening.

UGC George V: 144 & 146 Avenue des Champs-Elysées, 8th, M° George V, ☎ 08 92 70 00 00. Tickets €9.30 (big screen) and €8.70, or €4.90 for the first screening of the day. This is the largest cinema on the Champs-Elysées (split into two), recently remodeled to modern standards while retaining its historic mirrors and crystal wall sconces. There are two "salles prestiges" with balconies and digital sound. A very chic place to catch the latest flick.

MOVIEGOING TIPS

For non-French films, be sure to check if they are shown in *VO* (shown in their original language with French subtitles), or *VF* (dubbed over in French without subtitles). The least expensive time to see a film in Paris is before noon, when most theaters have half-price matinées. Most cinemas don't open their screening rooms until right before the film starts, so if you get there early be prepared to stand in a crowd waiting to get past the ticket checkers. In the smaller cinemas there are no ads, so the film starts right away. In larger cineplexes there are about 10 minutes of ads before the film.

■ Alternative & Arthouse Cinema

Forum des Images: in the Grande Galerie, Forum des Halles, 1st, M° Châtelet-Les Halles, ☎ 01 44 76 62 00, www.forumdesimages.net. Open daily except Monday, from 1 to 9pm; entry for the library and public screenings is €5.50, €4.50 if you're under 30. The Forum des Images has one of the largest film libraries in France, with many rare films, French classics, and international films available for private viewing or as part of their regular screenings. There are also regular film festivals such as the popular Cinéma d'Animation (International Animation Festival). There are no listings in *Pariscope*, so check the web site or stop by to find out what's on or to browse the movie catalog.

Le Lucernaire Forum: 53 Rue Notre-Dame-des-Champs, 6th, M° Vavin or Notre-Dame-des-Champs, ☎ 01 45 44 57 34, www.lucernaire.fr. Tickets €7 (€6 on Wednesday). This cultural center has three cinema screening rooms, a theater (where *Le Petit Prince* has been running for 20 years!), art gallery, rare-book shop, restaurant and bar, and a drama school. Definitely worth a detour, even if just for an *apéritif* at the bar.

L'Entrepôt: 7-9 Rue Francis-de-Pressensé, 14th, M° Pernety, ☎ 01 45 40 07 50, www.lentrepot.fr. Tickets €6.90. The Entrepôt is an arthouse cinema opened in a converted warehouse in 1977 by cinema fanatic and future French President François Mitterand. It houses three screening rooms, a bar and restaurant with one of the best garden terraces in Paris (see dining section, page 275). Films are often followed by debates, and there are regular live jazz and world music evenings throughout the year.

La Géode: Parc de la Villette, 19th, M°Porte-de-la-Villette, ☎ 08 92 69 70 72, www.cite-sciences.fr. Tickets €8.75, €6.75 for anyone under 25. This hemispherical theater with a 10,700-square-foot screen uses OMNIMAX technology (larger than IMAX), which make viewers feel they're in the middle of the film (the reclining chairs aren't bad, either). Films are made specifically for this format and run along the themes of nature and science, but they are not necessarily dry documentaries. Headphones for English translations are available for all screenings. It's possible to get combined tickets for the Géode and the Cité des Sciences et de l'Industrie (Science & Technology Museum) next door.

VIVE LE ROCKY HORROR PICTURE SHOW!

The **Studio Galande** (42 Rue Galande, 5th, M° St-Michel, ☎ 01 43 26 94 08, tickets €7) has been carrying the torch for loyal fans of the cult classic *Rocky Horror Picture Show* since 1980, with screenings every Friday and Saturday night at 10:30pm. Don't forget the rice!

■ Historic Movie Theaters

Max Linder Panorama: 24 Boulevard Poissonnière, 9th, M° Grands Boulevards, ☎ 08 36 68 50 52. Tickets €8.50 (€4.50 for the 12:15pm screenings). It's easy to walk right past the discreet façade of this historic theater, opened by the burlesque actor Max Linder in 1914. In the 1980s it was completely gutted and modernized with three seating levels, THX sound and a panoramic screen. All films are shown in their original version.

La Pagode: 57*bis* Rue de Babylone, 7th, M° Saint François Xavier, ☎ 01 45 55 48 48. Tickets €7.30 (€5.80 on Mondays and Wednesdays). A pagoda in Paris? It all started in 1895 when the owner of the Bon Marché department store purchased a pagoda in Japan and had it shipped to Paris, stone-by-stone, as a wedding gift to his wife. The marriage didn't last, however, and in 1931 the beautifully carved pagoda and its Japanese garden were transformed into a movie theater, conserving as much of the original décor as possible. Try to see a film in the Salle Japonaise instead of the modern Salle 2.

OPEN-AIR CINEMA FESTIVALS

Paris has two annual open-air cinema festivals each summer. The better known one is at the **Parc de la Villette**, every night at about 10pm except Monday, from mid-July through August (free entry, bring a blanket or rent a beach chair on site; schedule at www.la-villette.com), featuring classics and recent hits from around the world in their original language. Many English-language films are included.

The **Cinéma au Clair de Lune** is another free festival that takes place in public squares and parks all over Paris in mid-August, showing films set in Paris (from 9:30pm; chairs provided for limited number of people; www.forumdesimages.net).

Family Fun

 Families with young children will find plenty in Paris to keep them occupied, from marionnettes and pony rides to zoos and kid-friendly museums. The parks and gardens of Paris offer plenty of running space and playgrounds for small tots, while amusement parks and circuses can entertain the entire family.

■ Parks & Gardens

Public Spaces

Most parks in Paris have small playgrounds, sand pits or jungle gyms for children. **The Jardins du Luxembourg** (M° St-Michel or RER Luxembourg, 6th) has one of the largest children's playgrounds in the center of Paris, resembling a giant version of the McDonald's plastic playgrounds (small entry fee). There are also marionnettes (see page 312), pony rides and toy sailboats to push around in the large duck pond.

The **Jardin des Plantes** (M° Jussieu, 5th) has a small playground and one of the oldest zoos in the world (the *ménagerie*) with monkeys, bears, lions and a petting farm (€6 for adults, €3.50 for kids ages four to 16; open daily, 9:30am to 6pm in summer, 9:30am to 5pm in winter, ☎ 01 40 79 30 00).

If all the animals are hiding from sight, take the kids to the fascinating **Grande Galerie de l'Evolution** (open 10am to 6pm, closed Tuesday; tickets €7, €5 for students under 26, free for children under age four; www.mnhn.fr, ☎ 01 40 79 30 00). Here they can ogle all sorts of life-sized (and spookily alive-looking) animals from giraffes and elephants to wolves and penguins, as well as giant dinosaur fossils and extinct species.

The very modern **Parc André Citroën** (M° Javel, 15th) has a kid-friendly lawn (no dogs allowed), lots of jungle-like corners to explore, and smoothly paved paths for moms with strollers. There's an enormous hot-air balloon (open daily from 9am until 30 minutes before park closing time; €10-12 for adults, €5-10 for kids ages three to 17; ☎ 01 44 26 20 00, www.aeroparis.com) tethered firmly at the park gives panoramic views of Paris for up to 20 passengers at a time, with no danger of floating off. When the weather heats up, the park guards pretend they don't notice the children running through the playful water jets that spring up from the pavement next to the greenhouses (even though a big red sign says to keep out).

Families could easily spend the day at the **Parc de la Villette** (M° Porte-de-la-Villette, 19th). There's a series of playgrounds with cushioned flooring divided up by age group (the Jardin des Dunes), a winding 80m (220-foot) dragon slide, and eight other themed gardens such as the Jardin des Miroirs and the Jardin des Bambous, all set in a 69-acre park with lawns and the scenic Canal de l'Ourcq running through the middle (www.lavillette.com). Inside the imposing **Cité des Sciences & de l'Industrie** (Science Museum) is the **Cité des Enfants** (open Tuesday through Saturday, 10am to 6pm; Sunday until 7pm; entry €5 per person, children must be accompanied; ☎ 08 92 69 70 72, www.cite-sciences.fr). It's made up of two hands-on learning exhibitions, one for kids three to five years old and the other for kids ages five to 12 years. Young visitors get to work on a construction site, survey an ant colony, find out where electricity comes from, make a TV show, and discover how their counterparts in other countries live. Entrance is based on time-slots of 90 minutes, so try to arrive early in the day to avoid disappointment (especially in summer and on Wednesdays). The Cité des Sciences also has a planetarium, aquarium, and many temporary exhibitions for older children and adults. Museum Pass accepted. Just outside the museum is a real (retired) French naval submarine, *l'Argonaute* (open daily except Monday, 11am to 5:30pm; entry €3) and the mirror-ball **Géode Omnimax** cinema (see *Cinema* section, page 306).

Bois de Boulogne

The Bois de Boulogne (M° Porte Maillot or Sablons, 16th) is the largest green space within Paris, with three floral gardens, forested trails, bike paths, two lakes, tennis, horseracing stadiums and even a campsite on the Seine. But what kids really love is the **Jardin d'Acclimatation**, which combines a zoo, amusement park rides, museums, and playgrounds in a natural setting (open daily, 10am to 6pm, until 7pm from June through September; entry €2.50, free for kids under age three; ☎ 01 40 67 90 82, www.jardindacclimatation.fr). If arriving by métro, consider taking the mini-train from the station to the park entrance (€4.80 includes round-trip train ride and park entry). The entry fee covers the playgrounds, zoo, puppet theater, and infants' garden. The rides, targeted for children up to about 12 years old, require individual tickets (about €2.30 per ride, less if you buy a booklet of tickets), and include small rollercoasters, boat rides, trampolines, pony rides, merry-go-round and bumper cars. Older kids and adults can try the mini-golf, indoor bowling alley, billiards and arcade, and the remote-control boats on the lake.

There is also a separate entrance fee for three museums in the Bois de Boulogne. The **Musée en Herbe** (open daily in summer, 10am to 6pm, on Saturdays from 2 to 6pm; entry €3, ☎ 01 40 67 97 66, www.musee-en-herbe.com) is a children's museum (ages three and up) that uses hands-on activities to introduce kids to the art world. For kids who like to know how things work, the **Explor@dome** (entry €4.50, ☎ 01 53 64 90 40, www.exploradome.com) is a science and multimedia center with lots of hands-on experiments and activities. The **Musée des Arts et Traditions Populaires** (open 9:30am to 5:45pm, closed Tuesday; entry €4, Museum Pass accepted; ☎ 01 44 17 60 33) presents scenes of everyday life in villages throughout France over the past thousand years, from a fishing village in Brittany to a shepherd's hamlet in the Alps. All three museums are in French only, but are visual enough to be interesting even for those who don't understand a word. There are a number of restaurants, cafés and snack bars throughout the park, and a designated area for those who've packed a picnic. The Parc d'Acclimatation is perfect for families with small children looking for an alternative to Disney-style entertainment.

 AUTHOR'S NOTE: *See the* Adventures On Wheels *and* On Water *sections, pages 172 and 178, for more information about cycling and boating in the Bois de Boulogne and Bois de Vincennes.*

Bois de Vincennes

On the other side of Paris, the Bois de Vincennes (M° Château-de-Vincennes or Porte Dorée, 12th) is dominated by the imposing **Château de Vincennes**. The château is under long-term renovation, but it is surrounded by forest trails, and the grounds feature a lake where couples can row around in wooden boats. For €3 (€1.50 students ages seven to 26) you can explore the **Parc Floral de Paris** (M° Château-de-Vincennes; ☎ 01 73 04 75 75, www.parcfloraldeparis.com), open daily, 9:30am to 6pm in winter, until 8pm in summer. This is a floral garden with lawns for picnics; there is also a butterfly garden pavilion, puppet theater, playground, and a small children's amusement park (open daily, March through August, at 2pm, on weekends only in September; ride tickets €1 each). Free jazz and classical concerts take place on summer and fall weekends in the park's open-air concert pavilion. Children who love animals can visit the **Ferme de Paris**, formerly the Georges-Ville Farm, with dairy cows, veggie gardens, goats, pigs, chickens and rabbits. Located next to the hippodrome. Hours vary by season: from April through September it's open weekends and public holidays, 1:30pm to 6:30pm; in July and August, hours are Tuesday through Friday, 1:30 to 6pm; in October and March, 1:30 to 5:30pm; and from November to February, 1:30 to 5pm, closed public holidays; entry €2, €1 for ages seven to 26, ☎ 01 43 28 47 63). The **Parc Zoologique de Paris** (M° Port Dorée, open daily, 9am to 6pm in summer, 9am to 5pm in winter; entry €8, €5 for kids from age four to 16, ☎ 01 44 75 20 10) is the largest zoo in Paris, with requisite bears, giraffes, monkeys, hippos and seals. The Grand Rocher, a 215-foot man-made mountain, offers panoramic views of the Bois de Vincennes. Feeding time takes place in the afternoon. The welcome center *(acceuil)* has a large souvenir and bookshop with multilingual guides to Paris sights; it's open weekdays, 10am to noon and 1 to 5pm; ☎ 01 48 08 31 20.

MAGIC BAR

Right around the corner from the Place des Vosges, **Le Double-Fond** (1 Place du Marché St-Catherine, 4th, M° St-Paul, ☎ 01 42 71 40 20) presents regular magic shows in their atmospheric stone vaulted cellar (tickets €18 adults, €13.50 children), or you can simply order a drink on the terrace bar (open late afternoon through midnight) and the server will perform a trick at your table.

■ Marionettes & Guignols

Puppet shows, known as *marionnettes* or *guignols*, have hardly evolved over the centuries, and yet remain as popular as ever with young Parisian children. There's plenty of interaction at these shows as kids cheer for the heroes and boo at the villains in classics such as *Puss in Boots* and *Three Musketeers*. The shows are in French, but it's not too hard for even the youngest of children to figure out what's going on (and, for once, they can be as loud as they want).

Marionnettes du Champ-de-Mars: On the Champ-de-Mars between Avenue Risler and Avenue Motte Piquet, 7th. Shows Wednesday, Saturday, and Sunday at 3:15 and 4:15pm. Tickets €2.80.

Marionnettes des Champs-Elysées: You'll find this puppet stage at the Rond Point des Champs-Elysées, between Avenue Matignon and Avenue Gabriel, 8th. Shows Wednesday, Saturday and Sunday at 3, 4 and 5pm. Tickets €3.

AUTHOR'S NOTE: *Puppet shows have been performed at the Rond Point since 1818!*

Marionnettes du Luxembourg: Next to the playground at the Jardins du Luxembourg. Shows Wednesday at 3:15pm and 4:30pm, Saturday and Sunday at 11am, 3:15 and 4:30pm. Tickets €3.90.

■ Theme Parks

Aquaboulevard: 4-6 Rue Louis Armand, 15th, M° Balard, ☎ 01 40 60 10 00, www.aquaboulevard.com. Open Monday through Thursday, 9am to 11pm; Friday and Saturday, 9am to midnight; Sunday, 8am to 8pm. Entry €20, €10 for ages three to 12 (no children under age three are allowed in the water park; racing-style bathing suits required for the guys). This indoor water park maintains summer temperatures year-round, with water slides, wave pools and tropical décor under a gigantic glass atrium ceiling. Arrive early in the morning to avoid lines. Wednesday afternoons and weekends are the most crowded. The water park is attached to a commercial center with foodcourt, arcade, newsstand, cinema, and a sports shop where you can buy a bathing suit if you need one. Watch out for the extras: lockers €1, parasol €5, beach lounger €5. There's a bit of a walk from the métro, but Bus 38 (via Gare de l'Est and St-Germain-des-Prés) arrives right outside the entrance.

Parc Astérix: Plailly (north of Paris on the A1, between Roissy-CDG Airport and Senlis), ☎ 03 44 62 34 34, www.parcasterix.com. Open April to October, 9:30am to 7pm daily in high season, 10am to 6pm on Wednesdays and weekends in low season (September/October). Tickets €31 for visitors 12 and up, €23 for kids ages three to 11, and free for children under three. (Discounts for holders of two-day passes, hotel-park passes, or "Forfait Parc Astérix," which includes entry and train/bus ride to the park). Parking €5. There is a bus every half-hour from Roissy-CDG Airport (Gare Routière, Quai A3). From Paris, take the RER B3 to Roissy-CDG1 and transfer to the bus.

This popular amusement park is similar to its Disney competitor in style, the major differences being the theme (based on the French comic strip, *Astérix & Obelix*) and the rides (Parc Astérix has a seven-loop rollercoaster and a giant wooden rollercoaster). There are different areas of the park dedicated to Ancient Greece, Old Paris, and Gallic Village Life, and shows throughout the day, including live dolphins, falconry demonstrations, and Three Musketeers swordfights.

Restaurants in the park serve wild boar (*sanglier*), Obelix's favorite food. There is certainly a commercial side, with Astérix's winged helmet replacing the mouse ears, but it's not as omnipresent as at Disney. In the artisan's village you can watch real stone and wood carvers, stained-glass and pottery-makers. Aside from the map, there's nothing in English, so be prepared to learn a bit of French. Try to go weekdays outside French holidays (avoid August if possible). There's a three-star family hotel next door owned by the park: **Hôtel des Trois Hiboux**, from €81 (click on "Hotel & Shops" on the park web site).

■ The Disney Experience

Disneyland Paris & Disney Studios: Marne-la-Vallée (east of Paris on the A4, exit 14), ☎ 01 60 30 60 30, www.disneylandparis.com. Open daily, 10am to 8pm (opens at 9am on weekends, and park stays open until 11pm on summer weekends; Disney Studios closes at 6pm). One-day tickets for either Disneyland *or* Disney Studios are €39, €29 for ages three to 11, free for kids under three. The three-day pass, which allows access to both theme parks, is €107, €80 for kids ages three to 11. By RER A4 from Châtelet-Les Halles or Gare de Lyon to Marne-la-Vallée-Chessy (€12 round-trip, €6 for kids ages four to 10).

Disneyland Paris (formerly known as EuroDisney) received bad press when it opened in 1992, but today the park has more visitors than the Louvre and the Eiffel Tower combined (and more than half of them are French). If you're already familiar with the original Disneyland in California, this park will feel a bit smaller (no 'ToonTown, no Matterhorn, no New Orleans Square). The rides have been moved around a bit into Main Street and four "Lands" with a focus on the modern Disney characters (like Aladdin and Pocahontas). On the plus side, Discoveryland (Tomorrowland's French counterpart) has a slick, copper and turquoise Jules Verne décor with a vamped-up Space Mountain that even goes upside-down.

To avoid long lines, grab a free FastPass ticket, which lets you jump to the front of the line at designated times. Next door, the recently opened Disney Studios is still trying to establish itself. With a striking resemblance to a Southern California shopping mall (it's meant to look like a Hollywood studio), Disney Studios has a few "behind-the-scenes" attractions, one super-fast rollercoaster, an elaborate stunt show and Disney characters doing improvised "scenes" with audience participation. The predominant use of French in the parks is more obvious at Disney Studios, but they do their best to translate everything with very artful use of *Franglais*. It's possible to use a one-day ticket to visit Disney Studios with the option to visit Disneyland for the last three opening hours, but unfortunately it doesn't work the other way around. The parks are part of the Disneyland Paris Resort, with multiple theme-hotels, a golf course and the Disney Village (see below).

Disney After Dark

Just across the street from Disneyland (right at the entrance to the RER station) is **Disney Village**, an entertainment complex focusing on dining and nightlife with a Disney theme, and no entry fee. Try to ignore the Planet Hollywood, tired Rainforest Café and the golden arches. More worthy of your attention is **Buffalo Bill's Wild West Show** (with some spectacular horseback stunts), the **Hurricanes** nightclub, and **King Ludwig's Castle** restaurant. There's also a 15-screen cinema (English films Monday nights), Disney stores (same souvenirs sold inside Disneyland and Disney Studios), and the Disney Lake (pedal boats in summer and ice skating in winter). Most of the restaurants and bars are open until 1am, and Hurricanes stays open until 5am. Just don't forget the last train back to Paris is at 12:20am!

■ The Circus

Paris is a favored destination for international circus acts, and hosts the annual **Festival Mondial du Cirque de Demain** (a show of young new circus talent from around the world) each February. Two well-known Parisian circuses include the historic **Cirque d'Hiver Bouglione** (110 Rue Amelot, 11th, M° Filles du Calvaire, ☎ 01 49 29 09 78, www.cirque-dhiver.com), and the **Cirque Diana Moreno Bormann** (112 Rue de la Haie Coq, Porte d'Aubervilliers, 19th, Bus 63, ☎ 01 64 05 36 25, www.cirque-diana-moreno.com). Temporary big tops are often set up in the Parc de la Villette or the Bois de Vincennes. Check the children's section of *Pariscope* for the schedule of permanent and visiting shows.

CIRCUS CLASSES

Adults and children from age six and up can try out the flying trapeze (with safety harnesses, of course) at **Club Med World** (Bercy Village, Cour Saint Emilion 12th, M° Cour St-Emilion ☎ 0810 810 410). Hours are Wednesday, 2 to 4pm and 6:45 to 9:15pm; Thursday, 6:15 to 8:15pm; Friday, 5:30 to 7:30pm and 8:15 to 8:45pm; and Sunday for children's circus brunches, 2 to 4pm. *Baptêmes* (initiations) cost €6, and one-hour classes cost €12.

■ Gaming with the Parisians

Video game aficionados of all ages can test their mettle against the locals at **Xs-Arena** (two locations: 43 Boulevard de Sébastopol, 1st, M° Les

Halles; and 53 Rue de la Harpe, 5th, M° St-Michel; www.xsarena.com), a gaming network and Internet center open 24/7. Non-playing members of the family can check e-mails and upload vacation photos to send home.

Sports & Races

 Paris hosts many prestigious sporting events throughout the year, and tickets should be purchased as far in advance as possible. Free events include the **Marathon de Paris** (April) and the arrival of the **Tour de France** on the Champs-Elysées (end of July).

■ Annual Sporting Events

- **Grand Prix d'Amérique** (trotting world championship), Hippodrome de Vincennes, January.
- **Six Nations Rugby Tournament**, Stade de France, February to April.
- **Jumping International de Paris** (show-jumping competition), Palais Omnisports Paris-Bercy, March.
- **Steeple-Chase de Paris**, Hippodrome d'Auteuil, May.
- **Rolland Garros International Tennis**, Stade Roland Garros, May and June.
- **French Open** (PGA European Tour), www.opendefrance.fr, June.
- **Le Golf Nationale** (Guyancourt, page 351), www.golf-national.com, June.
- **Grand Prix de l'Arc de Triomphe Lucien Barrière** (world racing championship of thoroughbreds), Hippodrome de Longchamp, October.
- **Tennis Masters Series**, Palais Omnisports Paris-Bercy, October and November.
- **Trophée Lalique** (figure-skating championship), Palais Omnisports Paris-Bercy, October and November.

 AUTHOR'S NOTE: *See* Adventures, *page 167-170, for information on participating in Paris sporting events.*

■ Sports Venues

Equestrian Events

Hippodrome de Vincennes: 2 Route de la Ferme, Bois de Vincennes, 12th, ☎ 01 49 77 14 70, www.cheval-france.com. Trotting races (harness racing).

Hippodrome d'Auteuil: Bois de Boulogne, 16th, M° Porte d'Auteuil, ☎ 08 21 21 32 13, www.france-galop.com. Hunt racing and steeplechase competitions.

Hippodrome de Longchamp: Bois de Boulogne, 16th, M° Porte d'Auteuil, ☎ 08 21 21 32 13, www.france-galop.com. National and international thoroughbred racing (flat racing).

A DAY AT THE RACES

During the regular racing season (September through June), the two Bois de Boulogne hippodromes, Longchamp and Auteuil, are open to spectators even if you're not placing bets. Entry onto the lawn (*pelouse*) is free. Tickets for the stands are €3-€4 (€8 during the Steeple-Chase de Paris), free for children under 18. Both hippodromes offer a welcome service, restaurants, free babysitting on Wednesdays and weekends, and pony rides for kids ages three to 10 every Sunday. Racing schedules and information available at www.france-galop.com, or call ☎ 08 21 21 32 13.

Stadium Sports

Stade Rolland Garros: Bois de Boulogne, 16th, M° Porte d'Auteuil, ☎ 01 47 43 48 00, www.rolandgarros.com. International and national tennis tournaments.

Rolland Garros was once open only for those with tickets to the matches, but the **Tenniseum** (Tennis Museum), opened in 2003, offers a chance to tour the "off-limits" areas of the stadium (tours Tuesday through Sunday in French and English). There is also a boutique for picking up your own Rolland Garros logo tennis balls or clothing, and a gourmet restaurant with valet parking and garden terrace seating in the summer. Entry at Avenue Gordon Bennet (Porte Mousquetaires). ☎ 01 47 43 48 48. Combined tour and museum tickets €15, €10 for kids under 18.

Stade de France: La Plaine St-Denis (93), ☎ 01 55 93 00 00, www.stadefrance.com. Hosts many sporting events, including national and international soccer (called football in Europe) and rugby matches. Behind-the-scenes tours of the stadium in English are available during high season (except during tournaments) at 10:30am and 2:30pm daily (€10, €8.50 for students, €7 for kids under 12).

Palais Omnisports Paris-Bercy: 12th, M° Bercy, ☎ 08 92 69 23 00, www.parisbercy.fr. Sporting events include basketball, tennis, martial arts, equestrian competitions and ice-skating.

Nightlife

■ Live Music

Jazz

 Parisians have been loyal jazz lovers since the Americans first introduced it in the city's clubs in the 1920s. Today Paris is second only to New York in the number of jazz clubs, featuring both local jazz talent and the many international stars that return to Paris year after year.

Duc des Lombards: 42 Rue des Lombards, 1st, M° Châtelet-Les Halles, ☎ 01 42 33 22 88, www.jazzvalley.com/duc.

One of the top jazz venues in Paris for the past 15 years, with French and international jazz stars. This is one of the few jazz clubs that lets you reserve a table. Concerts at 9pm, tickets €16-€23.

New Morning: 7-9 Rue des Petites Ecuries, 10th, M° Château d'Eau, ☎ 01 45 23 51 41.

This is one of the more prestigious jazz clubs in Paris, a hot and smoky club featuring major names and serious young talent. Nightly concerts at 9pm, doors open at 8pm, tickets €15-€30. Get there early for a good seat.

Le Petit Opportun: 15 Rue des Lavandières-Ste-Opportune, 1st, M° Châtelet-Les Halles, ☎ 01 42 36 10 36. Open evenings from 6pm, concerts usually at 10pm.

With seating for just 45 in a 14th-century stone cellar, this venue fills up quickly! Well-known American and European musicians play jazz classics from every age to an audience of loyal regulars. Drinks from the bar on the ground floor can be taken downstairs.

Le Bilboquet: 13 Rue Saint Benoît, 6th, M° Saint-Germain-des-Prés, ☎ 01 45 48 81 84. Open nightly 8:15pm to 4am, tickets €21.

A jazz legend, the Bilboquet has an old Belle Epoque atmosphere with wood paneling, copper ceilings and a sunken bar/restaurant. Downstairs is the privately owned **Club St-Germain**, a popular dance club for the young locals (free entrance with purchase of a drink).

Sept Lézards: 10 Rue des Rosiers, 4th, M° St-Paul, ☎ 01 48 87 08 97. Restaurant/tearoom open daily, concerts nightly at 10pm, tickets €7-12.

This restaurant, tea room and jazz club in the heart of the Marais has its own house band, *Le Big Boeuf Orchestra* (and the more compact version called *Boeuf!*), who play free concerts on Monday nights to a hip, cosmopolitan crowd.

Club Music

 Harry's New York Bar – Piano Bar: 5 Rue Daunou, 2nd, M° Opéra, ☎ 01 42 61 71 14, www.harrys-bar.fr. Open Monday through Friday, 10pm to 2am, until 3am Saturdays.

Harry's New York Bar has been a Paris legend since Hemingway's day. The piano bar is downstairs, with comfy upholstered seating and pre-WWII caricatures decorating the walls. George Gerschwin supposedly annoyed the bar clients upstairs while composing "An American in Paris" on Harry's piano.

House of Live: 124 Rue de la Boétie, 8th, M° St-Philippe-du-Roule, ☎ 01 42 25 18 06. Open daily, 9am to 5am, free concerts Tuesday through Thursday at 10:30pm, Friday and Saturday at midnight.

Arrive early in the evening to avoid waiting in line for the free modern jazz, indie rock and French pop concerts at this laid-back spot. On Sunday there are live Gospel Brunches (from 2 to 5pm).

Opus Club: 167, Quai de Valmy, 10th, M° Louis Blanc, ☎ 01 40 34 70 00, www.opus-club.com. Open from 7:30pm, tickets €8-€18.

This large restaurant and club on the Canal St-Martin features live jazz, soul, pop, gospel, reggae and French chanson. The mezzanine restaurant (menus €40) features views over the concert stage.

Nouveau Casino: 109 Rue Oberkampf, 11th, M° Ménilmontant, ☎ 01 43 57 57 40, www.nouveaucasino.net. Open Tuesday through Sunday, 7pm to 2am (until 5am Friday and Saturday). Concerts €5-€20.

Located behind the Oberkampf HQ, Café Charbon, the Nouveau Casino is primarily known for its electronic music and clubbing after midnight. But they also host a number of live indie rock, punk and pop concerts from 7 or 8pm.

La Scène: 2*bis* Rue des Taillandiers, 11th, M° Ledru-Rollin, ☎ 01 48 06 50 70, www.la-scene.com. Concerts €10.

This former warehouse on the edge of the Bastille neighborhood has both live concert and clubbing nights, with an eclectic program of both unknown and popular electronic, hip hop and rock musicians. Their Sunday Brunch concerts are usually packed, so call and reserve a place in advance.

China Club' Sing-Song: 50 Rue de Charenton, 12th, M° Bastille, ☎ 01 43 43 82 02, www.chinaclub.cc. Open Wednesday and Thursday from 8pm, Friday and Saturday from 10pm. Entry €10-15 (many free concerts as well).

In the basement of the Colonial-style Chinese bar and restaurant is the Sing-Song, a sultry nightclub lounge featuring jazz, groove, and funk vocalists with piano accompaniment. Reservations are a good idea, since the place fills up quickly.

Guinguette Pirate: Quai François Mauriac (at the foot of the Bibliothèque François Mitterand), 13th, M° Quai de la Gare, ☎ 01 43 49 68 68, www.guinguettepirate.com. Open Wednesday through Sunday, most concerts start at 8pm, tickets €4.50-€8.

An old Chinese junk converted into a pirate ship, the Guinguette Pirate has live pop, acoustic and world music concerts, improv theater, free poetry readings and nostalgic French *chanson*. A charming venue unlike anything else in Paris!

Les Voûtes: at Les Frigos, corner of Quai Panhard & Levassor and Rue Neuve Tolbiac, 13th, M° Bibliothèque, www.les-frigos.com.

Located in the vaulted cellars of one of the city's legalized artists' squats, Les Voûtes has an eclectic offering of musical concerts and cultural events such as literature debates, traveling theater acts and international performance artists.

Glaz'Art: 7-15 Avenue de la Porte de la Villette, 19th, M° Porte-de-la-Villette, ☎ 01 40 36 55 65, www.glazart.com. Open from 8:30pm, tickets €9-€12.

This alternative artistic and cultural club has an eclectic, international program featuring everything from Indie rock, Cuban salsa, punk accordion, Brazilian orchestra, and African percussion. Tickets are also available from FNAC.

Flèche d'Or Café: 102*bis* Rue de Bagnolet, 20th, M° Alexandre Dumas, ☎ 01 43 72 42 44. Concerts from 9pm, tickets €2-€6.

Once an abandoned train station, the Flèche d'Or is now a bar-club-restaurant popular with a diverse crowd from students and locals to fashion groupies and artsy intellectuals. A great place to go if you're allergic to dress codes and €20 cocktails. It has the atmosphere of a squatted warehouse with a diverse live music program, and is often packed to the rafters for Tuesday open-mike nights (scènes ouvertes). The restaurant, in a glassed-in terrace, has a selection of hearty salads and light snacks for €7-€15; open Tuesday-Saturday from 8:30pm, brunch Sunday 11am-3pm. Call before heading all the way up there, since disputes between cranky neighbors, the artistic management and the café owners often result in unexpected closures.

■ Cabaret

There are two kinds of cabaret in France: the kind most tourists have heard of, featuring a perfectly choreographed troupe of identical topless dancers; and the intimate, artistic cabaret that celebrates French *chan-*

son, humorous wit, and artistic talent. You can enjoy both in Paris if you're willing to stand in line with tour groups for the former, and potentially understand very little of the French language in the latter.

Bal du Moulin Rouge: 82 Boulevard de Clichy, 18th, M° Blanche, ☎ 01 53 09 82 82, www.moulinrouge.fr. Dinner from 7pm, shows from 9pm and 11pm daily. Tickets from €82, dinner and show from €130. No kids under age six; formal attire requested.

Opened in 1889 to an enthusiastic public, the Moulin Rouge has remained the most famous cabaret in the world. Its trademark red windmill, lively French cancan, sumptuous décor and beautiful dancers have been immortalized in Toulouse Lautrec's paintings and, more recently, Baz Luhrmann's hit musical film starring Nicole Kidman. Catering to the visiting masses, the Moulin Rouge today feels a bit too commercial to be titillating, but there's no disputing the beauty and talent of the performers.

Le Paradis Latin: 28 Rue Cardinal Lemoine, 5th, M° Cardinal Lemoine, ☎ 01 43 25 28 28, www.paradis-latin.com. Show tickets €75 (includes champagne), dinner-show tickets €109-€200. Closed Tuesday. Dinner from 8pm, shows from 9:30pm.

Set in a theater built by Gustave Eiffel, the Paradis Latin calls itself the most Parisian of the Paris cabarets. Its Left Bank location gives it a bit of an off-the-beaten-track feel, but it has a similar show to the one at the Moulin Rouge, with dazzling choreographed dancing and music.

Crazy Horse: 12 Avenue George V, 8th, M° Alma-Marceau, ☎ 01 47 23 32 32 32, www.lecrazyhorseparis.com. Nightly shows at 8:30pm and 11pm, three shows on Saturday. Show with drinks only, €29-€110. Dinner shows €130-€160.

The relatively small theater of this cabaret allows for no elaborate special effects, just the enviable perfection of the 20 nude dancers and their elaborate *Teasing* show. Like other cabarets of its kind, there are also magic and comedy acts while the ladies change their barely-there costumes.

Au Lapin Agile: 22 Rue des Saules, 18th, M° Lamarck-Caulaincourt, ☎ 01 46 06 85 87, www.au-lapin-agile.com. Shows Tuesday through Sunday, 9pm to 2am. Entry €24 (includes first drink). Reservations recommended.

This tiny Montmartre country house has been a popular cabaret for over 150 years. The main room is low-lit, with red lampshades, dark walls covered in old paintings and drawings, and set with ancient wooden tables and benches to hold about 60 people. There is a piano, but no stage. The performers sing and play their instruments right in the center of the room, everything from old Edith Piaf songs with an accordion to piano-accompanied poetry. If you can imagine being in a small restaurant where suddenly the group at the next table starts singing – and expects you to join in – you have the idea. This is the perfect place to come if you really want to get a peek into old Montmartre. Make sure to eat first, then show

Paris

up anytime between 9pm and 2am. No one expects you to sit for five whole hours on a wooden bench, but you're more than welcome to try!

■ Bars & Clubs

After an embarrassingly stale showing in the 1990s, the Paris nightlife scene has experienced an exciting renaissance with an impressive line-up of newcomers to complement the classic favorites. The **Bastille**, once the only decent place to get a drink east of the Marais, has been upstaged by the edgy bars and clubs in the converted ateliers of **Belleville**, **Oberkampf**, and **Ménilmontant**. The once boring area around **métro Bonne Nouvelle** is now populated by some of the city's best clubs and stylish new restaurants. Parisians have rediscovered their waterways, with floating *péniche* clubs moored along the **Seine** and bohemian-bourgeois bars opening along the tree-lined **Canal St-Martin**. Of course, *plus ça change….* **St-Germain-des-Prés** has become one of the few Left Bank neighborhoods to attract the Gucci-clad stiletto wearers after dark, although the rest of the **Latin Quarter** remains prime stomping ground for students. The clubs and bars around the **Champs-Elysées** are still enamored with exotic Asian and Indian themes, although the most exclusive new venues are adopting a sleek, retro-futuristic décor reminiscent of Kubrick films. The **Marais** is still happily gay (although more mixed than before), while the titillatingly sleazy **Pigalle** has been somewhat tamed by the encroachment of artsy intellectuals (and busloads of tourists) from **Montmartre**. With a choice like this, it's hard to see how anyone could leave town disappointed.

IMPORTANT NOTE

The minimum legal drinking age in France for beer and wine is 16 years of age, 18 for stronger drinks and spirits. There are no "open container" laws (which is why it's perfectly okay to open a bottle of wine in the park), but walking around on the streets with a can of beer isn't exactly the done thing, and police can confiscate your booze if they think you're being too rowdy.

Talk of the Town

Stunning décor, absurdly expensive cocktails, exclusive door policies and an international jet-set of supermodels, rock stars and Saudi princes keeps these establishments in the society pages until the next flavor-of-the-month comes along. Dress your best and give it a go (but have a back-up plan just in case).

Man Ray: 32 Rue Marbeuf, 8th, M° Franklin-D-Roosevelt, ☎ 01 56 88 36 36, www.manray.fr. Bar open nightly, 7pm to 2am (drinks €15); dance club Friday and Saturday, 12:30am to 5am (entry €20).

Owned by stars Mick Hucknall, Johnny Depp, Sean Penn and John Malkovitch, the Man Ray is a hot nightspot, with a neo-Asian décor. Give the restaurant a miss and check out the bar scene of 20-something fashion models and sunglass-wearing men in designer suits. The schedule changes often to keep up with the trends, but there's usually a live DJ or jazz at the bar, and funky hip-hop or R 'n B on club nights.

La Suite – Sweet Bar: 40 Avenue George V, 8th, M° George V, ☎ 01 53 57 49 49. Open 8pm to 2am (4am Friday and Saturday), private parties on Thursday. Drinks €12-30.

La Suite is the Warhol-esque restaurant opened by the former soirée organizers of the Bains Douches. Needless to say, it's become *the* destination for every paparazzi-hunted star in town. The Sweet Bar is decorated in white leather booths with tropical fish tanks and colorful neon lighting.

Le Cabaret (Le Cab): 2 Place du Palais-Royal, 1st, M° Palais-Royal, ☎ 01 58 62 56 25. Club open nightly from midnight to 5am. Entry (Friday and Saturday only) €20.

This club tucked between the Louvre and the Palais Royal became the favorite new hangout for fashionistas as soon as it opened in 2001. Renamed Le Cab in 2003 (to avoid being continuously mistaken for an actual cabaret), the lower-level club features a retro-futuristic '60s-'70s décor and an intimate lounge room with beds instead of sofas (and a low ceiling so everyone sits down). If you want to get in during Fashion Week, book a table at the restaurant well in advance.

Bar du Plaza Athénée: 25 Avenue Montaigne, 8th, M° Alma-Marceau, ☎ 01 53 67 66 00, www.plaza-athenee-paris.com. Open daily, 6pm to 1:30am. Drinks €8 (coffee) to €20 (whisky).

Just inside and to the right of the hotel entrance, this designer bar is the perfect place to settle in for some star-spotting with an elaborate cocktail. There are cozy leather club chairs in the lounge and an iceberg-like bar that lights up when you touch it.

Nirvana Lounge: 3 Avenue Matignon, 8th, M° Franklin-D-Roosevelt, ☎ 01 53 89 18 91. Open daily, 8am to 4am (dance club Tuesday through Sunday from 11:30pm, entry €11 weekends). Drinks €6-15.

The neo-Indian kitsch décor, weekly tarot readings and meditation sessions of this restaurant-bar-club attract a crowd with slightly more bohemian leanings. Have a drink at the bar until the lower-level dance floor heats up with a mix of 70s and 80s hits.

VIP Room: 76 Ave des Champs-Elysées, 8th, M° George V, ☎ 01 56 69 16 66, www.viproom.fr. Open Tuesday through Sunday, midnight to 5am. Entry €20, drinks €15-30.

Paris

This is as close to the St-Tropez scene as Paris ever gets, with a steady flow of rock stars and French TV personalities that keep the mere mortals shivering out on the sidewalk. Music ranges from hip-hop and pop to house and techno.

Elegant Classics

The French have the Americans to thank for the genesis of the cocktail bar, but you've got to admit the Parisians have done a fabulous job creating elegant and welcoming havens for barflies from around the world. "Casual Friday" business to semi-formal attire is appropriate if you want to blend in.

Hemingway Bar: Hôtel Ritz, 15 Place Vendôme, 1st, M° Tuileries, ☎ 01 43 16 30 30, www.ritzparis.com. Open Tuesday through Saturday, 6:30pm to 2am.

Take a deep breath and make a beeline through the hotel's revolving doors, past the stuffy bar on the left, and all the way down the corridors of the shopping gallery to find one of the best little bars in Paris. "Liberated" by the famous author after WWII, the bar is decorated with his own photographs and cozy leather chairs. There's an impressive list of Champagne cocktails and single malt whiskies, and tapas are available if you have the munchies. Cigar aficionados welcomed on Wednesdays.

Harry's New York Bar: 5 Rue Daunou, 2nd, M° Opéra, ☎ 01 42 61 71 14, www.harrys-bar.fr. Open daily, 10:30am to 2am.

Harry's is a tourist attraction in its own right as birthplace of the Bloody Mary, Side Car and Blue Lagoon cocktails, among others. Opened in 1911, it has a cozy and intimate wood-paneled bar, covered in memorabilia, US collegiate sports pennants, and signed photos and drawings from some of the well-known clientele over the years. Harry's attracts a post-theater crowd, loyal locals, and tourists with guide books in tow. Follow the bar staff's gentle guidance if you're not sure what to order (just don't ask for celery in your Bloody Mary). Lunch served noon to 3pm.

China Club – Le Fumoir: 50 Rue Charenton, 12th, M° Bastille, ☎ 01 43 43 82 02, www.chinaclub.cc. Open daily, 7pm to 2am, Happy Hour 7 to 9pm.

Le Fumoir is up the stairs in the back of the restaurant, with a sultry colonial-style décor and a menu of aged liquors and Cuban cigars. Get there early in the evening or risk hanging around in the hall until a table opens up.

Closerie des Lilas: 171 Boulevard du Montparnasse, 6th, M° Vavin or RER Port-Royal, ☎ 01 40 51 34 50. Open daily, 11am to 1:30am, bar open from 7pm.

The bar at this elegant brasserie once welcomed the Paris Lost Generation of the 1920s. Less touristy than the nearby Café Deux Magots, it has an intimate atmosphere and lively buzz favored by writers, politicians and chic locals.

Mathis Bar: 3 Rue Ponthieu, 8th, M° St-Philippe-du-Roule, ☎ 01 53 76 01 62. Open Monday through Saturday from 11pm until dawn.

Most people haven't heard of the Mathis Bar, and that's just the way the clientele like it. Smartly dressed locals and society-page personalities come to this discreet, low-lit "after" bar to enjoy their cocktails in the deep velour sofas. Anyone asking for autographs or brandishing a camera will quickly find their way to the nearest exit.

The (See & Be) Scene

This is where stylish locals try hard to look like they're not trying to look cool. Think limited edition sneakers under custom-frayed jeans, the latest combination cell phone/camera/MP3 player on a necklace, and artfully mussed-up hair – you get the idea. Some serious DJ talent keeps it all real.

GETTING PAST THE BOUNCERS

A WORD TO
THE WISE

Whether it's "private party" or "we're full," Parisian doormen make it very clear when your attire isn't up to snuff. It's hard to overdress in this part of Paris, and a stroll down the Avenue Montaigne or Faubourg St-Honoré will give you an idea of what's in style. Men will have to make an extra effort if they expect to get in without female accompaniment. A pair of designer sunglasses (yes, at night) will help deflect the doorman's piercing stare, and a limo arrival will almost guarantee you entry (and it isn't much more expensive than a taxi; ask your hotel concierge). If you're willing to cough up the dough, a dinner reservation at any of these establishments will allow you access to the club afterwards.

De la Ville Café: 64 Boulevard Bonne-Nouvelle, 10th, M° Bonne-Nouvelle, ☎ 01 48 24 48 09. Open Monday through Saturday, 11am to 2am; Sunday, 2pm to 2am.

This former Belle Epoque bordello is one of the hippest hangouts of East Paris, combining industrial hard edges with the bordello's beautiful marble stair case, and a huge all-season terrace for people-watching on the boulevard. Live DJs Wednesday nights, with dancing upstairs. The period brasserie next door was recently annexed and given a face lift, so bar clientele don't have to go far when the hunger pangs set in.

La Mezzanine: 62 Rue Mazarine, 6th, M° Odéon, ☎ 01 55 42 22 00, www.alcazar.fr. Live DJ Tuesday through Saturday, 8pm to 2am.

The trendy mezzanine bar of the Alcazar Restaurant features some of the best DJs from France and the UK, mixing groove, lounge, electronic freestyle and European house (a disco-inspired style of dance music) for a chilled-out atmosphere.

Batofar: Quai François Mauriac (at the foot of the Bibliothèque François Mitterand), 13th, M° Quai de la Gare, ☎ 01 56 29 10 33, www.batofar.net. Open nightly from 7pm, until dawn on weekends. Concerts €5-€12.

The big red lighthouse boat is still going strong, with live DJs from all over Europe specializing in electronic music in every form. The terrace bar (free entry) on the quay opens evenings from May through September, with DJ accompaniment and a view of the passing river boats.

Sir Winston: 5 Rue de Presbourg, 16th, M° Etoile, ☎ 01 40 67 17 37. Open daily, 9am to 2am; until 4am on weekends. Restaurant noon to 3pm and 7:30 to 11:30pm, bar snacks all day.

Just around the corner from the Arc de Triomphe, this bar and restaurant, once a very British hangout, now has an Asian lounge atmosphere complete with statues of Buddha and fusion cuisine. Its intimate lower-level booths are the perfect place to take a date for cocktails and private conversation at 3am. A DJ provides the essential groovy chill-out tunes.

Le Costes Bar: 239 Rue St-Honoré, 1st, M° Tuileries, ☎ 01 42 44 50 25. Open daily, 7am to 2am. Drinks €6 (coffee)-€15 (whisky).

Located in the most fashionable hotel on the hippest shopping street in Paris, Le Costes is an ideal stopping point for an intimate afternoon coffee or an aperitif during Paris Fashion Week. With a best-selling series of Hôtel Costes electric lounge mixes, you know the music will be okay. The luxurious Napoleon III décor and groovy music is enough to make up for the chilly service.

Kong Bar: 1 Rue du Pont Neuf, 1st, M° Pont-Neuf, ☎ 01 40 39 09 00. Open daily, 10am to 2am. Happy hour, 6 to 8pm.

Opened in 2003 on the fifth and sixth floors of the Kenzo building, Kong has an over-the-top Philippe Starck-designed environment that combines Japanese *manga* kitsch and Fashion TV flash with views over Paris and the Samaritaine department store. Needless to say, more effort went into the look than the food, so stick to the bar. The Thursday night soirées tend to last well past the closing hour.

Andy Wahloo: 69 Rue des Gravilliers, 3rd, ☎ 01 42 71 20 38. Open Monday through Saturday, noon to 2am.

This kitsch Moroccan bar, under the same ownership as the chic 404 restaurant next door, has become one of the latest locales of the Paris jet-set. The cosmopolitan clientele sit on pop-art paint-can stools, eating tapas and drinking North African wines, cocktails and mint tea with the latest *raï* music mixes playing in the background.

Cool & Casual

For those seeking a watering hole with character, not hype.

L'Ile Enchantée: 65 Boulevard de la Villette, 10th, M° Colonel-Fabien, ☎ 01 42 01 67 99. Open Monday through Friday, 8am to 2am; Saturday from 5pm, Sunday from 10am.

Hidden between Belleville and the Canal St-Martin, the Ile Enchantée is an unpretentious East Paris café-bar with high ceilings and vast windows overlooking the boulevard. During the day it's mellow enough to hang out and read the paper. The service is friendly, the drinks affordable, and there are regular electro-soft DJ soirées upstairs on the weekends.

La Fourmi: 74 Rue des Martyrs, 18th, M° Pigalle, ☎ 01 42 64 70 35. Open daily, 8am to 2am, weekends until 4am.

This faux-industrial neo-bistro at the foot of Montmartre, with floor-to-ceiling windows overlooking the boulevard, is a quiet place to watch the world go by during the day, and so packed at night when the nearby concert halls empty out that there's barely room to move. In general, a sure bet for the Pigalle neighborhood.

Le Mecano: 99 Rue Oberkampf, 11th, M° Parmentier, ☎ 01 40 21 35 28. Open daily, 9am to 2am.

Located in an old factory, the Mecano is decorated with vintage tools, flea-market furniture and funky industrial artworks. There's a lively atmosphere at night, with groovy music, inexpensive drinks and dancing between the tables toward midnight.

La Maroquinerie: 23 Rue Boyer, 20th, M° Gambetta, ☎ 01 40 33 30 60. Open Monday through Saturday, 11am to 1am.

This laid-back literary café is in a former leather workshop (*maroquinerie*), and has become a popular neighborhood cultural center, with regular poetry readings, concerts, 35mm film screenings, and lively discussions and debates among the city's literati. The sunny inner courtyard is packed as soon as the weather warms up. Light meals available throughout the day.

Chez Prune: 71 Quai de Valmy, 10th, M° République, ☎ 01 42 41 30 47. Open Monday through Saturday, 8am to 2am; Sunday, 10am to 2am.

A typically *branché* (hip) East Paris institution, this bistro overlooking the Canal St-Martin is popular with bohemian intellectual types and not-quite-starving artists. Food is served at lunch, and bar snacks are available in the evening.

L'Imprévu: 7-9 Rue Quincampoix, 4th, M° Hôtel-de-Ville or Châtelet-Les Halles, ☎ 01 42 78 23 50. Open Monday through Saturday, noon to 2am; Sunday, 1pm to 2am.

Hidden on a quiet street between the Pompidou Center and Les Halles, this whimsical bar has different rooms to suit different moods, decorated

Paris

with flea-market antiques, vintage sofas, and elaborate wall murals. There's a non-smoking "tent" room in the back, a long list of cocktails, and friendly service.

Le Tribal Café: 3 Cour des Petites Ecuries, 10th, M° Strasbourg-St-Denis, ☎ 01 47 70 57 08. Open Wednesday through Saturday, 9am to 2am.

The Tribal Café is a bit of a scruffy bar with a great terrace on a pedestrian street off the busy Rue du Faubourg St-Denis. Come for the free *moules-frites* Wednesday and Thursday nights, or free couscous Friday and Saturday night, from 9pm.

Chez Georges: 11 Rue des Canettes, 6th, M° St-Sulpice, ☎ 01 43 26 79 15. Open Tuesday through Saturday, noon to 2am.

This tiny Left Bank pub with the legendry vaulted cellar has long been considered a student pub, but the crowd also includes an older mix of loyal locals and nostalgic tourists who love the old wooden tables, the charming décor and the inexpensive bottles of wine.

L'Entrepôt: 7-9 Rue Francis-de-Pressensé 14th, M° Pernety, ☎ 01 45 40 07 50, www.lentrepot.fr. Open daily, 9am to midnight, until 1am on concert evenings.

The roomy bar of the Entrepôt arthouse cinema (see *Cinema* section, page 306) was designed as a place where people could gather to debate, listen to live music concerts, and generally hang out in a culturally rich environment. There are regular jazz nights on Thursday and Artistic Brunches on Sunday. Families, local businessmen and students mix with the artsy types for morning coffee or an evening cocktail.

La Palette: 43 Rue de Seine, 6th, M° Odéon or Mabillon, ☎ 01 43 26 68 15. Open Monday through Saturday, 8am to 2am; food served from noon to 3pm.

This neighborhood artists' café is just far enough off the beaten path to feel secluded from the St-Germain-des-Prés crowds. Come after lunch to hang out with art students and gallery owners on the terrace, or later in the evening for a livelier crowd squeezed up against the old-fashioned zinc bar. The staff may seem a bit gruff at first, but they'll usually let you linger over a book and a coffee all afternoon without a word.

> **AUTHOR'S NOTE:** Café and wine bar listings can be found in the Where to Eat section, pages 282-287.

Parlez-Vous Anglais?

Being a cosmopolitan city with a large foreign student population, Paris has a healthy selection of "expat" pubs with English, Scottish, American, Australian, or Irish themes. Most people don't visit Paris to hang out in an English-speaking bar where Guinness, Budweiser, televised Cricket matches and pub quizzes are main staples. But they can be a relief for travelers too jet-lagged to attempt ordering anything *en français*, and they're quite popular with French people looking to practice their English with charming foreigners. Expect prices to be slightly higher than in their French counterparts (and the cocktails to be slightly stronger). Check the free monthly **Connexion Magazine** or the **Funky Paris Guide** (www.funkymaps.com) for the latest expat pub listings and their events. Here are a few notables:

The Auld Alliance: 80 Rue François Miron, 4th, M° St-Paul, ☎ 01 48 04 30 40, www.theauldalliance.com. An authentic Scottish pub with haggis on the menu and kilts behind the bar.

Café Oz: 18 Rue St-Denis, 1st, M° Châtelet-Les Halles, ☎ 01 40 39 00 18, www.cafe-oz.com. An Australian theme bar with Aboriginal décor and an elevated DJ platform.

The Frog & Rosbif: 116 Rue St-Denis, 2nd, M° Etienne-Marcel, ☎ 01 42 36 34 73, www.frogpubs.com. An English theme pub with televised sports, traditional Sunday brunch and beers brewed on the premises.

Klein Holland: 36 Rue du Roi de Sicile, 4th, M° Hôtel-de-Ville, ☎ 01 42 71 43 13, www.dutchbars.com. A mellow Dutch bar and restaurant with friendly staff and *bitterballen* (meatballs) on the menu.

The Shebeen: 16 Rue du Pot de Fer, 5th, M° Monge, ☎ 01 45 87 34 43, www.theshebeen.com. A friendly drinking hole with popular quiz nights and an insane-but-friendly South African/New Zealander/Irish/French staff.

Lizard Lounge: 18 Rue du Bourg-Tibourg, 4th, M° Hôtel-de-Ville, ☎ 01 42 72 81 34, www.hip-bars.com. A popular American cocktail bar with live DJ nights in the stone cellars.

Clubbing the Night Away

Pulp: 25 Boulevard Poissonière, 2nd, M° Grands Boulevards, ☎ 01 40 26 01 93. Open Wednesday through Saturday, midnight to 5am. Entry €12, free Wednesday and Thursday, when they play some of the city's best electronic, hip hop, rock and house music. Cheap drinks and a friendly, laid-back atmosphere.

Nouveau Casino: 109 Rue Oberkampf, 11th, M° Ménilmontant, ☎ 01 43 57 57 40, www.nouveaucasino.net. Midnight until dawn, Wednesday through Saturday, tickets €5-9 (most nights free, check the program).

This Oberkampf favorite is so popular that even the West Parisians make the trek across town for the quality techno, house and rock tunes in a funky, retro setting.

AUTHOR'S NOTE: *Pick up club flyers (many good for free entry) at the streetwear concept store Le Shop (3 Rue d'Argout, 2nd, M° Etienne-Marcel), the trendy vintage-clothing shop Kiliwatch (64 Rue Tiquetonne, 2nd M° Etienne-Marcel), or the DJ record shop Techno Import (16 Rue des Taillandiers, 11th, M° Bastille or Voltaire).*

Le Queen: 102 Avenue des Champs-Elysées, 8th, M° Georges V, ☎ 01 53 89 08 90, www.queen.fr. Open nightly 11pm to 6am. Entry €10, €12 Monday, €20 Friday and Saturday.

This gay club is one of the Grande Dames of Paris nightlife, still going strong after 12 years. Their biggest party of the week, Monday's Disco Inferno soirée, welcomes a mixed crowd. Their web site has a handy chart to show which nights are gay-only or mixed, and whether the music is disco, dance or house. Wear your most fabulous dancing shoes!

La Loco: 90 Boulevard Clichy, 18th, M° Clichy, ☎ 01 53 41 88 88, www.laloco.com. Open 11pm to 5am. Entry €10, €20 Friday and Saturday. Ladies free until 1am on Sunday.

Right next to the Moulin Rouge, La Locomotive has never been considered the trendiest club in town, but the young and lively crowd of students and tourists packed into the three floors don't seem to mind. There's different music on each floor, ranging from pop and disco to house and drum'n'bass.

Le Rex Club: 5 Boulevard Poissonière, 2nd, M° Bonne-Nouvelle, ☎ 01 42 36 10 96, www.rexclub.com. Open Wednesday through Saturday, 11:30pm to dawn. Entry €15 maximum, many free nights.

This temple of electronic music (everything from house and trance to drum'n'bass and hard-core) was where French DJ star Laurent Garnier made the *French Touch* famous, and its superior sound system attracts DJs from the UK and US.

Le WAGG: 62 Rue Mazarine, 6th, M° Odéon, ☎ 01 55 42 22 00, www.alcazar.fr. Open Wednesday through Sunday, 11:30pm to 5am. Entry €12.

This slick, UK-style club, opened by *Alcazar* owner Terence Conran in the former Whisky a GoGo club, is the only one of its kind on the Left Bank. The prices are a bit more Right Bank (drinks from €10), but the cosmopolitan clientele and quality house mixes make it all seem okay.

L'Elysée Montmartre: 72 Boulevard Rochechouart, 18th, M° Anvers, ☎ 01 42 23 46 50, www.elyseemontmartre.com.

Even though the Elysée Montmartre is primarily a concert venue, its monthly DJ soirées (such as Open House night) attract top talent from around the world. Try to get tickets in advance (€10-€18), or end up waiting in a line that stretches around the block.

The Alternative Scene

Those who've packed their Doc Marten's will be pleased to know that the Goth and punk scene is alive and well in Paris, if you know where to look. **Les Furieux** (74 Rue de la Roquette, 11th, M° Voltaire, ☎ 01 47 00 78 44, www.lesfurieux.fr), is open Tuesday through Saturday, 4pm to 2am; Sunday, 7pm to 2am). This bar near the Bastille features rock, metal, Gothic, industrial and punk music, as well as arts expositions and album launches. On the other side of town is the Transylvanian restaurant-bar **Le Comte Dracula** (9*bis* Cour des Petites Ecuries, 10th, M° Strasbourg-St-Denis, ☎ 01 47 70 97 85, www.comtedracula.org). Open Monday through Saturday, noon to 2am, it hosts weekly soirées dedicated to bands like Marilyn Manson or Dead Can Dance. Don't miss the annual Halloween party!

■ Dancing

Tango & Salsa

La Casa del Tango: 11 Allée Darius-Milhaud, 19th, M° Ourcq, ☎ 01 40 40 73 60, www.lacasadeltango.net.

For fans of Argentinean tango, La Casa del Tango has Thé Tango (afternoon tea and tango, €6) every Sunday afternoon, and Le Bal (evening tango ball, €7) on the last Friday of the month.

Bistro Latin (a.k.a. **Latina**): 20 Rue du Temple, 4th, M°Hôtel-de-Ville, ☎ 01 42 77 21 11.

Closer to the center of town, this Latin American cultural center and cinema holds regular Argentinean tango and Colombian salsa nights throughout the week (9pm to 1am; entry €9).

La Java: 105 Rue du Faubourg du Temple, 10th, M° Belleville ☎ 01 42 02 20 52. Salsa nights Friday and Saturday, 11:30pm to 5am. Entry €16 (includes drink).

La Java, where young and old, beginners and pros, locals and tourists dance in a 1920s retro dance hall, has been the hottest Latin club for over a decade now.

Swing, Bebop & Jazz

Le Caveau de la Huchette: 5 Rue de la Huchette, 5th, M° St-Michel, ☎ 01 43 26 65 05, www.caveaudelahuchette.fr.

This Left Bank temple of jazz is one of the oldest in Paris, with regular swing and bebop bands so the young, mostly student crowd can get up and dance. Concerts nightly at 9:30pm; tickets €8-€10.

Paris

FRENCH ROCK & ROLL DANCING

 One of the most popular types of dancing in France is called Rock & Roll, a swing variation used almost as a default for any fast jazz or rock music. Younger American and British tourists may find it odd to see the French dancing this way to modern music in clubs (even to U2 and Madonna). It's best to join in or get out of the way!

Le Slow Club: 130 Rue de Rivoli, 1st, M° Châtelet, ☎ 01 42 33 84 30.

This dance hall is one of the rare places in Paris with its own permanent orchestra. Soirées are dedicated to swing, lindy hop, jazz, big band and old '50s rock, with plenty of slow songs for happy couples. It's the larger and less-touristy sister club of the Caveau de la Huchette. Entry €10-13 depending on the night. Dancing Wednesday through Saturday, 10pm to 3am.

Bal de l'Elysée Montmartre: 72 Boulevard Rochechouart, 18th, M° Anvers, ☎ 01 42 23 46 50, www.elyseemontmartre.com.

The traditional ball at the Elysée Montmartre features a full orchestra playing popular hits (mostly from the 1980s) for up to 1,200 rock 'n roll dancers of all ages, followed by a DJ. Every other Saturday night, except in August. Entry €14.

> **AUTHOR'S NOTE:** *See the* Cultural Adventures *section, page 212, for more information on dance classes in Paris.*

OPEN-AIR DANCING

From mid-May through mid-September, the **Square Tino Rossi** (Quai St-Bernard, 5th, M° Jussieu) becomes an open-air dance hall with couples of all ages and nationalities dancing on the edge of the Seine. The largest section of the square is strictly tango, with smaller amphitheaters dedicated to salsa or swing. Even if you don't dance, it's a magical sight to see the spinning dancers with Notre-Dame illuminated in the background. Nightly (unless there's rain), 9pm-1am; €2 donation requested.

Old-Fashioned Guinguettes

History

In the early 20th century, working-class Parisians enjoyed their weekend afternoons at the guinguettes – restaurants, cafés and dancehalls – on the banks of the Marne. Free from the constraints of city life, they danced to the accordion, drank cheap wine and dined on little fried fish called *fritures*. There were almost 200 of these establishments at the height of their popularity, until in the 1960s when tastes in music changed and Parisians with cars were able to travel farther on weekends. A few of the old guinguettes have survived, and are popular escapes for Parisian families looking for a bit of old-fashioned afternoon entertainment. The atmosphere is casual, but men should avoid wearing shorts.

Chez Gégène: 162*bis* Quai Polangis, Joinville-le-Pont, ☎ 01 48 83 29 43, www.chez-gegene.fr (take RER A2 to Joinville-le-Pont then follow signs, or take Bus 101 to the end). Open mid-April through December, Friday and Saturday, 8pm to 2am; Sunday, noon to 7pm. Call to confirm times. Dinner and dancing €34-€40. Original '50s décor and terrace overlooking the Marne.

Le Petit Robinson: 164 Quai Polangis, Joinville-le-Pont, ☎ 01 48 89 04 39, www.guinguette.com (take RER A2 to Joinville-le-Pont then follow signs, or take Bus 101 to the end). Open all year, with Friday and Saturday evening dances and Sunday lunch dances. Dinner and dancing €50, dancing only €14-€16. Waltzes and tangos in a modern, upscale atmosphere with a 1907 Belle Epoque décor. Next door is mini-golf and a bowling alley.

Guinguette de l'Ile du Martin Pecheur: 41 Quai Victor Hugo, Champigny sur Marne, ☎ 01 49 83 03 02, www.guinguette.fr (take the RERA2 to Champigny, then cross the river by footbridge to the island). Open April through October, Thursday through Saturday, 8pm to 2am, Sundays and holidays, noon to 7pm. Dinner-dance €24-€28. Accordion or duets Thursday and Friday, traditional orchestra on weekends. The island has play areas for kids, swings, a puppet theater and a *boules* court.

BOAT CRUISES ALONG THE MARNE

 The best way to travel through the Marne valley is by boat. Three companies operating along the Marne are **Adam Croisières** (May to September, ☎ 01 48 71 02 98, www.adamcroisieres.com), **Paris Canal** (☎ 01 42 40 96 97, www.pariscanal.com) and **Canauxrama** (☎ 01 42 39 15 00, www.canauxrama.com).

Naughty Paris

Anyone who has heard of the Marquis de Sade or read the novel *Les Liaisons Dangereuses* knows that Paris has an established history of breaking every kind of sexual taboo. Most visitors can satisfy their curiosity about the naughtier side to the city by wandering through Pigalle or booking a show at the Moulin Rouge (see the *Cabaret* section, page 320). But those who are looking for something more interactive (without being illegal) can check out the many fetish and swingers' clubs (*échangists*) throughout the city. Some of the better-known ones are **Le Château** and **Le Donjon** (two clubs at one address: 103 Rue Marcadet, 18th, ☎ 01 42 58 13 01, www.chateau-donjon.com), and **Les Chandelles** (1 Rue Thérèse, 1st).

Call ahead to ask about dress codes and door policy (some clubs are couples-only). Listings can be found in the back of *Pariscope* under *Rencontres et Loisirs*.

LAP DANCING COMES TO PARIS

It may be hard to believe, but there were no lap-dancing bars in Paris until the 2001 opening of the British chain **Stringfellows Cabaret of Angels** (27 Avenue des Ternes, 17th, ☎ 01 47 66 45 00, entry €25). This was quickly followed by **Larry Flint's Hustler Club** (13-15 Rue Berri, 8th, ☎ 01 53 53 86 00) and a French version by the owners of La Suite, called **Pink Paradise** (49-51 Rue Ponthieu, 8th, ☎ 01 58 36 19 20, entry €25). Strangely enough, the French find the idea of "look but don't touch" to be a bit frustrating, so most of the clientele tend to be English and American tourists more accustomed to this particular style of entertainment.

Gay Paree

While the Marais and Les Halles districts remain the center of the city's gay community, it's getting harder and harder to define places as "gay" or "straight," since they mix so much. That's certainly the case when it comes to nightclubs, with **Queen** and **Pulp** (gay and lesbian, respectively) at the top of every clubber's list. Even bars that used to be strictly lesbian are slowly seeing a more mixed clientele. So take a stroll through the 1st, 3rd and 4th arrondissements (conveniently bunched together), and you'll find it hard to miss the rainbow flags and same-sex couples. For more detailed information on the gay community, check out the bilingual web site **www.paris-gay.com** for detailed listings and reviews of gay and lesbian bars, clubs, social groups, health services, clothing shops and bookstores. *Insider Paris Guides* (www.insiderparisguides.com) publishes the **Insider Guide to Gay Paris** (e-book) written by the American Schuyler Hoffman. Another surprisingly good source of information is on the web site of the **Paris Tourism Office** (www.parisbienvenue.com,

☎ 08 92 68 31 12), which posts information about gay and lesbian events such as the **Rainbow Attitude** trade show.

After-Dark Resources

All of the 24-hour news agents, pharmacies and *tabacs* tend to be concentrated around the Place de Clichy (9th/18th, M° Place Clichy) and the Avenue des Champs-Elysées (8th, M° George V). If you need a nicotine fix past midnight and aren't content to bum a few off of the passers-by, swing by the **Old Navy Bar** (150 Boulevard Saint-Germain, 6th) or **La Havane** (4 Place de Clichy, 9th). Those desperate to send a postcard or a fax at 4 am can go to the 24-hour **La Poste** at 52 Rue du Louvre, 1st. If you're up late because of a nasty travel bug or the flu, follow the nearest neon-green blinking sign to the **Pharmacie Dehry** (84 Avenue des Champs-Elysées, 8th) or the **Pharmacie Perrault** (6 Place Clichy, 9th) both open 24 hours. Those seeking supplies for a *soirée d'amour* who are too embarrassed to ask at the counter (they're called *préservatifs*) will be happy to find a dispenser box on the wall outside most pharmacies.

AUTHOR'S NOTE: *Check out the* Where to Eat *section, page 298, for listings of late-night, early-morning and 24-hour restaurants.*

Outside Paris

For some, Paris *is* France. Not only is it the administrative and political capital, but no other French city comes close to Paris in population size, tourism, or cultural diversity. And yet this makes Paris distinctly different than the rest of France. Many visitors would like to get a better sense of what lies beyond the

péripherique (besides Disneyland), but think they don't have the time to travel throughout the country. But you don't have to go far from Paris to discover the many cultural and natural treasures of the region once called the Garden of Kings. Those who venture just an hour outside the city will find stunning royal châteaux, humble country inns, village markets, and every kind of outdoor adventure from horseback riding and canoeing to mountain biking and rock climbing. And because the Ile-de-France region is still largely undiscovered by foreign tourists, it's much less crowded, less expensive, and more laid-back than Paris.

This section of the guide highlights the major historical, cultural and natural sights of four towns outside Paris and their surrounding villages and forests. Each section includes specific information on getting around, dining, shopping, adventures, sightseeing and accommodation. While it's possible to visit any of these towns on a day trip from Paris, it's best to stay at least two or three days to explore the countryside and rural villages at a more leisurely pace.

Versailles

Overview

Versailles is one of the most popular day-trips outside Paris, and indeed many visitors feel that it's a must-see, right up there with the Louvre and the Eiffel Tower. And, much as with these monuments, a visit to Versailles can be much more enjoyable with a bit of advance planning. It's not just a question of hopping on the RER and getting in line at the château entrance. There are many ways of getting here, and many different ticket combinations for entrance to the park, the gardens, the private guided tours, the audio tours, the stables and the shows. And that's just the château! The town itself has a variety of sights and shops worth visiting as well. It's certainly worth spending one or two nights in the town to really get to know the château, absorb the fascinating history, stroll the gardens and explore the open market and charming antiques shops.

Planning Your Trip

■ When To Go

The **Grandes Eaux Musicales** and night shows at the Château de Versailles take place from April through October, when the gardens are generally looking their best. June is the best summer month to visit, before the heat of July and the crowds of August arrive. The dry and mild days of September are also a good time to visit, when the town of Versailles hosts the annual **Marché des Potiers** (international pottery festival) and opens its museums and state-owned historic buildings to the public for the **Journées du Patrimoine.** In winter the gardens are a bit dreary (although the admission is free), and there are no particular events organized in town for the December holidays.

■ Tourism Offices

i

Versailles Tourism Office: 2*bis* Avenue de Paris (in the Sofitel building),☎ 01 39 24 88 88, fax 01 39 24 88 89, www.versailles-tourisme.com. Be sure to ask for a free map of the city of Versailles if they're not on display. There's an interactive information screen open 24/7 outside the door of the office. Open daily, 9am to 7pm (until 6pm November to March).

Mairie de Versailles: 4 Avenue de Paris, ☎ 01 30 97 80 01, www.mairie-versailles.fr. Get additional information on public transportation, local markets, history of the town and current events at this bilingual web site, or just stop by and admire the beautiful Mairie (Town Hall) built in 1900.

Tourism Office of the Yvelines Département (78): Hôtel du Département, 2 Place André-Mignot, ☎ 01 39 07 71 22, fax 01 39 07 85 05, www.cg78.fr. This regional tourism office can provide information for the entire Yvelines département. Free brochures can be ordered from the web site (look under the "Rubrique Tourisme" for the English version of the site).

■ Emergency Numbers

General Emergency . . . . ☎ 112 (toll free)
Municipal Police . . . . ☎ 01 39 50 25 48
SOS Médecin (doctors on-call). . . . . ☎ 01 39 58 58 58
Commissariat (info on all-night pharmacies). . . . . ☎ 01 39 24 70 00

Getting Here

Versailles is one of the easiest towns in Ile-de-France to reach from Paris on public transport, with several RER, train and bus links.

■ By Train

RER

The **RER C5** has daily service between Paris (any Left Bank RER C station) and **Gare Versailles-Rive Gauche** 5am to 11:30pm. Travel time is about 30 minutes from Invalides. Tickets cost €2.50 one-way (zone 4 *Carte Orange/Mobilis* passes accepted). Those planning on renting a bike should get off one station early, at **Gare Versailles-Chantiers** (15 minutes on foot to the château.

Those arriving at Roissy-CDG will have to change from RER B to RER C at St-Michel. Those arriving at Paris-Orly should check at the RATP information desk at the airport, since it may be faster taking the RER C directly to Versailles-Chantiers (with one transfer), depending on the time of day.

WARNING! *Not every train that stops on the platform goes to Versailles. Make sure the name of the train is Vick or Vero, or ask someone else on the platform if you're not sure (the destinations are usually displayed on the platform monitors).*

MONEY-SAVING TIP

If you're just coming in for the day to visit the Château de Versailles, you can pre-purchase the **Forfait Château de Versailles** for €20.80 (half-price for kids under 18), which includes round-trip on RER C and a Versailles Passport for entry to the château and gardens (see *Sightseeing*, page 344, for more information).

By Transilien

The SNCF (www.sncf.fr) *Transilien* trains have daily service between **Paris-Gare St-Lazare** and **Gare Versailles-Rive Droite** from 6am to 1am (5am to midnight toward Paris). Travel time is about 35 minutes. Tickets €3.20 one-way. On arrival at Versailles, turn left and continue straight along Avenue Foch (five minutes to the Marché Notre-Dame, 10 minutes to the tourism office and château). There are taxis and buses outside the station.

Another *Transilien* train has daily service between **Paris-Gare Montparnasse** and **Gare Versailles-Chantiers** 5am to 1am. Travel time is about 25 minutes. Tickets €2.50 one-way. The station at Chantiers is 15 minutes from the château and tourism office. Bike rental, taxis and buses are outside the station.

■ By Bus

Bus 171 (www.ratp.fr) has service Monday through Saturday between Paris Pont de Sèvres (end of métro line 9) to Versailles (direction Versailles-Place d'Armes), 7:30am to 8:30pm. Travel time is about 35 minutes. RATP tickets for zone 4 are valid (otherwise purchase a single ticket from the driver, €2.20 one-way).

The **Bus de Nuit - Line 2** (www.busdenuit.com) has nightly service midnight to 5am between **Paris Châtelet** and **Versailles-Rive Gauche** station (one per hour), travel time approximately 50 minutes. Tickets cost €6 one-way. Free transfers can be made at Châtelet to Line 1 (Orly Airport) or Line 1.2 (Roissy-CDG).

■ By Car

Versailles is 14 miles west of Paris via the A13 motorway, direction Rouen (exit the *périphérique* at Porte de St-Cloud or Porte d'Auteuil and follow signs). From Orly Airport take the A86 bypass directly to Versailles.

■ By Taxi

A taxi trip from central Paris or Orly Airport to Versailles in the day will cost about €35, €45 at night. From Roissy-CDG Airport a taxi will cost €60 during the day, €75 at night.

Skippy (☎ 01 39 55 22 22, www.skippy.fr) has private chauffeured car service between Paris, the airports and Versailles with fixed rates, and they accept credit cards. Call to reserve or look for their white cars with the blue kangaroo logo on the window at Paris train stations and airports.

Getting Around

Most of Versailles can be visited on foot, but it can be a bit exhausting. Unless you're going outside the town, take advantage of inexpensive local taxis and buses, or rent a bike if the weather is nice. Pick up a free map of the town at the tourism office.

■ By Bike

Compact in size and blessed with bike lanes on the major boulevards, Versailles is an easy town to explore by bicycle. Even if you
just go to the château, a bike will allow you to ride around the vast
park to the Trianons and Hameau instead of walking or taking the tourist
train. Be sure to ask for a lock and bungee cords when renting your bike.

Bike Rental

Bikes can be rented at the **RER Versailles-Chantier Station** (Place
Raymond Poincaré, ☎ 01 39 20 16 60) for €5/hour, €12/day, €16/week.
Open weekdays 7:15am to 7:45pm, weekends 11am to 5pm (closed holidays). For more info, stop by the **Phébus Office** across the street from
the RER Rive-Gauche station (Bus K has regular service between the stations).

Bikes can also be rented at the **Grand Canal** in the park of the Château
de Versailles (just outside the western entrance gate to the gardens).
Single-gear cruisers cost €5/hour or €3.30/half-hour, payable on return.
Photo ID required as deposit. To get to the canal without going through
the château gardens (which are only free in winter), take the Boulevard
de la Reine to the Avenue des Trianons, and turn left onto Avenue
St-Antoine. Or take **Bus P** (direction INRA) from the RER Rive-Gauche
station to the Porte de Matelots, just south of the canal.

■ By Bus

Local bus service, **Phébus** (☎ 01 39 20 16 60, www.phebus.tm.fr)
uses the same RATP tickets as the Paris métro (€1.30 each, €10
for a *carnet* of 10). Zone 4 *Carte Orange* and *Mobilis* passes are accepted. You can find bus route information for Versailles and purchase
tickets on weekdays at the **Phébus Kiosk** (12 Avenue de Gaulle, under
the arcades of the commercial center) or daily at the **Phébus Office** (Raymond Poincaré, near the Versailles Chartiers station).

On Sundays from April through October the Phébus **Petite Reine** bus
does a continuous circuit between the three train/RER stations, the
château, and the Trianons. Bikes are allowed on this bus, space allowing.
There is also a **Versailles Tour** bus that goes on a circuit through Versailles' St-Louis and Notre-Dame neighborhoods, to the château and to
the Rive Droite and Rive Gauche stations (daily all year long, except Monday). You can use individual bus/métro tickets used in Paris, or purchase
tickets on board (€1.30 each).

■ By Car

It isn't really necessary to have a car to get around within Versailles, and
parking can be difficult near the château. But for those who want to visit

sites farther away or to travel into Paris or the airports any time of the day, then a car can be convenient. Be sure to find out if your hotel has free parking.

Car Rental

Avis . . . . Gare Versailles Chantiers, ☎ 01 39 53 42 42

Citer . . . . 16 Rue des Chantiers, ☎ 01 39 50 62 20

Europcar . . . . 64 Rue des Chantiers, ☎ 01 39 07 16 80

Hertz. . . . . 1 Rue des Chantiers, ☎ 01 39 51 41 02

Rent a Car . . . . 18 Rue des Etats Généraux, ☎ 01 39 20 00 66

■ By Taxi

Taxis can be found outside the three stations and the château. Trips within town during the day are rarely more than €5. Be sure to ask in advance if they accept credit cards.

Skippy. . . . . ☎ 01 39 55 22 22

Affaires Taxi . . . . ☎ 06 07 42 32 62

Artisans Taxis Versailles . . . . ☎ 01 39 51 04 04

Espace Taxi Fabien . . . . ☎ 06 07 33 71 37

Taxi Ferreira. . . . . ☎ 06 08 71 85 21

Taxis Abeille . . . . ☎ 01 39 50 50 00

A Brief History

■ The Palace

Versailles was a real shooting star in French history, its dazzling brilliance cut short by the French Revolution barely a century after the Sun King unveiled it to the world. As a young king, **Louis XIV** dreamed of building a grand palace where he could escape the unpredictable Parisian mobs and keep an eye on his scheming nobles. So when the powerful chief minister Cardinal Mazarin died in 1661, the newly independent 22-year-old was ready to show his kingdom who was in charge. With magnificently bad timing, Louis's finance minister **Nicolas Fouquet** had just finished building his own opulent new palace, **Vaux-le-Vicomte**, and invited the king for a weekend of lavish entertainment. Feeling his authority undermined by this show of wealth, Louis had Fouquet imprisoned on trumped-up charges, then hired away his talented building team – the architect Louis Le Vau, the landscape designer André Le Nôtre, and the interior artist Charles Le Brun – to start work on a much grander château.

He was determined to create a symbol that would forever embody the divine majesty and absolute power of the French monarchy.

He chose to build the palace on the location of his father's hunting lodge in Versailles, a marshy woodcutters' village between Paris and the royal residence in St-Germain-en-Laye. For the next two decades the town became an enormous construction site. Le Vau added new wings and façades on every side until they completely enveloped the original hunting lodge. Le Nôtre completely altered the landscape by draining marshes and hauling in thousands of tons of earth for his gardens and elaborate canals. And Le Brun commissioned the kingdom's finest artists and craftsmen to create the sculptures, furnishings and dazzling interior décor. Le Vau was succeeded by Mansart in 1678, whose illustrious additions include the Sun King's magnificent bedroom (the **Chambre du Roi**), and the famous **Galerie des Glaces** (Hall of Mirrors). Louis wasn't content just to build his château. He also tried his hand at town planning, creating the trident-shaped boulevards emanating from the château, and checkerboard neighborhoods with aristocratic mansions among Mansart-style public buildings and workshops.

■ The Kings

 In 1682, the Château de Versailles was ready for Louis and his thousands of courtiers and government ministers to move in. Life inside this gilded heaven revolved around the Sun King's every movement, from his ceremonial "Rising" and "Setting" in the royal bedchamber to his musical and theatrical performances in the royal gardens. He controlled his nobles like puppets, keeping them in line with a complex system of court etiquette and a never-ending schedule of feasts and entertainment. These were the country's Golden Years of unmatched musical, theatrical and artistic glory. And, although the cost of maintaining Versailles occasionally caused a grumble among the nation's taxpayers, no other French king has ever matched the power that Louis XIV had over his kingdom. As he so confidently declared, *l'Etat, c'est moi* (I am the State).

His successors at Versailles, **Louis XV** and **Louis XVI**, were considerably less ostentatious. They ruled from behind closed doors and spent most of their days within the private apartments, remodeled to suit their personal tastes. Most of the changes during Louis XV's reign (such as the Petit Trianon) were designed to accommodate his mistress **Madame de Pompadour**, while the shy Louis XVI added an outdoor theater and rustic, lake-side house and dairy farm to entertain his demanding wife, **Marie Antoinette**.

On October 5, 1789, a revolutionary mob broke into the private apartments and forcibly escorted the royal couple back to Paris where they could keep an eye on them. It was the end of Versailles as the royal seat of power, and a year later the artworks and furnishing were auctioned off.

Napoleon was able to recover many of these lost treasures during his reign, but the château was falling into decline, and the town virtually deserted. The fate of Versailles was looking grim until the Restoration monarch Louis-Philippe used his own money to turn the château into a Museum of French History in 1830. It reappeared briefly in the limelight during the Franco-Prussian War of 1870, when the French government fled Paris and chose Versailles as their base of operations, and again in 1919 when the Treaty of Versailles put an end to World War I. The French state continued developing the museum collections, and in the 1920s began the long process of restoring the château itself, with extensive restorations of the gardens, galleries, stables and original royal apartments. Versailles continues to play an important role in the French Republic, with one wing reserved for joint Parliamentary sessions, and the Grand Trianon transformed into prestigious quarters for presidential guests such as Queen Elizabeth II, Ronald Regan, and Mikhail Gorbachev.

RECOMMENDED READING

Madame de Pompadour by Nancy Mitford (Random House, 1954; New York Review of Books, 2001)

Athénaïs: The Life of Louis XIV's Mistress, the Real Queen of France by Lisa Hilton (Little, Brown, 2002)

André Le Nôtre: Gardener to the Sun King by Erik Orsenna (George Braziller, Inc., 2001)

The Wicked Queen: The Origins of the Myth of Marie-Antoinette by Chantal Thomas (Zone Books, 1999)

Saint-Simon and the Court of Louis XIV by Emmanuel Le Roy Ladurie (University of Chicago Press, 2001)

Sightseeing

■ Guided Tours

French Links (☎/fax 01 45 77 01 63, www.frenchlinks.com) and **Paris Walkabout** (www.pariswalkabout.com) offer private guided tours of Versailles in English on foot or by minibus. **Fat Tire Bike Tours** (www.fattirebiketours.com) features group cycling tours in English that include entrance to the château (see the *Adventures – On Wheels* section, page 352, for more info).

The **Calèches du Château de Versailles** are the only way of seeing the château gardens without walking, via private guided tours by horse-drawn carriage. They charge by the trip (not by the person), for up to seven passengers (save money by finding other people to form a group): €45 for 15 minutes, €80 for 30 minutes, €120 for 45 minutes, €150 for an hour. They can be found at the Parterre Nord (the north entrance to the gardens) from Tuesday through Sunday, 10:30am to 5:30pm (October to March, 11am to 4:30pm).

ATTENTION: *The Calèches aren't the same as the horse-drawn wagons (with seating for 20) found at the top of the Grand Canal, which only go to the Trianon and Hameau and back, for €6.*

■ Practicalities

There's a **gift shop** next to Porte B-2, and a bookshop, **Librairie de l'Ancienne Comédie**, at the garden entrance. Pick up an English-language guide book on Versailles (about €15) before visiting the château (especially if you're not taking an audio tour), since there's minimal commentary or descriptions in the château or gardens.

Public restrooms are well hidden (there's one at Porte A, next to the downstairs café) and will cost you €0.40. Have loose change ready.

The underground **café** at the entrance of Porte A has a few tables and pre-packaged food "to go" (pre-made sandwiches, sodas, donuts, candy bars). Crowds at lunchtime are huge. The **snack bar** in the gardens is calmer, but serves the same fare. Opt for one of the many reasonable restaurants by the Grand Canal or in the town of Versailles (see *Where to Eat*, page 354), or pack a picnic to enjoy in the park.

■ The Château

It will require a bit of pre-planning to navigate the many different sections of the Château de Versailles successfully; each has its own entrance, ticket prices, and opening hours. Unlike many of the other royal châteaux in Ile-de-France, Versailles doesn't have a majestic garden leading up to a single entrance. It has a parking lot chock-full of tour buses, street entrepreneurs selling postcards and Eiffel Tower statues, and a confusing number of entrances. Not exactly the best way to see Versailles at first glance, but almost unavoidable. The best advice for visitors is to get there when the château opens and head directly to one of the many information kiosks (☎ 01 30 83 78 00 or 01 30 83 76 20), where you'll be given a map and an explanation of the different tickets and tour options for the day, before getting into any ticket lines. The web site (www.chateauversailles.fr) offers minimal practical information, but can give visitors an idea of what sections they want to see.

AUTHOR'S NOTE: *It's impossible to see everything at Versailles in one day, so decide ahead of time what you will leave out, or spread your visit over two days.*

Admission

The château is open Tuesday through Sunday, 9am to 6:30pm (until 5:30pm from October to April), last entrance a half-hour before closing. Regular admission includes independent access to the **Grands Appartements** (the King and Queen's State Apartments and Hall of Mirrors) and the **Hall of Battles**. Regular admission tickets are €7.50, €5.30 after 3:30pm, free for students and kids under 18, and everyone the first Sunday of the month from November to March. Museum Passes and Versailles Passports accepted (enter at Porte B-2). Those without passes need to line up with the masses at Porte A. There's no commentary or printed information in this section except for a map/brochure (pick it up at the top of the stairs on the right, just inside the chapel entrance). Audio guides can be rented for an additional €3.50. This is the most crowded section of the château, especially at 10am and 3pm. Try to visit at lunch or after 4pm.

WARNING! *Versailles is notoriously one of the least user-friendly places to visit in France, with long lines in an uncovered courtyard, inadequate restroom facilities, and a confusing jumble of entrances, tour schedules and multiple tickets. Much of this should be remedied by the Grande Versailles renovations (modeled on the successful transformation of the Grand Louvre). Unfortunately, the first phase of this 17-year project won't be completed until 2010, so be prepared for even more confusion and unexpected closures during the construction.*

Passes

The **Paris Museum Pass** (www.intermusees.com) allows free access to the main section of the Château de Versailles and the Grand et Petit Trianon in the château park without waiting in line, though it doesn't include add-on tours or access to the château gardens. For more information on the Museum Pass see page 77.

The **Versailles Passport à la Journée** allows free access without waiting in line to the main section of the Château de Versailles, the audio-guided tour of the Chambre du Roi, the Grand et Petit Trianon in the château park, entrance to the château gardens and Grand Eaux de Versailles (weekends only May to September), and the Coach Museum (weekends only April to October). It does not cover private guided tours. From April through October the Passport costs €20, €6 for kids 10-17, free for kids under 10. From November through March it costs €14.50, €4 for kids 10-17. Go directly to Porte C2 or D to purchase the Passport before 2pm. They can be pre-purchased at FNAC (stores throughout Paris) or tourism offices.

For those coming from Paris, the **Forfait Versailles** pass includes the Versailles Passport and round-trip RER transportation. Passes cost €24 from April to October, €17.70 from November to March (discounts for kids), and can be purchased at any RER ticket window.

Add-Ons

 An audio-guided tour of the **Chambre du Roi** (King's Bedchamber) costs €11.50 (regular admission + €4; free for kids under 10). Purchase your ticket at Porte D, and enter at Porte C (Passport holders go directly to Porte C). This ticket then allows you access to the **Grands Appartements** and **Hall of Battles** through Porte B-2. Note: The Chambre du Roi is only open until 5:30pm (until 4:30pm, October to April), and is closed the first Sunday of the month, November to March.

There are also **private guided tours** of sections normally closed to the public, including the Opera House, Marie Antoinette's private quarters, and the Royal Chapel. These cost €11.50-€15.50 (regular admission + €4-€8 for the tour, depending on length; discounts for visitors 11-17, free for kids under 10). It's absolutely essential to book these tours first thing in the morning at Porte D. Tours meet outside Porte F (get there a few minutes early). Tour tickets then allow you access to the **Grands Appartements** and **Hall of Battles** through Porte B-2 (N@vipasses – hand-held computer guides with color touch screens – and audio guides for the main section are not included in the price). There are no tours after 3:30pm or on the first Sunday of the month from November to March.

A WORD TO
THE WISE

AUTHOR'S NOTE: *The handheld N@vipass directs visitors around the château and offers images and commentary on the different rooms and artworks. Pick it up on the regular independent tour before going upstairs.*

In the Midi Wing of the château is the museum of the National Assembly, **Les Grandes Heures du Parlement** (☎ 01 39 25 70 70), a separate museum exploring the history of the French Parliament. Those interested in French political history can visit Tuesday through Sunday, 9am to 5:30pm. Tickets €3 (includes audio guide), €2.50 for visitors 18-25, free for kids under 18.

■ Château Park & Gardens

The château gardens (between the Grand Canal and the château) are open daily, from 7am in summer and 8am in winter until sunset (between 5:30pm and 9:30pm, depending on the season). Entrance is €3, €1.50 for kids 10-17, free for kids under 10 and for visitors with the Versailles Passport. Free in winter and after 6pm in high season (April to October). Consider visiting after the château itself has closed to maximize your time. Ask for the free garden brochure/map at any information kiosk before going into the gardens to avoid getting lost or missing all the good stuff hidden in unlikely places. The main section is quite manicured, and features the famous fountains and hedges of Le Nôtre. Off to the sides, amid the more natural trees and wild gardens, are the grottos with impressive Greek mythological sculptures. Keep your ticket stub if you want to re-enter the gardens later in the day. There's no entrance fee to the forested park surrounding the château gardens from the top of the Grand Canal. Here visitors can rent bicycles to explore the vast forest trails or row around the canal (see the *Adventures* section, page 352, for rental information).

THE GRANDES EAUX MUSICALS

Le Nôtre's grand water fountains come to life accompanied by classical music on Saturdays, July through September; and Sundays, April through mid-October. The shows take place at specific times throughout the day; ask at any information kiosk for the schedule. Park entrance on these days is €5, €3.50 for kids under 18, free for kids under 10 and Versailles Passport holders. Ask at any information kiosk for the brochure and schedule.

■ The Trianon & Hameau

The north end of the park is where the kings and queens created smaller havens where they could escape the oppressive court life of the château. The **Grand Trianon**, a marble palace and romantic garden built by Louis XIV, was completely redecorated in the First Empire style by Napoleon and Joséphine. One wing is reserved for the French President and visiting heads of state. The neoclassic **Petit Trianon** was built by Louis XV for his mistress Madame de Pompadour and later altered by Marie Antoinette, who hosted private plays and concerts in the garden theater. The Grand and Petit Trianon are open daily, noon to 6:30pm (until 5:30pm October to April). Combined tickets cost €5 (€3 after 3:30pm), free for kids under 18. Museum Passes and Versailles Passports accepted. Next door is Marie Antoinette's country **Hameau**, a lake-side hamlet and farm where she played at being a milkmaid. The grounds are free to explore, but the interior isn't open to the public.

> 🏛 **ATTENTION!** *Consider visiting the gardens and the Grand and Petit Trianon on Monday, when the rest of the château is closed.*

GETTING AROUND THE PARK & GARDENS

Rent a **bike** at the top of the Grand Canal to avoid the 30-minute walk from the château and gardens to the Trianon and Hameau. There's also a tiny **tourist train** that takes visitors in a loop from the Terrasse Nord (in the gardens next to the château) to the Grand Canal and the Grand and Petit Trianon for €5.40 (€3.30 for children ages three to 12). Bicycles and trains aren't allowed inside the actual gardens, but those too weary to explore on foot can take one of the private carriage rides (see page 345).

■ Beyond the Château

The Royal Stables

 Across from the château, framing the Place des Armes, are the **Grandes** and **Petites Ecuries**, the stables designed by Mansart to house the hundreds of royal horses, grooms and pages. In one wing of the Grandes Ecuries is the **Musée des Carrosses** (Coach Museum), a prestigious collection of historic carriages, sleighs, and sedans assembled by King Louis-Philippe. Open weekends only, April to October, 9am to 6:30pm. Entrance is €2, free for kids under 18 and Versailles Passport holders.

The other half of the Grandes Ecuries was completely restored to its former glory, and reopened in 2003 as the **Académie du Spectacle Equestre** (☎ 01 39 02 07 14, www.acadequestre.fr) under the direction of the famous circus-horse trainer, Bartabas. They present regular choreographed shows (*la Reprise Musicale*) in an elegant arena with the same sort of pageantry and equestrian artistry that Louis XIV once adored. They take place weekends at 2:15pm; reservations recommended. Tickets €15, €7 for students, free for kids under age five. It's also possible to visit during the morning practice sessions (the *Matinales*) although, without any commentary in English; this is better reserved for horse lovers who understand what's going on. These sessions take place in the arena, Tuesday through Friday, 9am to noon; and weekends, 11am to 2pm (visitors can come and go throughout the practice). Entrance is €7 (€3 for students, free for kids under age five), and includes access to the stables and a chic little café overlooking the château across the street.

The Tennis Court

Just to the southeast of the château is the **Jeu de Paume** court (on the tiny Rue Jeu de Paume), one of the only remaining royal "real tennis" courts left in France. This is where the Third Estate gathered in June 1789 to write up a constitution declaring the Universal Rights of Man – the birth of the French Revolution. It's open to visitors on weekends, April to October, 12:30 to 6:30pm.

The King's Garden

Around the corner is the **Potager du Roi** (10 Rue Maréchal Joffre, ☎ 01 39 24 62 62, www.potager-du-roi.fr), Louis XIV's historic kitchen gardens run today by the National Landscaping School. Those interested in seeing what interesting shapes pear and apple trees can be trained into can pay €6.50 to have a look around (€4.50 on weekdays, €3 for students, free for kids under age six). Or just buy some fresh veggies, fruit or conserves from the boutique. Open daily, April to October, 10am to 6pm. Free guided tours (in French only) on the weekends.

The Markets

Across from the Potager is the **Quartier Saint-Louis**, a neighborhood developed by Louis XV around the **Cathédral St-Louis**. Follow the Rue d'Anjou to the **Carré Saint-Louis**, four market squares surrounded by charming 18th-century shops with curving slate rooftops. These are now occupied by artists' galleries and antiques shops.

 The **Quartier Notre-Dame**, which lies to the northeast of the château, was a "new town" meticulously designed by Louis XIV. Begin at the elegant octagonal square known as Place Hoche, which has a lovely view of the château church, **Eglise Notre-Dame** (35 Rue de la Paroisse), whose registers recorded the births, deaths, marriages and baptisms of the royal family. Follow the Rue de la Paroisse to the **Marché Notre-Dame** (corner of Avenue Maréchal Foch), a market square created in 1671, with four covered market buildings reconstructed in 1841. Restaurants and cafés line the outside of the square. Cut through the **Passage de la Geôle**, a small passage lined with antiques shops on the northwest corner, to the **Musée Lambinet** (pictured, 54 Boulevard de la Reine, ☎ 01 39 50 30 32, www.musee-lambinet.com), a fascinating museum sadly ignored by most tourists. Set in a beautiful 18th-century mansion, the collections highlight the history of Versailles up through the French Revolution. There is also a room dedicated to religious art from the Middle Ages. Open Tuesday, Thursday, Saturday, and Sunday, 2 to 6pm; Wednesday, 1 to 6pm; and Friday, 2 to 5pm. Entrance €5, €2.50 for students.

The town of Versailles has many other historic buildings that can only be seen from the outside. Those interested in a self-guided architectural tour should ask for the free *Historical Places* brochure at the tourism office.

Adventures

■ On Foot

Hiking

Versailles has plenty of woodland forests where weary sightseers can escape the crowds and contemplate the countryside. The **Château Park**, open free to the public, is crisscrossed by wide alleys and small trails. The far end of the **Grand Canal** offers a fine view of the impressive château, with hardly another human to be seen (nature lovers might spot herons, swans, ravens, and even squirrels). There's also a nice forest for strolling around the **Pièce d'Eau des Suisses**, to the south of the château.

The **GR11** trail can be followed in a 7.5-mile loop from the Gare Versailles-Chantiers. Follow the red and white markers toward the château (turning left at the yellow markers when you see the sign for the St-Cyr train station). The Versailles Tourism Office has specific directions on their web site.

The **Randonneurs d'Ile-de-France** (www.rifrando.asso.fr) is a non-profit hiking association that specializes in day hikes outside Paris, including Versailles (with sightseeing stops at the château or Grandes Ecuries). Although it's normally only open to members, visitors are welcome to go on a free "sample hike" (participants pay their own train transportation and food costs). There are several hikes almost every day of the year to choose from. Check out their bilingual web site for more details, or simply call their friendly Paris office to sign up: 92 Rue du Moulin Vert, 14th, M° Pernety, ☎ 01 45 42 24 72.

Farm Visit

Gally Farms (☎ 01 30 14 60 60, www.gally.com) is a historic working farm dating back to the 11th century. There are two sections open to the public: a *Cueillette* (fresh fruit, veggie and flower picking) and the *Ferme* (an animal farm, garden shop, corn field labyrinth and activity area for kids). There's no information in English, so an adult who understands French would help. Entrance to the animal farm is €3.30 (€2.50 for kids). Open weekends and holidays 10am to 6pm; Wednesdays 10am to 12:30pm and 2-6pm. The corn labyrinth (open late June through October, call for the hours) costs €5 (€4 for kids 3-12). It's a

short drive north from Versailles on the D7 (Route de Bailly) just before
Cyr-St-Ecole. Free parking and picnic area.

Golf

 The **Golf National** (2 Avenue du Golf, Guyancourt, ☎ 01 30 43 36
00, www.golf-national.com), south of Versailles, is the training
center for the French national team, and host of the French Open.
It has two 18-hole courses for advanced golfers (greens fees €30-€49
weekday, €45-€63 weekends) and one nine-hole course open to all levels
(greens fees €19). Equipment can be rented for €16, golf cart rental €5.
Open 7:30am to 8pm on weekdays, 7am to 8pm on weekends (8am to 7pm
off-season).

The **Golf de Noisy-le-Roi** (1 Chemin de la Pièce, Noisy-le-Roi, ☎ 01 34 62
05 50) has a nine-hole course (par 27) for all levels, with a covered driving
range, clubhouse restaurant and equipment hire. Open daily, 9am to
8:30pm (from 10am on weekends). Located north of Versailles near
Marly-le-Roi. Greens fees €20 during the week, €25 on weekends.

■ On the Water

Boating

Row around the immense **Grand Canal** in a small wooden dinghy
(*barque*) for €11/hour or €8/half-hour (€10 deposit). Four passengers
max. The rental cabin is at the top of the Grand Canal in the Château
Park, across from the Flotille Restaurant. Open March to November,
10am to 7pm (shorter hours on off-season weekends). For more information contact the Château de Versailles, ☎ 01 30 83 78 00 or 01 30 83 76 20.

Fishing

 Fishing is permitted on the lake south of the château known as
the **Pièce d'Eau des Suisses**; simply set up your gear and purchase a permit (*carte de pêche*) when the park guard passes by. Or
stop by the fishing supply shop, **Articles de Pêche**, at 6 Rue Général
Leclerc (by St-Louis Cathedral, ☎ 01 39 50 33 33), for supplies and a permit.

■ On Wheels

Cycling

The **town** of Versailles has many tree-lined streets with bike lanes for leisurely exploration of the different neighborhoods and quiet side-streets.
The **Château Park** is open to cyclists (including the area around the
Grand Canal, Trianon, and Pièce d'Eau des Suisses). For cycling in the
surrounding **forests**, visitors can buy the VTT (all-terrain) **cycling**

guide (in French, with maps) at the tourism office for €5. Bikes can be **rented** at the Versailles-Chantiers station or at the top of the Grand Canal (see *Getting Around*, page 340, for detailed info).

Fat Tire Bike Tours (24 Rue Edgar Faure, M° Dupleix, 15th, ☎/fax 01 56 58 10 54, www.fattirebiketours.com) offers day-long guided bike tours in English that include entrance to the Château de Versailles, the Trianon and an optional garden visit, plus transportation to and from the office in Paris (on the RER) and bike rental. The tour costs €50 . Tours are available May to October, Sunday, Tuesday and Thursday from 10am. Reservations are required.

AUTHOR'S NOTE: *Bikes are allowed on the* Petite Reine *bus, which has Sunday service between the town's three train stations from April to October.*

A WORD TO THE WISE

■ In the Air

The **Aéro-Club de Versailles** offers flights over Versailles for two people in Robin DR-400 planes for 20 to 30 minutes, €30-€40. Meets at the Aérodrome de Versailles (St-Cyr-l'Ecole). For more information contact Philippe Krouch, ☎ 06 73 35 00 32.

Survol de Versailles offers helicopter flights above Versailles for €105-€185. A shuttle picks up passengers at the Versailles Tourism Office and takes them to the aerodrome in St-Cyr-l'Ecole. For more info, ☎ 01 39 24 88 88 or 01 39 42 05 75.

Where to Shop

Head to the **Quartier Notre-Dame** for the **Marché Notre-Dame**, a Provençal-style market with produce, flowers, herbs and spices, preserves, and local gourmet foods. The covered produce market, **Les Halles de Notre-Dame**, is open Tuesday through Saturday, 7am to 7:30pm; and Sunday, 7am to 2pm. The outdoor market, the **Carré de la Place Notre-Dame**, has a food market every Tuesday, Friday and Sunday, 7am to 2am, and an antiques and crafts market every Wednesday, Thursday and Saturday, 11am to 7pm.

Follow the **Passage de la Geôle** (on the northwest corner of the square) to the antiques shops opened inside the converted jailhouse, **Village des Antiquaires** (mostly open Friday through Sunday, 10am to 7pm). Another pedestrian-only passage worth visiting is the **Rue des Deux Portes** (accessible from the southwest corner of the market square), lined with boutiques selling wine, coffee beans, clothing, antiques and gifts. Don't miss the little side-passage across from #10.

Farther toward the Versailles-Rive Droite station are the **Cour Plessis Artisan Workshops** (at the very back of Passage Plessis, off 41 Avenue Foch), where visitors can see local artists and craftspeople at work. Open Monday through Saturday, 8am to 7pm.

In the **Quartier Saint-Louis**, don't miss the adorable antiques shops and boutiques around the **Carré St-Louis**. There's also an **open market** at the Place de la Cathédral St-Louis every Thursday and Saturday from 7:30am to 1:30pm.

A WORD TO
THE WISE

TIP: *Les Manèges is the commercial center of Versailles. It is right outside the RER exit at Versailles-Rive-Gauche. Aside from a bus ticket office, tourism office and newsstand, it has nothing much to offer.*

Where to Eat

RESTAURANT PRICE SCALE
The following price scale represents the cost of an average meal for one person, not including drinks.
€ . . . . Under €15
€€ . . . . €16-€25
€€€ . . . . €26-€40
€€€€ . . . . €41-€60
€€€€€ . . . . over €60

■ Near the Château

La Flotille: At the Grand Canal, Parc du Château de Versailles, ☎ 01 39 51 41 58. Casual family dining (€-€€).

This traditional French restaurant has a little bit of everything from hot sandwiches and pizza to steaks, fish and pasta dishes. Call ahead to reserve a spot on the large terrace overlooking the Grand Canal or to ask about nearby parking.

La Petite Venise: At the Grand Canal, Parc du Château de Versailles, ☎ 01 30 97 19 44. Traditional French (€€). Open daily for lunch and dinner.

This restaurant is set in the completely restored 19th-century stables built for King Louis-Philippe, with exposed wooden beams, stone walls and an outdoor terrace. Kids' menus available.

Le Café Trianon: 1 Boulevard de la Reine, at the Westin Trianon Hotel, ☎ 01 30 84 52 10. Fine dining (€). Open daily for lunch and dinner. Valet parking.

Enjoy traditional refined cuisine overlooking the Château Park from the elegant terrace of this luxury hotel restaurant. Relax by the fire afterwards at the Marie-Antoinette Bar next door.

■ In the Village

Potager du Roy: 1 Rue Maréchal Joffre, Quartier St-Louis, ☎ 01 39 50 35 34. French country (€€). Open Tuesday through Saturday for lunch and dinner.

This charming little restaurant right across from the King's Kitchen Gardens serves up fresh country cuisine in a friendly atmosphere.

Galler: 8 Rue des Deux Portes, Quartier Notre-Dame, ☎ 01 39 51 59 93. Tearoom (€).

Satisfy your sweet tooth with tea and cakes at this pretty tearoom and chocolate boutique on a pedestrian-only passage.

Fenêtres sur Cour: in the center of the Passage de la Geôle, Quartier Notre-Dame, ☎ 01 39 51 97 77. Restaurant and tearoom (€€). Closed August.

This small tearoom and restaurant is inside a modern glass pavilion overlooking the cobblestone courtyard and antiques shops of the Passage de la Geôle. They also have an excellent wine selection.

■ Around the Marché Notre-Dame

 Generally speaking, the restaurants at the northwest corner of the market square (near the Passage de la Geôle) are mostly fast-food, with the most expensive restaurants at the opposite, southeast corner of the square.

Boeuf à la Mode: 4 Rue au Pain, Marché Notre-Dame, ☎ 01 39 50 31 99. Authentic bistro (€€-€€€). Open daily for lunch and dinner.

A traditional 1930s bistro serving hearty fish and steak meals, with a large terrace overlooking the market. Kids' menu available.

Bistrot du Boucher: 12 Rue André Chénier, Marché Notre-Dame, ☎ 01 39 02 12 15. Fine dining (€€-€€€). Open daily for lunch and dinner.

Enjoy traditional French cuisine on a large terrace overlooking the market. Their €26 *menu* includes wine and cheese.

La Cameleone Café: 19 Rue de la Pourvoierie, Marché Notre-Dame, ☎ 01 30 21 90 90. Contemporary (€-€€). Open daily for lunch and dinner.

This funky restaurant has a modern, artsy atmosphere. They make their own fresh pasta on the premises.

Chien Qui Fume: 72 Rue de la Paroisse, Marché Notre-Dame, ☎ 01 39 53 14 56. Authentic bistro (€€). Open Monday through Saturday for lunch and dinner.

"The Smoking Dog" is a picturesque little bistro serving up smoked meats and surf-&-turf meals in a laid-back dining room. Closed August.

Where to Stay

The following price scale represents rates charged for a double room per night during high season, including taxes. Breakfast not included except where noted. All prices quoted in euros. Credit cards accepted unless otherwise noted.

MONEY-SAVING TIP

The **Bon Week End à Versailles** (www.bon-week-end-envilles.com) promotion provides two nights for the price of one in participating hotels, half-off on different sights around town (including bike or canal boat rental), and discounts at local restaurants. Valid for arrivals on a Friday or Saturday. Ask the tourism office for more information.

ACCOMMODATIONS PRICE SCALE	
€	Under €70
€€	€71-€100
€€€	€101-€150
€€€€	€151-€250
€€€€€	over €250

■ Hotels

Hôtel du Cheval Rouge: 18 Rue André Chenier, Marché Notre-Dame, ☎ 01 39 50 03 03, fax 01 39 50 61 27, www.chevalrouge.fr.st (€).

Built in Louis XIV's former livery stable, this hotel overlooking the Marché Notre-Dame is one of the most charming in Versailles. There are 38 rooms, all with private bathroom, satellite TV and direct-dial telephone. The hotel also has a cozy bar, restaurant, and free private parking. Five minutes' walk to the château or the Versailles-Rive Droite station. Quads from €86. Reserve early!

Hôtel Home St-Louis: 28 Rue St-Louis, Versailles, ☎ 01 39 50 23 55, fax 01 30 21 62 45, hotel.st.louis@free.fr (€).

This family-run budget hotel in the Quartier St-Louis (near the Carré St-Louis) has 25 rooms with private bath (shower or bathtub), TV and telephone. Just 10 minutes' walk to the château.

Hôtel Le Versailles: 7 Rue Sainte-Anne, Versailles, ☎ 01 39 50 64 65, fax 01 39 02 37 85, www.hotel-le-versailles.fr (€€).

Right across from the Château de Versailles, this modern hotel has 46 air conditioned rooms decorated in classic contemporary style, with modem jack, satellite TV and full bathroom with hair dryer. The hotel has a bar, lounge and garden terrace, and parking garage with direct access by elevator. They can also arrange for babysitting, car rental, and laundry service.

Hôtel de France: 5 Rue Colbert, Versailles, ☎ 01 30 83 92 23, fax 01 30 83 92 24, www.hotelfrance-versailles.com (€€€).

Set in an 18th-century townhouse across from the Château de Versailles, this classic hotel features 23 rooms decorated in period furnishings, with fabric wall coverings, satellite TV, direct-dial phone, marble bathroom with hair dryer, and air conditioning on request. Room service is available noon to midnight.

Westin Trianon Palace: 1 Boulevard de la Reine, Versailles, ☎ 01 30 84 50 00, fax 01 30 84 50 01, www.trianonpalace.fr or www.westin.com (€€€€-€€€€€).

Opened in 1910, this four-star luxury hotel on the edge of the Château de Versailles park was where the Treaty of Versailles was signed in 1919. It has 192 air conditioned rooms divided into two buildings: the original 1910 Palace and the Pavillon built in 1990. All rooms are soundproofed, have garden or park views, period furniture, pale walls and floral fabrics, white tile or pink marble bathrooms with heated towel racks, combined bath tub and shower, double basin sinks, bathrobes and hair dryer. Amenities include multi-line phone with modem jack, in-room safe, minibar, video on demand and videogames, satellite TV, and free daily paper. Both buildings are connected via an underground passage to the Trianon Spa, which has a large, heated indoor swimming pool, sun deck, fitness center, sauna, and hair and beauty salon. There are two haute-cuisine restaurants, a bar and a café, with views overlooking the Château de Versailles park. Pampering fit for a king....

Outside Paris

■ Camping

Camping International: 31 Rue Berthelot, Versailles, ☎ 01 39 51 23 61, fax 01 39 53 68 29, www.campint.com

This tranquil campsite is on the edge of the forest in Versailles, 20 minutes' walk to the château (in the Porchefontaine quarter). Tent pitches cost €11-€13, mobile home rental €28 (for up to two adults, €4 for each additional person). Facilities include children's play area, free hot showers, laundry machines, TV, pay phones, safe-deposit boxes, and Internet station (fee). Reservations recommended. Open April through October.

Entertainment & Nightlife

The recently renovated **Montansier Théâtre** (13 Rue des Réservoirs, ☎ 01 39 20 16 00, www.theatre-montansier.com) hosts a full season of theater, dance and musical concerts, both classics and contemporary works, from September through May. Tickets €12-€36. This stunning royal blue and gold theater was opened in 1777 by Louis XVI and Marie Antoinette as the town and court theater, and is considered one of the most beautiful in France.

The **Centre de Musique Baroque de Versailles** (www.cmbv.com) has an annual fall Baroque music festival, **Automne Musicale**, with concerts throughout October and November in the château's Opéra Royal and Salon d'Hercule. Tickets €13-€36. There are also regular Thursday recitals, **Les Jeudis Musicaux**, at the Chapelle Royale throughout the year. For information or reservations ☎ 01 39 20 78 10.

The **Château de Versailles** is the site of many concerts and shows throughout the year. Check the web site for the complete calendar, or ask about the **cultural program** at the Service d'Action Culturelle, ☎ 01 30 83 77 88.

Most of the nightlife takes place in the bars around the Marché Notre-Dame, although it can be pretty quiet off-season. There's a bar-club, **Les Caves du Roi** (5 Passage de la Geôle, ☎ 01 39 50 88 62) and a more laid-back Irish-themed pub (French owned) across from the château called **O'Paris** (15 Rue Colbert, ☎ 01 39 50 36 12).

Families with access to a car can check out **France Miniature** (☎ 01 30 16 16 30, www.franceminiature.com), just six miles from Versailles in the new town of Elancourt. The theme park is a 12-acre map of France with miniature representations of 140 major monuments by region, including Paris (the Eiffel Tower, Notre Dame Cathedral, Sacré-Coeur Basilica), Versailles, Mont St-Michel, the Loire Valley (Château Chenonceau, Azay-le-Rideau), the Roman Amphitheater in Arles, Lourdes Basilica, and the Port of St-Tropez. There are also miniature farms, landscaping, five acres of sea (the Channel), 10 rivers, a motorway with moving vehicles, an airport, and a miniature railway. Be sure to ask for the English pamphlet at the entrance to get the full explanations of the monuments. It's good fun for kids, and even adults can learn a lot about the different regions of France. There's a snack bar and restaurant (which gets very crowded at lunch), as well as picnic tables for those who've packed their own meal. Open daily from the end of March through mid-November, 10am to 6pm (until 7pm in July and August). Tickets €13, €9 for ages four to 14. Allow at least 90 minutes to see everything.

Fontainebleau

Overview

Fontainebleau is known throughout the world for its grand **château**, once home to France's kings and emperors, as well as for its vast **National Park forest** whose amazing geological formations make it one of the finest rock-climbing destinations in Europe. It's worth staying for several days, using the lively 19th-century town as a base for exploring the nearby artists' havens of **Barbizon** and **Milly-la-Forêt**, the medieval village of **Moret-sur-Loing**, and the majestic inspiration for Versailles, **Vaux-le-Vicomte**.

Planning Your Trip

■ When to Go

Fontainebleau is lively throughout the year, although outdoor activities are best enjoyed from May through October. Some of the smaller shops and restaurants close in August and around the December holidays, although hotel rooms are easier to find. Winter is even less crowded, perfect for visiting art and museum expositions in Fontainebleau and Barbizon. Fall is the most popular time to visit (and tends to be drier than spring), with the changing of the leaves in the forest and the excitement of various festivals and horse shows. Be sure to book hotel rooms well in advance!

■ Tourism Offices

Fontainebleau Area Tourism Office: 4 Rue Royale, Fontainebleau, ☎ 01 60 74 99 99; reservations ☎ 01 60 74 80 22; www.fontainebleau-tourisme.com. There's also an office at the

Outside Paris

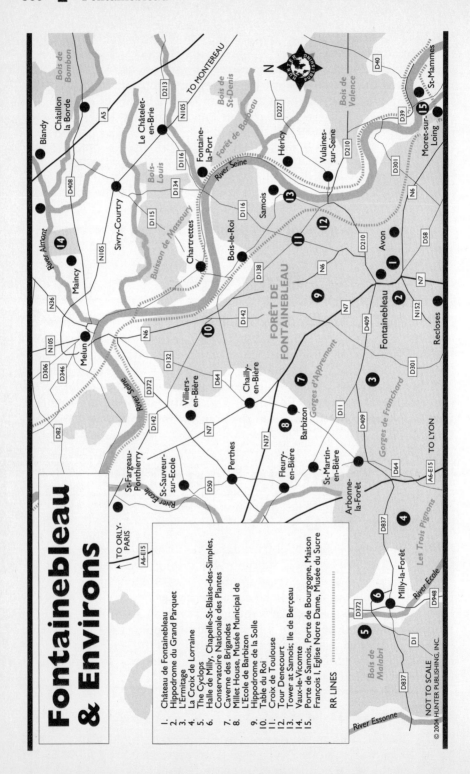

Fontainebleau & Environs

1. Château de Fontainebleau
2. Hippodrome du Grand Parquet
3. L'Ermitage
4. La Croix de Lorraine
5. The Cyclops
6. Halle de Milly, Chapelle-St-Blaise-des-Simples, Conservatoire Nationale des Plantes
7. Caverne des Brigands
8. Millet House, Musée Municipal de L'Ecole de Barbizon
9. Hippodrome de la Solle
10. Table du Roi
11. Croix de Toulouse
12. Tour Denecourt
13. Tower at Samois, Ile de Berçeau
14. Vaux-le-Vicomte
15. Porte de Samois, Porte de Bourgogne, Maison François I, Eglise Notre Dame, Musée du Sucre

RR LINES - - - - - -

NOT TO SCALE
© 2004 HUNTER PUBLISHING, INC.

SNCF station Fontainebleau-Avon, Quai #1. Visitors can find maps, rental bikes, Fontainebleau audio guides, accommodation reservations, ticket sales and information on nearby towns and villages. Open Monday through Saturday, 10am to 6pm; Sunday, 10am to 12:45pm and 3 to 5pm (10am to 1pm from November to March).

Office National des Forêts (ONF): Centre d'Initiation à la Forêt, Route Ermitage, Fontainebleau, ☎ 01 64 22 72 59. The ONF provides maps and information on the forests of the Gâtinas National Park, including the Forêt de Fontainebleau. They also organize regular activities and guided tours of the forests, in French. Open Wednesday from 9am to 5pm (information is available by phone Monday through Saturday).

Seine-et-Marne Regional Tourism Office: 9-11 Rue Royale, Fontainebleau, ☎ 01 60 74 99, www.Tourisme77.net. Get detailed information on the entire Seine-et-Marne département (includes Provins and Disneyland Paris), right around the corner from the Fontainebleau Tourism Office. Open weekdays 9am to 12:30pm and 2 to 5:30pm.

Mairie de Fontainebleau: 40 Rue Grande, Fontainebleau, ☎ 01 60 74 64 64, www.fontainebleau.fr. If the tourism office is closed, the *accueil* (welcome desk) at the Town Hall can usually provide a map of the town and answer basic questions about public transport or current events.

Barbizon Tourism Office: 55 Grande Rue, Barbizon, ☎ 01 60 66 41 87, www.barbizon-france.com. This tiny office, next to the Maison-Atelier de Theodore Rousseau and the church, has maps, books, postcards, and friendly advice on what to see and do in town. There are also automated public toilets here.

Milly-la-Forêt Tourism Office: 60 Rue Jean-Cocteau, Milly-la-Forêt, ☎ 01 64 98 83 17, www.millylaforet.fr, officetourismemillylaforet@wanadoo.fr. This tiny tourism office is in an old circular stone tower. Visitors can pick up a free map of the town, although there are no brochures in English (the staff are all multilingual if you have questions). Open daily except Wednesdays and Sunday afternoons, 10am to 1pm and 2 to 5:30pm.

Moret-sur-Loing Tourism Office: Place de Samois, Moret-sur-Loing, ☎ 01 60 70 41 66, www.ville-moret-sur-loing.fr. Located just outside the city gate, this tourism office is well-equipped with brochures and local maps. They also sell tickets, organize guided tours (in French), and help with local accommodations. Open Tuesday through Sunday, 10am to noon and 2:30 to 5:30pm.

Outside Paris

■ Annual Festivals & Events

Check the local tourism offices for more detailed information.

March

Les Journées Gourmandes (Fontainebleau): an annual three-day gourmet food and *terroir* festival held in the château's Cour Henri IV the first week in March.

April

Concours International des Poneys (Fontainebleau): International pony show and competition the third week in April.

May

Marché de l'Herboriste (Milly-la-Forêt): A large plant and medicinal-herb festival, with entertainment and local products to sample, held at the Place du Marché the last weekend in May.

June to September

 Festival Sons et Lumières (Moret-sur-Loing): A magical nighttime light and sound show recounting the history of Moret, held on the river each Saturday, mid-June through mid-September.

August

Fête de St-Louis (Fontainebleau): Three days of outdoor activities, fireworks and a carnival on the château's grounds, the last week in August.

September

Fête des Peintres (Barbizon): An annual festival of Barbizon painters held during the second week of September.

 Fête du Cheval et Patrimoine (Fontainebleau): Prestigious horse riding, racing, and show jumping events throughout the month of September, attracting equestrian fans and competitors from around the world. A steeplechase takes place in October.

November-December

Noël à Fontainebleau: Ice skating, Christmas markets and holiday lights from the last week in November through New Year's Day.

■ Emergency Numbers

General Emergency (toll-free) . . . . ☎ 112
Fontainebleau Police Station . . . . ☎ 01 60 71 58 00
Regional Gendarmerie . . . . ☎ 01 64 22 24 88

Night Doctor (7pm to 8am) . . . . ☎ 01 64 22 00 77
SOS Médecin (home/hotel visit) . . . . ☎ 01 64 10 38 38
Pharmacy . . . . ☎ 01 60 71 58 00

ATTENTION! *Most of the pharmacies in Fontainebleau are on the Rue Grande. There's always one open 24-hours or on-call* (pharmacie de garde), *and that information is posted daily on the door to every pharmacy.*

Getting Here

■ By Transilien

The Transilien regional train (SNCF) has a daily service between the Gare de Lyon and Fontainebleau between 6am and 12:30am (5:30am to 10:40pm toward Paris). The train's final destination will be listed as Montereau, Montargis, Sens or Laroche-Migennes (*Banlieue* lines), but get off at the station Gare de Fontainebleau-Avon (☎ 01 64 22 38 57). One-way tickets cost €9.05. Travel time is approximately 40 minutes. A regular bus, line AB, goes between the station and the Château de Fontainebleau (in the center of town) every 15 minutes, tickets €1.60 (or one RATP ticket).

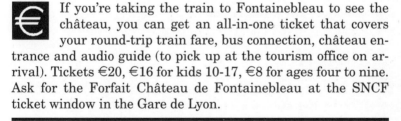

MONEY-SAVING TIP

If you're taking the train to Fontainebleau to see the château, you can get an all-in-one ticket that covers your round-trip train fare, bus connection, château entrance and audio guide (to pick up at the tourism office on arrival). Tickets €20, €16 for kids 10-17, €8 for ages four to nine. Ask for the Forfait Château de Fontainebleau at the SNCF ticket window in the Gare de Lyon.

AUTHOR'S NOTE: *There are no direct RERs from either airport to Fontainebleau. The fastest way to get to the Gare de Lyon (where you will transfer) from either international airport is to take the RER B to Châtelet-Les Halles and switch to métro line 14 (direction Bibliothèque).*

A WORD TO THE WISE

Outside Paris

■ By Car

Fontainebleau is 37 miles southeast of Paris on the A6 (direction Lyon), past Orly Airport, exit 37 to Fontainebleau. Travel time is approximately 75 to 90 minutes depending on traffic. Many locals work in Paris, so the traffic is heavier going toward Paris in the morning, and toward Fontainebleau in the evening.

■ By Taxi

A typical taxi ride to Fontainebleau from central Paris will cost €150 (during the day, in regular traffic). From Orly Airport the cost is approximately €45. There is a taxi rank outside the Gare de Fontainebleau-Avon.

Getting Around

The town of Fontainebleau is fairly compact, so it's no problem getting around on foot or bike. It's best to have a car or rent a bike to explore the forest (the best climbing spots are almost an hour's walk from the town center) and other towns in the area.

■ By Bus

Connex (☎ 01 64 45 55 55) provides a limited bus service in Fontainebleau. Line AB goes between the Gare de Fontainebleau-Avon and the center of town (in front of the château) every 15 minutes. Line 31 goes between the château and Barbizon, and Line 9a from the Mairie de Fontainebleau to Moret-sur-Loing.

Another bus company, **SAMTA** (☎ 01 64 98 85 21), provides infrequent service to Milly-la-Forêt. Ask at the tourism office for detailed schedules.

■ By Bike

As it is relatively flat, Fontainebleau is easy to explore by bike. It's best to have a good local map before venturing deep into the forest and neighboring towns. A round-trip to Barbizon or Moret-sur-Loing is about 12 miles, and it's 22 miles to Milly-la-Forêt. Remember to stay on designated cycle paths within the forests. See *Adventures – On Wheels*, page 352, for more information on cycling in the forest.

Bike Rental

A la Petite Reine: 32 Rue Sablons, Fontainebleau, ☎ 01 60 74 57 57, www.la-petite-reine.fr. Daniel's bike shop has been around for over 20 years. He rents out mountain bikes or city cruisers with locks and optional baby seats (€5) or helmets (€3). Weekend rentals are €5/hour,

€13/half-day and €16 for a full day (€13/full-day on weekdays). Passport or €300 deposit required. Closed on Monday.

Fontainebleau Area Tourism Office: 4 Rue Royale, Fontainebleau, ☎ 01 60 74 99 99, reservations ☎ 01 60 74 80 22, www.fontainebleau-tourisme.com. Open Monday through Saturday, 10am to 6pm; Sunday, 10am to 12:45pm and 3 to 5pm (10am to 1pm from November to March). Bike rentals €15/half-day, €19/full-day.

Location Mulots: Gare SNCF de Fontainebleau-Avon, Avon ☎ 01 64 22 36 14 or 01 60 72 14 45. VTT (all-terrain mountain bikes) available daily from 9am to 6pm.

M. Siméon: (inside the shoe shop) 31 Rue Grande, Barbizon ☎ 01 60 66 42 62. Bike rentals €13.72/day, €10.68/half-day, or €9.15/two hours.

AUTHOR'S NOTE: *If you've rented a bike in Paris, it's possible to bring it down on the train (for example from Motorail in the Gare de Lyon, open daily). See the* Paris – Getting Around *section (pages 58-59) for more information.*

■ By Car

If you rent a car, decide whether you want to pick it up in Paris or Fontainebleau (taking into account mileage and how much luggage you're hauling around). Find out if your hotel has free parking (many do), since there's no free parking in the center of Fontainebleau during the day, even on the street. The five **Vinci** parking garages (☎ 01 60 74 99 99, www.vincipark.com) provide their clients with free umbrellas and bicycles (while supplies last).

A WORD TO
THE WISE

TIP: *If you're driving between Fontainebleau and Paris, consider stopping at **Vaux-le-Vicomte** on the way, because it's out in the middle of nowhere with no public transport access.*

Car Rental

- ■ **Avis**: 185 Rue Grande, Fontainebleau ☎ 01 64 22 49 65
- ■ **Europcar**: 185 Rue Grande, Fontainebleau ☎ 01 64 22 42 62
- ■ **Hertz**: 232 Rue Grande, Fontainebleau ☎ 01 64 22 55 77
- ■ **Société Nouvelle Sud Automobiles (SNSA):** 177 Rue Grande, Fontainebleau ☎ 01 64 69 53 30
- ■ **Ada Locations**: 207 Rue Grande, Fontainebleau ☎ 01 60 71 08 81
- ■ **Rent-a-Car:** 49 Ave Franklin Roosevelt, Avon ☎ 01 60 72 75 75

■ By Taxi

Expect to pay between €8 and €10 for a taxi trip in-town.

Taxi Companies

Fontainebleau . . . . ☎ 01 64 22 00 06 or 01 64 22 26 03

Barbizon. . . . . ☎ 06 80 43 02 97

Milly-la-Forêt . . . . ☎ 01 64 98 75 75 or 01 64 98 95 45

Moret-sur-Loing . . . . ☎ 01 60 70 84 04 or 06 07 35 37 43

History & Sightseeing

■ Town & Forest

Deep in the heart of the forest, Fontainebleau became a favored hunting ground of the kings (poaching strictly *interdit*) where, during the reign of King François I, gentlemen came to practice the chivalrous lifestyle of the day – a men's club of sorts. The royal palace grew, and along with it the village of artisans and workers needed to keep the king's court running smoothly, including his military training grounds.

TOURS

Get a general introduction to the town with an **audio tour**, available at the tourism office for €4.60. It includes 90 minutes of commentary (in English) on the château's park and gardens, the town of Fontainebleau, and the *Gorges de Franchard* in the forest.

Three Paris-based companies offer **guided tours** in English to Fontainebleau, Barbizon, Moret-sur-Loing, Milly-la-Forêt and Vaux-le-Vicomte: **French Links** (☎/fax 01 45 77 01 63, www.frenchlinks.com), **Escapades** (www.webscapades.com) and **Paris Walkabout** (www.pariswalkabout.com).

Fontainebleau developed as a town in the 19th century, when the bourgeoisie's town houses with gardens were built across from the château (at today's Place Charles de Gaulle). Thanks to the mayor's tight control on urbanization, Fontainebleau remains relatively compact, with 19th-century architecture, pedestrian streets and, of course, the château and gardens that recall the town's prestigious royal history. But it's not a town content to rely on the past for its reputation. Today it's also home to one of

Europe's most prestigious business schools (INSEAD) and its annual horse shows and races attract equestrian fans from around the world. Fontainebleau's cosmopolitan population enjoys a large selection of restaurants and bars, making it a lively town at night, unlike many of its cute-but-sleepy neighbors.

■ The Château & Environs

Of course, the star of the town is the Château de Fontainebleau, home to 14 French sovereigns from François I to Napoleon III. Even when Louis XIV moved the court to Versailles, the royal family and the court would still return faithfully each year to Fontainebleau during the hunting season. Over the course of almost a millennium each king extended and changed certain aspects of the palace to suit the needs and the tastes of the time, prompting Napoleon to call it the *Maison des Siècles,* or House of Centuries. Although the château fell into disrepair during the Revolution, Napoleon restored many of the original furnishings and artworks, and transformed it into one of the most illustrious residences of the Empire. Unlike at many empty castles and palaces throughout the country, visitors to Fontainebleau can actually see the way the rooms appeared at the time of its royal use, including the king's bathing room, and, sadly, a bed made for **Marie Antoinette** that she never had the chance to use. Fontainebleau also has the only remaining furnished Throne Room in France, built for the Emperor Napoleon, in the former royal bedchambers.

ORIGIN OF THE NAME

Tourists can immediately incriminate themselves by mispronouncing the name of this regal town as *Fown-ten-Bloo*, when in fact it's pronounced *Fawn-tan-Blow* (accent on the last syllable). That last part of the name doesn't come from "blue," but "Bleau," which is said to have been the name of King Louis VII's hunting dog. The dog was supposedly found in the area drinking from a fountain during a hunt in the 12th century. So originally the château was named for the Fontaine de Bleau, and eventually became Fontainebleau.

Audio Tours & Guide Books

Begin your visit to the **Musée National du Château de Fontainebleau** (Place du Général de Gaulle, Fontainebleau, ☎ 01 60 71 50 70, www.musee-château-fontainebleau.fr) in the bookshop, just to the right of the grand horseshoe-shaped staircase. There's hardly any descriptive information inside the actual museum (even in French), so it's a good idea to buy a proper guide book (guides in English from €3-€12) or an audio guide (€3). The museum entrance and ticket windows are back through the courtyard to the left. Entrance is €5.50, €4 for visitors ages 18 to 25 and for everyone on Sundays, free for kids under 18 and for everyone on the first Sunday of the month. Museum Passes accepted.

The standard tickets give visitors independent access to the main rooms of the château (*Les Grands Appartements*), as well as the private salons and Empress Eugénie's *Musée Chinois*, although these are only open for short periods during the day (call in the morning to ask for the schedule). Be sure when you're walking around to look out the windows for magnificent garden views. Each room seems to be more magnificent than the one before it, even though the styles don't exactly match. The succession of French kings and emperors, being the earliest home-improvement addicts, couldn't leave anything the way it was when they found it. The plaque in front of a grand marble staircase mentions that there was once a beautiful room for the queen's ladies in that spot until the king needed a shortcut to his own room. The *Petits Appartements* and the popular *Musée Napoleon* can only be visited with a guide (in French, €3, €2.50 for students, free for kids under 14). Be sure to allow at least two hours to see everything. You can leave and come back on the same day using the same ticket if you decide to take a lunch break, but many rooms start closing an hour before official closing time, so don't wait until too late in the day to return. Open daily except Tuesday from 9:30am to 5pm (until 6pm June to September).

> **DID YOU KNOW?** *Napoleon Bonaparte said goodbye to his troops here on April 20, 1814, before going into exile at Elbe Island.*

The Gardens of Fontainebleau

There's no entrance fee to stroll through the **château gardens**, including the formal *Grand Parterre* of hedges and fountains designed by Le Nôtre, the tiny *Jardin de Diane* courtyard garden, and the informal *Jardin Anglais* with its romantic carp pond. To the east are the vast lawns and *Grand Canal* of the *Parc du Château*, where locals picnic and walk their dogs in almost complete solitude from the outside world. The park and gardens are open daily from May to September, 9am to 7pm (until 5pm in winter). See the *Adventures* section (page 378) for information on carriage rides in the park, boat rentals on the lake, and fishing in the canal.

Fontainebleau Forest

Aside from its royal hunting heritage, the 42,000-acre **Forêt de Fontainebleau** is known for its strange and dramatic geological formations, including sandy stretches of "desert," limestone formations, caves, and towering boulder mountains that attract expert climbers from around the world. It's considered one of the most beautiful forests in France, popular with Parisian day-trippers looking to escape the hectic city. The forest also hides over 6,500 species of wildlife, including **deer**, **wild boar**, **foxes**, **rabbits**, and **squirrels**. Visitors can enjoy the forest scenery from their car when driving to Barbizon or Milly-la-Forêt, but the best scenery can only be seen off the main roads. See the *Adventures* sections of this chapter for different ways of exploring the forest on foot, on bicycle or on horseback.

CONSERVATION NOTE

Even when used as the royal hunting grounds, only 10% of the Forêt de Fontainebleau was forested. It was Louis XIV who had Colbert plant more than 1,400 acres of trees in 1716. When the forests were opened to the public in the 19th century, Parisians began to arrive by the new railways, including the Barbizon painters, who were the first to lobby Napoleon and local officials to preserve the beauty of the forests. In 1830 over 15,000 acres of pines alone were planted. Today the biodiversity of the forest is closely monitored in order to create a balance between nature and the millions of annual visitors.

■ Outside Fontainebleau

Barbizon

The picturesque town of Barbizon, 5½ miles northwest of Fontainebleau off the N7, was once a humble woodcutter's village. Landscape painters fell in love with the area in the 19th century and came from all over the world to set up their easels right out in the forests, painting simple country scenes. These painters, including masters such as Théodore Rousseau, Camille Corot and Jean-François Millet, became known as the **Barbizon School**, and are considered precursors to the Impressionist movement. Today Barbizon is a postcard-perfect village full of art galleries, gourmet restaurants and charming luxury inns, with many of the original artist studios converted into museums. It's the ideal place to eat and sleep if money is no object, although it costs nothing to drool over the expensively restored "country homes" for sale in the real estate office windows. The town is full of smartly dressed tourists in Range Rovers and coach parties during the high season, so try to visit early in the morning or during the off-season to get a glimpse of the authentic village atmosphere.

Most of the town can be seen from the main street, the Grande Rue. At the top of the street is **Jean-François Millet's House & Studio** (27 Grande

Rue, Barbizon, ☎ 01 60 66 21 55), where the artist lived and worked on his masterpieces, including *The Angelus*, *The Gleaners* and *The Sower*, from 1849 until his death in 1875. One room is reserved for contemporary art exhibitions. Free entry, open daily from 9:30am to 12:30pm and 2pm to 5:30pm.

 DID YOU KNOW? *Barbizon wasn't popular only with painters in the 19th century. The Scottish author of* Treasure Island, **Robert Louis Stevenson**, *came to Barbizon in 1875 to write his* Forest Notes *at the Hôtellerie du Bas Bréau (22 Grande Rue).*

The **Musée Municipal de l'Ecole de Barbizon** (☎ 01 60 66 22 27) is made up of two museums, the **Auberge Ganne** (92 Grande Rue) and the **Maison-Atelier Théodore Rousseau** (55 Grande Rue). The Auberge Ganne, restored in 1995, was a popular inn for landscape painters from all over the world, who came to check out the action in the forests around Barbizon and Fontainebleau from 1837 until 1870. The scenes on the walls and furniture painted by guests are still intact, and the museum houses a collection of over 400 paintings and masterpieces from the Barbizon school, including works by Camille Corot, Jules Dupré and Ferdinand Chaigneau. Rousseau's house and studio, a tiny space made up of two rooms next to a chapel, is now a museum dedicated to the artist and his work. There's also a room dedicated to the artist **Rosa Bonheur**. Open daily except Tuesday, 10am to 12:30pm and 2 to 5:30pm. Tickets (valid for both museums) are €4.50, €2.30 for students, children under 12 free. There's no information in English except a guide on sale in the gift shop for €9.50.

For those who want to see where the Barbizon painters found their inspiration, stop by the tourist information center (55 Grande Rue) and ask for the free English brochure, *Barbizon Painters Discovery Trail*, which maps out a two- to three-hour walk through the forest highlighting eight of their favorite painting spots. It's an easy trail, perfect for a casual, non-strenuous stroll.

Milly-la-Forêt

The sleepy little village of **Milly-la-Forêt**, 11 miles west of Fontainebleau (off the D837 via D409), can be visited in a half-day. The best time to visit is during the Thursday afternoon market, which takes place under the huge wooden **Halle de Milly** (Place du Marché) built in 1479. Right in the heart of the village, the market is surrounded by small shops selling local farm products and medicinal herbs, bakeries, butcher shops, gift boutiques, cafés and restaurants. An **antiques fair** takes place at La Halle the second Sunday of every month from March through November. Parking in the center of town may be difficult, so try parking by the tourism office (60 Rue Jean-Cocteau, Milly-la-Forêt, ☎ 01 64 98 83 17), just a short walk from the Place du Marché.

It's best to visit the other main sights by car or bicycle, since they are all outside the town center. Follow the Route de la Chapelle St-Blaise across from the tourism office, and immediately on the right you'll see the tiny **Chapelle St-Blaise-des-Simples**. The interior of this 12th-century chapel was decorated in 1959 by the artist, poet and filmmaker, Jean Cocteau. He was buried in the chapel cemetery in 1963, surrounded by an herb garden containing medicinal plants cultivated in the village for centuries. Open daily except Tuesday, Easter through November 1st, 10am to noon and 2:30 to 6pm; open weekends and holidays November 1st through Easter, 10:15am to noon and 2:30 to 5pm; entry €2. There's a guide in English available for €6.

A WORD TO
THE WISE

AUTHOR'S NOTE: *The house in Milly-la-Forêt where **Jean Cocteau** lived from 1947 to 1963, at the end of Rue de Lau, will be open to the public beginning in the fall of 2004. Contact the tourism office for more information.*

Milly-la-Forêt is historically associated with medicinal herb cultivation, drawing visitors from around the world for its annual **Marché de l'Herboriste** the last week in May. Garden center addicts can get their fix at the town's own national plant conservatory. Continue past the chapel along the Route de Nemours, and look for signs on the right pointing to the **Conservatoire National des Plantes** (☎ 01 64 98 83 77), where over 200,000 types of aromatic and medicinal plants and herbs are grown on five acres. It has a 19th-century drying room, a collection of antique garden tools, and a greenhouse full of exotic plants. There's also a plant shop and picnic tables set up in the garden. Open weekdays, April through October, 9am to 5pm; and weekends, May through September from 2 to 5:30pm. Closed October to March; entry €4, €2.50 for kids.

The town has gained fame in recent years for a bizarre monument hidden in the forest to the north of the town. Measuring almost 75 feet high, **Le Cyclop** was created by contemporary sculptors Jean Tinguely and his wife, Niki de Saint Phalle, with the help of Arman, César, Marcel Duchamp and JR Soto. Started in 1969, and taking over 20 years to finish, the whimsical sculpture is made of 300 tons of metal, mirrors, and a waterfall. Staircases and catwalks allow visitors to explore the inside of Tinguely's complex mechanical universe. Donated to the state, it opened to the public in 1994, and can only be visited between May and October, with a guide. On Saturdays tours are every 45 minutes from 2 to 5pm; on Sundays, every 45 minutes from 11am to 12:30pm and 2 to 5:45pm (confirm tour times with the tourism office). The tour costs €5.50, €4.50 for students. Kids under 10 aren't allowed into the sculpture for safety rea-

sons. To find the sculpture, drive or cycle to the northwest of town on the
Avenue de Ganay (D948) and turn left at the roundabout onto the D837. A
sign marks the turnoff to the right into the forest. You'll need to leave
your car at the parking lot and walk along a wide cycle path for about
three minutes. A sign on the left leads to the sculpture, barely visible
through the trees, and surrounded by a tall security gate.

Moret-sur-Loing

 Moret-sur-Loing is seven miles southeast of Fontainebleau off the
N6 (south of the château gardens), via Veneux-les-Sablons. It's
also possible to take the train from the Gare de
Fontainebleau-Avon (or even direct from Paris' Gare de Lyon) in the direction of Monterau/Laroche or Montargis/Nevers, and get off at the station
Gare de Moret – Veneus-les-Sablons. It's a 15-minute walk into the center
of town from the station (taxis are usually available).

Moret-sur-Loing's heyday was in the Middle Ages, when it was the main
crossing point of the River Loing on the route between Paris and Lyon.
Heavily fortified to protect the French kingdom from insurrection by the
Dukes of Burgundy, the village still boasts over 4,500 feet of walls, two
fortified gateways and 20 towers. It's one of the few towns in
Ile-de-France, along with Senlis, that has retained its medieval structure.
In the 19th century, Impressionist painter Alfred Sisley fell in love with
the narrow cobblestoned streets, fortifications and romantic riverbanks.
He created over 400 paintings of Moret-sur-Loing over a decade, but
didn't receive any recognition until after his death.

Today's visitors can easily explore the compact village and its riverbanks
on foot. And unlike Barbizon, Moret-sur-Loing still feels like a real town
with down-to-earth prices, despite its popularity with Parisian
weekenders. The main axis is along **Rue Grande**, flanked on both ends
by 12th-century towers, the **Porte de Samois**, overlooking the tourism
office (☎ 01 60 70 41 66), and the **Porte de Bourgogne**, which guards the
bridge over the River Loing. Hardly changed over the centuries, the village's narrow, winding streets still hide a number of half-timbered houses
and even a Renaissance façade on the **Maison François I** behind the
Mairie (on Rue du Pave Neuf).

Follow the Rue de l'Eglise uphill to the early Gothic **Eglise Notre-Dame**,
altered several times over the centuries. Inside is a beautifully carved Renaissance organ loft. Next to the church on the corner of Rue Grez is the
original medieval hospice where the local nuns invented the famous bar-
ley sugar candies. Those with a sweet-tooth may want to stop by the
Musée du Sucre d'Orge des Religieuses de Moret (5 Rue Puits du
Four, Moret-sur-Loing, ☎ 01 60 70 35 63), in the converted sugar house
just around the corner, where you can learn all about the centuries-old
tradition (video in English) – and to try the candy, of course!

Cut back toward the river and walk up the Rue de l'Est to the Rue du Donjon. Sisley lived in the house at the corner of Rue Montmartre from 1889 until his death in 1899. Farther up the street is the 12th-century Donjon (castle keep), where Louis XIV imprisoned his finance minister Nicolas Fouquet, whose extravagant Château de Vaux-le-Vicomte had enraged the king. Both buildings are closed to the public.

Walk back down to the Porte de Bourgogne and get a glimpse of the town from the historic tanning mill in the middle of the bridge. This is the view that has attracted attracted so many painters to Moret-sur-Loing since the 19th century. Have a stroll along the riverbank paths or rent a canoe to explore the shallow river and the town's scenic ramparts. See the *Adventures – On the Water* section, page 379, for more details.

Vaux-le-Vicomte

 The sprawling Château de Vaux-le-Vicomte has a bittersweet place in Ile-deFrance's history. The Lord High Treasurer, **Nicolas Fouquet**, had it built in 1653 to show how successful he was, hiring the "dream team" of the period: architect Louis Le Vau, garden designer André Le Nôtre, and painter Charles Le Brun. It was the building masterpiece of the 17th century, and made many of Fouquet's contemporaries very jealous. Days after the Sun King, Louis XIV, attended a spectacular party at Vaux-le-Vicomte, complete with fireworks and entertainment by Molière, Fouquet was arrested by d'Artagnan and imprisoned for life (on falsified evidence given by the minister Colbert). The king then had Le Nôtre, Le Brun and Le Vau build him a bigger and more spectacular version of Vaux-le-Vicomte – at Versailles. Vaux-le-Vicomte has changed hands many times over the centuries, but still remains a privately owned château.

Vaux-le-Vicomte (☎ 01 64 14 41 90, www.vaux-le-vicomte.com) is out in the middle of the countryside in Maincy, off the N36 and D215 east of Melun. The château and gardens are open from Easter through November, 11am to 6pm. Entrance is €12, €9.50 for kids under 16, free for kids under six. Be sure to ask for the free discovery guide for children. No baby strollers are allowed inside. There is a small, but very nice bookshop in the château, and a larger gift shop you have to pass through on your way out of the property (souvenirs include Vaux-le-Vicomte jams and copies of prints displayed in the château).

Guests visit the château independently, following a set itinerary to avoid getting lost. Start off with a walk through the old stables, now a museum of horse-drawn carriages brought to life with wax-figure horses and passengers. At the main entrance to the château visitors can pick up audio guides for €1.50 and books in different languages about the château. Similar to the Château de Fontainebleau, Vaux-le-Vicomte is furnished and finely decorated with statues, tapestries and paintings, with mood lighting and Renaissance-style music piped in for added atmosphere. If you're confused by the "King's Room," don't worry – the king never lived here, but had his own private quarters when he visited. Halfway through the tour you have the option of visiting the dôme for another €2 (no children under 10), where you get a panoramic view over the château's grounds.

The 70 acres of gardens, although slightly altered from Le Nôtre's time, still retain many of his clever tricks of perspective. Stroll the different *parterres*, or sections, and notice how things seem closer than they really are as you walk toward the grottos. On a clear day, standing at the far side (south) of the *Grand Miroir Carré*, you can see the château reflected in the water, even though it's just over 1,300 feet away. If you aren't up for the 30-minute walk from one end of the garden to the other, you can rent electric golf carts (Club Cars) for up to four people, €13 for 45 minutes (only for licensed drivers at least 18 years old). Gadget-lovers can rent the GPS guide, which not only directs you to all of the good spots, but also provides commentary in English (€20 on top of the Club Car rental).

SPECIAL EVENTS

The historic fountains are turned on for the **Jeux d'Eaux** every second and last Saturday of the month. **Candlelit tours** of the grounds and château take place every Saturday night from May through October from 8pm to midnight, with a Champagne bar and classical music in the gardens. Entry for the Candlelit Evenings is €15, €13 for kids under 16. Open-air opera performances take place in September (very popular, so book in advance, ☎ 08 92 70 18 04), usually featuring classics such as *Don Giovanni* or *The Marriage of Figaro*.

The château's restaurant, **l'Ecureuil** (the Squirrel), is quite reasonable for breakfast (€3-5), lunch (*carte* €12, kids' menu €6) or snacks without leaving the château. It's self-service, with seating on a large terrace in the summer. Outside food isn't allowed inside the château grounds, but guests can picnic in the parking area (the shady parts are past the chain link fence, in the forest). Try to avoid going into Melun, the large city next door, whose mildly interesting historic center is spoiled by the ugly tower blocks and industrial buildings surrounding it.

Adventures

■ On Foot

Hiking

The Forêt de Fontainebleau surrounds the town of Fontainebleau and stretches all the way to the edges of Barbizon, Milly-la-Forêt and Moret-sur-Loing, making it possible to hike from town to town without leaving the forest. Its 42,000 acres are crisscrossed with trails and forest roads, with a number of clearly marked one-way and circular circuits. Those who prefer to do less walking can drive to forest parking areas closer to the trailheads and rock climbing formations. It may not look like there's much to see from the roads, but this forest has many hidden surprises for first-time visitors. Expanses of sandy desert, limestone grottos and bizarre rock formations (called *chaos* in French) emerge from dense forest groves, and steep plateaus reward hikers with panoramic views and historic monuments.

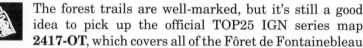

BE PREPARED

The forest trails are well-marked, but it's still a good idea to pick up the official TOP25 IGN series map **2417-OT**, which covers all of the Fôret de Fontainebleau (including the *Trois Pignons*), and highlights climbing sites, campsites, and picnic areas. The map can be purchased at local tourism offices, news agents, and many gas stations in the area. A compass is handy for those who like to wander off the marked trails. Be sure to carry plenty of drinking water and wear proper hiking shoes. If you're hiking alone, tell someone where you're going and when you plan to return. And remember the forest can be a few degrees cooler than in town.

 WARNING! *The forest parking areas in Fontainebleau are prime targets for thieves, so be sure not to leave anything valuable inside your car.*

Major Trails & Areas of Interest

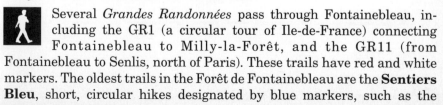 Several *Grandes Randonnées* pass through Fontainebleau, including the GR1 (a circular tour of Ile-de-France) connecting Fontainebleau to Milly-la-Forêt, and the GR11 (from Fontainebleau to Senlis, north of Paris). These trails have red and white markers. The oldest trails in the Forêt de Fontainebleau are the **Sentiers Bleu**, short, circular hikes designated by blue markers, such as the

Outside Paris

Sentier Denecourt. The **Tour Denecourt**, just to the north of Fontainebleau (between the D116 and the D138), has an orientation table at the top of the tower that shows just how immense the forest really is.

The **Gorges d'Apremont** has many interesting natural sights, such as the rock sculptures in the **Caverne des Brigands** and the **Rocher d'Eléphant** (which resembles...). There are panoramic views from the **Chaos d'Apremont**. To reach this area, leave Barbizon by the Allée aux Vaches and continue until the trailhead at the Carrefour du Bas Bréau. The **Gorges de Franchard**, below the Gorges d'Apremont and directly to the west of Fontainebleau, has dramatic granite cliffs with views over the 12th-century **Ermitage**. To get there, take the D409 west from town and turn left onto the Route Ronde (D301). Turn right into the forest at the Croix de Franchard.

WHO WAS DENECOURT?

In the early 19th century, Claude François Denecourt, one of Napoleon's retired soldiers, traced the first hiking trails through the forests around Fontainebleau (*les Sentiers Bleu*). The trails were designed to guide visitors to the most picturesque areas of the forest – a revolutionary idea, since the forests were not considered places of leisure at that time.

The **Massif des Trois Pignons**, named for the three giant rock formations resembling pine cones. This area is quite rugged, with heather moors and pine trees punctuated by hills and boulder formations. Look out for the famous sands of the **Cul de Chien**, which have exhausted countless unsuspecting hikers. The Trois Pignons area is near Milly-la-Forêt. To reach the main trailhead at the Noisy Cemetery, head south out of town on the D142/D16 in the direction of Nemours, and the parking lot is on the left just before Noisy-sur-École.

FRENCH RESISTANCE MEMORIAL

Climb up to the Croix de Lorraine, where resistance fighters during WWII used to signal Allied airplanes at night for weapons drops. There are great panoramic views overlooking the Vallée Close.

Climbing

The Fôret de Fontainebleau has over 200 listed climbing sites, and although many of them are reserved only for very experienced climbers, there are also several circuits for beginners and even kids. The tourism office in Fontainebleau sells a climbing guidebook in English for those who want to do some serious bouldering. Otherwise the 2417-OT map mentioned in the previous section is adequate for locating the top sites, including **Les Rochers du Cuvier**, **Les Rochers des Demoiselles**, **Le Cul de Chien**, **Le Diplodocus**, **La Tortue** and **Le Reptile**.

Climbing circuits are marked with colored arrows indicating the average difficulty, from white, yellow, orange, blue, red and black. White marks indicate either extremely difficult circuits, or ones dedicated for kids – the difference should be obvious. Only the most difficult circuits require rope; otherwise it's all free-climbing.

ESSENTIAL CLIMBING GEAR

 Aside from a good pair of climbing shoes, local experts recommend bringing along a towel or something else to stand on (to keep the sand off your shoes before trying a boulder). Using chalk (magnesia) is a no-no; use rosin instead (called "pof" in Europe), which can be purchased at Au Vieux Camper stores in Paris or at SOS Escalade (open every Sunday at the Cimetière de Noisy parking lot). Bring plenty of drinking water and cold food (no barbecues, fires or stoves allowed in the forest).

Tree-Walking

ArbrenArbre (☎ 01 69 68 04 33, www.arbrenarbre.com) offers tree-walking outings in which participants traverse the forest canopy using climbing equipment such as ropes, harnesses, rope ladders and pulleys. Open year-round to anyone age seven and up (special Baby Tarzan activities for kids from three to six years old). Call for pricing and meeting places.

Golf

Golf de Fontainebleau: Route d'Orléans, RN152, Fontainebleau, ☎ 01 64 22 22 95. This is one of the most prestigious golf courses in France, and to play as a guest you'll have to come during the week or daily during July and August, and be able to prove a handicap of 24. They have one 18-hole course (par 72, 103 bunkers) in the center of the forest, and a clubhouse bar and restaurant. Greens fee €75 during the week, €100 on weekends. Closed Tuesday.

Cély Golf Club: Le Château, Route de St-Germain, Cély-en-Bière ☎ 01 64 38 03 07. This 18-hole course (for all levels) is on the grounds of an impressive château surrounded by a Japanese garden. The holes and groomed fairways are tucked into a forest of oak trees. There's a bar and cafeteria. Greens fees during the week are €40, €60 on weekends. It's necessary for non-members to reserve 48 hours in advance. Golf carts can be rented for €16. Look for signs from the village of Cély-en-Bière, traveling northwest of Fontainebleau just off the A6 and the D372. Closed the last two weeks in December.

Golf de la Forteresse: Located at Thoury-Ferrotte (southeast of Fontainebleau on the D22), ☎ 01 60 96 95 10, www.golf-forteresse.com. On the site of an old fortified farm, this 18-hole course (par 72) is in a forested valley of lakes and rivers. Greens fees €20-€30 weekdays, €45-€60 weekends. Clubs can be rented for €12, and a golf cart €30. The club house, restaurant and golf shop are in the converted stone farmhouse. Open 8:30am to 7pm (6pm in winter), closed late December.

■ On Horseback

Guided Horseback Rides

La Belle Aventure: 35 Route de Montargis, Souppes-sur-Loing, ☎ 01 60 55 02 64, http://la.belle.aventure.free.fr. This equestrian farm run by Bruno Voirin organizes regular half-day (€23-€28), full day (€65) and weekend rides (€182-€210) in the Fontainebleau region. Casual riding, helmet and boots not necessary. Open for all levels, although it's best to have some experience for longer rides. They also have horse-drawn carriage rides (*attelages*), by the half-day (€20 per person) or full day (€54 per person). Located south of Fontainebleau off the N7. Call for details or check the web site for the scheduled rides.

Le Relais du Picotin: Château St-Louis, Route de Sens, Poligny, ☎ 01 64 38 84 16, http://lerelaisdupicotin.free.fr. Located in a 19th-century hunting lodge south of Fontainebleau, this equestrian center organizes half-day (€38), full-day (€70-€80) or weekend rides (casual riding, for all levels). Discount rates for young riders. They also have moonlit rides and horse-drawn carriages. Be sure to look at their map online, they are actually off the road toward Sens, not in Poligny.

Centre Equestre de Recloses: Chemin du Clos de la Bonne, Recloses, ☎ 01 64 24 21 10, http://cheval-en-foret.ifrance.com. Annie Durieux runs this equestrian center to the southwest of Fontainebleau (off the N152). There are several two-hour-long rides a day (€19), and a one-hour ride at the end of each day. Open to all levels, riders are split into groups according to ability. Half-day and full day rides have to be arranged in advance (for experienced riders), from €48-€86.

La Bleausière: 11 Allée Odette Dulac, Barbizon, ☎ 06 82 01 21 18, http://la.bleausiere.free.fr. Open year-round in the heart of the Forêt de Fontainebleau just outside Barbizon, this riding center organizes short and long guided tours for adults and children of all levels (casual riding), mostly on weekends (call to reserve). Good shoes and long pants are necessary for the ride, and wear a hat if it's sunny. Call or stop by for rates and scheduled rides.

AUTHOR'S NOTE: *Racing events are held throughout the year in Fontainebleau, but September is the month of the* **Cheval & Patrimoine**, *with many events from racing, costumed parades and the* **Fête du Cheval** *horse show, which attracts equestrian fans from around the world.*

Donkey-Trekking

Ane en Forêt: 20 Allée de l'Ecureuil, St Fargeau Ponthierry, ☎ 01 64 09 91 37, www.ane-et-rando.com. Want to go hiking but don't want to carry all of your stuff? Pascal and Marie-Claud Bureau offer their docile donkeys for forest trekking (packs and kids only, up to 40 kilos/88lbs) from €50 for a day to €150 for two days with transport of overnight materials. Call at least a week in advance to reserve.

■ On the Water

The Loing River at Moret-sur-Loing is perfect for canoeing and rowing in small boats. For some scenic houseboating, head upriver to the village of St-Mammès, which sits at the fork in the river where the Loing splits off from the Seine. The shallow Loing splits off again to the Canal Loing, where a system of locks keeps the water level deep enough for houseboats and transporters to float all the way to the Mediterranean Sea.

Boat Rental

Bâteaux du Confluent: 6 Quai de Seine, St-Mammès, ☎ 01 64 23 25 59. Located just up the river from Moret-sur-Loing, this company offers self-drive houseboats, rented by the day or week (no permit needed, 10 passengers maximum). Open April to October, possibly other months if reserved. From €190/day to €732/week in summer. Also, low-horsepower motorboat rental with a maximum capacity of five to six passengers, available by the hour (from €30/hour). Open afternoons from May to September, and all day weekends and holidays. There's no web site, but the company is run by an Englishman and his bilingual wife, so don't be afraid to call for more info.

Seine et Loing Rivières: 1 Rue du Port de Valvins, Avon, ☎ 01 64 22 51 34. Self-drive houseboats, by the weekend or week (week minimum in July and August), no permit needed, accommodating from two to a maximum of 10 passengers. The houseboats are equipped with linen and kitchen utensils. Bike rental possible as well. From €400/weekend.

L'Armada du Loing: 23 Route de St-Mammès, Moret-sur-Loing, ☎ 06 07 21 38 15. Motorboat rental by the hour, no permit needed. Open daily April to October, 10am to 7pm (also by reservation).

Top Loisirs: 16 Rue Sylvain Colinet, Fontainebleau, ☎ 01 60 74 08 50, www.toploisirs.fr. This company provides canoes and kayaks for un-guided or guided paddling down the Loing from Grez-sur-Loing or La Genevraye to Moret-sur-Loing for a day (€50 per canoe, €26 per kayak) or half-day (€35/canoe, €18/kayak), with return shuttle. From May to September.

Escale Forme Canoë-Kayak: ☎ 01 60 70 90 77 or 06 70 07 16 79. You can rent these hybrid canoe-kayaks for €50/day, or €35/half-day, for a guided or independent ride down the Loing from Grez and Montigny to Moret-sur-Loing.

O'Vive Canoë: 8 Rue Ernest Bouquot, Moret-sur-Loing, ☎ 06 86 83 88 76. Canoe trips in a group for the day (€18) or half-day (€15). A shuttle takes passengers from Moret-sur-Loing to the starting point in Grez or Montigny. Safety equipment provided, passengers need to bring sturdy shoes that can get wet, and a change of clothing in case you go in. Call to reserve.

Le Loing en Barque: Dinghy (*barque*) rental on weekends only, mid-June through September, from the banks of the Loing River at Moret-sur-Loing. For more information contact the tourism office, ☎ 01 60 70 41 66.

Promenade en Barque à l'Etang aux Carpes: Château de Fontainebleau, ☎ 01 60 66 43 21 or 06 81 50 09 20. Float around in a small wooden rowboat on the calm lake at the Château de Fontainebleau and get a close-up view of the giant carp colony. €9/half-hour, €15/hour, four people max in each boat. Open daily (except Tuesday), May through September from 2 to 6pm (7pm in summer).

Sightseeing Cruise

Larguez Les Amarres – Bâteau *Renoir*: 5 Quai du Loing, St-Mammès, ☎ 01 64 23 16 24 or 06 87 75 41 18, www.saint-mammes.com. Three-hour guided tours of the villages along the Seine and Loing Canal, with refreshments. €20 (€10 for children under 12). Every Sunday at 3pm, April to October, reservations necessary.

Swimming

Léz'Art Café: Route de la Bonne Dame, Fontainebleau (just up the hill above the Avon-Fontainebleau train station), ☎ 01 64 22 38 14, www.lezart-cafe.fr. A large outdoor diving pool in a tropical-island setting, with a bar, restaurant and lounge chairs. There are also circus activities (minimum age five years) such as the flying trapeze, "tree-walking" using harnesses and pulleys, and a giant trampoline (with harness). At night there is dancing and music (sometimes live shows) from 11pm. Pool entrance €6-€10, trapeze class €23, tree-walking €21. Free parking from 7pm to 1am. Lunch menus from €12.

Bois le Roi: *Base de Pleine Air*, Rue de Tournay, Bois-le-Roi, ☎ 01 64 81 33 00. This leisure park has a sandy beach with an area for swimming. There's also beach volleyball, golf driving range, walking and cycling trails, picnic areas and snack bar. There's no fee to enter, but it gets unbearably crowded in August. Open all year.

Fishing

 Fishing is permitted in the **Grand Canal** inside the château park (not the Etang aux Carpes in the gardens). Simply set up your line and purchase a permit (*carte de pêche*) from the park guard when he comes around. Get more information on local fishing, permits and a large selection of equipment at **JM Sporting Pêche** (Butte Montceau Commercial Center in Avon, just past the train station, open daily, ☎ 01 64 22 93 80).

Carp, black bass, perch and rainbow trout are just a few of the species of fish in the **Loing River**. Permits, info, equipment and bait can be purchased at fishing shops in St-Mammès (**Coupery**, 44 Quai de Seine, ☎ 01 60 74 44 27) and in Moret-sur-Loing (**Crucifix**, 15 Rue de l'Eglise, ☎ 01 60 70 55 31).

■ On Wheels

 There are over 700 miles of cycling trails in the Fontainebleau forests (designated with green trail markers). Don't go off-trail or onto trails reserved for hikers or horse riders. The ONF and tourism offices can provide detailed maps with cycling itineraries, including the *Tour du Massif en Velo*, which covers all of the main cycling sites in the forest on two looping 30-mile trails, and the Fontainebleau-Barbizon loop.

The tourism office in Fontainebleau can indicate places around Fontainebleau (you'll need a good map) where the forest trails are flat and paved (but closed to traffic), perfect for easy walking with baby strollers, wheelchairs, skates, or light cycling. In French, these trails are called *routes goudronnées*.

The **Barbizon-Fontainebleau Trail** (aka *le FB*) is a popular five-mile signposted cycle trail through the forest between Barbizon and Fontainebleau. You can pick up and drop off rental all-terrain bikes (VTT) at either town's tourism office. Get the map at the tourism office in Fontainebleau. It's in French, but easy to follow.

Guided Bike Tours

Profil Evasion (☎ 01 69 68 04 33, www.profil-evasion.com) offers guided bike tours for all ages in the Gâtinas Forest (Milly-la-Forêt) or Fontainebleau Forest. Two-hour rides cost €13, including bike and licensed guide plus insurance. VTT (mountain bike) lessons are also available. Call for the schedule and meeting places.

The **Association des Amis de la Forêt de Fontainebleau – AAFF** (☎ 01 60 72 08 72, www.aaff.org) organizes free half-day cycling outings in Fontainebleau (except in the winter), always in French, but visitors are welcome. Call or check the web site for the schedule.

> **AUTHOR'S NOTE:** *See the* Getting Around *section of this chapter, page 364, for local bike rental companies.*

Horse-drawn Carriages

Les Attelages de la Forêt de Fontainebleau: 66 Rue Gambetta, Avon, ☎ 01 64 22 92 61 or 06 81 50 09 20. This company offers carriage rides by the hour or for a whole day, with the option of a forest picnic. They also do daily tours in the Fontainebleau Château Park from Easter until November, every 15 minutes from 10:30am to 1pm and 2:30 to 5pm, at the Porte Dorée. €4 per person.

■ In the Air

The **Relais du Couvent** (☎ 01 64 38 75 15, fax 01 64 38 75 75, www.lafermeducouvent.com) offers hot-air balloon and helicopter tours of the region, including over Vaux-le-Vicomte. Open all year, weather permitting. From €160 per person.

France Montgolfières (www.franceballoons.com) organizes hot-air balloon trips from Moret-sur-Loing for €165 on weekdays, €380 for couples any day of the week (€145 for ages six to 12 years old).

Where to Shop

■ Fontainebleau

The best shopping street in Fontainebleau is the **Grande Rue**. There are a number of clothing and gift shops, as well as a **Monoprix** (grocery/department store) at #58, **Nicolas** wine shop at #108, and the **F. Cassel** chocolate boutique at #71. The prized local cheese, *Le Fontainebleau*, can be found at the **Barthélemy Fromager**, #92. It's also worth checking out the boutiques on the **Rue des Sablons**, and the **Reelbooks English Bookshop** at #9 Rue de Ferrare. There's an **open market** every Tuesday, Friday and Sunday morning at the Place de la République, with local food products, clothing and crafts.

■ Barbizon

Barbizon is well known for its art galleries (many are in the former studios of artists of the Barbizon school), and also has galleries offering contemporary art, antiques shops and gift boutiques, all along the main street, **Grande Rue**. Don't miss **La Forêt des Arts** at #16 (bookshop, art gallery, tearoom), ☎ 01 60 69 24 63.

■ Milly-la-Forêt

In Milly-la-Forêt, all of the shops are at the **Place du Marché**. There's a mix of food shops, gift boutiques and *herboristes* (selling local aromatic and medicinal herbs) such as **L'Herbier de Milly** and **Millymenthe**, specializing in peppermint and mint products since 1934. Market day under the historic Halles is every Thursday afternoon, with an antiques fair every second Sunday from March through November.

Where to Eat

RESTAURANT PRICE SCALE
The following price scale represents the cost of an average meal for one person, not including drinks.
€ . . . . Under €15
€€ . . . . €16-€25
€€€ . . . . €26-€40
€€€€ . . . . €41-€60
€€€€€ . . . . over €60

Outside Paris

■ Fontainebleau

 La Petite Alsace: 26 Rue Ferrare, ☎ 01 64 23 45 45. Alsatian specialties (€€). Open daily for lunch and dinner. This friendly restaurant serves regional dishes, such as sauerkraut and pork. Lunch menus from €10.

Au Bureau: 12 Rue Grande, ☎ 01 60 39 00 01. Family restaurant/pub (€-€€). Open daily, non-stop, 10am to 1am. This cozy pub and restaurant serves many American Tex-Mex specialties, *flammekeuchen*, and beers from around the world. A young and lively clientele usually arrive after dark for the DJs and live music. Air conditioning and comfy booths.

Le Montijo: 27 Place Napoleon Bonaparte (next to the Aigle Noir Hôtel), ☎ 01 60 74 60 54. Bar/café (€-€€). Open daily, 11:30am to 1am. This elegant, low-lit cocktail bar with glassed-in terrace seating serves light meals and a large selection of beverages and cocktails. Occasional live piano music.

Croquembouche: 43 Rue France, ☎ 01 64 22 01 57. Traditional French (€€-€€€). Open for lunch Friday through Tuesday, dinner Monday, Tuesday, and Thursday through Saturday. Closed August. Fresh, gourmet French cuisine served in a laid-back dining room decorated in pastel fabrics. Popular with the local business school students.

Le Caveau des Ducs: 26 Rue Ferrare, ☎ 01 64 22 05 05. Traditional French (€€€). Open daily for lunch and dinner. Enjoy traditional French gourmet cuisine in a 17th-century stone vaulted dining room decorated with tapestries and heavy oak tables, or outside on the summer terrace. There's a good "all inclusive" weekday lunch *menu* for €29.

Beauharnais: 27 Place Napoleon Bonaparte (in the Hôtel de l'Aigle Noir), ☎ 01 60 74 60 00. Fine dining (€€€€-€€€€€) Open Wednesday through Sunday for dinner, lunch on Sunday only. Closed three weeks in August and the last week in December. This elegant restaurant is considered one of the best in Fontainebleau, with contemporary French cuisine and a large wine cellar. The dining room is decorated in Empire style with beautiful frescoes on the walls. Brunch is served on Sunday afternoons.

■ Barbizon

L'Ermitage St-Antoine: 51 Grande Rue, ☎ 01 64 81 96 96. Bistro/wine bar (€). Open Wednesday through Sunday for lunch and dinner. This lovely bistro has delicious, simple cuisine served in either the cozy dining room with paintings decorating the wooden walls, or in the renovated stone and glass room that opens up to an interior courtyard. There's also a vaulted stone cellar where films are shown at night.

L'Orée du Bois: 5 Grande Rue (in the Hostellerie de la Dague), ☎ 01 60 66 40 49, www.ladague.com. Traditional French (€€€). Open for lunch and dinner. This cozy restaurant serves traditional French cuisine in a laid-back dining room with a winter fireplace, or on the flowered terrace in summer.

Hôtellerie du Bas-Bréau: 22 Grande Rue, ☎ 01 60 66 40 05, www.bas-breau.com. Classic fine dining (€€€€-€€€€€). The *haute cuisine* restaurant of this four-star hotel on the main street has a comfortable, almost rustic décor with a fireplace and a large, shady terrace for dining poolside in the summer. The cooking focuses on seasonal themes, with fresh fish and game, an extensive wine list, and a cheese menu that includes the local specialty, *La Fontainebleau*.

■ Moret-sur-Loing

Les Impressionistes: 47 Avenue Jean-Jaurès (in the Hostellerie du Cheval Noir), ☎ 01 60 70 80 20, www.chevalnoir77.com. Creative cuisine (€€€€). Open Wednesday through Sunday for lunch and dinner. Closed mid-July to mid-August. This inventive restaurant in an 18th-century coach house has a bright dining room and a fresh, contemporary menu.

Relais de Pont-Loup: 14 Rue Peintre Sisley, ☎ 01 60 70 43 05. Traditional French (€€€). Open Tuesday through Sunday afternoon. This charming restaurant just across the river from Moret-sur-Loing has an inviting dining room of brick walls, exposed wooden beams, fireplace and open grill. In the summer guests can dine in the garden terrace overlooking the river. Be sure to reserve in advance for weekends!

Where to Stay

ACCOMMODATIONS PRICE SCALE
The following price scale represents rates charged for a double room per night during high season, including taxes. Breakfast isn't included except where noted. All prices are quoted in euros. Credit cards accepted unless noted.
€ . . . . Under €70
€€. . . . . €71-€100
€€€ . . . . €101-€150
€€€€ . . . . €151-€250
€€€€€. over €250

NOTE: *To dial French telephone/fax numbers from abroad, drop the "0" and add the country code, "33."*

■ Hotels & Inns

Fontainebleau

 Hôtel Victoria: 112 Rue de France, ☎ 01 60 74 90 00, fax 01 60 74 90 10, www.hotelvictoria.com (€). This simple but charming hotel dating back to the early 19th century (George Sand and Alfred de Musset were once guests), has 20 rooms with satellite TV, direct-dial telephone, and private bathroom. A few have parquet floors and fireplace mantels. The hotel also offers private parking, a garden terrace, and bar.

Hôtel de Londres: 1 Place Général de Gaulle, ☎ 01 64 22 20 21, fax 01 60 72 39 16, www.hoteldelondres.com (€€-€€€). This charming hotel in a historic townhouse has just 11 rooms of different sizes, each elegantly decorated and soundproofed, with satellite TV, telephone, and private bathroom. Some rooms have views of the château. See the photos of each room on the web site. There's no restaurant, but the hotel has a comfortable lobby lounge, bar and private parking.

Hôtel Napoleon: 9 Rue Grande, ☎ 01 60 39 50 50, fax 01 64 22 20 87, www.hotelnapoleon-fontainebleau.com (€€€). A former 19th-century post house near the château with 57 rooms overlooking an interior garden, each decorated in simple, refined fabrics and dark wood furnishings. All are equipped with a private bathroom, hairdryer, telephone, satellite TV with video and minibar. The hotel also provides 24-hour room service, private parking, laundry service, an Internet station, safe-deposit box, and gourmet restaurant, La Table des Maréchaux.

Grand Hôtel de l'Aigle Noir: 27 Place Napoleon Bonaparte, ☎/fax 01 60 74 60 00, www.hotelaiglenoir.fr (€€€€). This historic hotel in a former private mansion across from the château has just 56 rooms, each personalized with different fabrics and period furnishings, private bathroom, satellite TV, direct-dial phone and air conditioning. The hotel has all of the services that you would expect with its four-star status: private car park, elevator, indoor swimming pool, sauna, fitness center, garden terrace, *haute cuisine* restaurant and bar.

Barbizon

Auberge Les Alouettes: 4 Rue Antoine Barye, ☎ 01 60 66 41 98, www.barbizon.net (€). This small hotel, one of the least expensive in Barbizon, has 22 simple but comfortable rooms with private bathroom (bath or shower), cable TV and telephone. The hotel, set in a leafy garden, has private parking, a gourmet restaurant, bar and a huge outdoor terrace.

Hostellerie de la Dague: 5 Grande Rue, ☎ 01 60 66 40 49, fax 01 60 69 24 59, www.ladague.com (€-€€). A three-star hotel in a quaint manor house in the center of Barbizon with 25 rooms, all decorated with wicker furnishings, striped wallpaper and floral fabrics, and equipped with TV, phone, and private bathroom (shower or bath). The hotel also has a gourmet restaurant, bar with terrace, private parking, and garden. Quads with bath available for €105.

Hôtellerie du Bas-Bréau: 22 Grande Rue, ☎ 01 60 66 40 05, fax 01 60 69 22 89, www.bas-breau.com (€€€€). This four-star *Relais et Châteaux* hotel on the main street in Barbizon has 20 elegant rooms, each decorated in pale colors, discreet floral fabrics, and period furnishings, with air conditioning, private bathroom, satellite TV and direct-dial phone with modem jack. Many of the rooms are in a second building in the hotel's garden (a park, really). The hotel also has a cozy lounge with fireplace and exposed wooden beam ceilings, haute cuisine restaurant, outdoor pool, tennis court and garden terrace. *Treasure Island* author Robert Louis Stevenson stayed here in 1875 while writing his *Forest Notes*.

Moret-sur-Loing

Auberge de la Terrasse: 40 Rue due la Pêcherie, ☎ 01 60 70 51 03, fax 01 60 70 51 69, aubergedelaterrasse@wanadoo.fr (€). The Auberge is a charming hotel overlooking the Loing River. It has 17 rooms, with country-style décor and private bathroom, TV, and telephone. There's a traditional French restaurant with fireplace, and a large terrace facing the river. Closed for one week in February and two weeks in late October.

Hostellerie du Cheval Noir: 47 Avenue Jean-Jaurès, ☎ 01 60 70 80 20, fax 01 60 70 80 21, www.chevalnoir77.com (€€). This former coach house has just eight rooms with private bathroom, satellite TV and telephone. Rooms are comfortable, decorated with an Impressionist painters theme, some with exposed wooden beams. The hotel also has a bright, light-filled restaurant and breakfast room overlooking the garden. Closed for two weeks in August.

■ Bed & Breakfast

 Gîtes de France (www.gites-seine-et-marne.com) has listings for *chambres d'hôtes* (bed & breakfasts), self-catering cottages and farm campsites in the Fontainebleau area. The bilingual web site is searchable by location, number of guests and ratings (ears of corn instead of stars). Typical bed & breakfast accommodation for a couple costs €50. Visitors can also contact specific tourism offices for information on local chambres d'hôtes in Fontainebleau, Moret-sur-Loing, Milly-la-Forêt and Barbizon.

■ Camping

 Camping Les Courtilles du Lido: Chemin du Passeur, Veneux-les-Sablon, ☎ 01 60 70 46 05. No credit cards. This campsite is situated between Fontainebleau and Moret-sur-Loing. It has a bar, pizzeria, TV, hot/cold showers, small pool and playground. Also tennis and mini-golf (for a small fee).

Camping La Belle Etoile La Rochette, ☎ 01 64 39 48 12, www.camp-la-belle-etoile.com. This campsite just south of Melun (on the Seine) is grassy, but lacks shade in high summer. There's a large playground, small swimming pool, café and shop. You can bring a tent or rent a bungalow or tented pavilion (€67-€77, sleeps six). Not within walking distance of anything. Follow camping signs from La Rochette.

Entertainment

Check with the **Fontainebleau Tourism Office** (☎ 01 60 74 99 99, www.fontainebleau-tourisme.com) for the current schedule of shows, concerts, races and other events during your stay.

■ Nightlife

Fontainebleau has a relatively lively nightlife scene compared to most Ile-de-France towns outside Paris, frequented by a large grad-student population. There are about two dozen music bars, cocktail lounges and pubs along the Rue Grande and its side-streets. Three of the more popular nightspots include the chic lounge/bar **La Villa** (10 Rue Montebello, ☎ 01 60 72 04 05), the gay disco bar/club **Le Diam's** (7 Rue Denecourt, ☎ 01 64 22 83 53), with a friendly, mixed clientele, and the British-style beer pub **Au Bureau** (12 Rue Grande, ☎ 01 60 39 00 01), with regular DJs and live music.

There are regular shows and concerts at Fontainebleau's two local theaters, **La Halle de Villars** (☎ 01 64 22 26 91) and the **Théâtre des Sablons** (☎ 01 64 22 97 39), as well as two cinemas, **L'Ermitage** (6 Rue de France, ☎ 08 36 68 69 22) and **Le Sélect** (23 Place Napoleon Bonaparte, ☎ 01 64 22 28 18).

■ Sporting Events

Equestrian fans have a choice of watching the races at **the Hippodrome de la Solle** (Route de Melun, ☎ 01 64 22 29 37), entrance €4.50, free for children under 16, or watching one of the prestigious annual horse shows at the historic **Parc Equestre du Grand Parquet** (RN152, Route d'Orléans, ☎ 01 64 23 42 87).

Haute Vallée de Chevreuse

Overview

Just an hour southwest of Paris is one of the more bucolic regional parks in Ile-de-France, the Haute Vallée de Chevreuse. One of the best-kept secrets of Parisian weekenders, this rural countryside features vast forests full of wildlife and cycling trails, with picturesque villages, historic châteaux, and rustic farms selling fresh regional products. Nearby is the elegant town of **Rambouillet**, with its presidential château, historic royal forest and wildlife preserve. With fewer foreign visitors than Fontainebleau, this peaceful region steeped in history is the perfect place to combine cultural sightseeing with outdoor adventure.

Planning Your Trip

■ When To Go

 Public transportation links facilitate quick day-trips from Paris, but it's worth staying a night or two in one of the charming inns to get the most out of your visit. Like much of Ile-de-France, the Haute Vallée de Chevreuse is at its best between April and October. Many of the country châteaux are closed in winter, and the damp forest trails lose much of their charm. Rambouillet is an exception; it is lively throughout the year, and even small villages usually have holiday markets and cultural events in the colder months.

Spring events include the March **Tonte des Moutons Mérinos** (sheep shearing festival), the April **Salon des Antiquaires** (antiques fair), and the May **Fête des Jardins & Grand Marché Fermier** (an annual farm and garden festival and food market). In June local farmers throughout the Haute Vallée de Chevreuse open their doors to the public for the **Fête des Fermes**. October is a busy month, with the annual **Salon National d'Art** art fair in Rambouillet, the **Rallye Pédestre** 7.5-mile walk from Senlisse to a festival in Dampierre-en-Yvelines, and the **Quinzaine Gastronomique d'Automne**, when the region's restaurants feature special hunting-themed menus of local game. No matter when you visit, it's always a good idea to call local tourism offices in advance to confirm opening hours and check for any unexpected closures.

■ Tourism Offices

i **Maison du Parc Naturel Régional**: Château de la Madeleine, Chemin Jean Racine, Chevreuse, ☎ 01 30 52 09 09, fax 01 30 52 12 43, www.parcnaturel-chevreuse.org. This office inside the historic **Château de la Madeleine** provides information for the entire Haute Vallée de Chevreuse, including hiking maps, guide books, hotel and camping listings, and local event information. Ask for the English information booklet, usually kept behind the desk. Open Monday through Friday, 2 to 5:30pm; Saturday, 2 to 6pm; Sunday and holidays, 10am to 5:30pm.

Rambouillet Tourism Office: Place de la Libération, Rambouillet, ☎/fax 01 34 83 21 21, www.ot-rambouillet.fr. This office has free guides, detailed maps, and information on the lively town as well as the surrounding areas and the regional park. Open daily, 9:30am to noon and 2:30 to 5:30pm (until 6pm in July and August).

Outside Paris

Tourism Office of the Yvelines Département: Hôtel du Département, 2 Place André-Mignot, Versailles, ☎ 01 39 07 71 22, fax 01 39 07 85 05, www.cg78.fr. This regional tourism office can provide information for the entire Yvelines département, including Versailles. Free brochures can be ordered from the web site (look under the "Rubrique Tourisme" for the English version of the site).

Chevreuse Tourism Office: 12 Place des Luynes, Chevreuse, ☎/fax 01 30 52 02 27, www.ville-chevreuse.fr. Chevreuse is one of the small villages in the Haut Vallée de Chevreuse, and home to the Maison du Parc Naturel Régional. This small tourism office can provide maps and accommodation information, and an audio guide for local sightseeing. The web site is in French only, so call for assistance in English. Limited opening hours: Wednesday and Saturday, 10am to noon and 2 to 5pm; and Sunday, 10am to noon.

St-Rémy-lès-Chevreuse Tourism Office: 1 Rue Ditte, St-Rémy-les-Chevreuse, ☎ 01 30 52 22 49, www.saintremyleschevreusetourisme.com. An RER station is located in this large village on the edge of the forest. The tourism office can provide information on hotels, restaurants and forest trails, as well as transportation links to Rambouillet and other villages in the regional park. Open Wednesday and Saturday, 9am to 12:45pm and 1:30 to 3:45pm; Sunday and holidays, 10am to 12:45pm and 1:30 to 4:45pm.

Dampierre Tourism Office: Hôtel de Ville, Dampierre-en-Yvelines, ☎ 01 30 52 57 30. This small village dominated by the Château de Dampierre has a few inns and hiking trails. The tourism information office is open limited hours from April to October, weekends and holidays 10am to 1pm.

A WORD TO
THE WISE

AUTHOR'S NOTE: *The new urban center of* ***St-Quentin-en-Yvelines****, set between the motorway and the regional park, is an ugly blot on the landscape and holds no interest for visitors to this region. Try to avoid it.*

■ Emergency Numbers

General Emergency (toll-free) . . . . ☎ 112
Rambouillet Police Station . . . . ☎ 01 30 46 27 54
Gendarmerie. . . . . ☎ 01 34 83 87 81
SOS Médecin. . . . . ☎ 01 43 37 77 77

Getting Here

■ By Train

RER

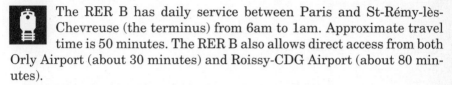 The RER B has daily service between Paris and St-Rémy-lès-Chevreuse (the terminus) from 6am to 1am. Approximate travel time is 50 minutes. The RER B also allows direct access from both Orly Airport (about 30 minutes) and Roissy-CDG Airport (about 80 minutes).

Transilien

The Transilien regional train (SNCF) has a daily service between the Gare de Montparnasse in Paris and Rambouillet (direction Chartres) 5:30am to 12:30am (4:30am to 11:45pm toward Paris). One-way tickets cost €6.40. Travel time is approximately 50 minutes. Gare de Rambouillet, ☎ 01 34 83 84 45.

TRAVEL OPTIONS

Other stations in the area include **SNCF Gare de la Verrière** and **RER Gare de St-Quentin-en-Yvelines**, which have links to the RER and regional buses, but no direct service to Paris, so expect to make one or more transfers at other stations along the way.

■ By Bus

Anyone desperate to get to the airport or Paris once trains and RERs have stopped running can try the **Bus de Nuit Line 2** (www.busdenuit.com), which runs nightly between Gare de la Verrière and Paris (change buses at Châtelet to reach both airports) from 12:30am to 3:40am. Tickets cost €6, and approximate travel time is 80 minutes.

■ By Car

The Haute Vallée de Chevreuse is about 30 miles southwest of Paris. To go directly to Rambouillet, take the A13 from Porte St-Cloud to A12/N12, then turn down the D191 to join the N10 (this avoids the ugly industrial towns). Travel time is about 55 minutes depending on the traffic. To go directly to St-Rémy-lès-Chevreuse, exit the

Outside Paris

A12 at the "Parc Naturel Régional" and follow the D58 and D13, toward Chevreuse.

From Orly Airport take the A6 to the A10, exit "Orsay," and follow the RN188, D95, and the D906. From Versailles take the D91 (direction Dampierre) or the D938 (direction Châteaufort).

■ By Taxi

A taxi ride to Rambouillet from central Paris will typically cost €75 (during the day, in regular traffic).

Getting Around

The villages of the Haute Vallée de Chevreuse are pretty easy to explore by car, bike or bus. Forest trailheads are within a short walking distance of train stations. Visitors to Rambouillet can get around to the major sights within the town on foot or using the local bus network. A good map (such as the Michelin 106 Environs de Paris 1/100,000), available at any news agent's shop or gas station, shows all of the smaller routes and shortcuts through forest roads.

■ By Bus

The **Baladobus** (☎ 01 30 52 09 09, www.parc-naturel-chevreuse.org) sightseeing shuttle operates every Sunday from May through mid-October, going in a continuous loop between public transport stations and major sites, including the RER St-Rémy-lès-Chevreuse, SNCF Gare de la Verrière, Château Dampierre, Abbaye de Cernay, Chevreuse, Château de Breteuil, Granges de Port-Royal, and the Château de la Madeleine. Tickets cost €3.50, €2 for children and students.

The **R Bus** (☎ 01 30 59 84 33, www.monbus.com) operates several lines within Rambouillet from the SNCF station. Bus 71 gets closest to the Espace Rambouillet, and Bus 74 goes past the château and tourism office on the main street. The buses accept the same RATP tickets used in Paris (€1.30 each), or transportation passes for zone 5.

SAVAC (☎ 01 30 52 45 00, www.savac.fr) operates several bus lines from the Gare de St-Rémy-lès-Chevreuse to Rambouillet (line 039-303), Versailles (line 262-01), or the Gare de la Verrière (line 039-017). Service is limited, mostly weekdays 7am to 7pm. The buses accept the same RATP tickets used in Paris (€1.30 each), or transportation passes for zone 5.

■ By Bike

Sporty types can take advantage of the many forest and roadside cycle paths by renting a bicycle from one of the local agencies or bring one down on the train from Paris. It's about 22 miles round-trip (on the relatively flat D906) between the two farthest towns in this section, Rambouillet and St-Rémy-lès-Chevreuse. Don't forget that bikes are not allowed on the bus.

Bike Rental

Loca Cycles: Maison Forestière de la Porte de Saint-Léger, Rambouillet, ☎ 01 34 86 84 54 or 06 07 64 15 87, www.locacycles.com. Mountain bikes and cruisers are €4.40/hour or €15.40 for a full-day rental. Children's bikes and infant seats are available. The Maison Forestière is just to the north of Rambouillet off the D936 (direction Houdan/St Léger), or, when coming into town from the N10, exit at Poigny la Forêt and turn right at each intersection until you arrive. Open weekends, 9am to 7pm, March through October.

Loisirs VTT: 1 Sente de la Brèche, Dampierre-en-Yvelines, ☎ 01 30 52 56 40, www.loisirs-VTT.com. Mountain bike rentals from €6/hour to €19/day. Possibility of delivery to St-Rémy-lès-Chevreuse station. Open weekends all year, reservations recommended. Maps provided.

Location de Cycles Vautrin: Etangs de Hollande, St-Léger-en-Yvelines, ☎ 01 34 86 33 30. Bikes for kids and adults can be rented at the *Base de Loisirs* for cycling around the large lake, Etangs de Hollande.

■ By Car

Traveling by car offers the most freedom in this region, and the country roads are quite enjoyable to navigate. Parking is usually not too difficult, and even Rambouillet has several free parking areas in the town center. Cars can be rented in Paris, at both airports, or in Rambouillet.

Car Rental

- **Avis:** Massoutre Location, 4 Place de la Gare, Rambouillet, ☎ 01 34 83 35 36
- **Europcar:** Continentale Auto, 122 Rue Claire Fontaine, Rambouillet, ☎ 01 30 59 24 70
- **Hertz:** Sopres, 75 Rue Sadi Carnot, Rambouillet, ☎ 01 34 83 15 08

■ By Taxi

Taxis can be found outside any train or RER station. Most of these local taxis will go to Paris and both airports, and accept credit cards (ask about American Express). Always ask for a general quote (*un dévis*) on the price before going outside town.

Rambouillet . . . . ☎ 06 08 71 92 04 or 06 09 22 82 77

St-Rémy-lès-Chevreuse . . . . . . ☎ 06 11 27 20 00 or 01 30 52 59 88

Chevreuse . . . . ☎ 06 07 47 91 10

Taxi Bleu (all Ile-de-France) . . . . ☎ 08 25 16 66 66

History & Sightseeing

■ La Haute Vallée de Chevreuse

This region, with its aristocratic châteaux, ancient churches, and vast forests that were once the favorite hunting grounds of the French sovereigns, has always been a prestigious and highly coveted region of Ile-de-France. With its proximity to Paris and convenient public transport links, the Haute Vallée de Chevreuse began attracting an urban exodus of daily commuters. To protect its rural heritage of forests, farms and small villages from modern overdevelopment, the **Parc Naturel Régional de la Haute Vallée de Chevreuse** was created in 1985.

Today the park has over 71,000 acres of protected forests, wetlands, farms and rural villages, with 150 miles of newly created trails and carefully restored historic monuments to welcome visitors. Foreign tourists have been slow to discover the many historic and natural sights of the region, but there's much to see and do. Avoid the mistake of seeing this area as just a collection of historic monuments and forests. The Haute Vallée de Chevreuse is also an area rich in agricultural tradition, with lively country festivals and local farms where visitors can sample homemade cheeses and cured meats. So enjoy the sightseeing suggestions in this guide, but don't be afraid to go off the beaten trail (map in hand, of course) to discover the region's many hidden treasures and simple delights.

MONEY-SAVING TIP

Anyone planning on visiting more than one château or site in the area should pick up one of the free multi-site brochures. The *Route Historique du Roy Soleil* pass includes the châteaux at Rambouillet, Breteuil, Dampierre and Maintenon, and the *Carte Multi-Site Rambouillet* includes La Bergerie Nationale, the Château de Rambouillet, La Laiterie, L'Espace Rambouillet, the Musée Rambolitrain, the Palais du Roi de Rome, and the Musée du Jeu de l'Oie. Get the brochure stamped at the first location you visit and you'll receive discounts on admission at each subsequent site, and free entry for children. For more information, contact the Rambouillet Tourism Office, ☎ 01 34 83 21 21.

AUTHOR'S NOTE: *Because this region remains relatively undiscovered by foreign tourists, many of the major sights and tourism offices have limited opening hours and very little information in English. This is likely to change as more independent travelers venture into the region, but until then trailblazers can enjoy the cultural immersion!*

Chevreuse

Begin your visit in Chevreuse, a prosperous medieval village formerly protected by the bishops of Paris and known for its tanneries and popular fairs. The town has many ancient buildings, including the 10th-century **Prieuré de St-Saturnin** and the 12th-century **Eglise St-Martin**, which has a Cliquot organ dating back to Louis XIV's reign. Have a stroll along the charming **Chemin des Petits Ponts**, which gets its name from the tiny bridges connecting a row of back gardens to the ancient mills and wash houses along the left bank of the Yvette Canal.

Head up the hill to the imposing ruins of the **Château de la Madeleine** (Chevreuse, ☎ 01 30 52 09 09), a towering fortress that has overlooked the Chevreuse Valley since the 11th century. It was modified several times over five hundred years by successive lords, and heavily fortified after falling into English hands during the Hundred Years' War. It was eventually abandoned in the 17th century by the Duc de Luynes, who moved into more comfortable quarters in the Château de Dampierre. The sisters of St-Cyr then occupied the château until the Revolution, when it eventually fell into ruin. Purchased by the Yvelines département in 1981, the Château de la Madeleine is currently undergoing extensive renovations, so only a small part of the interior is open to the public. But it's worth the steep climb for the panoramic views. Stop by the **Maison de la Parc** offices inside the château to pick up maps and information about the regional park (ask for the English brochure if you don't see it). Open Monday to Saturday, 2pm-5:30pm; Sunday and holidays, 10am-5:30pm.

Port-Royal-des-Champs

Just to the north of Chevreuse is the **Abbaye de Port-Royal-des-Champs** (☎ 01 30 43 74 93, D91, Magny-les-Hameaux), which played an important role in French religious and philosophical history as one of the major centers of Jansenism in the 17th century. The writer Jean Racine, cousin of the Duc de Luynes, studied Greek and Roman classics with the *Solitaires* of the abbey for four years, until Louis XIV, who was against the Jansenist teachings, had the small school closed in 1660, and the abbey completely razed in 1709. Visitors can stroll the 24 acres of peaceful abbey grounds, climb the 100 stairs (*Cent Marches*) up to the Granges Plateau, or pay respects at Racine's original resting place (he was reburied in the Eglise St-Etienne-du-Mont, Paris). Open daily except Tuesday from 2 to

5pm, Sundays from 11am to noon and 2 to 5pm. Entrance €3, €2.30 for students, free for kids under 18.

LITERARY TRAIL

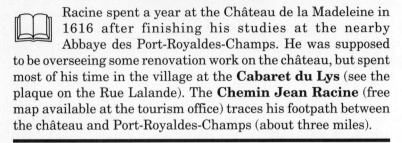 Racine spent a year at the Château de la Madeleine in 1616 after finishing his studies at the nearby Abbaye des Port-Royaldes-Champs. He was supposed to be overseeing some renovation work on the château, but spent most of his time in the village at the **Cabaret du Lys** (see the plaque on the Rue Lalande). The **Chemin Jean Racine** (free map available at the tourism office) traces his footpath between the château and Port-Royaldes-Champs (about three miles).

Those who want to find out more about the controversial Jansenists can also visit the **Musée National des Granges de Port-Royal** (☎ 01 39 30 72 72) on the other side of the abbey's grounds. The museum is inside the "Petites Ecoles" where the Solitaires used to teach their classes, and features religious paintings, ancient books and portraits of the leading Jansenists of the time, including Pascal, who spent much of his time at Port-Royal. Open March 15 to November 9, daily except Tuesday, 10:30am to 6:30pm. Open in winter (except December holidays) on weekends only, 10:30am to 6pm. Entrance €3, €2.30 for students, free for kids under 18. Visit to the gardens only, €1.

Dampierre-en-Yvelines

South of the Abbey on the D91 is the tiny village of Dampierre-en-Yvelines, dominated by the Mansart-designed **Château de Dampierre** (☎ 01 30 52 53 24), built in the 17th century for the Duc de Luynes and still inhabited by his descendents. The interior has a few well-preserved architectural features and sculptures, with intricately carved woodwork and a mural by the painter Ingres representing the Golden Age. The château sits smack in the middle of parklands and formal gardens designed by the prolific Le Nôtre, with a lake, Grand Canal, and tiny islands set throughout the waterways. Open daily from April 1 to October 15, 2 to 6:30pm (park open 11am to 6:30pm). Entry to the park and château costs €9.50, €7.50 for students. Entrance to the park and gardens only is €6, €4.50 for students (picnics allowed). There is also a gourmet restaurant, **Les Ecuries du Château** (closed in August, see page 408 for details), in the château's former stables.

> **TIP:** *Climb up the hill across the street from the château gates for a free bird's eye view of the estate and its gardens.*

Château de Breteuil

Set in the middle of farmlands four miles south of Chevreuse, the château (in Choisel, off the D906, ☎ 01 30 52 05 02, www.castle-france.com) is the isolated but charming estate of the aristocratic Breteuil family, who served the Kings of France as military officers, ambassadors and ministers throughout the 17th and 18th centuries. Built during the reign of Henri IV in the early 1600s, the Breteuil has hosted many prestigious guests, including the Empress Maria-Teresa, Gambetta, King Edward VII of England, and Marcel Proust. The château, empty for much of the 20th century, was renovated in the late 1960s by its current owner, the 10th Marquis de Breteuil. If you only visit one château in the region, this should be it. The décor is heavily influenced by Versailles, with waxwork characters recreating historical scenes in each room. Although this can feel a bit Disney-ish, it's well-done and gives the château a unique lived-in feel, as if the daily life was frozen at some point in the 18th century. The château can only be visited with the guide, in French, but there's an English brochure available on request. Visits start at 2:30pm (every 15 minutes), with the last tour at 5:30pm. Entrance for the château and grounds costs €9.90, €7.90 for students and kids.

There are 200 acres of parkland and formal gardens dotted with stables, carriage buildings and even a medieval pigeon tower. These are also brought to life by waxwork figures, including scenes from Charles Perrault's fairy tales (you'll recognize *Sleeping Beauty*, *Puss in Boots* and *Red Riding Hood*, among others). In addition to the formal hedges, rose gardens, fountains and labyrinth, there are also children's playgrounds and picnic areas, quiet forest paths, and even a family of goats grazing in the grassy moat. Entrance to the grounds only (open daily from 10am) costs €6.80, €5.40 for students and kids and also allows you into the château kitchens, where you can read what was on the menu for King Edward VII of England's visit in 1905. Plan on spending at least a half-day or longer at the château to see everything. A crêpe stand is open in the picnic area on Sundays from April through October. Pack a lunch if you come on any other day, since there are no cafés or shops nearby.

Abbaye des Vaux-de-Cernay

Cross back over the D906 on the D24 to the Abbaye des Vaux-de-Cernay (outside Cernay-la-Ville, ☎ 01 34 85 23 00, www.abbayedecernay.com), six miles west of Breteuil. This 12th-century abbey was one of the most important in Ile-de-France, with considerable support from the Pope and local lords. The monks cleared the land for cultivation, built canals and cloisters, and created one of the largest libraries in the country. The abbey was abandoned after the Revolution and used as a quarry until 1873, when the Baroness Nathaniel de Rothschild bought and restored the main buildings and part of the grounds. She also added the lodgings, which are now a four-star hotel. For a complete history of the abbey a

Outside Paris

38-page guide in English is available for €4.60 at the front desk. The grounds are open daily for visits from 9am to 5pm, €4 on weekends and holiday, free entrance on weekdays. Picnics are not allowed, but the hotel tearoom (open 3 to 6pm) has a €13 *formule*, which includes entry to the grounds. Modern additions include a second hotel (three-star) and gourmet restaurant.

■ Rambouillet

Much like Fontainebleau, the 20,000-acre **Forêt de Rambouillet** was one of the favorite royal hunting spots due to its abundant stocks of **wild boar**, **roe deer**, **stags** and **rabbits**. Although the Château de Rambouillet didn't become a royal residence until 1783, when it was acquired by Louis XVI, the estate regularly hosted French kings, including François I, who died in the tower during a hunting trip in 1547. The town developed significantly during the 18th century, with the construction of the **Mairie**, the **Palais du Roi de Rome**, the *Sous-Préfecture* (a regional administrative office), and the opening of the national sheep farm, the *Bergerie Nationale*. Other additions during the Second Empire and the 1920s contributed to the elegant architectural layout of the town center and parklands. Today Rambouillet has more of a chic, upscale atmosphere closer to that of Versailles than the villages of the Haute Vallée de Chevreuse, with the added cachet of being the official summer residence of the French presidents.

Hunting is no longer the main activity in the Forêt de Rambouillet, which now attracts hikers, riders, cyclists and nature lovers, and the forest critters continue to thrive. The **Espace Rambouillet** wildlife preserve offers a protected habitat to many species, including birds of prey such as falcons and eagles. And although Rambouillet is technically outside the Haute Vallée de Chevreuse Regional Park limits, they remain connected by dozens of cycle paths, *Grandes Randonnées* hiking trails, and tree-lined country roads.

All of the interesting sights in Rambouillet are on or just off the town's pleasant main street, **Rue du Général de Gaulle**. Given a face lift in the late 1990s, the street's wide sidewalks are lined with brasseries, gift boutiques, restaurants and real-estate agencies. Head to the Place de la Libération, a square (used as a parking lot) just outside the entrance to the château grounds. The tall building on the left is the **Hôtel de Ville** (Town Hall, www.rambouillet.fr), built in 1786 as a grain storage center and bailiff's courthouse. The façade is actually made out of stone and plastered to look like brick. Napoleon officially handed over the building to the local authorities in 1809, an event commemorated by a small inscription on the pediment.

Stop into the small tourism office next door to pick up local maps, sightseeing multi-site brochures, and information on current events taking place around town. Ask for the English brochure, *Rambouillet: From One Garden to Another*, for a self-guided, 90-minute walking tour of the town's main buildings and sites, with historical commentary.

> **TIP!** *Public toilets can be found around the corner from the tourism office.*

The Château

The Château de Rambouillet (☎ 01 34 83 00 25 or 01 34 94 28 79, www.monum.fr) was originally a manor house built in 1368 by the Provost of Paris. It was altered considerably as it passed through successive aristocratic hands, slowly being transformed from a medieval fortress into an impressive royal château. Some of the older architectural features remain, such as the 14th-century **François I Tower** where the king died in 1547. The hunting enthusiast Louis XVI spent more time at Rambouillet than any other monarch, making several changes to make the château more attractive to his wife, Marie Antoinette. The entire left wing of the château was demolished under Napoleon's over-enthusiastic renovations. It was here that he courted his second wife, Marie-Louise, the archduchess of Austria, and the balcony connecting his office to her bedroom still exists. In 1815 Napoleon signed his second and final abdication in the Château de Rambouillet after his defeat at Waterloo. The Restoration monarch, Charles X, signed his abdication in the same place 15 years later, and the château became state property under Napoleon III. It has been an official presidential residence since 1883, and has hosted several heads of state and international summits. The interior has an interesting Rococo and neo-Pompeian décor, with elaborate **Gobelins tapestries**, painted wall panels and a *Salle de Marbre* (marble room) dating back to the Renaissance. Those who have been to Malmaison or the Musée Napoleon at Fontainebleau may recognize the Emperor's personal decorating style in the *Cabinet de Bain*; the *Salle de Bain* of the Comte de Toulouse is covered in Delft faience tiles. The current presidential quarters are, for obvious reasons, closed to the public. Allow about an hour to visit the whole château. Open daily (except Tuesday), 10am to 11:30am and 2 to 5:30pm (until 4:30pm October to March); entry €5.50 (€4 with a stamped multi-site brochure), €3.50 for visitors 18-25, free for kids under 18. Museum Passes accepted.

A WORD TO
THE WISE

ATTENTION: *The Château de Rambouillet is closed to the public during presidential visits. These are usually only announced a day or two in advance, so it's best to call ahead to avoid disappointment.*

The Château Park

The vast château park is open to the public, and includes traditional formal fountains and hedges closest to the château, with a series of six grand canals and forested islands emanating outwards like a fan. Beyond the canals is a vast lawn called the **Tapis Vert,** where locals picnic and walk their dogs. The **Jardin Anglais** to the west is more relaxed, with a picturesque landscape of winding rivers and two charming 18th-century follies: **la Chaumière aux Coquillages** (shell cottage) is intricately covered on the inside with thousands of tiny shells and mother of pearl, and **la Laiterie de la Reine** (the queen's dairy), built for Marie Antoinette in the style of a classical temple, complete with marble statues and a man-made grotto. These are open daily (except Tuesday and during presidential visits) from 10am to noon and 2 to 5:30pm (until 3:30pm, October to March). Those planning on visiting the Laiterie and the Chaumière aux Coquillages in addition to the château should be sure to purchase a combined ticket for €6 (€5 with a stamped multi-site brochure), free for kids under 18.

The Village

Walk east along the Rue du Général de Gaulle to the **Palais du Roi de Rome** (on the Place du Roi de Rome). This once-grand palace was built by Napoleon in 1812 (significantly modifying the existing 18th-century mansion) for his son, the King of Rome. The young king, known as *l'Aiglon* (the Little Eagle), only spent a short time in the palace before his exile to Austria with his mother, Marie-Louise. The main part of the building no longer exists, and what remains has been split into two wings by the courtyard. The Rambouillet town council purchased one of the wings in 1989, and uses it today to host free temporary exhibitions (☎ 01 34 83 10 31). Don't miss the romantic garden hidden around the back, open daily, 2 to 8pm (until 5pm, October to March).

Specialty Museums

Rambouillet has three museums that appeal to kids (of all ages). At the far western edge of the château grounds is the **Bergerie Nationale** (☎ 01 61 08 68 00, www.bergerienationale.educagri.fr), a working farm built by Louis XVI, with cowsheds, stables, pigs, buffalos and the world-famous Rambouillet **Merino sheep**. Visitors can sample the fresh farm cheese, munch on lamb burgers in the snack bar, or learn about the history of sheep herding in the farm museum. Open Wednesday through Sunday and holidays, 2 to 5pm; entry €4.50, €3 for ages six to 12, free for kids under age six (reduced rates with a stamped multi-site brochure). Although the farm is in the château grounds, it's easier to reach by bicycle or car than through the park (from town turn left on Rue Raymond Poincaré; free parking).

Back in town, turn left off the main street toward the church to the **Musée Rambolitrain** (4 Place Jeanne d'Arc, Rambouillet, ☎ 01 34 83 15 93). This unique museum and garden features more than 4,000 miniature train models, many dating back to the 19th century, and over 1,300 feet of track. Open Wednesday through Sunday and holidays, 10am to noon and 2 to 5:30pm; entry €3.50, €2.50 for ages four to 12, free for kids under age four (€0.50 off with a stamped multi-site brochure).

Cross back over the Rue du Général de Gaulle to the **Musée du Jeu de l'Oie** (Place du Roi de Rome, Rambouillet, ☎ 01 30 88 73 73) a museum opened in 2001 featuring a collection of over 2,500 "Goose Games" (snakes-and-ladders-type board games) displayed in chronological order from the 17th century to the present. It's fascinating to see how board games in the past were not only entertaining, but beautifully crafted as well. A gaming room and kids' booklet add to the interactive aspect of the visit, but information in English is limited. Open Tuesday through Sunday, 2 to 6pm, entrance €3.50, €2.50 for ages four to 12 (€0.50 off with a stamped ulti-site brochure).

MONEY-SAVING TIP

Those who plan on visiting both the Musée du Jeu de l'Oie and the Musée Rambolitrain can get a combined entrance ticket for €4.50, or €3.50 with a stamped multi-site brochure (see page 394).

Adventures

■ On Foot

L'Espace Rambouillet

 Although the region's forests are teeming with wildlife, visitors are guaranteed a front row view at the Espace Rambouillet (Route de Clairefontaine, Rambouillet, ☎ 01 34 83 05 00, www.onf.fr/espaceramb/), a 615-acre wildlife preserve that allows visitors to observe deer and wild boar in a natural forest habitat. There are also over 100 birds of prey in aviaries, which are released throughout the day during scheduled flight demos. For smaller visitors there's a playground and pony rides (weekends April to October only). Dress for a forest hike, with backpack, hiking shoes and binoculars (you can rent these at the gift shop), pack a lunch to eat in the picnic area if you want to avoid the snack-bar food. Count on at least four hours for a full visit. All descriptions in French (but it's pretty obvious what everything is). Open daily, 9am to 6pm, April through October; and Tuesday through Sunday, 10am to 5pm, November through March. Closed mid-December through mid-January. Entrance €7.80, €6.20 for ages three to 12 (€1 off the regular fare with a stamped multi-site brochure).

TREE-WALKING

Randonnée Arbricole, or tree-walking, is offered through the **Aye-aye Club** (☎ 01 44 52 11 21, www.ayeaye.org) within the Espace Rambouillet (fee includes wildlife park entrance). Open to anyone in good health from eight years old and up, participants use a series of pulleys and climbing equipment to move through the forest canopy. Half-day initiation and tree-walk costs €55. Open weekends only, reservations necessary.

Hiking

There are over 27,000 acres of forest throughout the Haute Vallée de Chevreuse, and another 36,000 acres in the Fôret de Rambouillet, connected via the tree-lined D906. Hikers will find it easy to reach trails on foot from the RER station in St-Rémy-lès-Chevreuse, where many paths connect the small villages and sightseeing areas. Those who get off at the SNCF station in Rambouillet can reach the forest in about 15 minutes on foot (or get there faster with a local bus ride from the station). Casual hikers who don't want to venture too far into the forests can explore the vast park grounds of the Château de Rambouillet, Château de Breteuil, Abbaye de Port-Royal-des-Champs, or the Espace Rambouillet.

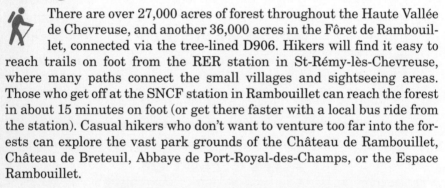

TIP: *Anyone planning on some serious hiking should purchase the TOP25 IGN series map* **2215-OT***, which shows even the smallest trails in the Forêt de Rambouillet and the regional park.*

There are many different types of trails in the region, including *Grandes Randonnées* (GR), which cross Ile-de-France; shorter *Petites Randonnées* (PR); and the regional circular hikes (PNR) that can usually be done in one day or less. Local trails, called *sentiers*, are usually themed hikes that follow a specific historic or cultural route. All of these trails are clearly marked, but those who want it mapped out should stop by the Maison du Park at the Château de la Madeleine, which sells a number of maps (text in French) that focus on specific areas, such as the guide *Les Vallées Confidentes* (€4), which shows 16 circular trails under six miles long.

PREVENT FOREST FIRES

Remember that campfires and barbeques are forbidden in the forests, and cigarette butts shouldn't be discarded on the ground (pack them out with the rest of your litter).

Primary Trails

The **Sentier Jean Racine** is a three-mile one-way trail from the parking lot at the Château de la Madeleine in Chevreuse to the Abbaye de Port-Royal.

The **Sentier de Maincourt** is a 1.2-mile circular wildlife walk from south of Mesnil-St-Denis along the Yvette River and across one of the largest wetlands in the park (boots recommended). Park on the D58 between Lévis-St-Nom and Maincourt.

The **Sentier des Maréchaux** is a three-mile circular trail around the Etang de Cernay, a lake that attracted many landscape painters in the 19th century. It follows the old trail used by quarry workers. Park at the end of the Route Forestière des Franchises (via the D202 from Senlisse, direction Essarts-le-Roi).

ATTENTION! *Never park your car in front of the forest trailhead barriers – these are access routes for emergency vehicles.*

Pick up the GR11 just outside the RER St-Rémy-lès-Chevreuse (turn left exiting the station and look for the red and white trail markers), which passes through Chevreuse, Choisel (Château de Breteuil) and Dampierre-en-Yvelines before continuing in a northwesterly direction.

Exit the SNCF Gare de Rambouillet to the left to follow the GR1 (red and white markers) on a five-mile trail around the château park grounds. To go all the way to the Espace Rambouillet and the Etang D'Or, follow the GR1 from the Rondeau (the round water basin on the far eastern end of the formal château gardens) and across the train tracks, and bearing right after crossing the RN10.

The trail splits at the Etang D'Or, with the GR1 heading east toward the D906 (to Chevreuse), and the PR4 (yellow markers) continuing to the Espace Rambouillet, looping back along the cycling trail.

The GR1C goes one way from Dampierre-en-Yvelines to Senlisse, Cernay-la-Ville, past the Abbaye Les-Vaux-de-Cernay to Auffargis.

Outside Paris

AROUND LES-VAUX-DE-CERNAY

This forested valley is popular with weekend hikers and picnickers for its lake, waterfalls and rugged landscape crisscrossed by hiking trails. There are even a few roadside snack bars in case you've forgotten to pack a lunch.

The **Randonneurs d'Ile-de-France** (www.rifrando.asso.fr) is a non-profit hiking association that specializes in day hikes outside Paris, including the forests of Rambouillet and the Haute Vallée de la Chevreuse. Although it's normally only open to members, visitors are welcome to go on a free "sample hike" (participants pay their own train transportation and food costs). There are several hikes almost every day of the year to choose from. Check out their bilingual web site for more details, or simply call their friendly Paris office to sign up: 92 Rue du Moulin Vert, 14th, M° Pernety, ☎ 01 45 42 24 72.

■ On Horseback

Centre Equestre de Chevreuse: 36 Route de la Brosse, Chevreuse, ☎ 01 30 52 49 66, fax 01 30 52 40 79. Located just outside the Château de la Madeleine, this equestrian center welcomes riders of all levels from the age of four and up. They organize rides from one hour (*promenades*) on Sundays as well as rides that last all day or several days (*randonnées*), for more experienced riders. Call for more information (open daily, 9am to 9pm).

Poney Club et Centre Equestre: Route de Bullion, Bonnelles, ☎ 06 82 37 47 22. This pony club in the southern end of the Haute Vallée de la Chevreuse has regular Sunday rides (spring through fall) for all levels through the regions forests. They also have pony riding for kids during the school holidays. Call for more information and the schedule. Open Tuesday through Sunday, 9am to 8pm (until 10pm Thursdays).

Poney Club de Rambouillet: 86 Rue de Groussay, Rambouillet, ☎ 01 30 88 74 33 (office) or 01 34 83 90 62 (stables). Located on the edge of the forest just outside town, this pony club organizes short rides for children ages four and up, as well as horseback rides for all ages from Easter through fall. Open daily, 9am to noon and 2 to 6pm.

 AUTHOR'S NOTE: *There are pony rides for kids at the* **Bergerie Nationale** *in the Château de Rambouillet Park, and accompanied horseback promenades organized on request for adults. For more information call the Poney Club, ☎ 01 61 08 68 46; or the Equestrian Center, ☎ 01 61 08 68 47.*

■ On Wheels

The Haute Vallée de Chevreuse Regional Park and Rambouillet have numerous cycling trails through the forest as well as bike lanes along roads such as the D906 (between Rambouillet and Cernay-la-Ville) and D936 (north from Rambouillet). There are also several paved cycling paths around the *Etangs de Hollande* (see below) that are particularly adapted for young cyclists (see *Adventures on Water*).

> **ATTENTION!** *Cyclists should remember not to go off the designated trails in the forest.*

See the *Getting Around* section of this chapter, page 391, for local bike rental information. Those arriving from Paris with a bicycle will find a cycle trail just outside the RER St-Rémy-lès-Chevreuse station (on the left), which leads to Chevreuse.

📖 *Ask for the free* Randonnée à Vélo *guide from any tourism office in the Park or in Rambouillet for detailed cycling itineraries between major sites and villages, an be sure to have a good map (either the Michelin 106* **Zoom Environs de Paris** *or the* **TOP25 IGN** *series map 2215-OT).*

■ On the Water

Boating

The largest lake in the region is the **Etang de Hollande** (☎ 01 34 86 30 50), created in the 17th century in the Forêt de Rambouillet just outside St-Leger-en-Yvelines. Known as a *base de loisirs* (leisure center), the lake has many activities such as swimming, pedal boats (*pédalos*), bike rental, windsurfing and sailing (*la voile*). There's a sandy beach and a brasserie, as well as a new miniature port, the **Cap Rambolitain**, where the family can ride around on motorized miniature versions of fishing trawlers and Mississippi river boats (open daily, July through August, 2 to 7pm).

Fishing

There's also a small lake outside the Espace Rambouillet called **l'Etang d'Or**, a popular fishing location (get a day permit – *carte de pêche* – from the campsite overlooking the lake).

Swimming

 It's possible to swim year-round at the **Piscine Intercommunale de Rambouillet** (36 Rue des Fontaines, ☎ 01 30 41 13 38), with several indoor and outdoor pools for infants,

Outside Paris

children and lap swimmers, including a giant outdoor waterslide, an indoor aquatic climbing wall, a volleyball court, sauna and bar. Open daily throughout the year but opening hours vary, so call ahead or check the schedule on their web site. Entrance €4.25, €3.05 for students, free for kids under age four (sauna, €6.10, adults only).

> **ATTENTION:** *Boys and men are required to wear fitted, racing-style bathing suits in public pools.*

■ In the Air

Hot-air balloon rides are available from **Air Atmosphère** (☎ 01 46 05 91 25, fax 01 48 25 37 42, www.air-atmosphere-dirigeable.fr) or **Mayerhoeffer Montgolfière** (☎/fax 01 45 57 20 53, mobile 06 16 11 05 07, www.mayerhoeffer-montgolfiere.com) from €150-€220 per person (hour flight) spring through fall.

Where to Shop

■ Specialty Stores

In Rambouillet, the Rue du Général de Gaulle has many shops and gourmet boutiques. You can find clothing, chocolates, jewelry and farm products here. Don't miss the antiques shops and decorative tile boutique **Dames de Faïence** around the corner on Rue Raymond Poincairé.

Antique hunters should make the effort to go to the **Bois l'Epicier** (☎ 01 30 46 12 12, www.boislepicier.fr), an antiques village housing about 20 boutiques all together in an old farm property with a 1950s-vintage bistro in the center. Open daily, 10am to 6:30pm; bistro open Tuesday through Sunday for lunch, Wednesday through Saturday for dinner. It's just off the D61 from Houdan (from Paris on the RN12 direction Dreux, exit Houdan center, then at the first roundabout take the direction ZA Bois l'Epicier).

■ Outdoor Markets

There's an outdoor market every Saturday in Rambouillet at the Place de la Libération and Place Félix Faure. An indoor and outdoor market takes place every Wednesday and Saturday morning in St-Rémy-lès-Chevreuse at the **Espace Jean Racine** (Rue Ditte), featuring clothing, food, flowers and local crafts.

■ Farm Produce

 The **Ferme de Coubertin** (off the D906, St-Rémy-lès-Chevreuse, ☎ 01 30 52 00 19) sells cheese and fresh milk, chickens and eggs. Open daily, 9am to 10:30am and 5 to 7pm (closed in the morning on Tuesdays and in July and August).

The **Ferme de la Noue** (on the D61, La Celle des Bordes, ☎ 01 34 85 16 17) is an old-fashioned farm that sells cheeses, cured meats, lamb meat, seasonal fruits and vegetables, and honey. Open March through November, Monday, Thursday and Friday from 6 to 7:30pm, and weekends from 4 to 7:30pm.

The **Ferme de la Villeneuve** (60 Rue du Champ de Courses, Rambouillet, ☎ 06 11 50 33 87) is just off the Route de Clairfontaine. The family-run farm has cows, goats, sheep and all sorts of fowl for fresh milk, cheese, and eggs.

Where to Eat

RESTAURANT PRICE SCALE
The following price scale represents the cost of an average meal for one person, not including drinks.
€ . . . . Under €15
€€ . . . . €16-€25
€€€ . . . . €26-€40
€€€€ . . . . €41-€60
€€€€ . . . . over €60

■ Chevreuse

Auberge du Moulin: 56 Rue de la Porte de Paris, Chevreuse, ☎ 01 30 52 16 45. Traditional French (€-€€). Closed all day Monday and Tuesday night.

A pleasant little restaurant with a large summer terrace and home-style cooking.

Le Normand: 31 Rue de Rambouillet, Chevreuse, ☎ 01 30 52 09 93. Traditional French (€-€€). Closed Sunday night and Monday.

Another adorable village restaurant popular with locals, serving traditional French country favorites. Large garden open in nicer weather.

■ Rambouillet

A la Biche: 48 Rue de Groussay, Rambouillet, ☎ 01 34 83 00 67. Traditional country cuisine (€€). Open weekdays only. Closed August.

The menu at this traditional restaurant with a rustic dining room features foie gras, game, and homemade terrines.

Bisson: 1 Rue du Général de Gaulle, Rambouillet, ☎ 01 34 83 23 82. French-Norwegian (€€€). Closed Sunday night.

Nordic and French dishes, such as *Canard à l'Orange* and Norwegian omelets, are the specialties here. Bisson is a cozy restaurant across from the château, with a terrace for outdoor dining in warmer weather.

La Poste: 101 Rue du Général de Gaulle, Rambouillet, ☎ 01 34 83 03 01. French brasserie (€€€, children's menu €12). Closed Monday, Thursday night and Sunday night.

This small, traditional brasserie and tearoom serves food from lunch through the evening non-stop. Tables are tightly packed together.

Le Cheval Rouge: 78 Rue du Général de Gaulle, Rambouillet, ☎ 01 30 88 80 61, www.cheval-rouge.com. Gourmet French cuisine (€€€). Closed Tuesday night and Wednesday.

The horse-themed menus ("Menu Galop," "Menu Trot") can be a bit disturbing, but don't worry, there's no horsemeat in the kitchen. Just gourmet French steak and fish specialties deliciously prepared and served in a rustic, laid-back atmosphere. On cool nights be sure to reserve a table next to the fireplace in the winter garden.

■ Dampierre

Les Ecuries du Château: Château de Dampierre, Dampierre-en-Yvelines, ☎ 01 30 52 52 99. Traditional country cuisine (€€€). Open for lunch Thursday through Monday, for dinner weekends only.

The focus is on game and traditional cuisine at this small restaurant in the château's former stables, set within the rampart walls. Closed August and February.

■ Cernay-la-Ville

 La Table du Prieur: Abbaye des Vaux-de-Cernay, on the D24, Cernay-la-Ville, ☎ 01 34 85 23 00, www.abbayedecernay.com. Haute cuisine (€€€€). Open daily for lunch and dinner.

Fine French cuisine in an amazing 12th-century abbey refectory with Gothic stone arches. Weekday lunch menus are available for under €30.

Where to Stay

ACCOMMODATIONS PRICE SCALE		
The following price scale represents rates charged for a double room per night during high season, including taxes. Breakfast isn't included except where noted. All prices are quoted in euros. Credit cards accepted unless noted.		
€		Under €70
€€.		€71-€100
€€€		€101-€150
€€€€		€151-€250
€€€€€.		over €250

To dial French telephone / fax numbers from abroad, add the country code "33" and drop the first "0."

■ Hotels & Inns

Au Bord du Lac: 2 Rue de la Digue, St-Rémy-lès-Chevreuse, ☎ 01 30 52 00 43, fax 01 30 47 14 84, www.auborddulac.com (€).

Just five minutes on foot from the RER station, this peaceful inn overlooking a lake has eight comfortable guest rooms with private bathroom (shower or bathtub), TV and telephone. There's also a rustic restaurant serving traditional French cuisine and a large garden terrace.

A la Biche Hôtel: 48 Rue de Groussay, Rambouillet, ☎ 01 34 83 00 67, fax 01 30 46 21 20 (€).

This hotel-restaurant has four rooms with simple, old-fashioned décor, exposed wooden beams and TV. The restaurant is open weekdays only. If you can get a room here, it's a good deal and within easy walking distance of the Château de Rambouillet.

Hôtel Le St-Charles: 15 Rue de Groussay, Rambouillet, ☎ 01 34 83 06 34, fax 01 30 46 26 84 (€).

The St-Charles is a modern, two-star hotel; the 14 rooms have telephone and satellite TV, and the hotel has free parking. It doesn't look like much from the outside, but the rooms are pleasant enough, with classic décor of pale walls and pastel print fabrics.

Le Chêne Pendragon: 17 Rue de la Croix Blanche, St-Léger-en-Yvelines, ☎ 01 34 86 30 11, fax 01 34 86 35 08 (€-€€).

Outside Paris

This lovely 18th-century coach house hotel has a cozy bar and dining room with fireplace, a garden terrace, and swimming pool. The 18 rooms, decorated with period furnishings and romantic canopy beds, are equipped with private bathroom, hair dryer, satellite television and direct-dial telephone. Private parking. About five minutes from Rambouillet by car.

Auberge du Château: 1 Grande Rue, Dampierre-en-Yvelines, ☎ 01 30 47 56 56, fax 01 30 47 51 75 (€€).

The Auberge has 12 rooms, each with fine antiques and charming country-home décor, private bathroom, TV and telephone. There's a lovely terrace overlooking the Château de Dampierre, a bar and a cozy restaurant, Les Tables des Blot, with a fireplace and home-style cooking. Free parking.

Hôtel de l'Abbaye and **Hôtel des Haras:** In the Abbaye des Vaux-de-Cernay, Cernay-la-Ville, ☎ 01 34 85 23 00, fax 01 34 85 11 60, www.abbayedecernay.com (€€-€€€€€ Abbaye; €€ Haras).

The four-star Hôtel de l'Abbaye, built by the Rothschilds in the 12th-century Abbaye des Vaux-de-Cernay has 58 rooms, from €90 (the Monk's room) to €590 (the Rothschild's room). The three-star Hôtel des Haras was built on the same property at the beginning of the 20th century, with a simpler décor of wood-paneled walls and rattan furniture in its 62 rooms. The grounds have a heated swimming pool, small sauna and Jacuzzi, tennis courts, and boating on the lake. Rooms are equipped with telephone and private bathrooms with hair dryer. Free parking. Both hotels are quiet and peaceful, in the center of a private forest.

> **AUTHOR'S NOTE:** *Rambouillet doesn't have many hotels, but there are a few families in town offering comfortable* chambres d'hôtes *(bed & breakfasts) at reasonable prices. For more information contact the Rambouillet Tourism Office (☎ 01 34 83 21 21) or the Maison du Parc (☎ 01 30 52 09 09).*

■ Camping

Camping Etang d'Or: Route du Château d'Eau, Rambouillet, ☎ 01 30 41 07 34, fax 01 30 41 00 17.

This campground between the Etang d'Or and the Espace Rambouillet has tent and caravan spaces under pine trees, a large playground, and coin-op laundry machines, and there are a number of cycle paths and trails accessible from the campgrounds. The restaurant is open in July and August. A car or bike is needed to get to the center of Rambouillet. Open February through November.

Gîte d'Etape de la Maison de Fer: On route D58, Dampierre-en-Yvelines, ☎ 01 39 56 09 45.

Gîtes are rural cabins or structures built to accommodate hikers or other travelers overnight in simple, yet comfortable quarters. These are run by the Maison du Parc, and reservations are necessary (☎ 01 30 52 09 09). This gîte, the House of Iron, was built originally for the Universal Exposition in 1889 by a colleague of Gustave Eiffel as a demonstration of housing that comes in a kit. Its current location is in an exotic garden overlooking the Yvette River valley with 18 beds available in rooms for two, four or six people. Open all year except the end of December.

Entertainment

 Rambouillet and the Haute Vallée de la Chevreuse don't have much in the way of clubs or bars, since most locals go into Paris for the nightlife. But there's always something going on, from festivals and concerts to exhibitions or art markets, so be sure to stop into the local tourism offices for the latest news.

There's one movie theater in Rambouillet, the **Cinéma Vox** (71 Rue du Général de Gaulle, ☎ 01 30 88 78 78), which shows films recently released in France, tickets €7. Don't forget that for English-language films, *VF* means it's dubbed in French and *VO* means it's the original-language version with French subtitles. There are also regular concerts, theater and events at Rambouillet's cultural center, **Le Nickel** (50 Rue du Muguet, ☎ 01 34 94 82 77).

Trotting fans can catch the horse races at the **Hippodrome de la Villeneuve** (Rue du Petit Grill, Rambouillet, ☎ 01 30 41 00 97) from mid-March through mid-September; tickets €5 (free entry and pony rides for kids).

Chantilly

Overview

Set within a large forest less than one hour north of Paris, Chantilly is known internationally for its prestigious equestrian events and living horse museum, as well as the impressive art collections of the Musée Condé, housed in the princely Château de Chantilly. The cultural, architectural and natural heritage of Chantilly, owned for centuries by the princes of Condé, has been wonderfully preserved. Six miles to the east is the ancient Gallo-Romain town of Senlis, a picturesque maze of cobblestoned streets and Gothic churches enclosed within third-century ramparts. Together, they offer visitors a unique perspective on French history in an exceptional forest setting.

A WORD TO
THE WISE

PRONUNCIATION TIP: *No one is going to put down Elvis for mispronouncing the town's name in his famous song* Chantilly Lace, *but don't you make the same mistake! Pretend there's no "l" and pronounce it shawn-tee-ee (emphasis on the third syllable).*

Planning Your Trip

■ When to Go

It's possible to visit Chantilly's prestigious museums year-round, but the best time to come is from April through October, when the lovely gardens look their best. Spring is the time for the **Daffodil** and **Chick & Egg** festivals at the Potager des Princes, and the annual **Chantilly Sculpture Festival**. June is the most exciting month in the racing season, with the **French Derby** and **Prix de Diane** attracting an international audience to the Hippodrome de Chantilly. The **Nuits de Feu** (International Fireworks Festival) also takes place in June, but only in even years. Chantilly celebrates the annual **Fête de la Music** (June 21) and **Bastille Day** (July 13-14) with traditional concerts and parades. After a quiet August, Chantilly and Senlis reveal their hidden treasures for the **Journées du Patrimoine** (Heritage Days) in September, and visitors feast on goodies at Chantilly's annual **Salon du Chocolat** (Chocolate Fair) in November. There are many events for the December holidays, including the **Marché du Noël**, the children's **Fairytale Horse Show** at the Musée Vivant du Cheval, and the **New Year's Eve Parade** through town. Try to reserve at least two days to see everything in Chantilly, and perhaps even a third to explore the medieval town of Senlis.

■ Tourism Offices

i **Chantilly Tourism Office**: 60 Avenue Maréchal Joffre, Chantilly, ☎ 03 44 67 37 37, fax www.chantilly-tourisme.com. The tourism office is in a large white house across from the forest, on the main road going into town from Paris, just a block from the train station and one mile from the center of town. There are maps and guide books available, as well as basic information on sights, local events and accommodations. Open May to September, weekdays, 9am to 12:30pm and 1:30 to 6pm (5pm on Friday); Saturday, 10am to 12:30pm and 1:30 to

5pm; Sunday, 10am to 1:30pm. From October to April it's open Monday through Saturday only, from 9:30am to 12:30pm and 1:30 to 5:30pm.

ATTENTION! *Chantilly and Senlis are actually just outside Ile-de-France, in the Oise département of the Picardie region. The telephone prefix for this region is "03" (instead of "01" for Ile-de-France).*

Senlis Tourism Office: Place du Parvis Notre Dame, Senlis, ☎ 03 44 53 06 40, fax 03 44 53 29 80, www.ville-senlis.fr. Located in the center of town across from the Eglise Notre-Dame, the Senlis Tourism Office can provide maps and information on accommodation, events, and guided visits through the town. Ask for the free self-guide brochure *Senlis: Royal City*. The boutique sells books, videos and decorative gifts. Open March through October, Monday through Saturday, 10am to 12:30pm and 2 to 6:15pm; Sunday, 10:30am to 1pm and 2 to 6:15pm. From November through February, open Monday through Saturday, 10am to 12:30pm and 2 to 5pm; Sunday, 11:15am to 1pm and 2:30 to 5pm.

Oise Département Tourist Board: ☎ 03 44 45 82 12, fax 03 44 45 16 19, www.oisetourisme.com This office can provide information on sightseeing and accommodation in the entire Oise département, including Chantilly and Senlis.

■ Emergency Numbers

General Emergency . . . . ☎ 112 (toll free)
Municipal Police . . . . ☎ 03 44 58 15 91
Gendarmerie . . . . ☎ 03 44 57 33 17
Médecins de Garde (doctors on-call) . . . . ☎ 03 44 66 44 66
Pharmacie Dubois . . . . ☎ 03 44 57 04 50
(occasionally open all night)

Getting Here

■ By Train

SNCF

The SNCF *Grandes Lignes* has daily services between Paris-Gare du Nord and Gare Chantilly-Gouvieux (direction Gare de Creil), 5am to 11:30pm (until 9:45pm toward Chantilly). At Gare du Nord, look for the Creil-23 train, on tracks (*voie*) 41-44. Approximate travel time is 30 minutes.

Outside Paris

ATTENTION: *Some trains actually go to Creil first, then loop back to Chantilly. Tickets cost €6.50 one-way.*

RER

RER D1 has limited service between Châtelet-Les-Halles and Orry-la-Ville-Coye (just south of Chantilly), travel time about 45 minutes. Passengers can then continue to Chantilly by train (one stop), bus, or taxi (ten-minute drive).

■ By Bus

The Picardie-Roissy bus has daily service, 5am to 11:30pm from the *Gare Routière* at Roissy-CDG airport to Senlis (the local Bus 15 runs regularly between Chantilly and Senlis). You can buy tickets on the bus or at the SNCF office in Senlis (€4.40 one-way), ☎ 08 10 60 00 60 or 03 44 53 25 38.

■ By Car

Chantilly is 30 miles north of Paris. The fastest way to get there is to avoid St-Denis and take the A1/E19 past Roissy-CDG airport to exit 7 (Survilliers), and follow the signs to Chantilly. Stay on the A1/E19 to go directly to Senlis (6.5 miles east of Chantilly).

Getting Around

All of the main sights in Chantilly are within a mile from the train station and tourist office (with a nice forest road in between), making it easy to get around on foot or by bike. If the weather isn't at its best, then opt for the local buses or taxis if you don't have a car. Senlis is even more compact than Chantilly, and is best seen on foot since the cobblestoned streets can be rough on bike tires.

■ By Bus

The local **Cariane** bus has a free shuttle that goes from the station to the center of town and the château. Line 15 runs between Chantilly and Senlis. Ask at the station or contact the tourism offices for detailed information.

■ By Bike

 It's a pleasure cycling around Chantilly's flat, tree-lined streets, many of which have designated bike lanes. Sportier types can brave the 13-mile round trip between Senlis and Chantilly on the scenic D 924, but look out for those cobblestones in Senlis!

The only place to rent bikes is **Orry Cycles** (5 Rue Neuve, Orry-la-Ville ☎ 03 44 58 04 03), a block from the train station in Orry-la-Ville (the RER D stops here). They rent all-terrain bikes for all ages by the hour or day, with or without a guide. Open daily, 8am to 8pm, but reservations are best (they can sometimes deliver bikes to Chantilly). If you bring a bike from Paris, they are allowed on the RER D and designated SNCF trains (ask when purchasing your ticket). Bike-friendly compartments are designated by a bicycle symbol, but ask the platform guard if you can't see it.

■ By Car

Chantilly is easy to navigate once you figure out that all roads lead back to the two main roads: Avenue Maréchal Joffre (north-south) and Rue Connetable (east-west). Parking isn't free in town (metered street parking), although the two large parking lots between the hippodrome and the château only cost €1-€2 for the day. It's almost impossible to park in town on any race days, particularly in June. It's handy to have a car to get to Senlis, but you'll have to park outside the city walls (two public parking lots are situated on the south side of the town).

Only **Avis** has a local rental agent (Locanor Location: 2 Rue Victor Hugo, Chantilly, ☎ 03 44 57 98 69). It may be more convenient to pick up a rental car from Roissy-CDG Airport (15 miles from Chantilly). See *Getting Around* in the *Paris* chapter for agencies.

■ By Taxi

Local Taxis

Taxi Bruno Chantilly . . . . ☎ 06 74 67 01 57

Allo Taxis Chantilly . . . . ☎ 06 07 19 99 93

Taxis de la Gare de Chantilly . . . . ☎ 03 44 57 10 03

Taxi Alexandre Senlis . . . . ☎ 06 07 21 55 86

Allo Taxi Senlis . . . . ☎ 06 07 82 62 35

Taxi Jean-Michel Senlis . . . . ☎ 06 80 70 10 31

Taxi Orry-la-Ville . . . . ☎ 03 44 58 93 38

A Brief History

The princely domain of Chantilly has a unique history, passing through the same family, the cousins of the Kings of France, from the 14th century until 1897. Its first period of greatness came during the Renaissance, when the **Connétable** (Constable) **de Montmorency** replaced the ancient medieval fortress with the twin châteaux on the lake, the Grand Château and the Petit Château (also known as the *Capitainerie*). His grandson, **Henri II de Montmorency**, lost the domain – and his head – when he was caught conspiring against Louis XIII in 1632. The king confiscated Chantilly and used it for his own private hunting excursions. It was returned to the family eleven years later, during the regency of the young Louis XIV, and passed on to Henri's nephew, **Louis II de Bourbon** (known as the Grand Condé) in 1660. He had Le Nôtre design the château's formal gardens and Grand Canal that became the centerpiece for his elaborate festivals. A great patron of the arts and literature, the Grand Condé entertained some of the 17th century's leading writers and philosophers at Chantilly.

SEE THE FILM

 Get an idea of 17th-century Chantilly in the 2000 film *Vatel*, starring Uma Thurman and Gerard Depardieu, a historical epic based on the elaborate party and feast that the Prince of Condé threw for King Louis XIV at the Château de Chantilly in 1671.

The domain was eventually inherited by his grandson, **Louis-Henri de Bourbon** (the 7th Prince of Condé). Louis-Henri believed he would be reincarnated as a horse, so he had the architect Jean Aubert build the magnificent **Grandes Ecuries**, a masterpiece of 18th-century architecture housing 240 horses and 500 hunting dogs in proper princely style. He also redecorated the apartments of the Petit Château, created Chantilly's famous porcelain factory, and imposed the town's first building codes defining acceptable architectural style. His son **Louis-Joseph de Condé** had the Château d'Enghien built in 1769 as overflow guest quarters, and added a rustic Hamlet to the Château Park, which inspired Marie Antoinette to build her own *Hameau* in Versailles. He emigrated at the outbreak of the Revolution to form a Loyalist army, after which the Grand Château was pillaged, turned into a prison, and eventually razed. The Grandes Ecuries, occupied by the army, were spared this grim ending.

When Louis-Henri returned to Chantilly during the Restoration in 1815, he managed to recover many of the artworks (which had been transferred to the Louvre) and had the apartments of the Petit Château completely restored. His heir, the Duc d'Enghien, had been executed by Napoleon in 1804 for organizing a royalist uprising, so in 1830 the domain was left to his grand-nephew, **Henri d'Orléans, Duc d'Aumale** (son of the last French king, Louis-Philippe). He breathed new life and prestige into Chantilly with the creation of the Hippodrome, one of the finest horseracing tracks in Europe, but was forced to leave during the Revolution of 1848, spending the duration of the Second Empire in England. The Duc d'Aumale returned to Chantilly in 1870, widowed and without an heir after the deaths of his two sons. He decided to rebuild the Grand Château as a showcase for the prized art collection amassed during his years in exile. Upon his death in 1886, the Duc d'Aumale donated the entire Domaine de Chantilly to the Institut de France – including the Grandes Ecuries, the hippodrome and the 15,000-acre forest – on the condition that the château be opened to the public as the **Musée Condé**, and that none of the artworks would be moved around or loaned to other museums.

DID YOU KNOW? *The residents of Chantilly are known as* Cantiliens.

Chantilly continues to flourish today by making the most of its three inherited treasures. On the artistic and cultural front is the Château de Chantilly, with one of the most important art collections in France and its elegantly restored park and **Le Nôtre gardens**. Its equestrian heritage includes the historic **Hippodrome de Chantilly**, which plays a leading role in the prestigious world of horse racing, and the renovated Grandes Ecuries, which have been transformed into a living horse museum, the Musée Vivant du Cheval. The third treasure is the 15,000-acre **Forêt de Chantilly**, providing a scenic backdrop to the town and over 100 miles of hiking and equestrian trails.

PARLEZ-VOUS ANGLAIS?

Don't be surprised to hear English spoken around town. The British arrived in Chantilly when the Hippodrome opened in 1834 to offer their expert services. Today the horse training center employs over 1,000 stable boys (even the French refer to them as "lads").

Sightseeing

■ The Town & Environs

The small town of Chantilly has fervently resisted modern over-development, preserving its 18th-century architecture and Haussmann-era mansions, many of which can be seen (from the outside, of course) along the **Avenue du Maréchal Joffre** and the **Rue du Connétable**. Many of these historic buildings are opened to the public during the annual Journées du Patrimoine (September).

The Princes of Condé carefully arranged their domain to be seen by visitors from a certain perspective at the **Rond-point des Lions**. So if you arrive from the train station or the main road from Paris, stop into the tourism office at the Avenue du Maréchal Joffre (for a map), and from the Rond-point de Sylvie, follow the Route de l'Aigle through the forest. The Hippodrome, Grandes Ecuries, and Château de Chantilly will suddenly appear on the left in all their glory.

■ Château & Parc de Chantilly

The **Château de Chantilly** (☎ 03 44 62 62 62, www.chateaude-chantilly.com) is actually made up of two conjoined châteaux, the 15th-century Petit Château and the 19th-century Grand Château. They house the **Musée Condé**, featuring the Duc d'Aumale's beautifully decorated private apartments and internationally renowned collection of old master paintings and rare books. The museum is open Tuesday to Sunday, 10am to 6pm, from March through October; from November to February it's open weekdays, 10:30am to 12:45pm and 2 to 5pm; weekends, 10:30am to 5pm. Tickets are €7, €6 for kids 13-17, €2.80 for kids ages four to 12, free for kids under four. Museum Passes accepted. This ticket includes access to the **Galeries de Peintures** and an accompanied tour of the **Grands Appartements** and **Chapelle**. The **Petits Appartements** private housing quarters of the Duc d'Aumale can only be visited with a guide on weekends and holidays (approximately 30 minutes). Tickets cost €6.50 (on top of the regular entrance fee). There's an English brochure at the entry with map and brief descriptions of each room, and there are also plasticized information sheets in multiple languages in each room, but these are hard to find when the museum is crowded. Audio guides are available for €2 at the boutique (next to the *Capitainerie*). Guidebooks in English can be purchased there for €5-€10. Be sure to ask at the main entrance when the free tour takes place (they last about 30 minutes). Allow *at least* 90 minutes to see the entire museum.

A WORD TO THE WISE

ATTENTION: *The Château d'Enghien is used by the château administrative office (closed to the public).*

MONEY-SAVING TIP

Check with the Chantilly Tourism Office (☎ 03 44 67 37 37, www.chantilly-tourisme.com) for the latest weekend packages that include hotel, museum passes and a day at Parc Asterix.

Entrance

The **Paris Museum Pass** (www.intermusees.com) is good for entry into the Château and Parc de Chantilly (Musée Condé)

Combination passes for the Domaine du Chantilly include the **Pass Culture** (Château et Parc de Chantilly and the Musée Vivant du Cheval; €14, €12 for kids 13-17, €8 for ages four to 12), **Journée dans les Communs Princiers** (Musée Vivant du Cheval and Potager des Princes; €14, €13 for kids 13-17, €10 for kids four to 12), **Pass Nature** (Parc du Château and Potager des Princes; €9, €7 for kids four to 12), and **Un Weekend à Chantilly** (Château et Parc de Chantilly, Musée Vivant du Cheval and Potager des Princes; €20, €18 for kids 13-17, €12 for kids four to 12). These passes are available through the participating museums.

The museum ticket includes entrance to the **Château Parc et Jardins** (the park ticket alone costs €3.50, €2 for kids four to 12). From the terrace outside the château, visitors can see the formal **French Gardens** and **Grand Canal** designed by Le Nôtre. But this is only a small fraction of the park grounds. Off to the left is the romantic-style **Jardin Anglais** with its newly restored Temple of Venus and Ile d'Amour. To the right of the formal gardens are the country Hameau, labyrinth and children's playground. The forested section of the park to the south hides the new **Kangaroo Park** and secluded trails where you may see deer or rabbits. It would take a few hours to see all of this on foot, so opt for a silent, electric-powered **boat ride** (€5) along the canal (about 30 minutes), available daily except Tuesday, March 15 to October 15, from 10am to 6pm (operates every day July-August). There are also 25-minute forest tours on the tiny **train** (€5, €3 for kids four to 12), running daily, April to October, 1:30 to 6pm (11am to 7pm in July and August). A combined ticket for the museum, park, boat and train costs €15, €13 for kids 13-17, €9 for kids four to 12. A horse-drawn-carriage tour (€6, €4.50 for kids four to 12) for up to 10 passengers is available weekends and holidays from May through mid-October. The park and gardens are open daily from 10am to 7pm, March through October (the park closes Tuesday at lunch 12:45 to 2pm), and daily except Tuesday, 10:30am to 5pm, November through February.

THE FAMOUS CHANTILLY WHIPPED CREAM

 The Hameau restaurant, **Aux Goûters Champêtres** (☎ 03 44 57 46 21), has a terrace in the gardens that serves traditional local specialties (menus €17-€35). You can also stop in just for the afternoon tea and desserts with the famous Chantilly whipped cream (supposedly invented here by the Prince de Condé in the late 1700s). Open daily, noon to 6pm, mid-March through mid-November.

Musée Vivant du Cheval

As part of the Domaine de Chantilly, the Grandes Ecuries were donated to the Institut de France, and used for many years by the local riding academy. The respected riding master Yves Bienaimé began his equestrian career there in 1959, and was struck by both the stables' splendor and its relative neglect. He returned to Chantilly with his wife Annabel two decades later and, after four years of negotiations with the Institut de France, opened the Musée Vivant du Cheval (☎ 03 44 57 40 40, www.musee-vivant-du-cheval.fr) in 1982. The Bienaimé family completely renovated and restored the 18th-century stables without subsidies, creating a living museum that shares not only the magnificent setting and history, but also gives visitors an inside peek into the horse world. Visitors are not just entertained with magical horse riding shows, but also shown the training techniques used for the performance. There's a series of exhibition rooms, each focusing on a different aspect of the equestrian world such as the role of horses in art and literature, the history of horse racing, or a collection of antique riding equipment.

Half-hour performances take place in a compact circular arena under the grand Dôme at 4:15pm daily, with music, lights and costumes. There's a children's pony show in the morning and educational demonstrations (in French and English) three times a day with Q&A sessions afterward (call or check web site to confirm the seasonal schedule). All members of the Bienaimé family participate in every show. It's hard not to notice how their passion and dedication really comes through in every aspect of the museum, making it a truly unique place to visit. Allow at least two hours if you plan on watching a performance. Open daily except Tuesday, April through October, 10:30am to 6:30pm (until 7pm on weekends); and November through March, weekdays 2 to 6pm, weekends 10:30am to 6:30pm. The museum is open on Tuesdays only in May and June, 10:30am to 5:30pm, and July and August, 2 to 5:30pm. The ticket window closes one hour before the museum. Tickets €8, €6.50 for kids 13-17, €5.50 for kids ages four to 12. The gift boutique by the entrance has guides to the museum in English for €5-€10.

EQUESTRIAN SHOWS

There's a schedule of elaborate shows such as the **Rêve & Poésie** (every first Sunday of the month, tickets €17, €16 for ages four to 12), **Polo Tango** (shows in May and October; tickets €24, €21 for kids), and **Noël, Le Cheval et l'Enfant** (shows throughout December; tickets €15, €14 for kids ages six to 12, €12 for kids two to five, including museum entrance. Be sure to book in advance, ☎ 03 44 57 91 79.

Potager des Princes

The **Parc de la Faisanderie** (Pheasant Park) was once part of the Château Park, with formal gardens designed by Le Nôtre and kitchen gardens that provided the Princes of Condé with their fresh produce. It was sold off during the French Revolution, and remained hidden from the public until 2002, when it was purchased by the Musée Vivant du Cheval and reopened as **La Potager des Princes** (17 Rue de la Faisanderie, Chantilly, ☎ 03 44 57 40 40, www.potagerdesprinces.com). It's strange to walk out of the town center right into the middle of these tranquil gardens, with sweeping views over a lake and the carefully planted beds of flowers and herbs, trained fruit trees and vegetable plots. Kids love the farmyard, with its chickens, ducks, goats and rabbits. Events in the park include live classical musical performances and a spring Chick & Egg Festival for kids. It's still a "work in progress," with plans for an educational garden museum and open-air theater.

■ The Hippodrome

There's no fee to watch a race from the lawn area of the 19th-century **Hippodrome de Chantilly**, completely renovated in 2003. It's a particularly lovely racetrack, framed by the château, the Grandes Ecuries and the Chantilly forest. Free "behind-the-scenes" guided tours are available every Sunday afternoon at 3pm, 4pm and 5pm from the Point Accueil (Welcome Desk). For more information contact **France Galop**, ☎ 08 21 21 32 13. **Clemence Services** (☎ 03 44 57 51 51, www.ccioise.fr/clemence, nicole.braem@wanadoo.fr) offers personalized, private tours of Chantilly's Hippodrome and race-horse training center, with an opportunity to meet professionals in the stables. Contact the bilingual guide, Nicole Braem for more information.

■ Senlis

Just six miles east of Chantilly is the remarkable town of Senlis, surrounded by **Gallo-Roman ramparts** built during the third century. It was once a powerful city in the French kingdom, hosting many important historical events such as the election of the first Capetian king, **Hugues (Hugh) Capet** in 987 AD, but later lost its royal-residence status to Fontainebleau, after which its château eventually fell into ruin.

Senlis and its religious community continued along quietly, constructing several of the town's most impressive monuments such as the 10th-century **Eglise St-Frambourg**, the 11th-century **Abbaye St-Vincent**, and 12th-century **Cathédral Notre-Dame**, with a 255-foot-tall Gothic steeple. To the south of the old town is another set of ramparts built along the Nonette River during the 12th and 13th centuries, which designate the current city limits. In the 15th century the town was at the center of civil strife, enduring a siege by the Armagnacs in 1418 and the capture of Joan

Outside Paris

of Arc after her victorious battle in 1429. Senlis was declared a historic town in 1965 to save it from modern development. Today it's a quiet, almost provincial town that seems to exist in a time warp. There are four museums, but the real draw is the town itself, which is so quaintly picturesque that it might be a movie set if it weren't for the local teenagers zipping around the narrow streets on their scooters.

It's best to explore the town's maze of cobblestoned roads and passageways on foot, although a horse-drawn carriage ride is a great way to get an overview of the major sights. **Senlis en Calèches** (☎ 03 44 53 10 26, www.senlis-en-caleche.com) has four 40-minute open carriage tours per day (except Tuesday and Friday morning), April through December, leaving from the Place du Cathédral. Call in advance to reserve a spot during high season.

Your first stop should be at the **Senlis Tourism Office** (Place du Parvis Notre-Dame, ☎ 03 44 53 06 40), across from the Cathédral Notre-Dame, for a detailed map of the town and information on any walking tours taking place that day (usually in French).

The **Cathédral Notre-Dame** is the town's most impressive sight, and one of the earliest examples of Gothic architecture. Many people come to admire the cathedral's western portal, which features the first stone representation of the Virgin's Ascension to Heaven. Just outside this portal is the **Musée de l'Hôtel de Vermandois**, a museum dedicated to the history of Senlis set inside a 12th-century private residence. The **Palais Episcopal** (former bishop's residence) is built into the ramparts on the south side of the cathedral, and houses the town's **Musée d'Art**, with examples of Gallo-Roman *ex-votos* (votive offerings), medieval sculptures, and paintings from the 17th through the 20th centuries.

MUSEUMS OF SENLIS

The town's four museums are actually run as one, with the same opening hours: Monday, Thursday and Friday, 10am to noon and 2 to 6pm; Wednesday, 2 to 6pm; weekends and holidays, 11am to 1pm and 2 to 6pm. A single ticket (€4, €2 for students) is good for entrance to all four.

The **Château Royal** was built by Louis VI in 1130. Although it's in ruins today, visitors can see many beautiful sections of the chapel and tower in the **Château Park** (entry €1). Part of the **Priory St-Maurice**, originally built in the 13th century, still stands on the far end of the château, its 18th-century extension is now home to a unique hunting museum, the **Museé de la Vénerie**. Next door is the town's fourth museum, the **Musée des Spahis**, dedicated to the history of the French Army's North African Cavalry.

To get a good look at the old **Gallo-Roman ramparts**, follow the Rue de Villevert and turn left onto the Rue du Chat Haret to the **Jardin du Roy** (King's Garden). Originally over three miles in circumference, 16 of the 28 original towers still stand along the 12-foot-thick walls, many incorporating the buildings constructed during the 17th and 18th centuries.

Stroll at your own pace through the old streets of the town, with its ivy-covered façades, half-timbered houses, and decoratively restored gables. The four most interesting streets in terms of old architecture are the **Rue de la Treille**, **Rue de la Chancellerie**, **Rue St-Frambourg**, and **Rue St-Péravi**. The **Place Gérard de Nerval** and the **Rue de Beauvais** have the best examples of private mansions built during the 17th and 18th centuries. Don't miss the15th-century **Hôtel de Ville**, on the **Rue du Chatel**, still in use today.

Adventures

■ On Foot

Hiking

The **Château Park & Gardens** in Chantilly are big enough to allow for at least a half-day of comfortable walking for casual hikers, with the benefit of a snack bar for those who don't want to venture too far from civilization. Another pleasant place for walking close to the town is along the **Grand Canal**, either on the **Chemin du Canal St-Jean** (behind the Potager des Princes), or on the **Sentier Botanique** (from the Parc Watermael Boitfort).

> **AUTHOR'S NOTE:** *See* Out-Of-Doors *in the* Glossary, *page 443, for useful adventure vocabulary.*

With over 15,500 acres, the **Forêt de Chantilly** is the largest privately owned forest in France. For centuries it was the private hunting grounds of the Domaine de Chantilly, surpassing even Versailles for its abundance of **deer** and **wild boar**. The Grand Condé commissioned Le Nôtre to create the long, rectilinear alleys and star-shaped crossroads in the 17th century to open the forest up for the large horseback hunting parties.

Today the long sandy alleys are used for training the racehorses (mornings until 1pm), and twice a week in season for traditional hunting (Tuesday and Wednesday). But the majority of the forest is now enjoyed by hikers, with hundreds of trails maintained by the Office National des Forêts (ONF). Before setting out for a hike, stop by the Maison Forestière (1 Avenue de Sylvie, ☎ 03 44 57 03 88, www.onf.fr) on the south side of the

Outside Paris

roundabout by the Chantilly Tourism Office, for details on the many marked trails and natural sights.

LOCAL MAPS

The best map for independent hikers is the TOP25 IGN series map 2412-OT, which covers the Forêt de Chantilly as well as the two adjoining forests, **Halatte** and **Ermenonville**. This map shows the sections of the Grandes Randonnées trails GR11 and GR12, which pass through the forest between Chantilly and Senlis. The Chantilly Tourism Office also sells a forest hiking guide (in French), *Promenons-nous dans les forêts de Picardie: Chantilly, Halatte, Ermenonville*.

There are several enjoyable hikes around the town of Senlis. Enjoy a scenic view of the 12th-century outer ramparts on the south side of the town by following the trail between the Nonette River and the Rampart Bellevue. Nature lovers can hike through the 17-acre **Parc Ecologique de Bon-Secours** (follow signs from the Avenue Maréchal Foch, northeast of the town), with a landscaped garden zone around a series of lakes, and a wilder, wetland preservation zone with wildlife observation platforms. Stop by the Senlis Tourism Office in the town center for more information on local trails.

The **Randonneurs d'Ile-de-France** (www.rifrando.asso.fr) is a non-profit hiking association that specializes in day hikes outside Paris, including the forests around Chantilly. Although it's normally only open to members, visitors are welcome to go on a free "sample hike" (participants pay their own train transportation and food costs). There are several hikes almost every day of the year to choose from. Check out their bilingual web site for more details, or simply call their friendly Paris office to sign up: 92 Rue du Moulin Vert, 14th, M° Pernety, ☎ 01 45 42 24 72.

Golf

Golf de Chantilly: Allée de la Ménagerie, Chantilly, ☎ 03 44 57 04 43. This historic course in the heart of the Chantilly forest has two 18-hole courses, par 73 and par 71. Open to non-members during the week (closed Thursday). Greens fees €80, €90 on Friday.

Golf d'Apremont: Follow signs in Apremont, ☎ 03 44 25 61 11, www.golf-apremont.com. Located in the forest between Senlis and Chantilly, this club has a regal country estate overlooking the 18-hole (par 72) course. There's also an elegant restaurant, La Tour d'Apremont. Open daily in high season (March through October, closed August). Greens fees €32-€40 during the week, €53-€75 on weekends.

International Club du Lys: Rond Point du Grand Cerf, Lamorlay, ☎ 03 44 21 26 00, www.golf-lys-chantilly.com. This family country club just to the west of Chantilly has two 18-hole courses (par 66, par 71) in the center of the forest. Greens fees are €46 weekdays, €77 weekends. They also have swimming, tennis, and horseback riding. Closed Tuesday.

■ On Wheels

Cycling

There are many scenic traffic roads through the forests around Chantilly for cyclists who like to stick to smooth surfaces. From the **Route de l'Aigle** (south of the Hippodrome), follow the **D924** to the **D138** for a casual ride toward Senlis through two tiny villages. Sportier types can follow the designated forest trails from the **Carrefour des Lions** all the way down to the **Coye-la-Forêt**, passing through one of the most beautiful sections of the forest, the **Etangs de Commelles**. There's only one bike rental company in the area (just below Coye-la-Forêt, see *Getting Around*, page 415), so be sure to make reservations in advance or bring a bike up from Paris.

ATTENTION! *Be sure to stay clear of the sandy alleys while the race horses are training (mornings), as they can get spooked by cyclists.*

Horse-Drawn Carriage

Senlis en Calèches: Place du Cathédral, Senlis, ☎ 03 44 53 10 26, www.senlis-en-caleche.com. There are regular 40-minute sightseeing tours of Senlis in the open-top carriages April to December, except on Tuesday and Friday mornings. Four passengers max, from €30. Daniel Compiègne, whose family has lived in Senlis for over 400 years, provides fascinating commentary on the history and architecture of the town. He can also arrange for day-trips through the surrounding forests with picnic lunch.

Super Seven Car

Cat-Seven Tours (www.cat-seven.com, www.cat-seven-fr): Take a unique tour as the driver of a Caterham Super Seven "four-wheeled motorcycle," invented as a racing car in the 1960s, with a co-pilot to navigate through the region's sights. From €120 for an hour's drive, or €300 for half-day sightseeing tours. Check out their web site or call for more information.

AUTHOR'S NOTE: *See* Sightseeing, *page 417, for information on boat, train and carriage rides around the park and gardens of the Château de Chantilly.*

■ On Horseback

There are several riding schools in and around Chantilly that organize rides through the forest (*promenades à cheval*). There are obviously more opportunities for experienced riders who are comfortable at a full gallop. For detailed information, contact the schools directly.

- **Centre Equester de Coye la Forêt**: Château de Coye, ☎ 03 44 21 41 12
- **Cercle Hippique de Chantilly**: 36 Avenue de Montmorency, ☎ 03 44 58 04 75
- **International Club du Lys**: Rond Point du Grand Cerf, Lamorlaye, ☎ 03 44 21 41 12

Those who'd like to try their hand at a bit of polo can take lessons at the **Polo Club du Domaine de Chantilly** (at the Ferme d'Apremont, ☎ 03 44 64 04 30 www.poloclubchantilly.com), hosts of the 2004 Polo World Championships, from €60/hour (less for group lessons). Call for details.

AUTHOR'S NOTE: *See* Entertainment, *page 430, for information on races at the Hippodrome de Chantilly or Polo Matches in Apremont.*

■ In the Air

Hot-air balloon (*montgolfière*) flights are available through **Picardy's Balloons** (☎ 03 44 71 70 95, fax 03 44 74 16 50, ballon@wanadoo.fr) or **Euro Balloon** (☎ 06 81 24 71 27 or 06 80 27 39 52, fax 01 45 91 05 96, www.euroballoon-snc.com); from €260 per person.

Where to Shop

Most of the boutiques in Chantilly can be found along the **Rue du Connétable**, **Avenue du Maréchal Joffre**, and the **Place Omer Vallon**. Reproductions of Chantilly porcelain can be found at the boutique in the Musée Condé, and the famous Chantilly lace at the boutique of the Musée de la Dentelle et du Patrimoine de Chantilly (Place Omer Vallon). The **open market** takes place at the Place Omer Vallon every Wednesday and Saturday morning.

Where to Eat

RESTAURANT PRICE SCALE	
The following price scale represents the price of an average meal for one person, not including drinks.	
€	Under €15
€€	€16-€25
€€€	€26-€40
€€€€	€41-€60
€€€€€	over €60

■ Chantilly

Belle Bio: 22 Rue du Connétable, Chantilly, ☎ 03 44 57 02 25. Organic French (€€-€€€). This comfortable restaurant and tea room serves traditional French cuisine made only from organically grown ingredients. Large summer terrace. Open for lunch through dinner, non-stop.

Auberge la Vertugadin: 44 Rue du Connétable, Chantilly, ☎ 03 44 57 03 19. Traditional French (€€€). This large but cozy bar and restaurant specializes in rich, country cooking. Fireplace inside, private garden terrace in the back. Kids' menu available. Open Monday through Saturday for lunch and dinner.

Le Goutillon: 61 Rue du Connétable, Chantilly, ☎ 03 44 58 01 00. Wine bistro (€-€€). This cozy bistro is decorated with red-checked table cloths and vintage prints and posters on the walls. Friendly atmosphere, tightly packed tables, and home-style cooking. Try the white wines and onion soup. Lunch *menu* €15.

The English Shop & Tearoom: 96 Rue du Connétable, Chantilly, ☎ 03 44 57 22 20. British tearoom (€). Popular with both the large population of British residents and the locals for its weekend English Brunch (€8), pots of tea and hot chocolate, and home-made cakes and scones. You can also pick up English-language newspapers and magazines. Open Tuesday through Sunday, 10am to 7pm.

■ Senlis

Hostellerie de la Porte Bellon: 51 Rue Bellon, Senlis, ☎ 03 44 53 03 05. Traditional French (€€€). Located in a converted post office, this hotel restaurant serves traditional French cooking in a warm and cozy atmo-

Outside Paris

sphere. There's a lovely garden terrace open during warmer weather. Open for lunch and dinner (except Sunday evening).

Feuilles et Grains: 1 Rue de l'Apport au Pain, Senlis, ☎ 03 44 60 95 06. Modern tearoom (€). A good place to stop for Mariage Frères gourmet teas and ice cream. They also serve club sandwiches and salads. There's extra seating downstairs if the main room is full. Open Tuesday through Saturday.

Where to Stay

ACCOMMODATIONS PRICE SCALE
The following price scale represents rates charged for a double room per night during high season, including taxes. Breakfast isn't included except where noted. All prices are quoted in euros. Credit cards accepted unless noted.
€ . . . . Under €70
€€. €71-€100
€€€ . . . . €101-€150
€€€€ . . . . €151-€250
€€€€€. . . . . over €250

NOTE: *To dial French telephone/fax numbers from abroad, drop the "0" and add the country code "33."*

Chantilly

Hôtel du Parc Best Western: 36 Avenue du Maréchal Joffre, Chantilly, ☎ 03 44 58 20 00, fax 03 44 57 31 10, www.hotel-parc-chantilly.com (€€). Guarded parking €8/night. This modern Best Western is comfortable and centrally located, if lacking in charm. Rooms are equipped with private bathrooms (shower and bath), direct telephone line, TV and hair dryer.

Relais d'Aumale: 37 Place des Fêtes, Montgresin, ☎ 03 44 54 61 31, fax 03 44 54 69 15, www.relais-aumale.fr (€€€). Located in the Forêt de Chantilly just five minutes' drive to the center of town, this country inn features two restaurants and a fireplace lounge, terrace, garden and private tennis court. There are 24 rooms with private bathrooms, direct telephone line, and TV.

Dolce Chantilly: Route d'Apremont-Vineuil St Firmin, Chantilly, ☎ 03 44 58 47 77 or 03 44 58 50 11, http://chantilly.dolce.com (€€€-€€€€).

This modern country-club resort is in the center of the forest, just a five-minute walk from the center of Chantilly. It has an 18-hole golf course, tennis, fitness center, indoor and outdoor pool, spa facilities, free parking, local shuttle, childcare, and a *haute-cuisine* restaurant. The 200 air conditioned guest rooms have a classic contemporary décor, with cable TV, Play Station, dual phone lines for Internet access, minibar, in-room safe, hair dryer, and ironing board. Check out their seasonal package deals that combine hotel, dinner and sightseeing or golf.

Château de la Tour: Chemin de la Chaussée, Chantilly-Gouvieux, ☎ 03 44 62 38 38, fax 03 44 57 31 97, www.lechateaudelatour.fr (€€€€). Breakfast included. A charming Anglo-Norman country estate built in 1913, the château features 41 spacious, air conditioned rooms decorated in warm colors and dark wood furnishings. They're equipped with private bathroom, direct-dial phone with modem jack, satellite TV and minibar. The hotel has an outdoor swimming pool, laundry service, Internet station, safe-deposit box and an elegant restaurant with an outdoor terrace. The town center of Chantilly is just a few minutes away on foot.

Château de Montvillargenne: Avenue François-Mathet, Chantilly-Gouvieux, ☎ 03 44 62 37 37, fax 03 44 57 28 97, www.chateaudemont-villargenne.com (€€€€). This authentic Anglo-Norman château built by the Rothschild family is the largest of its kind in France. Completely renovated in 2003, it has 120 themed rooms with styles ranging from Empire and Venetian to English country and Directoire; they feature en-suite bathrooms with whirlpool bath, direct-dial telephone with modem jack, satellite TV with video-on-demand and minibar. The hotel is equipped with a new fitness center, small indoor pool and sauna, and a gourmet restaurant. The least expensive rooms are actually in the new building near the fitness center, so opt instead for the next category up (Junior Executive) for a room in the château.

Senlis

Hostellerie de la Porte Bellon: 51 Rue Bellon, Senlis, ☎ 03 44 53 03 05, fax 03 44 53 29 94, www.portebellon.com (€). Three blocks from the center of Senlis, this charming hotel and restaurant has 18 comfortable guest rooms with simple, old-fashioned furnishings, TV, telephone, and a private bathroom with shower or bath. The restaurant serves traditional country cooking and local game, and has its own wine cellar. There's also a large garden courtyard for outdoor dining, and a cozy, wood-paneled lounge with fireplace for chilly winter nights. The bus station with service to Chantilly is right around the corner. Be sure to book rooms well in advance. Closed mid-December to mid-January.

AUTHOR'S NOTE: *The tourism offices in Chantilly and Senlis can provide a list of current chambres d'hôtes (bed & breakfasts) according to location and budget (most are about €45-€65 for a double).*

Camping

Campix: St-Leu d'Esserent (take the D44 north from Chantilly, and follow signs), ☎ 03 44 56 08 48. Just 15 minutes' drive from Chantilly, this heavily wooded campsite is perfect for those who want to feel as if they're camping in the wild (even in high season there's plenty of space, so campers get a bit of privacy from each other, unlike most campsites in Europe). There are adequate facilities and bread delivered in the morning, and there's a shortcut on foot to the sleepy medieval town of St-Leu d'Esserent and its towering cathedral. Bungalows available for up to four people, from €45/night.

Entertainment

Most of the action in town takes place during the racing season at the **Hippodrome de Chantilly** (April through June). Entrance to the lawn is free, and places in the stands cost €3-€8 (free for kids under 18). Over 2,500 horses train at Chantilly throughout the year. They can be seen running each morning on the sandy alleys crisscrossing the Forêt de Chantilly. For more information contact France Galop (www.france-galop.com, ☎ 03 44 62 41 00 or 08 21 21 32 13).

HIPPODROME RENOVATIONS

The Hippodrome first opened in 1834, but the current stands were rebuilt to accommodate larger crowds in 1880. Current renovations to bring the stadium into the 21st century (while still preserving its historic character) should be completed by the end of 2004.

Visitors can watch polo matches at the **Polo Club de Domaine de Chantilly** (☎ 03 44 64 04 30, www.poloclubchantilly.com) in Apremont, five minutes from Chantilly. Most matches take place on Saturday or Sunday at 3 pm, from April to mid-July and from September through October. Opened in 1995, this relatively new polo club is hosting the **2004 Polo World Cup** in September.

There are also regular events and shows at the **Musée Vivant du Cheval** and the **Potager des Princes**. Classical music concerts usually take place in the fall and winter at the **Eglise Notre-Dame de Chantilly** and the **Jeu de Paume**. Check with the tourism office for more information.

Parc Astérix (www.parcasterix.fr, ☎ 03 44 62 34 34), is on the A1, between Senlis and Roissy-CDG Airport. Open April through October. Hours are 9:30am to 7pm daily in high season, 10am to 6pm on Wednesdays and weekends only in low season (September/October). Tickets €31 for visitors age 12 and up, €23 for kids ages three to 11, and free for children under three; parking €5. (Discounts for two-day passes, hotel-park passes, or *Forfait Parc Astérix*, which includes entry and train/bus ride to the park).

Glossary
English to French

COMMON PHRASES

Yes/no	*oui / non*
Big/small	*grand(e) / petit(e)*
With/without	*avec / sans*
I speak (a little) French	*Je parle (un peu de) français*
Do you speak English?	*Parlez-vous anglais?*
What does _ mean?	*Que veut-dire _?*
How do you say _?	*Comment dit-on _?*
Please repeat that	*Répétez, s'il vous plaît*
More slowly	*plus lentement*
One more time	*encore une fois*
I don't understand	*Je ne comprends pas*
I don't know	*Je ne sais pas*
I have a question	*J'ai une question*
I have a problem	*J'ai un problème*
Where (is)?	*où (est)?*
Why (not)?	*pourquoi (pas)?*
Who (is it/are you)?	*qui (est-ce / êtes vous)?*
How? (What?)	*Comment?*

REMEMBER YOUR MANNERS

Please	*s'il vous plaît*
Thank you (very much)	*merci (bien / beaucoup)*
You're welcome	*de rien*
It was my pleasure	*Je vous en prie*
Pardon me	*Pardonnez-moi*
Excuse me	*Excusez-moi*
I'm sorry to disturb you	*Excusez-moi de vous déranger*
I'm sorry	*Je suis désolé*
Cheers	*A votre santé*
Enjoy your meal	*Bon appétit!*
Sir, Mr.	*monsieur*
Ma'am, Mrs.	*madame*
Miss	*mademoiselle*

Hello/Good evening . . . . *bonjour / bonsoir*
Goodbye . . . . *au revoir*

AROUND TOWN

Map . . . . *la carte*
Where is _?. . . . . *où se trouve _/ où est _?*
I would like _ . . . . *Je voudrais _*
How much does _ cost?. . . . . *Combien _ coûte?*
I can't find _ . . . . *Je ne peux pas trouver_*
I'm lost . . . . *Je suis perdu*
Can you help me? . . . . *Pouvez-vous m'aider?*
Help! . . . . *Au secours! Aidez-moi!*
Watch out! . . . . *Attention!*
Open/closed . . . . *ouvert(e) / fermé(e)*
Forbidden . . . . *interdit*
Do not enter . . . . *défense d'entrer*
No smoking . . . . *défense de fumer*
Out of service . . . . *hors service / en panne*
Right/left. . . . . *droite / gauche*
Straight ahead. . . . . *tout droite*
Stairway. . . . . *escalier*
Push/Pull . . . . *pousser / tirer*
Elevator. *ascenseur*
Restrooms . . . . *toilettes / WC*
Entrance/exit. . . . . *entrée / sorti*

TIME & DATE

Hour . . . . *heure*
One o'clock . . . . *une heure*
One-thirty . . . . *une heure et demi*
Late . . . . *en retard*
Early . . . . *tôt*

DAYS

Monday . . . . *lundi*
Tuesday. . . . . *mardi*
Wednesday. . . . . *mercredi*
Thursday. *jeudi*
Friday . . . . *vendredi*
Saturday. *samedi*
Sunday . . . . *dimanche*

Week . . . . *semaine*
Day/night . . . . *jour/soir*
Morning. . . . . *matin*
Noon . . . . *midi*
Midnight . . . . *minuit*
Today . . . . *aujourd'hui*
Tomorrow . . . . *demain*
Yesterday . . . . *hier*
Spring . . . . *printemps*
Summer. . . . . *été*
Fall . . . . *automne*
Winter . . . . *hiver*

AUTHOR'S NOTE: *The days of the week are not capitalized in French, nor are the months.*

MONTHS

January . . . . *janvier*
February . . . . *février*
March . . . . *mars*
April . . . . *avril*
May . . . . *mai*
June. . . . . *juin*
July . . . . *juillet*
August . . . . *août*
September . . . . *septembre*
October. . . . . *octobre*
November. . . . . *novembre*
December . . . . *décembre*

NUMBERS

first . . . . *premier*
second . . . . *deuxième*
third . . . . *troisième*
fourth. . . . . *quatrième*
fifth . . . . *cinquième*
sixth . . . . *sixième*
one . . . . *un*
two . . . . *deux*
three . . . . *trois*
four . . . . *quatre*

five . . . . *cinq*
six. . . . . *six*
seven . . . . *sept*
eight. . . . . *huit*
nine . . . . *neuf*
10. . . . . *dix*
11 . . . . *onze*
12 . . . . *douze*
13 . . . . *treize*
14. . . . . *quatorze*
15 . . . . *quinze*
16 . . . . *seize*
17 . . . . *dix-sept*
18 . . . . *dix-huit*
19 . . . . *dix-neuf*
20. . . . . *vingt*
30 . . . . *trente*
40 . . . . *quarante*
50 . . . . *cinquante*
60 . . . . *soixante*
70 . . . . *soixante-dix*
80. . . . . *quatre-vingt*
90 . . . . *quatre-vingt-dix*
100; 200 . . . . *cent; deux cent*
1,000; 2,000 . . . . *mille; deux mille*

IN A RESTAURANT

The bill . . . . *l'addition*
To eat . . . . *manger*
Plate. . . . . *assiette*
Organically grown . . . . *bio/bilologique*
Menu (from the menu) . . . . *carte (à la carte)*
Hot . . . . *chaud*
Included. . . . . *compris*
Counter/bar . . . . *comptoir/zinc*
Knife . . . . *couteau*
Fork. . . . . *fourchette*
Spoon . . . . *cuillère*
Tasting/sampling. . . . . *dégustation*
Starter/appetizer . . . . *entrée*

Two-course meal (set price) . . . . *formule*
Three-course meal (set price). . . . . *menu*
Cold. . . . . *froid*
Free . . . . *gratuit*
Tip included . . . . *service compris*
Main dish (of the day) . . . . *plat (du jour)*
Fixed price . . . . *prix-fixe*
Savory/sweet. *salé / sucré*
Server . . . . *serveur / serveuse*
Napkin . . . . *serviette*
Warm . . . . *tiède*
Glass . . . . *verre*
Drinks . . . . *boissons*
Acidic/sour . . . . *acidulés*

BEVERAGES

Drinks (pre-dinner) . . . . *apéritifs*
Alcoholic/non-alcoholic . . . . *alcool / non-alcoolisé*
Beer . . . . *bière*
Lager/dark beer . . . . *bière blonde / brune*
Draft beer . . . . *pression*
To drink/drinks . . . . *boire / boissons*
Coffee . . . . *café*
Hot chocolate . . . . *chocolat chaud*
After-dinner drinks, liqueurs . . . . *digestifs*
Water (tap water) . . . . *eau (du robinet)*
Herbal tea . . . . *infusion / tisane*
Milk . . . . *lait*
Citrus-based soft drink . . . . *limonade*
Tea (iced tea). *thé (glacé)*
Linden flower tea . . . . *tilleul*
Verbena tea. . . . . *verveine*
With whipped cream (Viennese-style) . . . . *viennois*
Wine . . . . *vin*
Take out/take away/to go . . . . *à emporter*
Eat in . . . . *sur place*

WHERE DOES IT HURT?

Doctor. . . . . *médecin*
Medicine . . . . *médicament*
Prescription. . . . . *ordonnance*

Dentist . . . . *dentiste*
Night Pharmacy/Doctor . . . . *pharmacie / médecin de garde*
Emergency Room . . . . *urgences*
Sick . . . . *malade*
Injury . . . . *blessure*
Allergic to . . . . *allergique à*
Sting (insect bite) . . . . *piqûre*
Blister . . . . *ampoule*
Itch . . . . *démangeaison*
Burn . . . . *brûler*
Sunburn . . . . *coup de soleil*
Diarrhea/constipation . . . . *diarrhée / constipation*
Cramp . . . . *crampe*
Condoms . . . . *préservatifs*
Band-aid . . . . *pansement*
Headache . . . . *mal à la tête*
Sore throat . . . . *mal à la gorge*
Cough (dry) . . . . *toux (sec)*
Runny nose . . . . *nez qui coule*
Motion sickness . . . . *mal de la route*
Fever . . . . *fièvre*
Head cold . . . . *rhume de cerveau*
Sinuses . . . . *sinus*
Upset stomach . . . . *maux de ventre*
Heart attack . . . . *crise cardiaque*
Toothache . . . . *mal aux dents*
It hurts here . . . . *ça fait mal ici*

IN THE SHOPS

Open/Closed . . . . *ouvert / fermé*
Register . . . . *caisse*
Shopping Bag . . . . *un sac*
Credit Card . . . . *carte bancaire* (or *CB*)
Cash . . . . *espèces*
Change . . . . *monnaie*
More/Less . . . . *plus / moins*
Store . . . . *magasin*
Magazine . . . . *magazine*
Clothing . . . . *vêtements*
Shoes . . . . *chaussures*

Clothing size . . . . *taille*
Shoe size . . . . *pointure*
Dressing room . . . . *cabine d'essayage*
Labels (*griffes*) removed . . . . *dégriffé*
Consignment store . . . . *dépôt-vente*
Secondhand clothes . . . . *vêtements d'occasion*
Used clothing (slang) . . . . *fripes* and *friperi*
Items left from last year . . . . *stock*

French to English

IN THE KITCHEN & ON THE MENU

Abats . . . . offal
Agneau . . . . lamb
Agrumes . . . . citrus fruits
Aigre doux/douce . . . . bitter/sweet
Ail . . . . garlic
Ailloli . . . . garlic mayonnaise
Ananas . . . . pineapple
Anchois . . . . anchovies
Andouille (andouillette) . . . . tripe sausage
Aubergine . . . . eggplant
Au four . . . . oven baked
Bar . . . . sea bass
Bavette . . . . undercut of sirlion
Betterave . . . . beetroot
Beurre . . . . butter
Bifteck haché . . . . hamburger
Bifteck . . . . steak
Bisque . . . . seafood soup
Boeuf (Bourguignon) . . . . beef (Burgundian, with red wine)
Bouillabaisse . . . . Mediterranean fish/shellfish soup
Brochette/kebab . . . . served on a skewer
Brouillé . . . . scrambled
Brûlé . . . . toasted
Caille . . . . quail
Campagnarde . . . . country/provincial
Canard . . . . duck
Carré d'agneau . . . . rack of lamb

Cassis	blackcurrant
Cassoulet	meat and bean stew
Cerises	cherries
Champignons	mushrooms
Charcuterie	cold meats
Chèvre, fromage de chèvre	goat, goat cheese
Choucroute	sauerkraut
Chou-fleur	cauliflower
Choux	cabbage
Citron	lemon
Cochon	pig
Compote	stewed fruit
Concombre	cucumber
Confiture	jam
Consommé	clear soup
Coq	rooster
Coquilles St-Jacques	scallops
Cornichons	pickles
Crêpe	flat pancake
Crevette	small shrimp
Croque-monsieur	toasted ham & cheese sandwich
Croquet-madame	toasted ham, egg & cheese sandwich
Crudités	fresh, raw vegetables
Crustacés	shellfish
Cuisse	thigh
Cuit	cooked
Daube	meat cooked slowly in red wine sauce
Daurade	sea bream
Dinde	turkey
Entrecôte	rib or rib-eye steak
Epaule	shoulder
Epicé	spicy
Epinards	spinach
Escalope	boneless chop
Escargots	snails
Farcie / farci	stuffing/stuffed
Faux-filet	sirloin
Filet mignon	tenderloin
Foie de veau	calf's liver
Foie gras	goose liver

Fromage de chèvre	goat cheese
Fraises	strawberries
Framboises	raspberries
(Pommes) frites	fries (fried potatoes)
Friture	whitebait
Fromages	cheeses
Fruit de mer	shellfish/sea food
Fumé	smoked
Galette	buckwheat pancake
Gamba	large prawn
Gaufres	waffles
Gelée	frozen
Gésier	gizzard
Gigot	leg
Gingembre	ginger
(Crème) glace	ice cream
Glacé(e)	frozen
Gras	fatty
Grillades	grilled meat
Grillé	grilled
Garicots	beans
Gomard	lobster
Guître	oyster
Jambon (cru)	ham (cured)
Jus	juice
Langouste	spiny lobster, rock lobster (crawfish)
Langue	tongue
Lapin	rabbit
Lardons	bits of bacon
Légumes	vegetables
Magret de canard	duck breast
Mesclun	mixed salad leaves
Miel	honey
Mille feulles	puff pastry
Morceaux	pieces
Moules marinières	mussels in white wine sauce
Oeuf	egg
Oie	goose
Os (de moelle)	bone (marrow)
Pain	bread

Glossary

Pain au chocolat . . . . croissant with chocolate center
Pain au Levain / l'Ancienne . . . . sourdough bread
Pain aux noix . . . . walnut bread
Pain campagne . . . . country-style bread with thick crust
Pain de mie . . . . sliced bread
Panier . . . . basket
Parfum . . . . flavor
Persil . . . . parsley
Piment . . . . pepper or chili
Pistou . . . . pesto
Poisson . . . . fish
Poitrine . . . . brisket (of beef)
Pomme (de terre) . . . . apple (potato)
Pot-au-feu . . . . beef and vegetable stew
Potiron . . . . pumpkin
Poule au pot . . . . chicken and vegetables stewed in broth
Poulet rôti . . . . chicken (rotisserie)
Poulpe . . . . octopus
Provençal . . . . with garlic, olives, tomatoes, onions anchovies
Ris d'agneau (de veau) . . . . lamb (veal) sweetbreads
Rognons . . . . kidneys
Rôti . . . . roasted/rotisserie
Rumsteck . . . . rump steak
Salade de chèvre . . . . goat cheese salad
Sanglier . . . . wild boar
Saumon . . . . salmon
Soja . . . . soy
Soupe de poissons . . . . fish soup
Suprême de volaille . . . . chicken breast in white sauce
Tapenade . . . . black olive and caper paste
Tartare . . . . minced raw meat (steak, salmon, tuna)
Tartine . . . . buttered baguette or open sandwich
Terroir . . . . regional specialties
Tête de veau . . . . veal's head
Thon . . . . tuna
Tripes . . . . tripe
Truffle . . . . truffles, gourmet fungus
Truite . . . . trout
Vapeur . . . . steamed
Veau . . . . veal

Velouté de tomates . . . . cream of tomato soup
Velouté de volaille . . . . cream of chicken soup
Viande . . . . meat

ON THE ROAD

Voiture d'occasion . . . . rental car
Stationnement interdit . . . . no parking
Vous n'avez pas la priorité . . . . yield
Sens unique . . . . one way
Carrefour . . . . intersection
Permis de conduire . . . . driver's license/permit
Assurance . . . . insurance
Carte Grise . . . . vehicle registration
Freins . . . . brakes
Avertisseur . . . . horn
Éclairage/phares . . . . lights/headlights
Démarreur . . . . starter
Roues/pneus . . . . wheels/tires
SOS Dépannage . . . . breakdown assistance

OUT-OF-DOORS

Randonnée (rando) . . . . long hike
Marcher/à pied . . . . to walk/on foot
Promenade/balade . . . . stroll
Courir . . . . to run
Course . . . . a race
Sentier . . . . trail/path
Carte/plan . . . . map
Balisage . . . . signage/marker
Piscine . . . . pool
Plage . . . . beach
Bonnet . . . . swimming cap
Slip de bain . . . . Speedo-type swimsuit
Douche . . . . shower
Cabine . . . . changing room
Vestiere . . . . coat/baggage check
Nager . . . . to swim
Plonger . . . . to dive
Bâteau . . . . boat
Croisière . . . . cruise

Barque	dinghy/rowboat
Patiner / patinoire	to skate/skating rink
Patins	skates
Glace	ice
Pêche / pêcher	fish/fishing
Vélo	bicycle
Vélo tout-terrain (VTT)	mountain bike
Vélo tout-chemin (VTC)	hybrid bike
Vélo de ville	city cruiser bicycle
Roller	roller skating
Casquet	helmet
Anti-vol	anti-theft lock
Panier	basket
Location / louer	rental/to rent
Cheval / poney	horse/pony
Rando Equéstre / Promenade à cheval	horseback rides
Ecuries	stables
Attelage/calèche	horse-drawn carriage
Grimper	to climb
Escalade	a climb
Mur	wall
Montgolfière	hot-air balloon
Cerf-volant	kite
Voler	to fly

Index